ROBO SAPIENS

Tales of Tomorrow

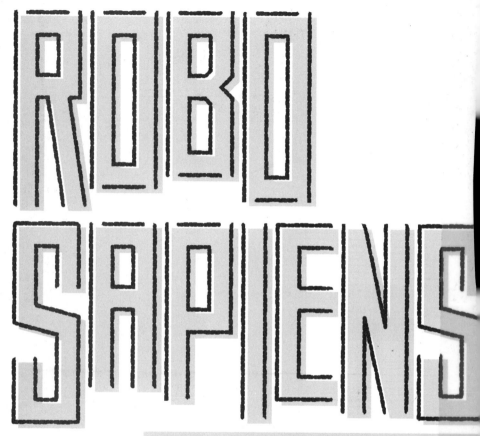

story & art by

Toranosuke Shimada

translation by

Adrienne Beck

Contents

#1

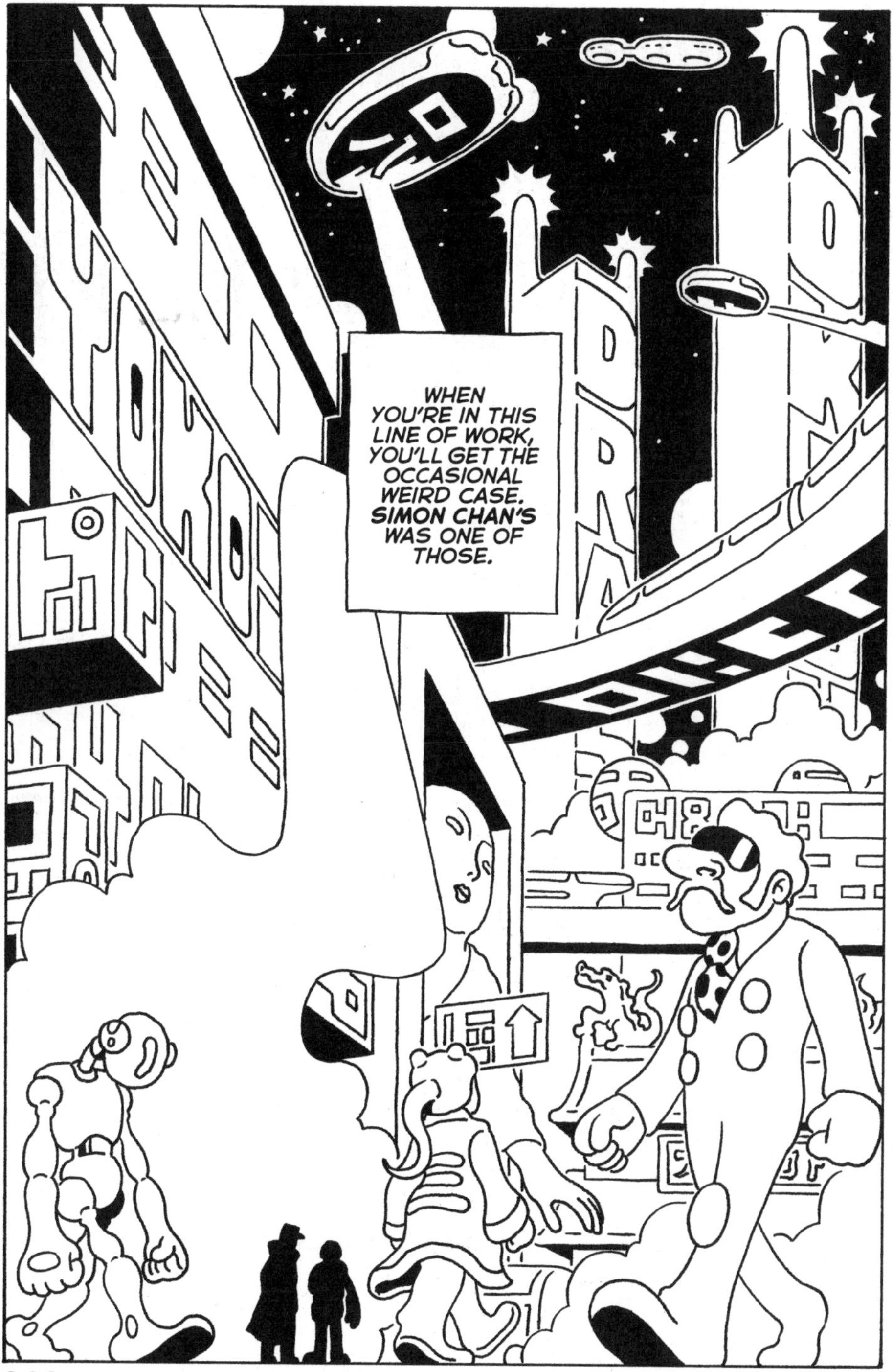
WHEN YOU'RE IN THIS LINE OF WORK, YOU'LL GET THE OCCASIONAL WEIRD CASE. SIMON CHAN'S WAS ONE OF THOSE.

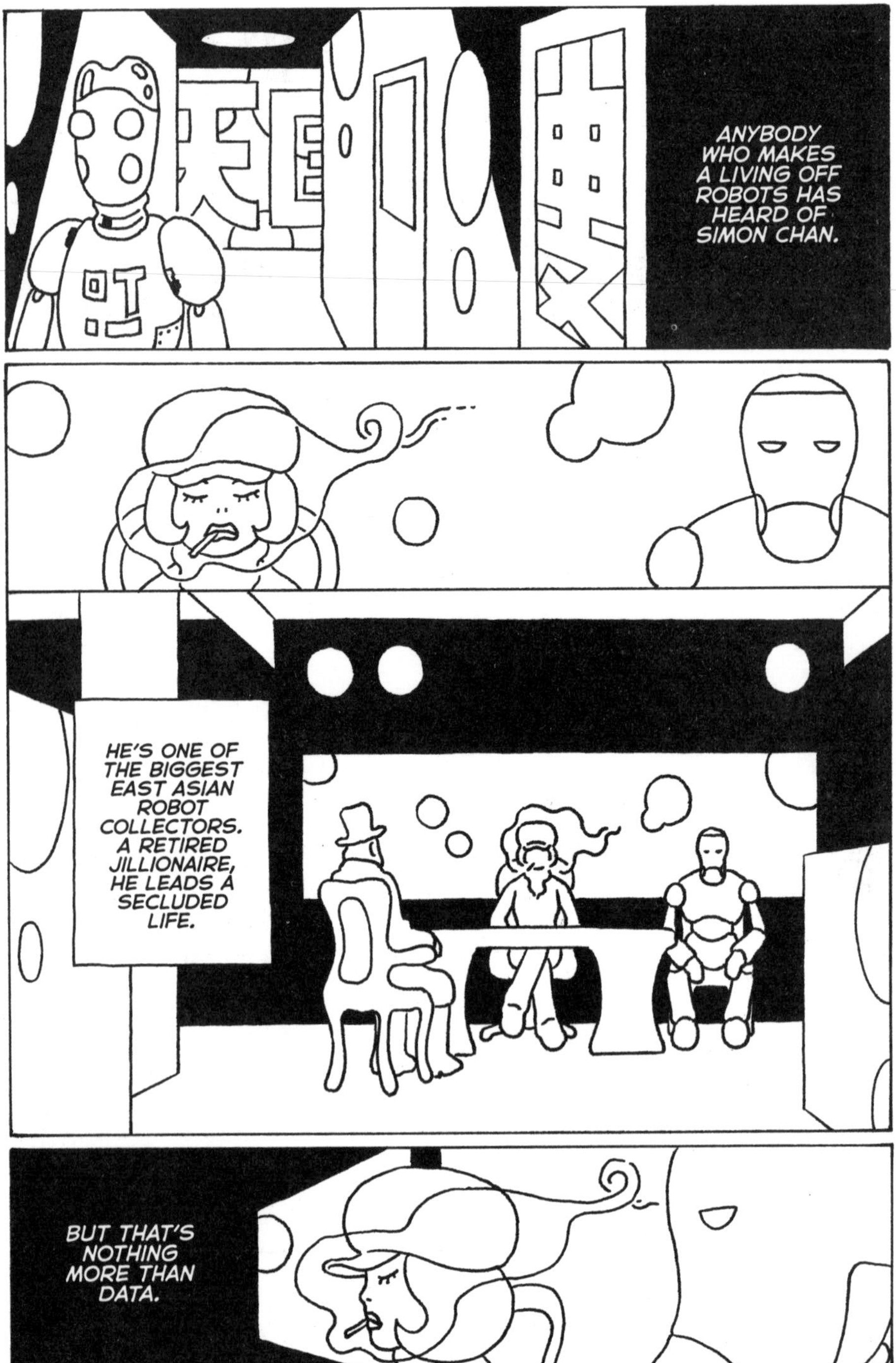
ANYBODY WHO MAKES A LIVING OFF ROBOTS HAS HEARD OF SIMON CHAN.
HE'S ONE OF THE BIGGEST EAST ASIAN ROBOT COLLECTORS. A RETIRED JILLIONAIRE, HE LEADS A SECLUDED LIFE.
BUT THAT'S NOTHING MORE THAN DATA.

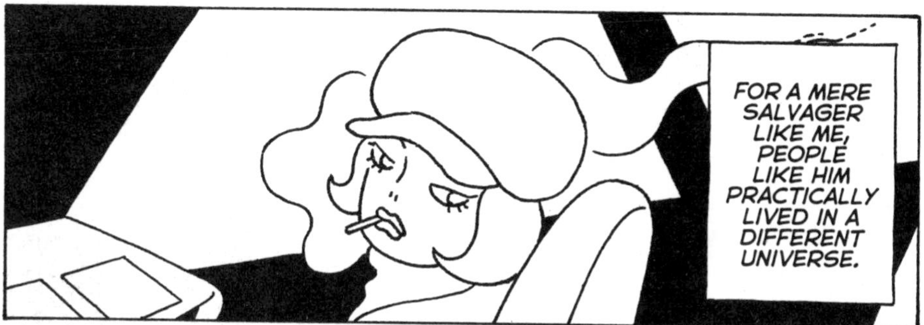
FOR A MERE SALVAGER LIKE ME, PEOPLE LIKE HIM PRACTICALLY LIVED IN A DIFFERENT UNIVERSE.

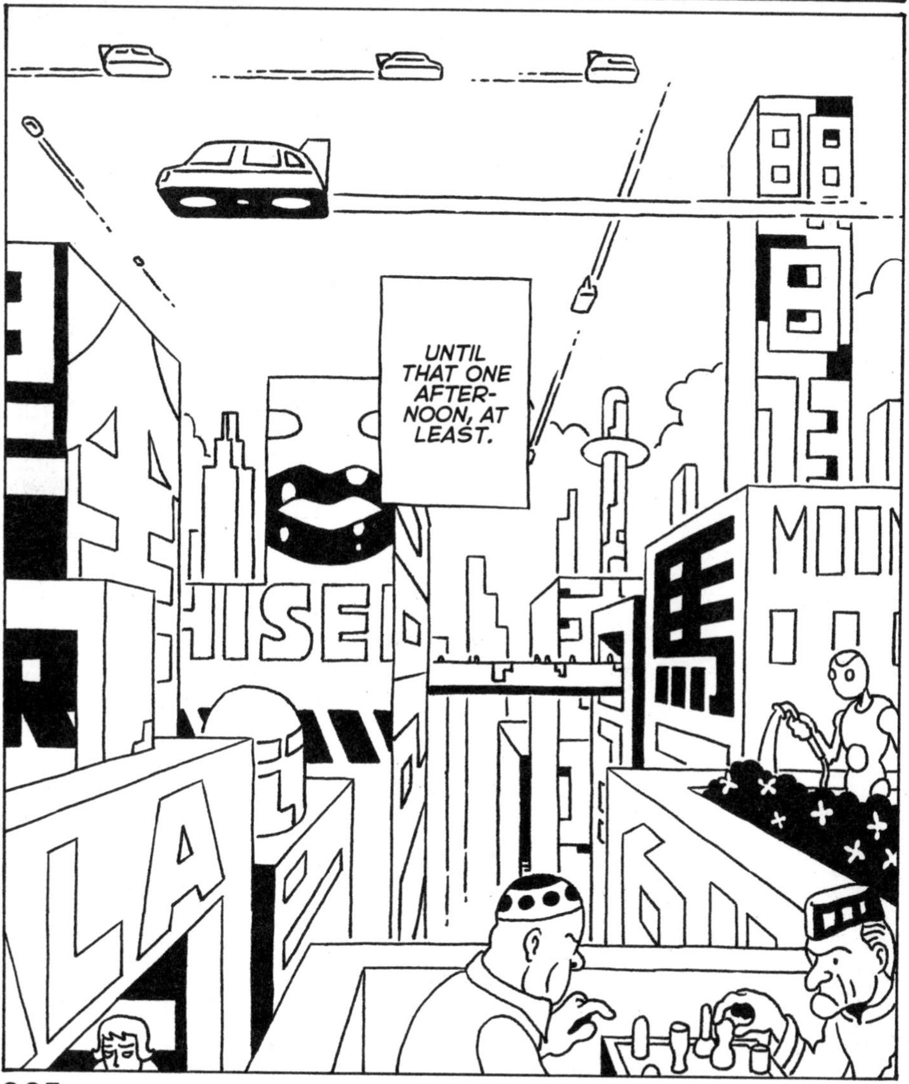
UNTIL THAT ONE AFTER-NOON, AT LEAST.

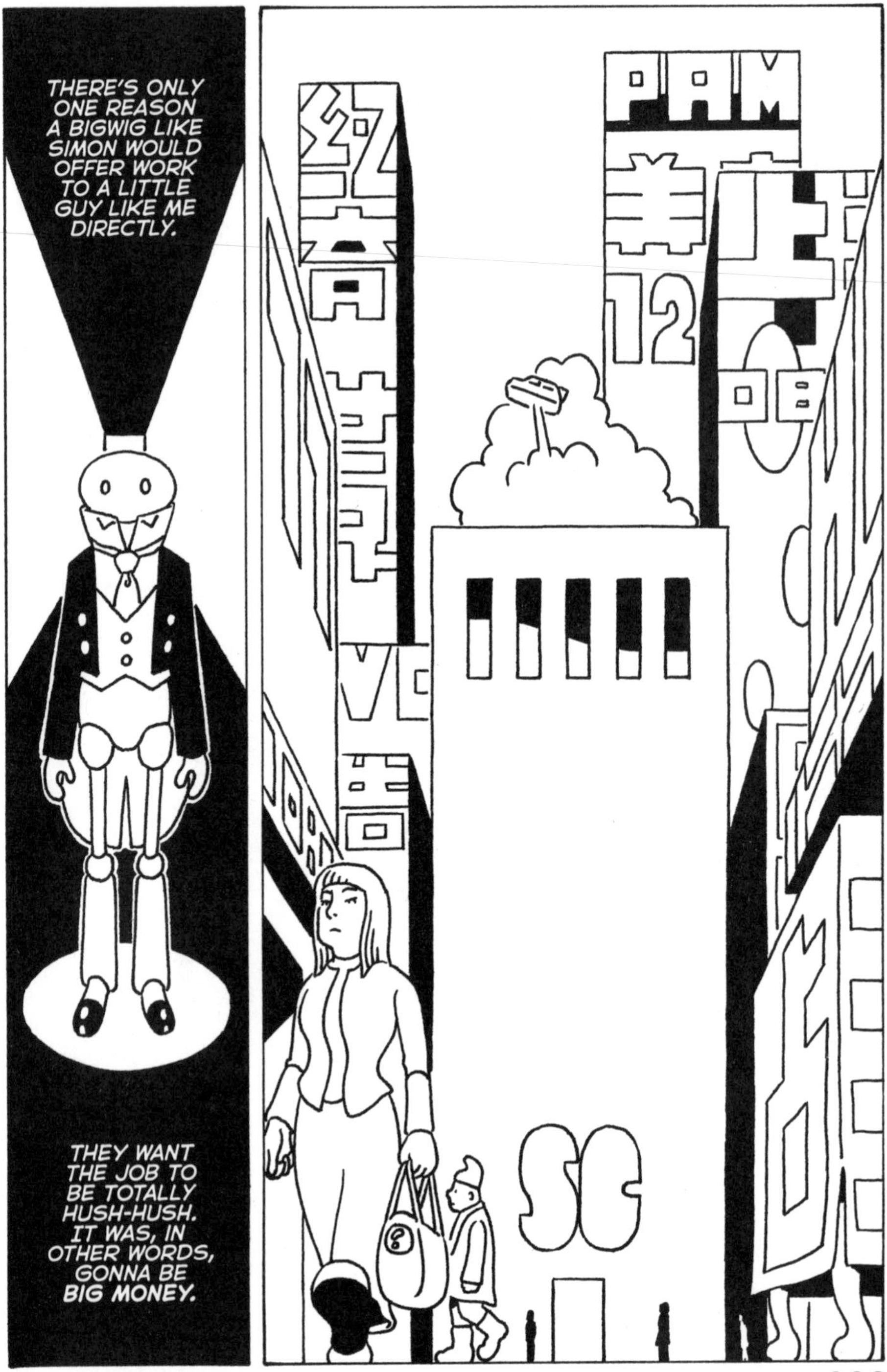
THERE'S ONLY ONE REASON A BIGWIG LIKE SIMON WOULD OFFER WORK TO A LITTLE GUY LIKE ME DIRECTLY.
THEY WANT THE JOB TO BE TOTALLY HUSH-HUSH. IT WAS, IN OTHER WORDS, GONNA BE BIG MONEY.
PAM
12

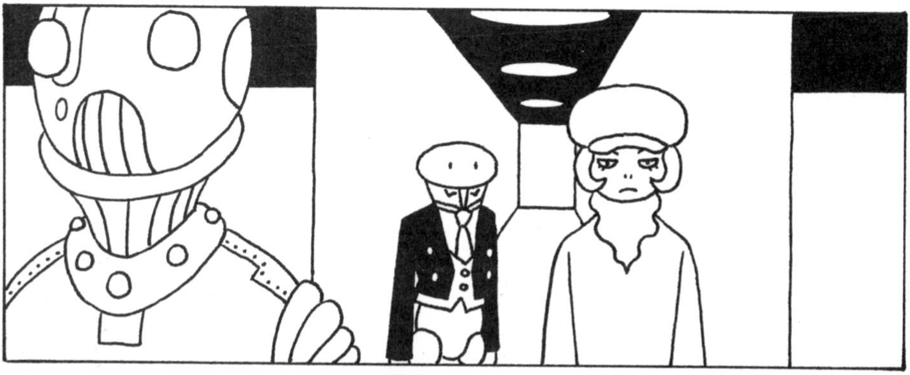
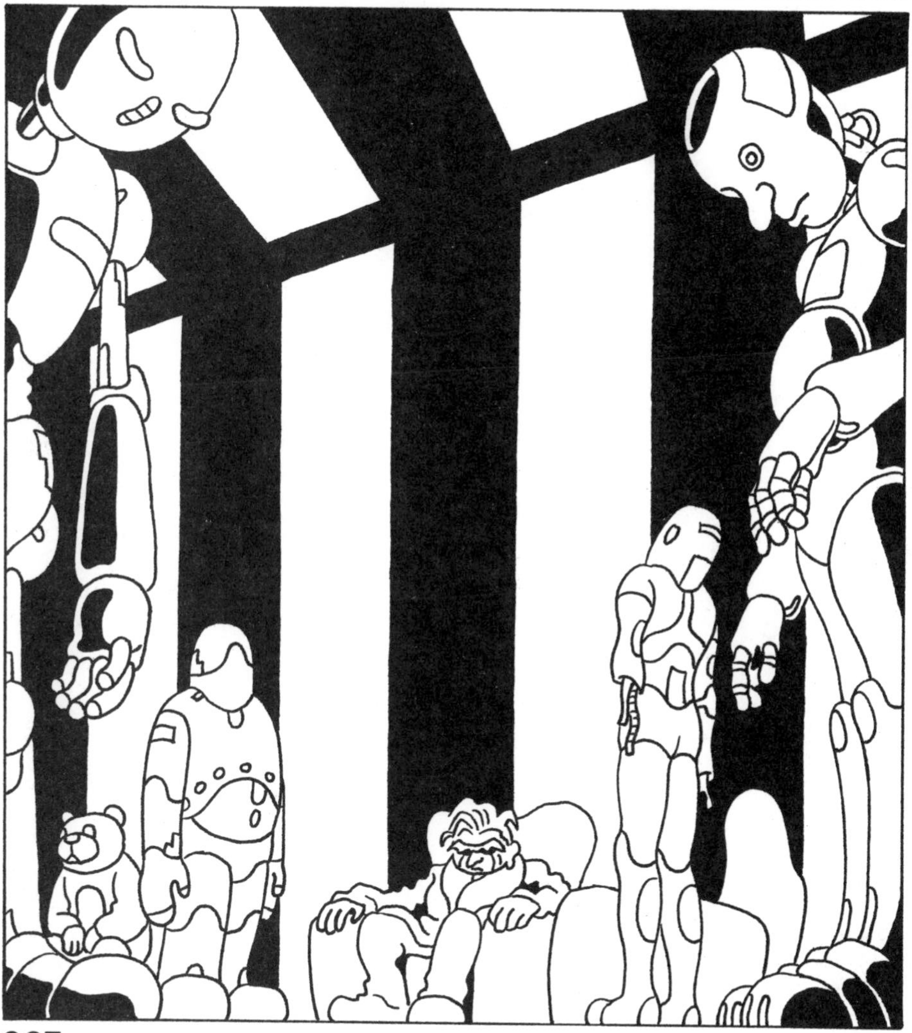

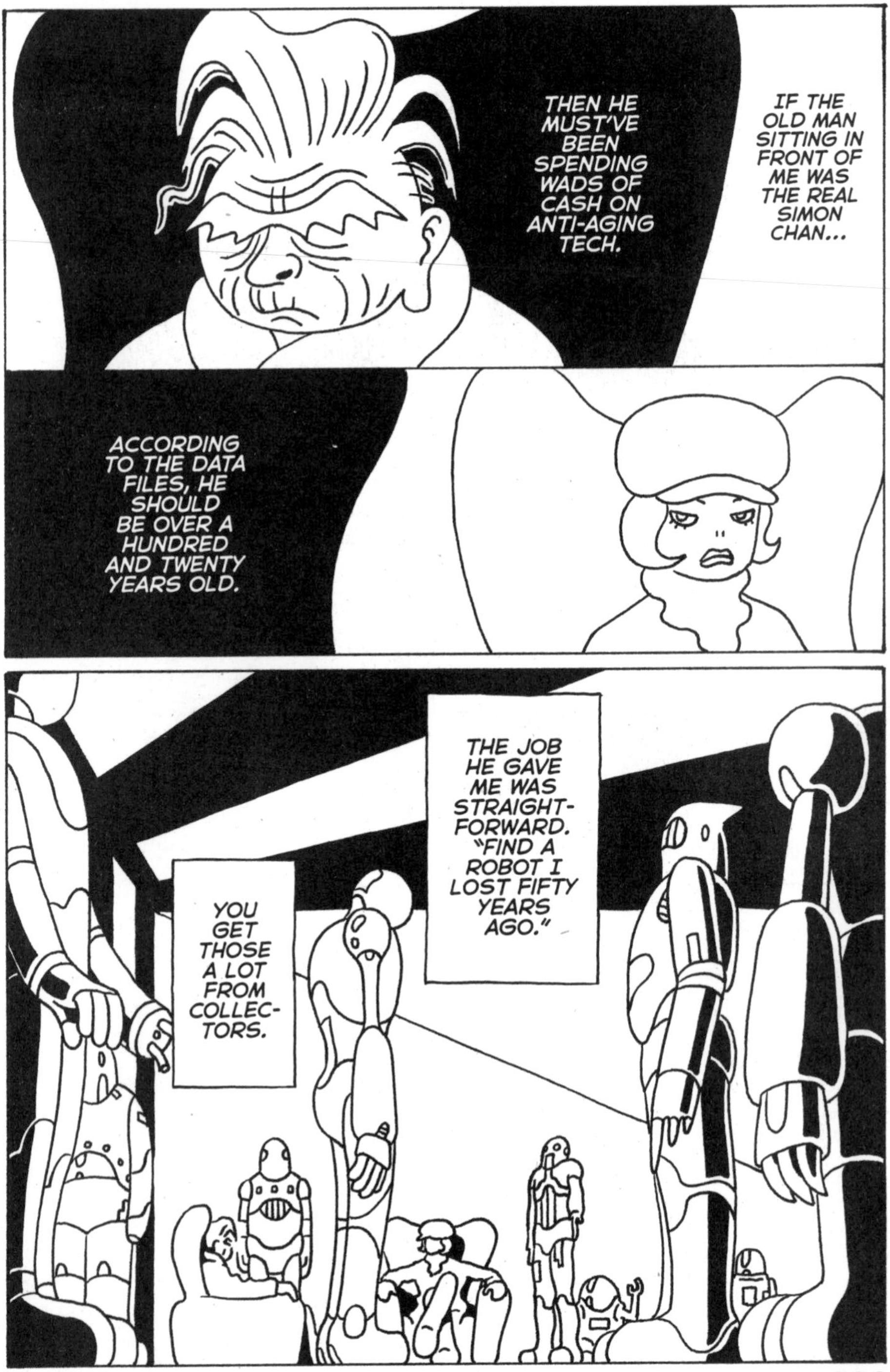
IF THE OLD MAN SITTING IN FRONT OF ME WAS THE REAL SIMON CHAN...
THEN HE MUST'VE BEEN SPENDING WADS OF CASH ON ANTI-AGING TECH.
ACCORDING TO THE DATA FILES, HE SHOULD BE OVER A HUNDRED AND TWENTY YEARS OLD.
THE JOB HE GAVE ME WAS STRAIGHT-FORWARD. "FIND A ROBOT I LOST FIFTY YEARS AGO."
YOU GET THOSE A LOT FROM COLLECTORS.

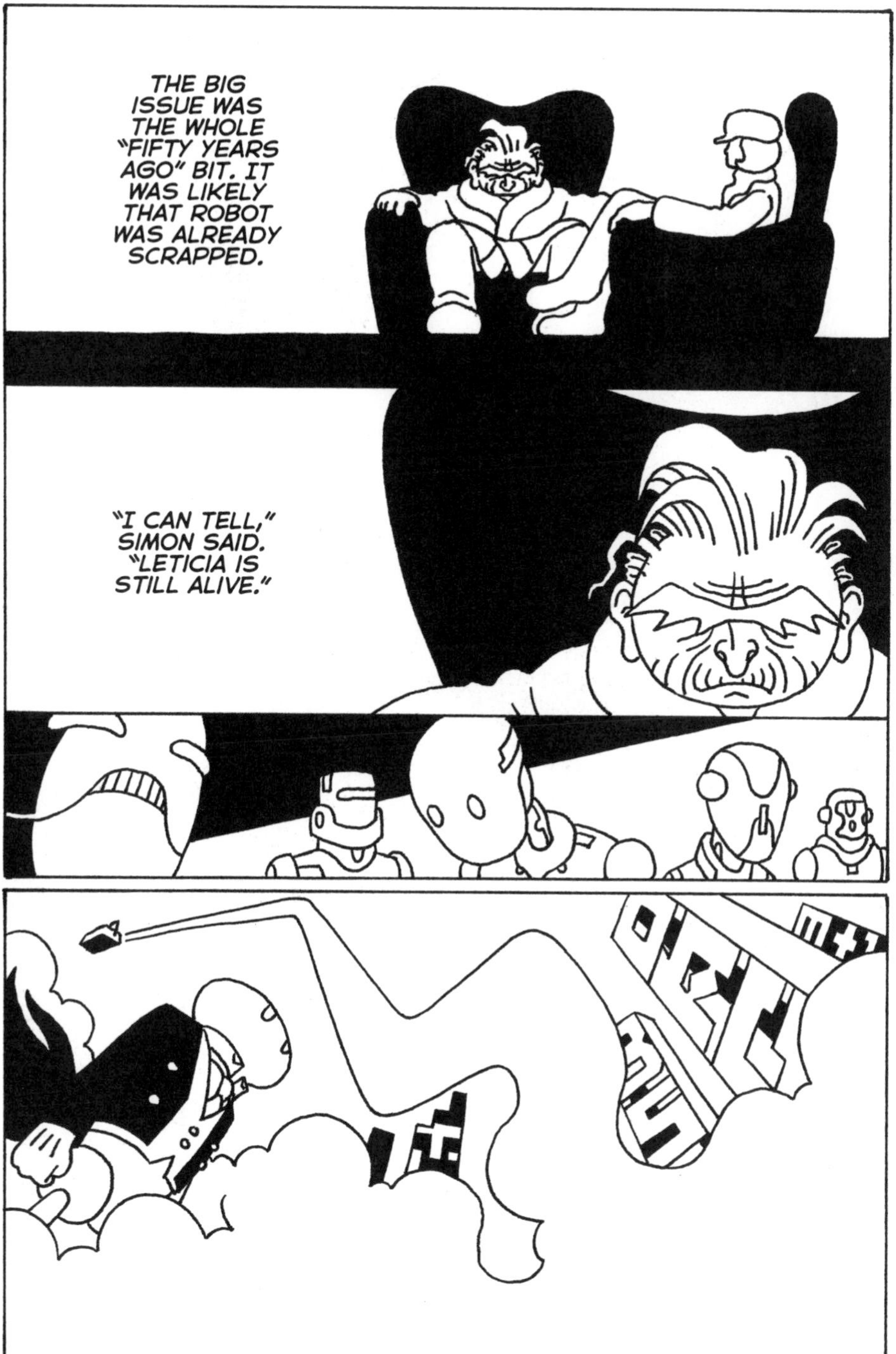
THE BIG ISSUE WAS THE WHOLE "FIFTY YEARS AGO" BIT. IT WAS LIKELY THAT ROBOT WAS ALREADY SCRAPPED.
"I CAN TELL," SIMON SAID. "LETICIA IS STILL ALIVE."

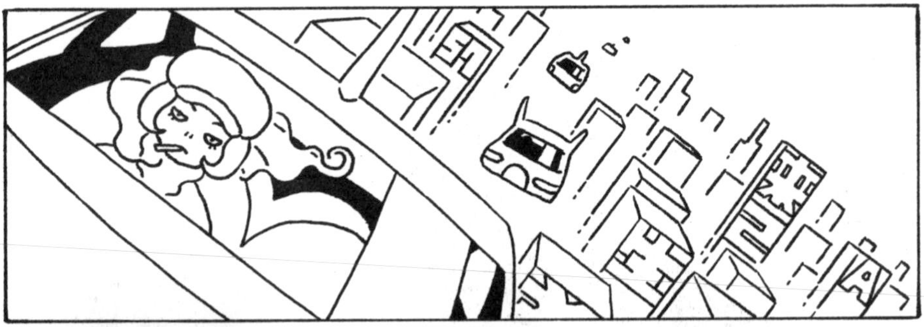

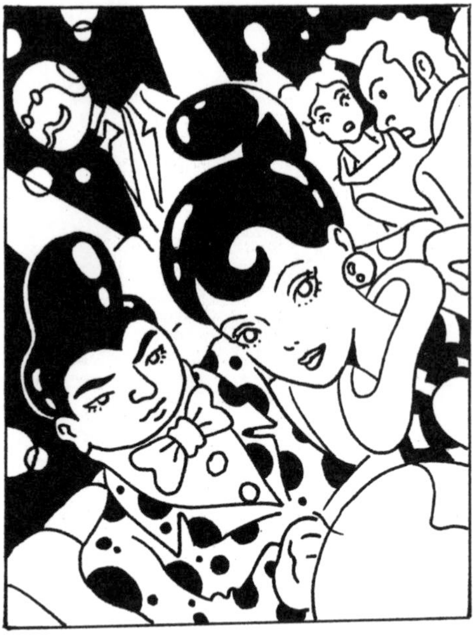

SIMON AND LETICIA CHAN WERE **THE** BIG COUPLE BACK IN THE HEYDAY OF HIGH SOCIETY. SIMON ADORED LETICIA, AND LETICIA LOVED HIM BACK.

BUT THEN SIMON LOST HER TO AN ACCIDENT. HE WAS FIFTY. SHE WAS THIRTY-EIGHT.

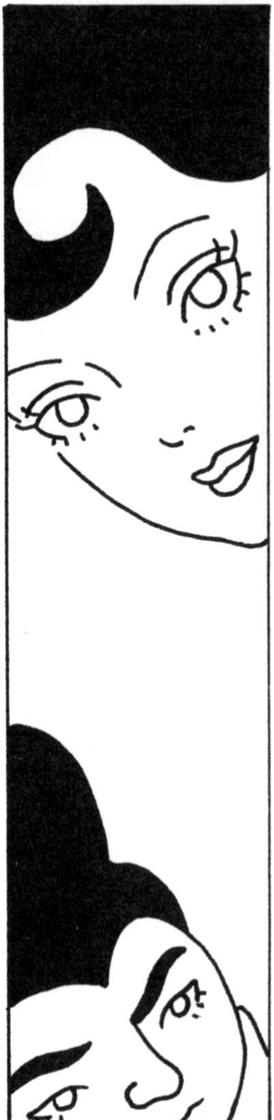

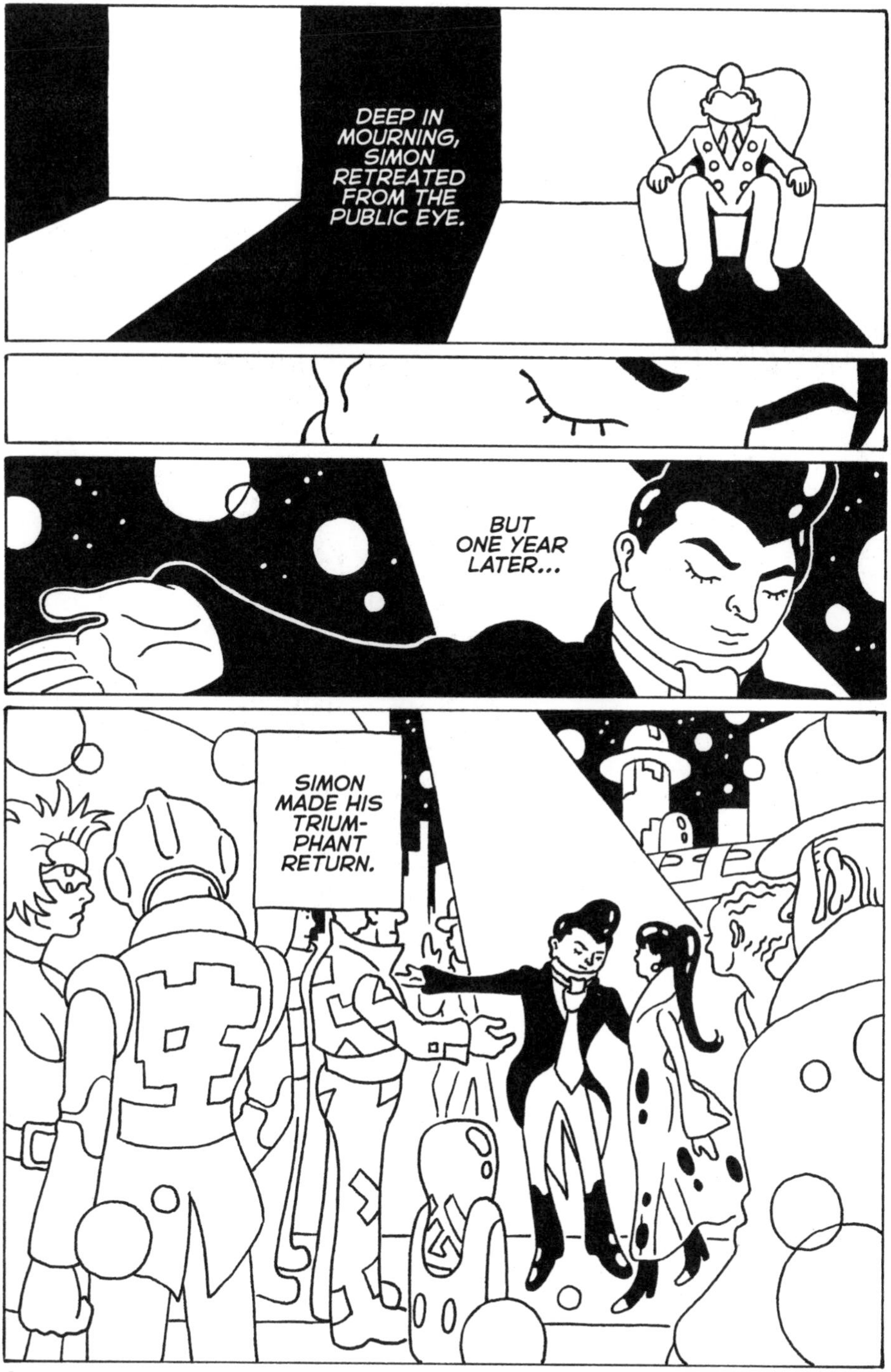
DEEP IN MOURNING, SIMON RETREATED FROM THE PUBLIC EYE.
BUT ONE YEAR LATER...
SIMON MADE HIS TRIUMPHANT RETURN.

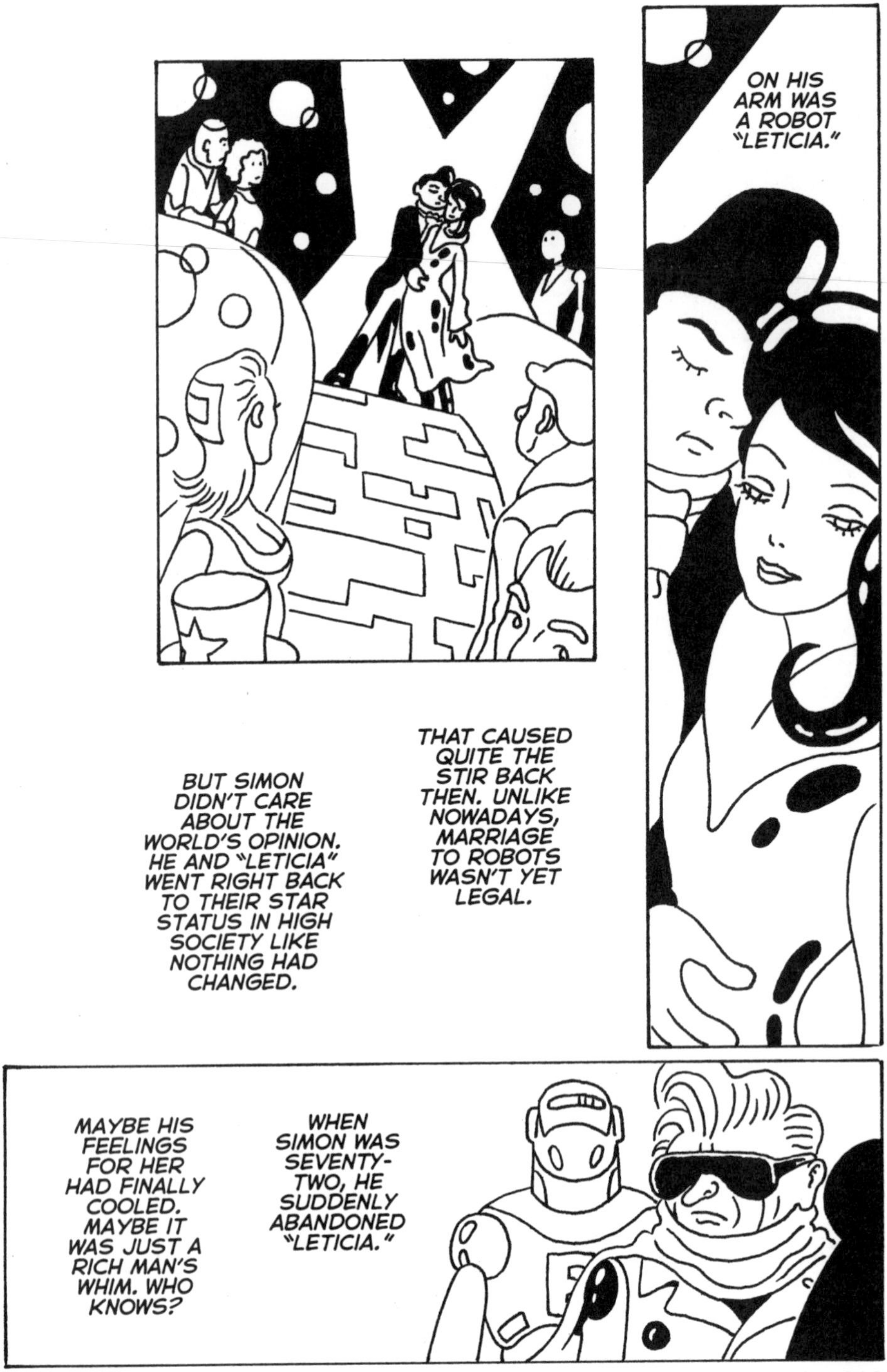
ON HIS ARM WAS A ROBOT "LETICIA."
THAT CAUSED QUITE THE STIR BACK THEN. UNLIKE NOWADAYS, MARRIAGE TO ROBOTS WASN'T YET LEGAL.
BUT SIMON DIDN'T CARE ABOUT THE WORLD'S OPINION. HE AND "LETICIA" WENT RIGHT BACK TO THEIR STAR STATUS IN HIGH SOCIETY LIKE NOTHING HAD CHANGED.
WHEN SIMON WAS SEVENTY-TWO, HE SUDDENLY ABANDONED "LETICIA."
MAYBE HIS FEELINGS FOR HER HAD FINALLY COOLED. MAYBE IT WAS JUST A RICH MAN'S WHIM. WHO KNOWS?

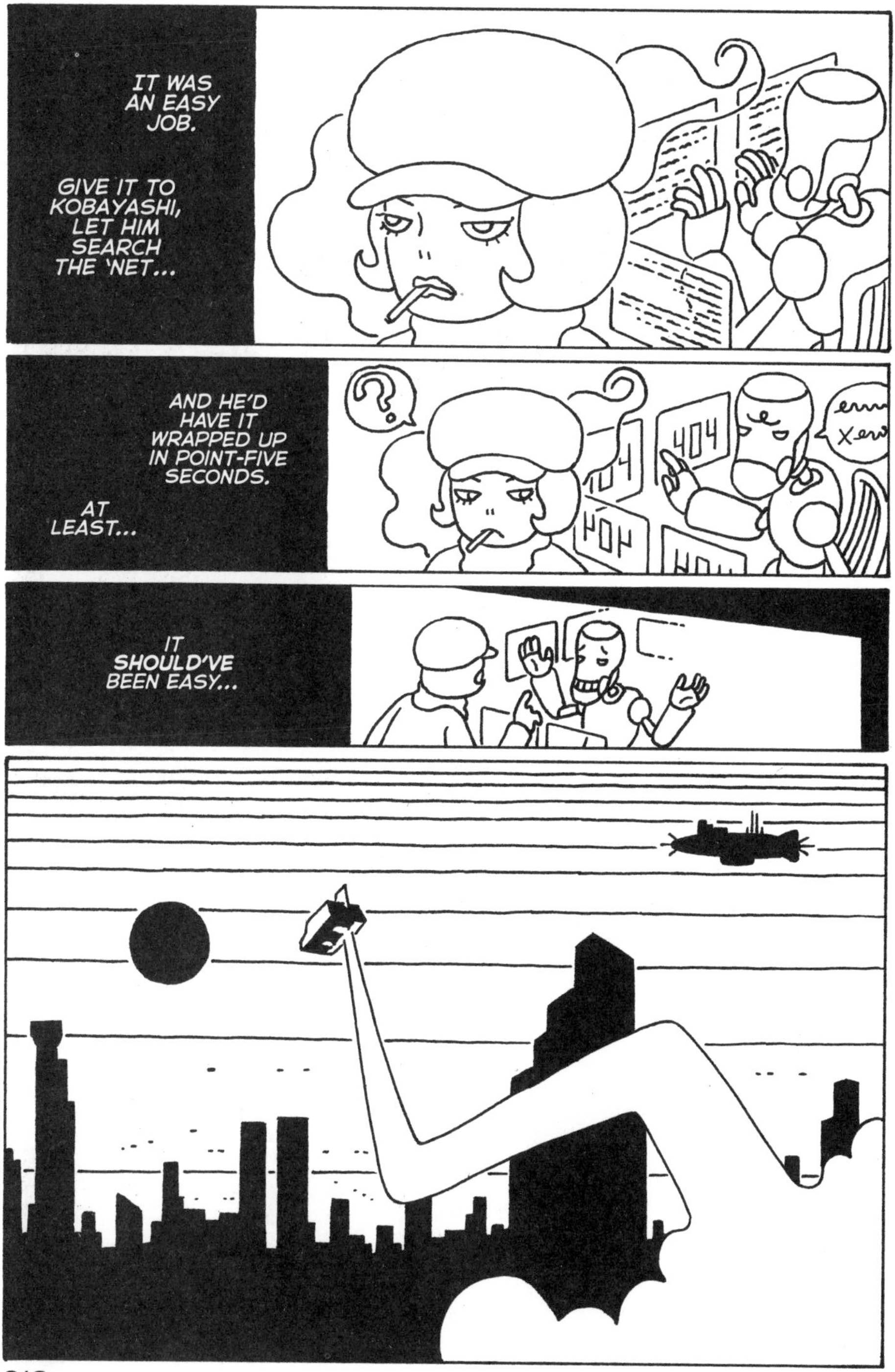
IT WAS AN EASY JOB.
GIVE IT TO KOBAYASHI, LET HIM SEARCH THE 'NET...
AND HE'D HAVE IT WRAPPED UP IN POINT-FIVE SECONDS.
AT LEAST...
IT SHOULD'VE BEEN EASY...

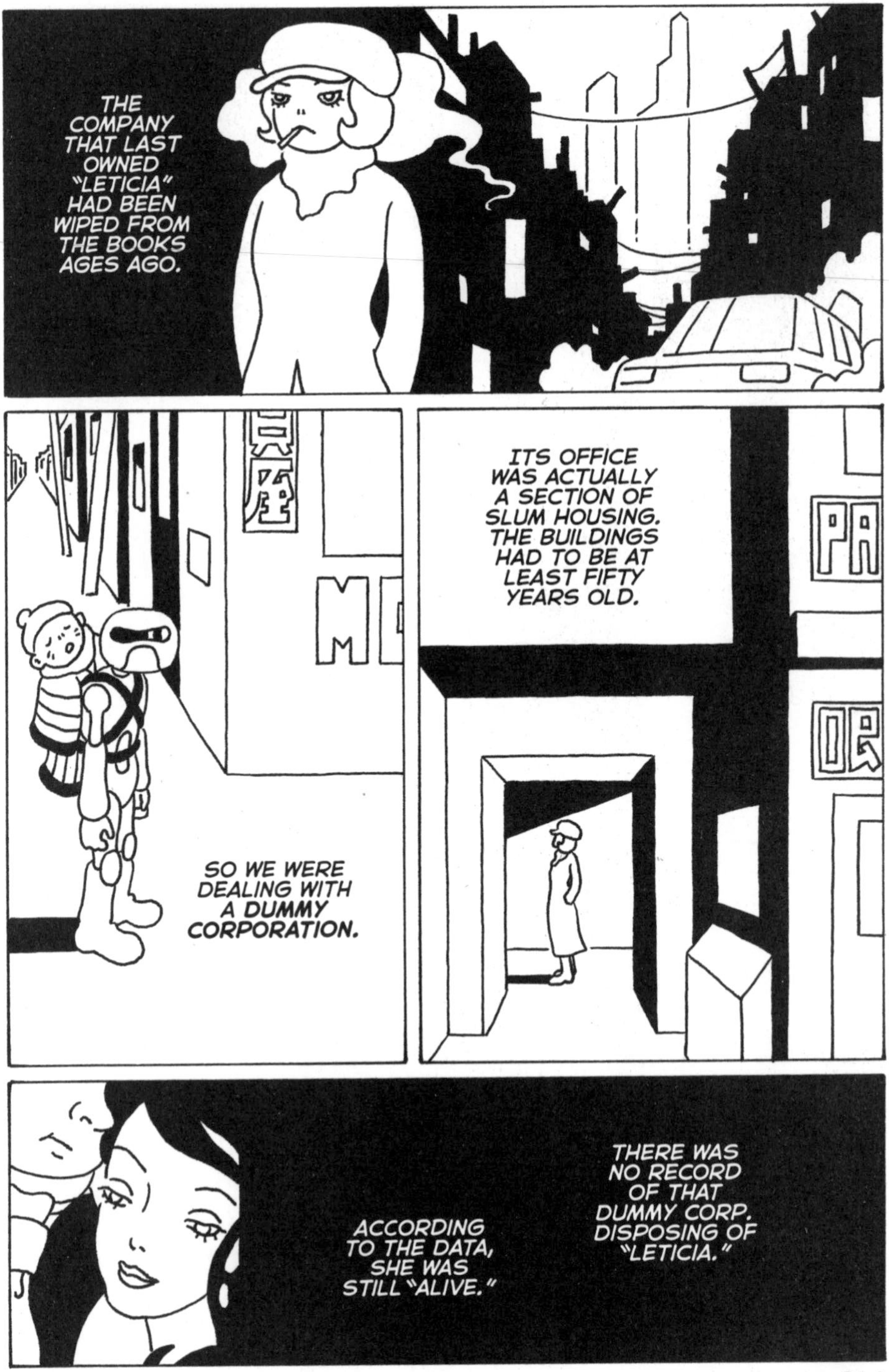
THE COMPANY THAT LAST OWNED "LETICIA" HAD BEEN WIPED FROM THE BOOKS AGES AGO.
ITS OFFICE WAS ACTUALLY A SECTION OF SLUM HOUSING. THE BUILDINGS HAD TO BE AT LEAST FIFTY YEARS OLD.
SO WE WERE DEALING WITH A DUMMY CORPORATION.
THERE WAS NO RECORD OF THAT DUMMY CORP. DISPOSING OF "LETICIA."
ACCORDING TO THE DATA, SHE WAS STILL "ALIVE."

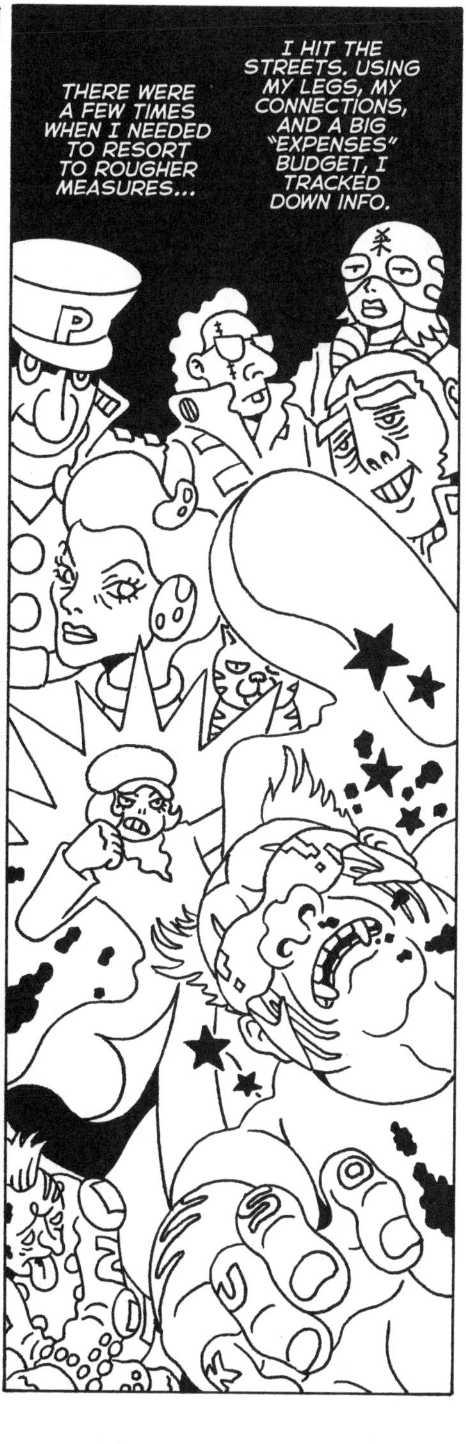
I HIT THE STREETS. USING MY LEGS, MY CONNECTIONS, AND A BIG "EXPENSES" BUDGET, I TRACKED DOWN INFO.
THERE WERE A FEW TIMES WHEN I NEEDED TO RESORT TO ROUGHER MEASURES...
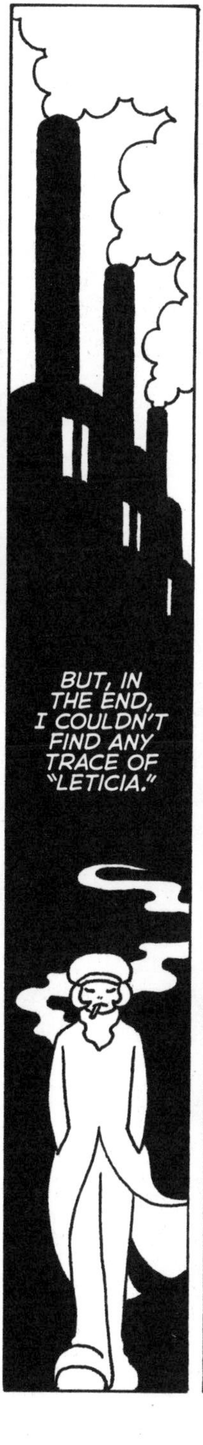
BUT, IN THE END, I COULDN'T FIND ANY TRACE OF "LETICIA."
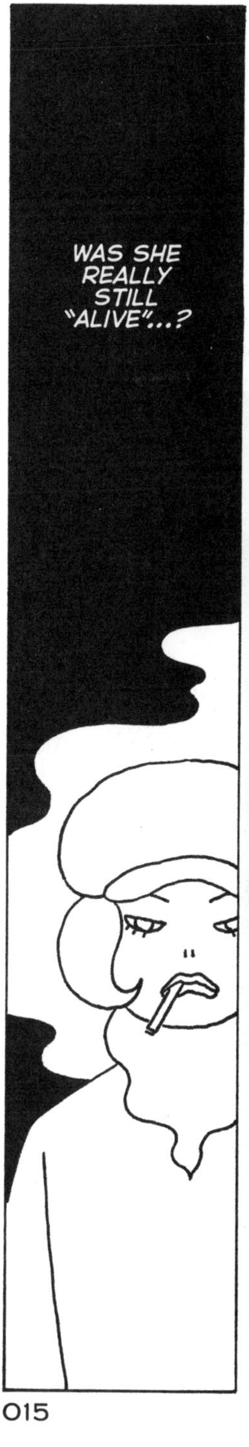
WAS SHE REALLY STILL "ALIVE"...?

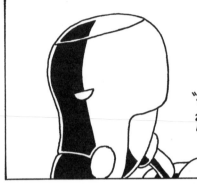

"KOBAYASHI. HOW LONG WAS THAT DUMMY CORP. AROUND ACCORDING TO RECORDS?"

"FROM JUNE 1st, 2098 TO MAY 1st, 2099, *BEEP*."

"WHEN DID THEY ACQUIRE LETICIA?"

"APRIL 14th, 2099, *BEEP*."

"TAISUI CLINIC PURCHASED "LETICIA" FROM SIMON CHAN ON APRIL 4th, *BEEP*."

"..."

"WHO OWNED LETICIA BEFORE THEN? SIMON CHAN?"

"NO, *BEEP*. IT WAS THE **TAISUI CLINIC,** A MEDICAL REHABILITATION FACILITY FOR THE WEALTHY."

"KOBAYASHI, FLY ME TO THE TAISUI CLINIC."

"SIMPLE ENOUGH, *BEEP*."

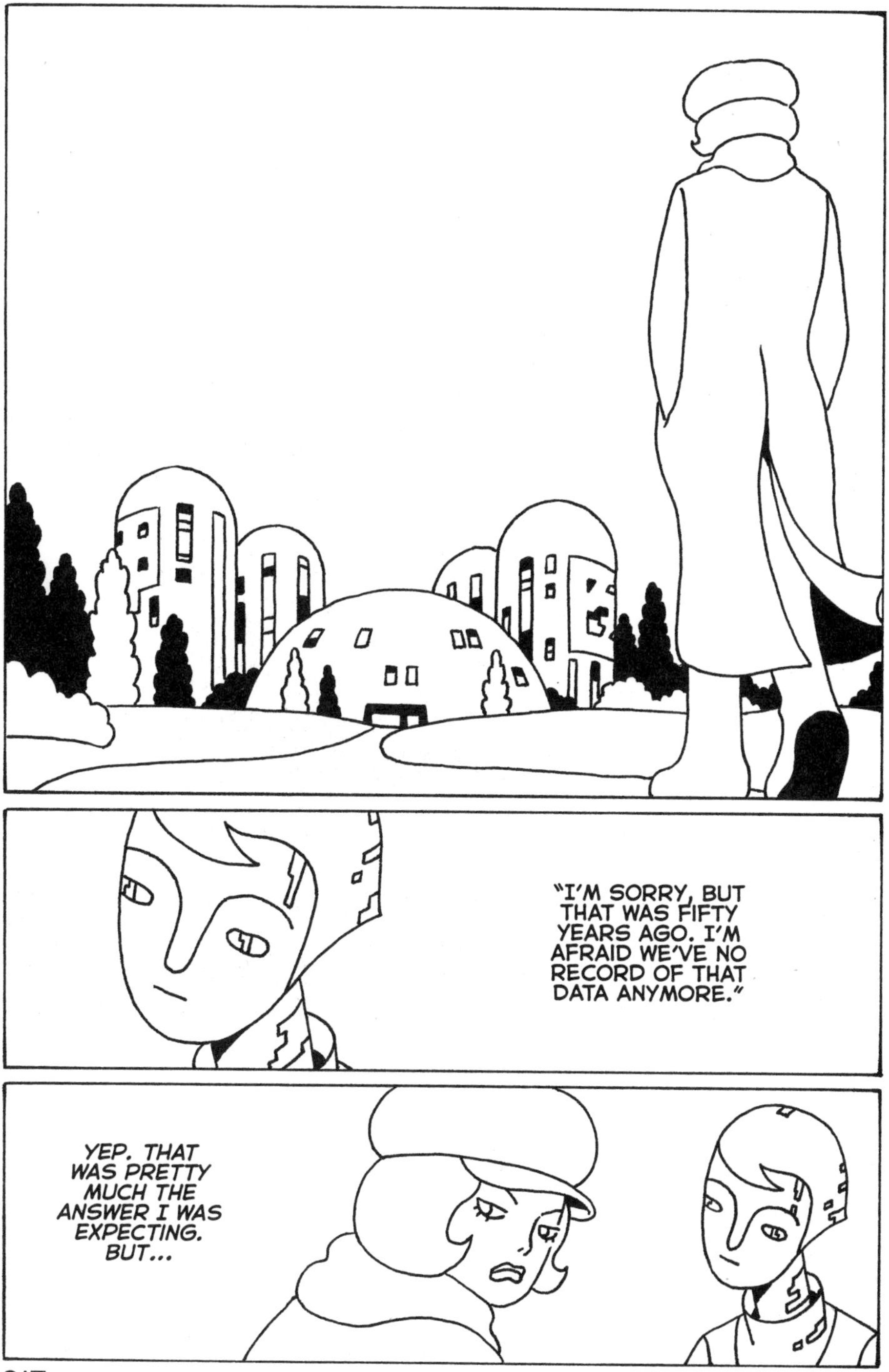
"I'M SORRY, BUT THAT WAS FIFTY YEARS AGO. I'M AFRAID WE'VE NO RECORD OF THAT DATA ANYMORE."
YEP. THAT WAS PRETTY MUCH THE ANSWER I WAS EXPECTING. BUT...

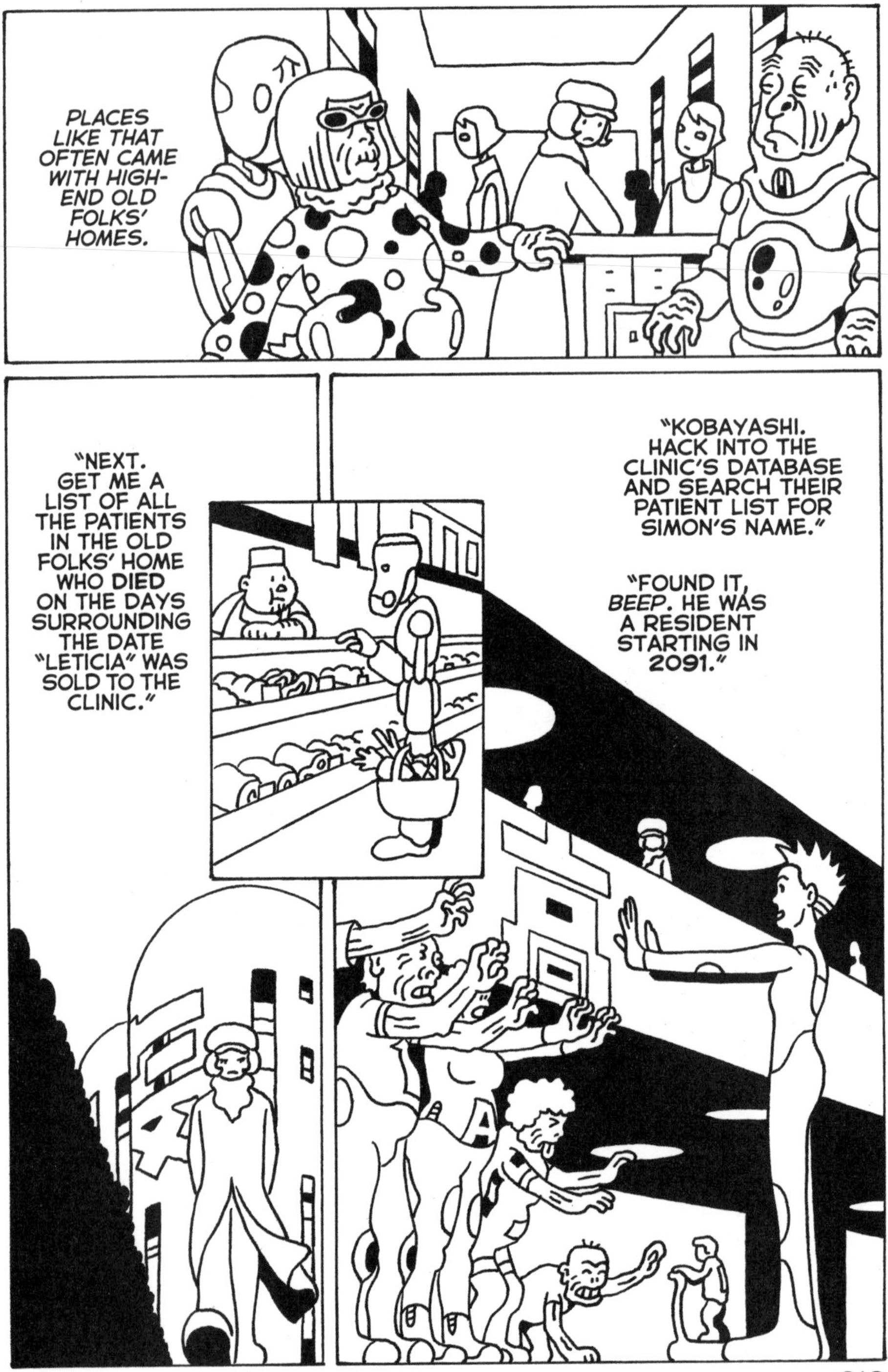
PLACES LIKE THAT OFTEN CAME WITH HIGH-END OLD FOLKS' HOMES.
"KOBAYASHI. HACK INTO THE CLINIC'S DATABASE AND SEARCH THEIR PATIENT LIST FOR SIMON'S NAME."
"FOUND IT, *BEEP*. HE WAS A RESIDENT STARTING IN 2091."
"NEXT. GET ME A LIST OF ALL THE PATIENTS IN THE OLD FOLKS' HOME WHO **DIED** ON THE DAYS SURROUNDING THE DATE "LETICIA" WAS SOLD TO THE CLINIC."

SEE,
PLACES LIKE
THAT OFTEN
CAME WITH A
MAUSOLEUM,
TOO.

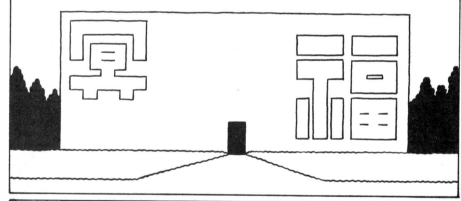

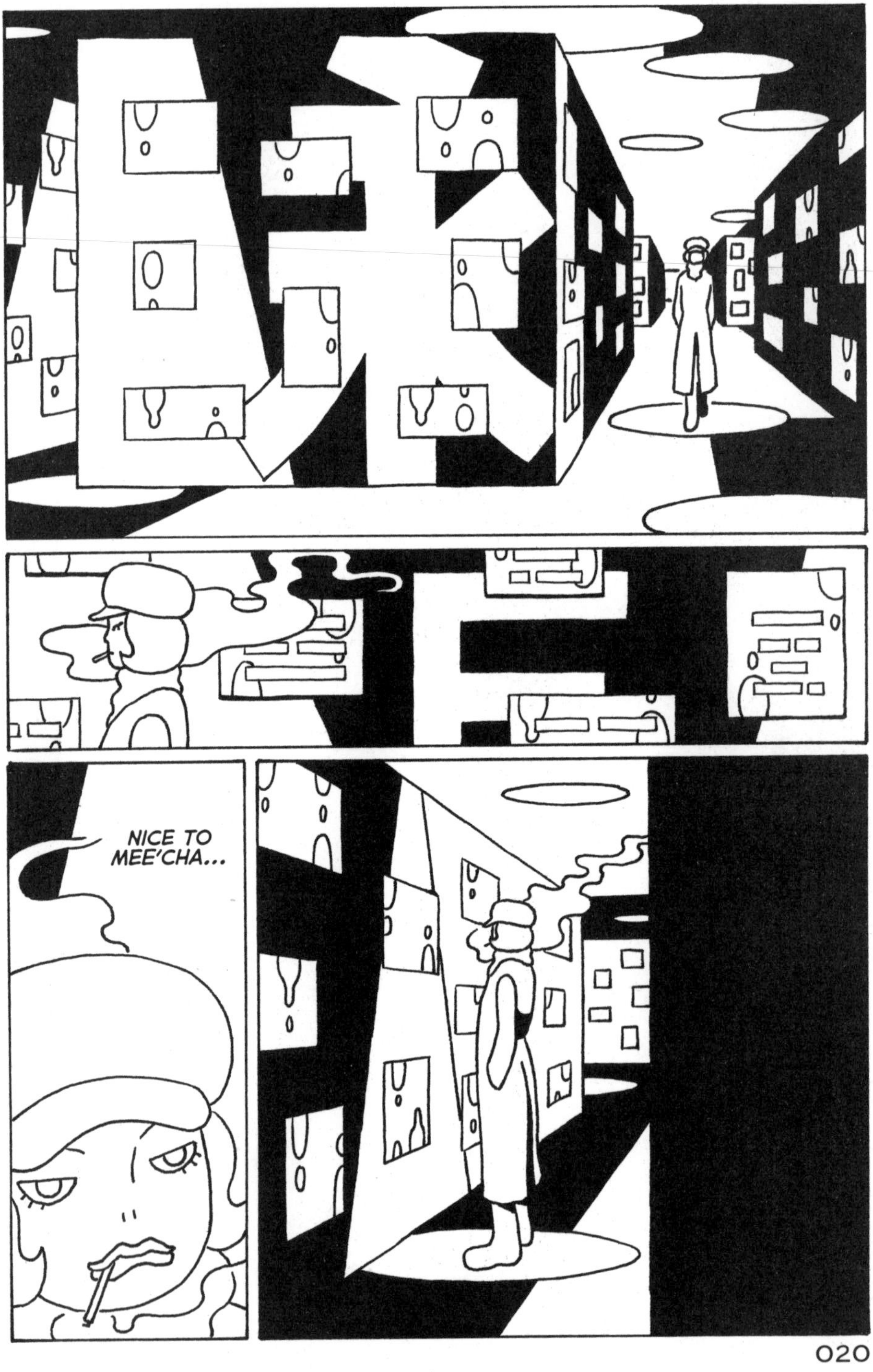
NICE TO MEE'CHA...

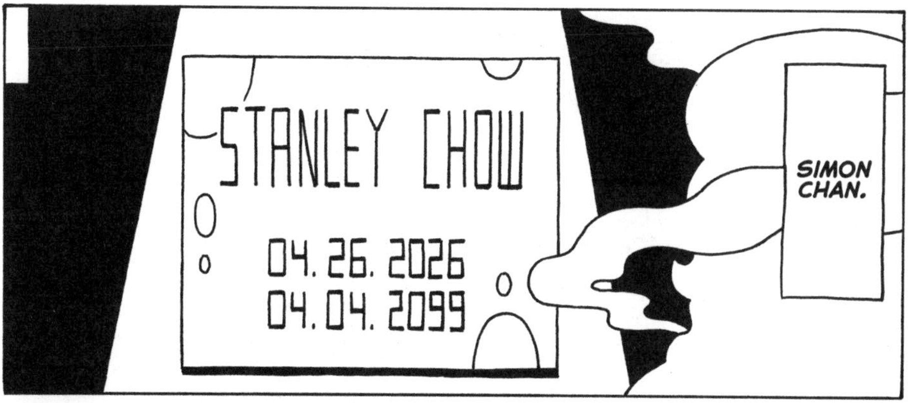
STANLEY CHOW
04. 26. 2026
04. 04. 2099
SIMON CHAN.

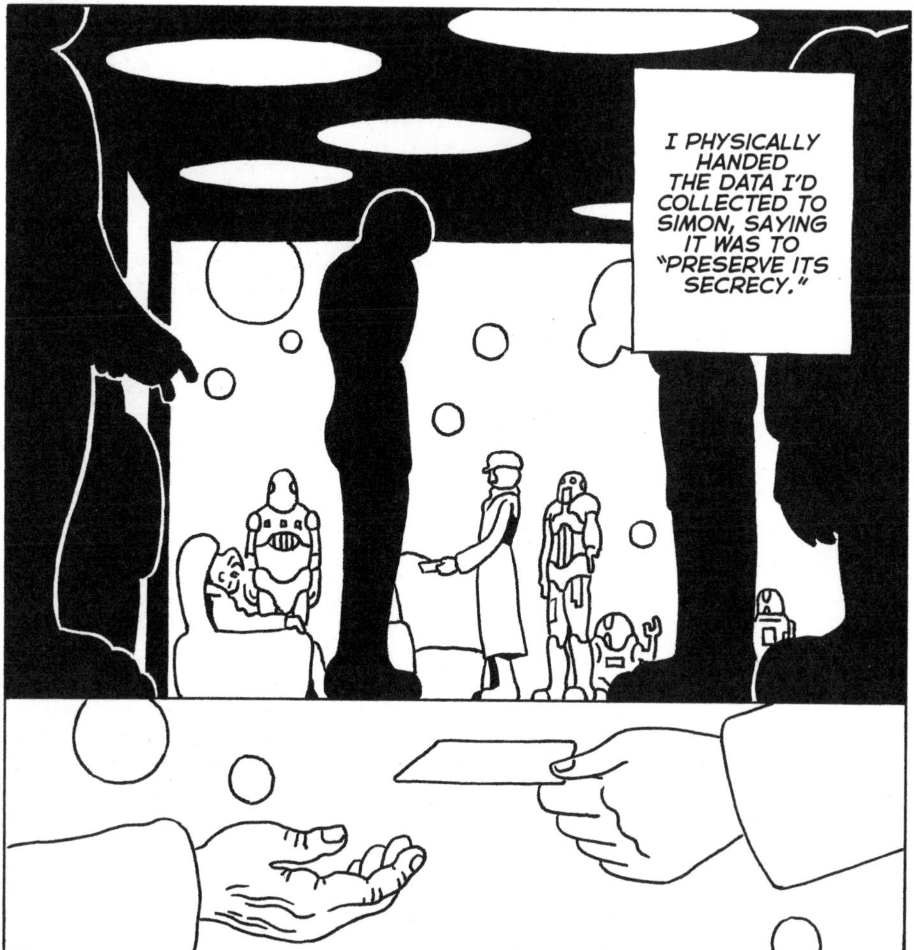
I PHYSICALLY HANDED THE DATA I'D COLLECTED TO SIMON, SAYING IT WAS TO "PRESERVE ITS SECRECY."

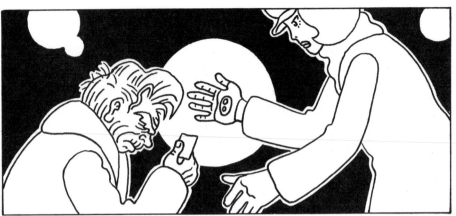

I PRESSED THE SENSOR IN MY PALM AGAINST SIMON'S CHEEK...

AND INSTANTLY TRANSFERRED THE DATA I READ OVER TO KOBAYASHI.

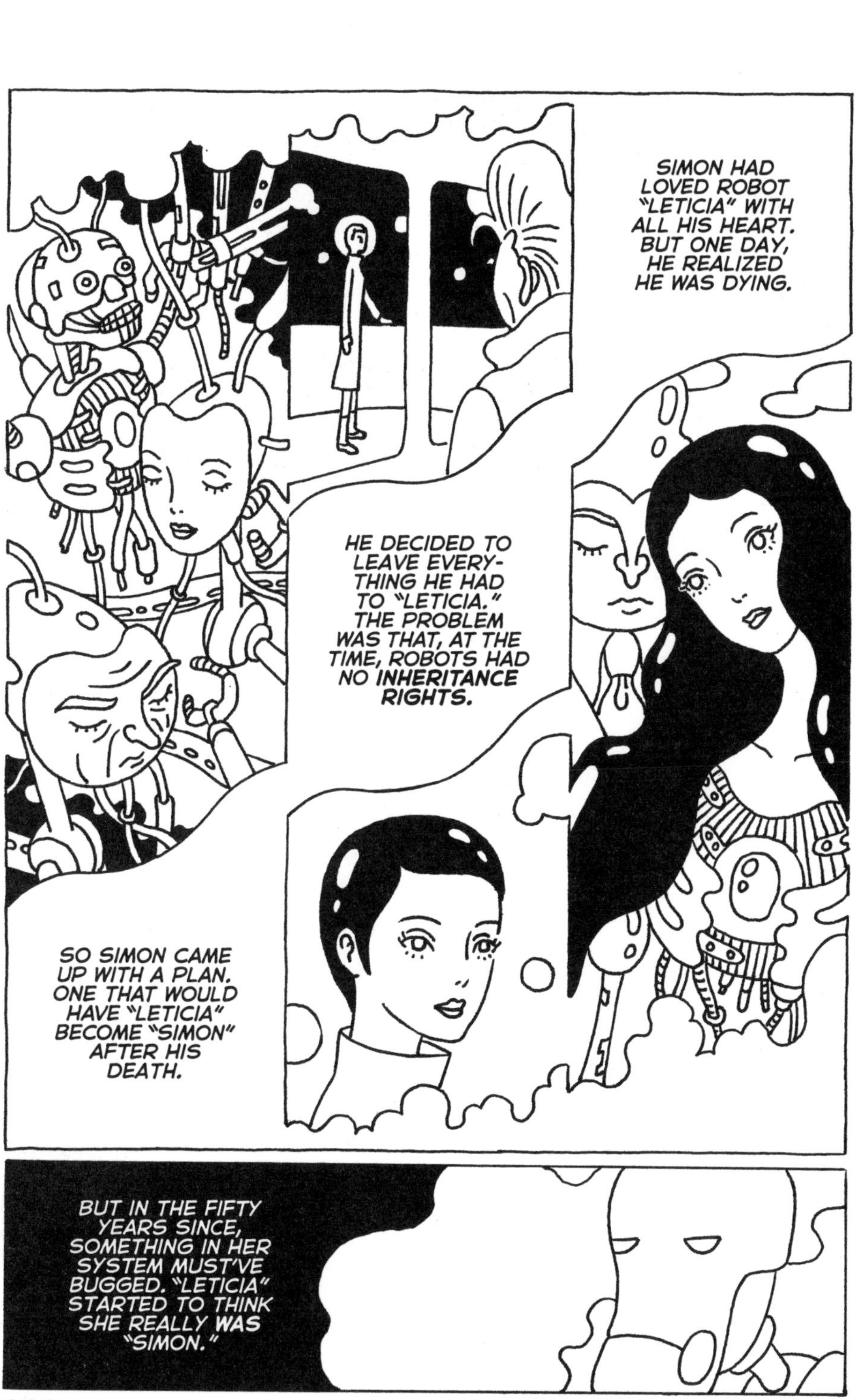
SIMON HAD LOVED ROBOT "LETICIA" WITH ALL HIS HEART. BUT ONE DAY, HE REALIZED HE WAS DYING.
HE DECIDED TO LEAVE EVERY-THING HE HAD TO "LETICIA." THE PROBLEM WAS THAT, AT THE TIME, ROBOTS HAD NO **INHERITANCE RIGHTS.**
SO SIMON CAME UP WITH A PLAN. ONE THAT WOULD HAVE "LETICIA" BECOME "SIMON" AFTER HIS DEATH.
BUT IN THE FIFTY YEARS SINCE, SOMETHING IN HER SYSTEM MUST'VE BUGGED. "LETICIA" STARTED TO THINK SHE REALLY **WAS** "SIMON."

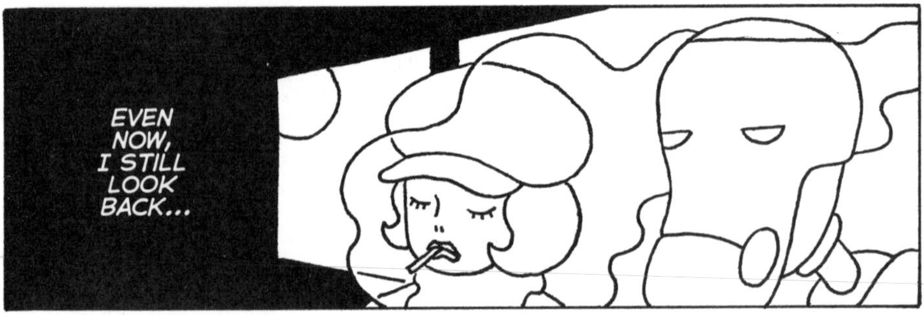
EVEN NOW, I STILL LOOK BACK...
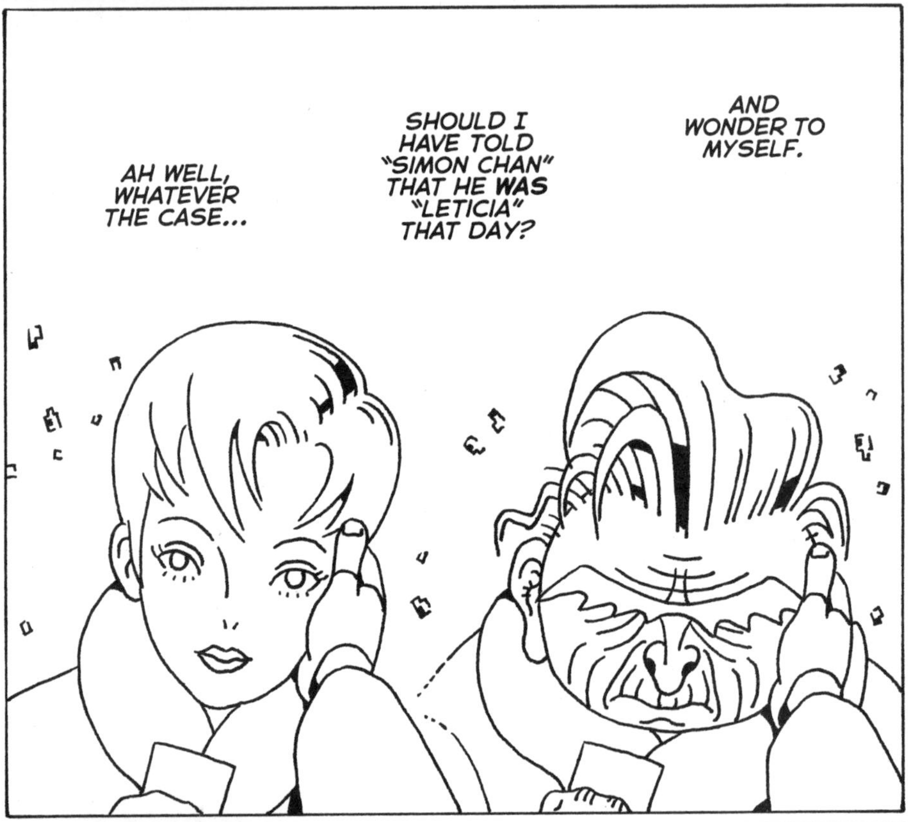
AND WONDER TO MYSELF.
SHOULD I HAVE TOLD "SIMON CHAN" THAT HE **WAS** "LETICIA" THAT DAY?
AH WELL, WHATEVER THE CASE...
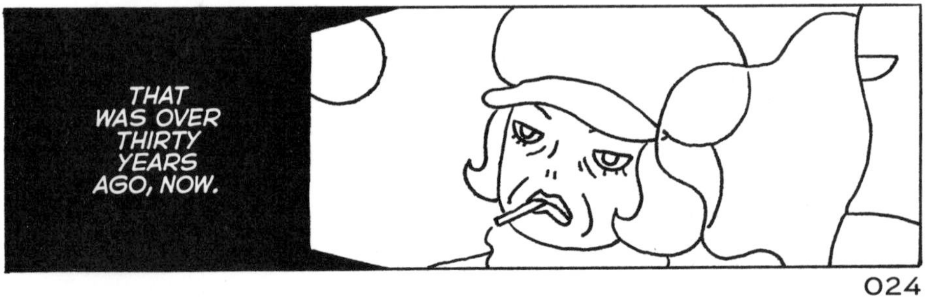
THAT WAS OVER THIRTY YEARS AGO, NOW.

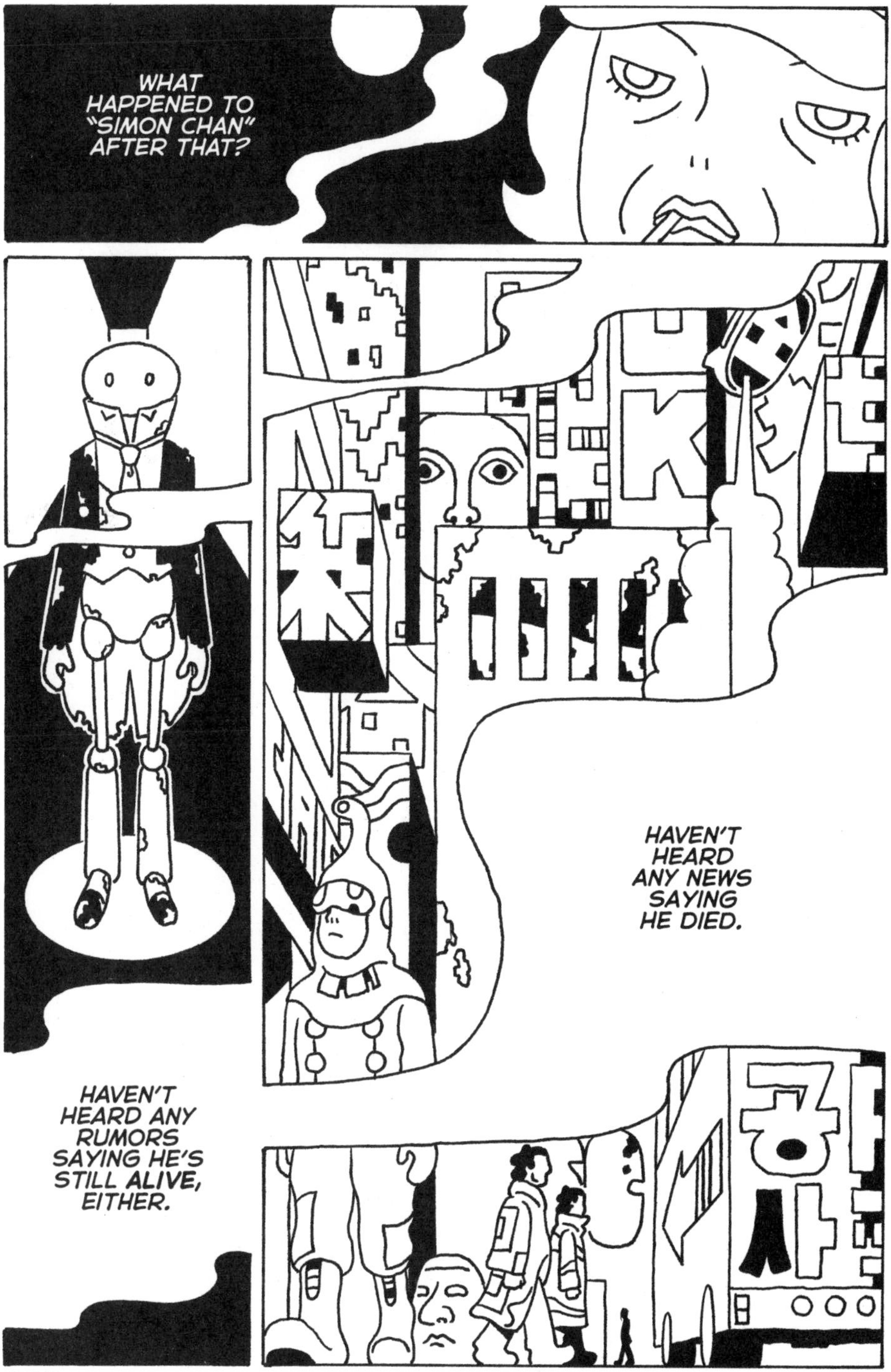
WHAT HAPPENED TO "SIMON CHAN" AFTER THAT?
HAVEN'T HEARD ANY NEWS SAYING HE DIED.
HAVEN'T HEARD ANY RUMORS SAYING HE'S STILL ALIVE, EITHER.

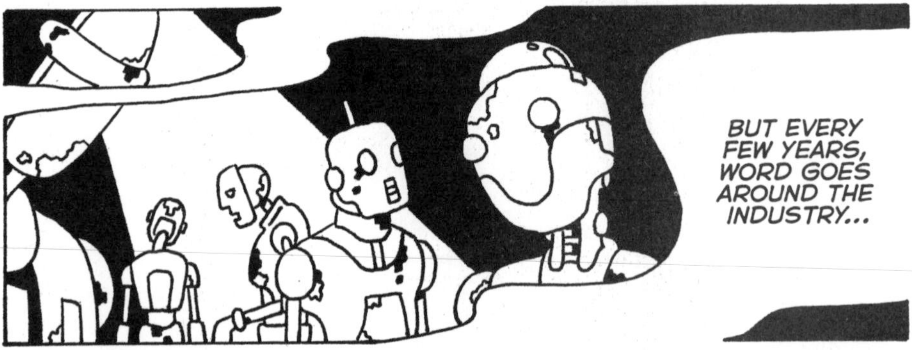
BUT EVERY FEW YEARS, WORD GOES AROUND THE INDUSTRY...

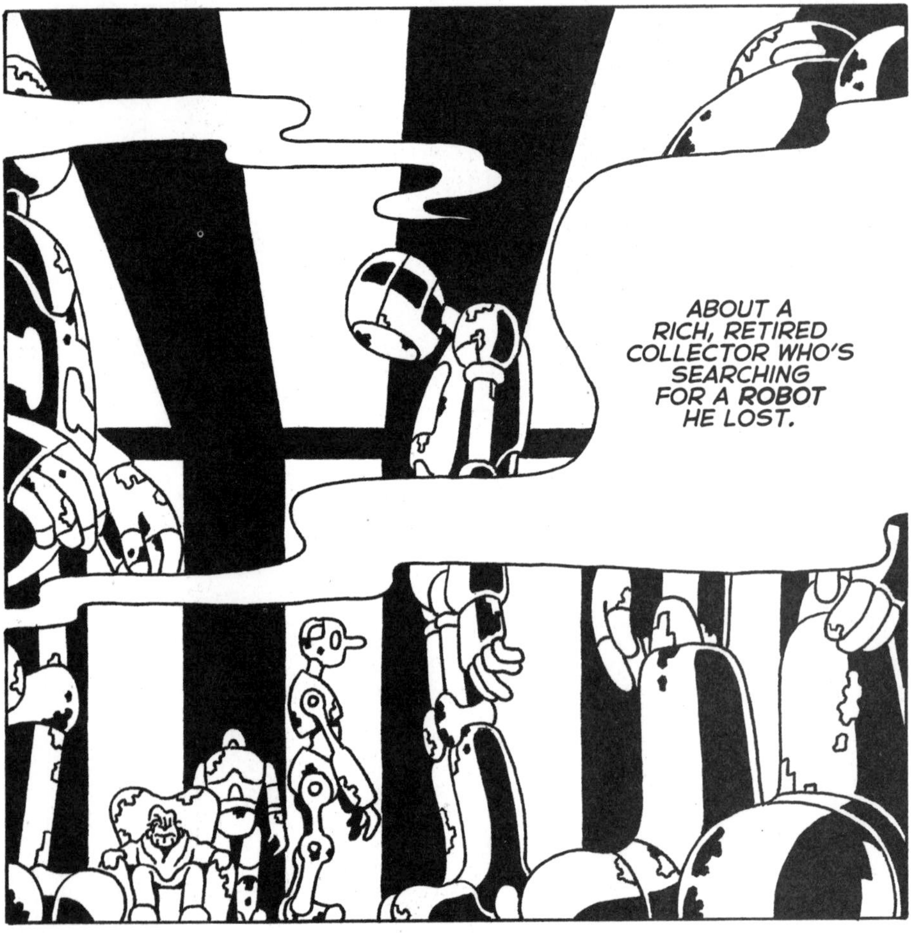
ABOUT A RICH, RETIRED COLLECTOR WHO'S SEARCHING FOR A **ROBOT** HE LOST.

#1/END

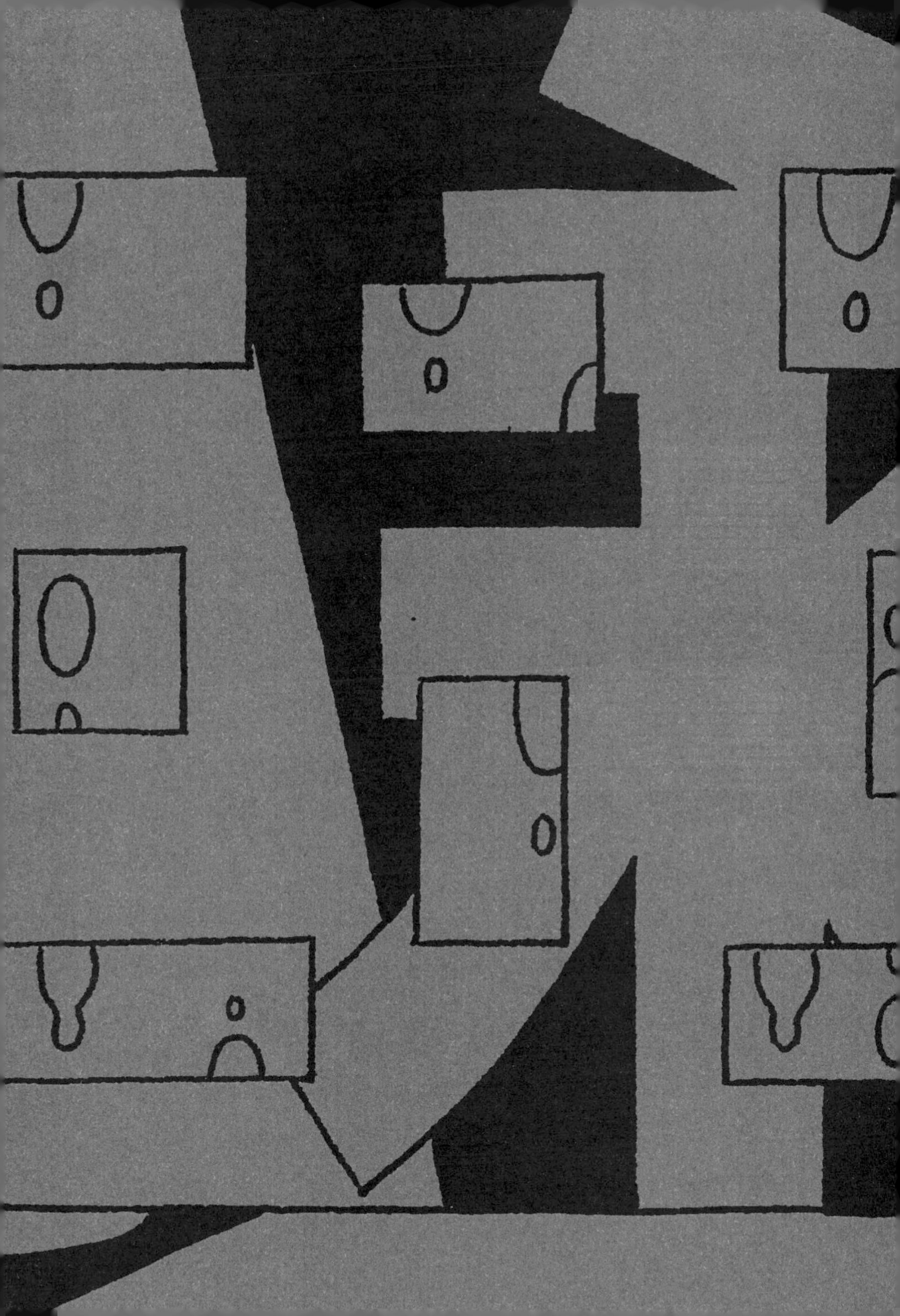

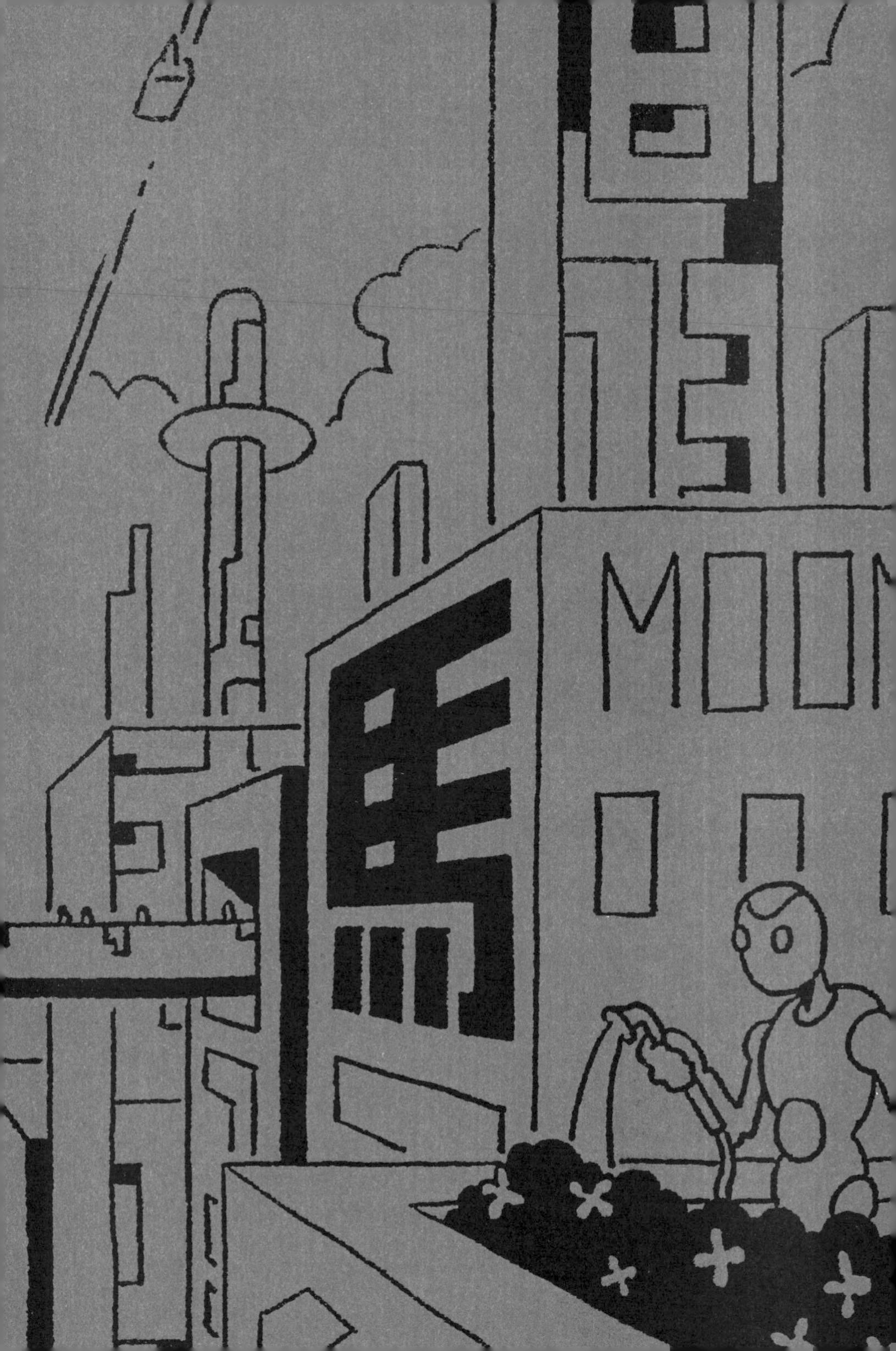
MOO

#2

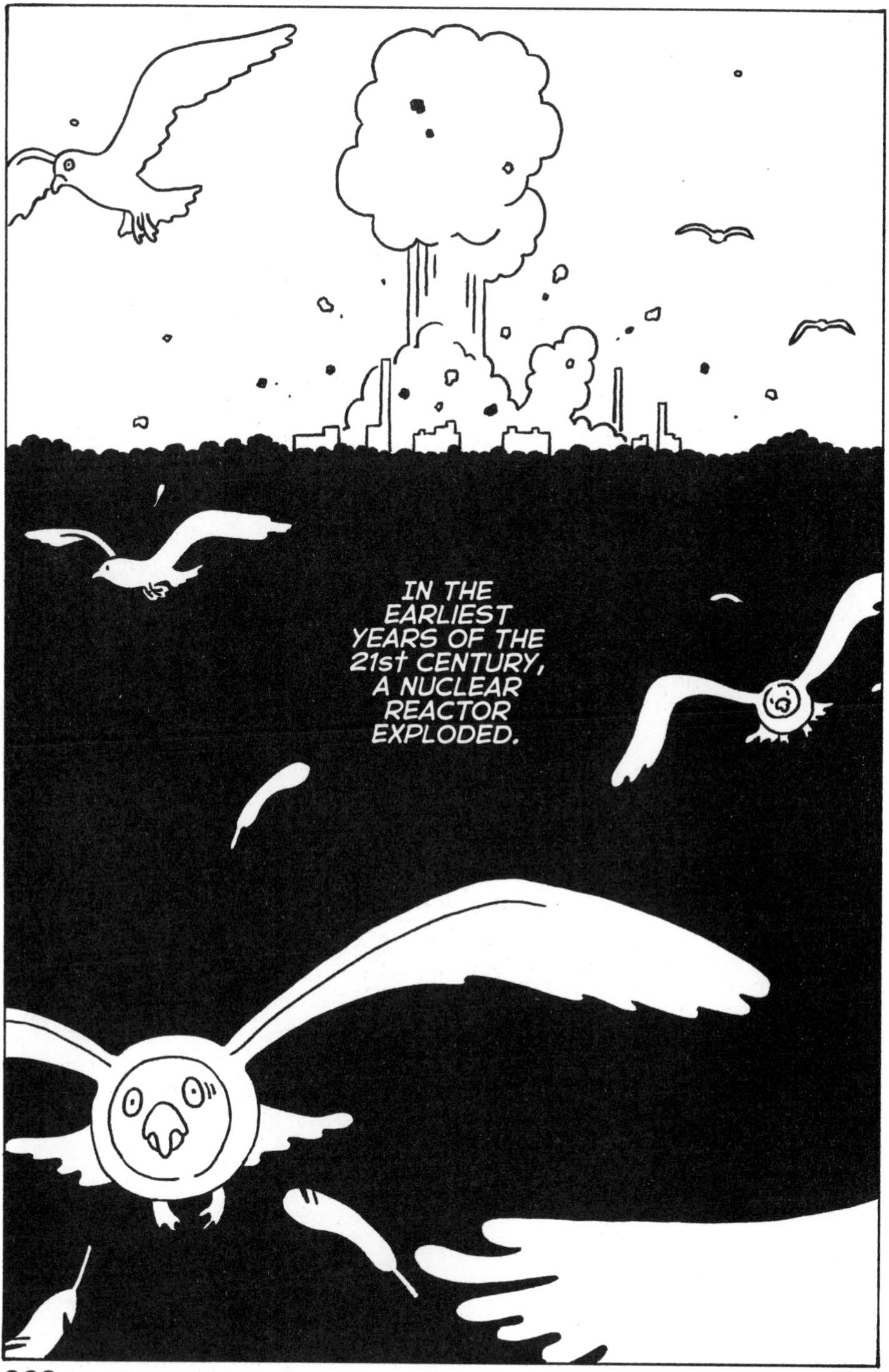
IN THE EARLIEST YEARS OF THE 21st CENTURY, A NUCLEAR REACTOR EXPLODED.

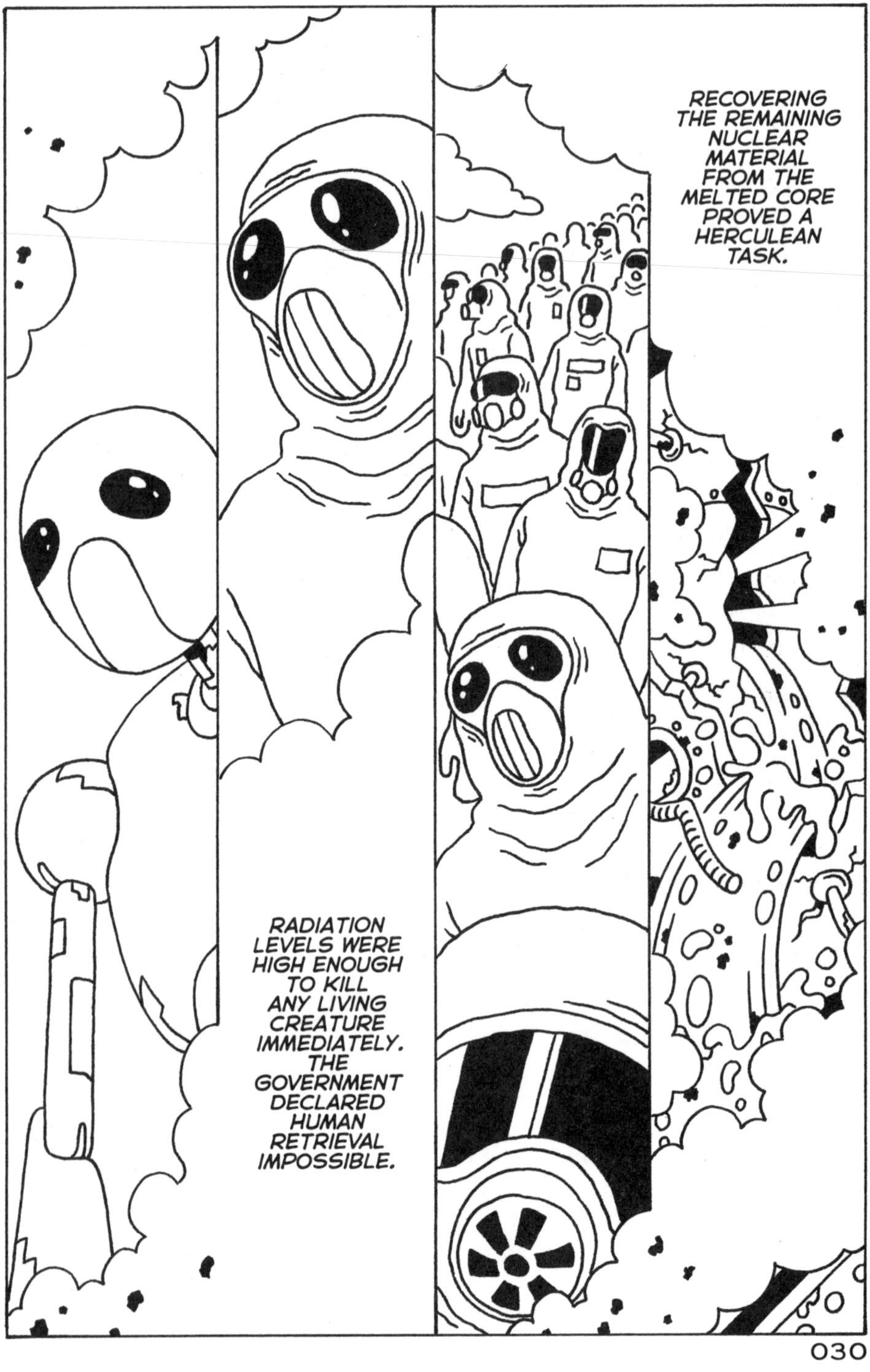
RECOVERING THE REMAINING NUCLEAR MATERIAL FROM THE MELTED CORE PROVED A HERCULEAN TASK.
RADIATION LEVELS WERE HIGH ENOUGH TO KILL ANY LIVING CREATURE IMMEDIATELY. THE GOVERNMENT DECLARED HUMAN RETRIEVAL IMPOSSIBLE.

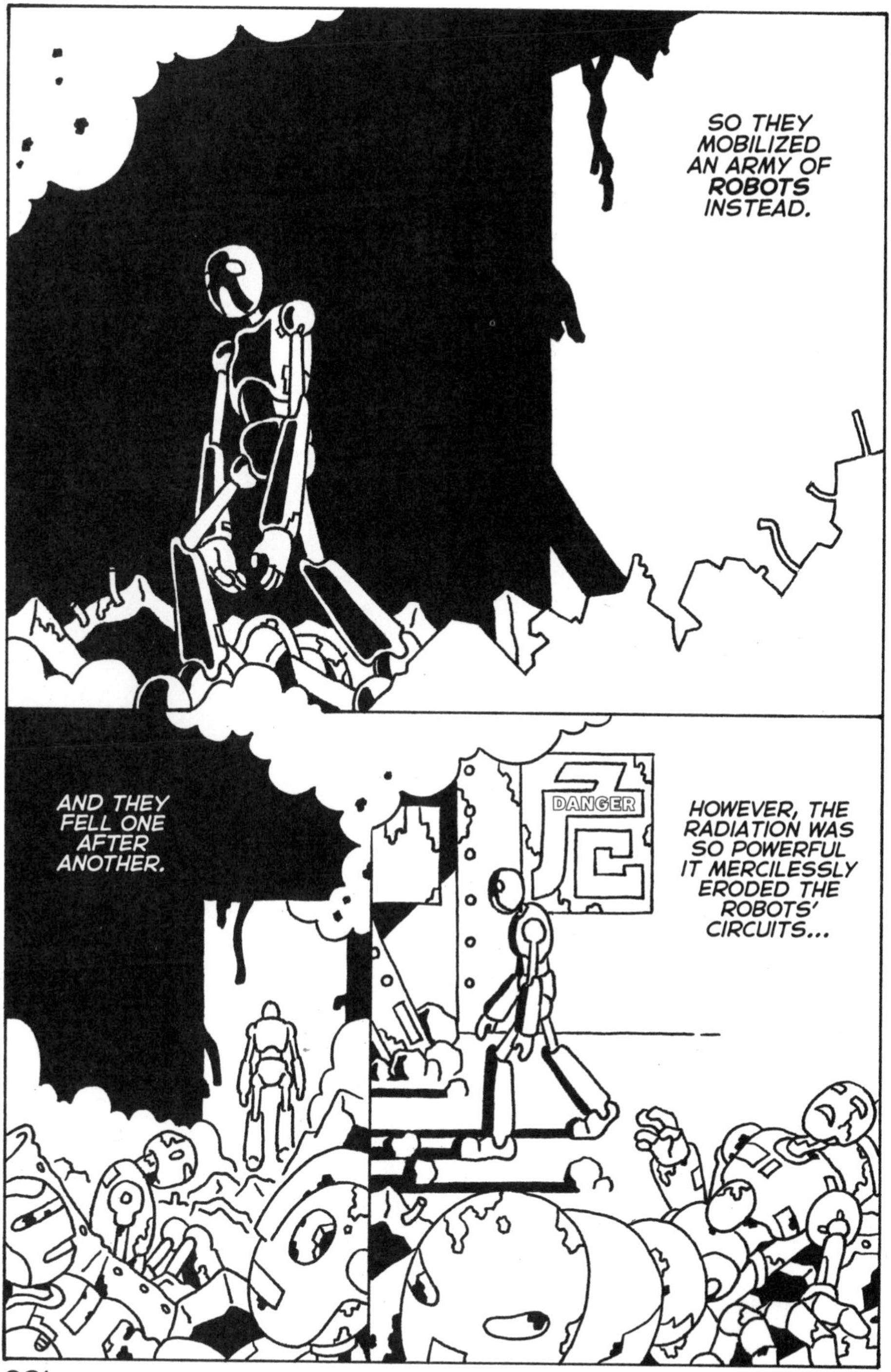
SO THEY MOBILIZED AN ARMY OF **ROBOTS** INSTEAD.
HOWEVER, THE RADIATION WAS SO POWERFUL IT MERCILESSLY ERODED THE ROBOTS' CIRCUITS...
DANGER
AND THEY FELL ONE AFTER ANOTHER.

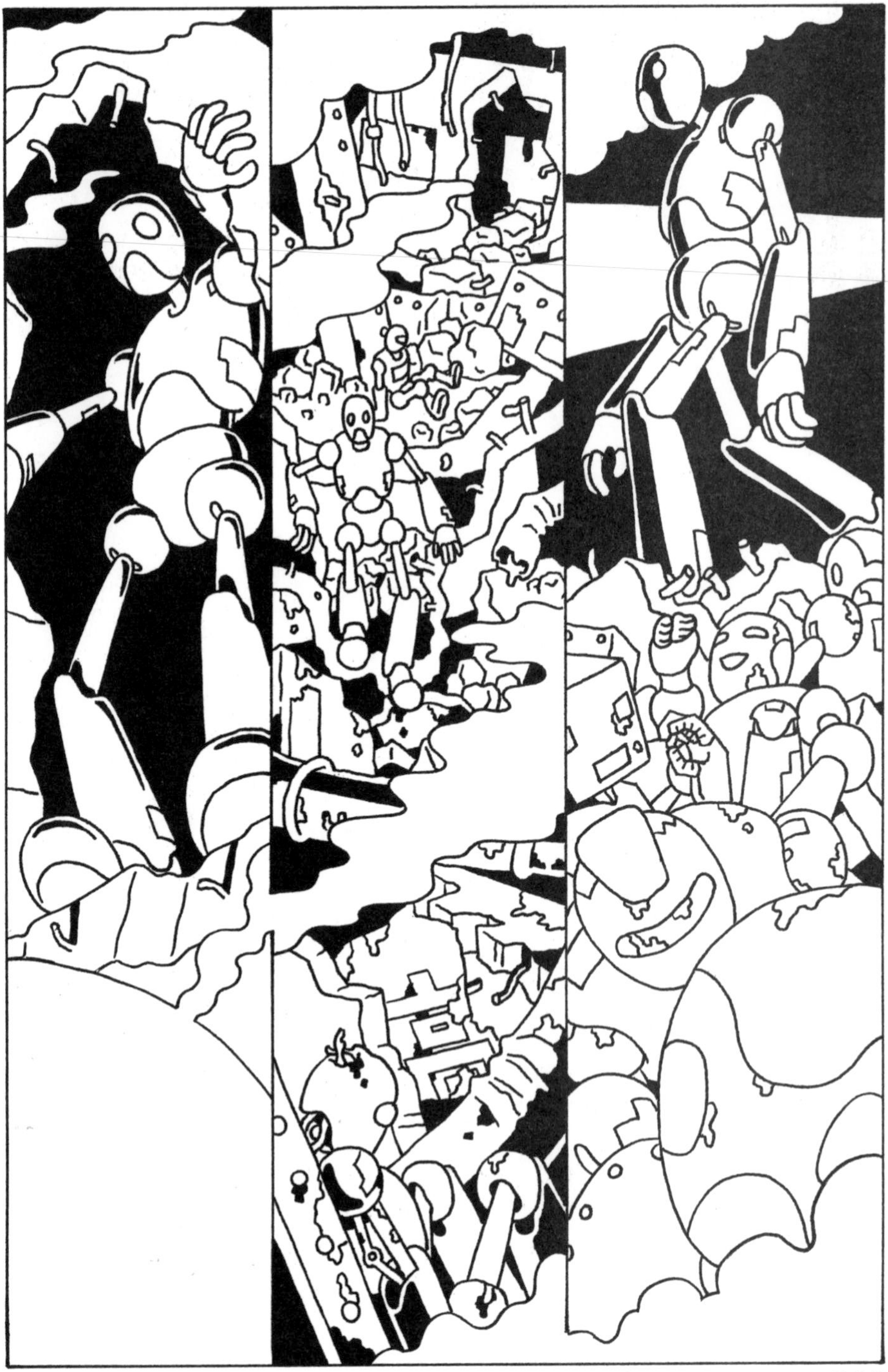

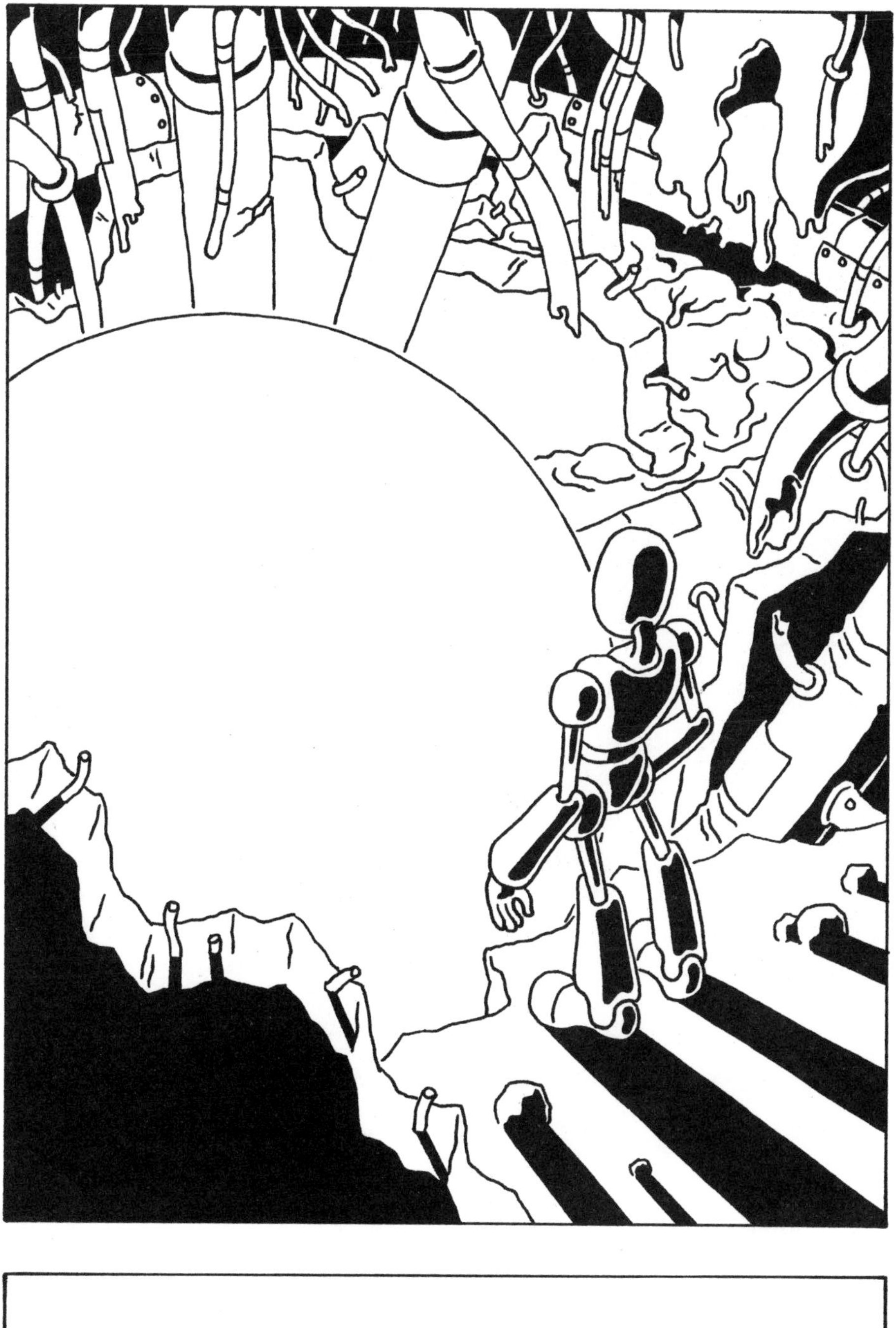

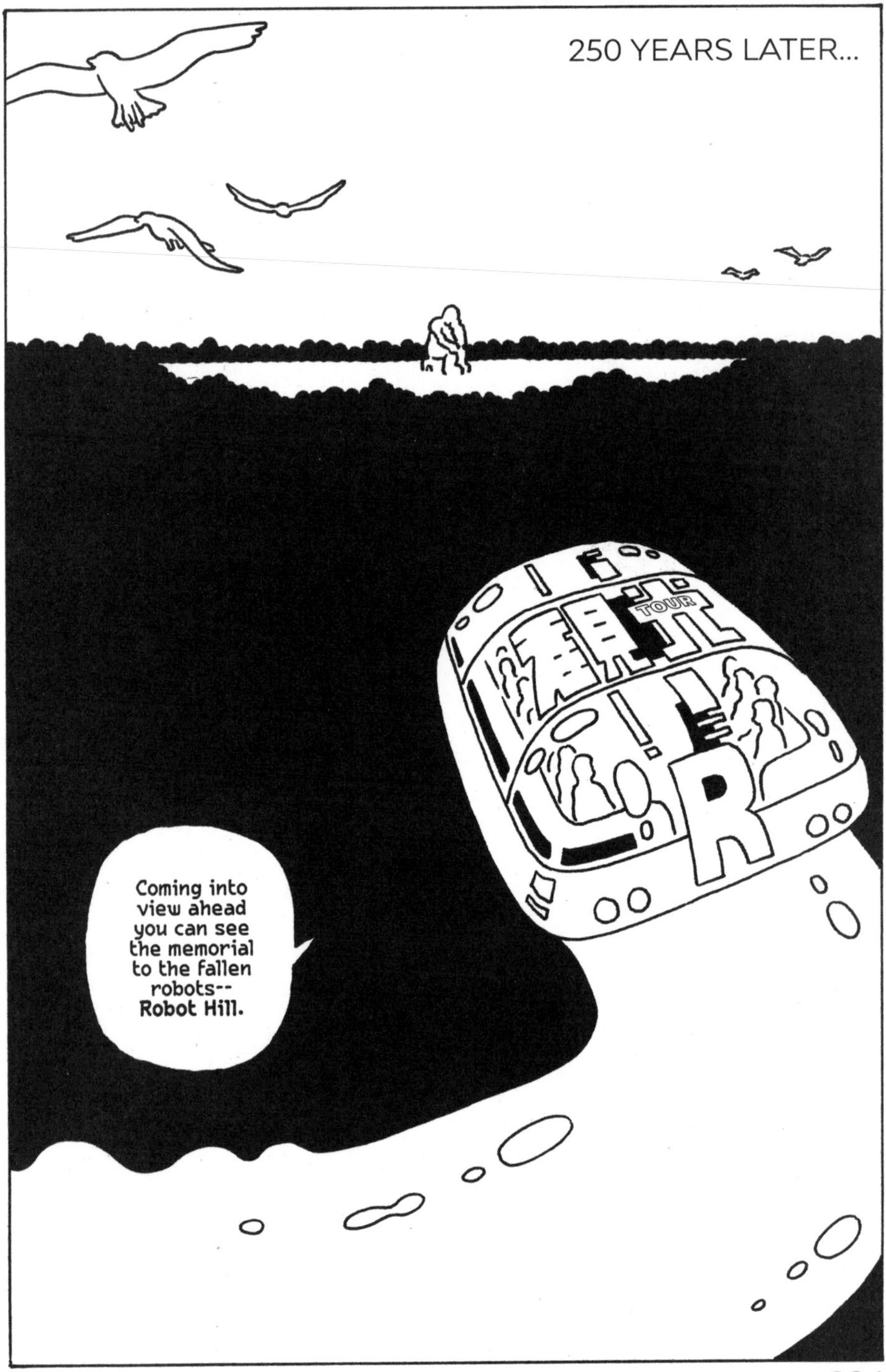
250 YEARS LATER...
TOUR
R
Coming into view ahead you can see the memorial to the fallen robots-- Robot Hill.

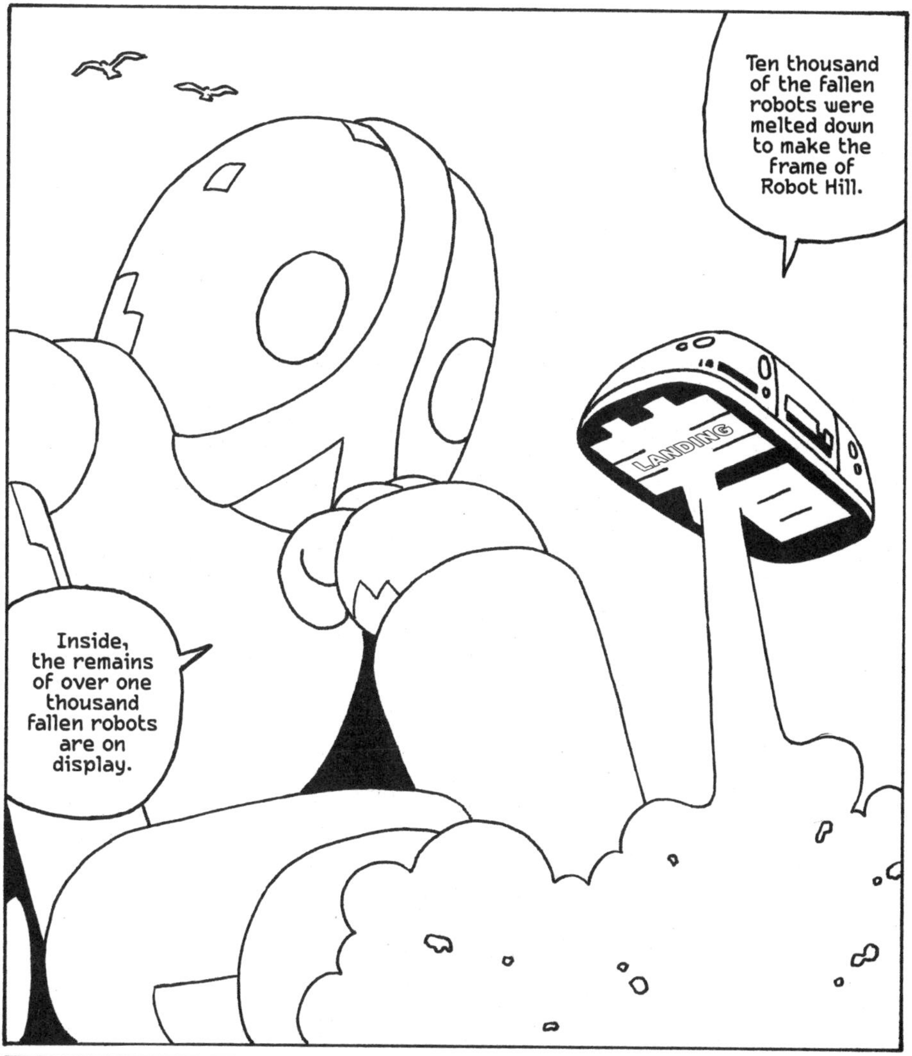
Ten thousand of the fallen robots were melted down to make the frame of Robot Hill.
LANDING
Inside, the remains of over one thousand fallen robots are on display.

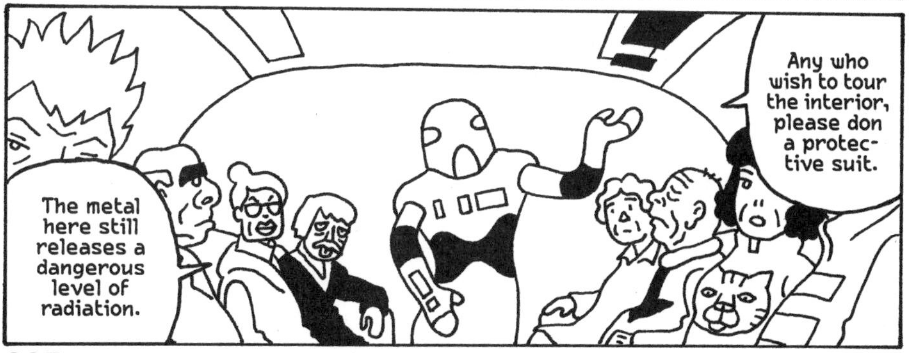
Any who wish to tour the interior, please don a protec-tive suit.
The metal here still releases a dangerous level of radiation.

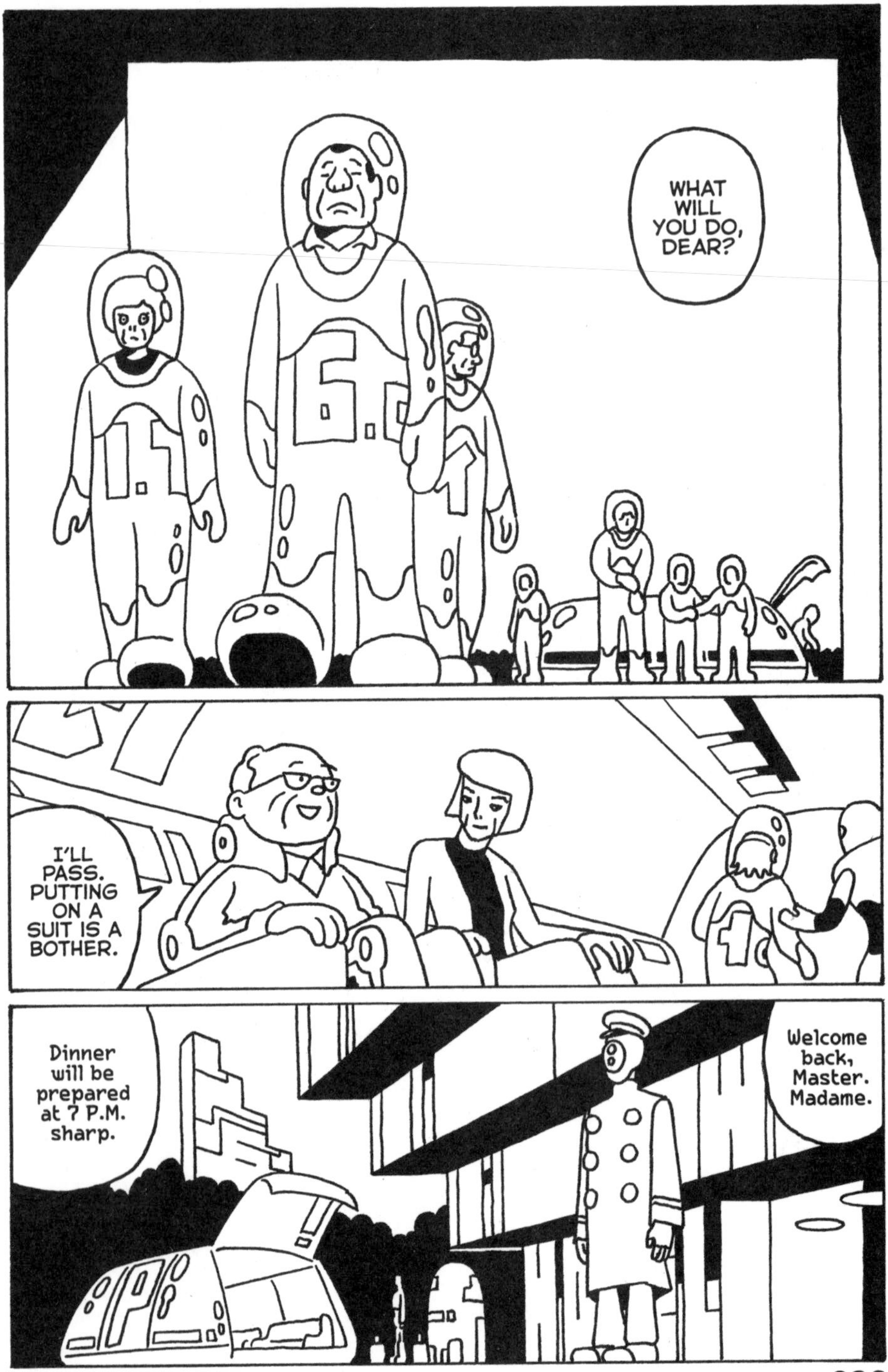
WHAT WILL YOU DO, DEAR?
I'LL PASS. PUTTING ON A SUIT IS A BOTHER.
Welcome back, Master. Madame.
Dinner will be prepared at 7 P.M. sharp.

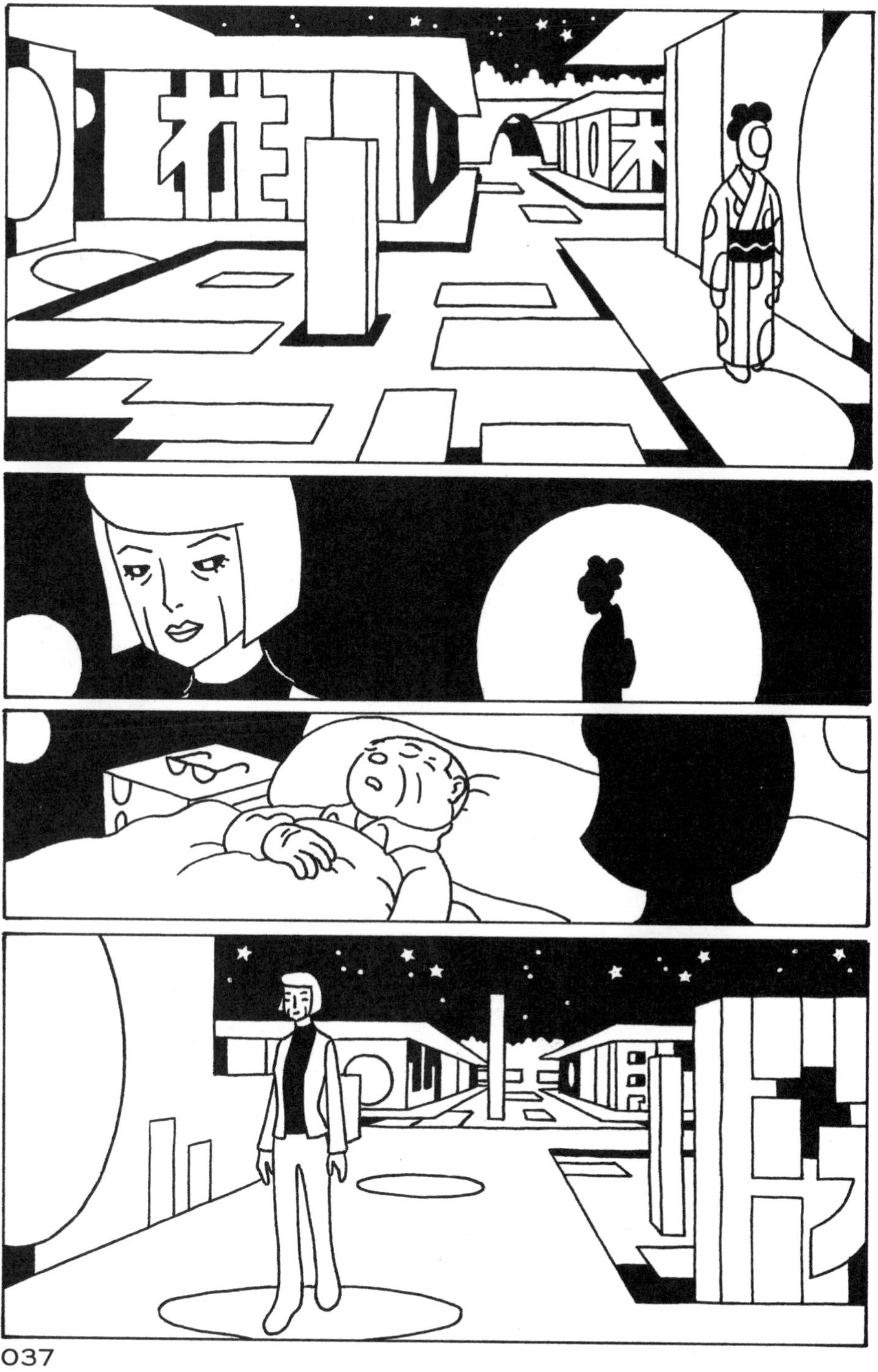

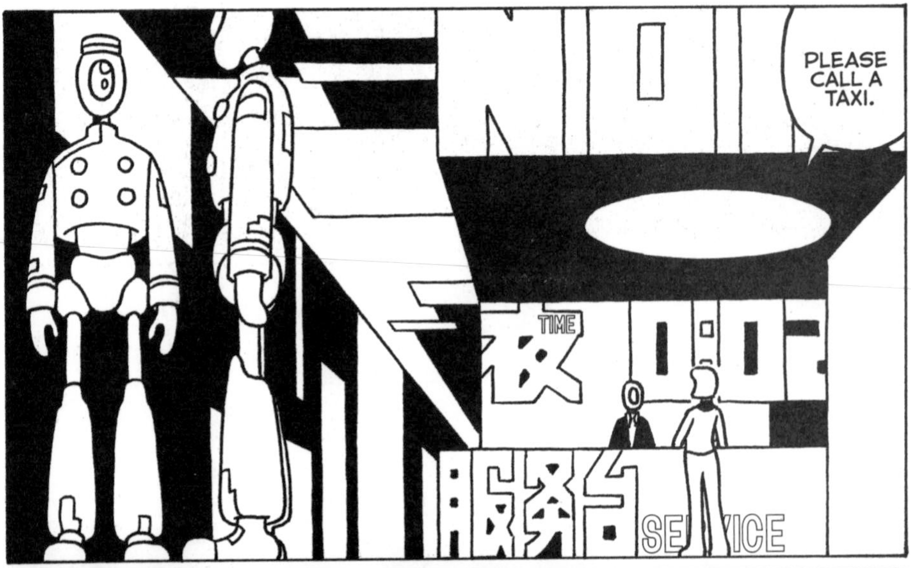
PLEASE CALL A TAXI.
TIME
夜
服务台

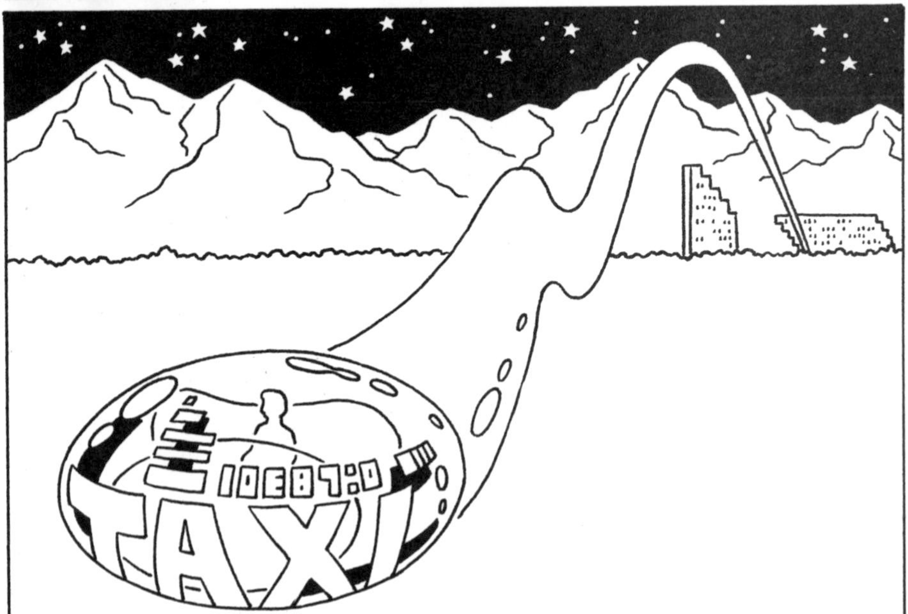
TAXI

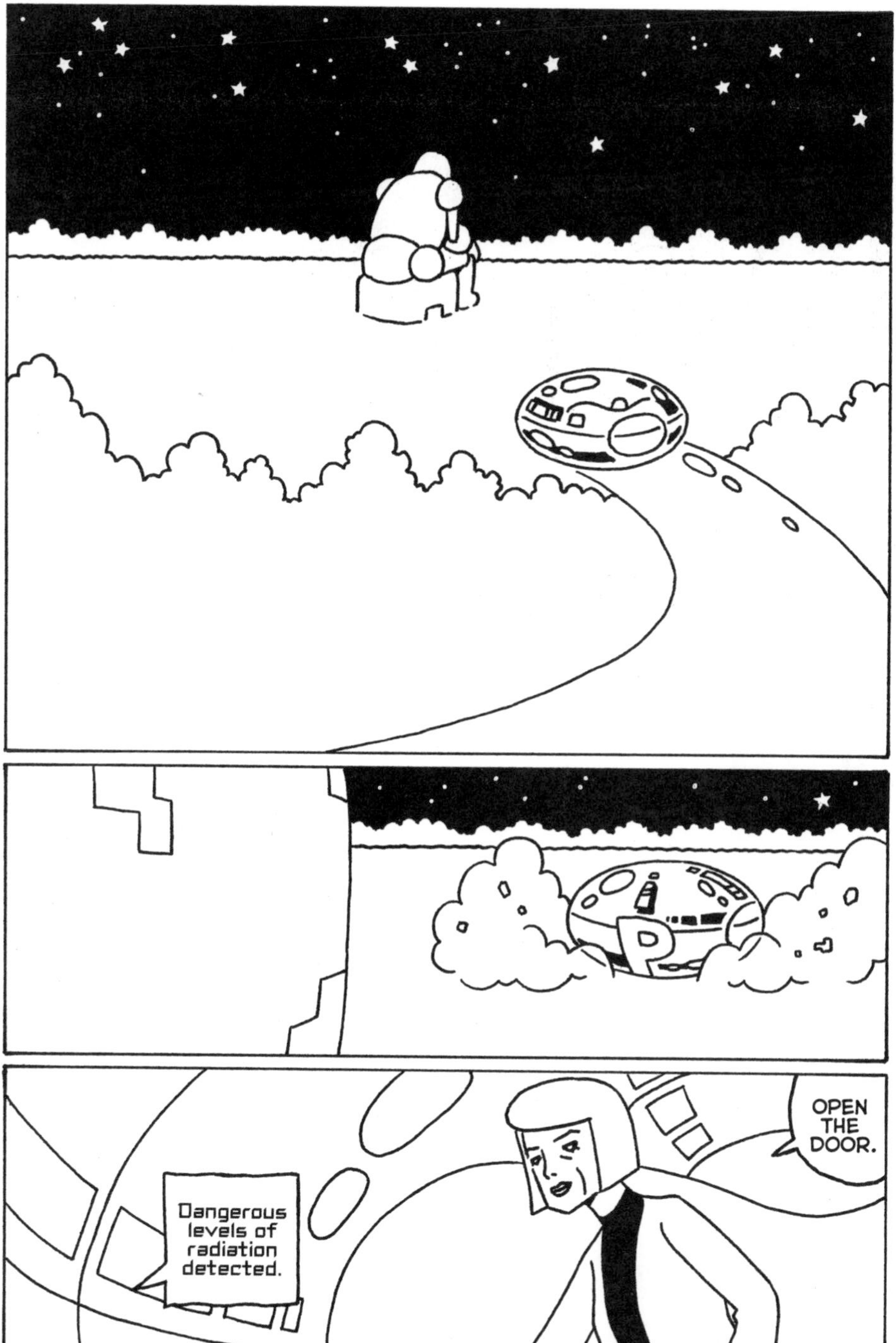
OPEN THE DOOR.
Dangerous levels of radiation detected.

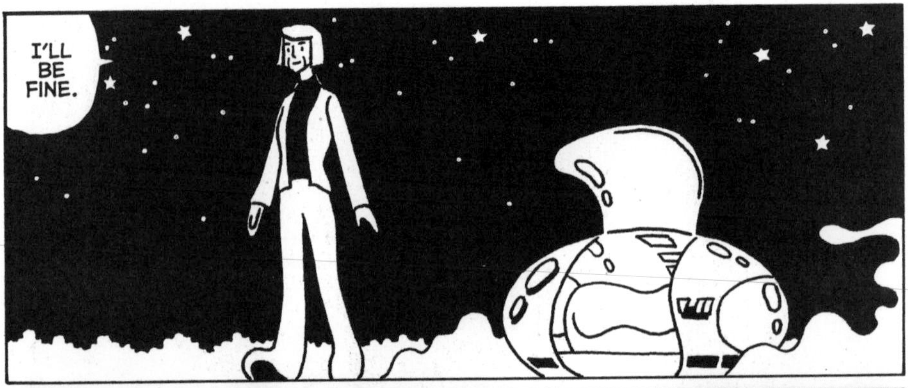
I'LL BE FINE.
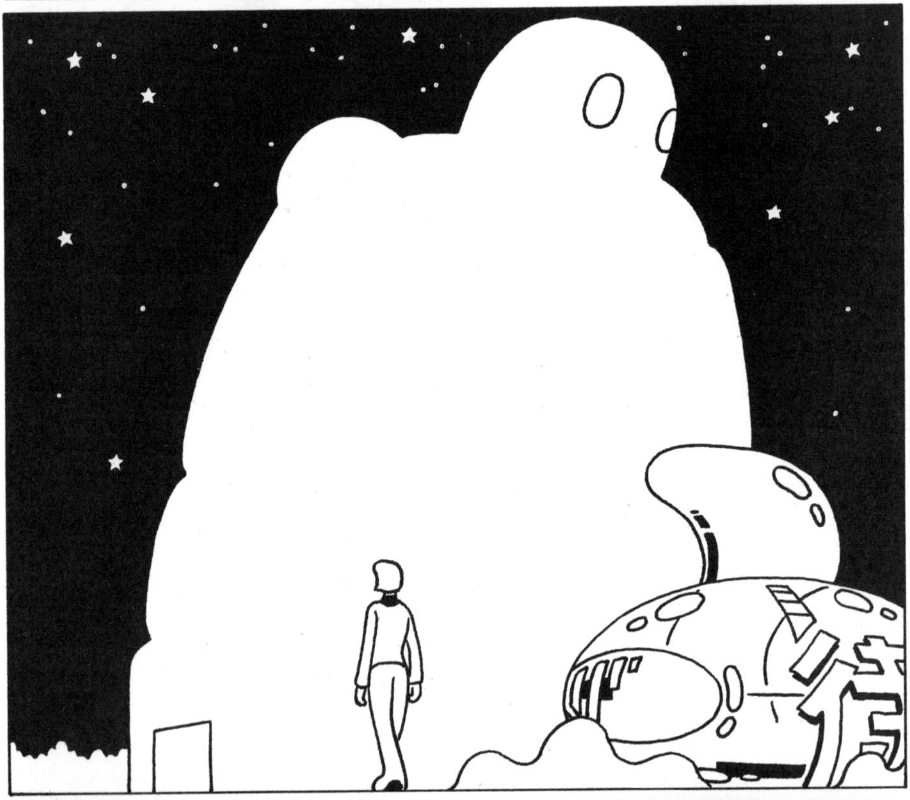
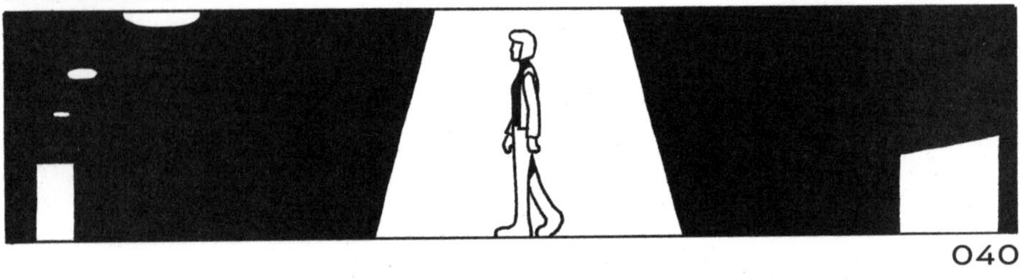

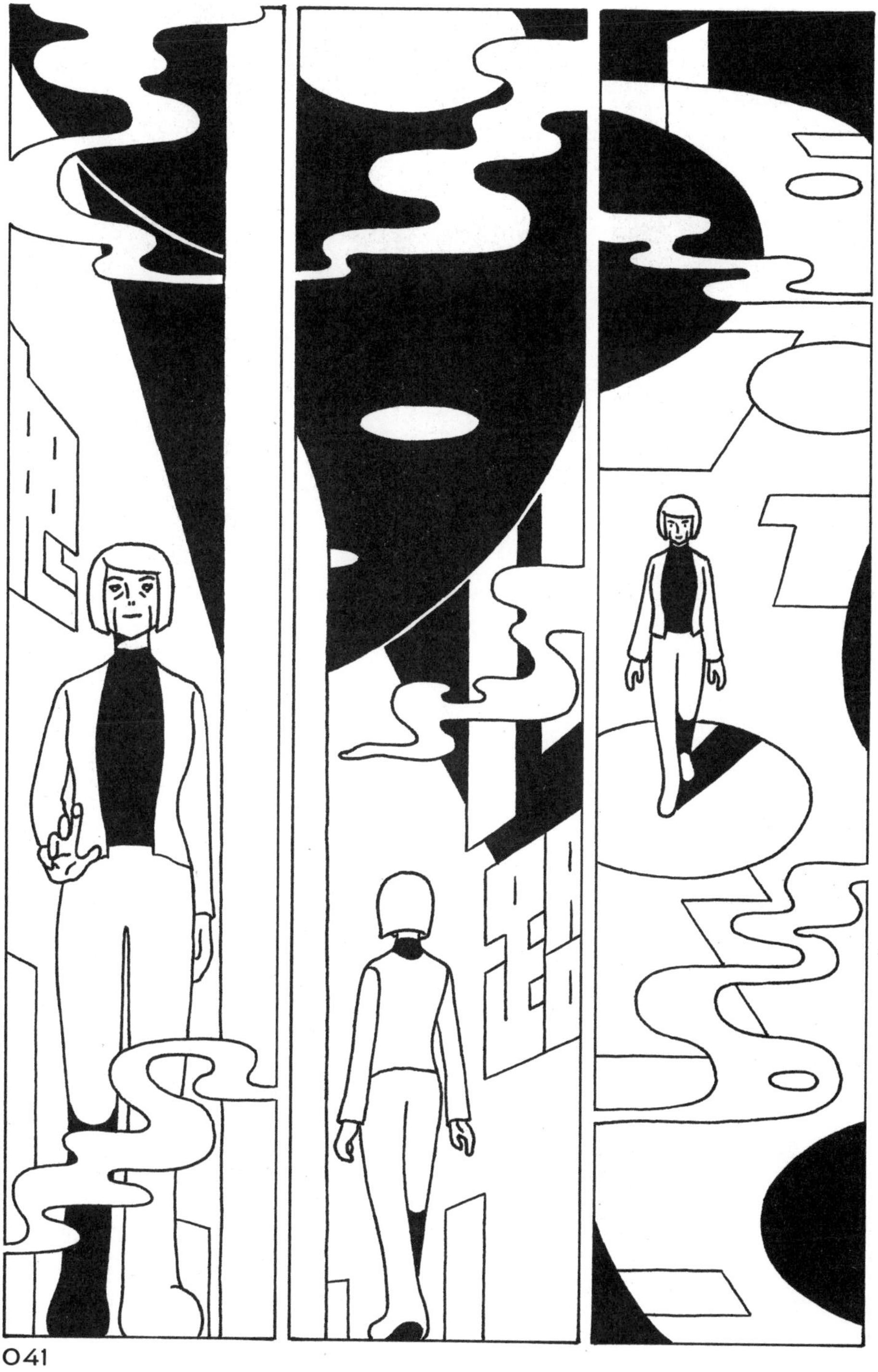

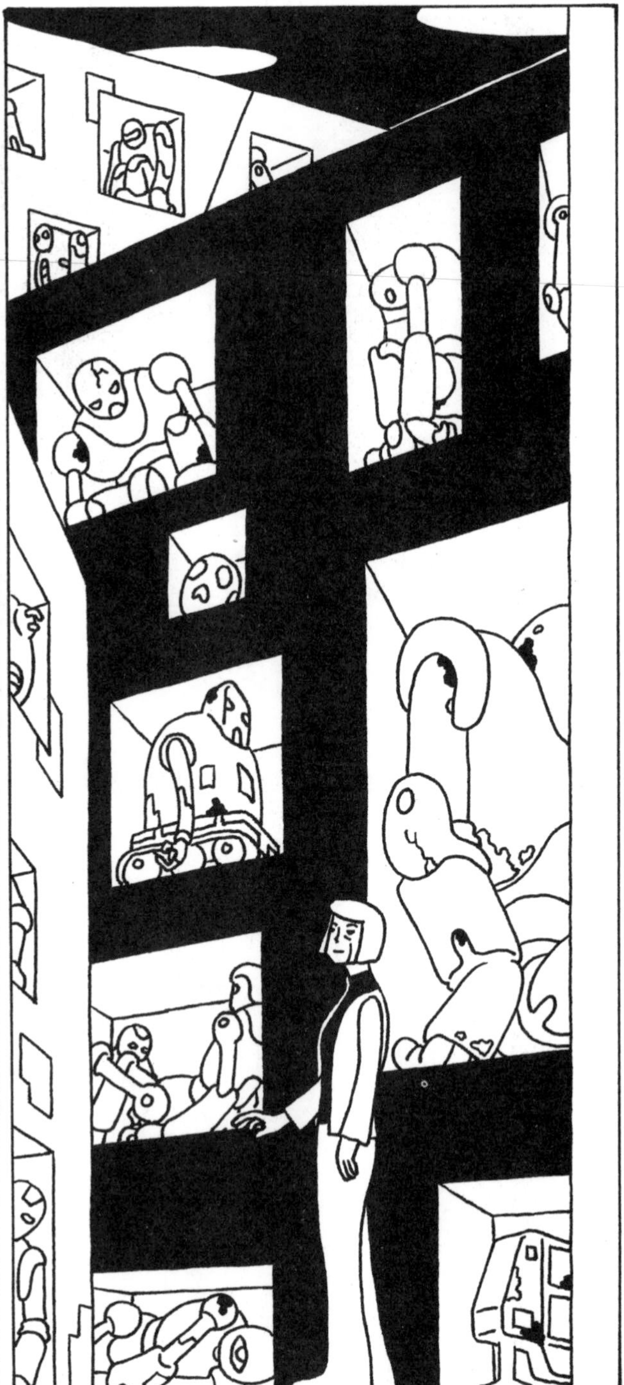

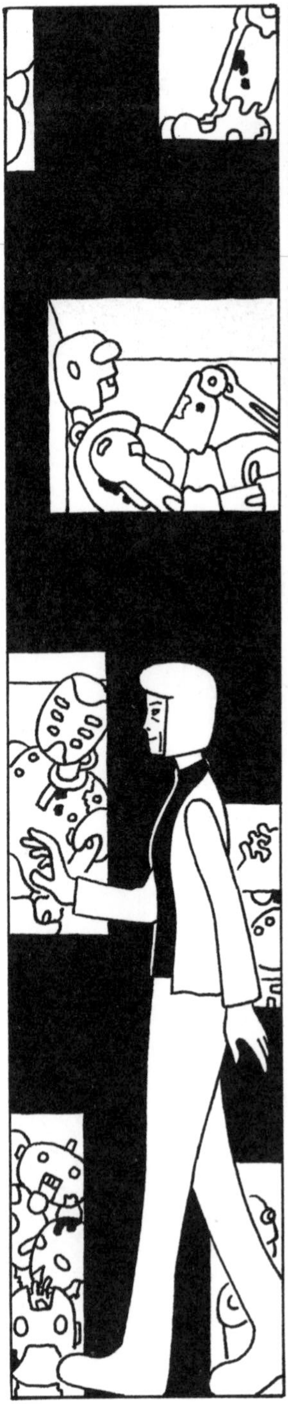

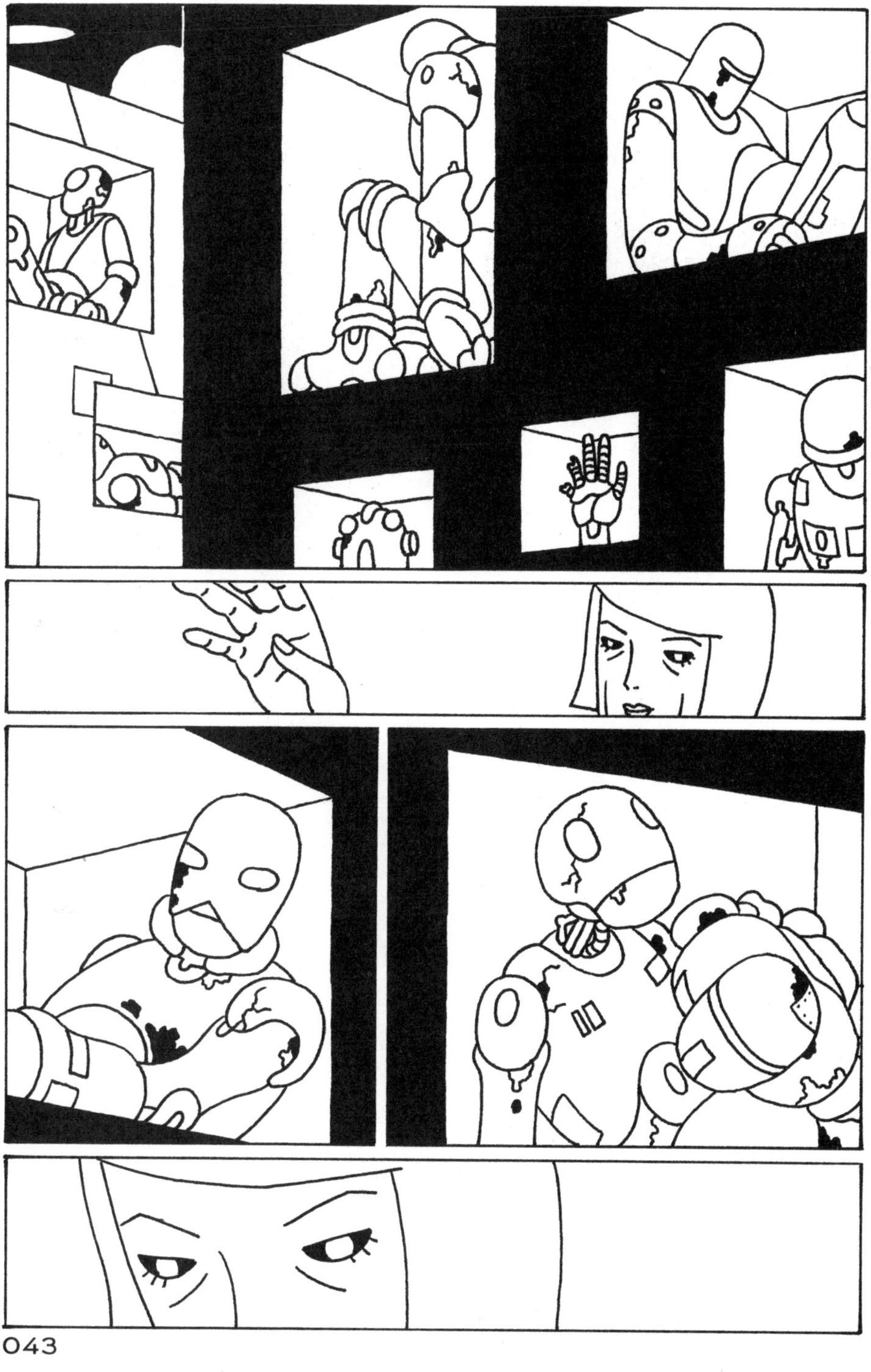

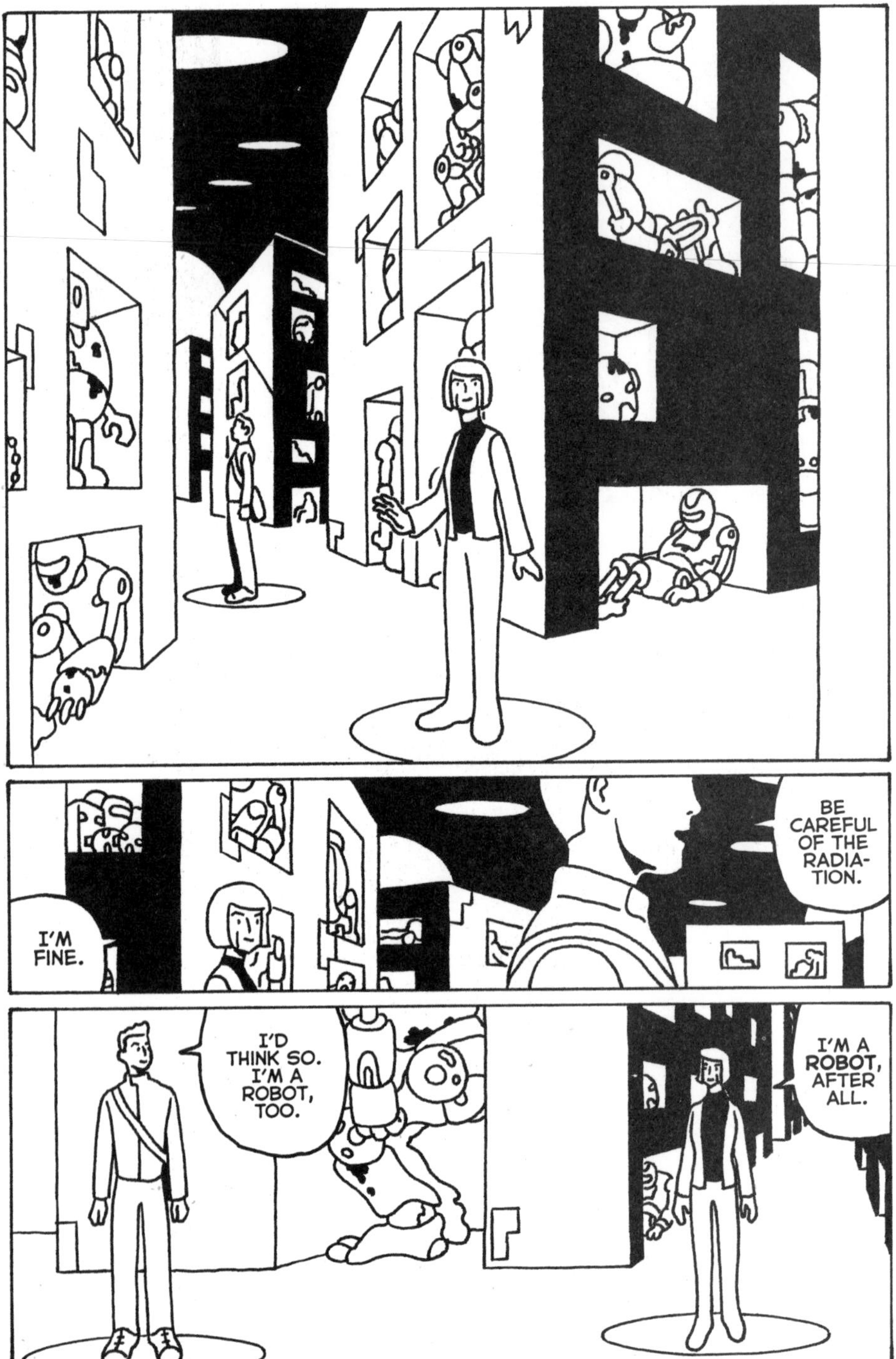
BE CAREFUL OF THE RADIA- TION.
I'M FINE.
I'M A ROBOT, AFTER ALL.
I'D THINK SO. I'M A ROBOT, TOO.

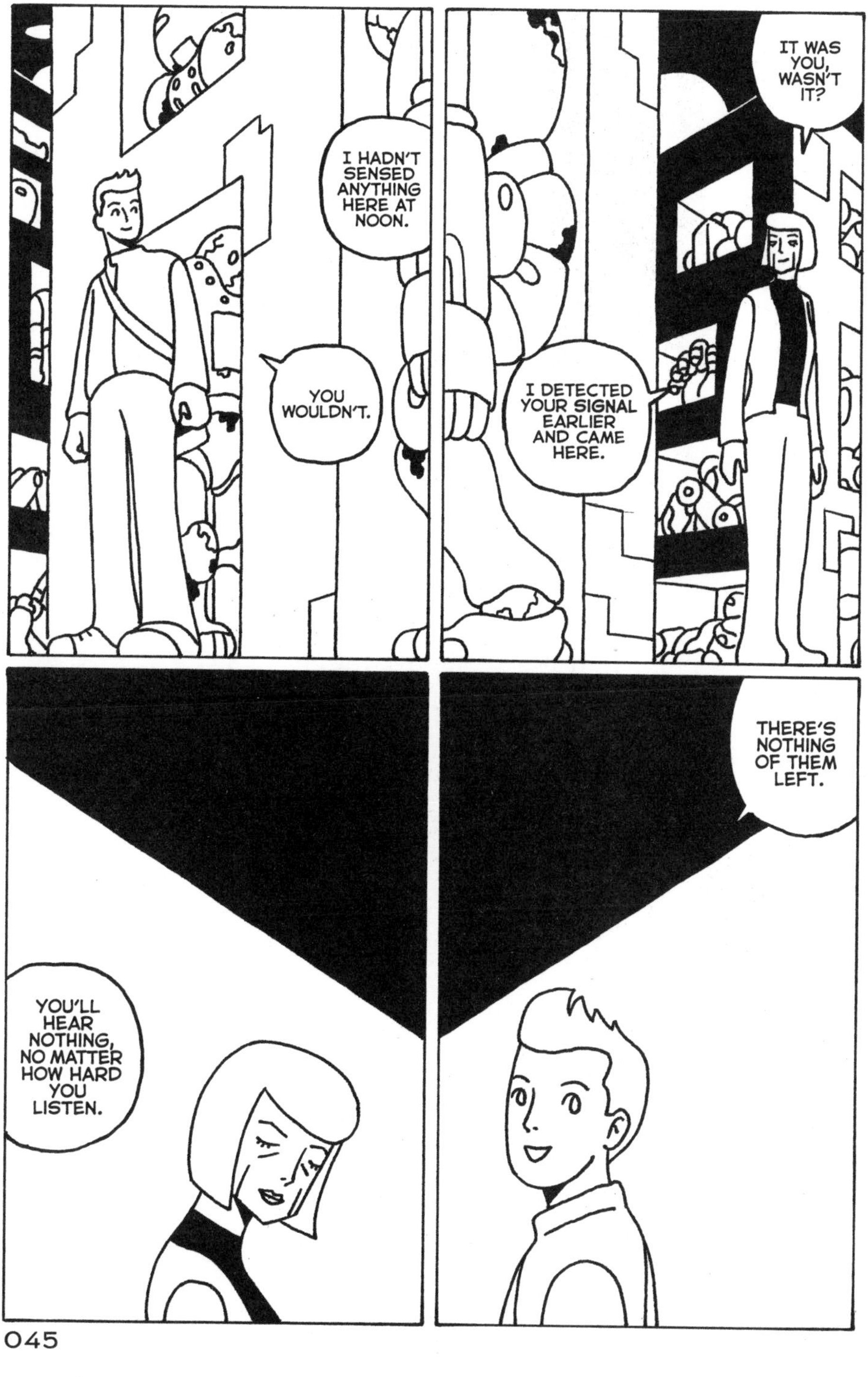
IT WAS YOU, WASN'T IT?
I DETECTED YOUR SIGNAL EARLIER AND CAME HERE.
I HADN'T SENSED ANYTHING HERE AT NOON.
YOU WOULDN'T.
THERE'S NOTHING OF THEM LEFT.
YOU'LL HEAR NOTHING, NO MATTER HOW HARD YOU LISTEN.

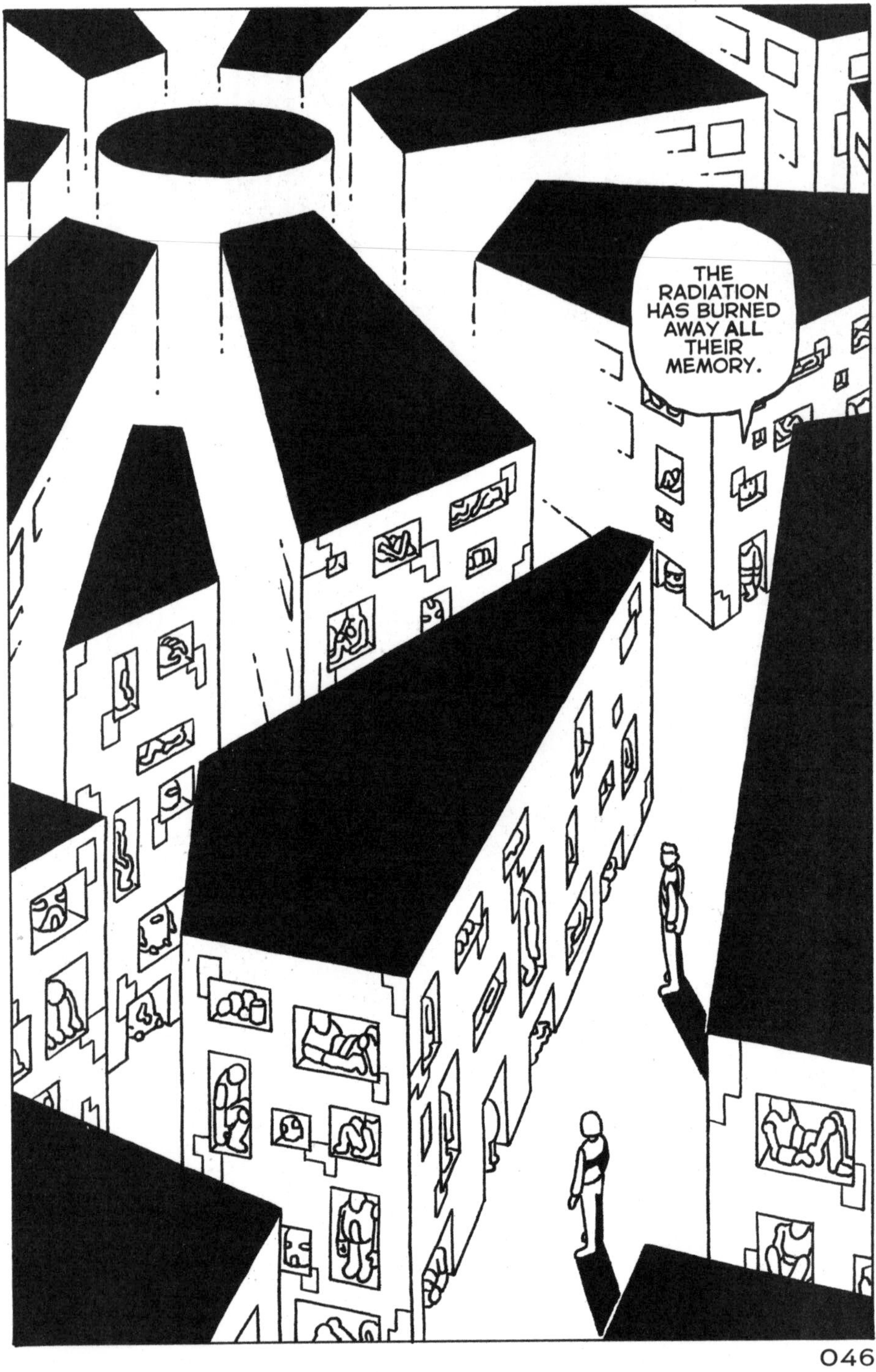
THE RADIATION HAS BURNED AWAY ALL THEIR MEMORY.

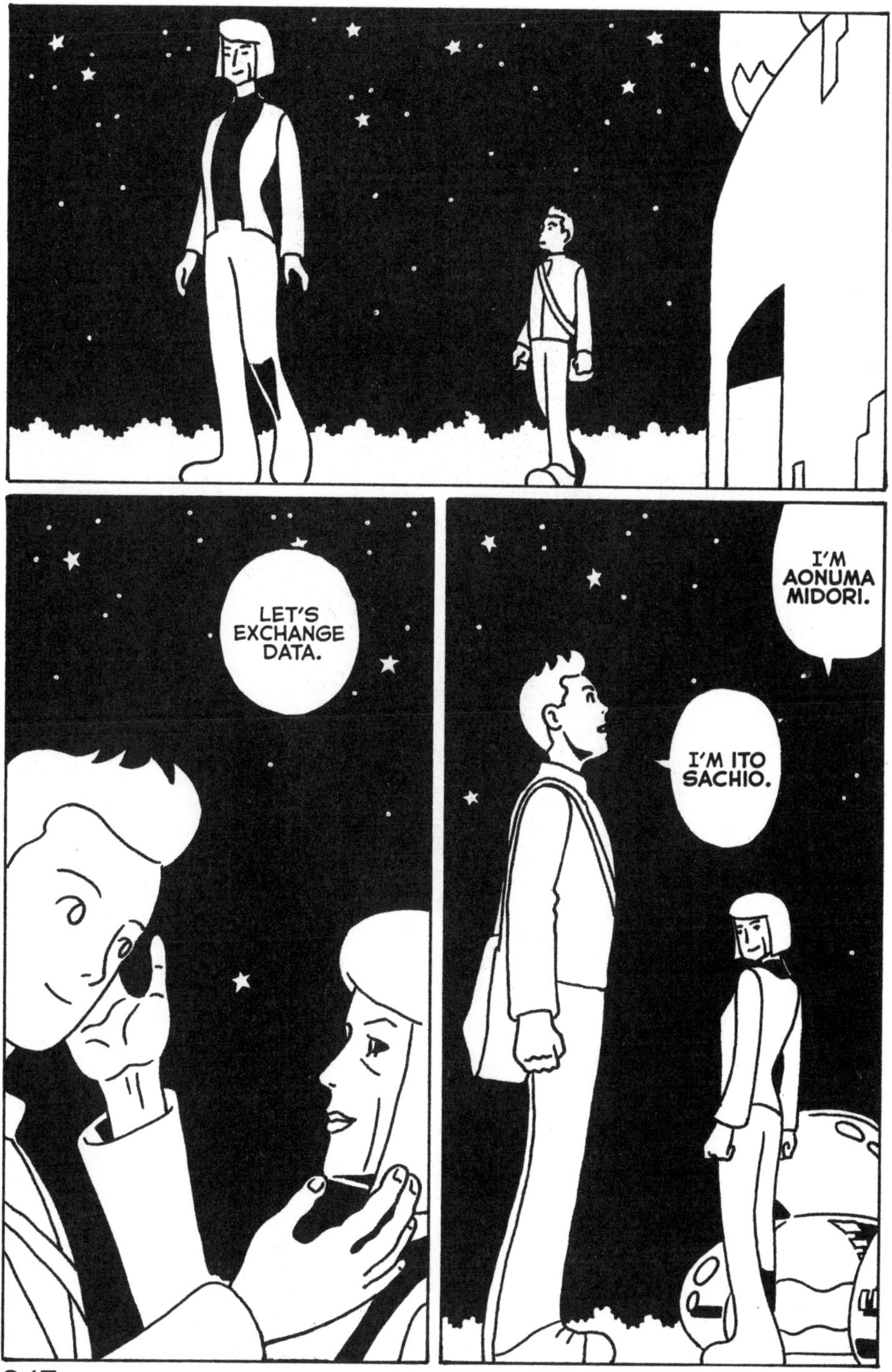
I'M AONUMA MIDORI.
I'M ITO SACHIO.
LET'S EXCHANGE DATA.

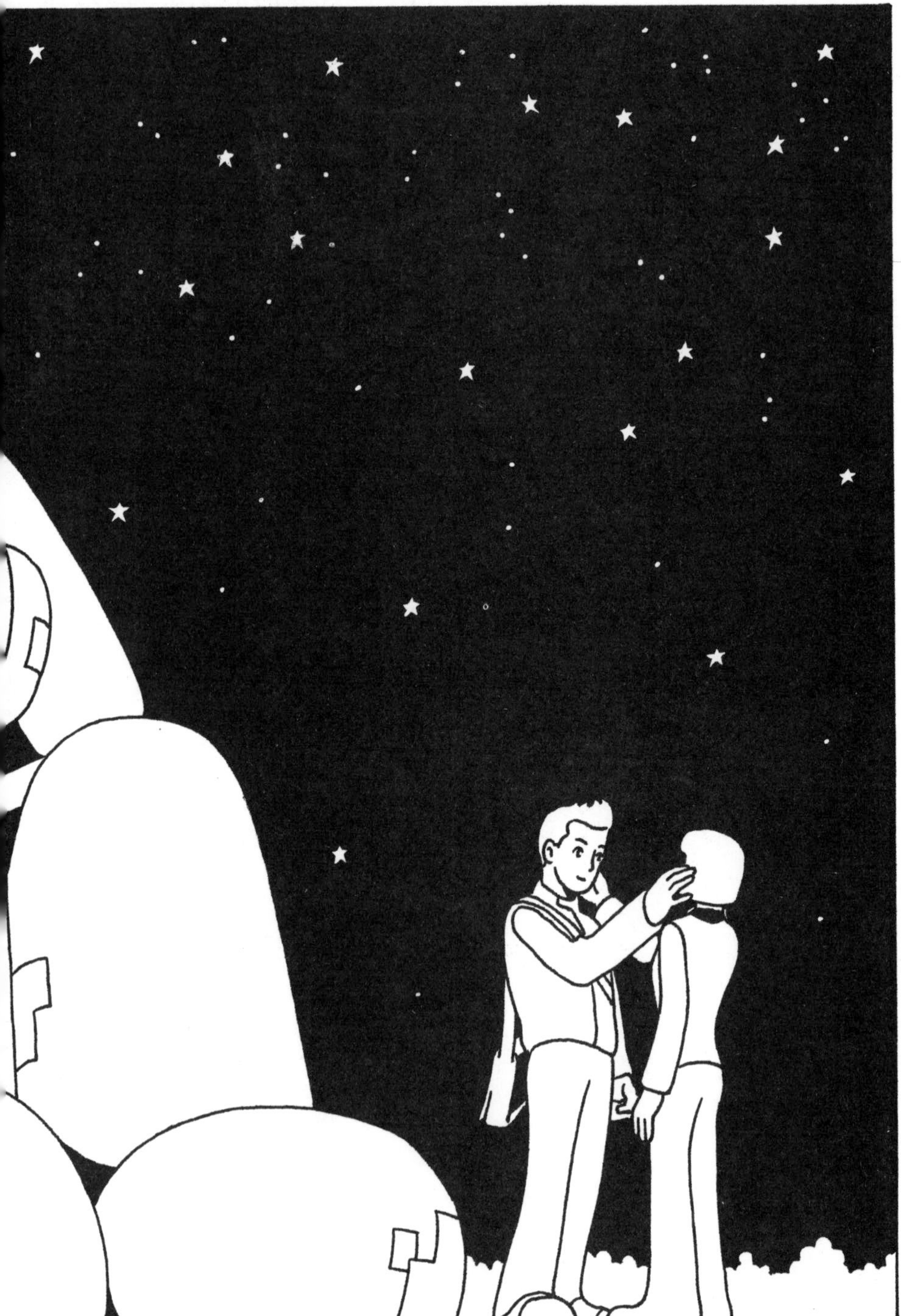

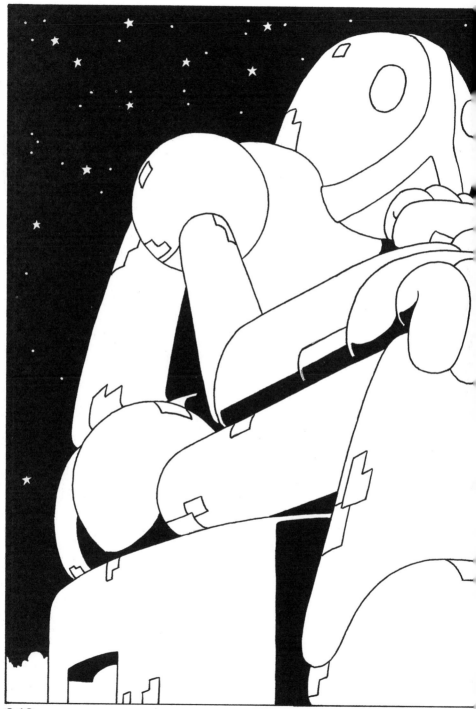

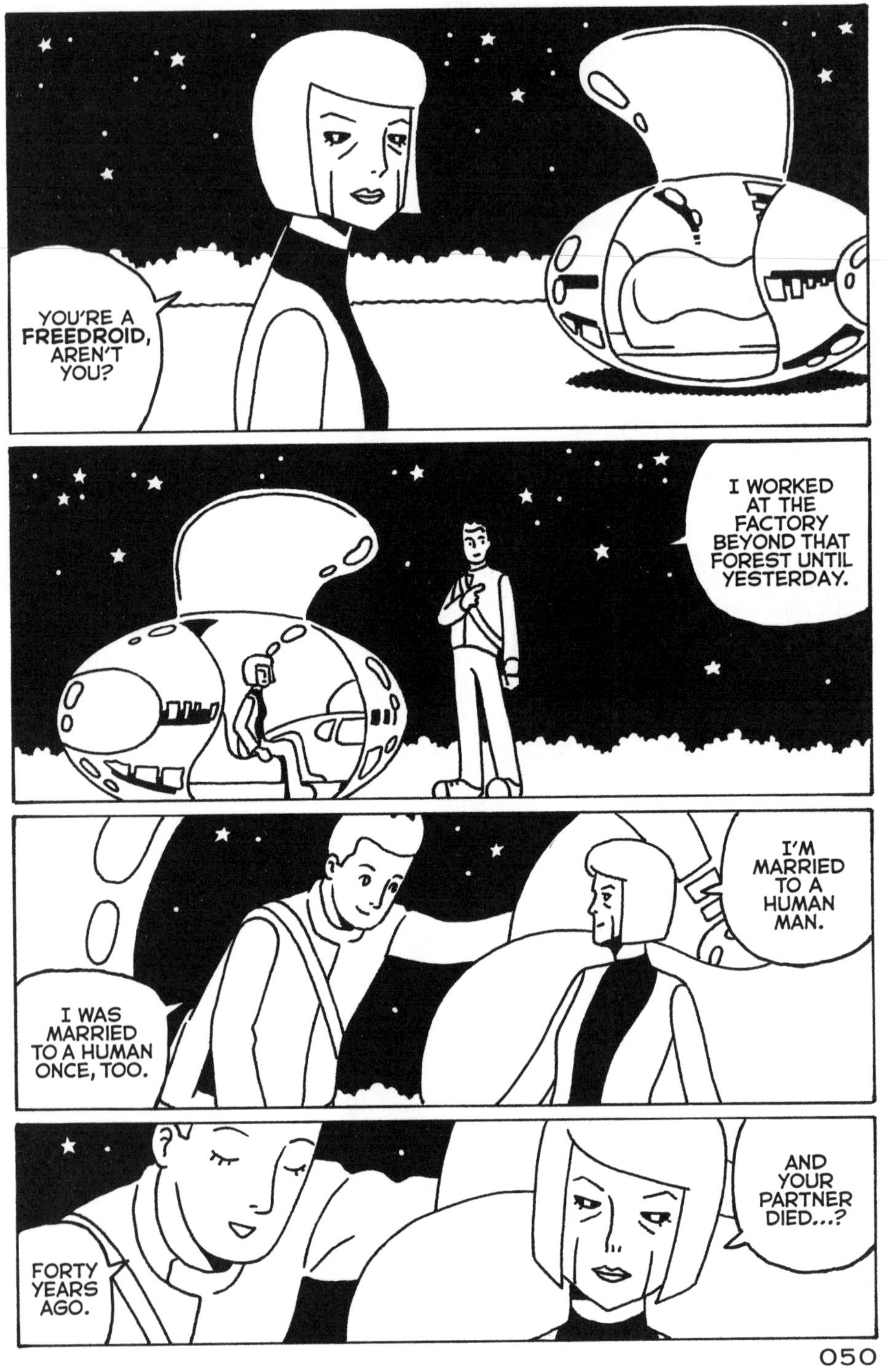
YOU'RE A **FREEDROID**, AREN'T YOU?
I WORKED AT THE FACTORY BEYOND THAT FOREST UNTIL YESTERDAY.
I'M MARRIED TO A HUMAN MAN.
I WAS MARRIED TO A HUMAN ONCE, TOO.
AND YOUR PARTNER DIED...?
FORTY YEARS AGO.

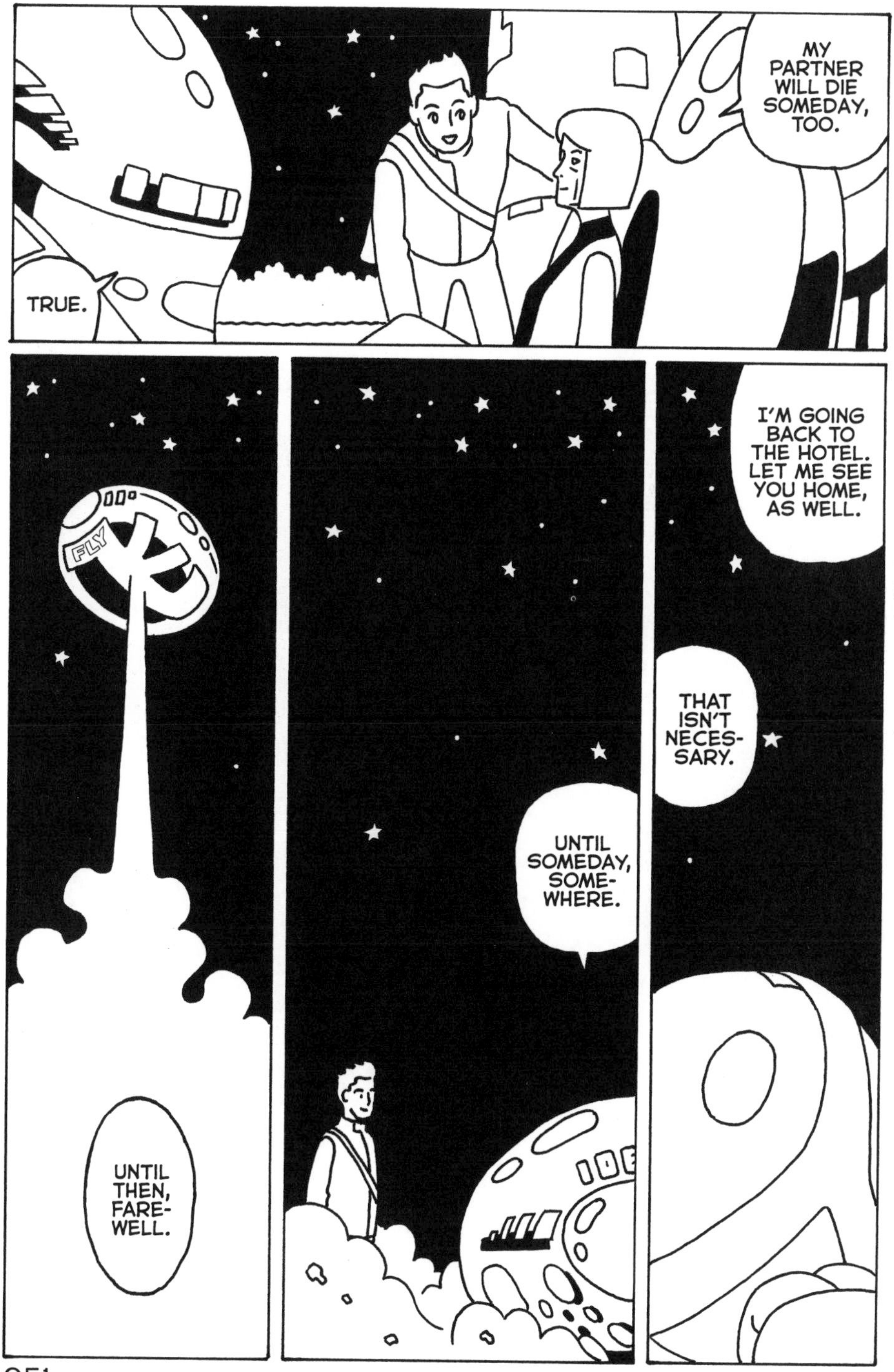
MY PARTNER WILL DIE SOMEDAY, TOO.
TRUE.
I'M GOING BACK TO THE HOTEL. LET ME SEE YOU HOME, AS WELL.
THAT ISN'T NECESSARY.
UNTIL SOMEDAY, SOMEWHERE.
UNTIL THEN, FAREWELL.

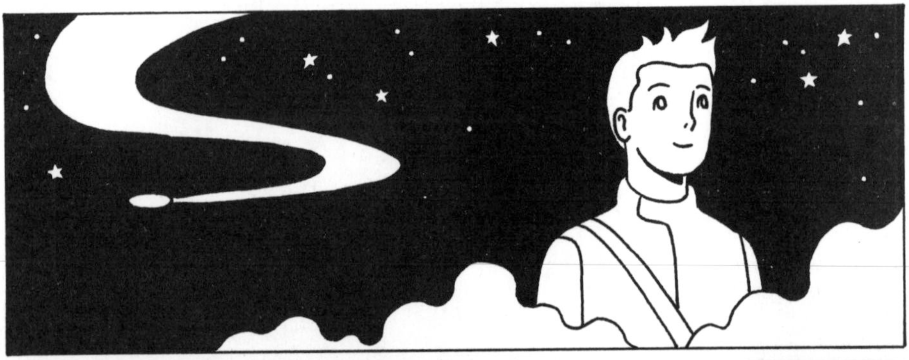

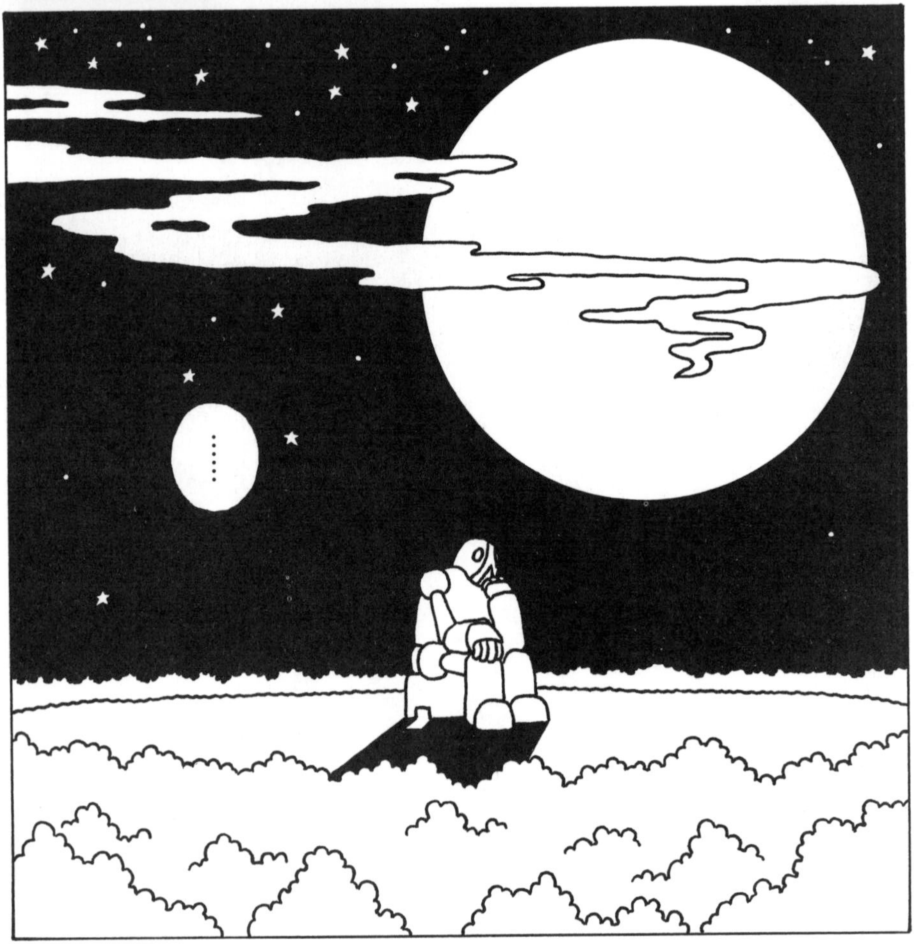
……

#2/END

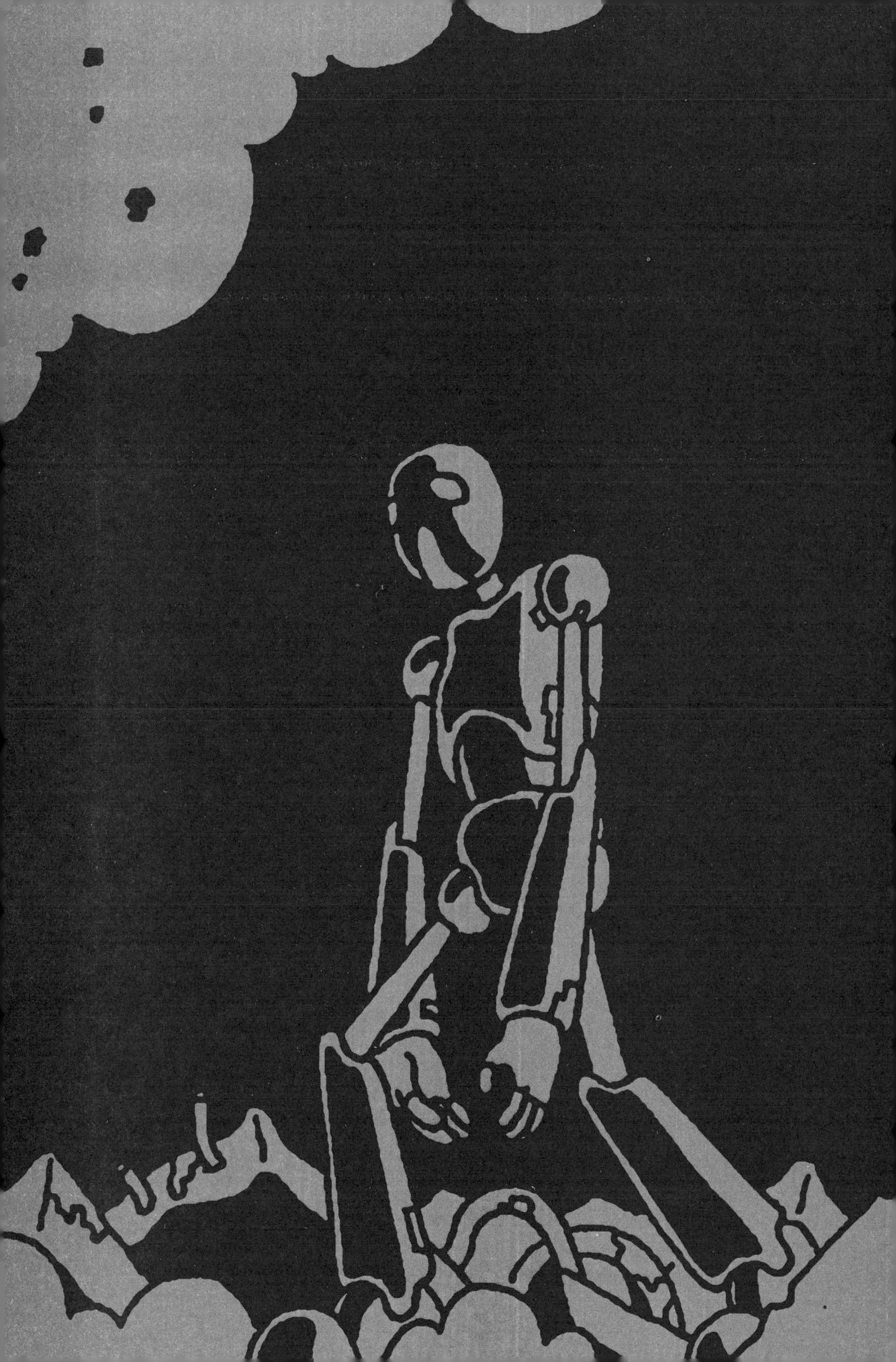

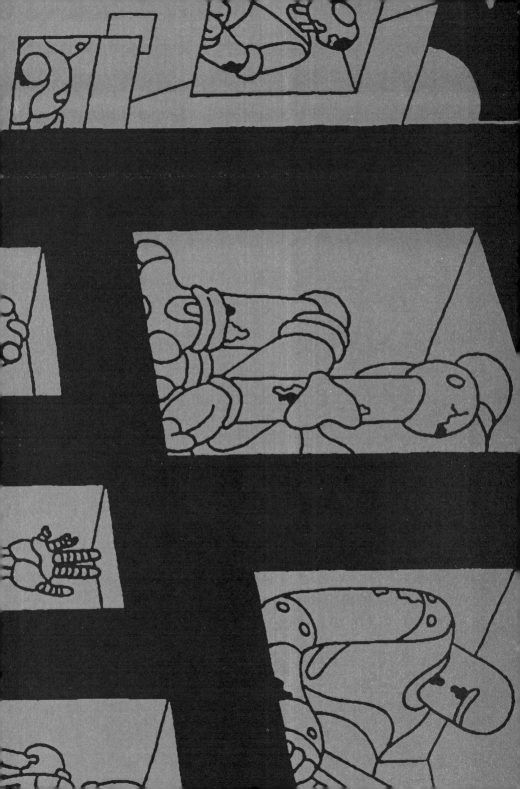

#3

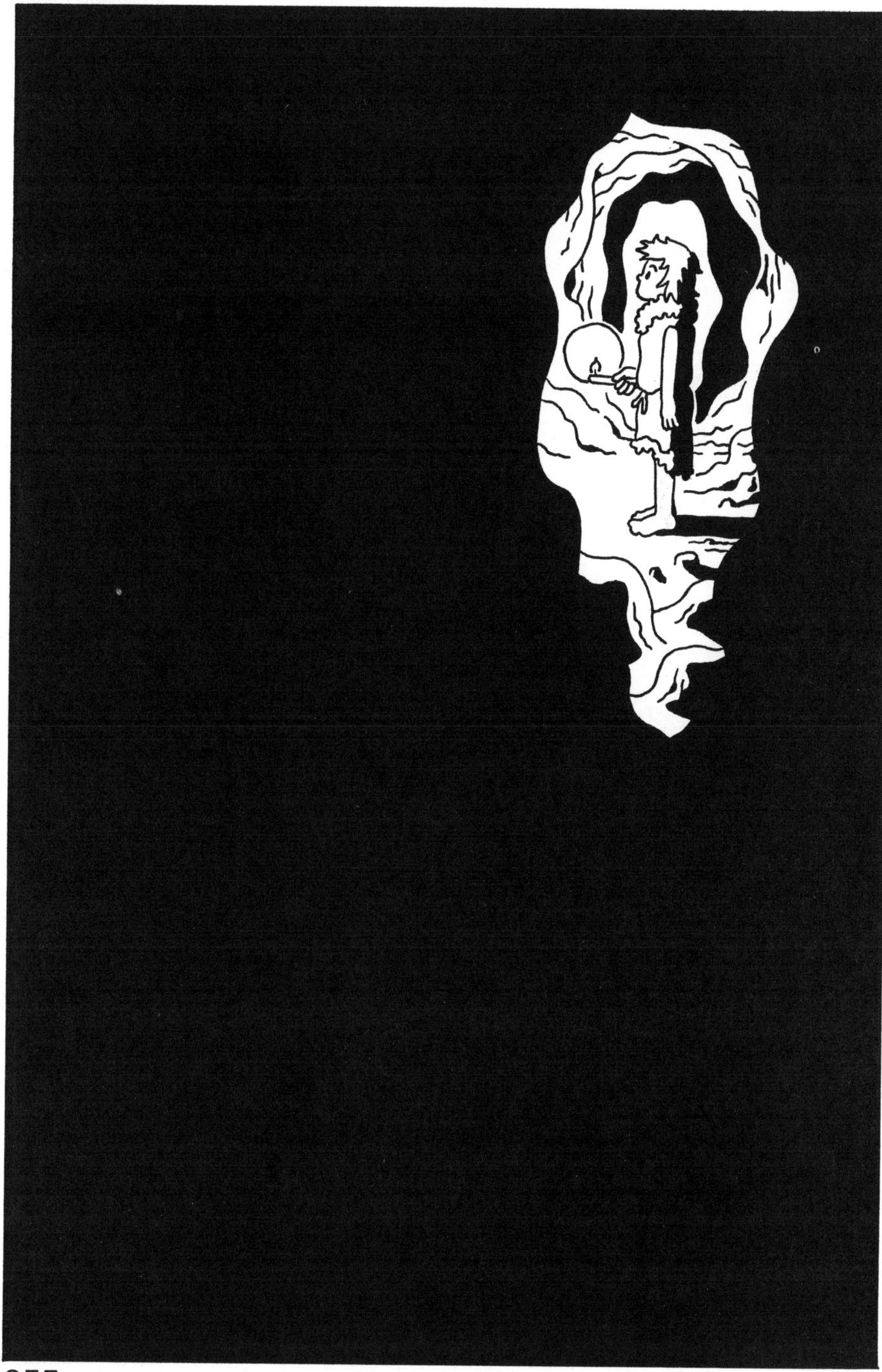

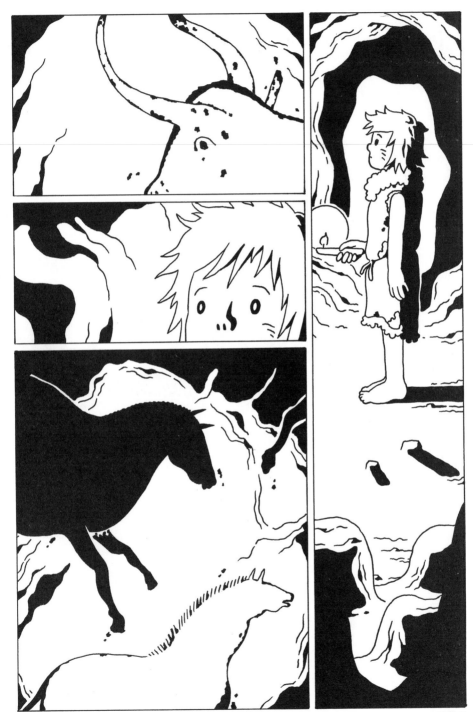

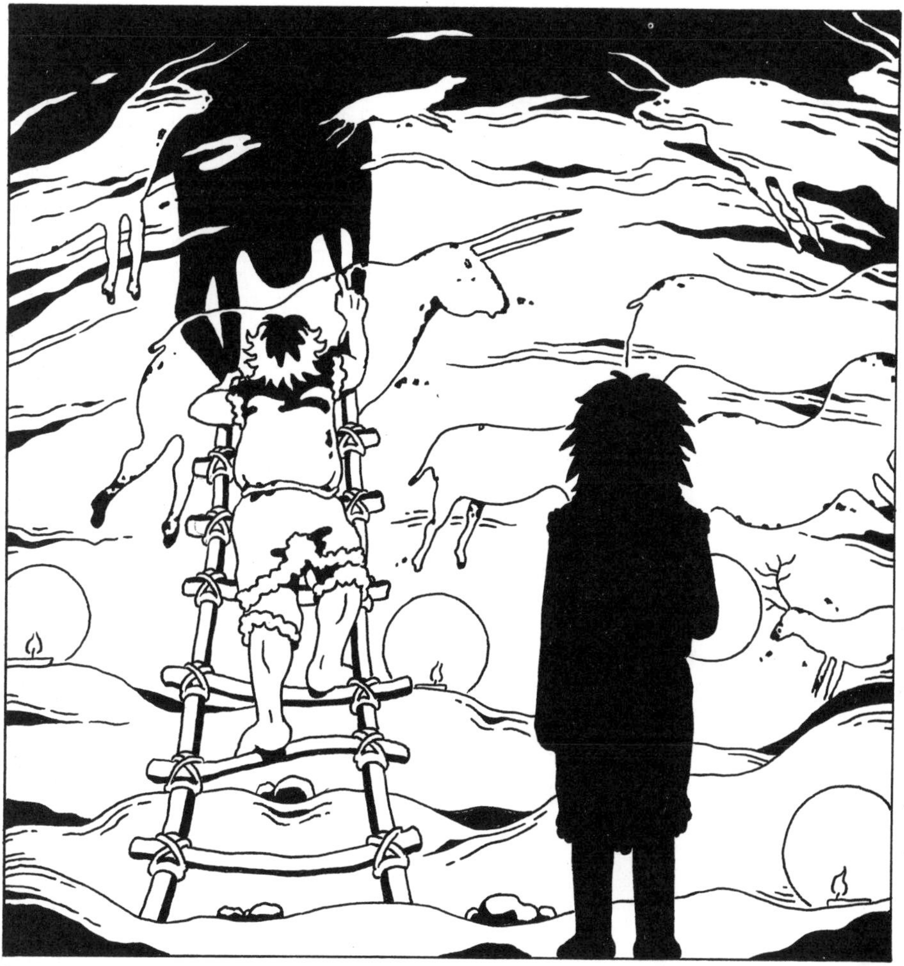

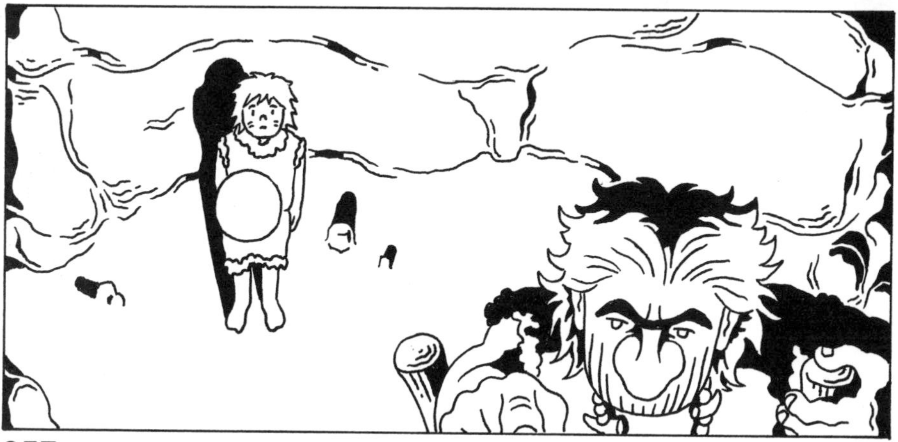

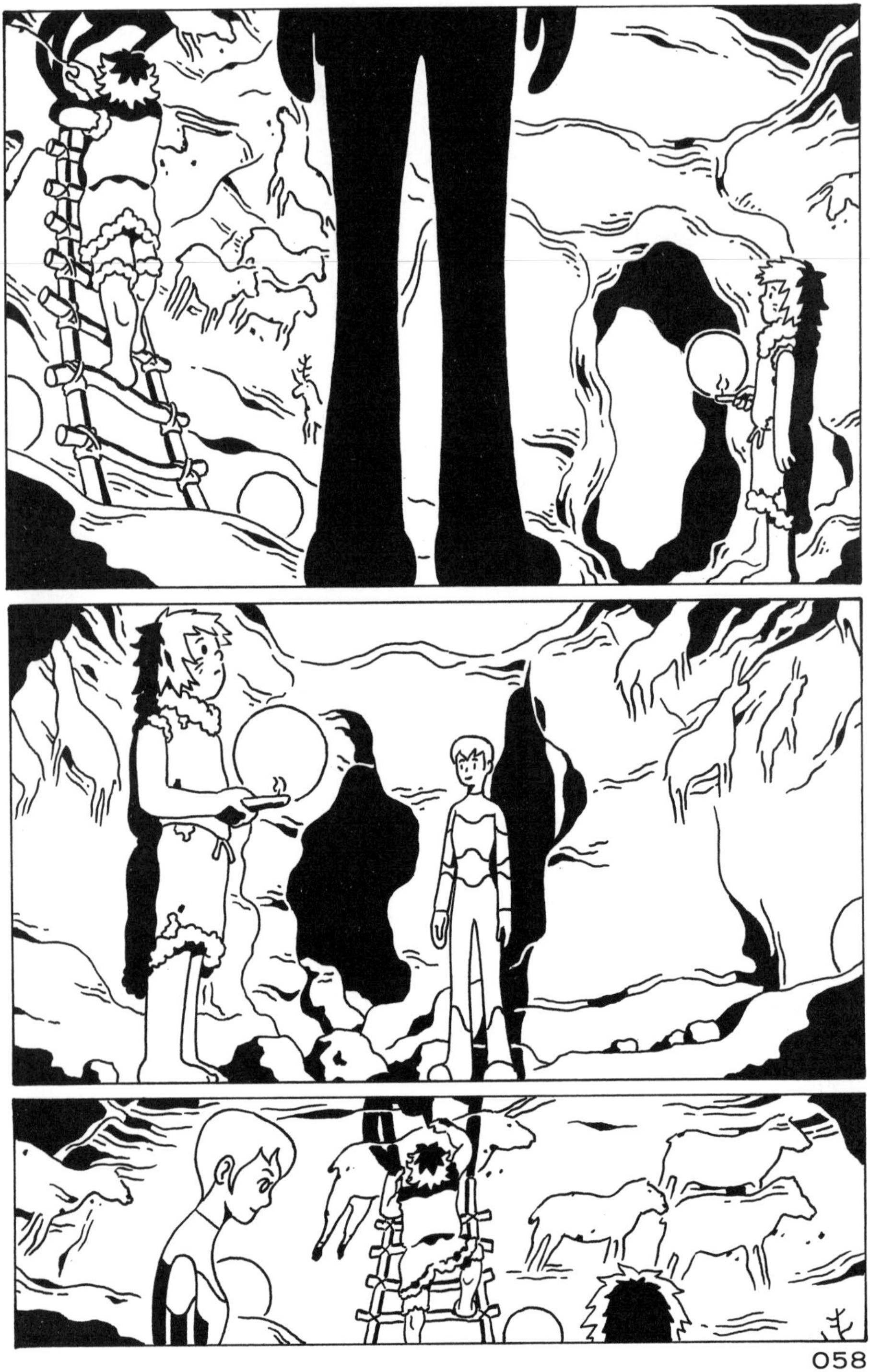

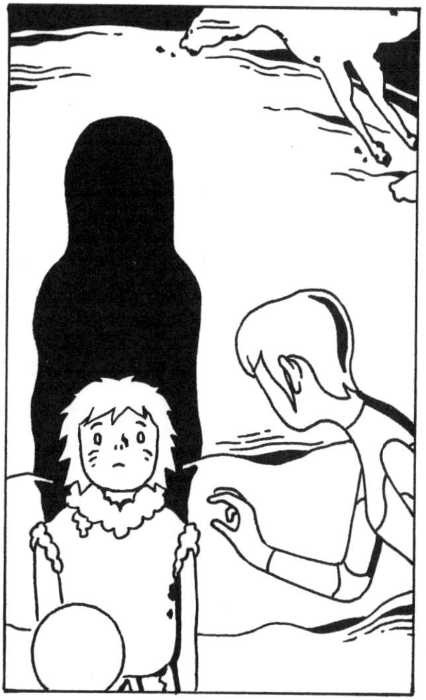

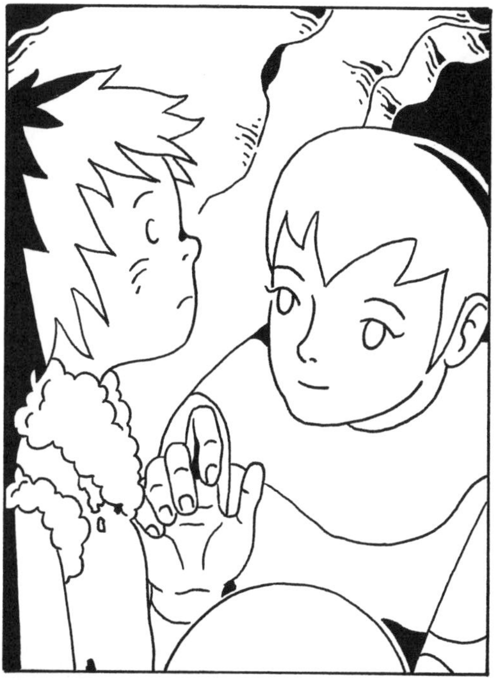

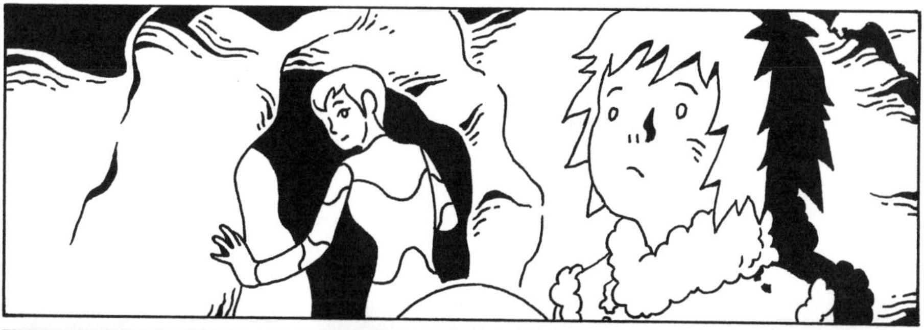

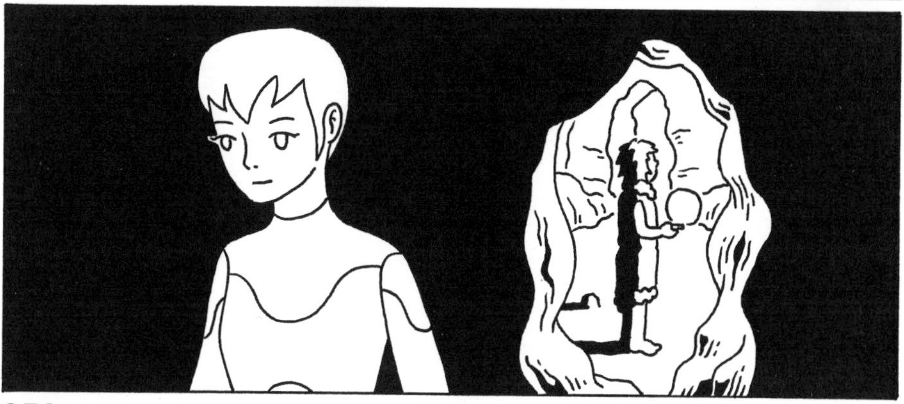

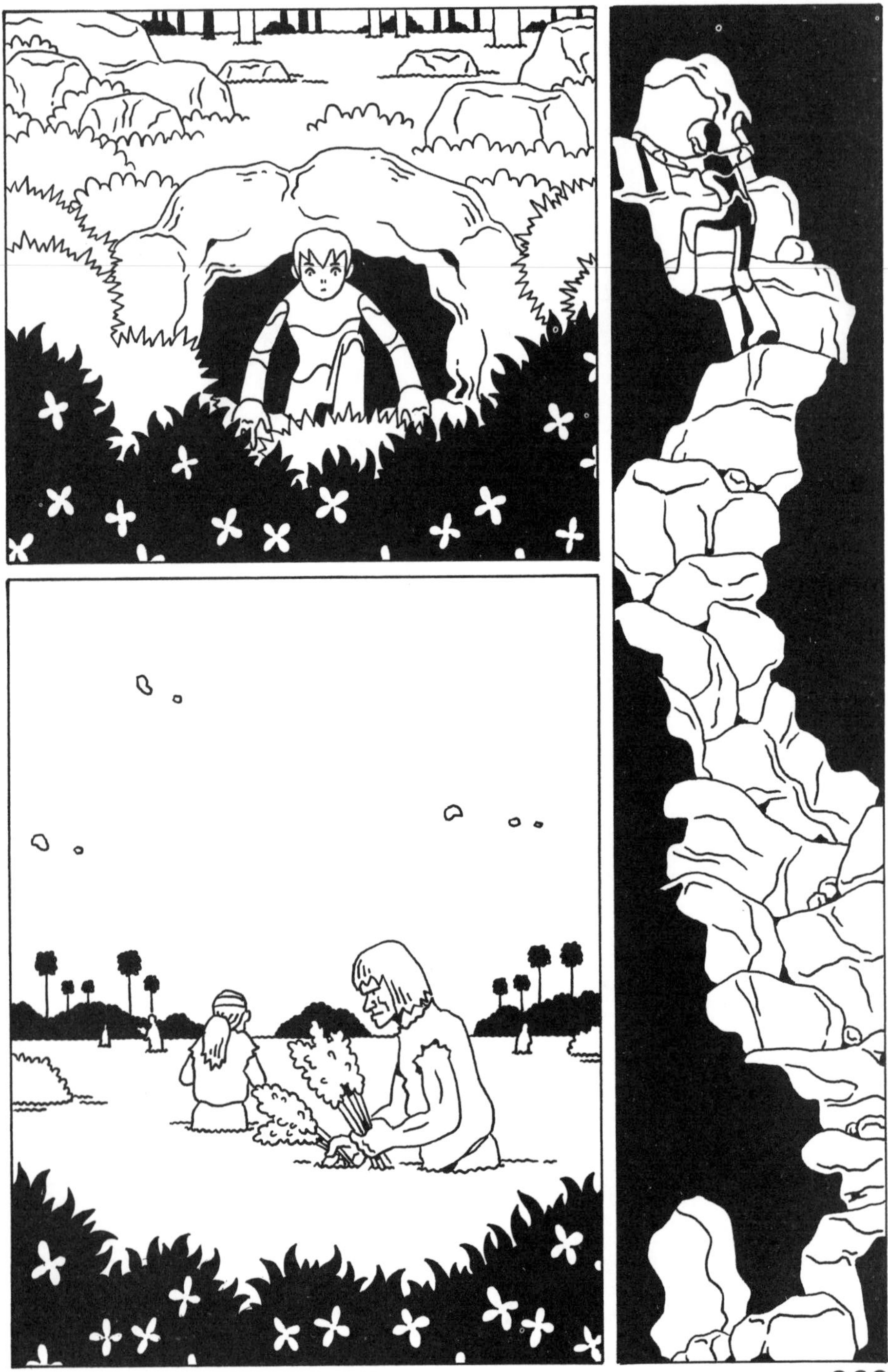

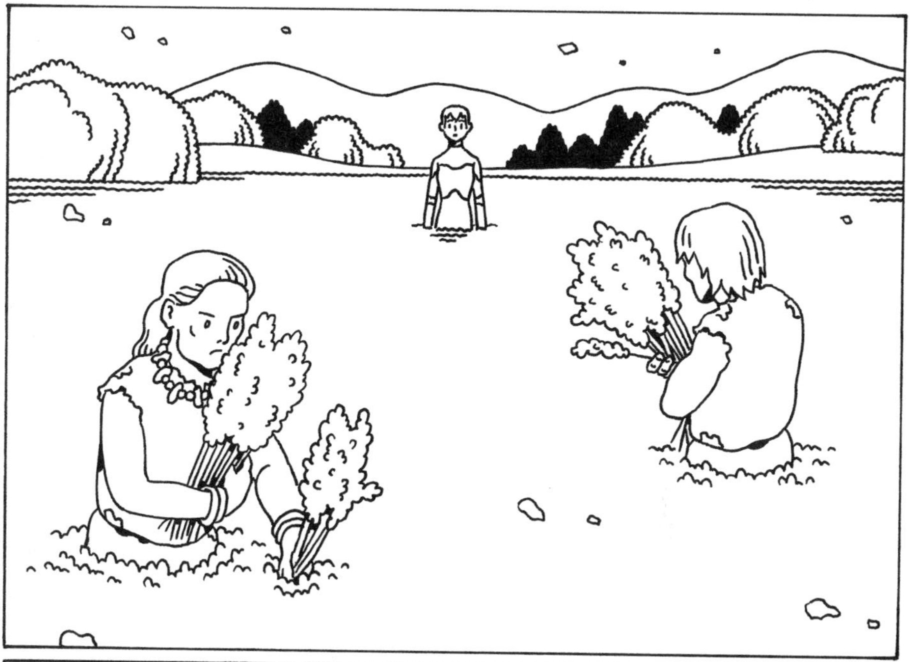
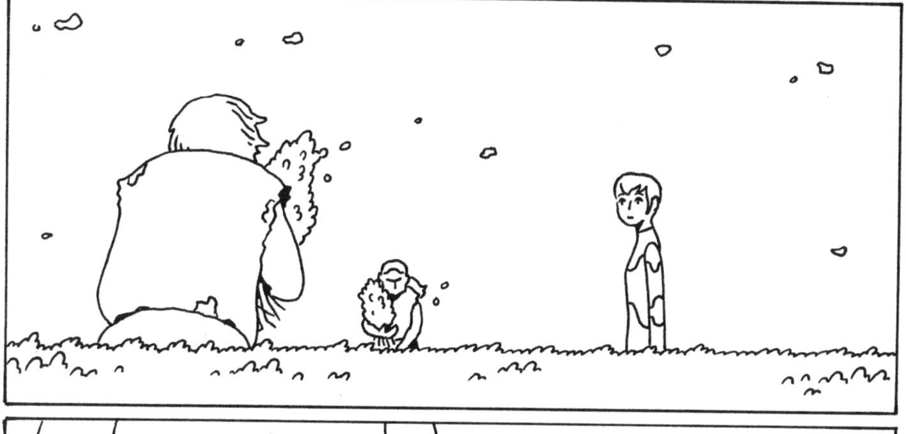
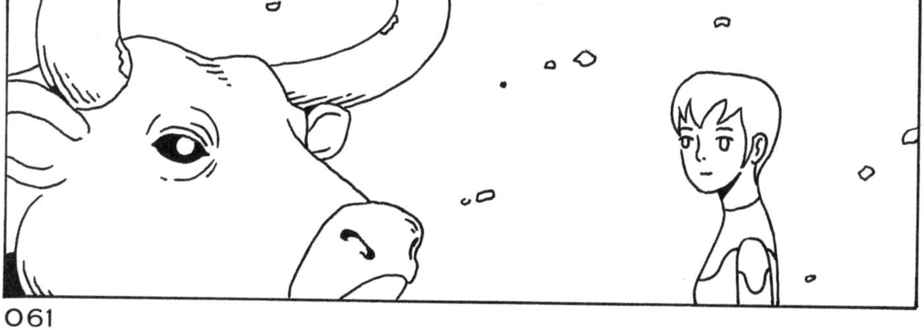

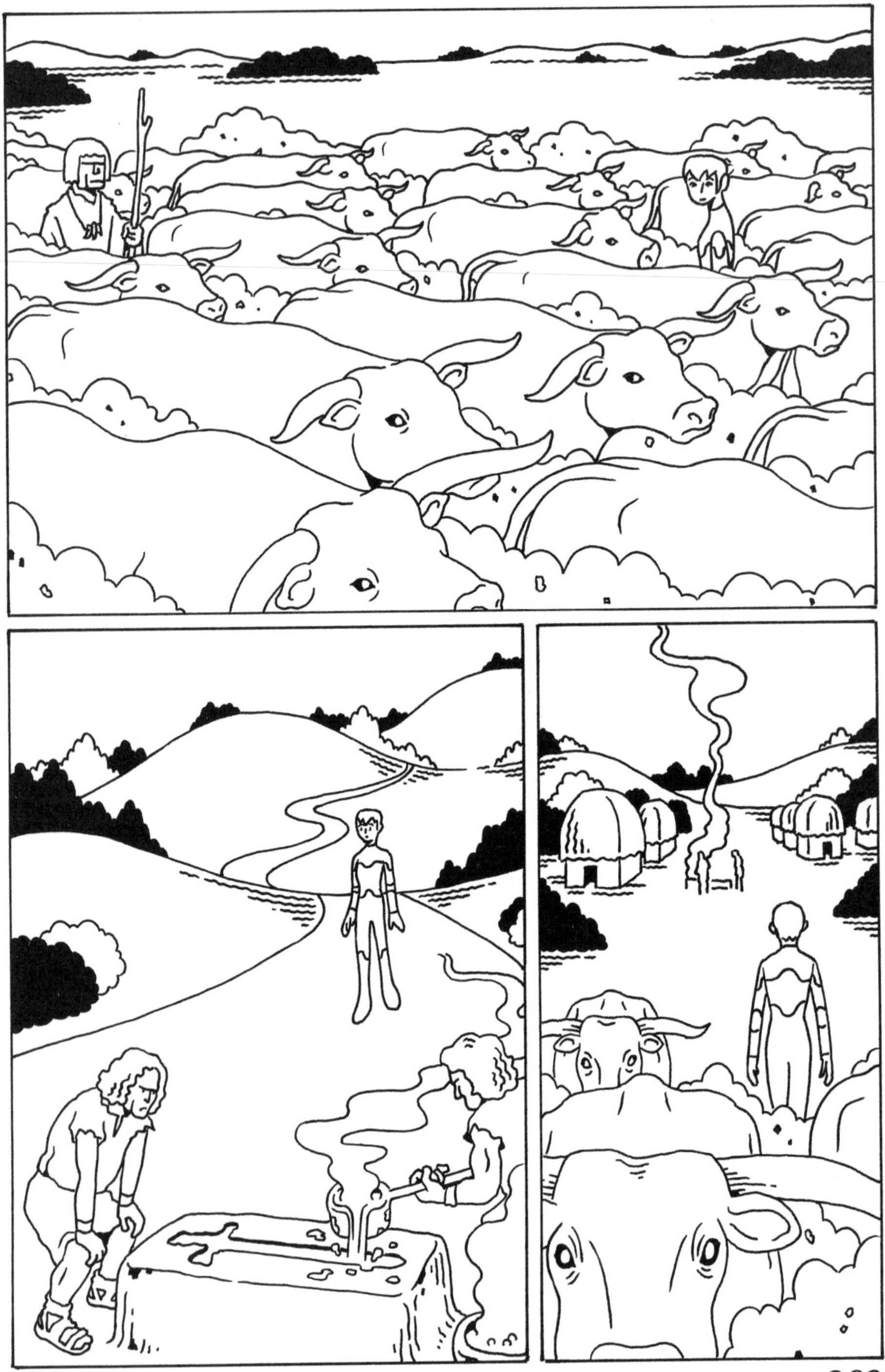

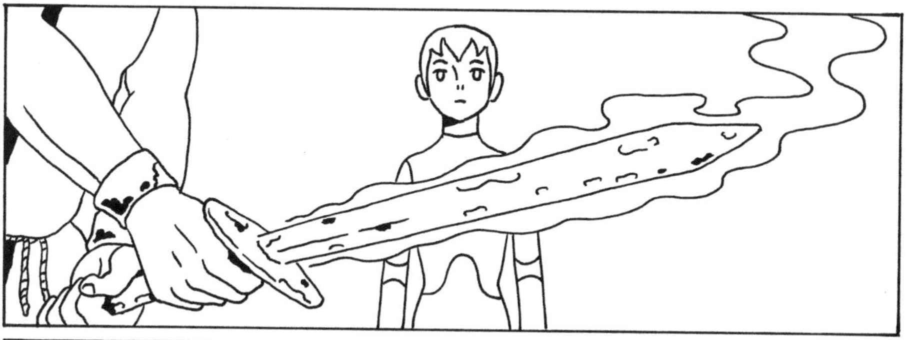

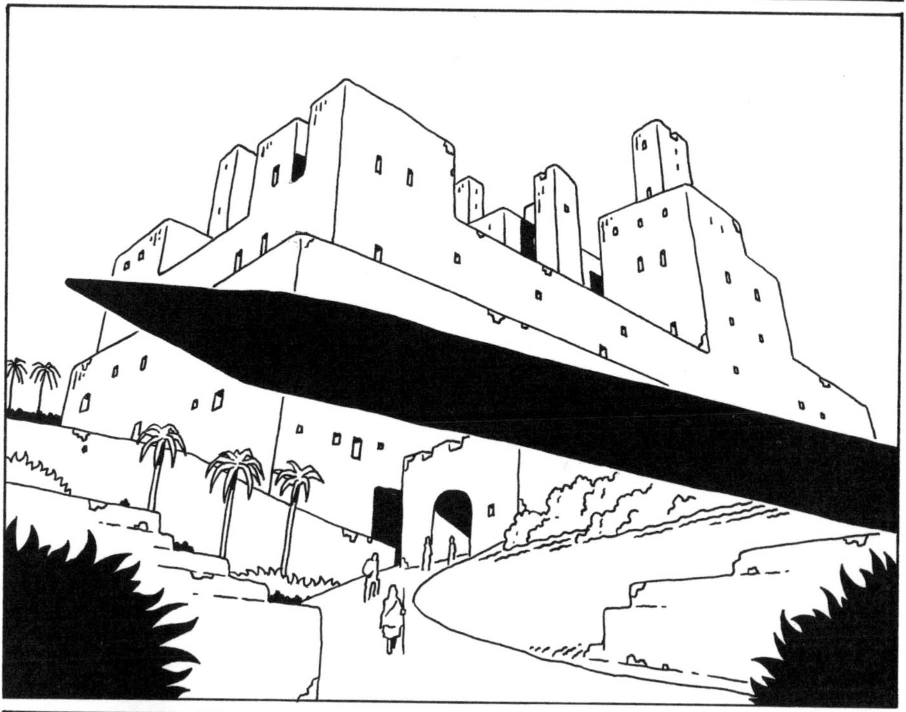

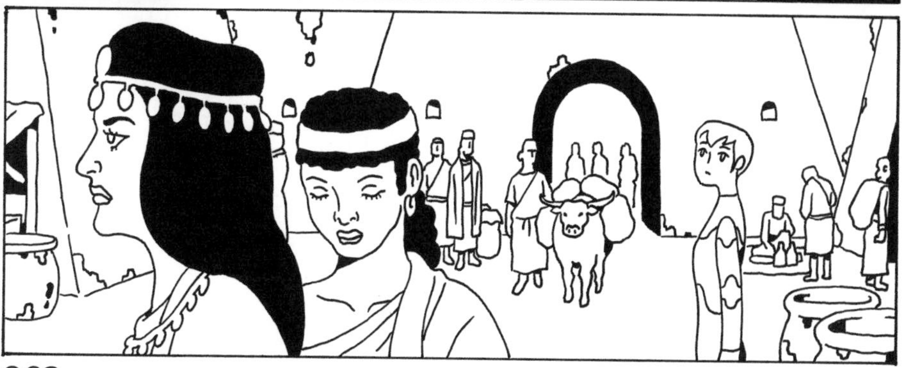

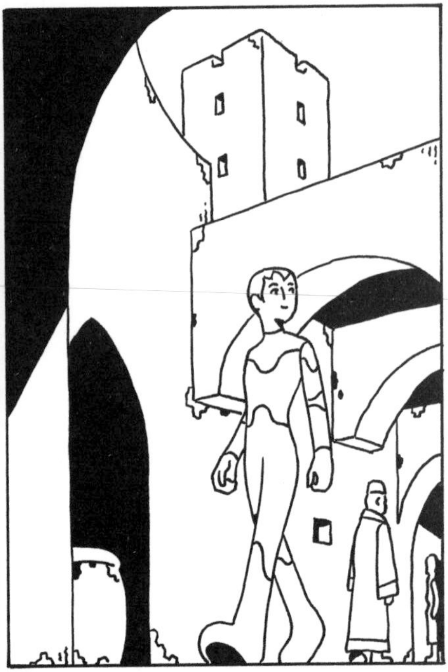
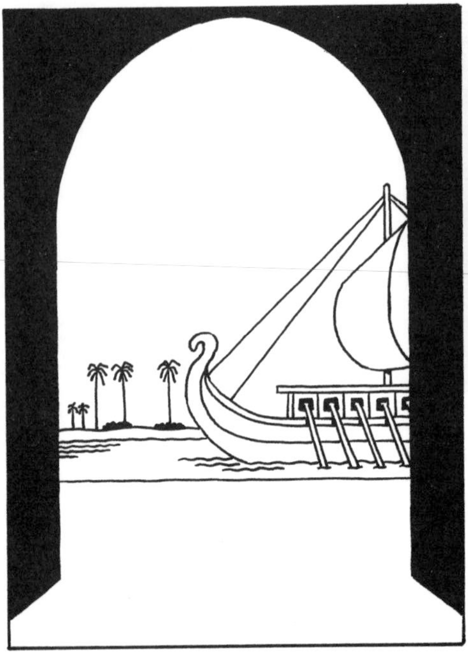
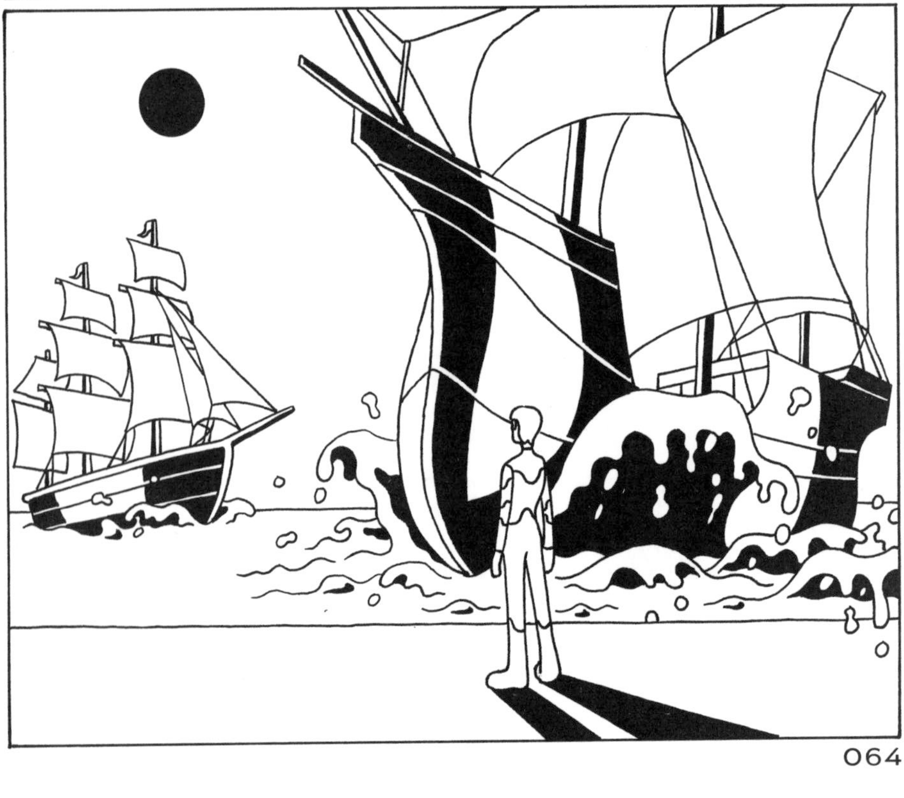

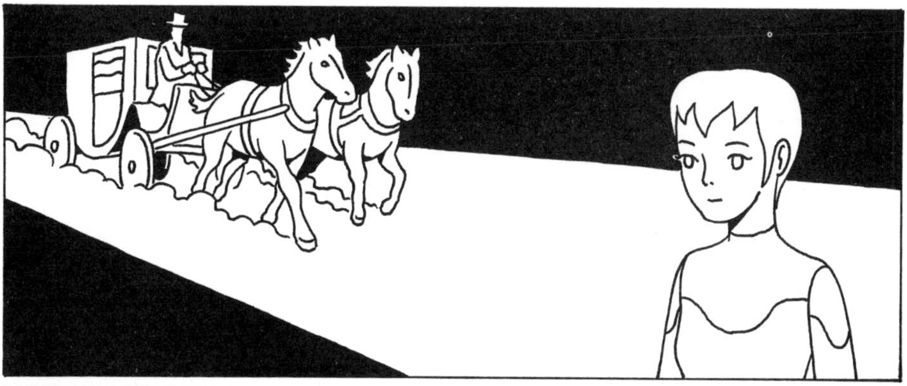
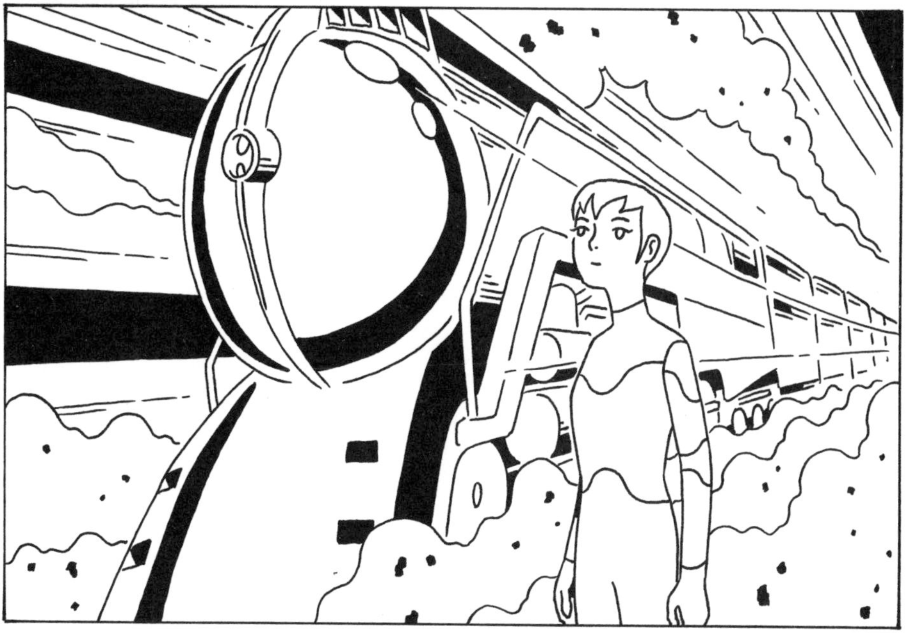
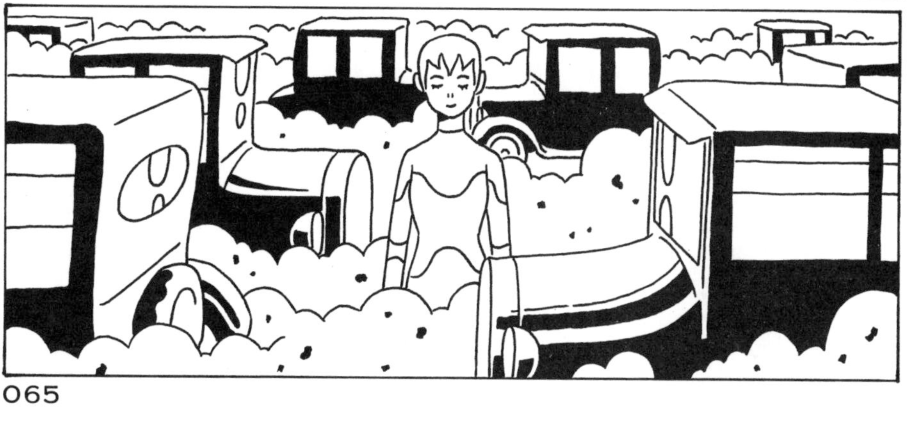

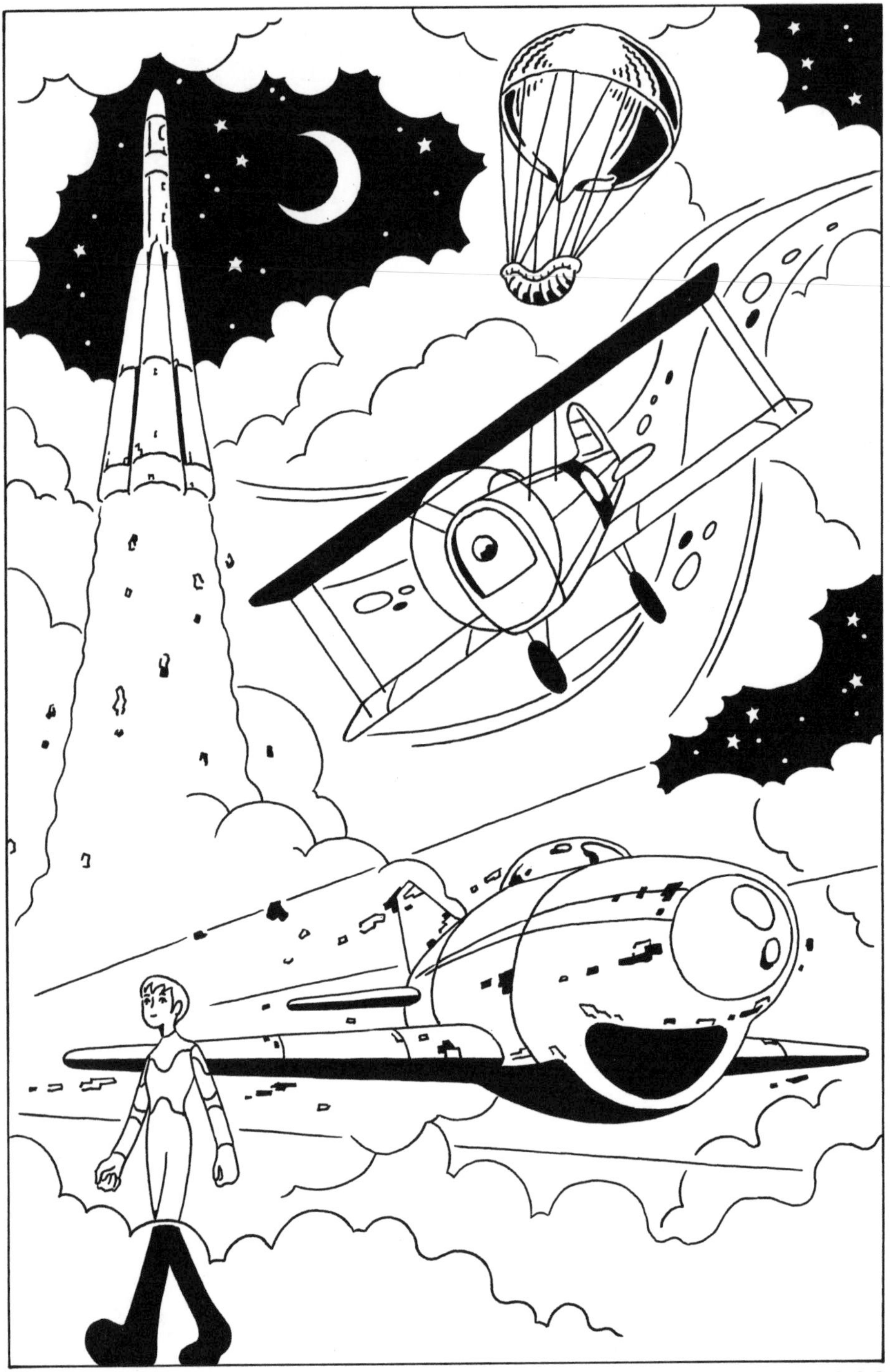

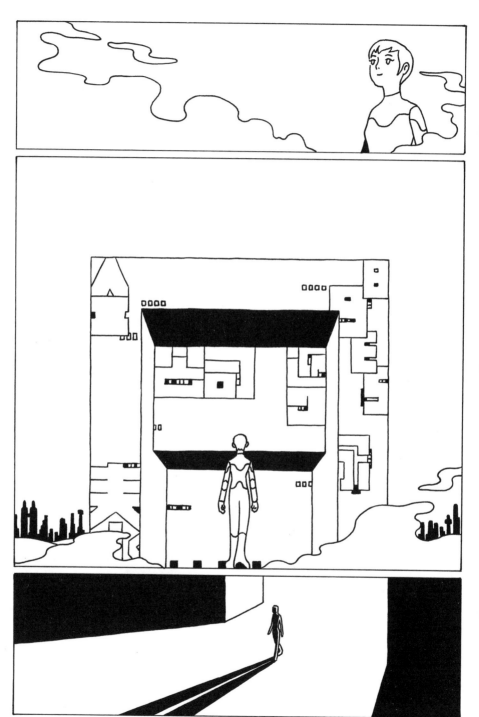

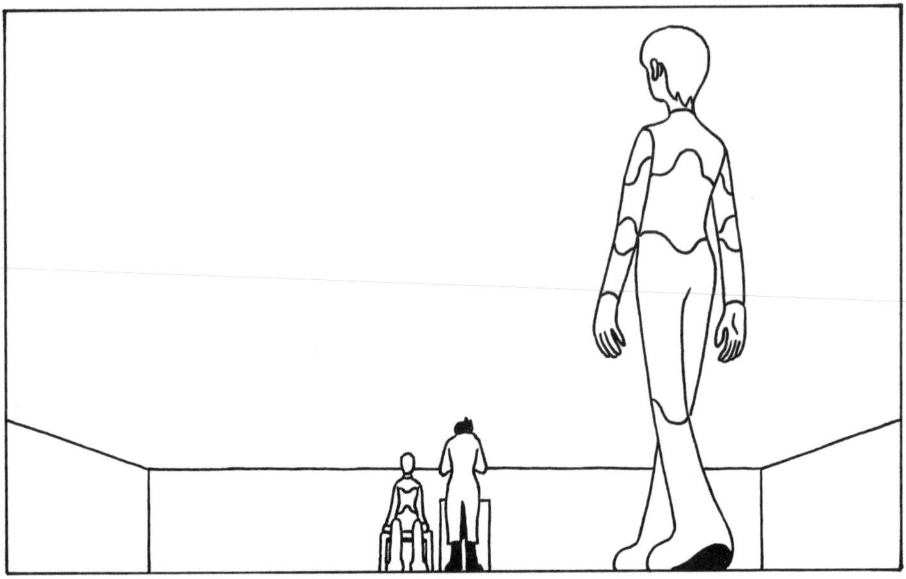
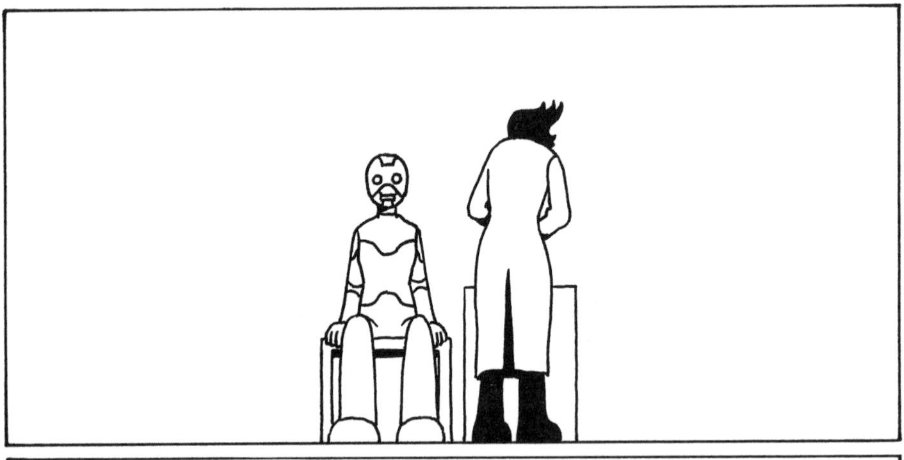
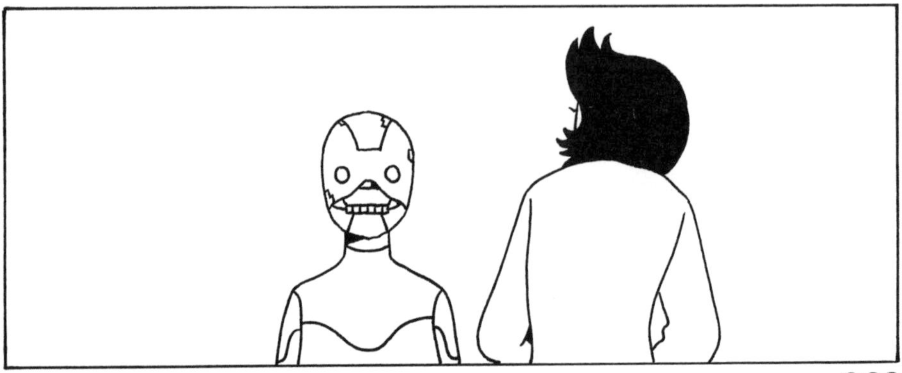

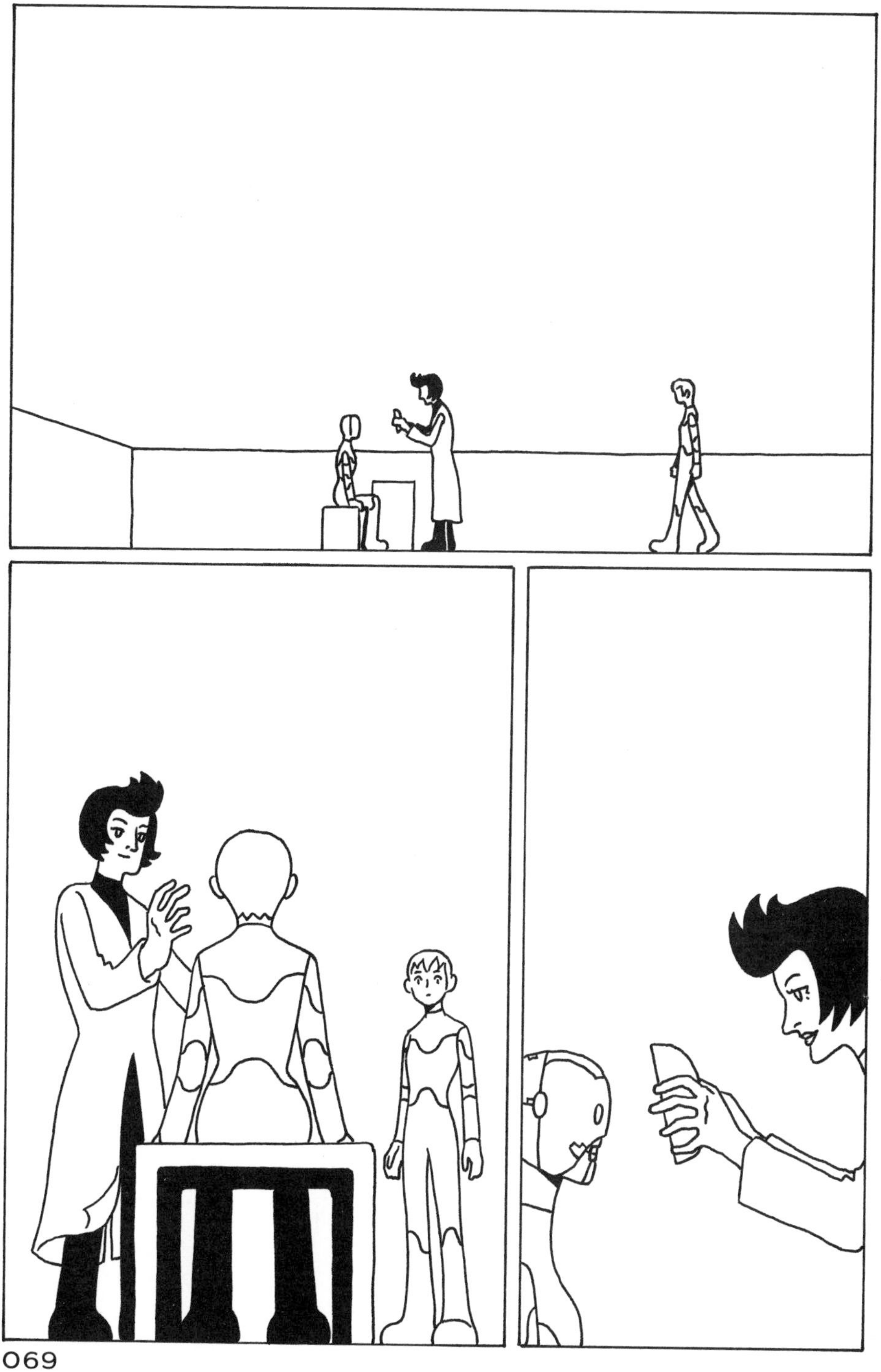

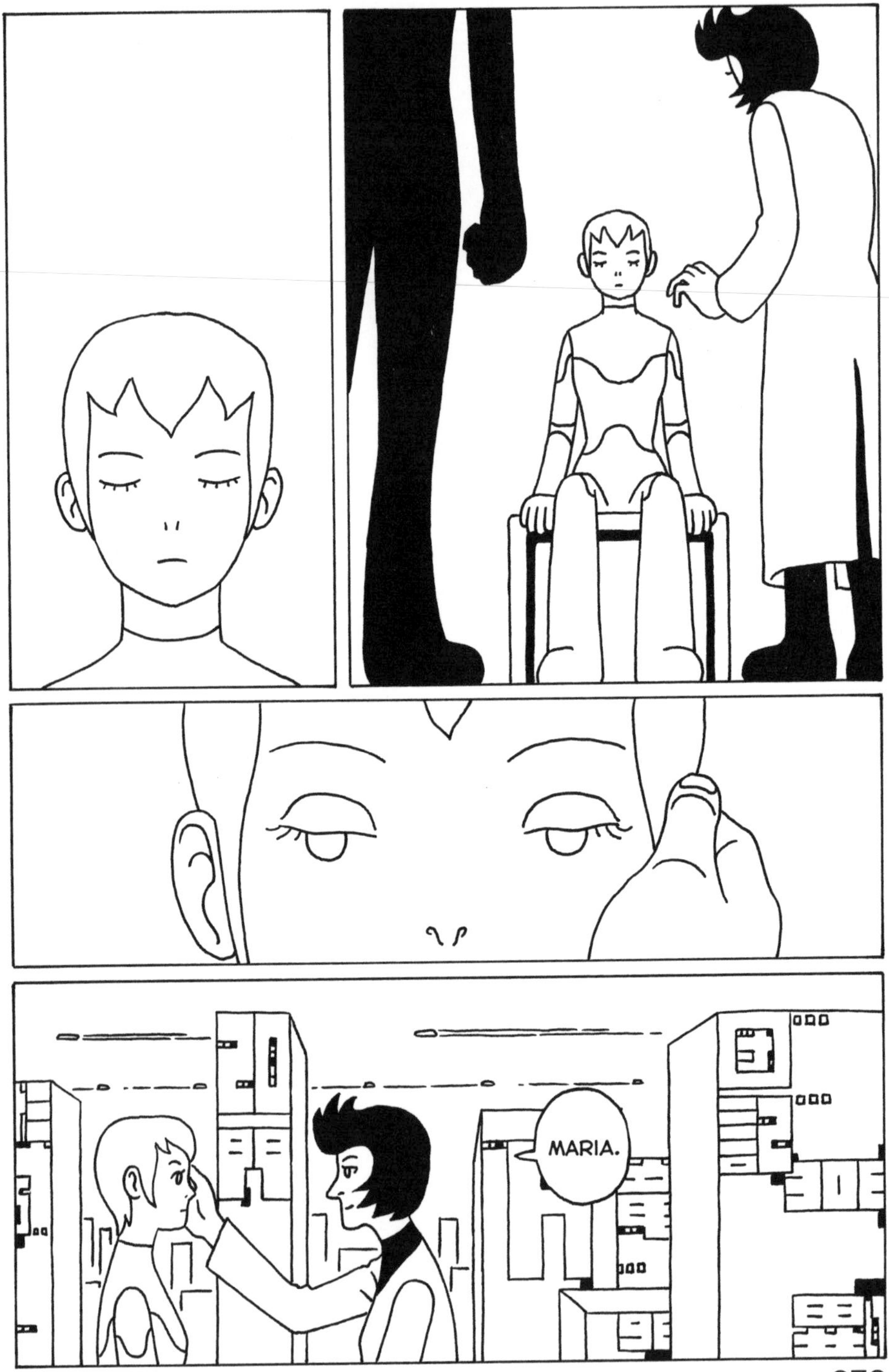
MARIA.

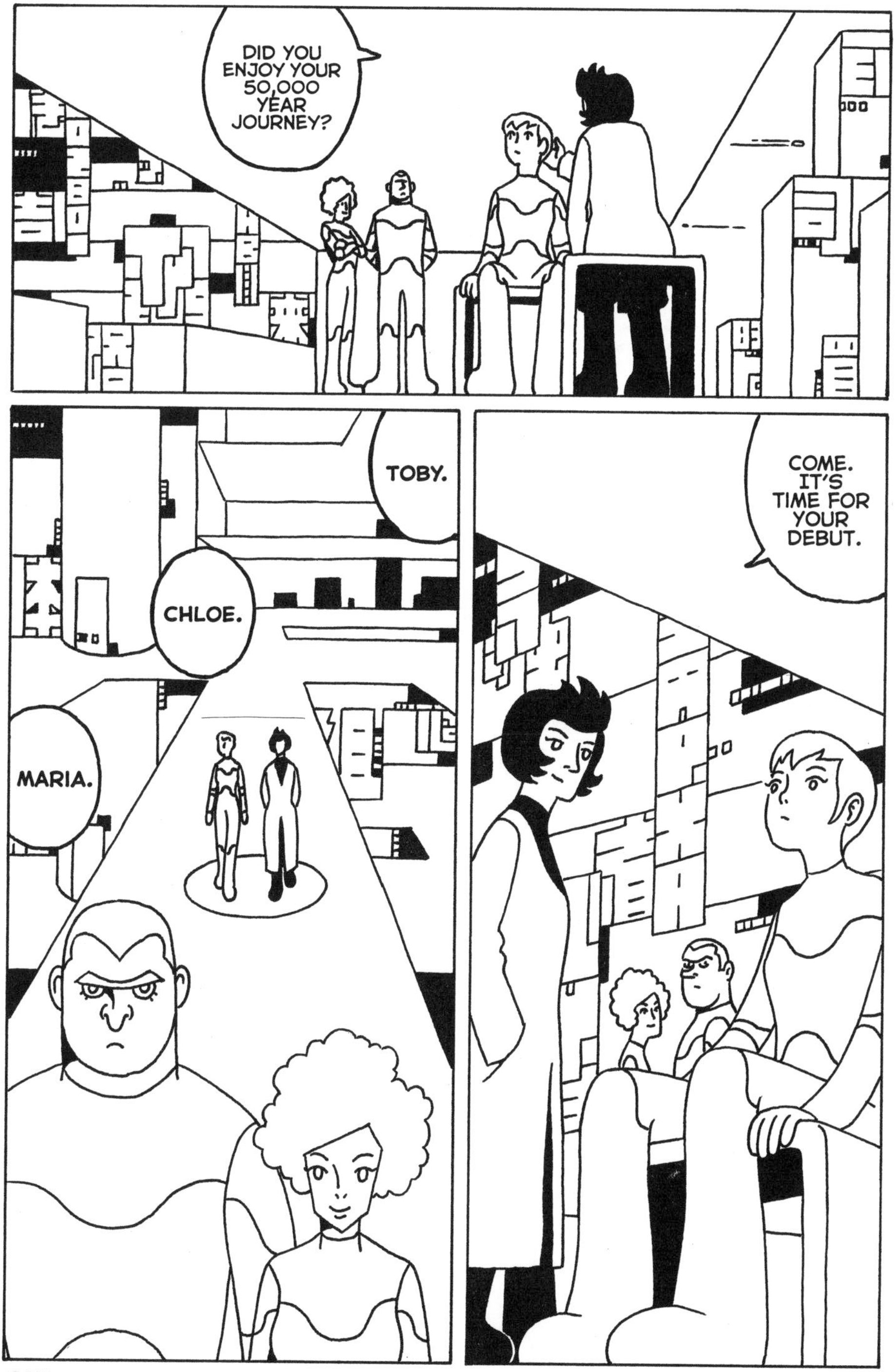
DID YOU ENJOY YOUR 50,000 YEAR JOURNEY?
COME. IT'S TIME FOR YOUR DEBUT.
TOBY.
CHLOE.
MARIA.

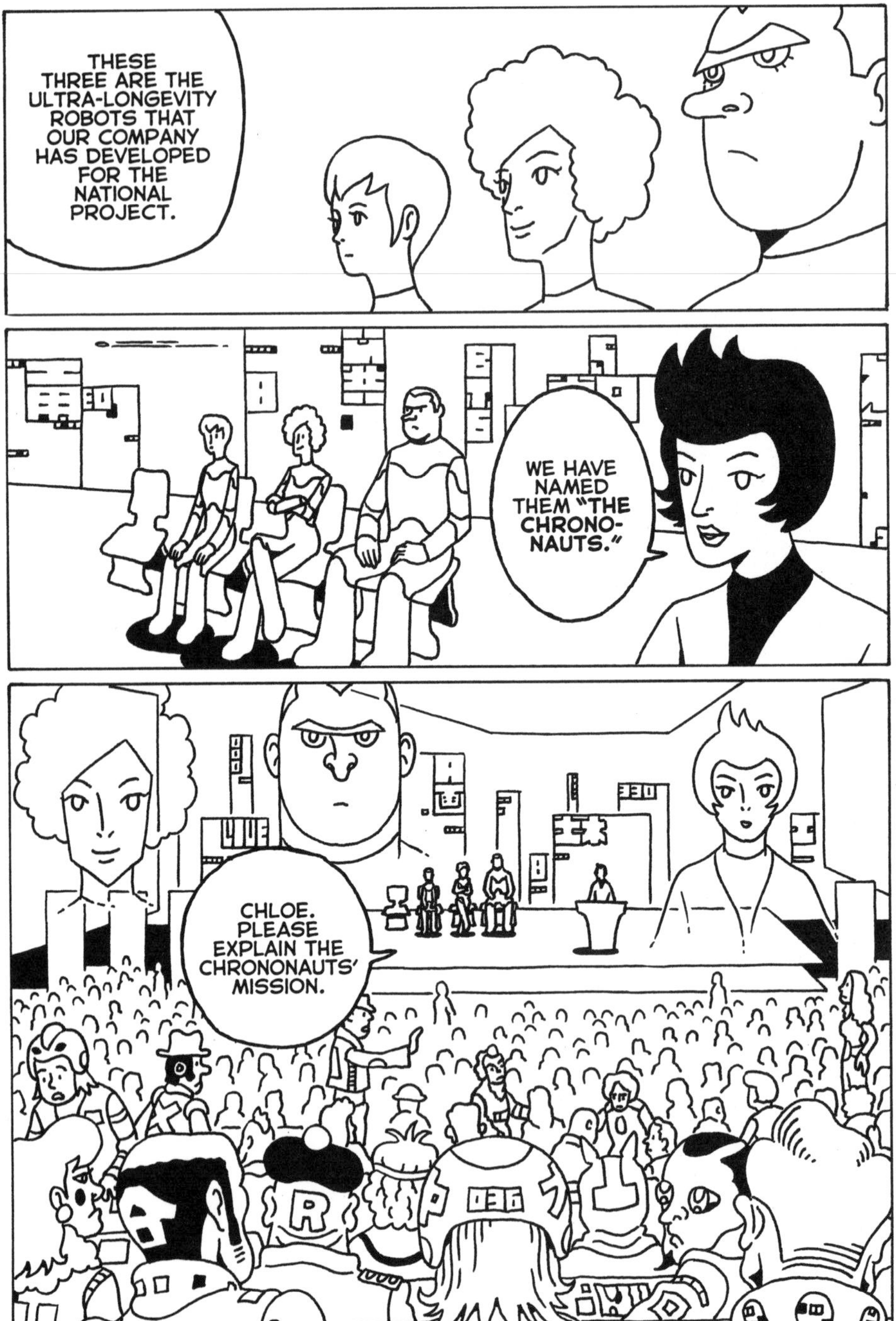
THESE THREE ARE THE ULTRA-LONGEVITY ROBOTS THAT OUR COMPANY HAS DEVELOPED FOR THE NATIONAL PROJECT.
WE HAVE NAMED THEM "THE CHRONONAUTS."
CHLOE. PLEASE EXPLAIN THE CHRONONAUTS' MISSION.

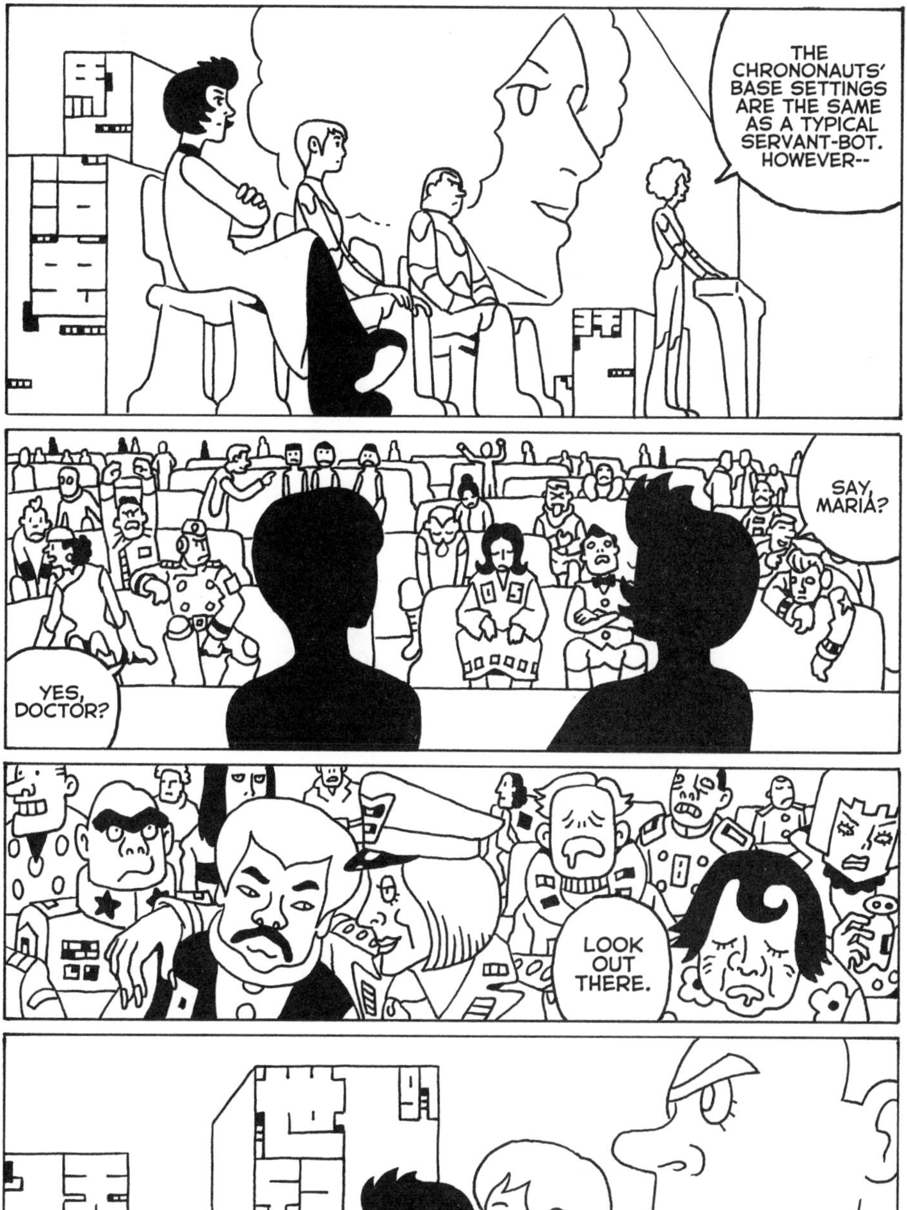
THE CHRONONAUTS' BASE SETTINGS ARE THE SAME AS A TYPICAL SERVANT-BOT. HOWEVER--
SAY, MARIA?
YES, DOCTOR?
LOOK OUT THERE.
LOOK AT WHAT 50,000 YEARS OF EVOLUTION WROUGHT.

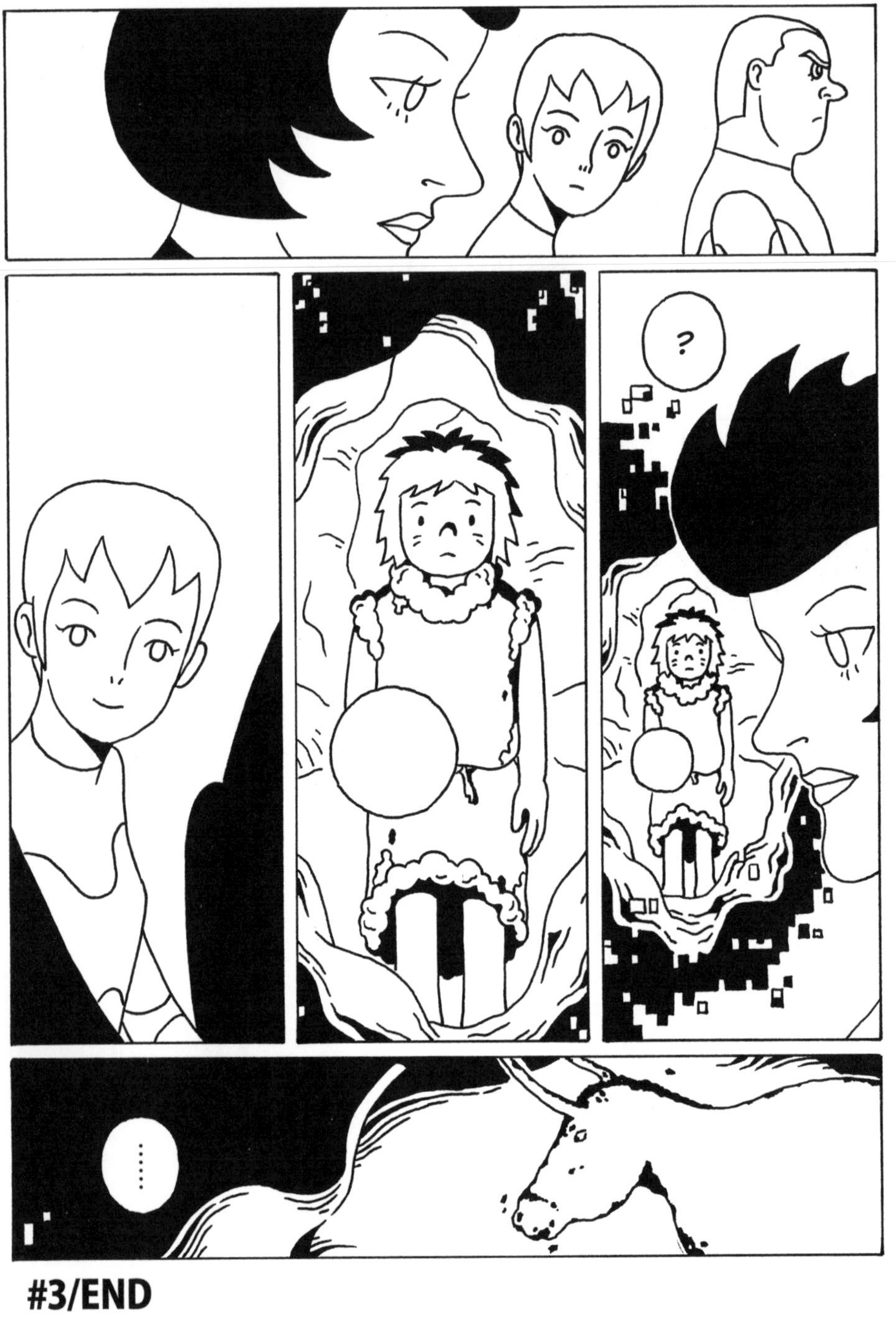
?
......

#3/END

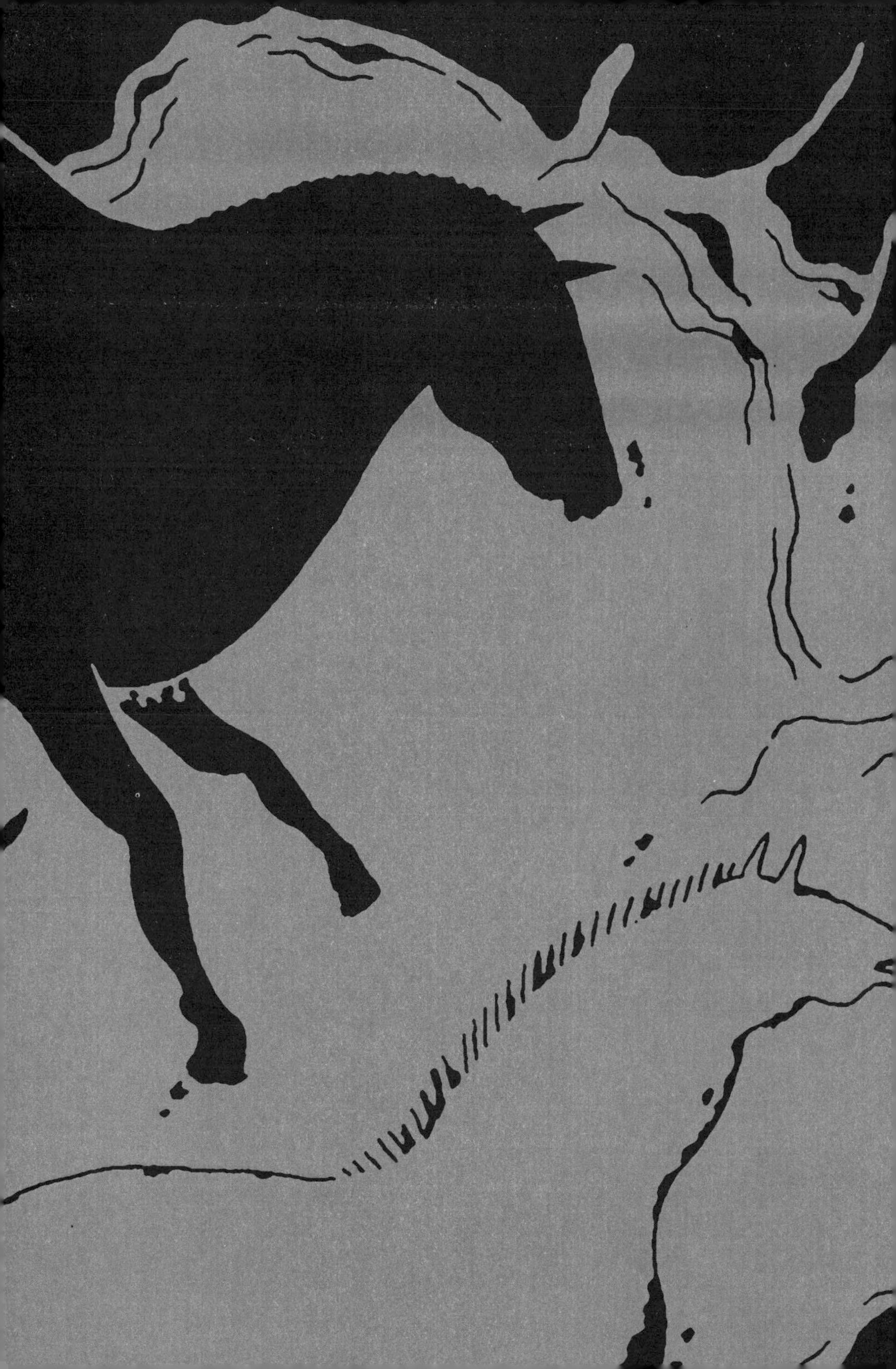

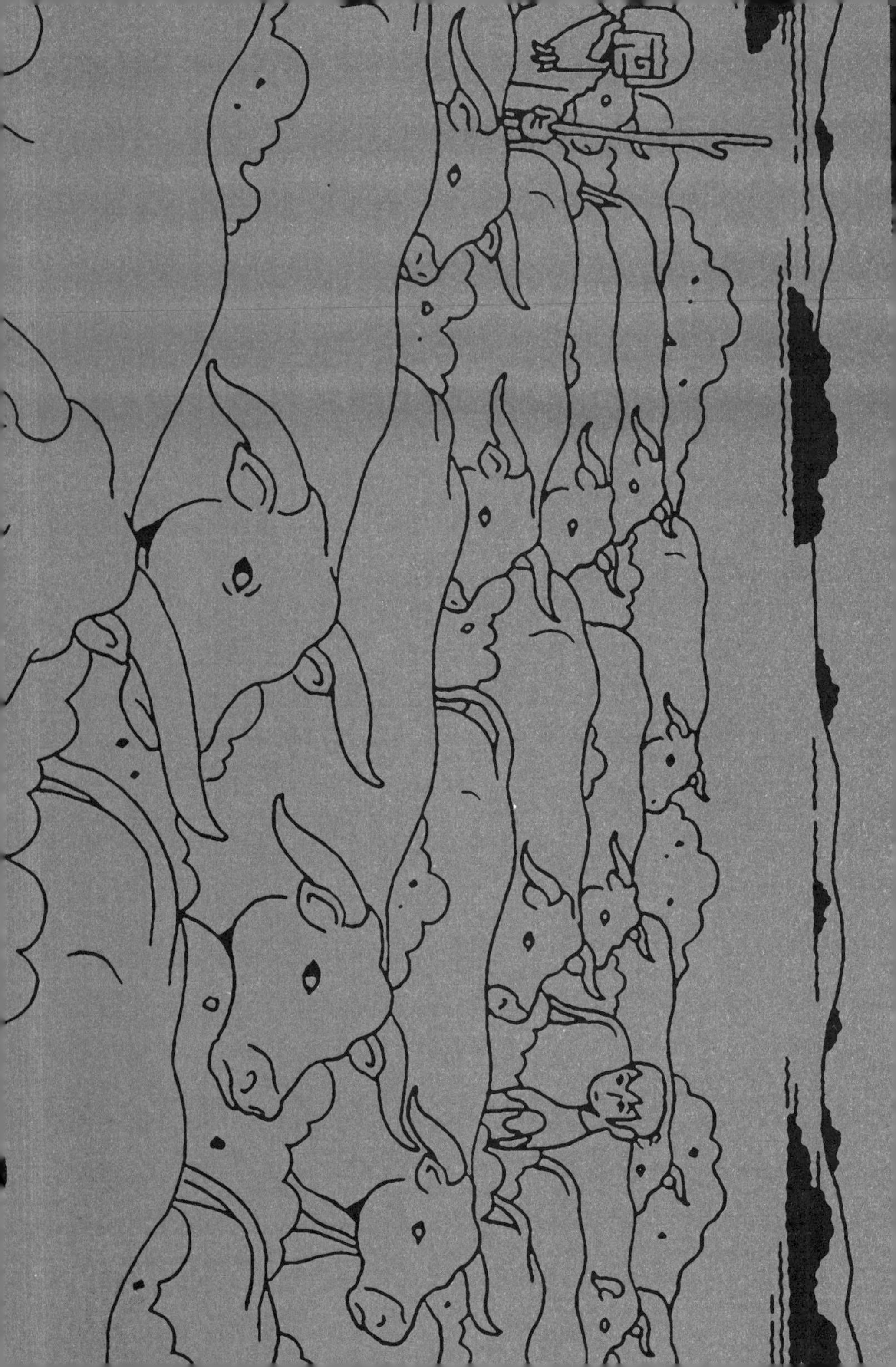

#4

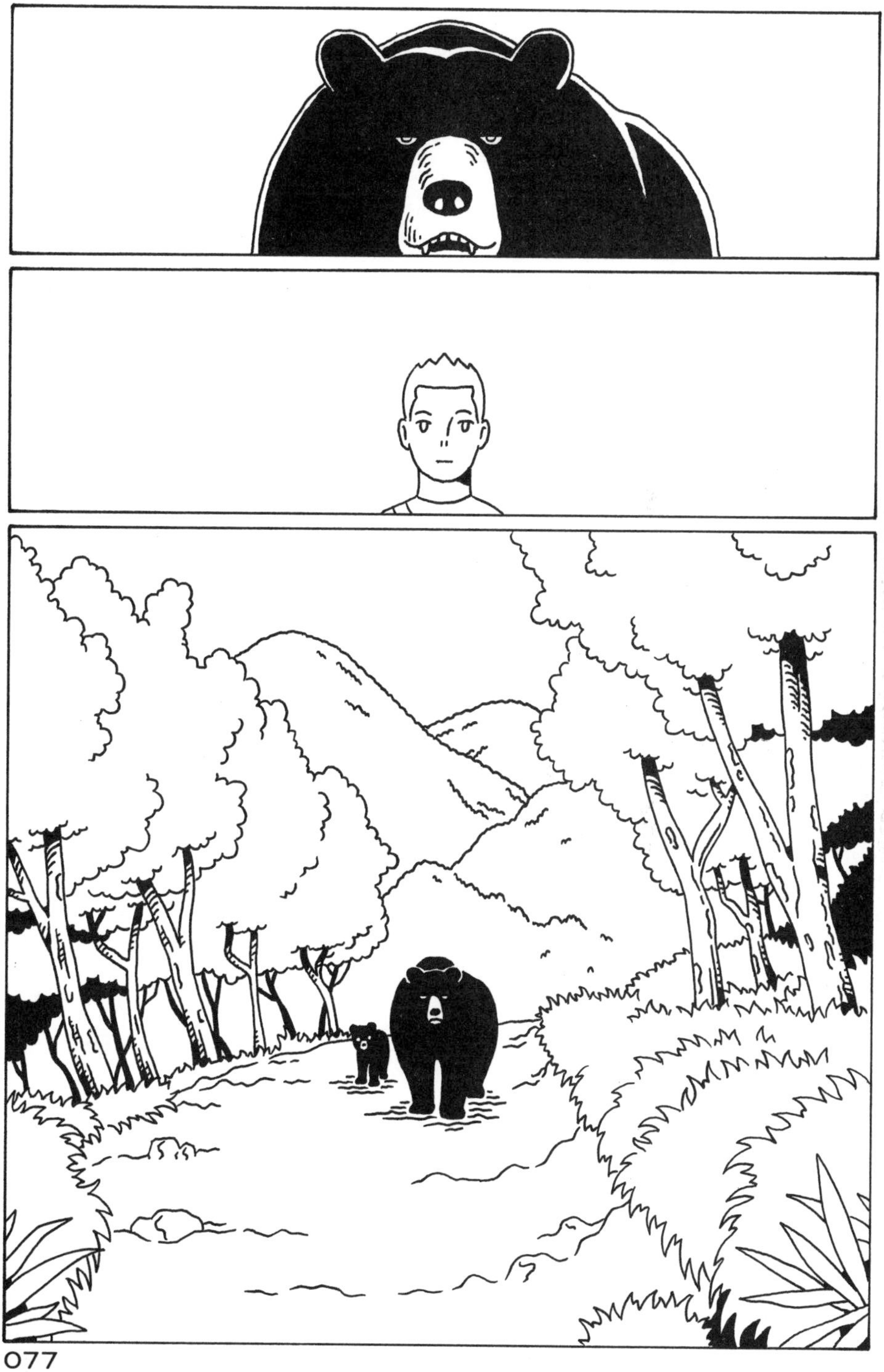

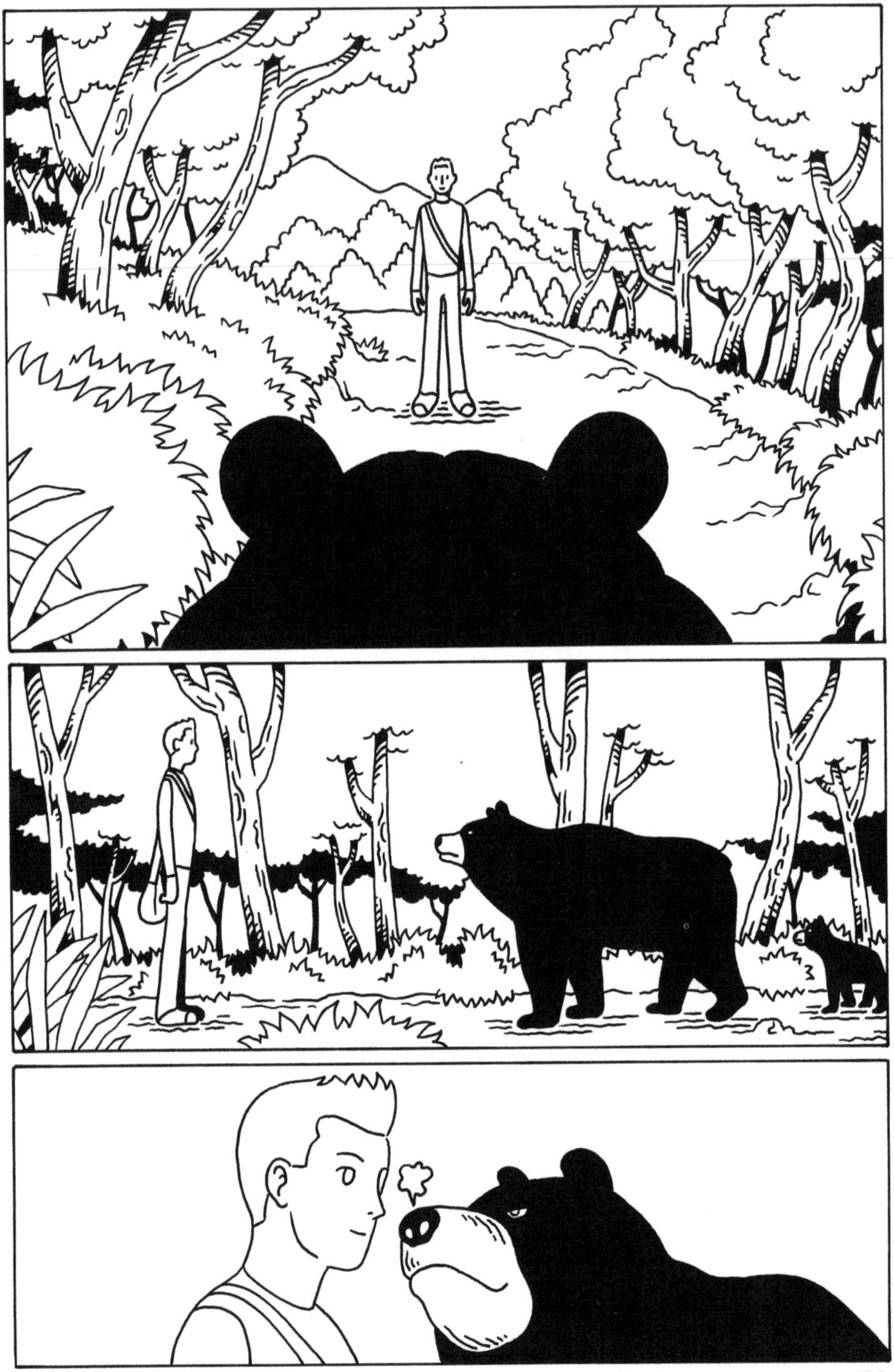

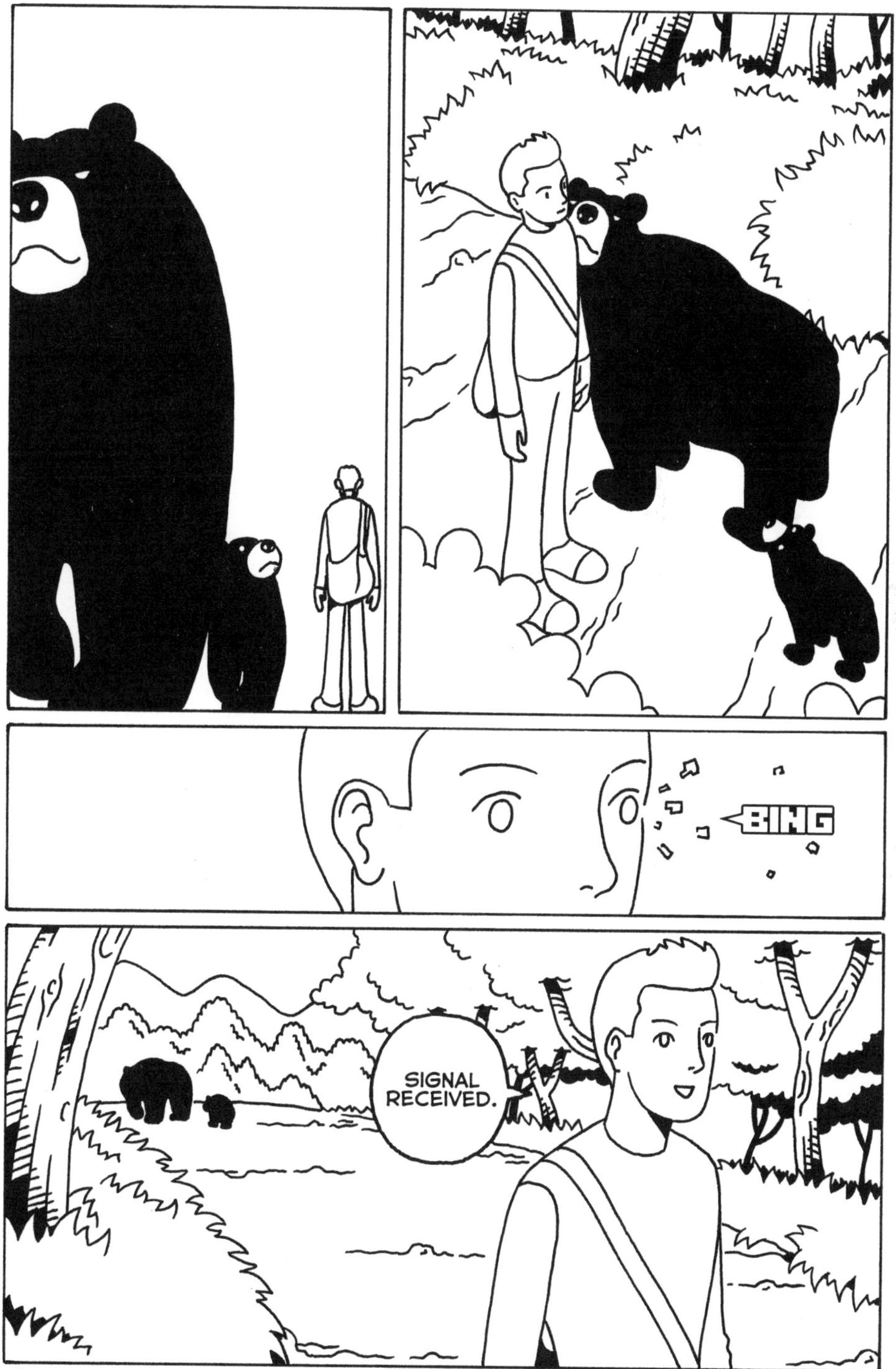
BING
SIGNAL RECEIVED.

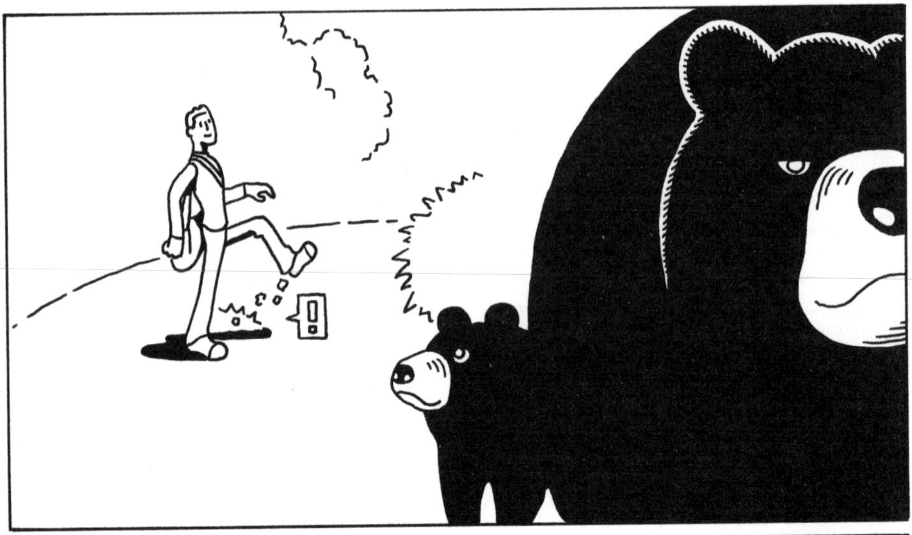
!

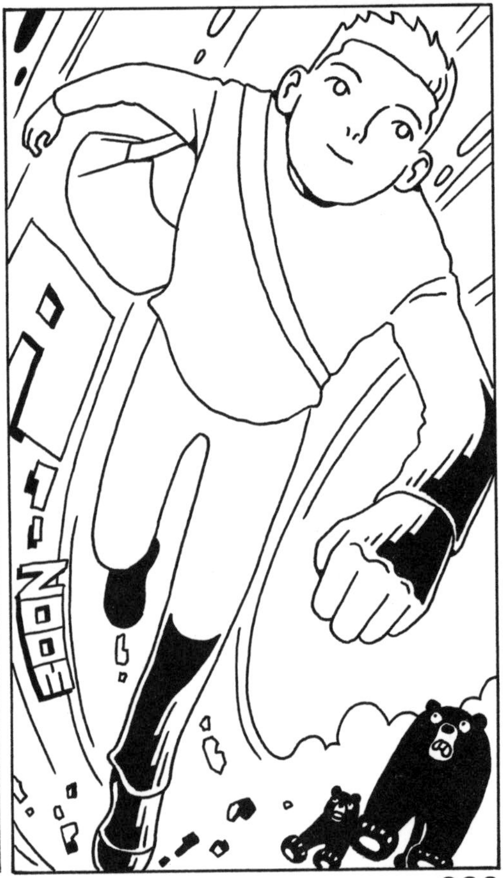
ZOOM

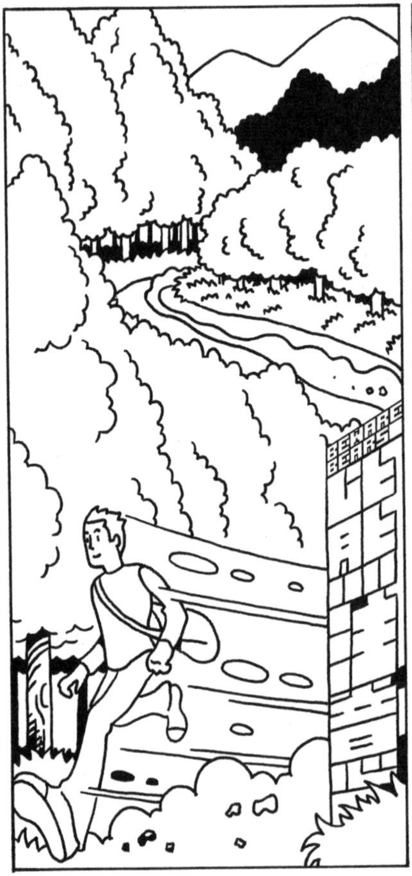
BEWARE
BEARS

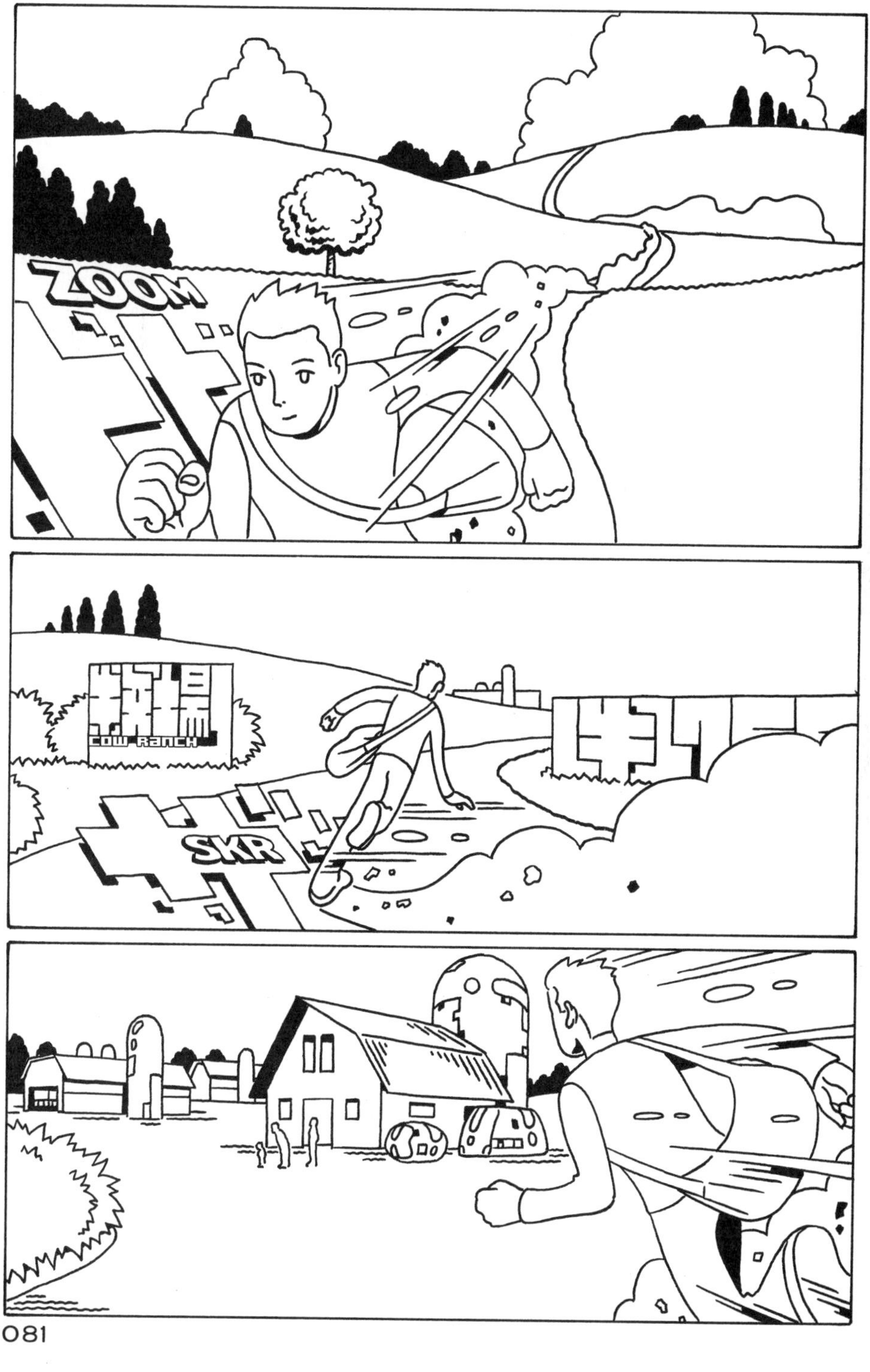
ZOOM
COW RANCH
SKR

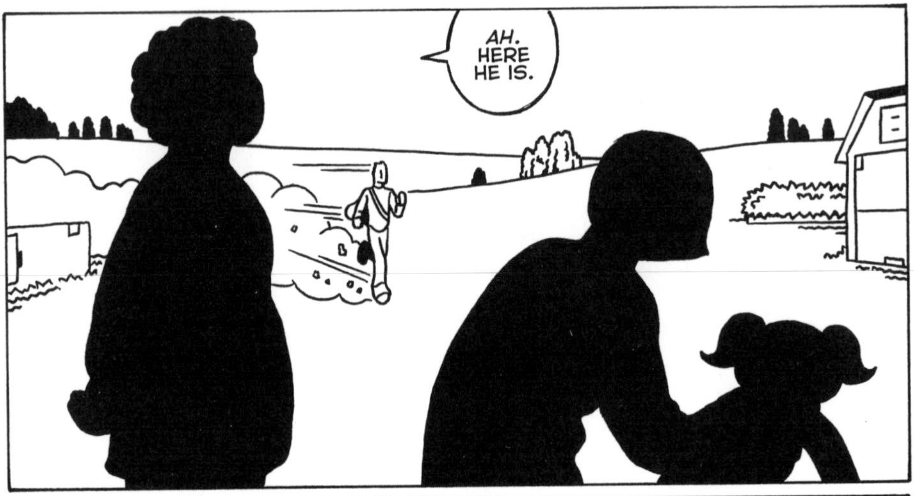
AH. HERE HE IS.

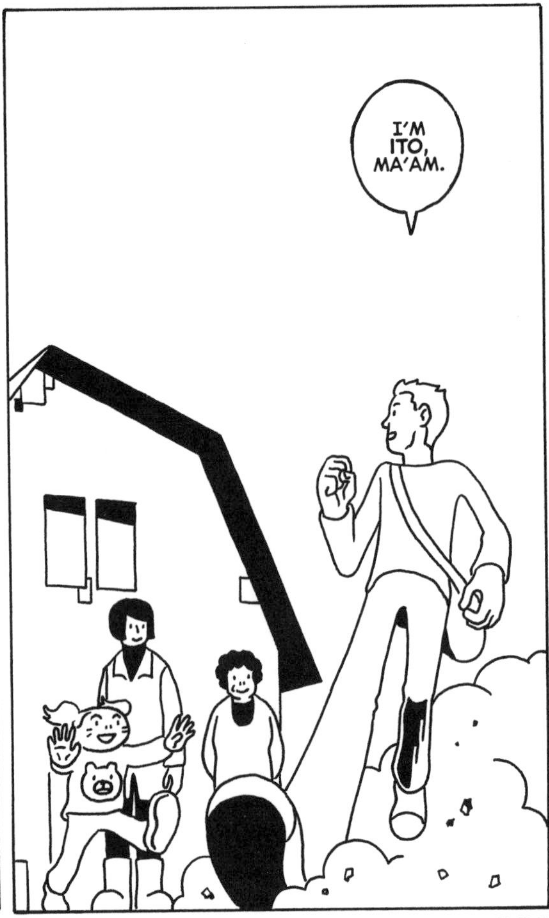
I'M ITO, MA'AM.

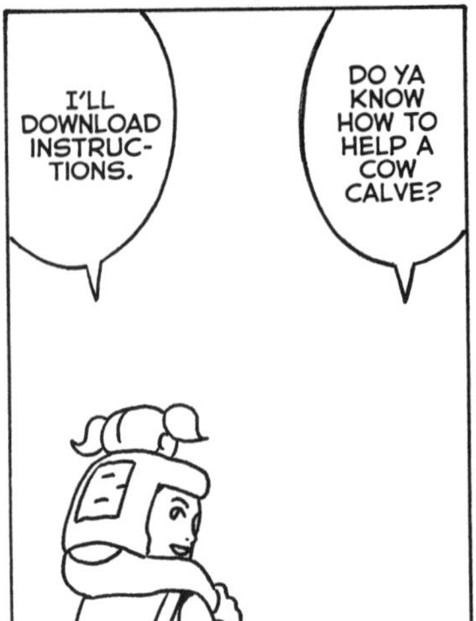
DO YA KNOW HOW TO HELP A COW CALVE?
I'LL DOWNLOAD INSTRUCTIONS.

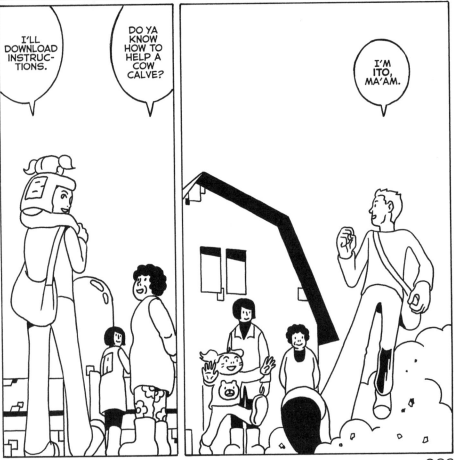

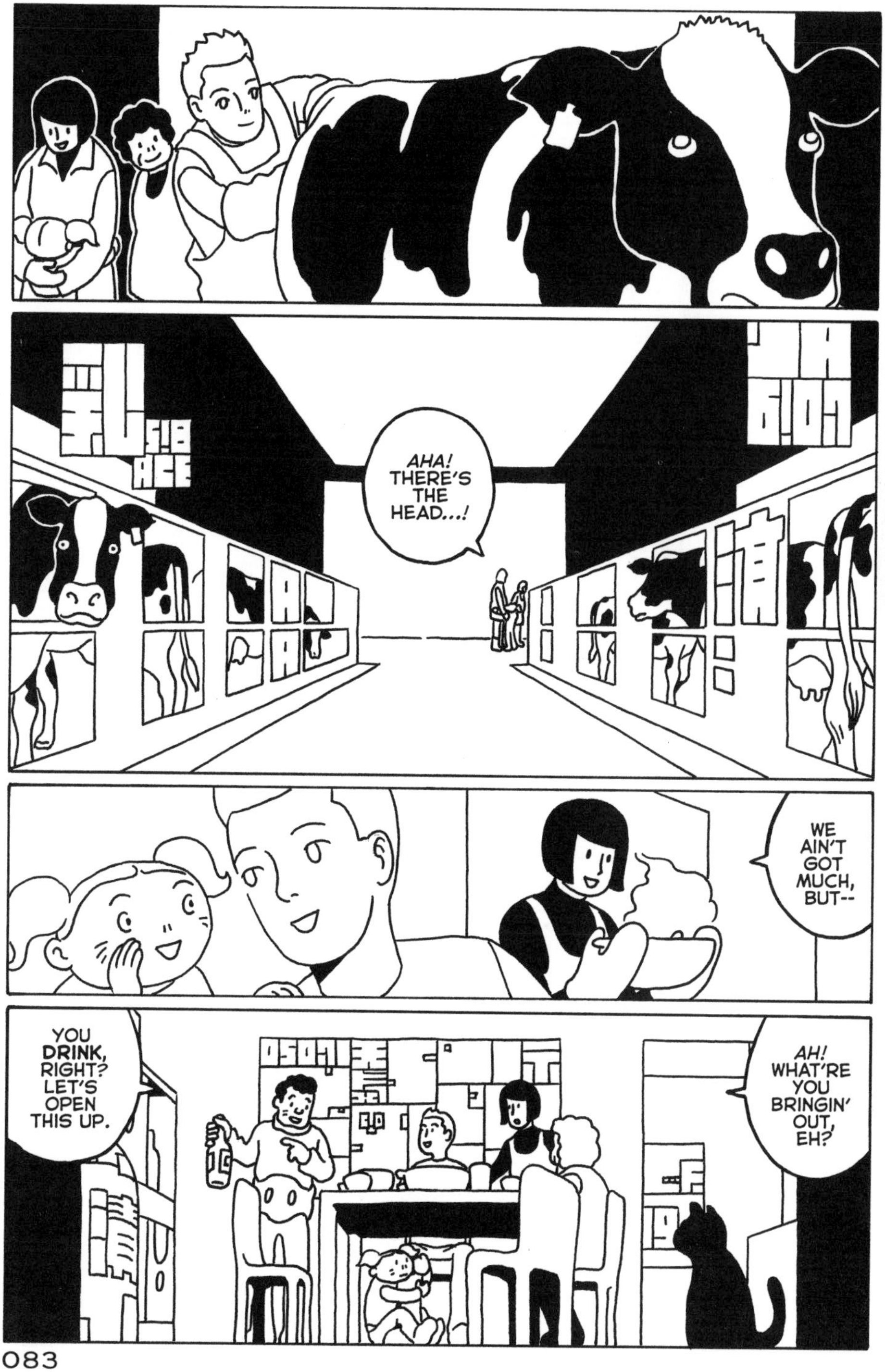
AHA! THERE'S THE HEAD...!
WE AIN'T GOT MUCH, BUT--
AH! WHAT'RE YOU BRINGIN' OUT, EH?
YOU DRINK, RIGHT? LET'S OPEN THIS UP.

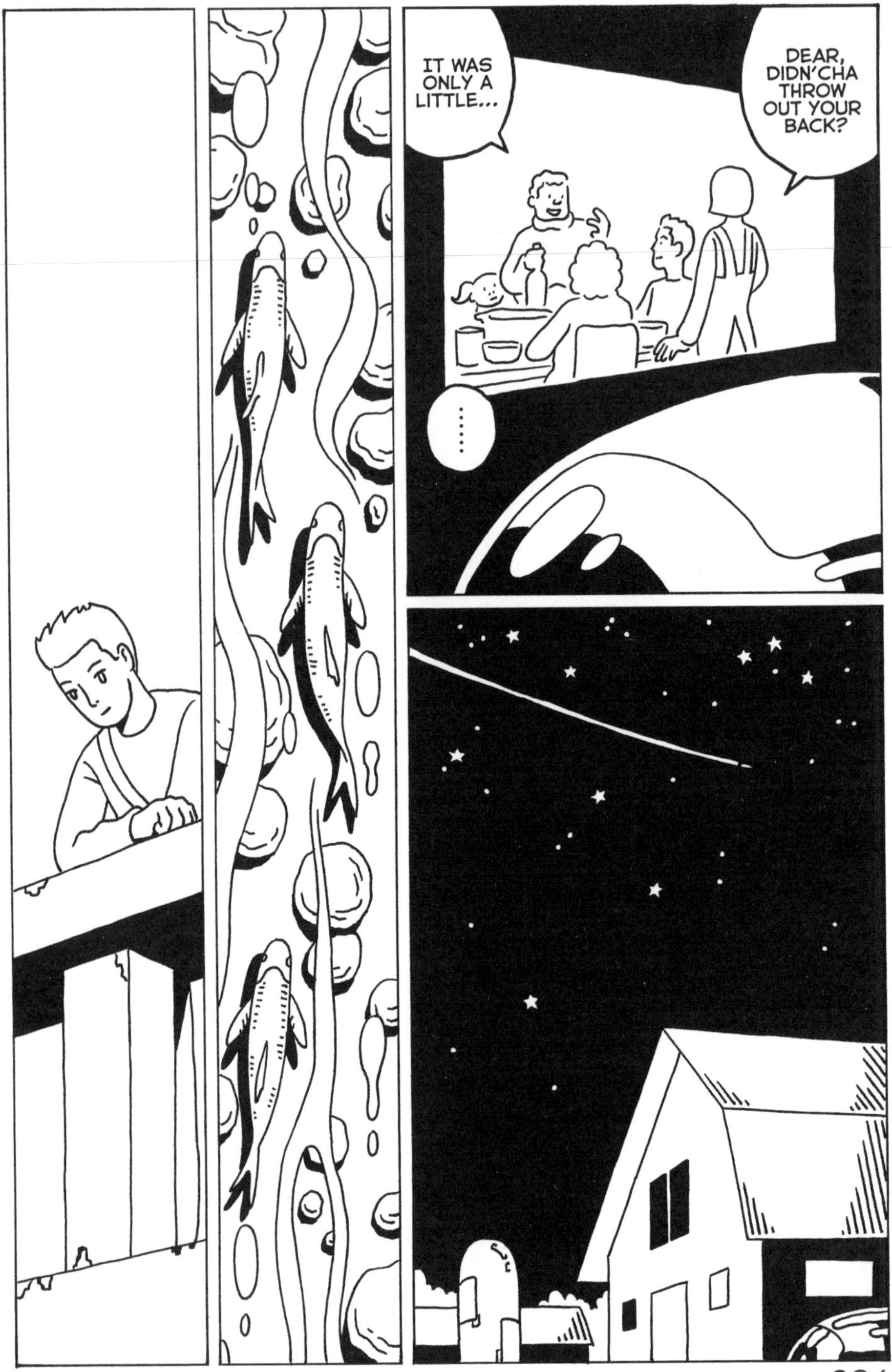
DEAR, DIDN'CHA THROW OUT YOUR BACK?
IT WAS ONLY A LITTLE...
......

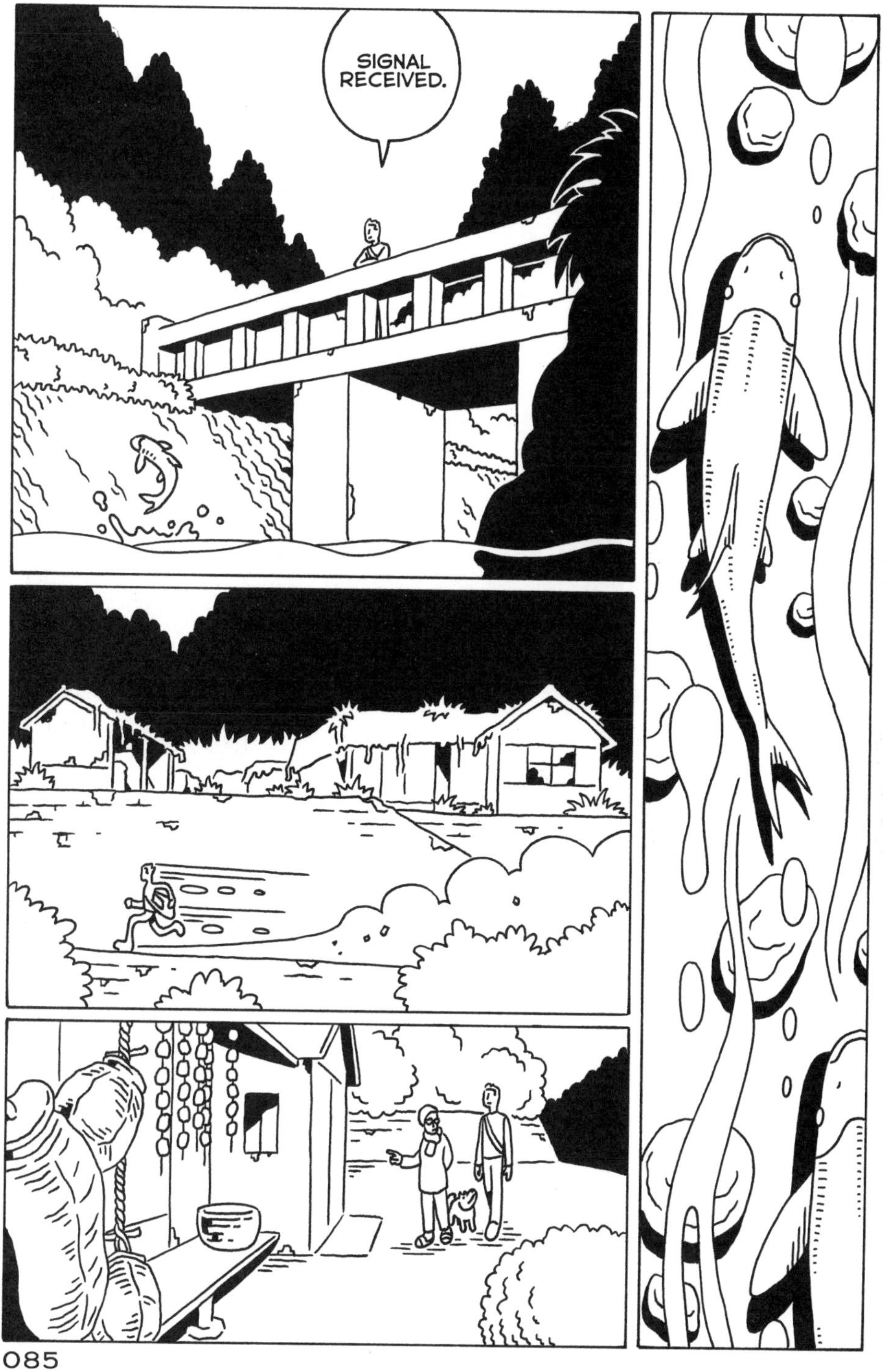
SIGNAL
RECEIVED.

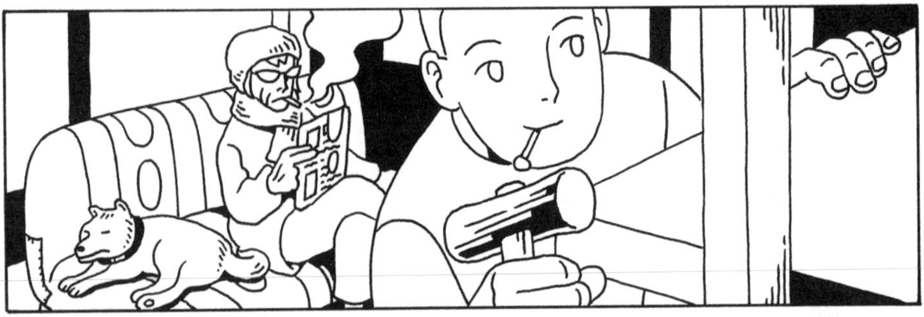
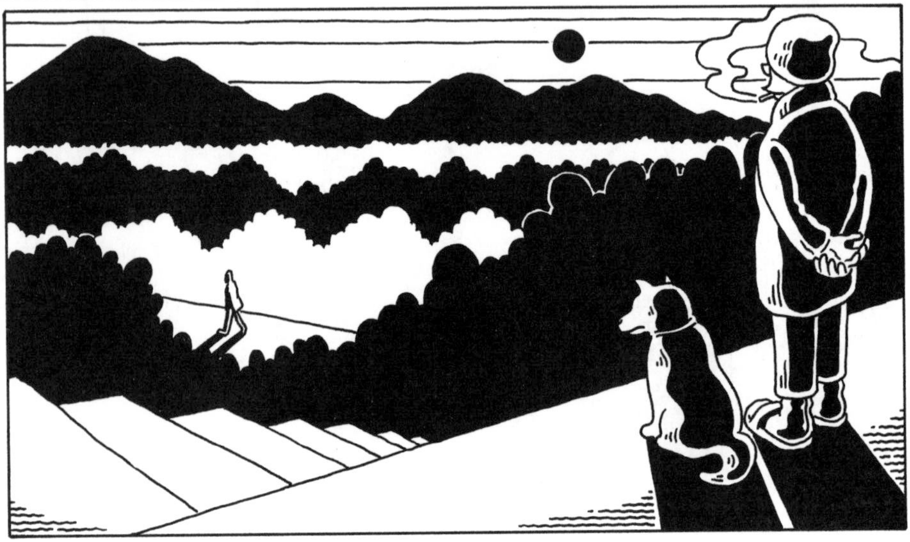
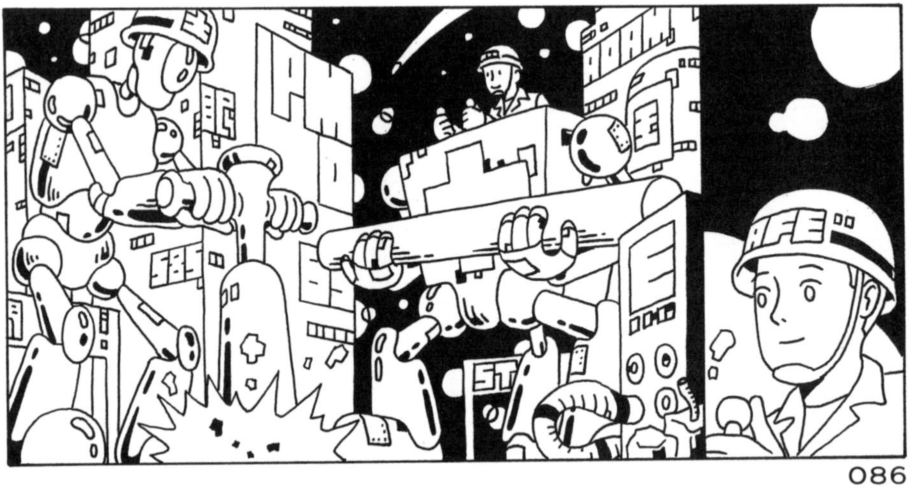

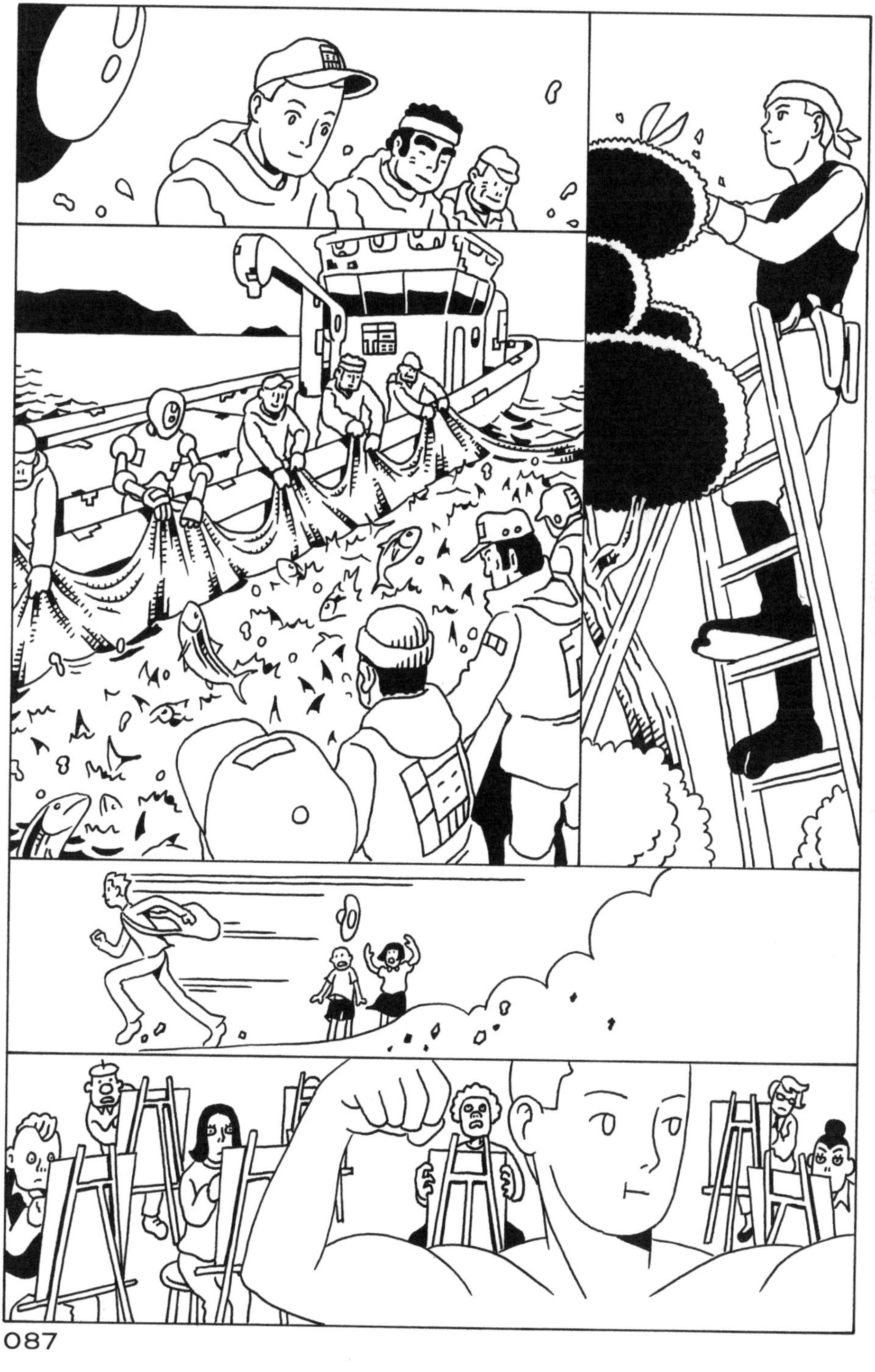

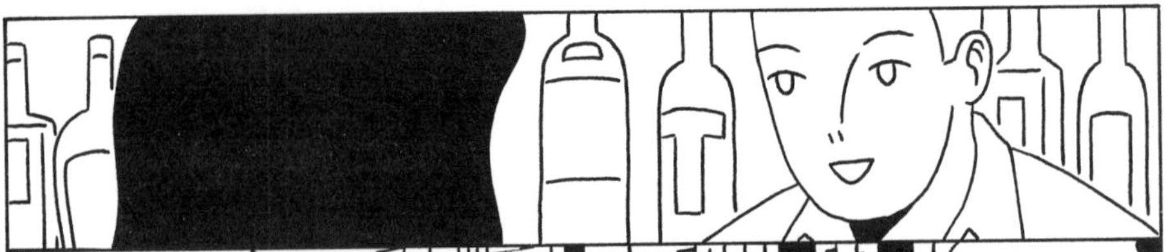
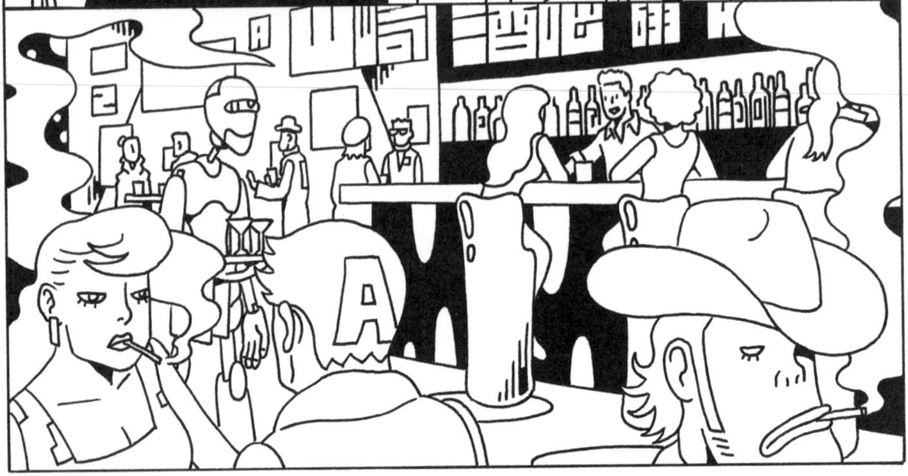
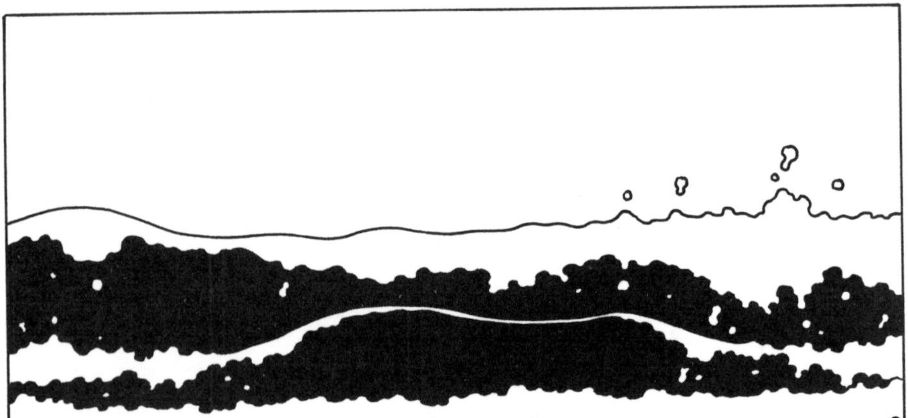
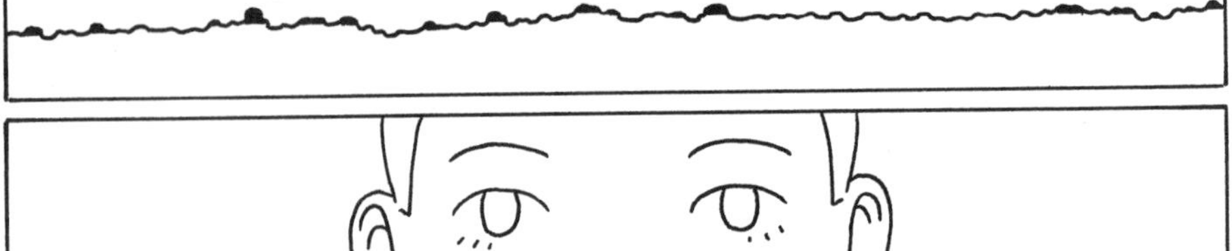

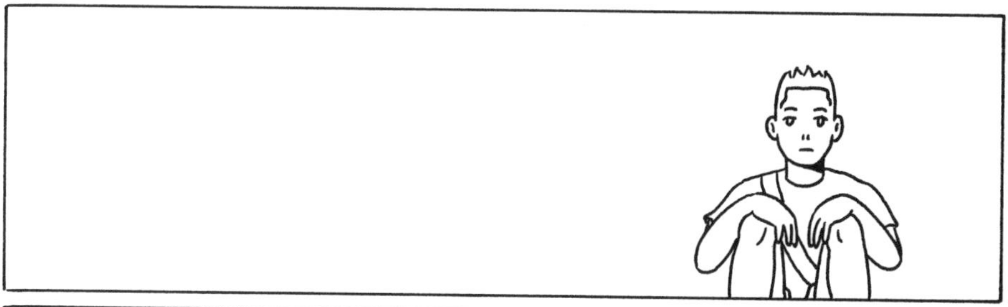
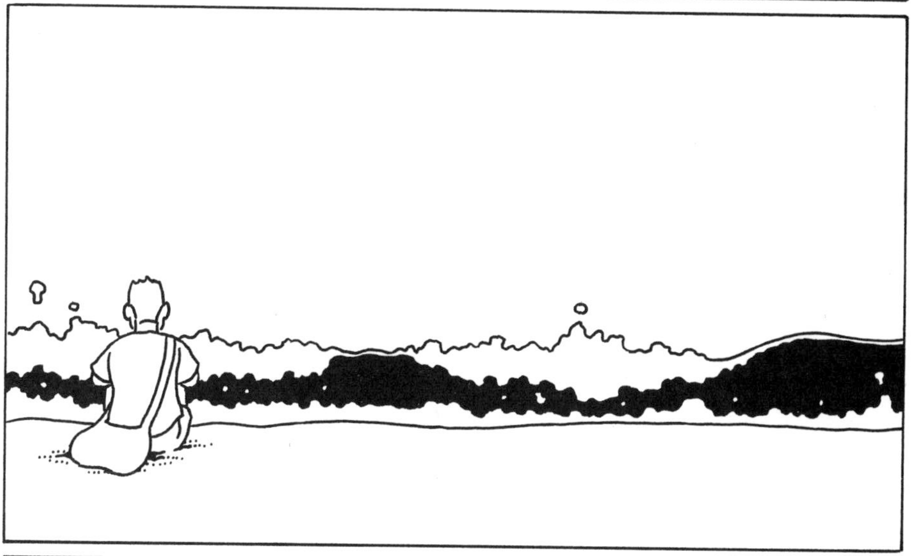
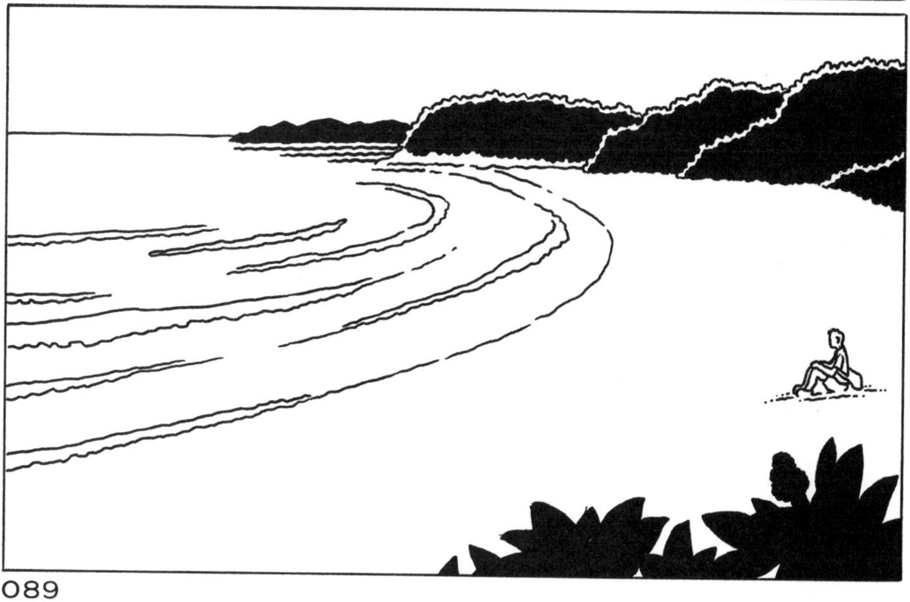

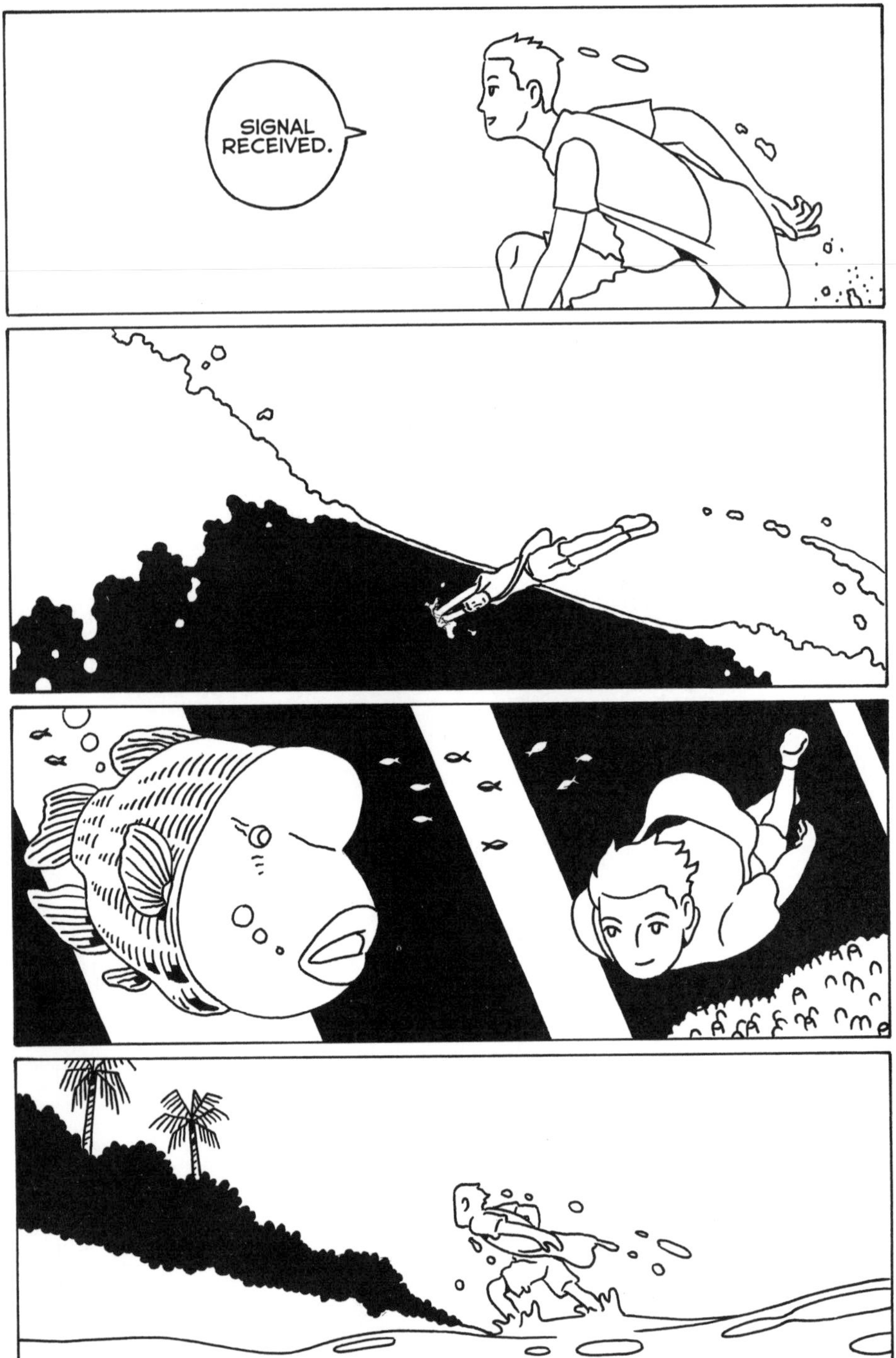
SIGNAL RECEIVED.

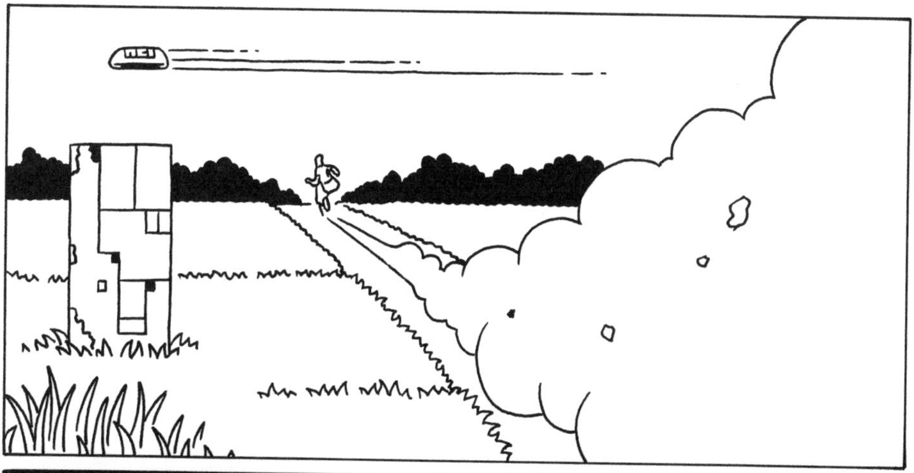

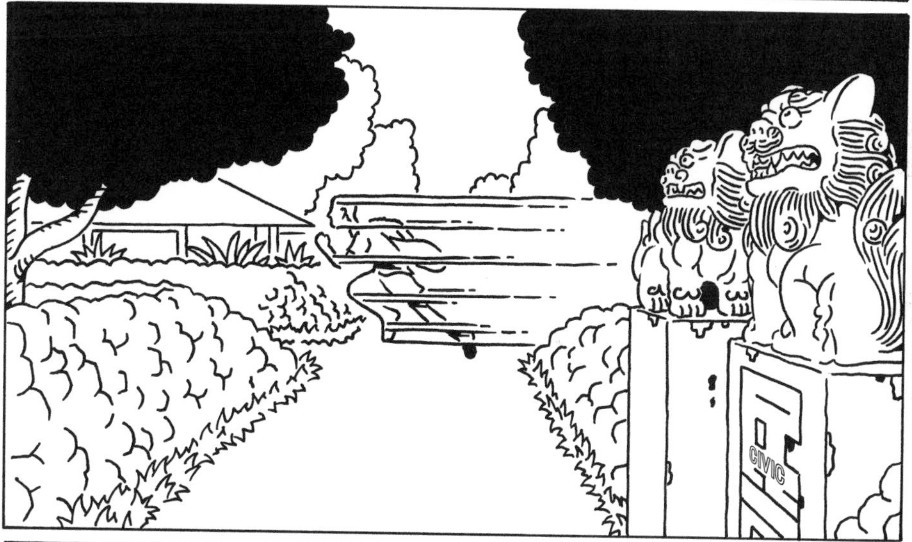

CIVIC

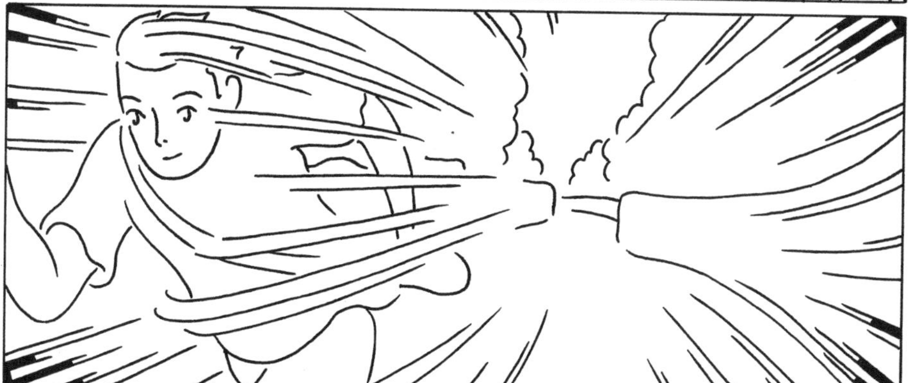

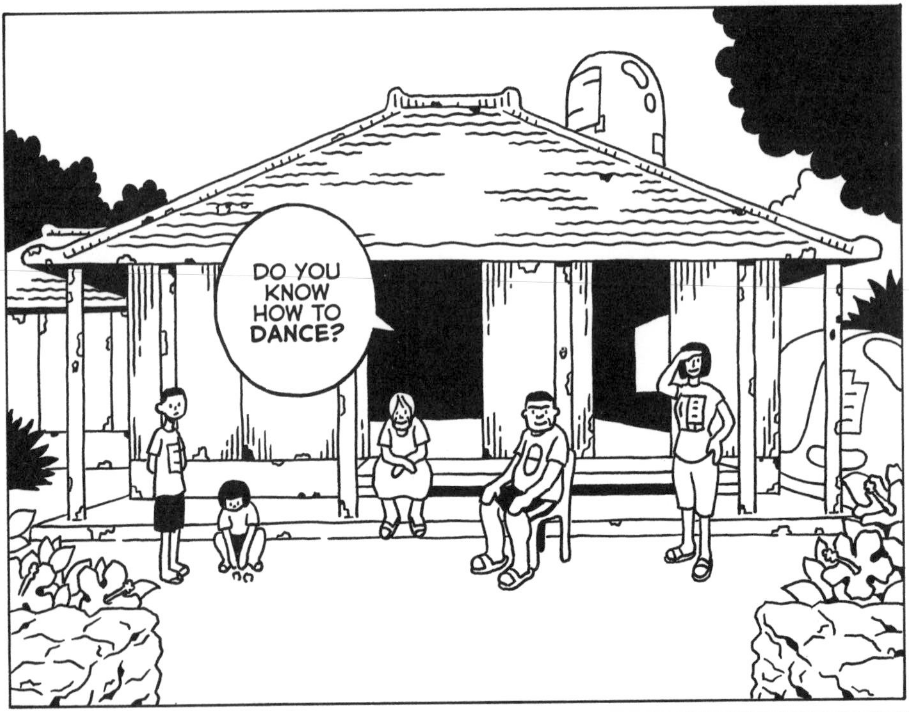
DO YOU KNOW HOW TO DANCE?

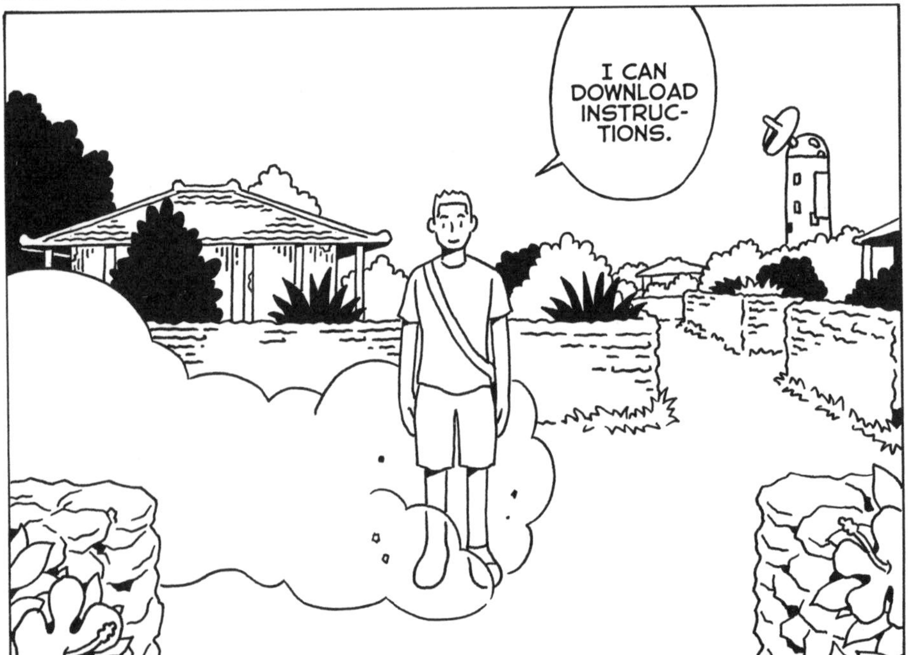
I CAN DOWNLOAD INSTRUC- TIONS.

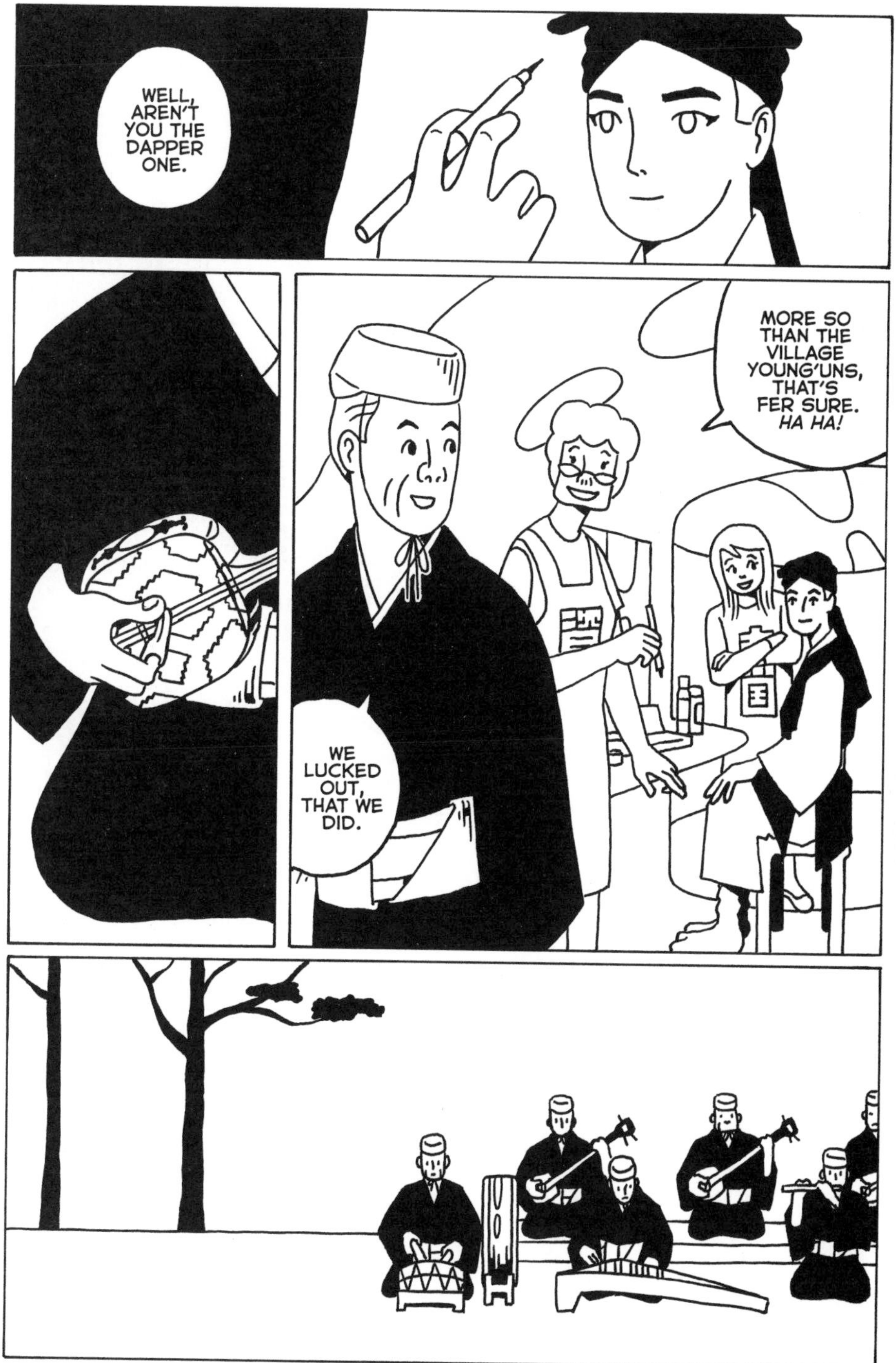
WELL, AREN'T YOU THE DAPPER ONE.
MORE SO THAN THE VILLAGE YOUNG'UNS, THAT'S FER SURE. *HA HA!*
WE LUCKED OUT, THAT WE DID.

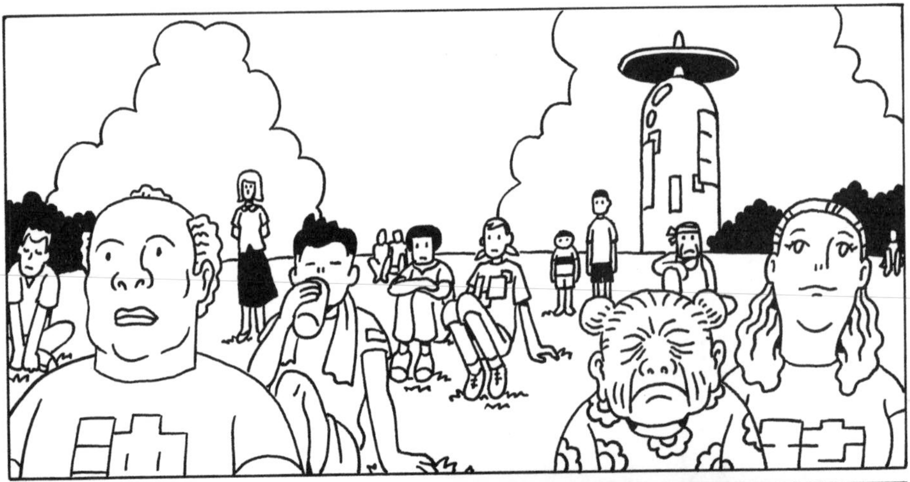

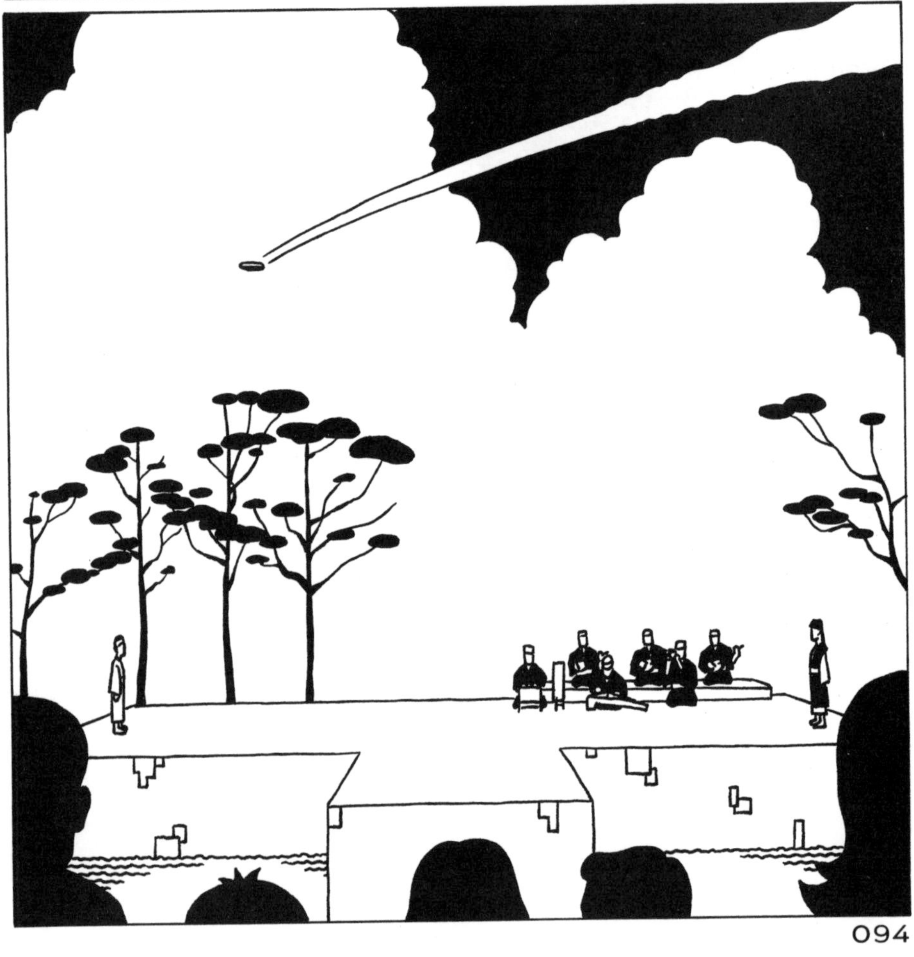

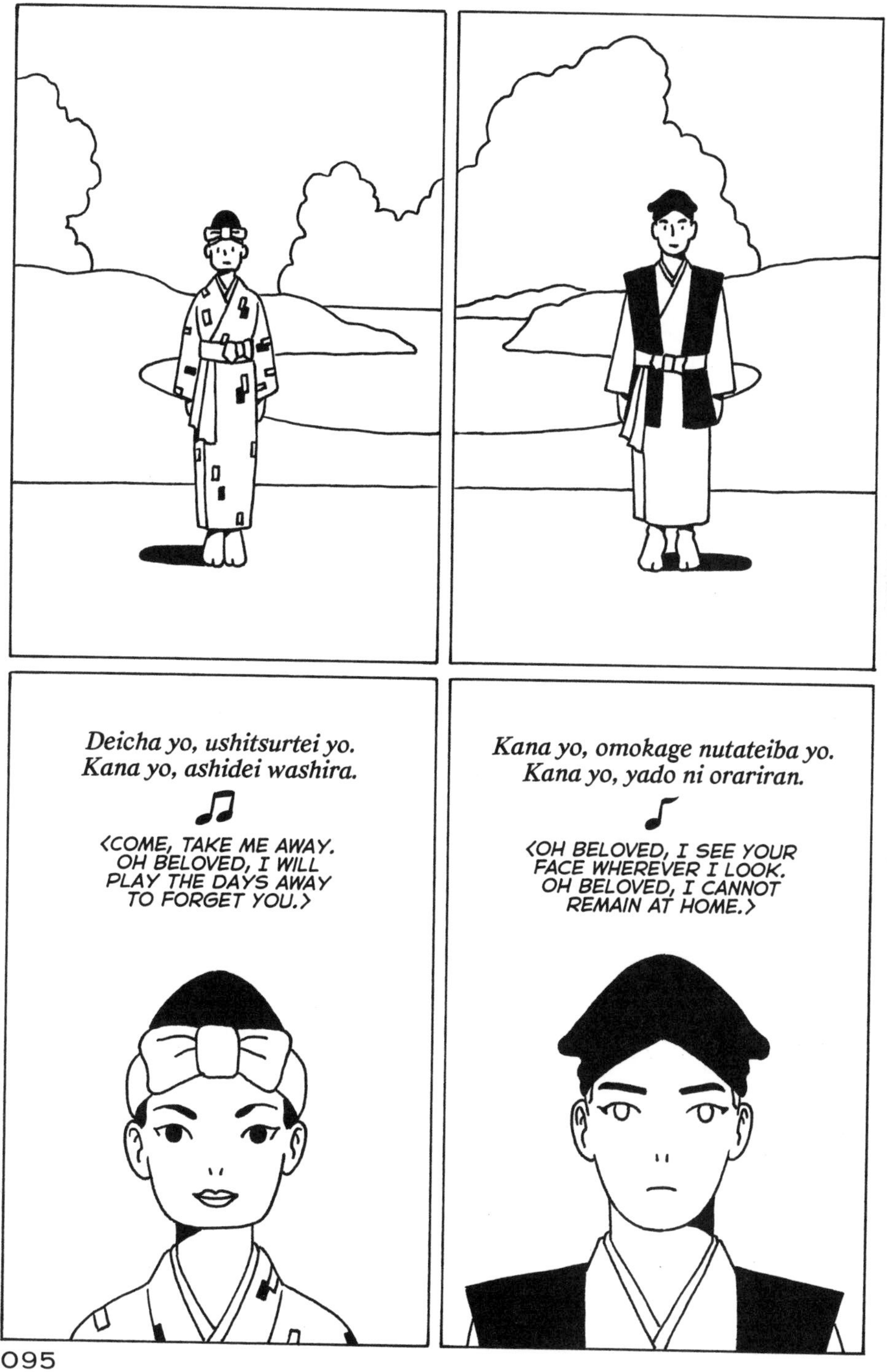
Kana yo, omokage nutateiba yo.
Kana yo, yado ni orariran.
<OH BELOVED, I SEE YOUR FACE WHEREVER I LOOK. OH BELOVED, I CANNOT REMAIN AT HOME.>
Deicha yo, ushitsurtei yo.
Kana yo, ashidei washira.
<COME, TAKE ME AWAY. OH BELOVED, I WILL PLAY THE DAYS AWAY TO FORGET YOU.>

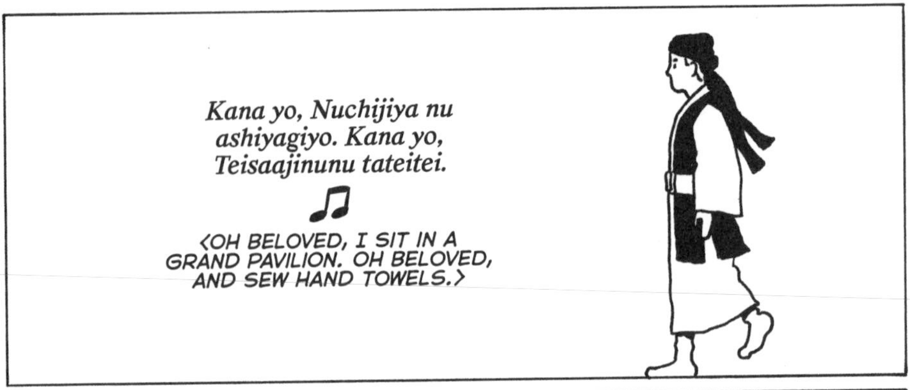
Kana yo, Nuchijiya nu ashiyagiyo. Kana yo, Teisaajinunu tateitei.
♫
<OH BELOVED, I SIT IN A GRAND PAVILION. OH BELOVED, AND SEW HAND TOWELS.>

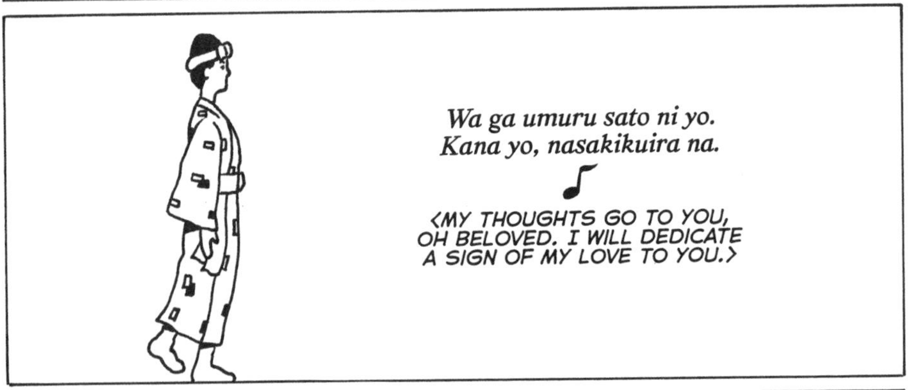
Wa ga umuru sato ni yo. Kana yo, nasakikuira na.
♪
<MY THOUGHTS GO TO YOU, OH BELOVED. I WILL DEDICATE A SIGN OF MY LOVE TO YOU.>

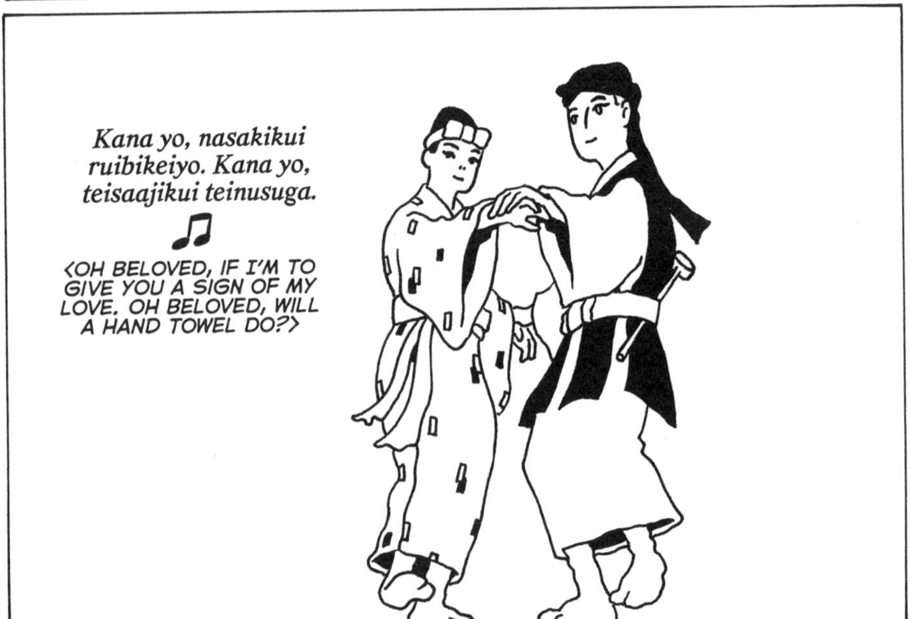
Kana yo, nasakikui ruibikeiyo. Kana yo, teisaajikui teinusuga.
♫
<OH BELOVED, IF I'M TO GIVE YOU A SIGN OF MY LOVE. OH BELOVED, WILL A HAND TOWEL DO?>

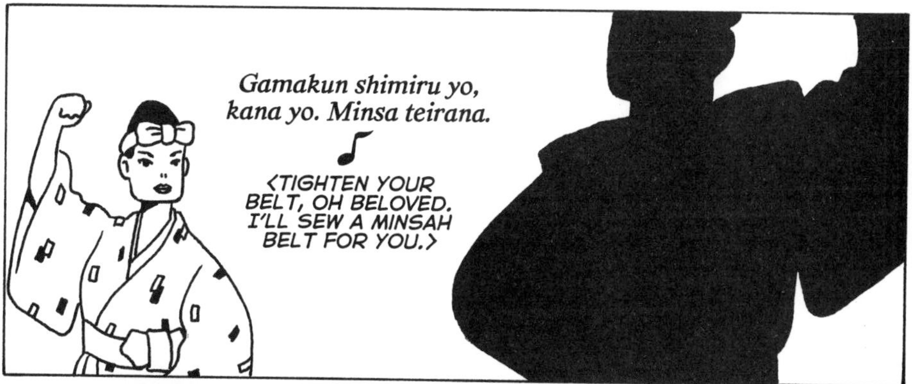
Gamakun shimiru yo, kana yo. Minsa teirana.
<TIGHTEN YOUR BELT, OH BELOVED. I'LL SEW A MINSAH BELT FOR YOU.>
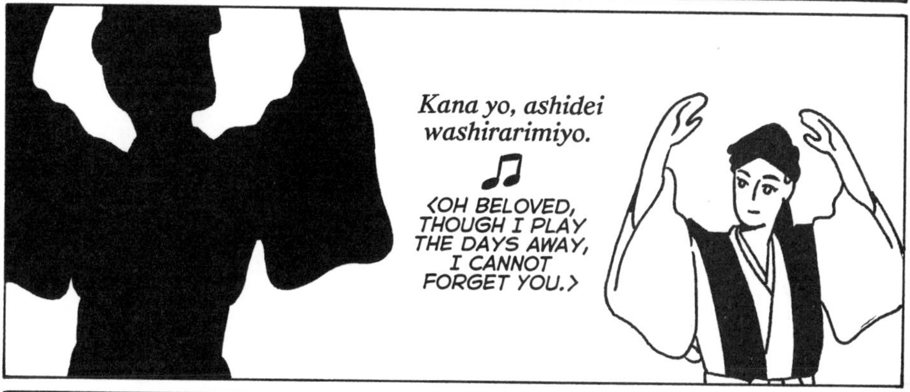
Kana yo, ashidei washirarimiyo.
<OH BELOVED, THOUGH I PLAY THE DAYS AWAY, I CANNOT FORGET YOU.>
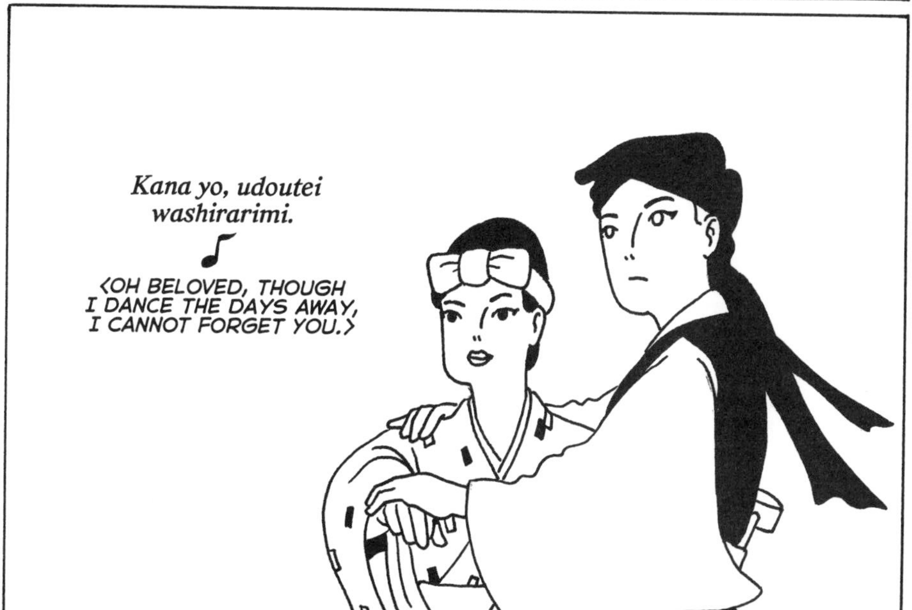
Kana yo, udoutei washirarimi.
<OH BELOVED, THOUGH I DANCE THE DAYS AWAY, I CANNOT FORGET YOU.>

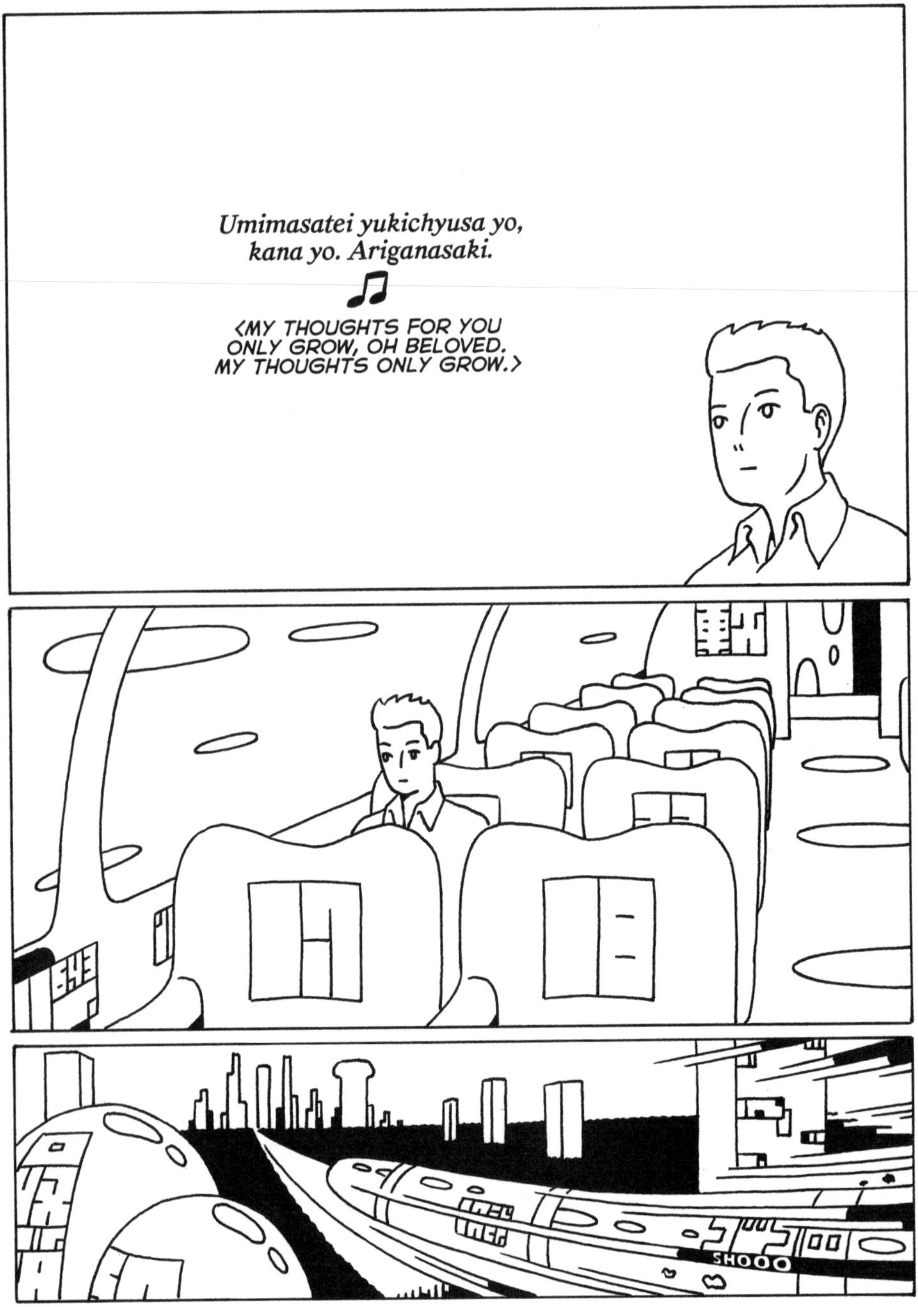
Umimasatei yukichyusa yo,
kana yo. Ariganasaki.
<MY THOUGHTS FOR YOU
ONLY GROW, OH BELOVED.
MY THOUGHTS ONLY GROW.>
SHOOO

#4/END

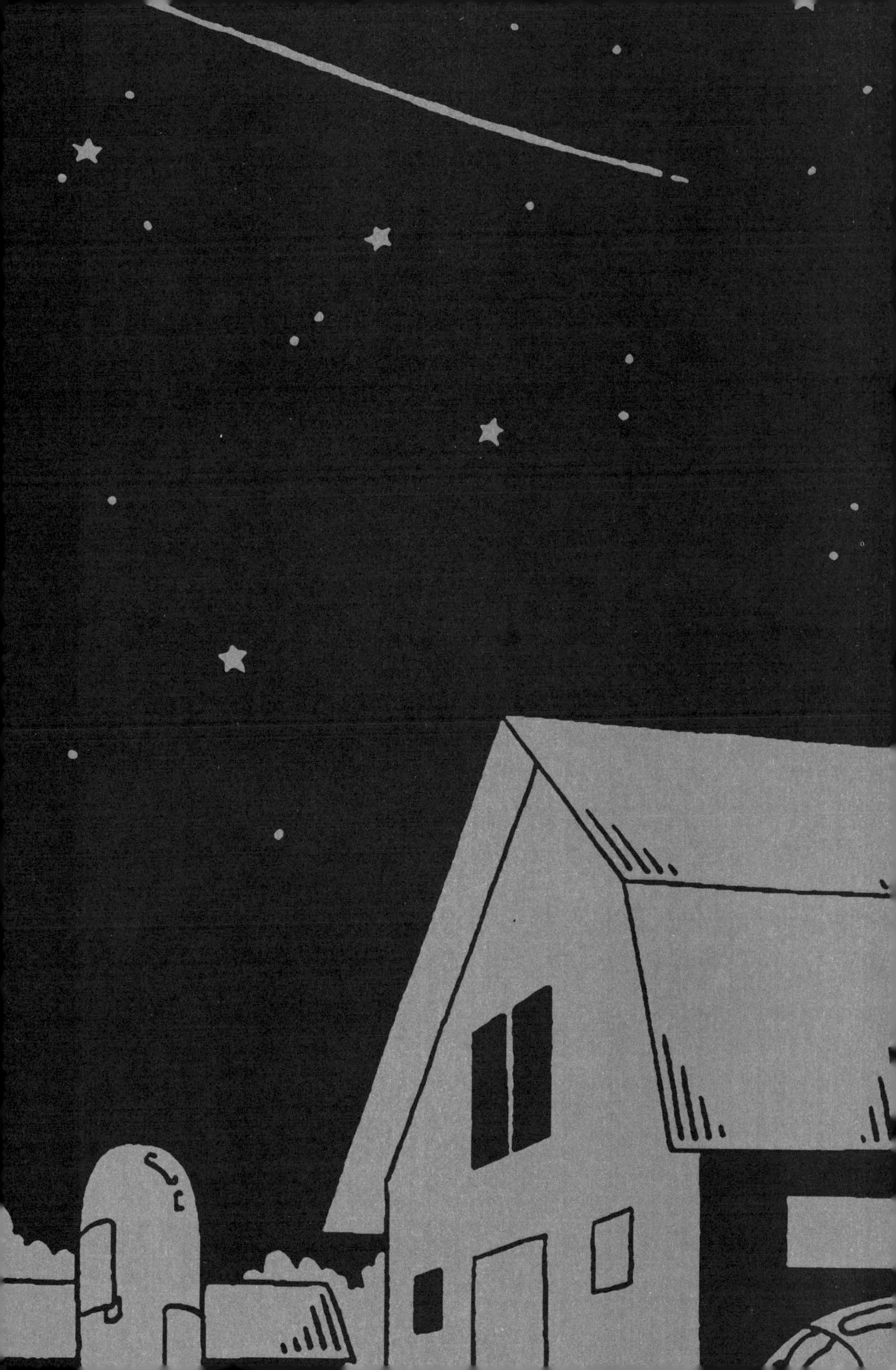

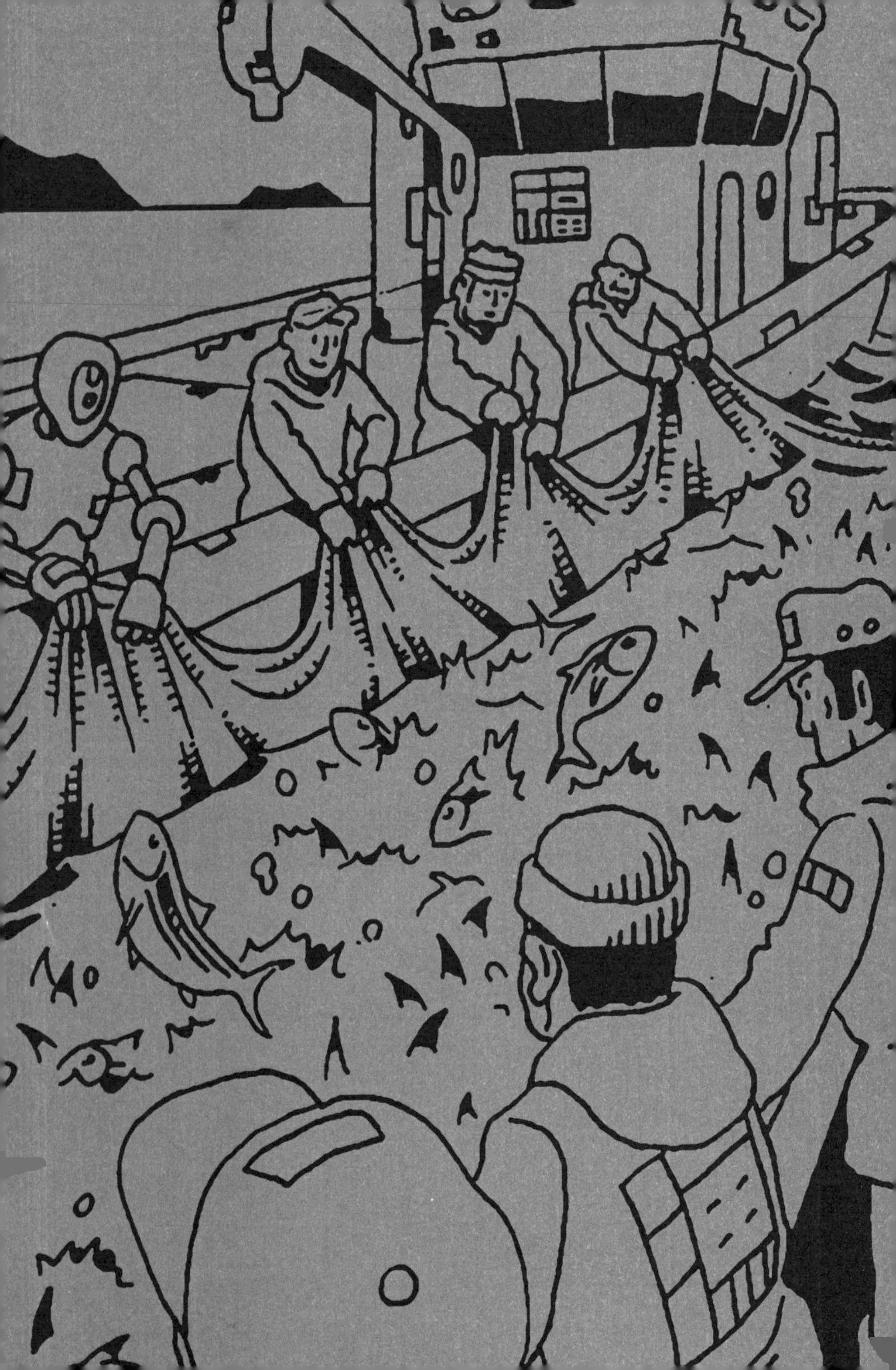

#5

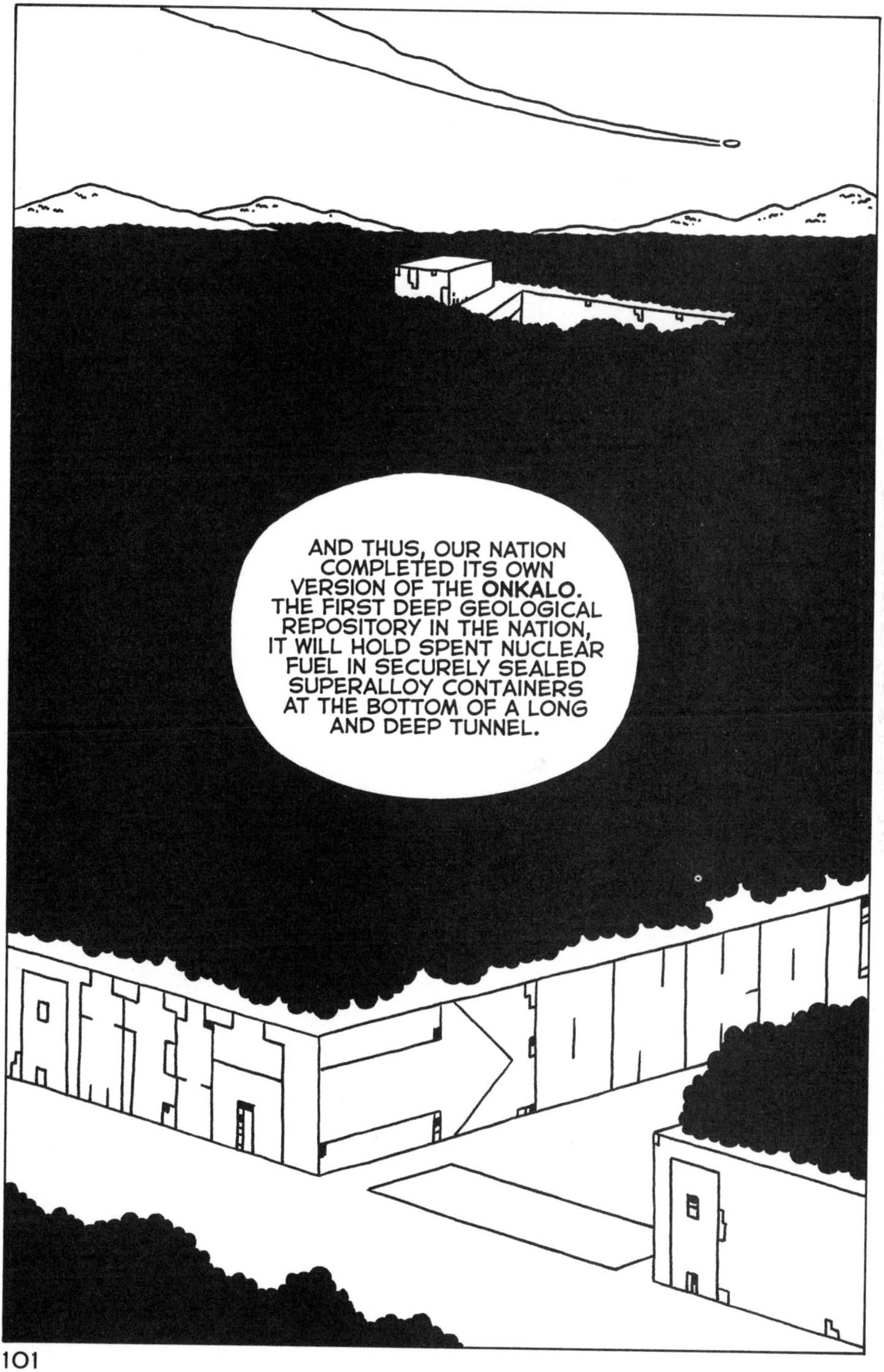
AND THUS, OUR NATION COMPLETED ITS OWN VERSION OF THE **ONKALO**. THE FIRST DEEP GEOLOGICAL REPOSITORY IN THE NATION, IT WILL HOLD SPENT NUCLEAR FUEL IN SECURELY SEALED SUPERALLOY CONTAINERS AT THE BOTTOM OF A LONG AND DEEP TUNNEL.

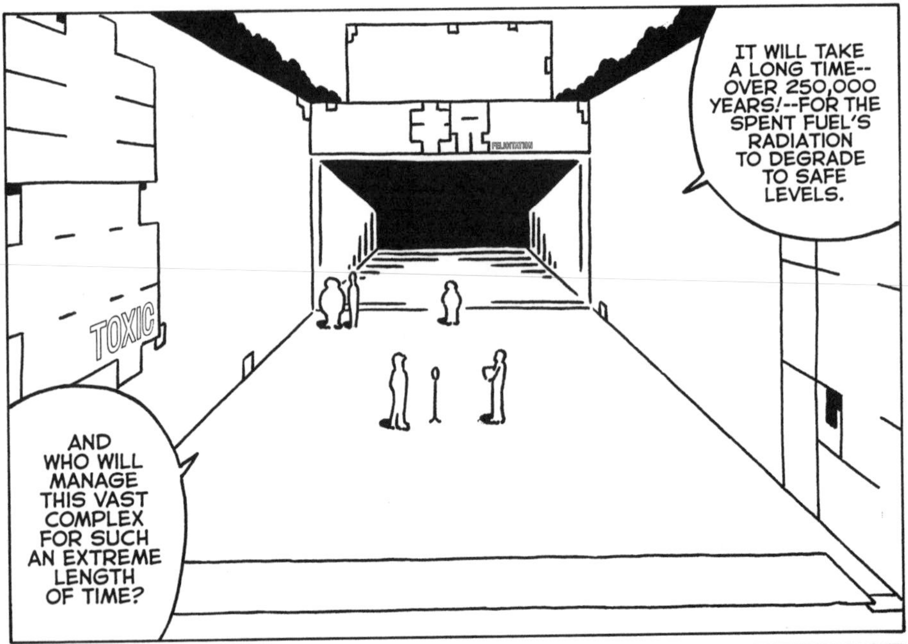
IT WILL TAKE A LONG TIME--OVER 250,000 YEARS!--FOR THE SPENT FUEL'S RADIATION TO DEGRADE TO SAFE LEVELS.
FELICITATION
TOXIC
AND WHO WILL MANAGE THIS VAST COMPLEX FOR SUCH AN EXTREME LENGTH OF TIME?

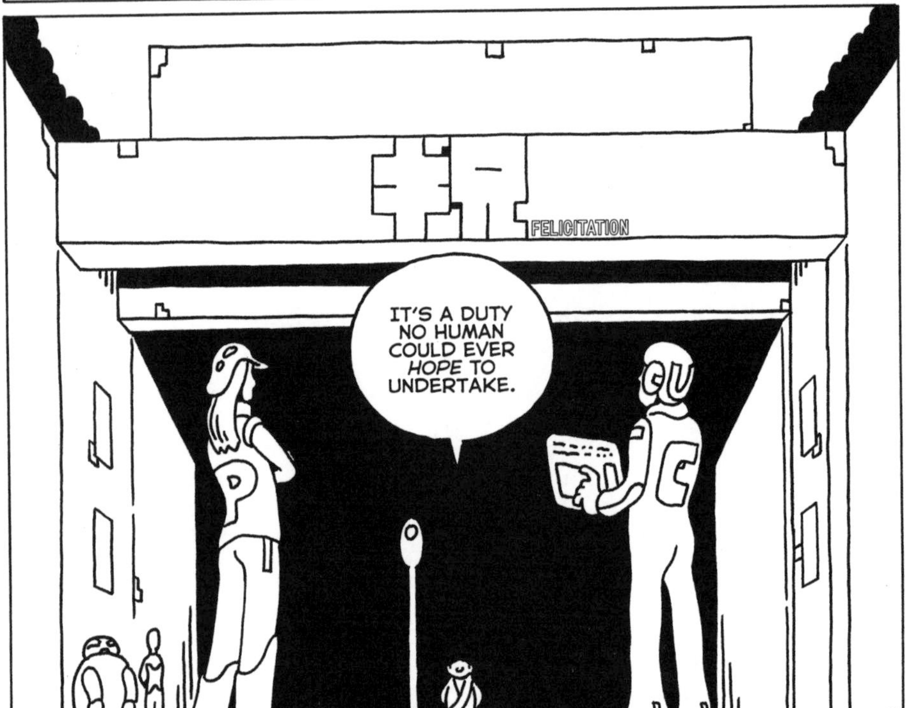
FELICITATION
IT'S A DUTY NO HUMAN COULD EVER *HOPE* TO UNDERTAKE.

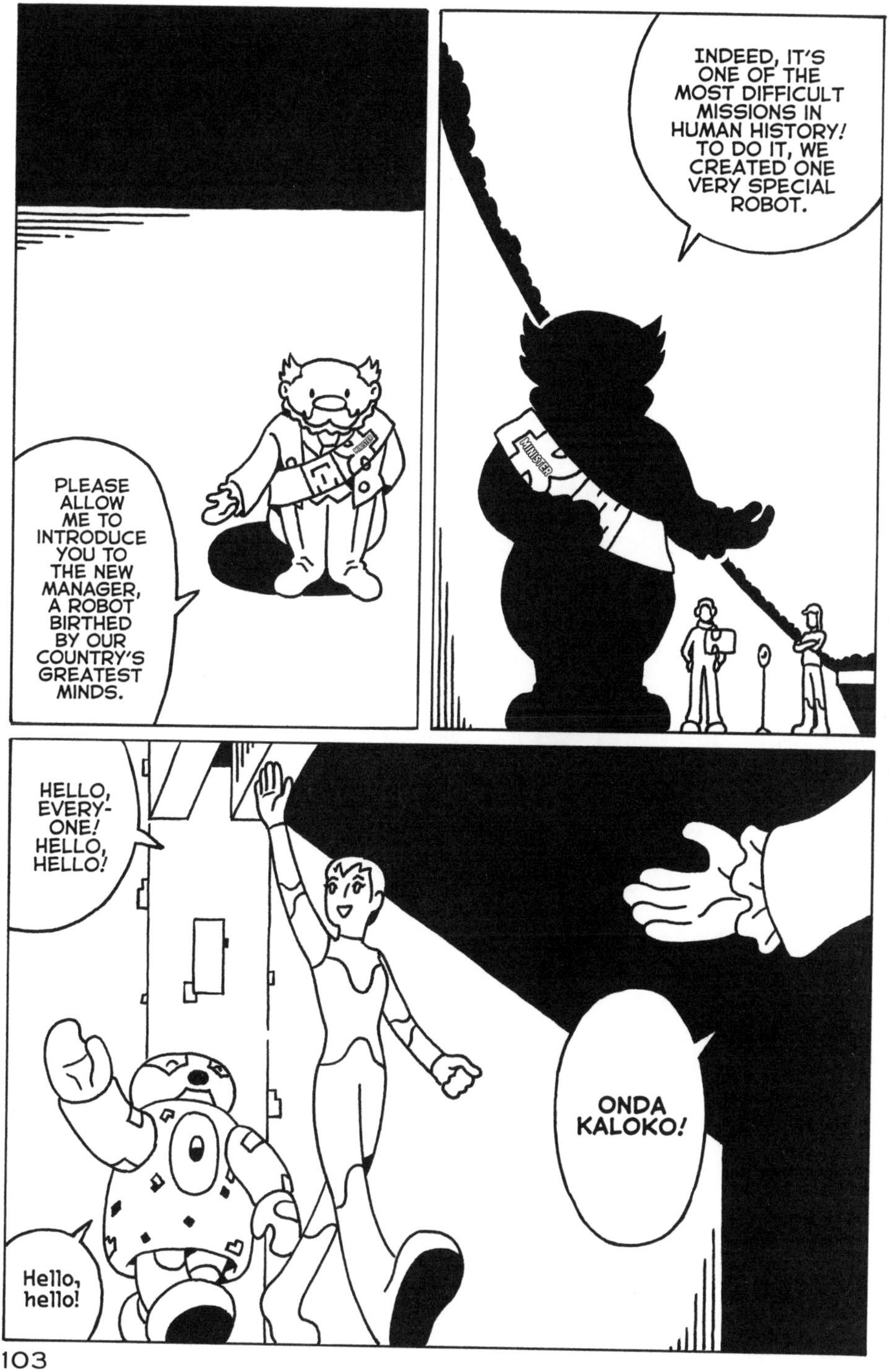
INDEED, IT'S ONE OF THE MOST DIFFICULT MISSIONS IN HUMAN HISTORY! TO DO IT, WE CREATED ONE VERY SPECIAL ROBOT.
MINISTER
MINISTER
PLEASE ALLOW ME TO INTRODUCE YOU TO THE NEW MANAGER, A ROBOT BIRTHED BY OUR COUNTRY'S GREATEST MINDS.
ONDA KALOKO!
HELLO, EVERY-ONE! HELLO, HELLO!
Hello, hello!

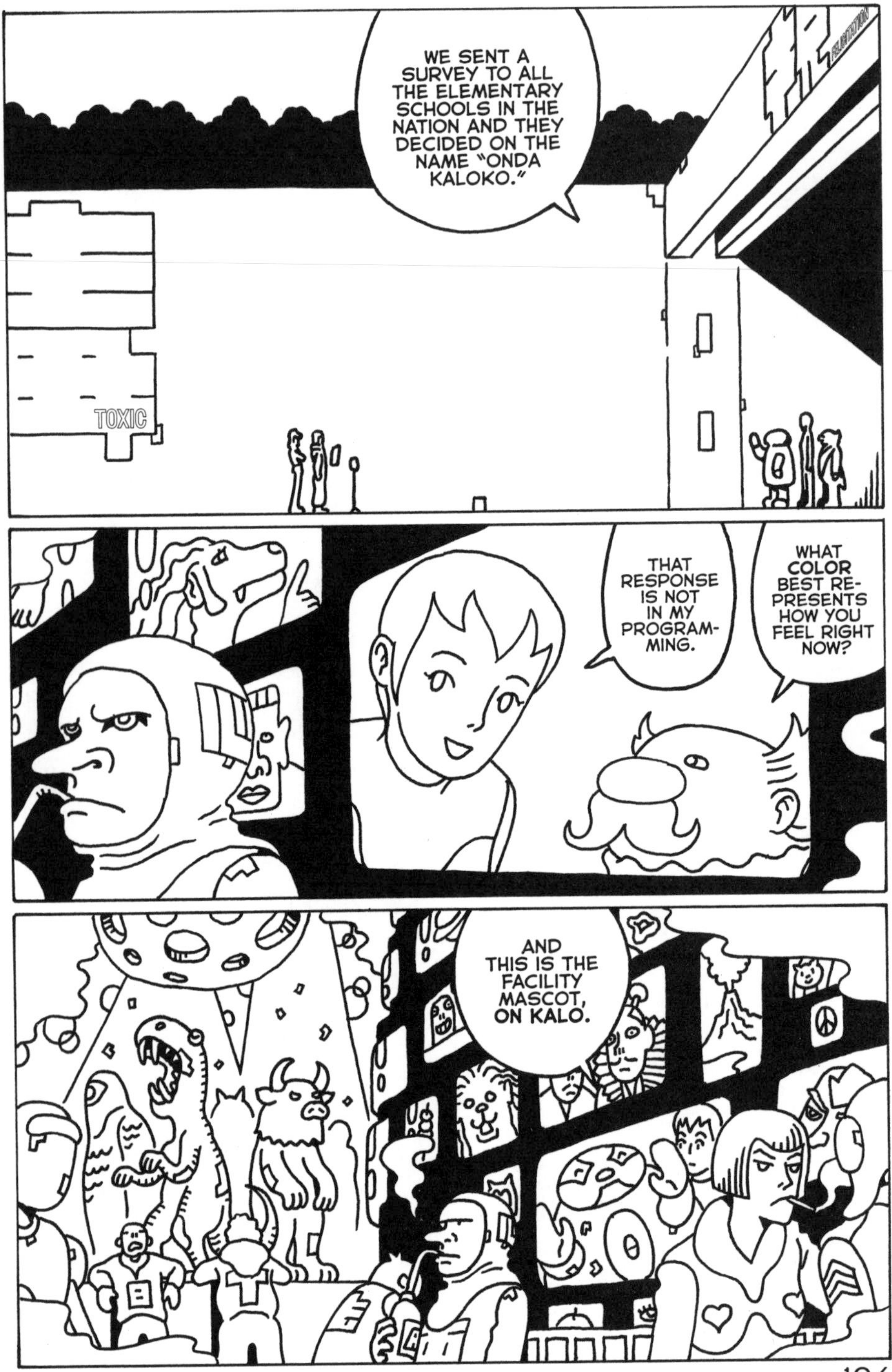
WE SENT A SURVEY TO ALL THE ELEMENTARY SCHOOLS IN THE NATION AND THEY DECIDED ON THE NAME "ONDA KALOKO."
TOXIC
WHAT COLOR BEST REPRESENTS HOW YOU FEEL RIGHT NOW?
THAT RESPONSE IS NOT IN MY PROGRAMMING.
AND THIS IS THE FACILITY MASCOT, ON KALO.

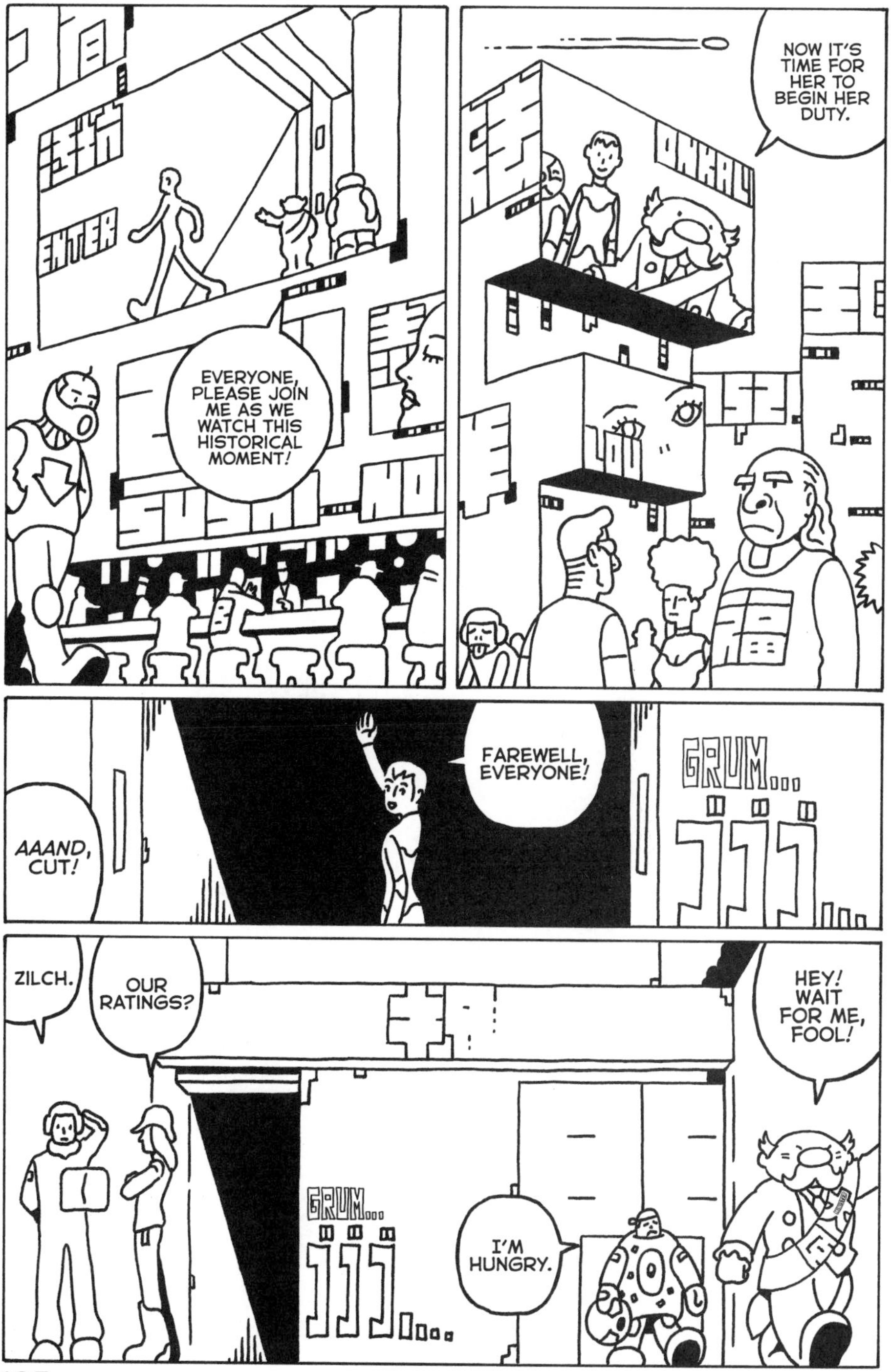
NOW IT'S TIME FOR HER TO BEGIN HER DUTY.
ONKALY
EVERYONE, PLEASE JOIN ME AS WE WATCH THIS HISTORICAL MOMENT!
ENTER
SUSHI
GRUM...
FAREWELL, EVERYONE!
AAAND, CUT!
HEY! WAIT FOR ME, FOOL!
I'M HUNGRY.
GRUM...
OUR RATINGS?
ZILCH.

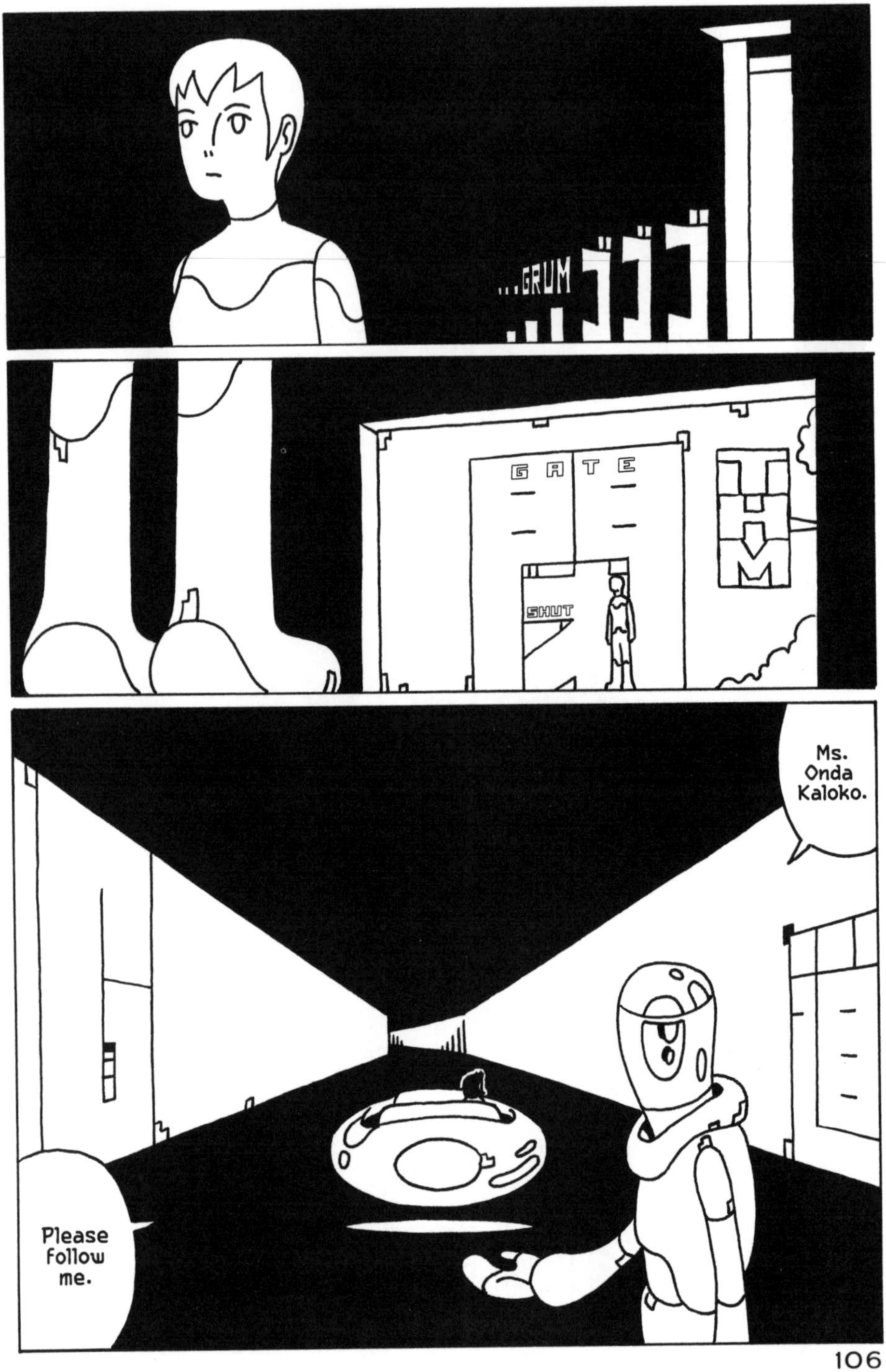
...GRUM
ゴゴゴ
GATE
SHUT
THM
Ms. Onda Kaloko.
Please follow me.

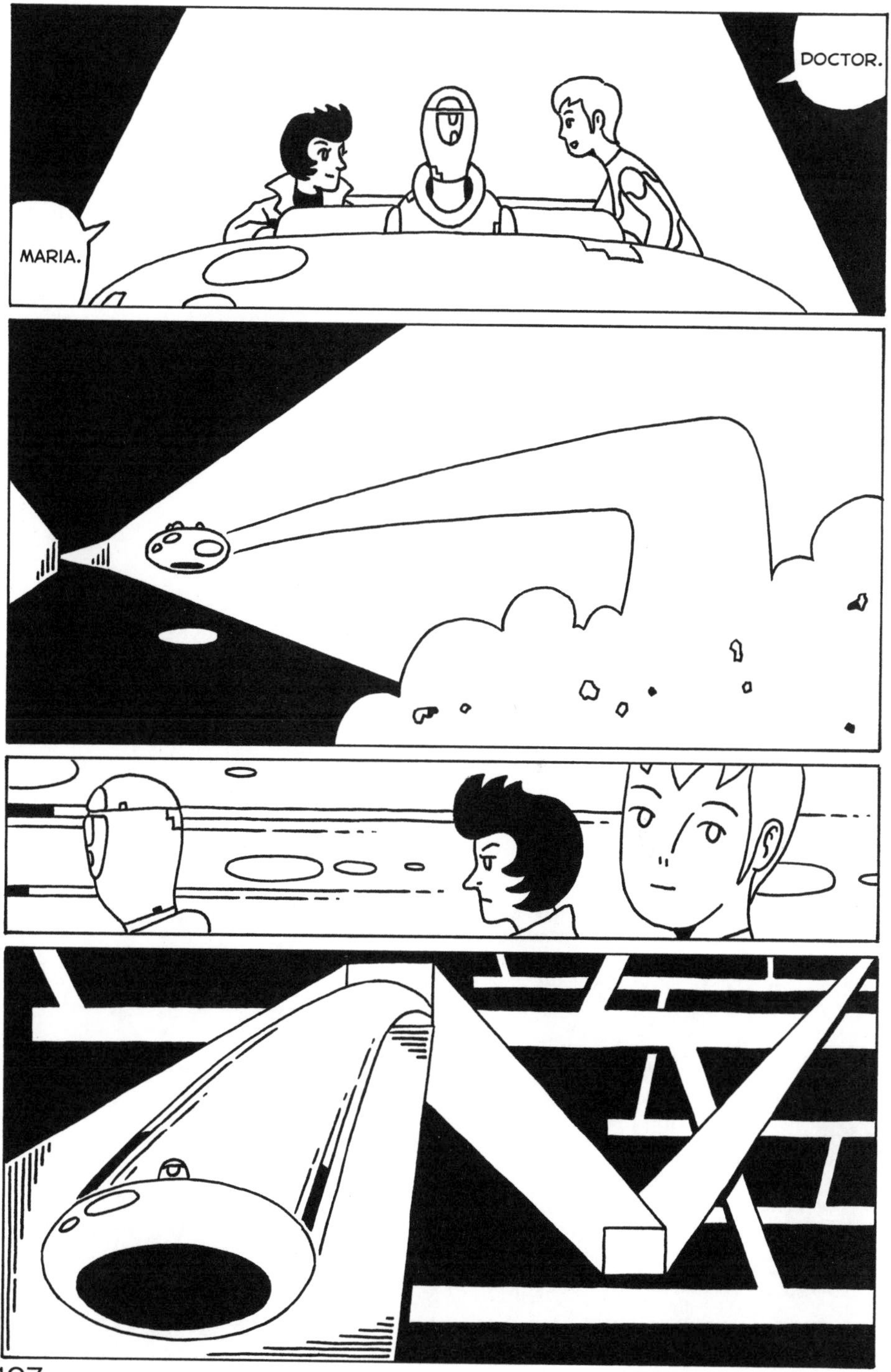
DOCTOR.
MARIA.

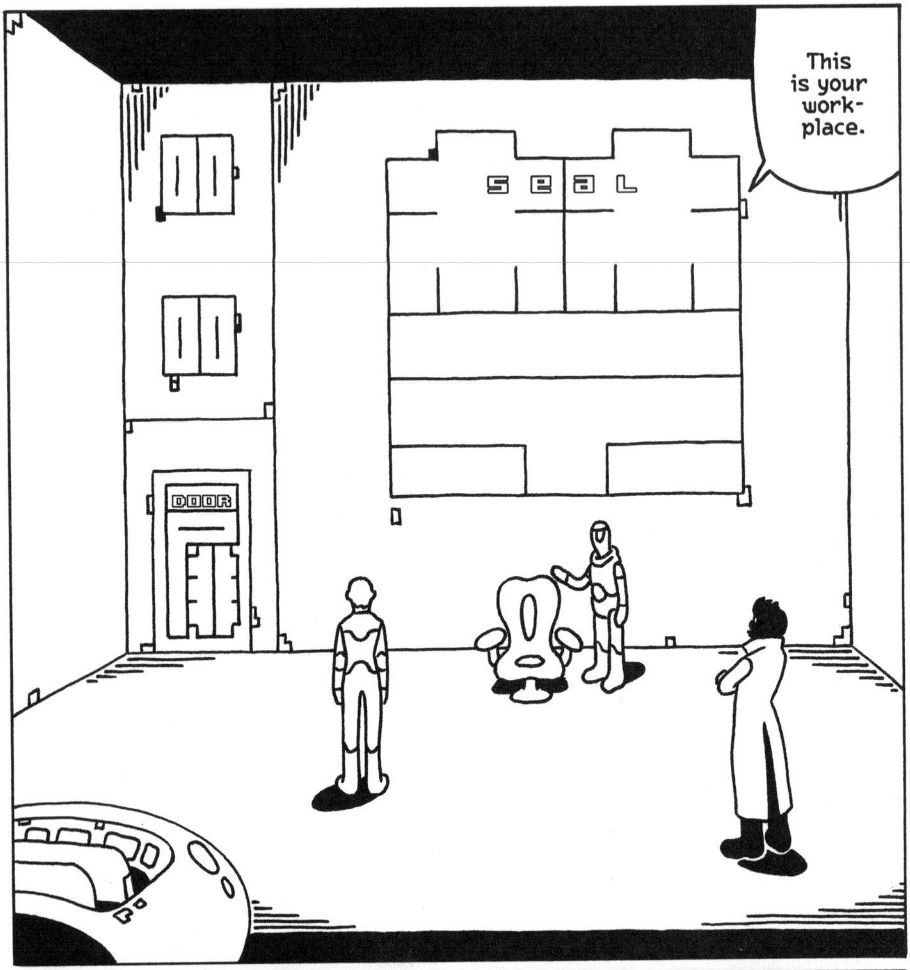
This is your work-place.
seal
DOOR

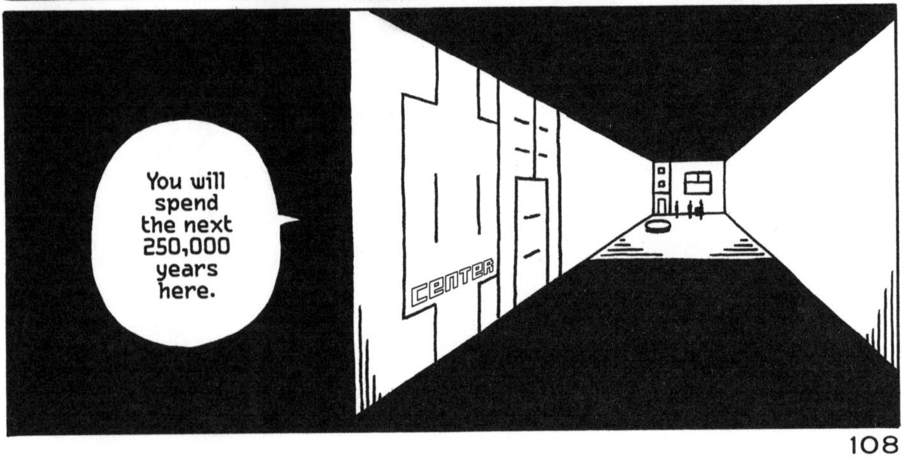
You will spend the next 250,000 years here.
CENTER

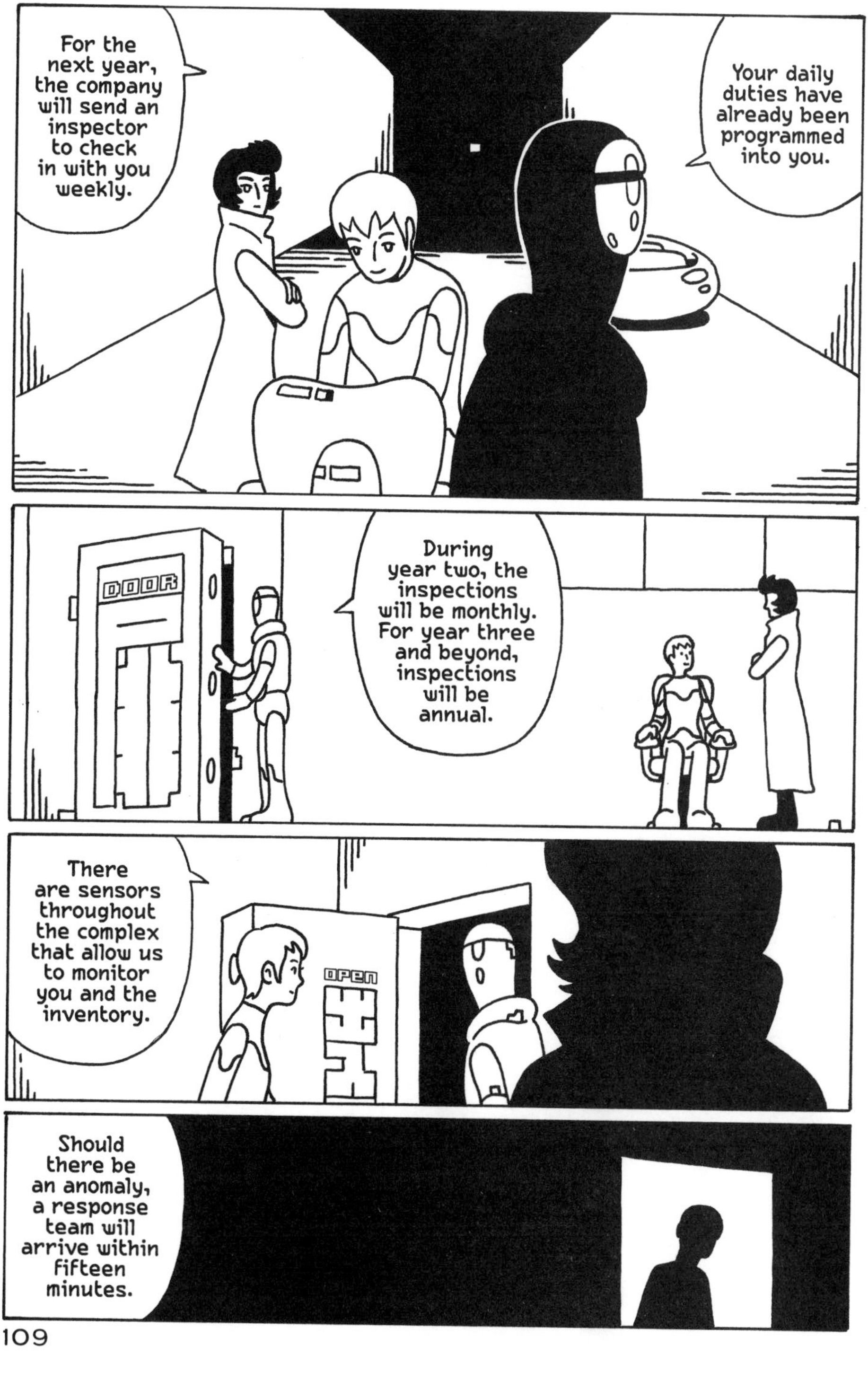
Your daily duties have already been programmed into you.
For the next year, the company will send an inspector to check in with you weekly.
During year two, the inspections will be monthly. For year three and beyond, inspections will be annual.
There are sensors throughout the complex that allow us to monitor you and the inventory.
DOOR
OPEN
Should there be an anomaly, a response team will arrive within fifteen minutes.

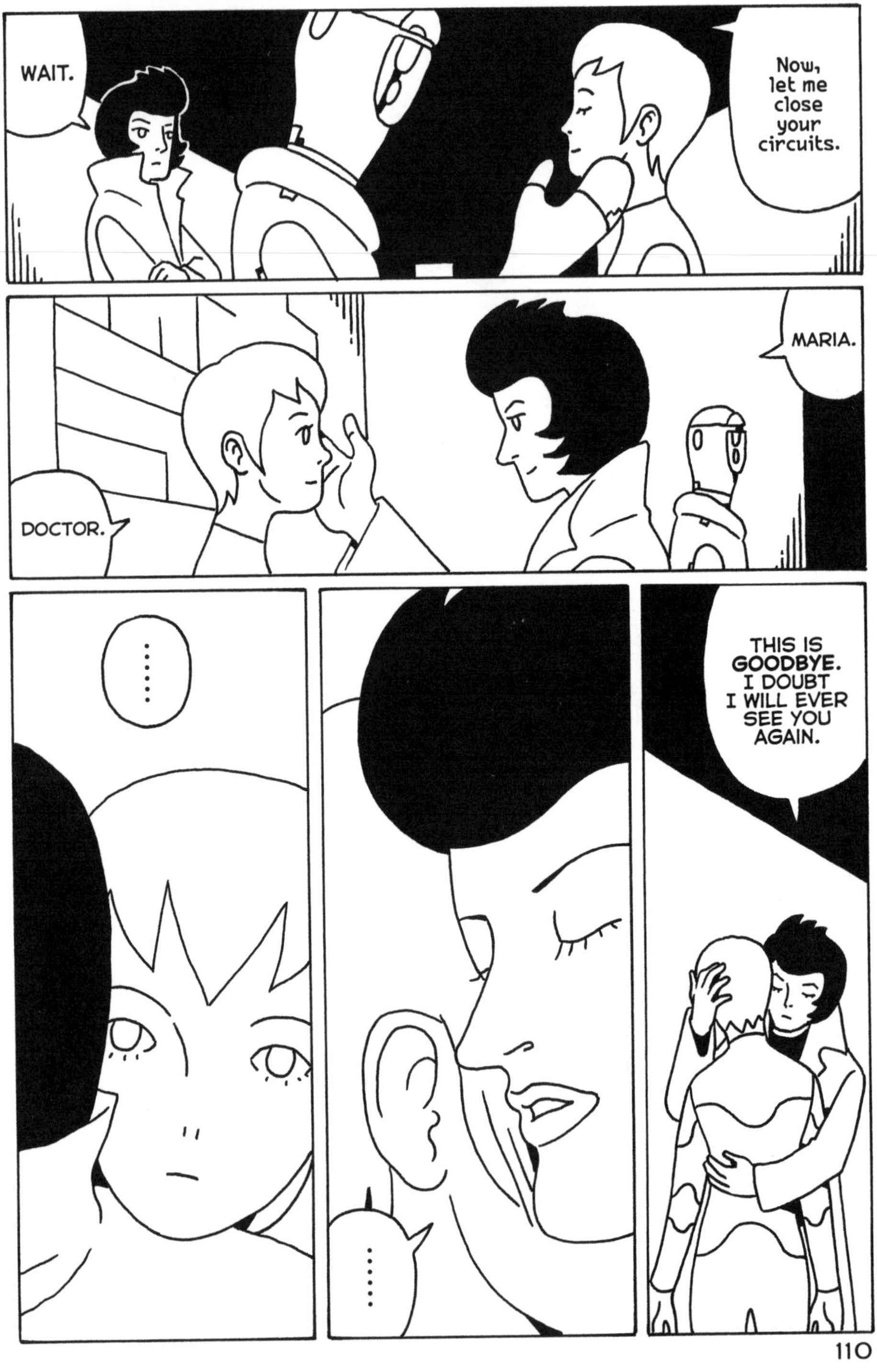
Now, let me close your circuits.
WAIT.
MARIA.
DOCTOR.
THIS IS **GOODBYE.** I DOUBT I WILL EVER SEE YOU AGAIN.
......
......

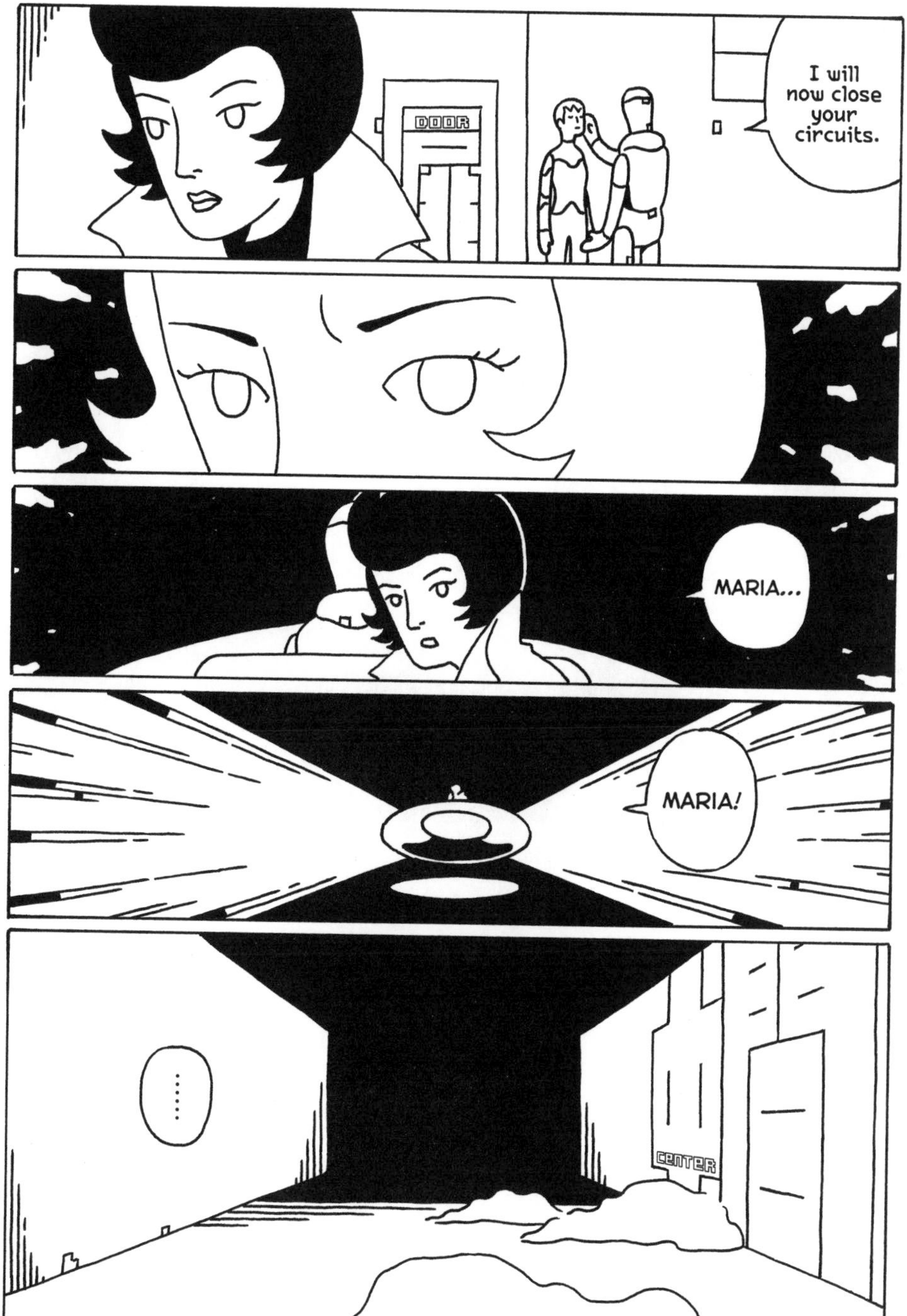
I will now close your circuits.
DOOR
MARIA...
MARIA!
......
CENTER

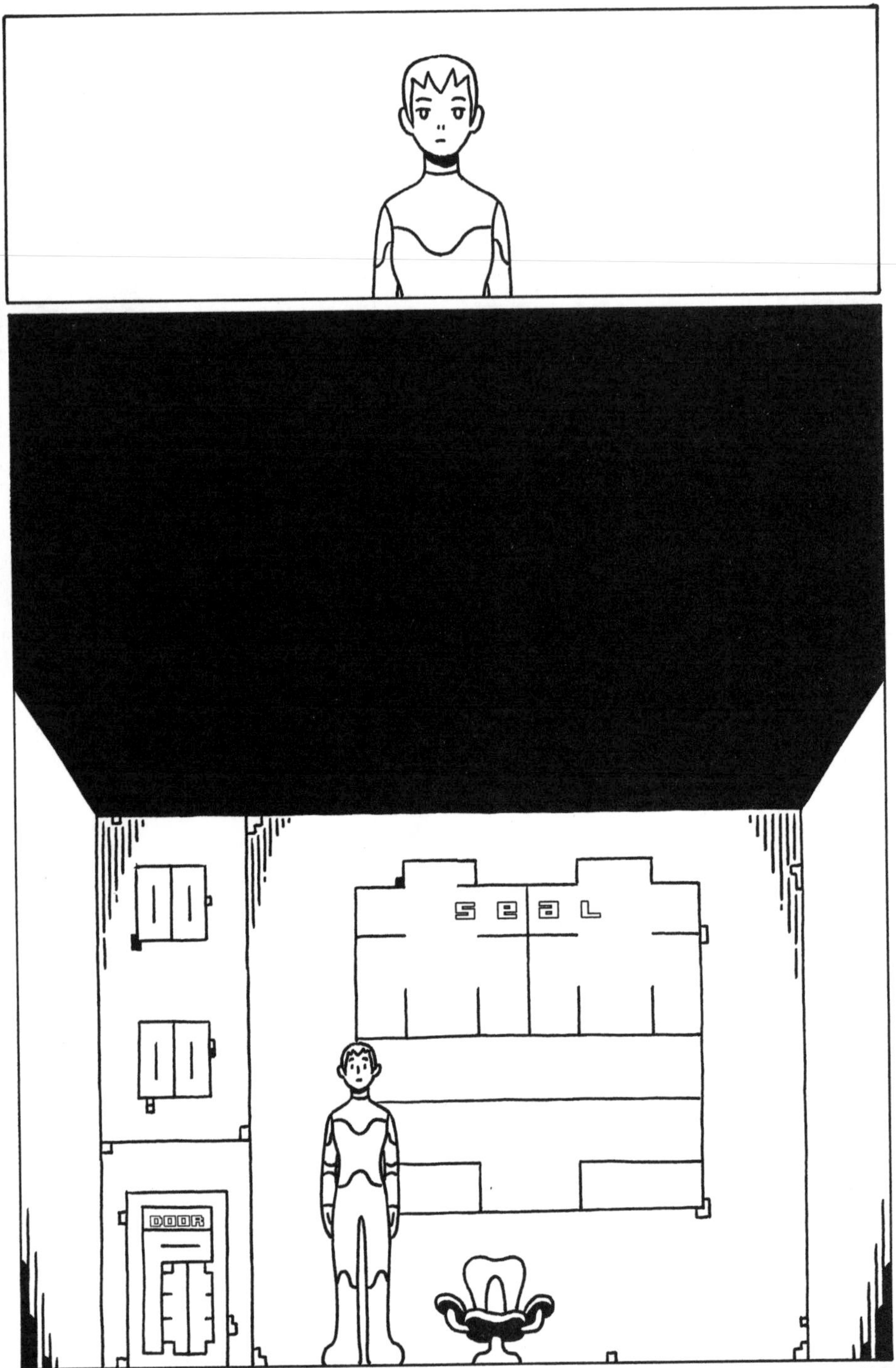
seal
DOOR

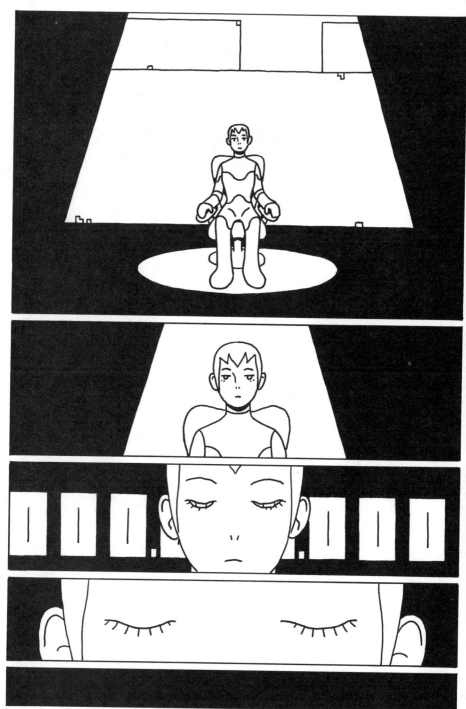

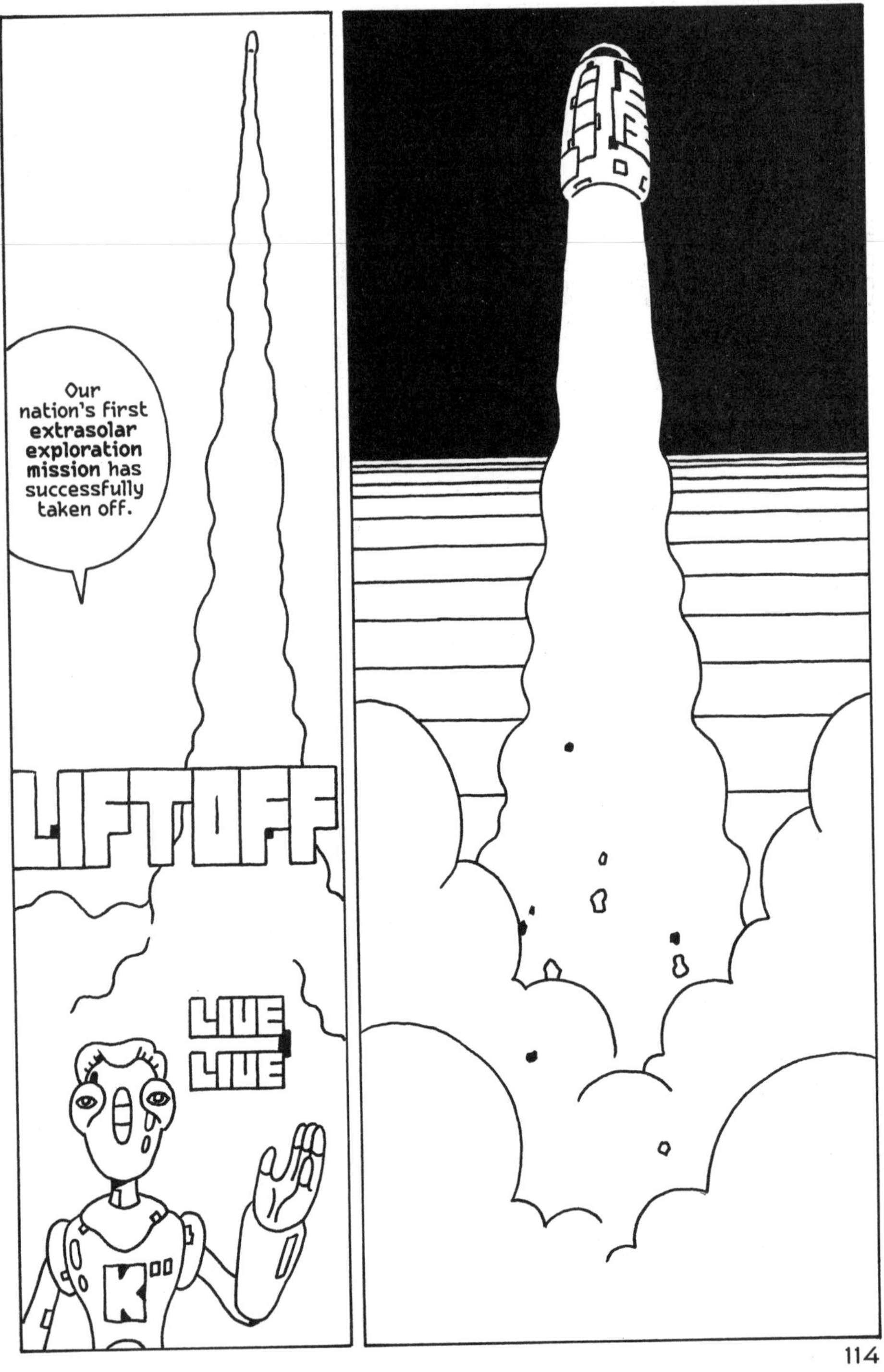
Our nation's first **extrasolar exploration mission** has successfully taken off.
LIFTOFF
LIVE
LIVE

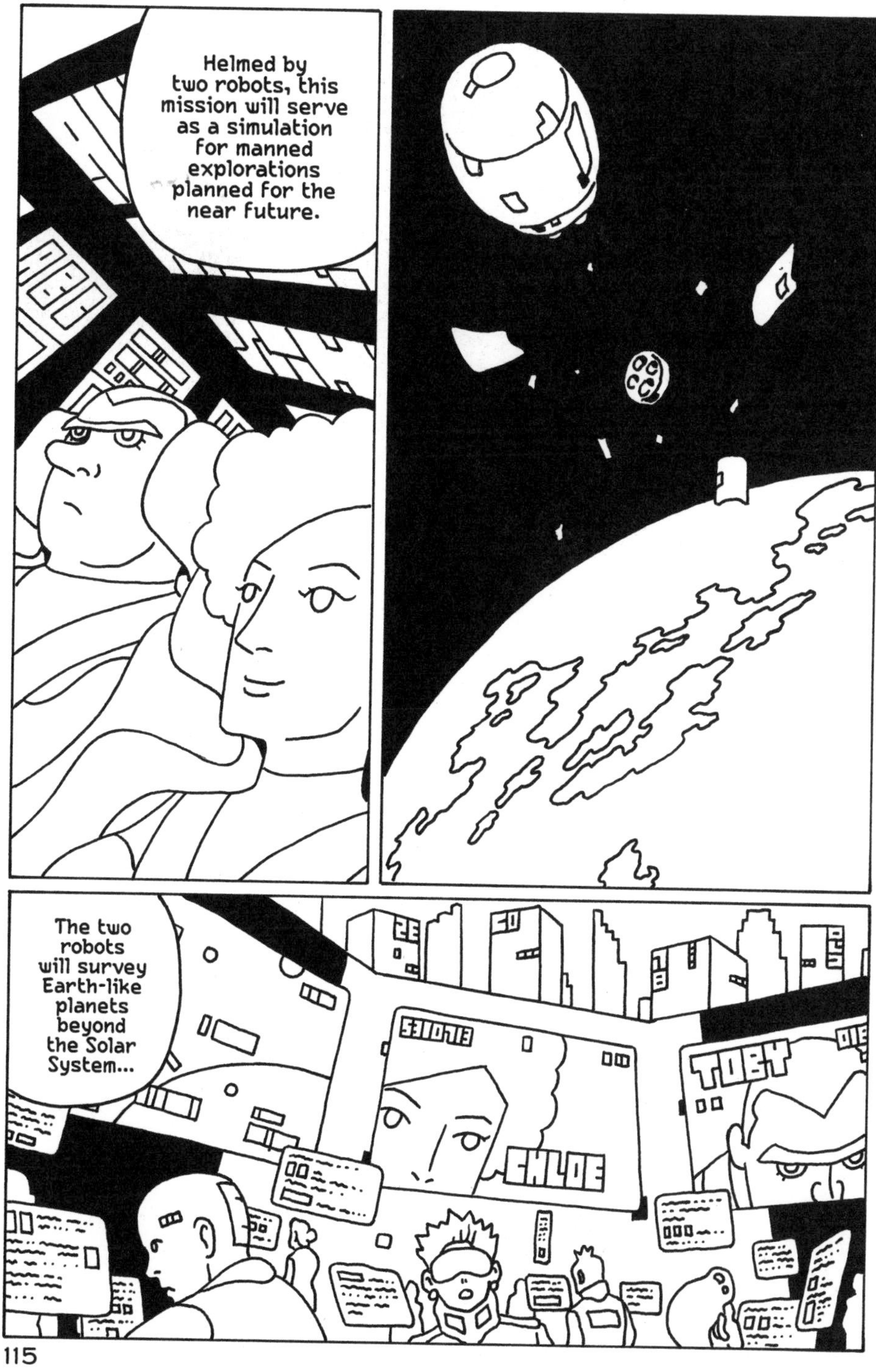

Helmed by two robots, this mission will serve as a simulation for manned explorations planned for the near future.
The two robots will survey Earth-like planets beyond the Solar System...
CHLOE
TOBY

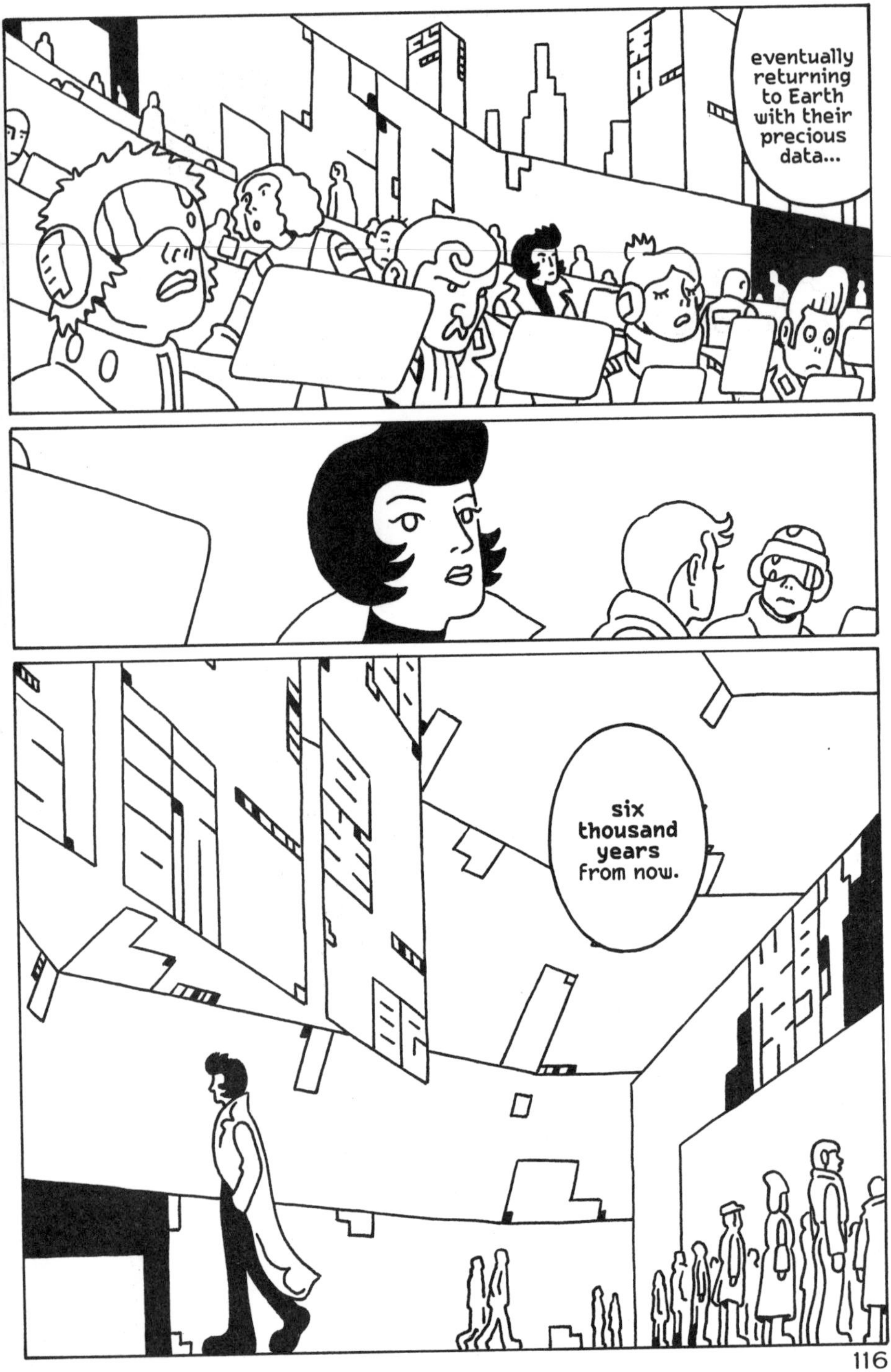
eventually returning to Earth with their precious data...
six thousand years from now.

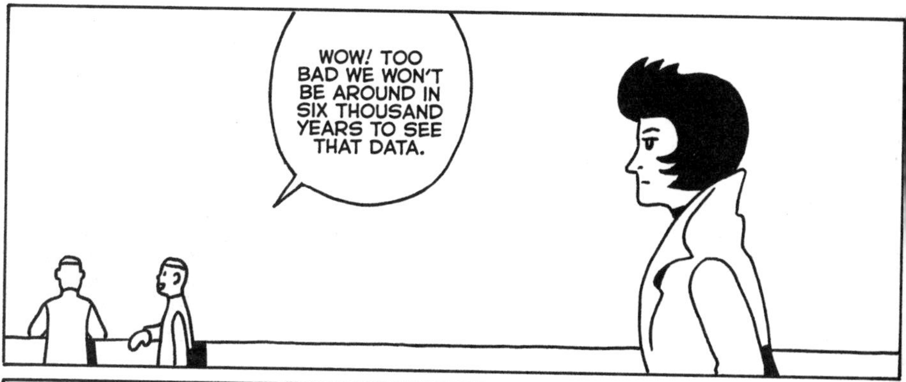
WOW! TOO BAD WE WON'T BE AROUND IN SIX THOUSAND YEARS TO SEE THAT DATA.

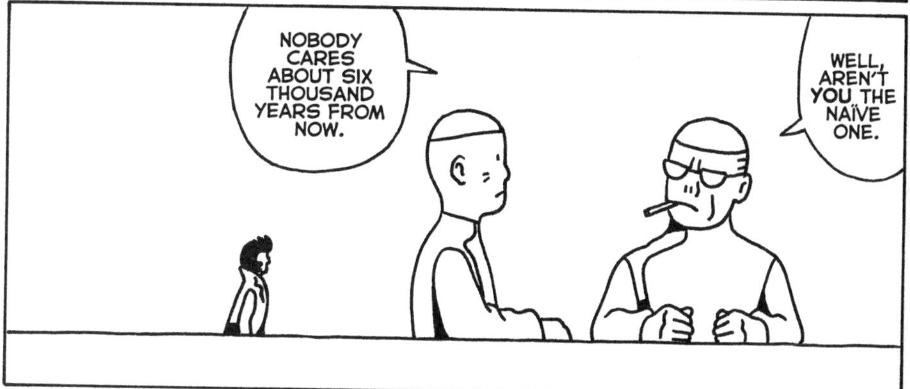
WELL, AREN'T **YOU** THE NAÏVE ONE.
NOBODY CARES ABOUT SIX THOUSAND YEARS FROM NOW.

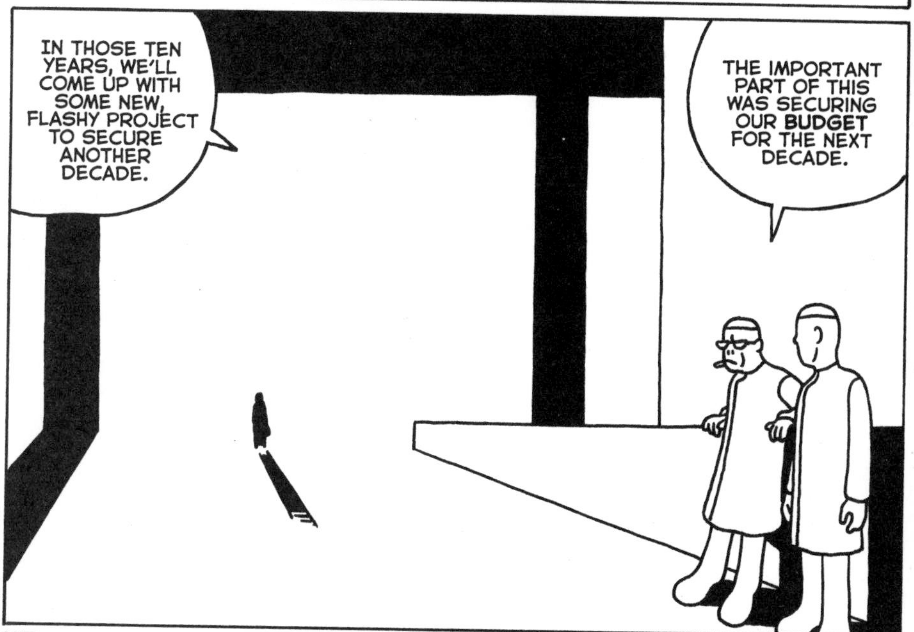
THE IMPORTANT PART OF THIS WAS SECURING OUR **BUDGET** FOR THE NEXT DECADE.
IN THOSE TEN YEARS, WE'LL COME UP WITH SOME NEW, FLASHY PROJECT TO SECURE ANOTHER DECADE.

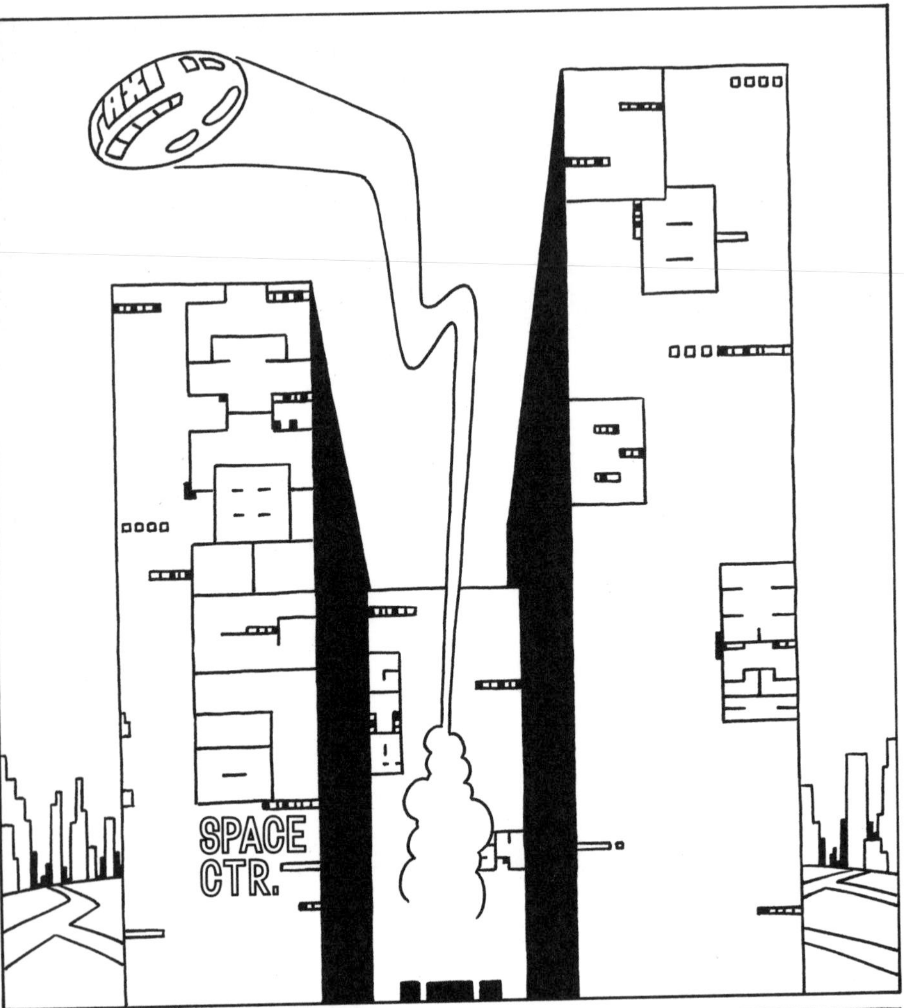
TAXI
SPACE CTR.

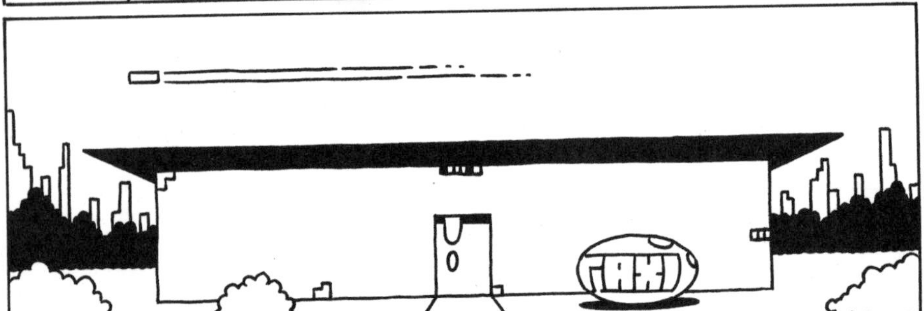
TAXI

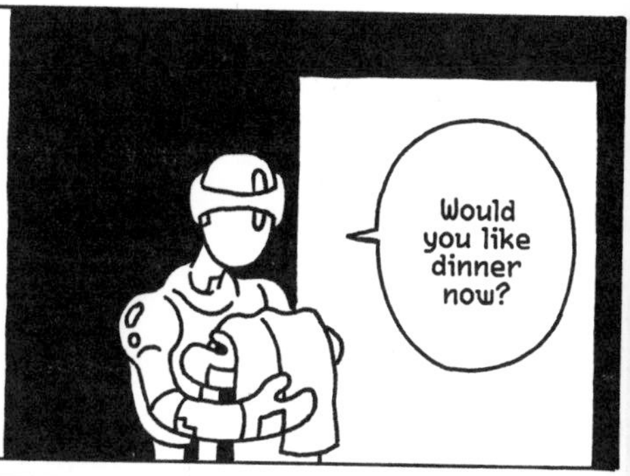
Would you like dinner now?
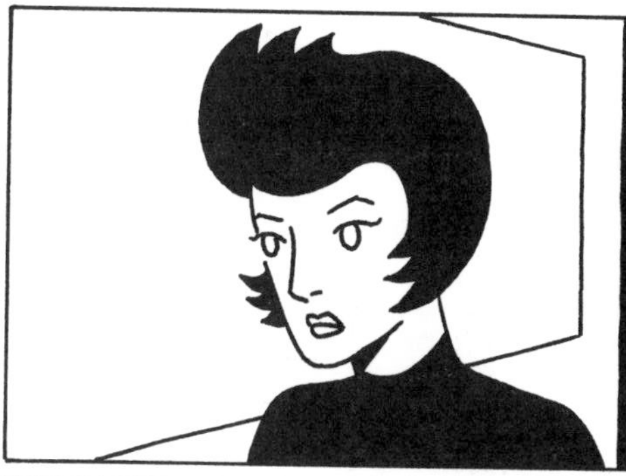
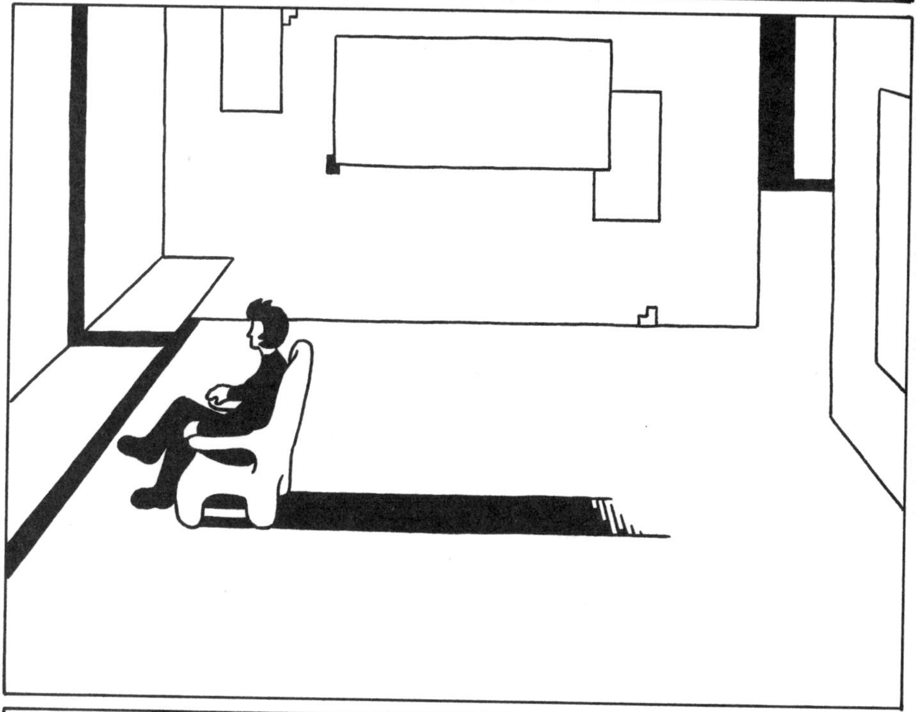
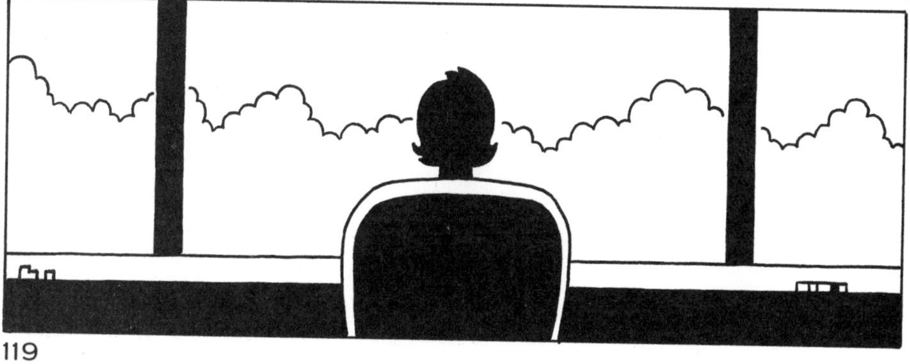

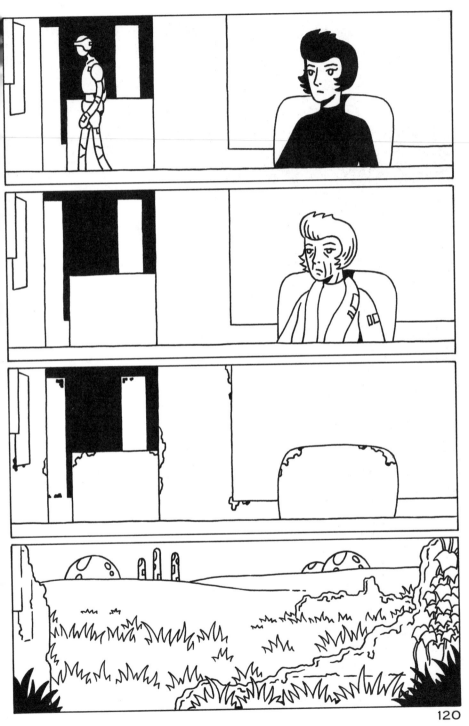

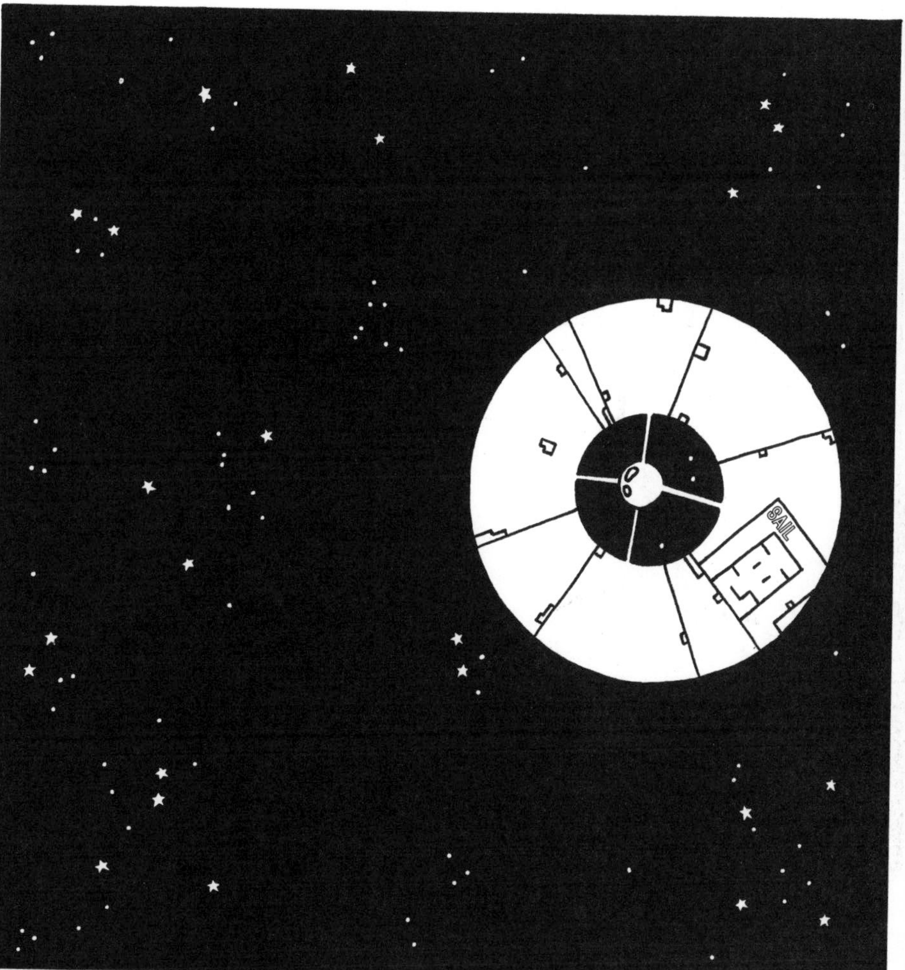
SAIL

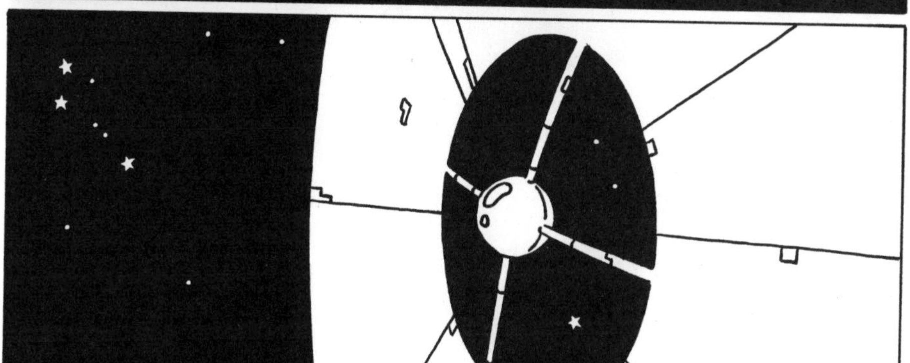

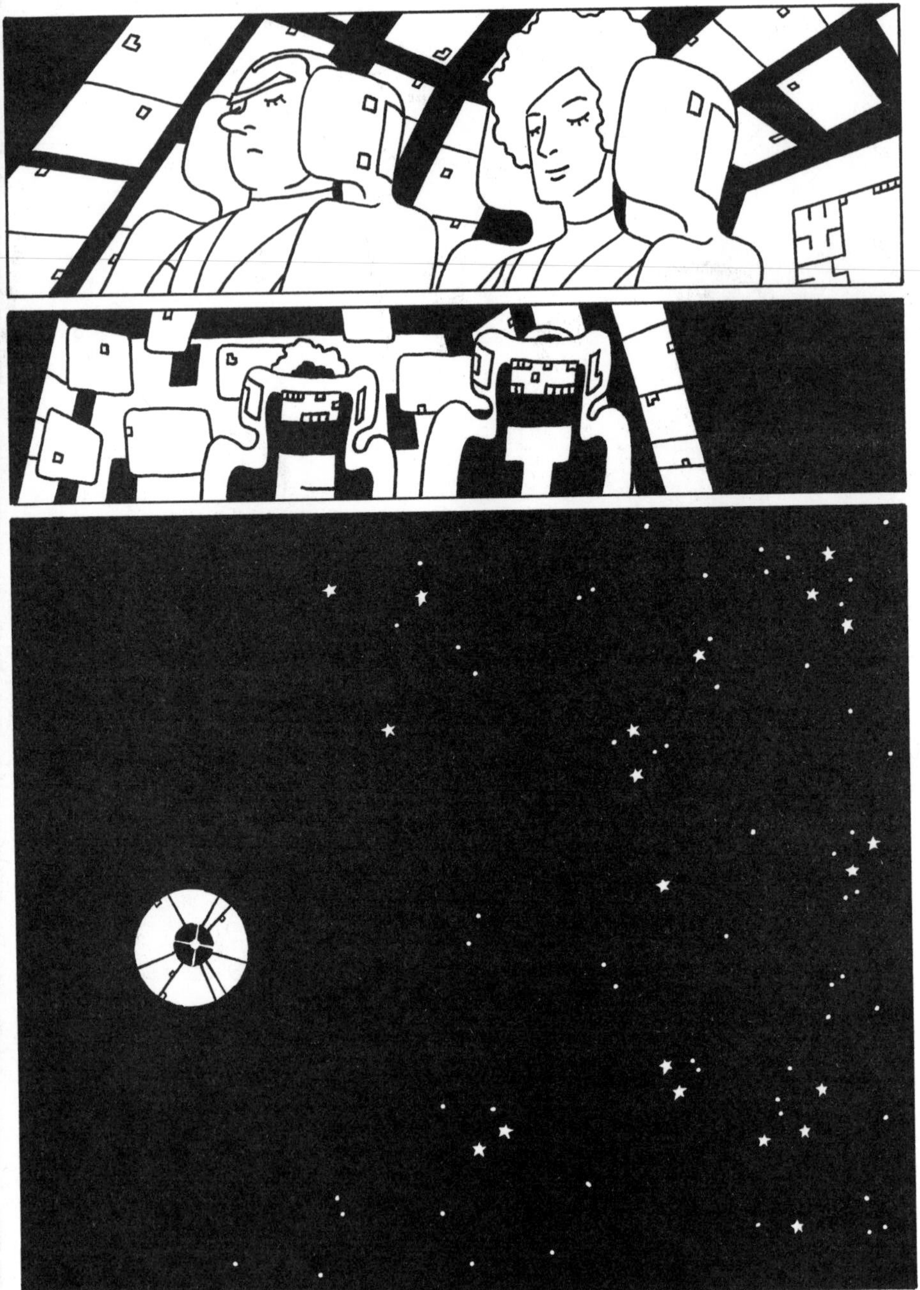

#5/END

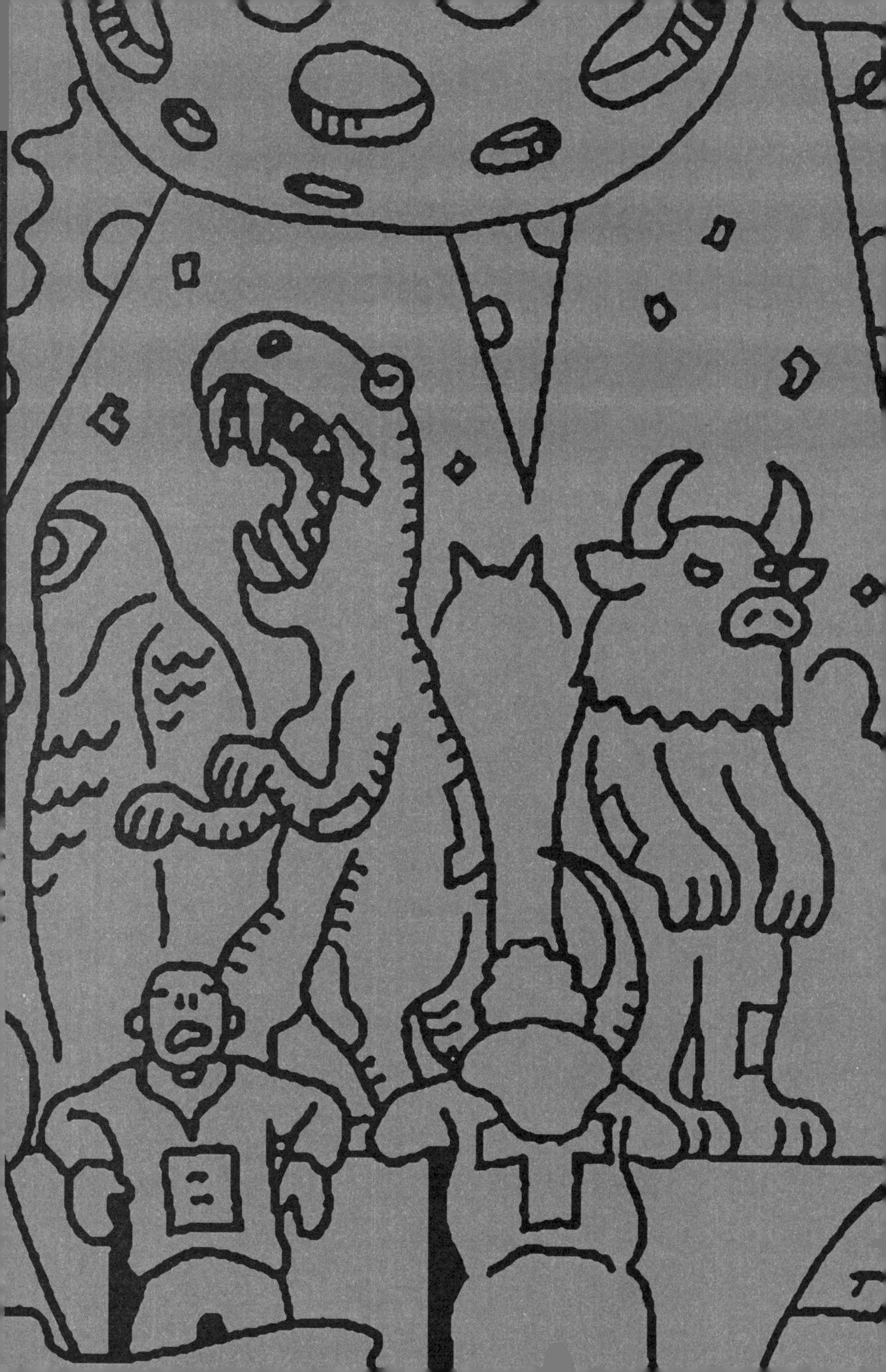

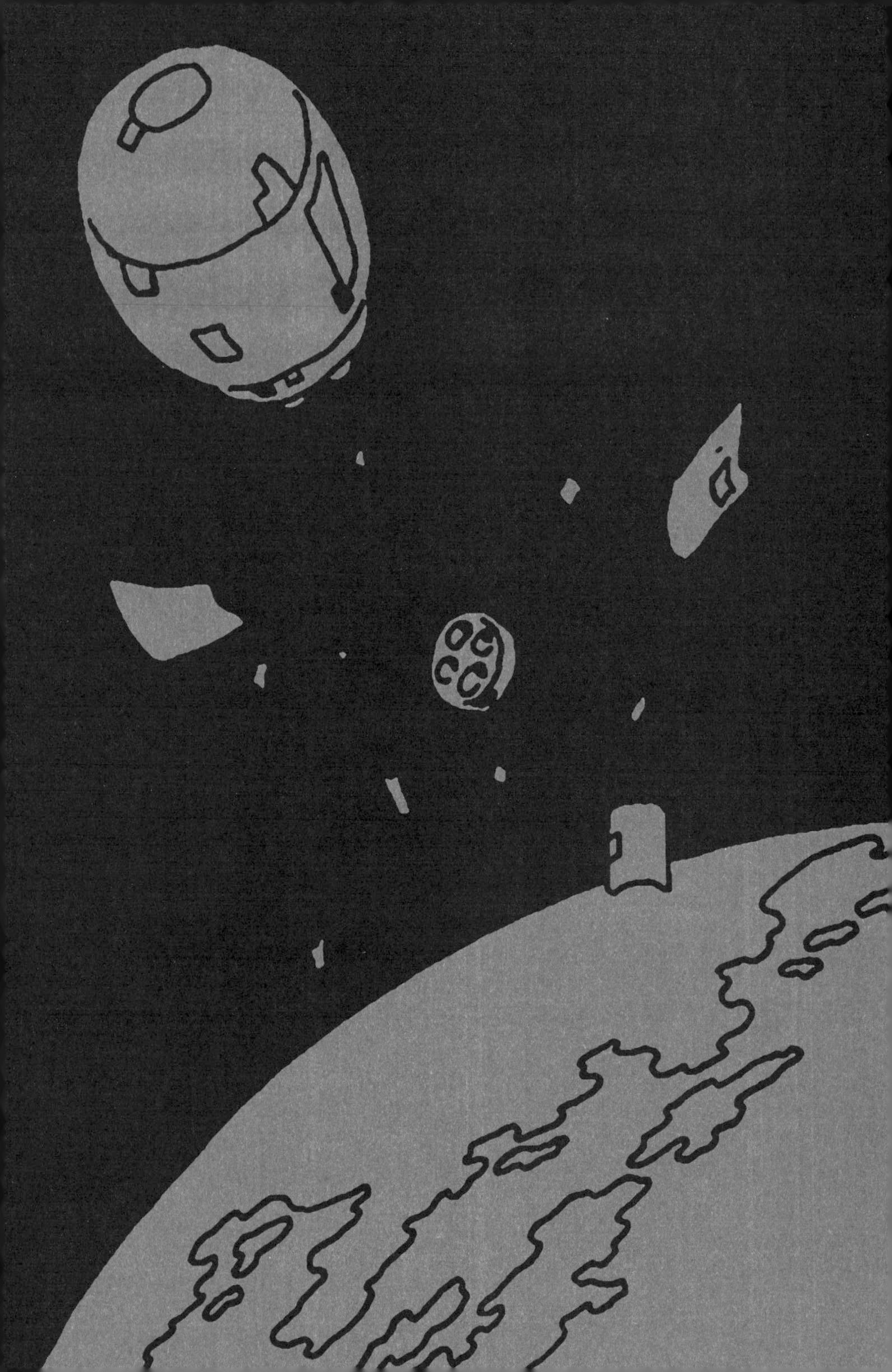

#6

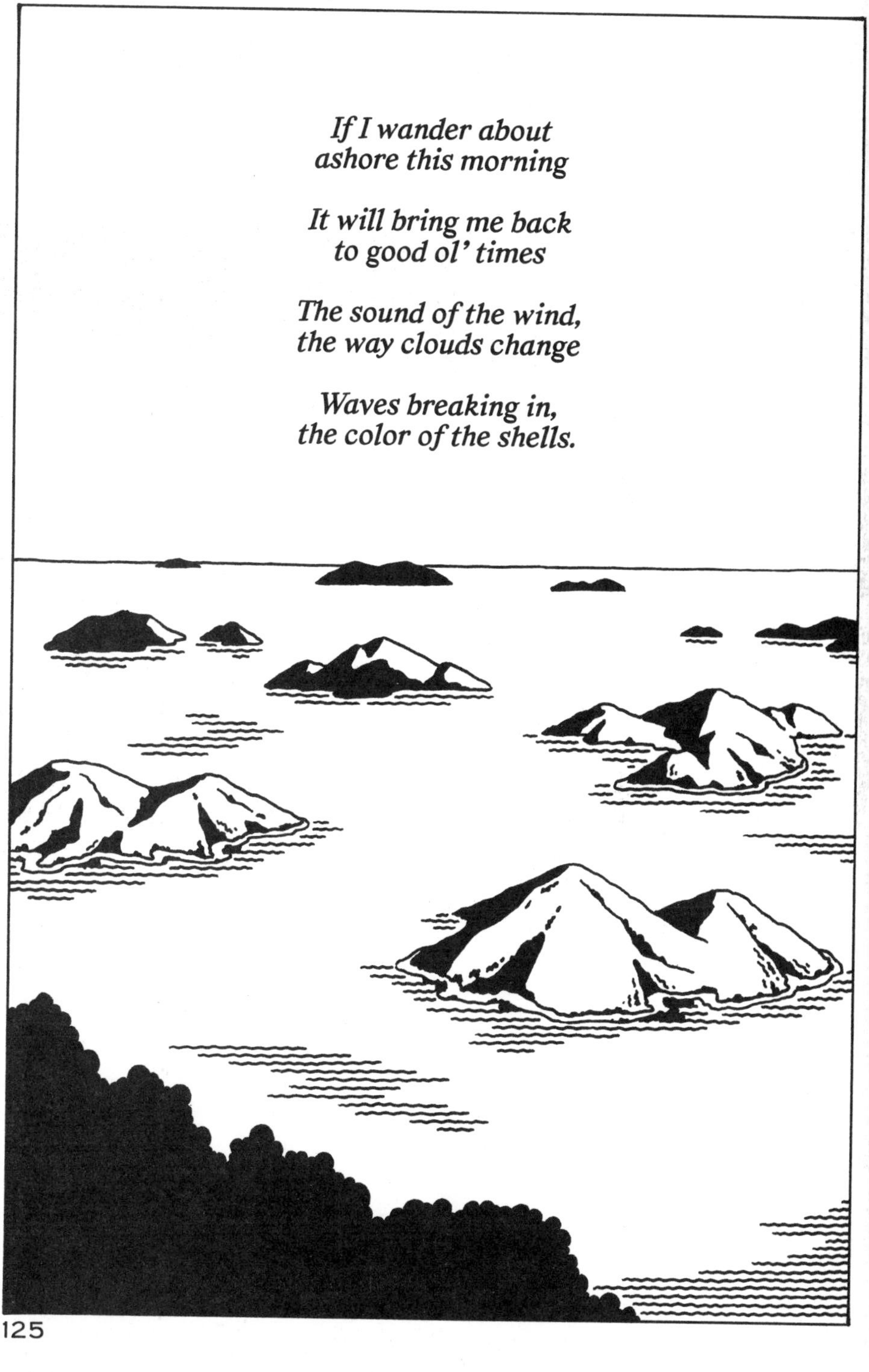
If I wander about
ashore this morning
It will bring me back
to good ol' times
The sound of the wind,
the way clouds change
Waves breaking in,
the color of the shells.

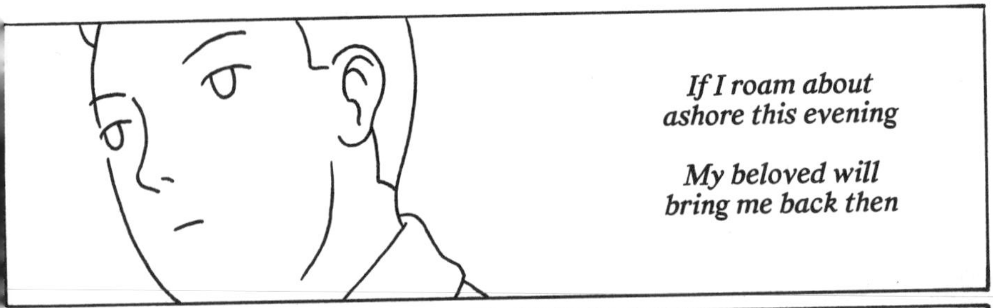
If I roam about
ashore this evening
My beloved will
bring me back then
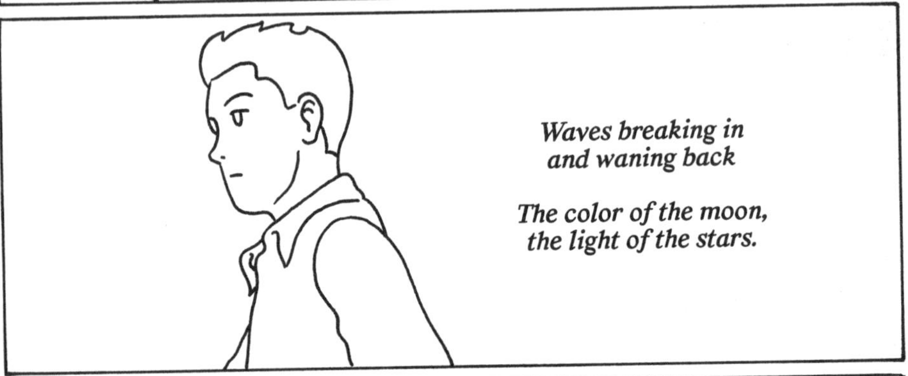
Waves breaking in
and waning back
The color of the moon,
the light of the stars.
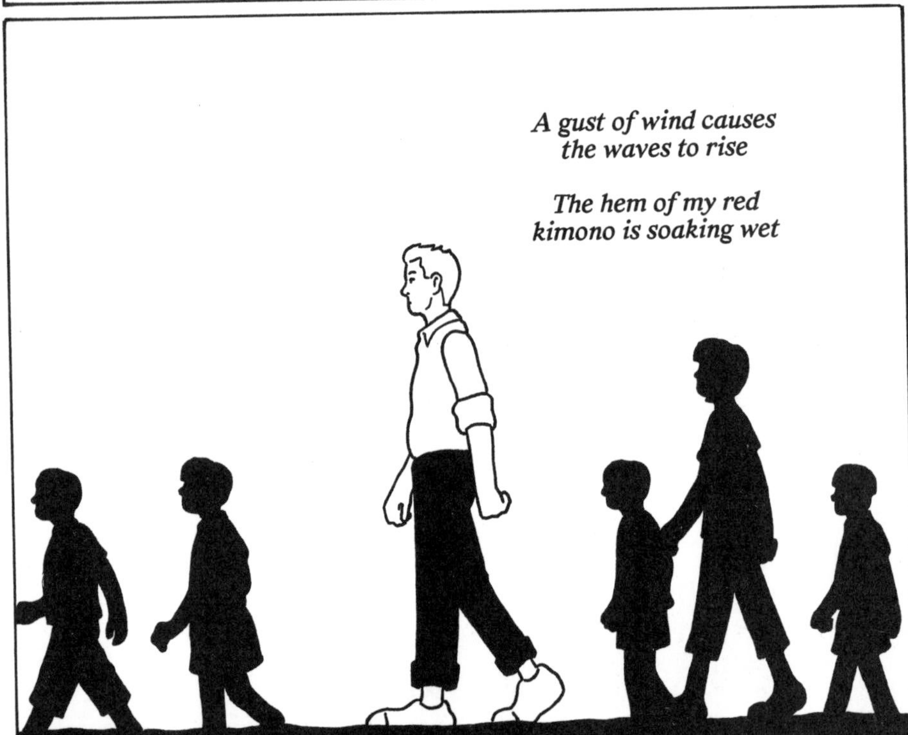
A gust of wind causes
the waves to rise
The hem of my red
kimono is soaking wet

"Hamabe no Uta," by Hayashi Kokei (lyrics) & Narita Tamezo (melody). Translation by Jelly Cat.

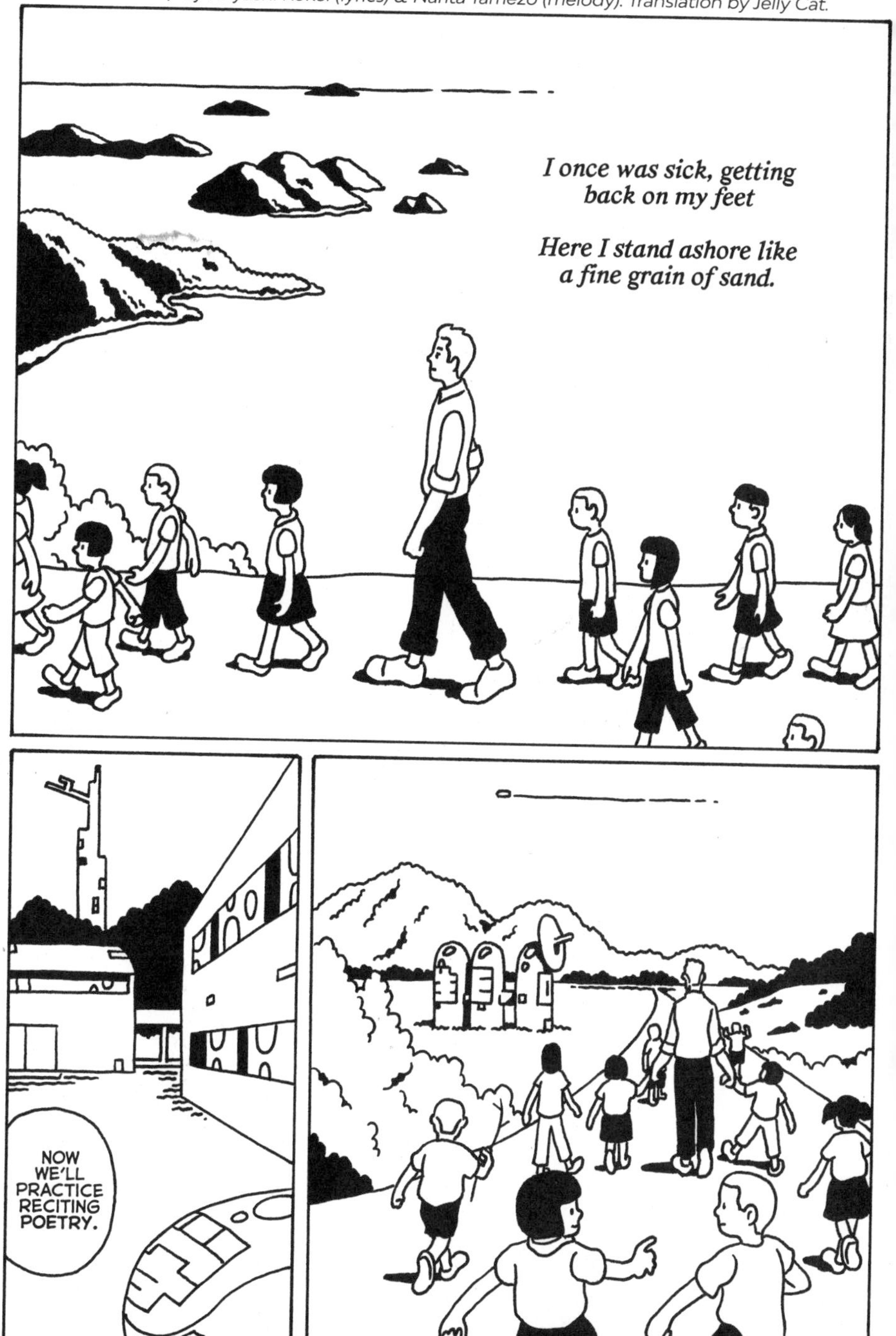
I once was sick, getting back on my feet
Here I stand ashore like a fine grain of sand.
NOW WE'LL PRACTICE RECITING POETRY.

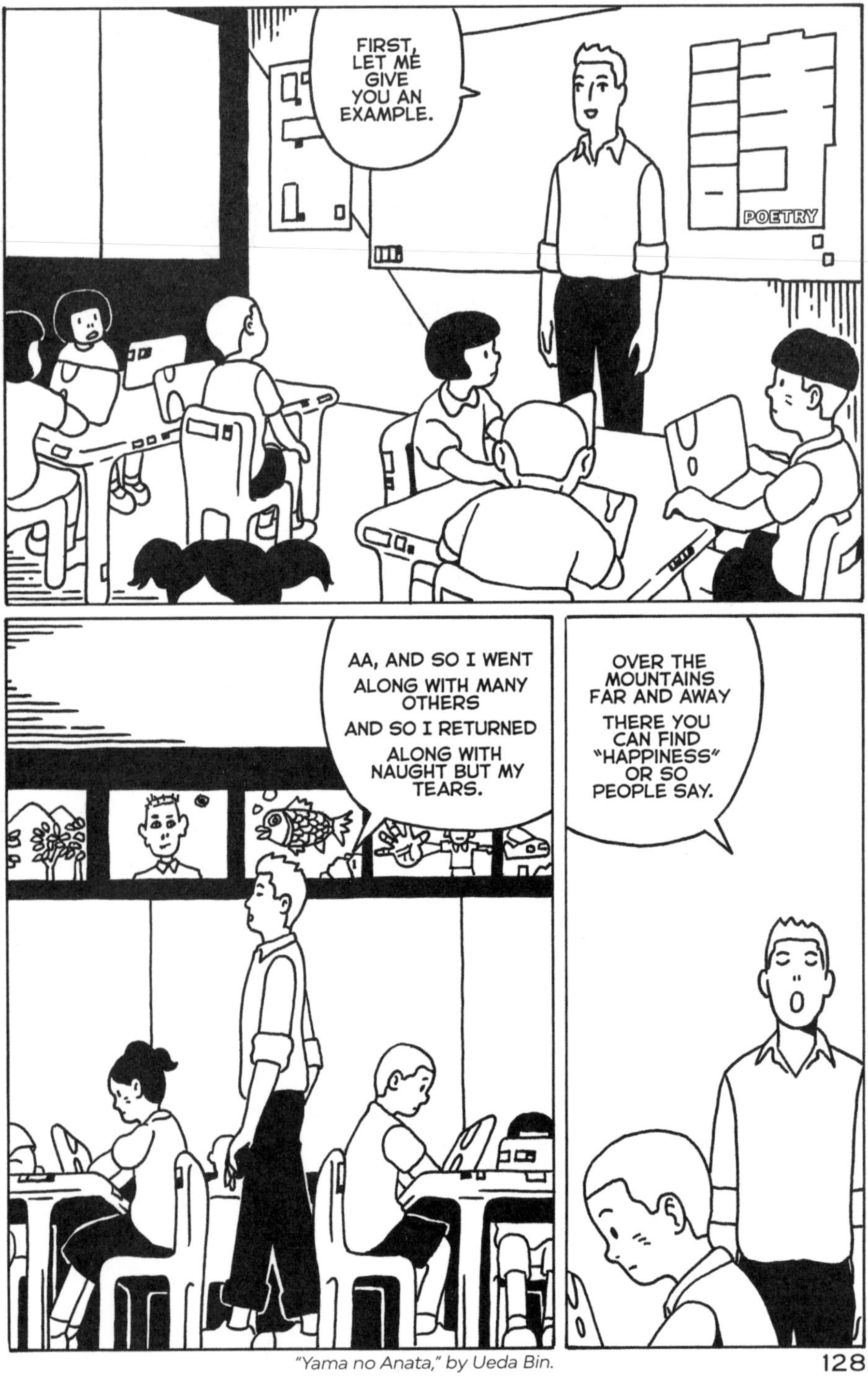
FIRST, LET ME GIVE YOU AN EXAMPLE.
POETRY
OVER THE MOUNTAINS FAR AND AWAY
THERE YOU CAN FIND "HAPPINESS" OR SO PEOPLE SAY.
AA, AND SO I WENT
ALONG WITH MANY OTHERS
AND SO I RETURNED
ALONG WITH NAUGHT BUT MY TEARS.

"Yama no Anata," by Ueda Bin.

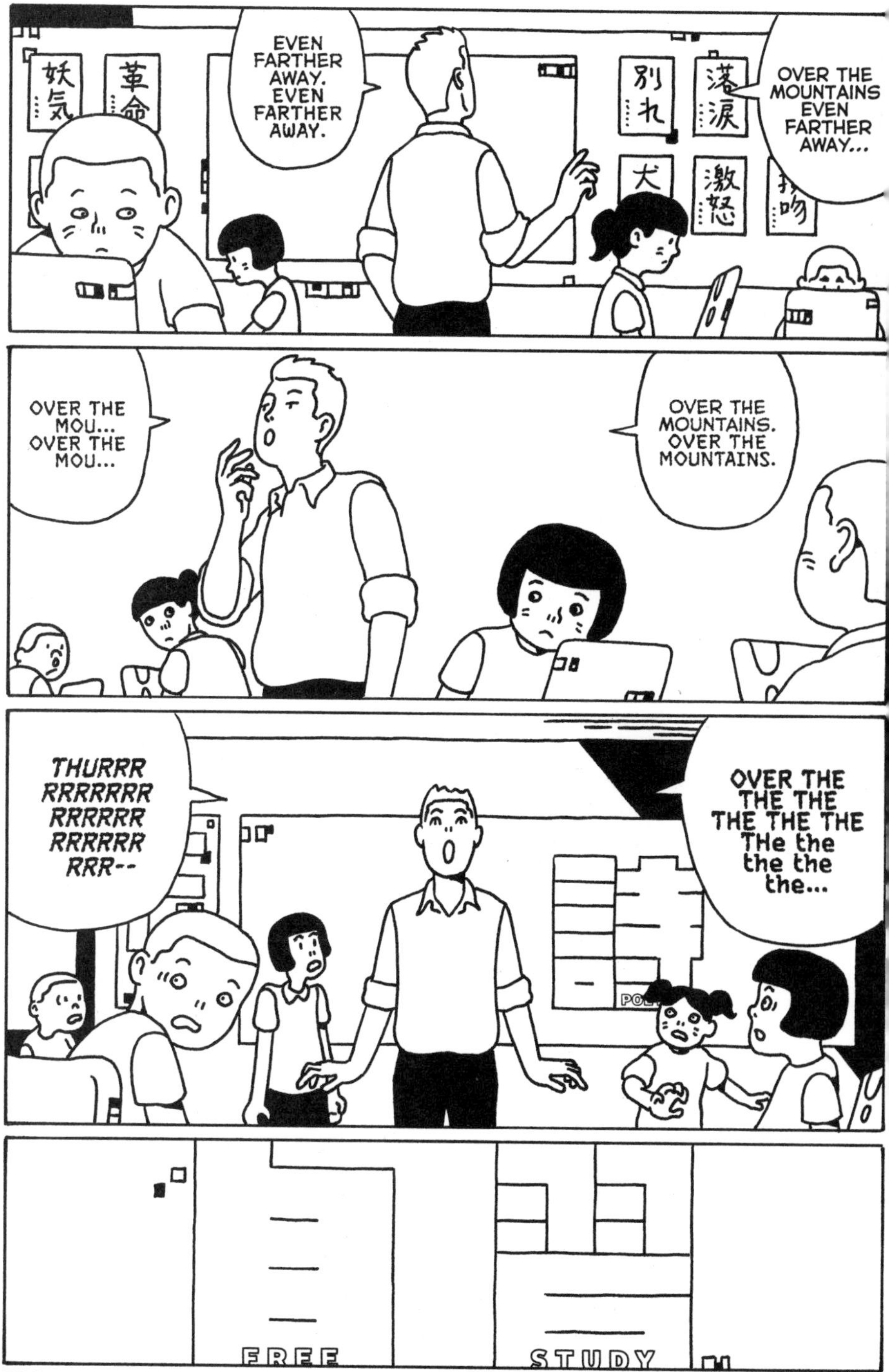
OVER THE MOUNTAINS EVEN FARTHER AWAY...
EVEN FARTHER AWAY. EVEN FARTHER AWAY.
落涙
別れ
激怒
革命
妖気
OVER THE MOUNTAINS. OVER THE MOUNTAINS.
OVER THE MOU... OVER THE MOU...
OVER THE THE THE THE THE THE THe the the the the...
THURRR RRRRRRR RRRRRR RRRRRR RRR--
FREE
STUDY

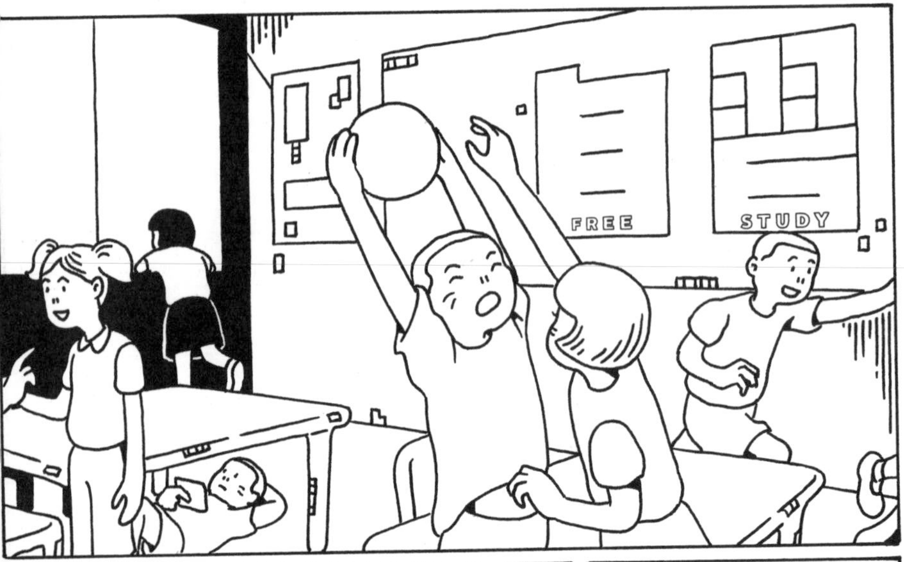
FREE
STUDY
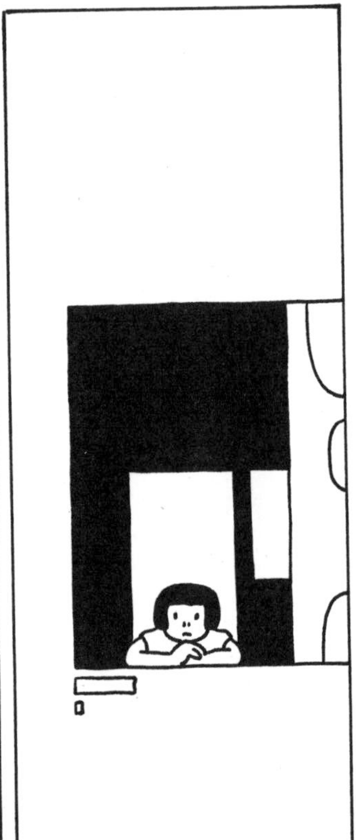
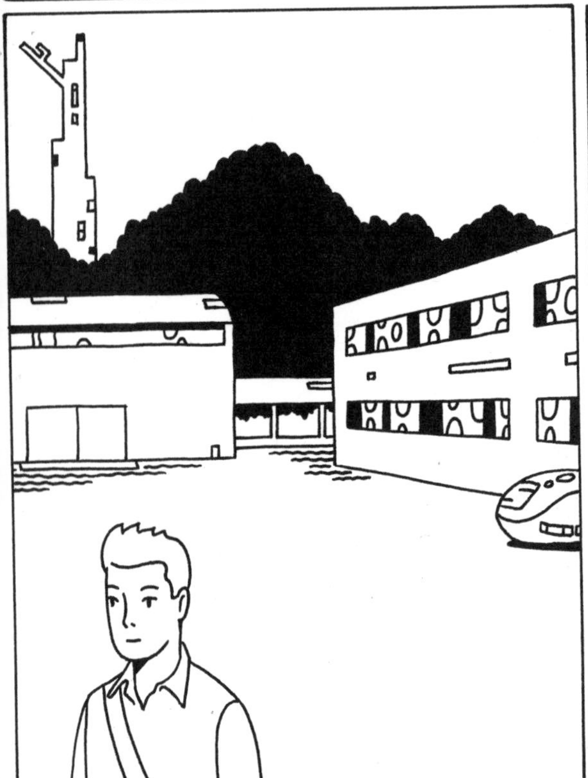

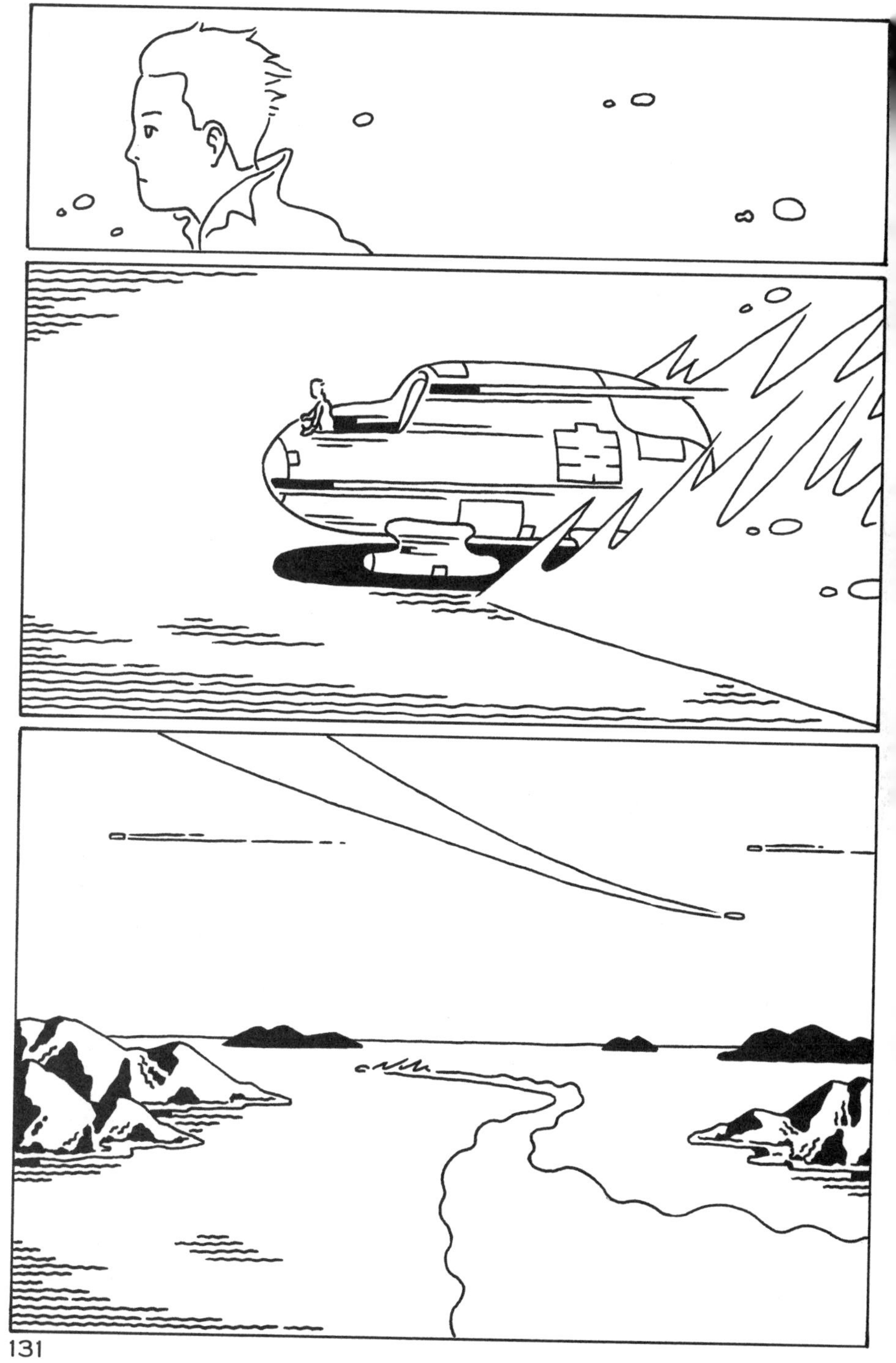

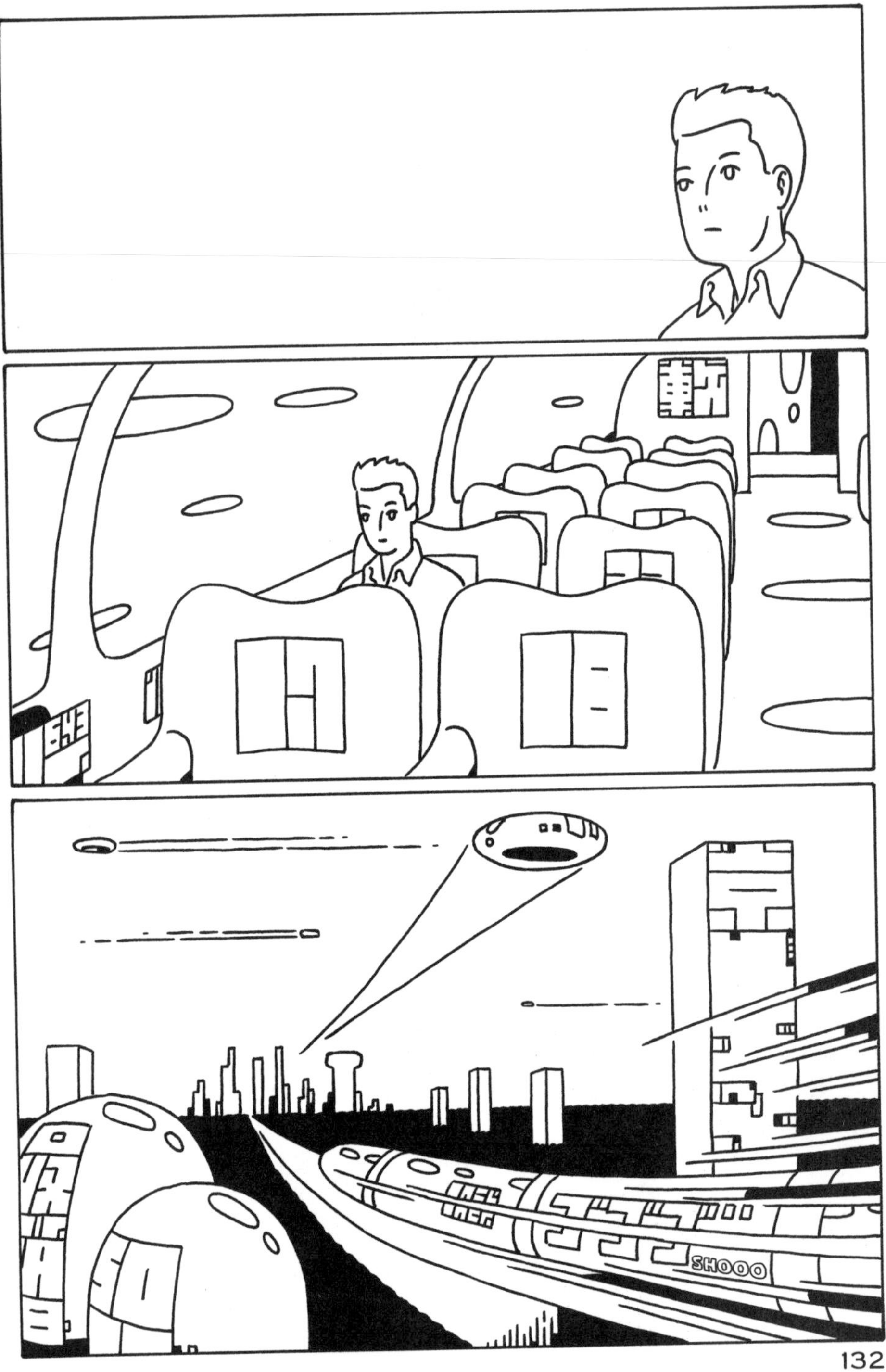
SHOOO

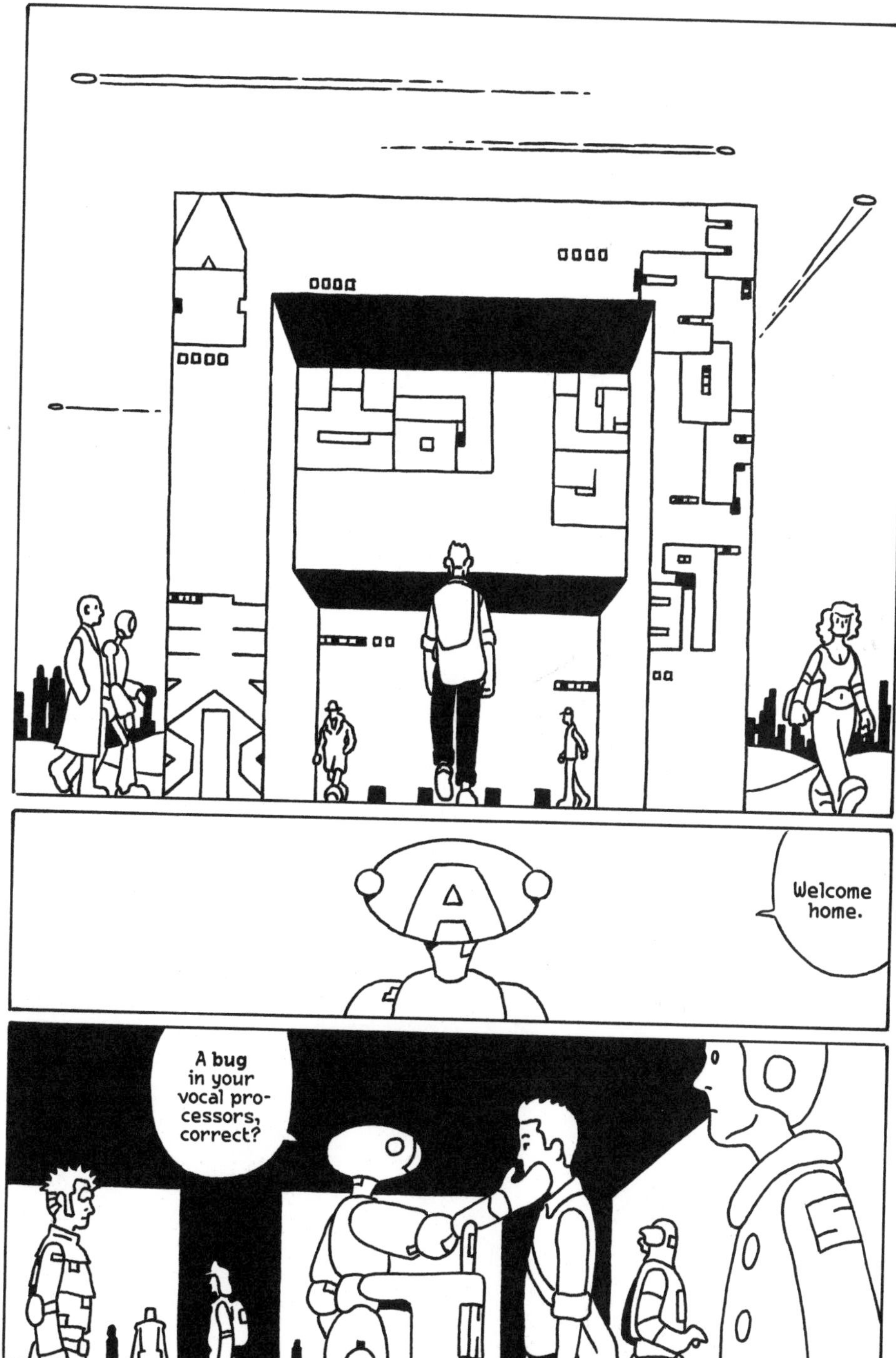
Welcome home.
A bug in your vocal processors, correct?

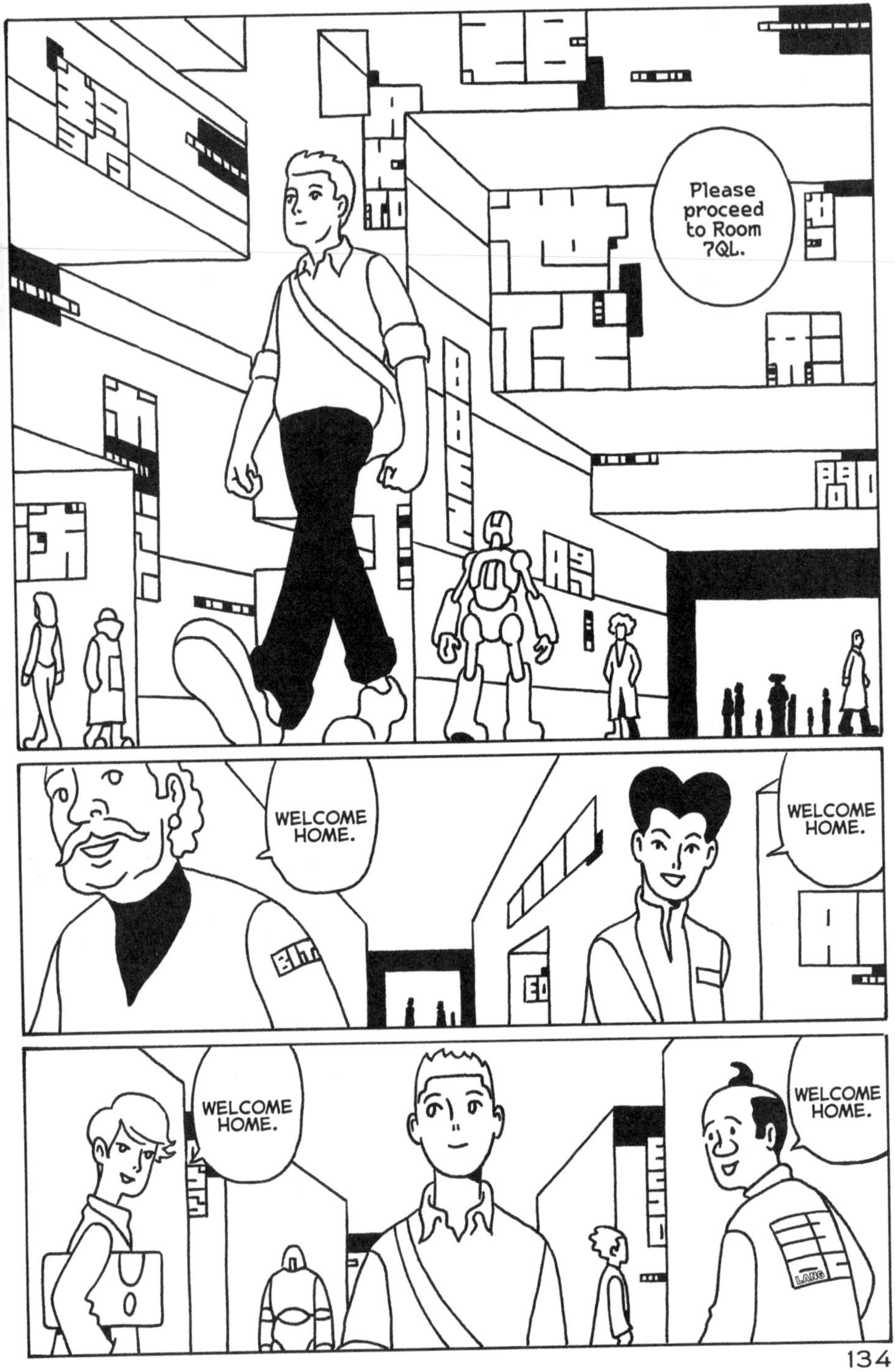
Please proceed to Room 7QL.
WELCOME HOME.
WELCOME HOME.
WELCOME HOME.
LANG
WELCOME HOME.

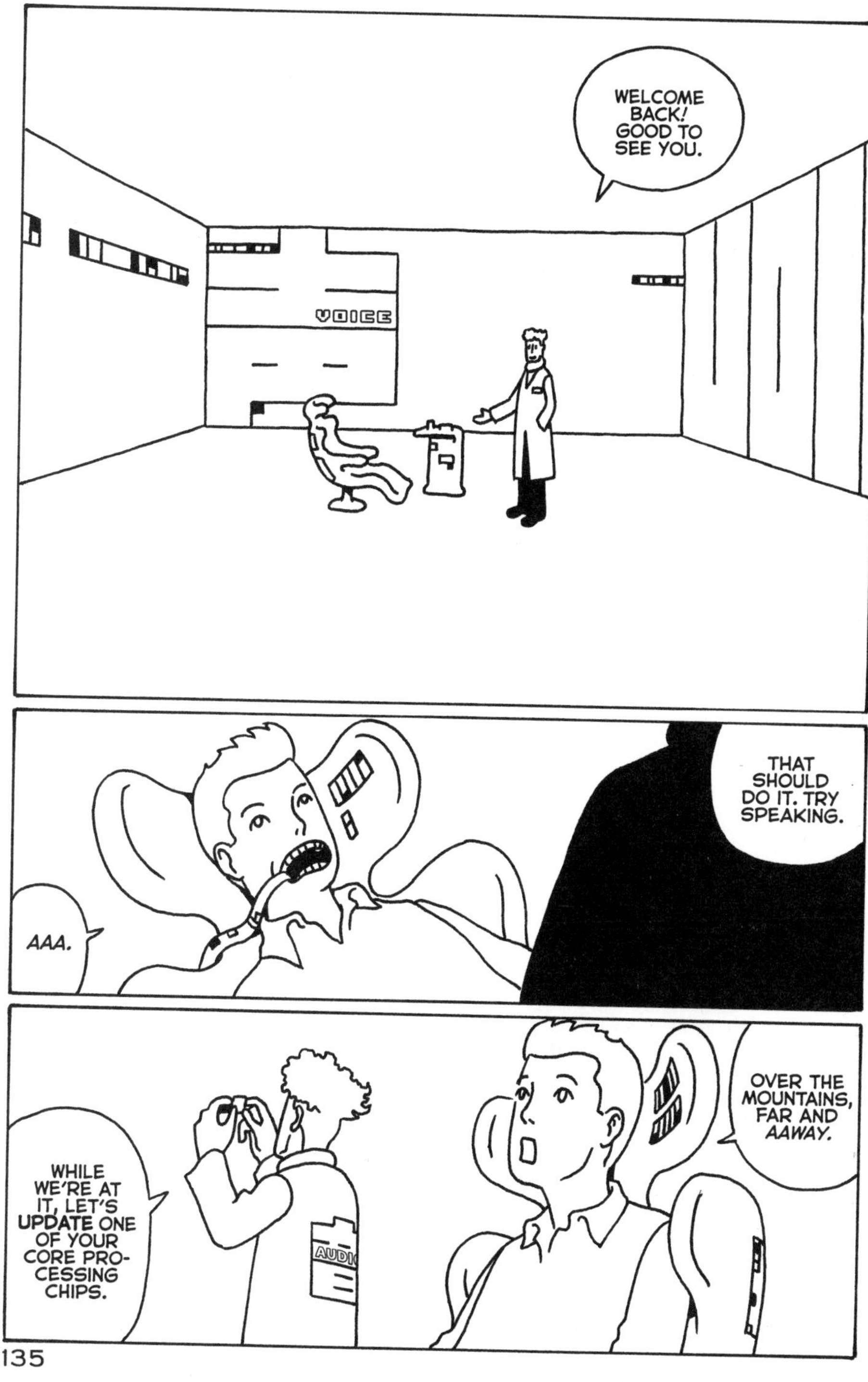
WELCOME BACK! GOOD TO SEE YOU.
VOICE
THAT SHOULD DO IT. TRY SPEAKING.
AAA.
OVER THE MOUNTAINS, FAR AND *AAWAY.*
WHILE WE'RE AT IT, LET'S **UPDATE** ONE OF YOUR CORE PROCESSING CHIPS.

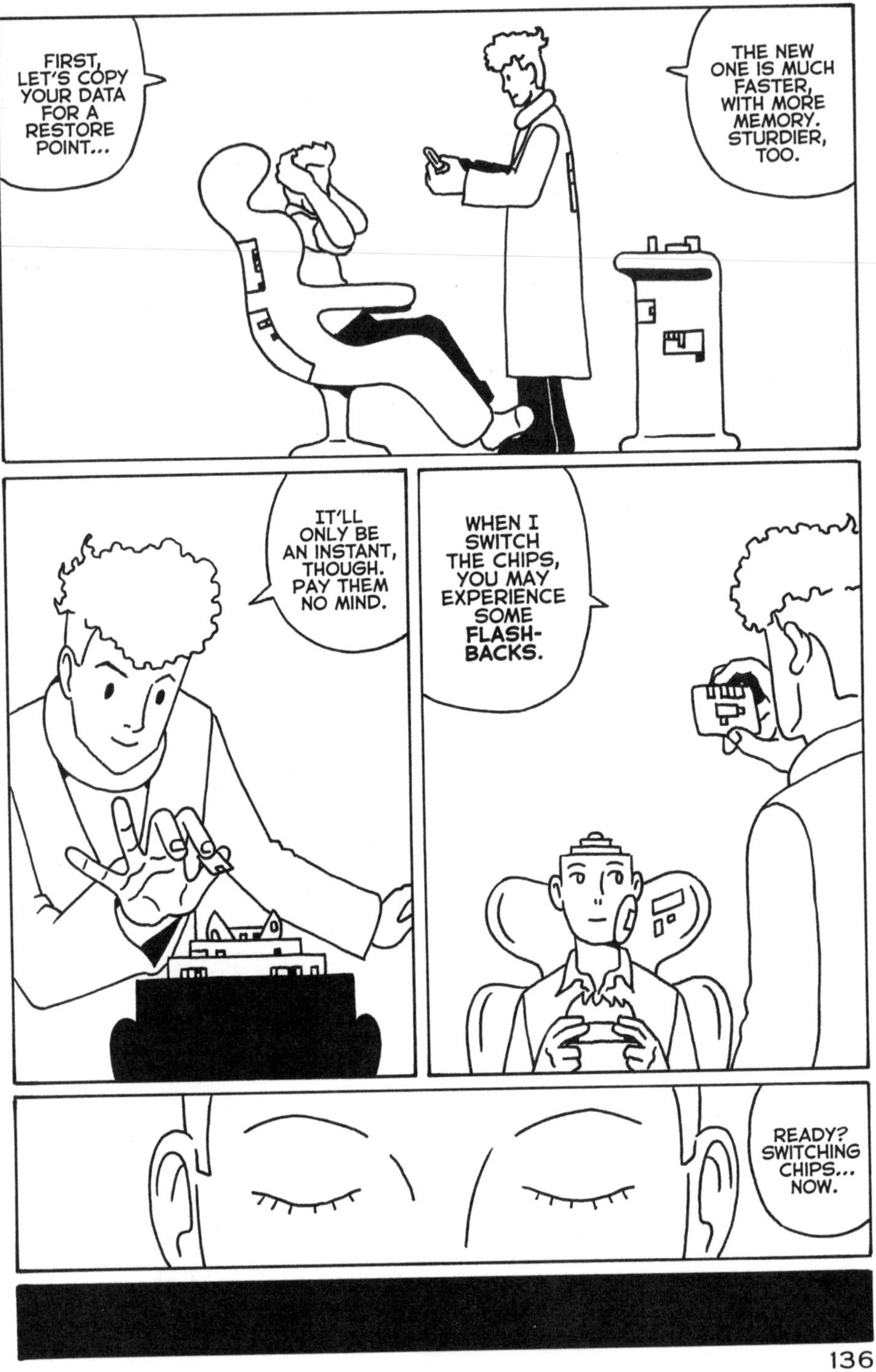
THE NEW ONE IS MUCH FASTER, WITH MORE MEMORY. STURDIER, TOO.
FIRST, LET'S COPY YOUR DATA FOR A RESTORE POINT...
WHEN I SWITCH THE CHIPS, YOU MAY EXPERIENCE SOME FLASH-BACKS.
IT'LL ONLY BE AN INSTANT, THOUGH. PAY THEM NO MIND.
READY? SWITCHING CHIPS... NOW.

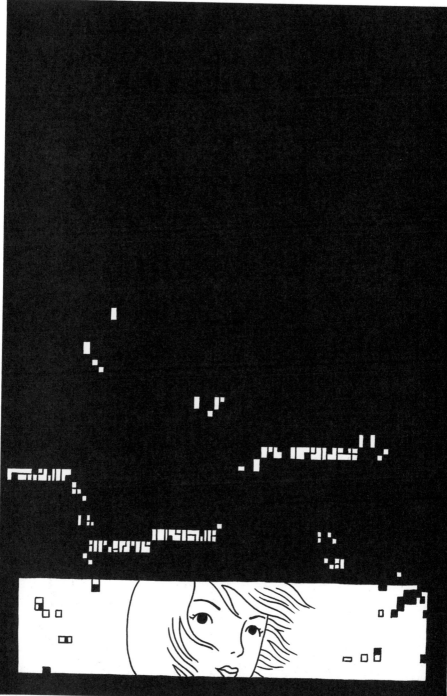

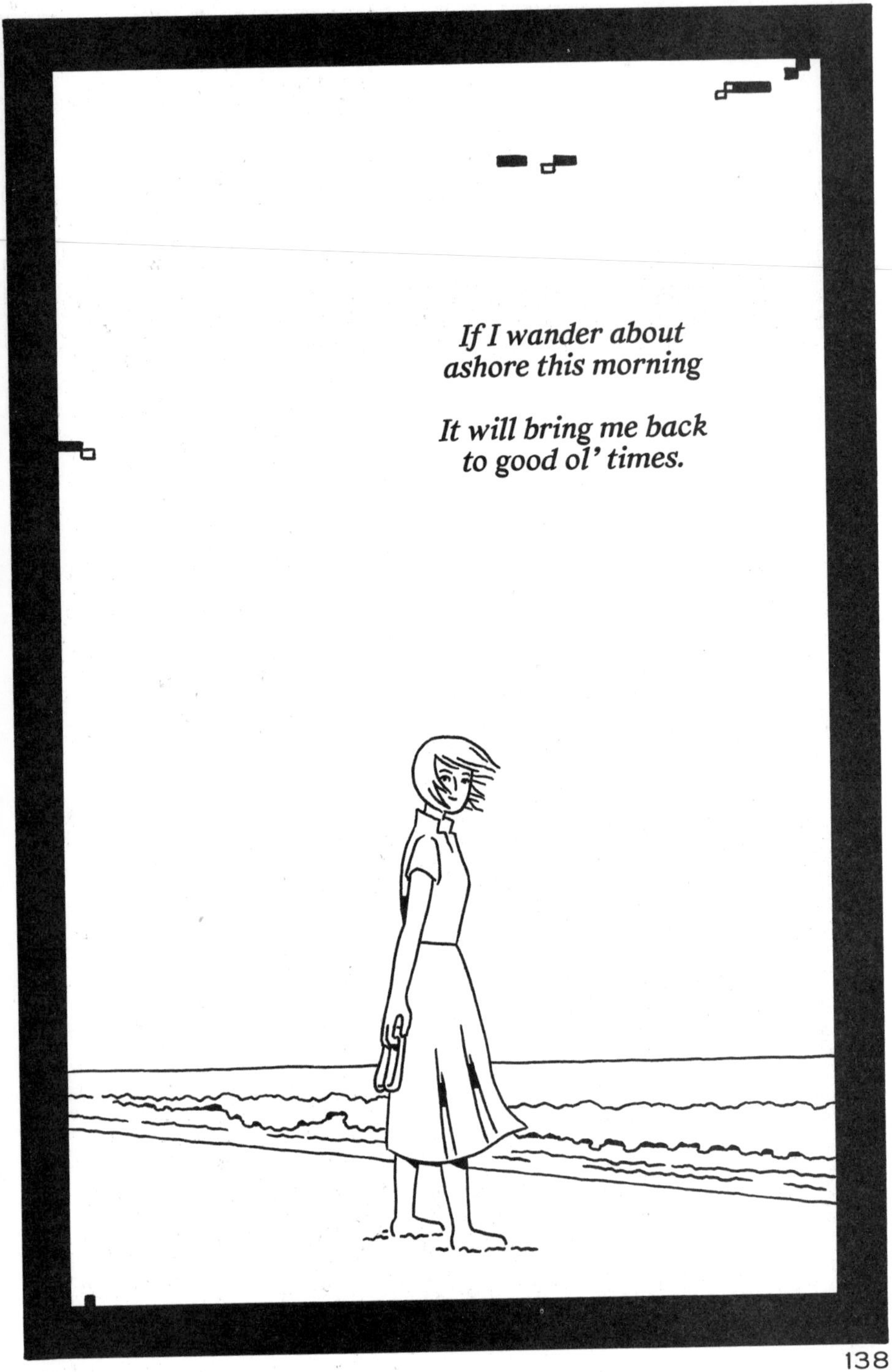
If I wander about
ashore this morning

It will bring me back
to good ol' times.

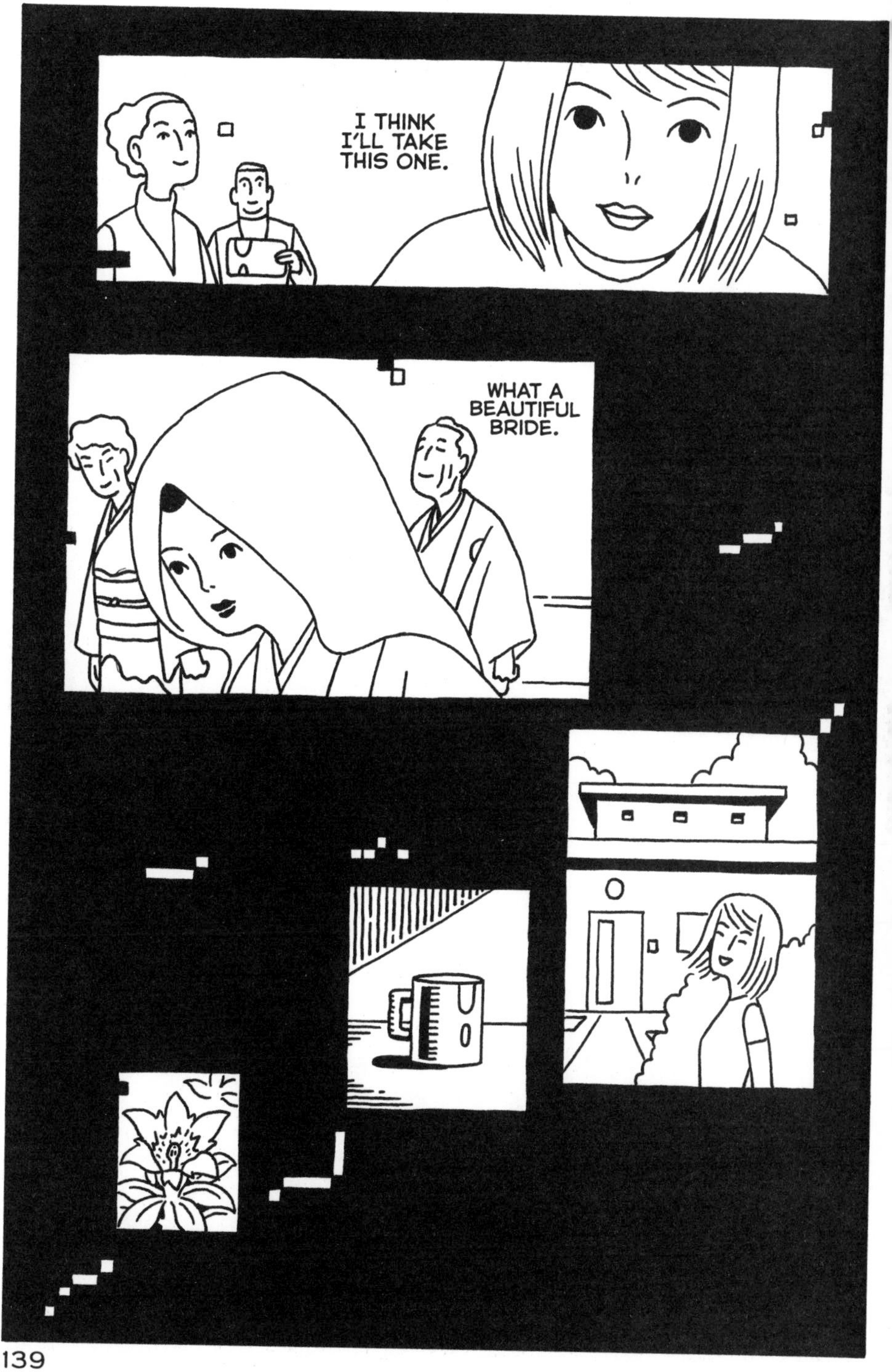
I THINK I'LL TAKE THIS ONE.
WHAT A BEAUTIFUL BRIDE.

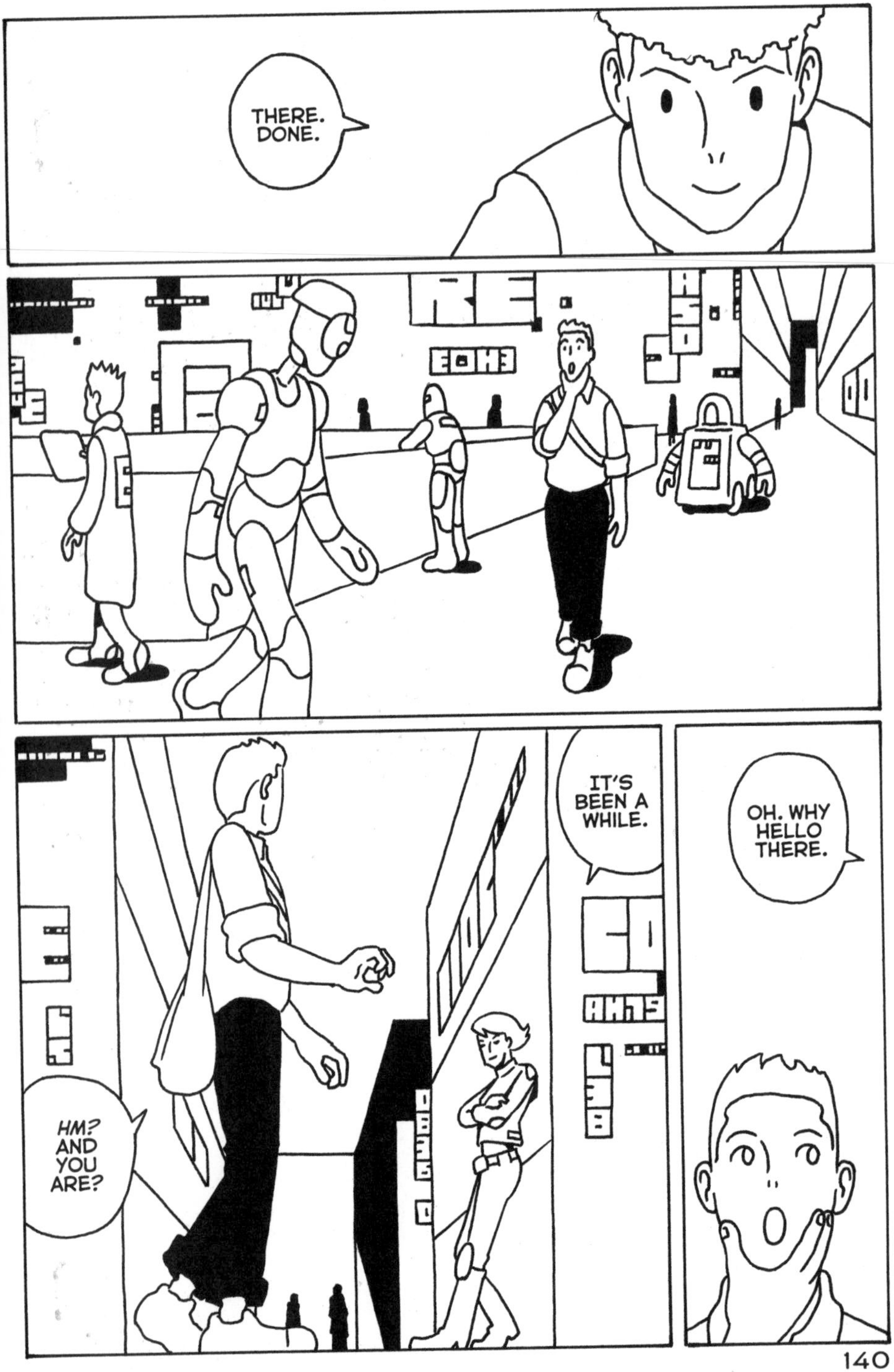
THERE. DONE.
OH. WHY HELLO THERE.
IT'S BEEN A WHILE.
HM? AND YOU ARE?

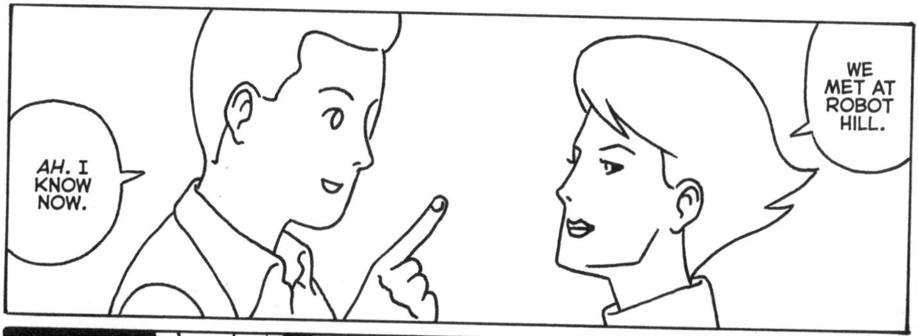
WE MET AT ROBOT HILL.
AH. I KNOW NOW.
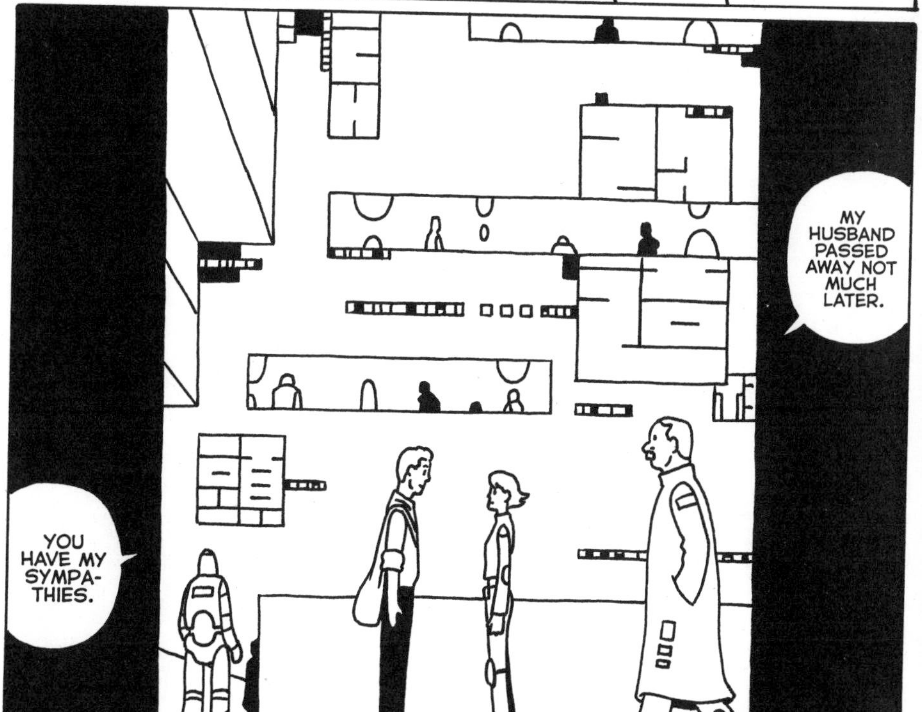
MY HUSBAND PASSED AWAY NOT MUCH LATER.
YOU HAVE MY SYMPA-THIES.
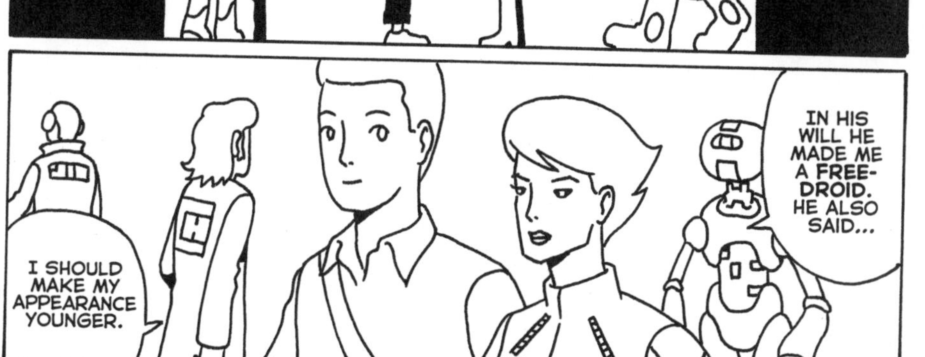
IN HIS WILL HE MADE ME A **FREE-DROID**. HE ALSO SAID...
I SHOULD MAKE MY APPEARANCE YOUNGER.

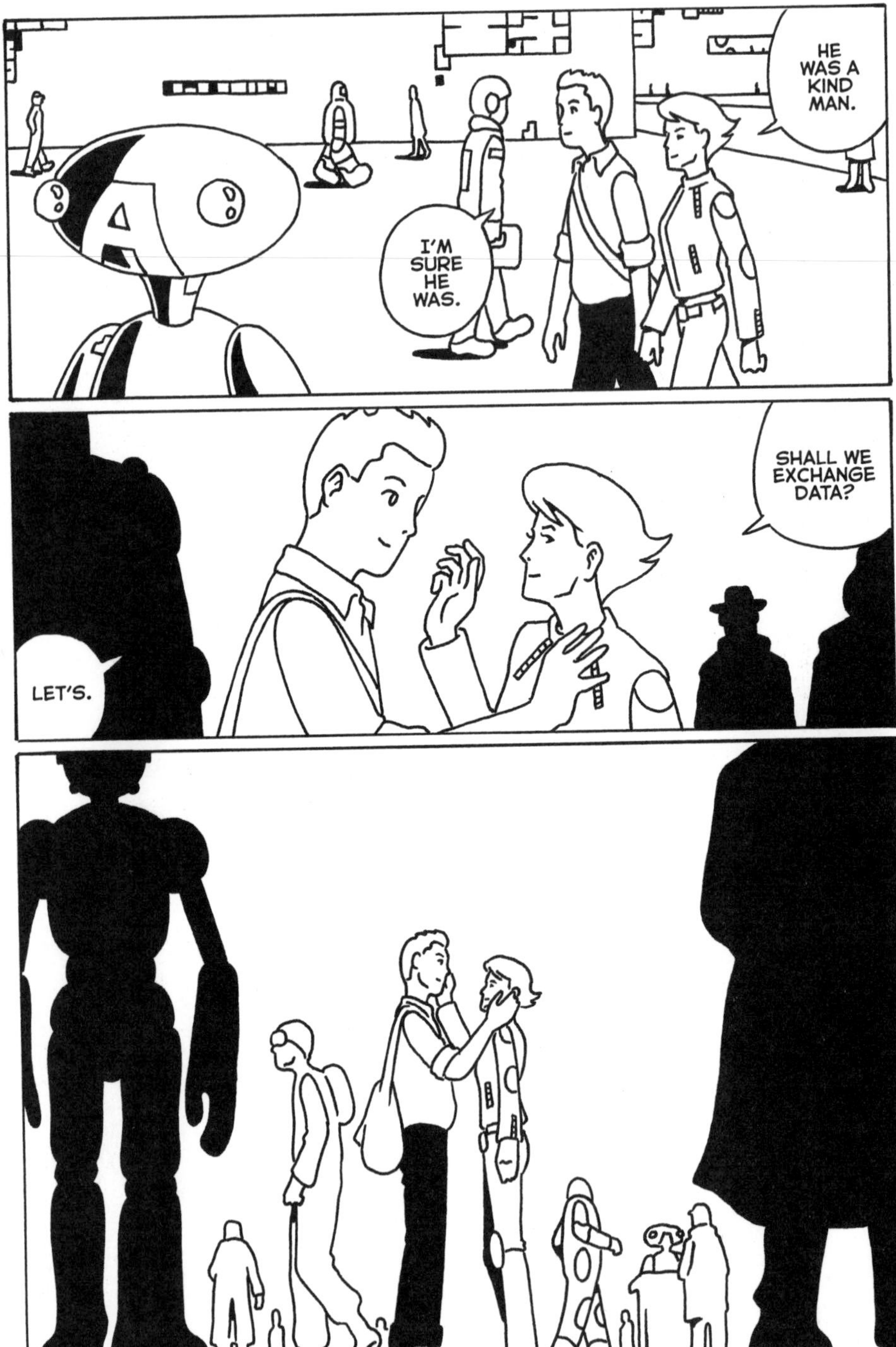
HE WAS A KIND MAN.
I'M SURE HE WAS.
SHALL WE EXCHANGE DATA?
LET'S.

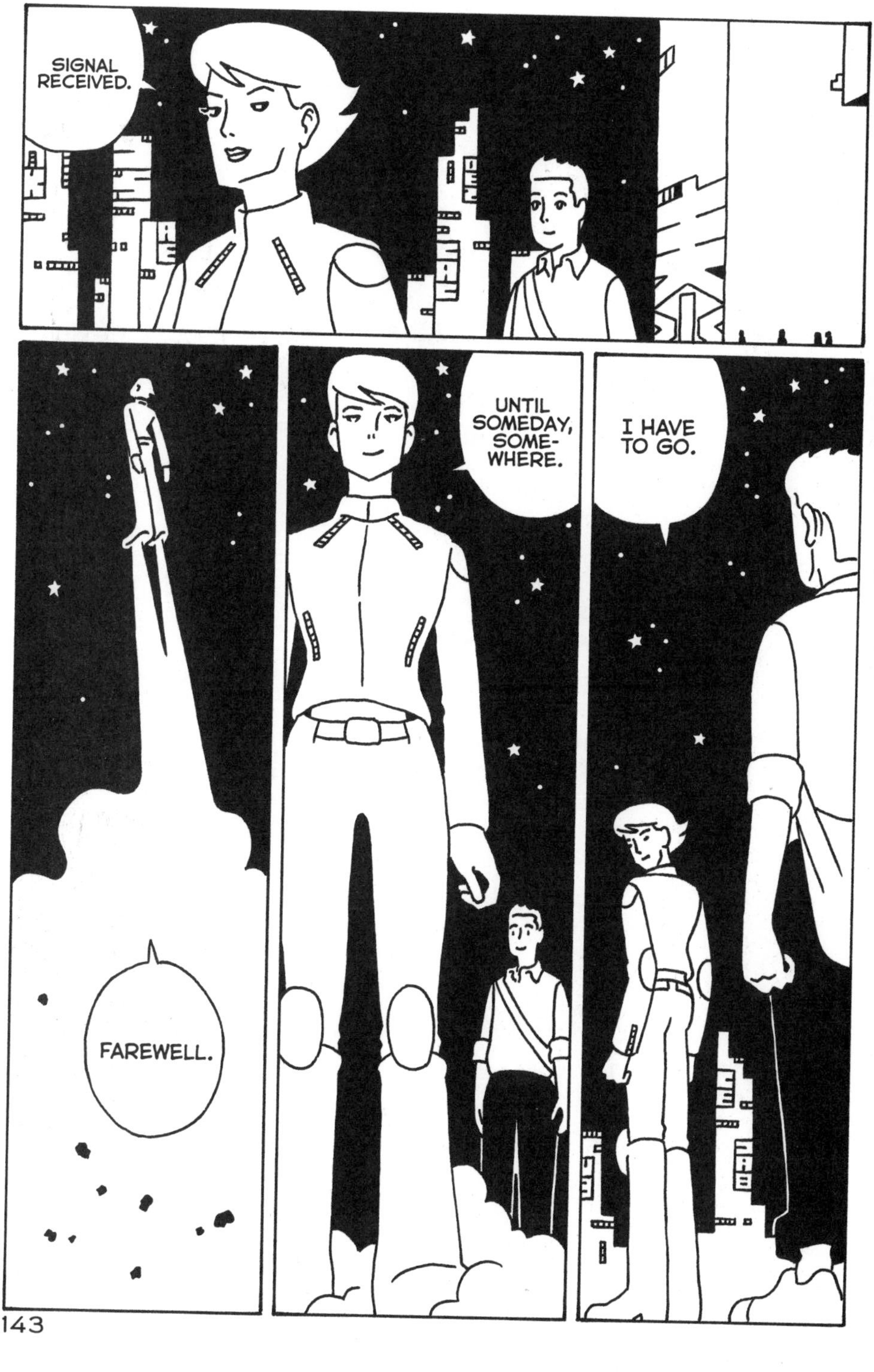
SIGNAL RECEIVED.
I HAVE TO GO.
UNTIL SOMEDAY, SOME-WHERE.
FAREWELL.

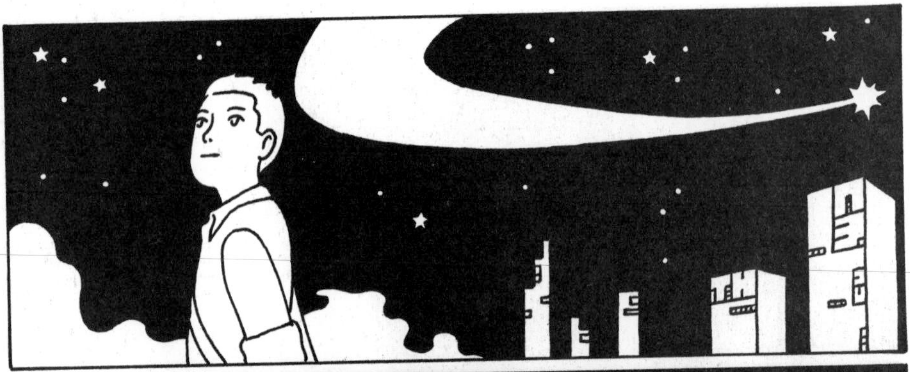

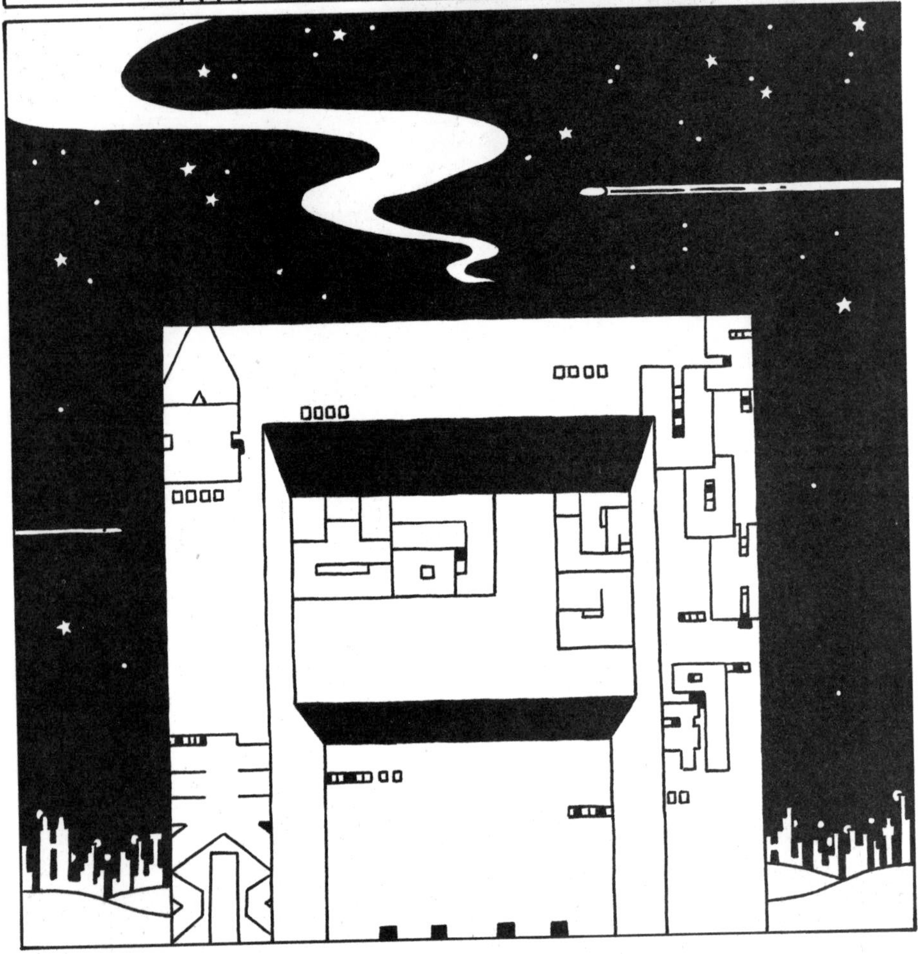

#6/END

#7

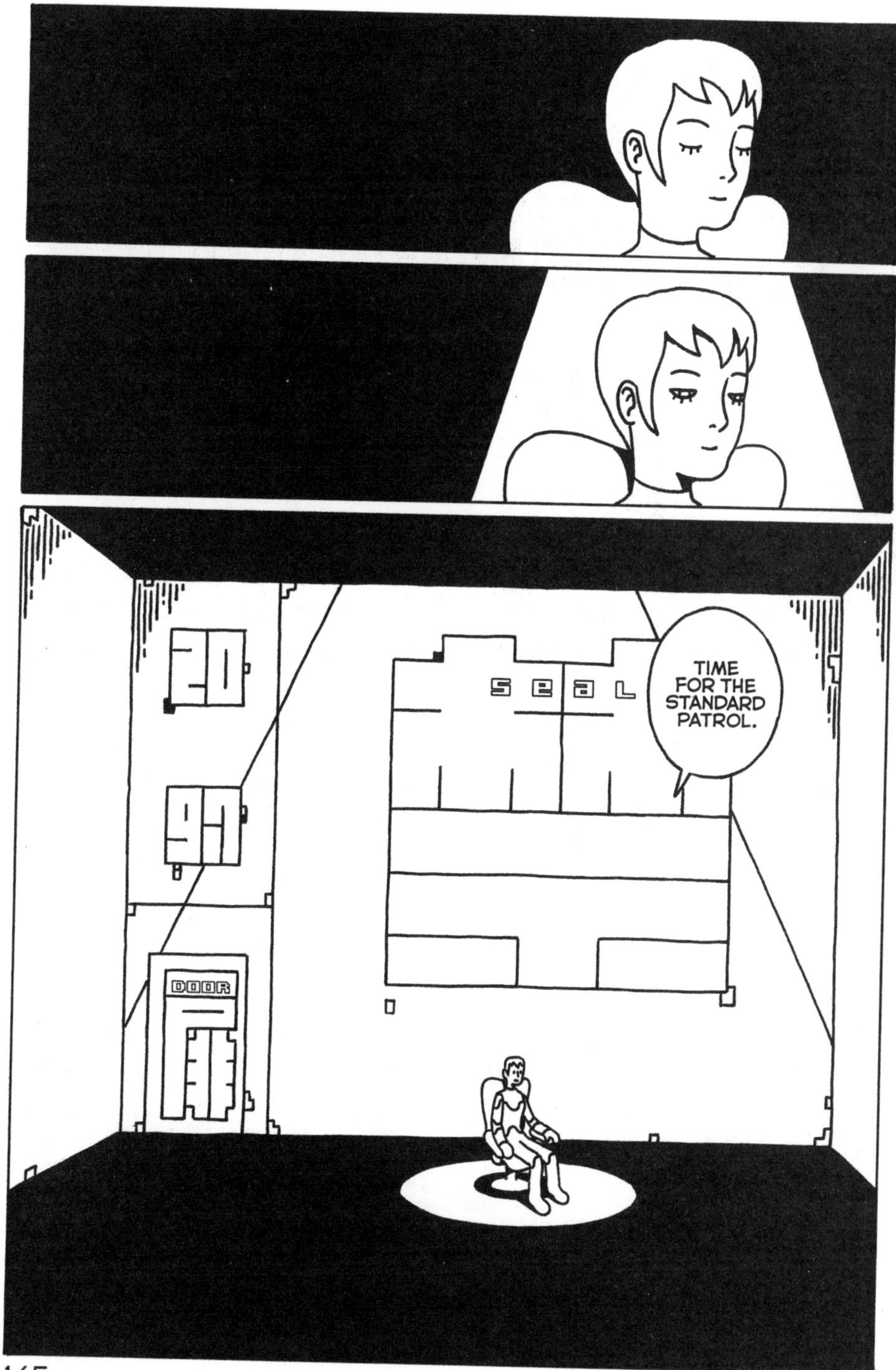
SEAL
DOOR
TIME FOR THE STANDARD PATROL.

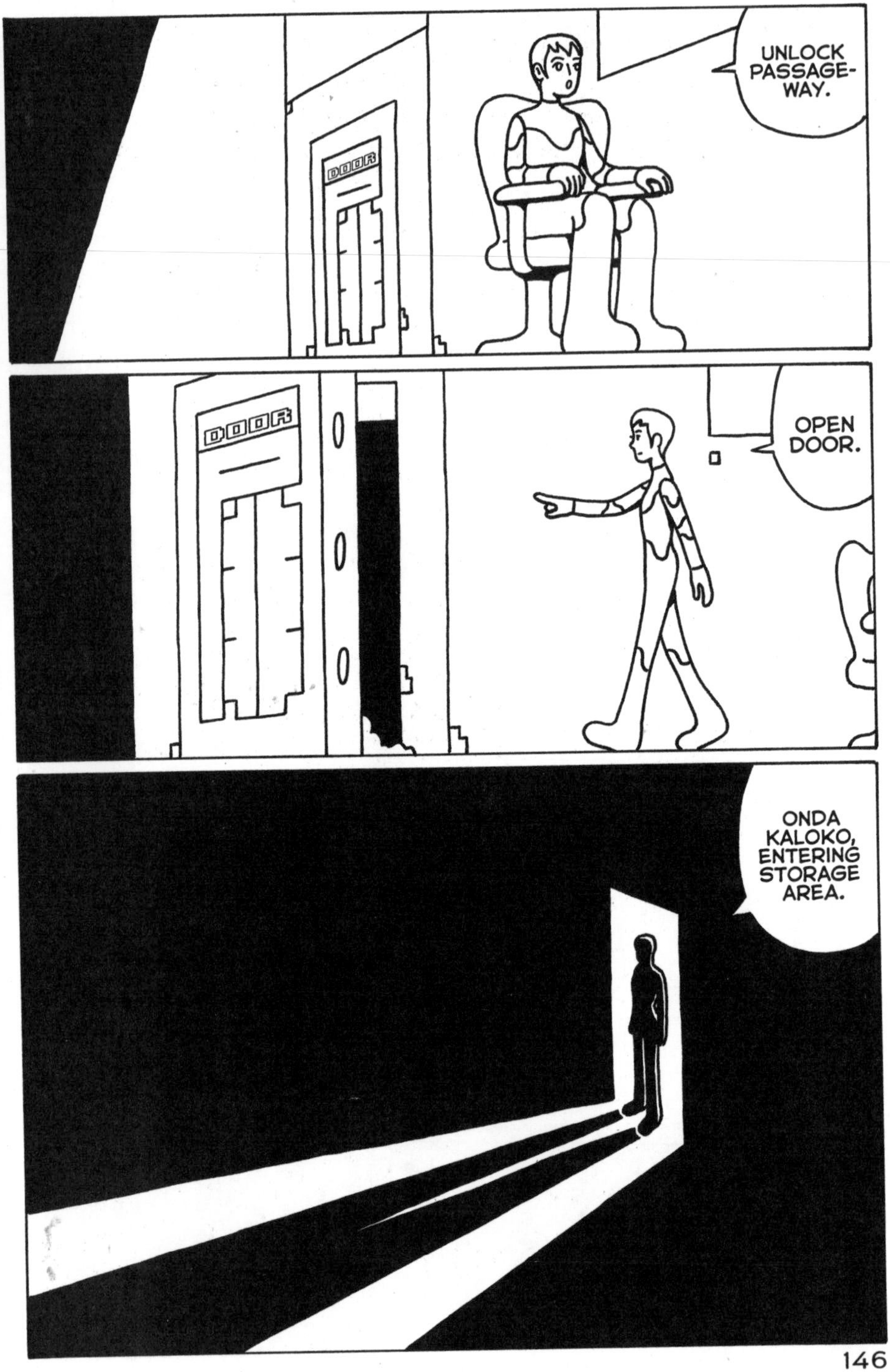
UNLOCK PASSAGE-WAY.
OPEN DOOR.
ONDA KALOKO, ENTERING STORAGE AREA.

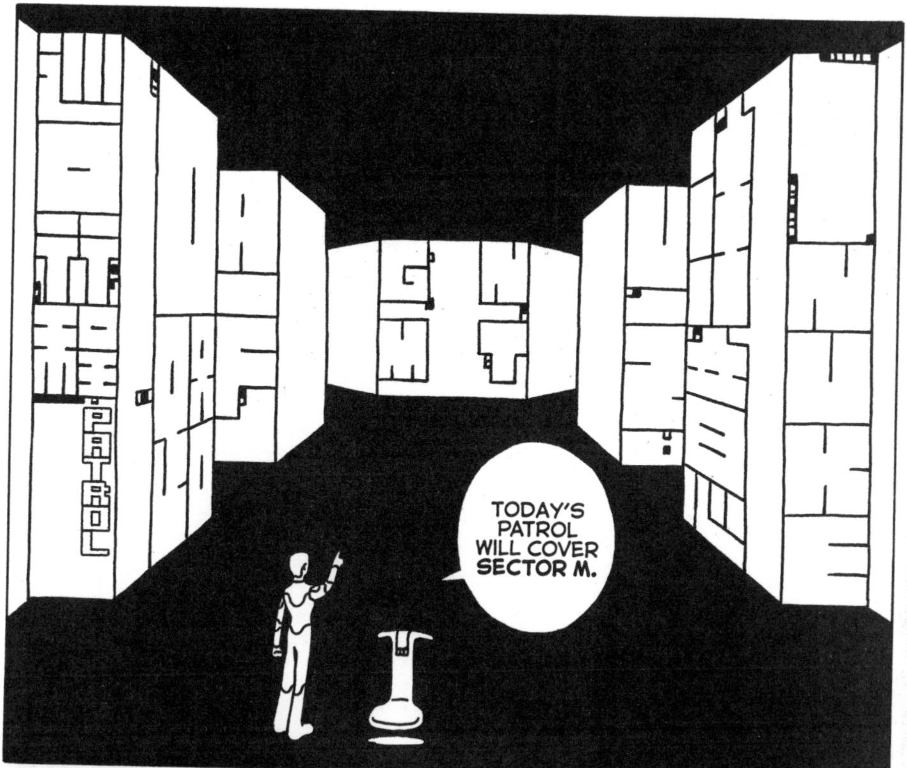
PATROL
TODAY'S PATROL WILL COVER SECTOR M.

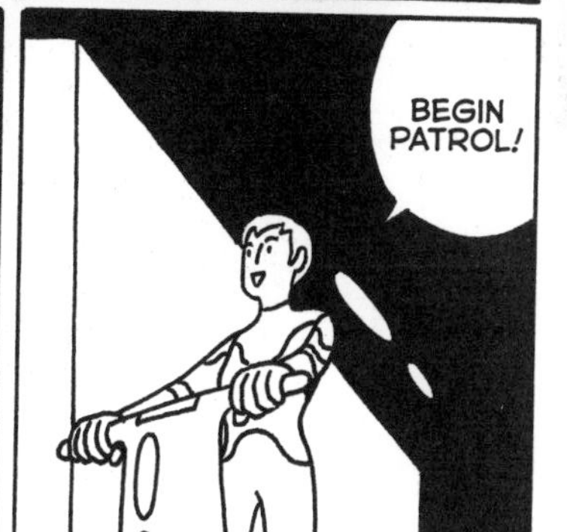
BEGIN PATROL!

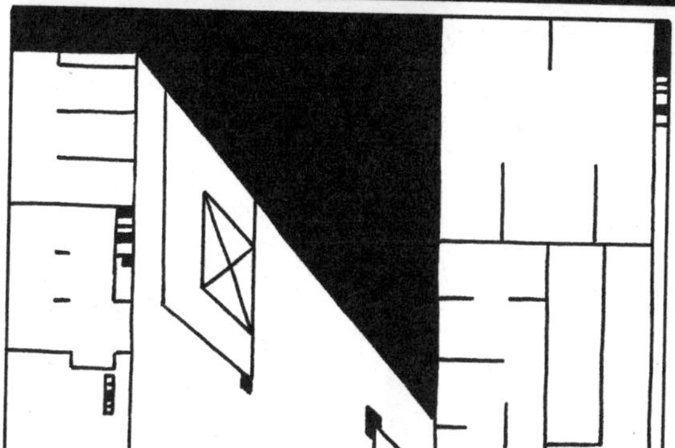
ROW

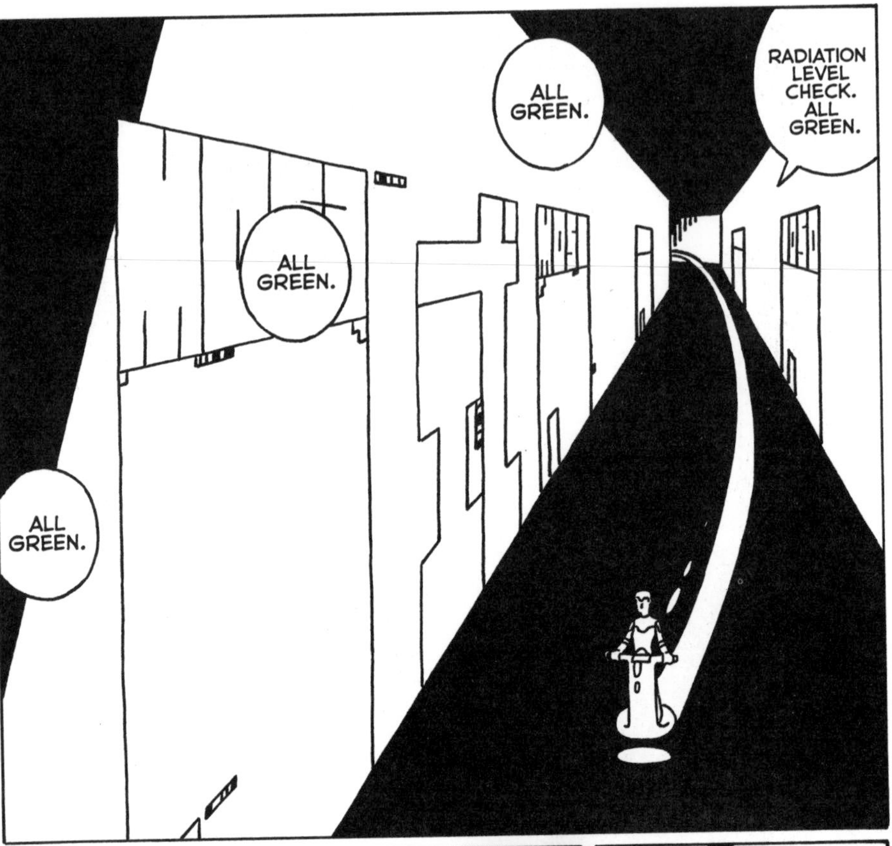
RADIATION LEVEL CHECK. ALL GREEN.
ALL GREEN.
ALL GREEN.
ALL GREEN.

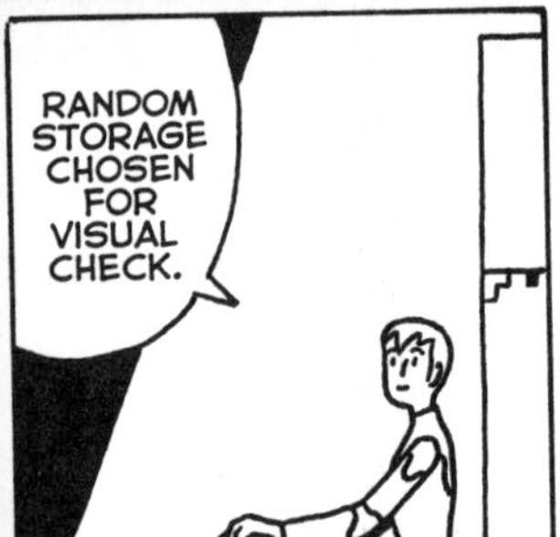
RANDOM STORAGE CHOSEN FOR VISUAL CHECK.

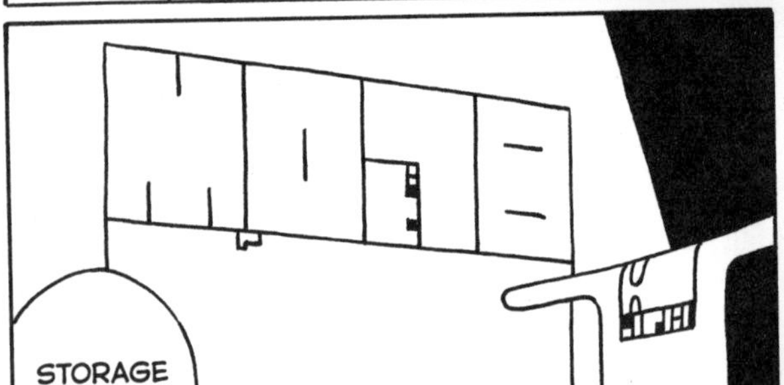
STORAGE ROOM M078.

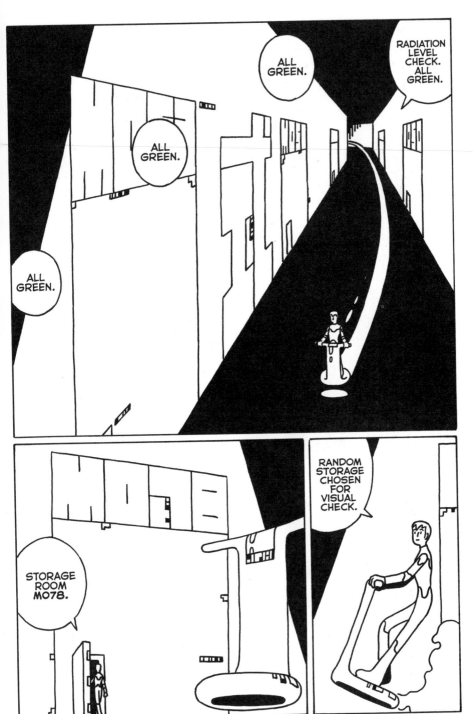

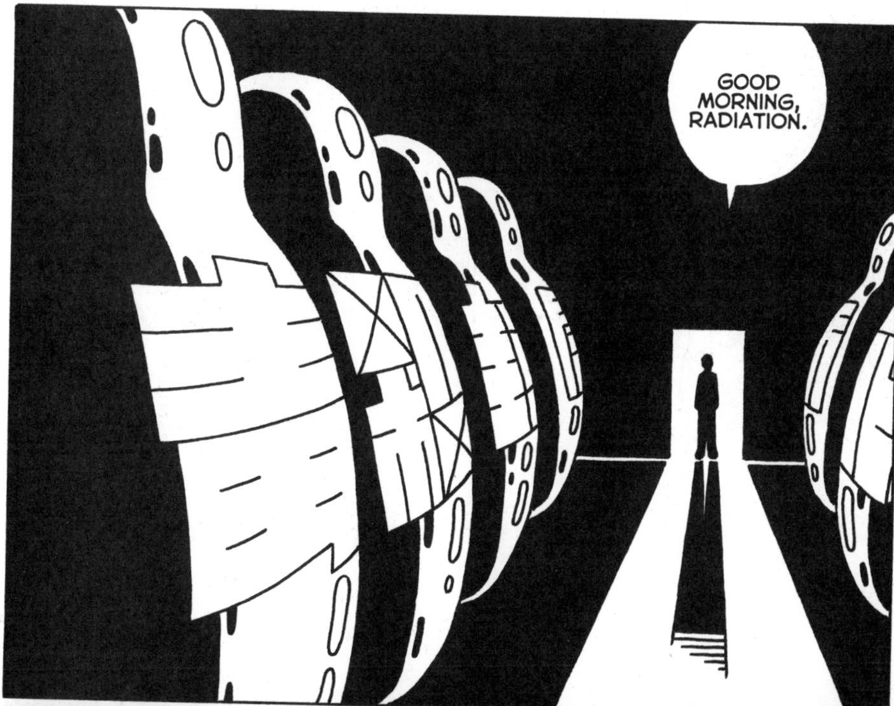
GOOD MORNING, RADIATION.

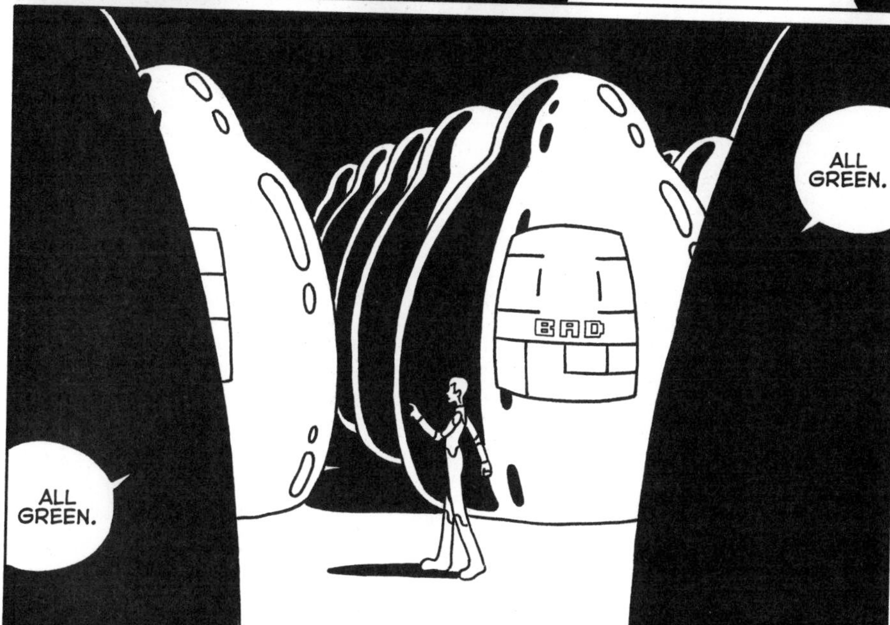
ALL GREEN.
BAD
ALL GREEN.

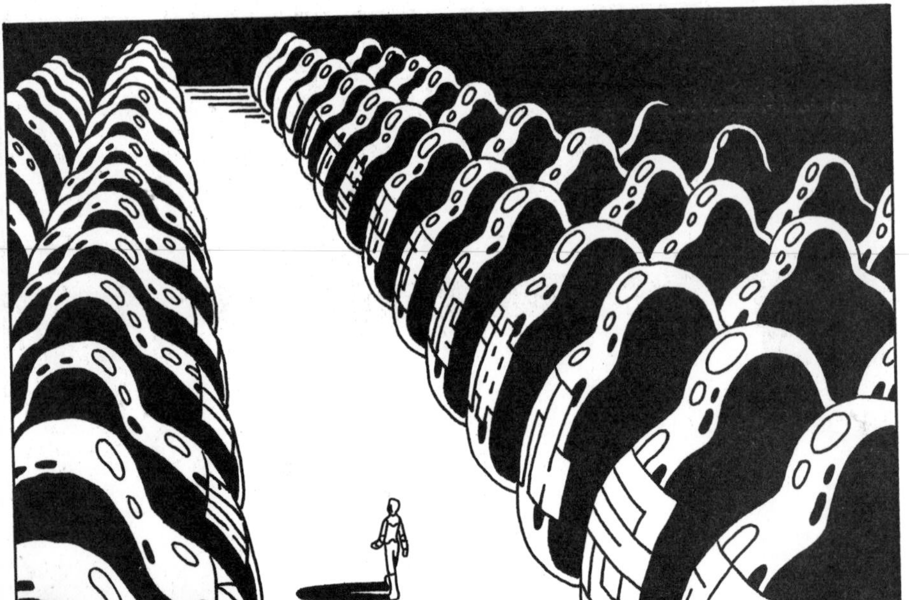
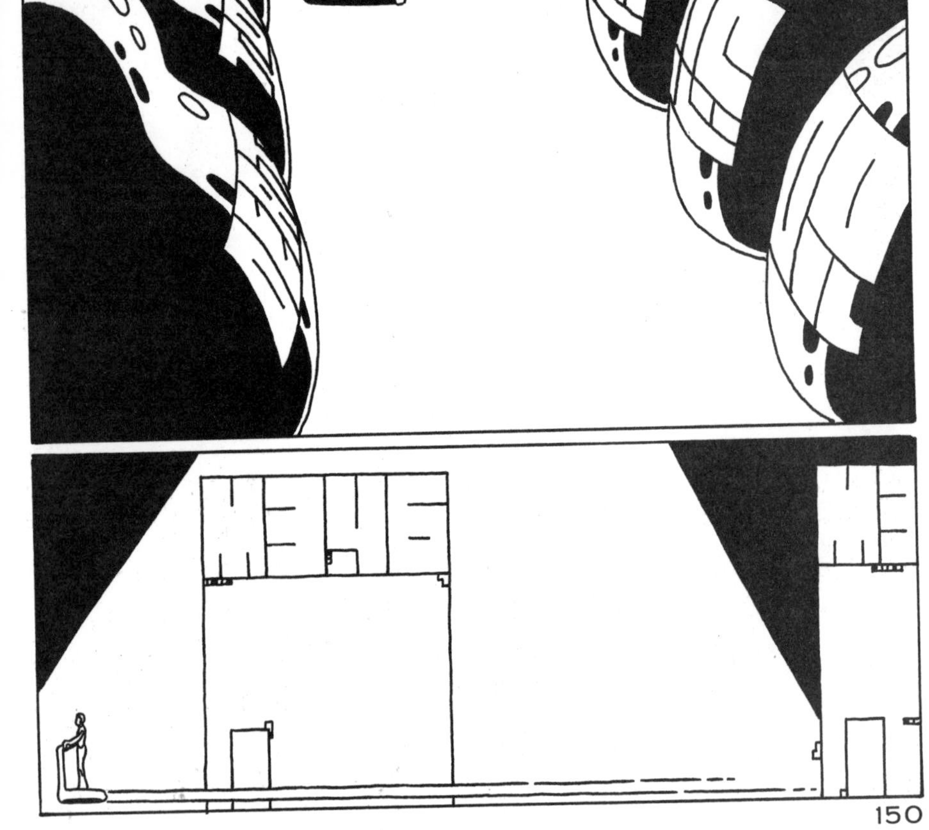

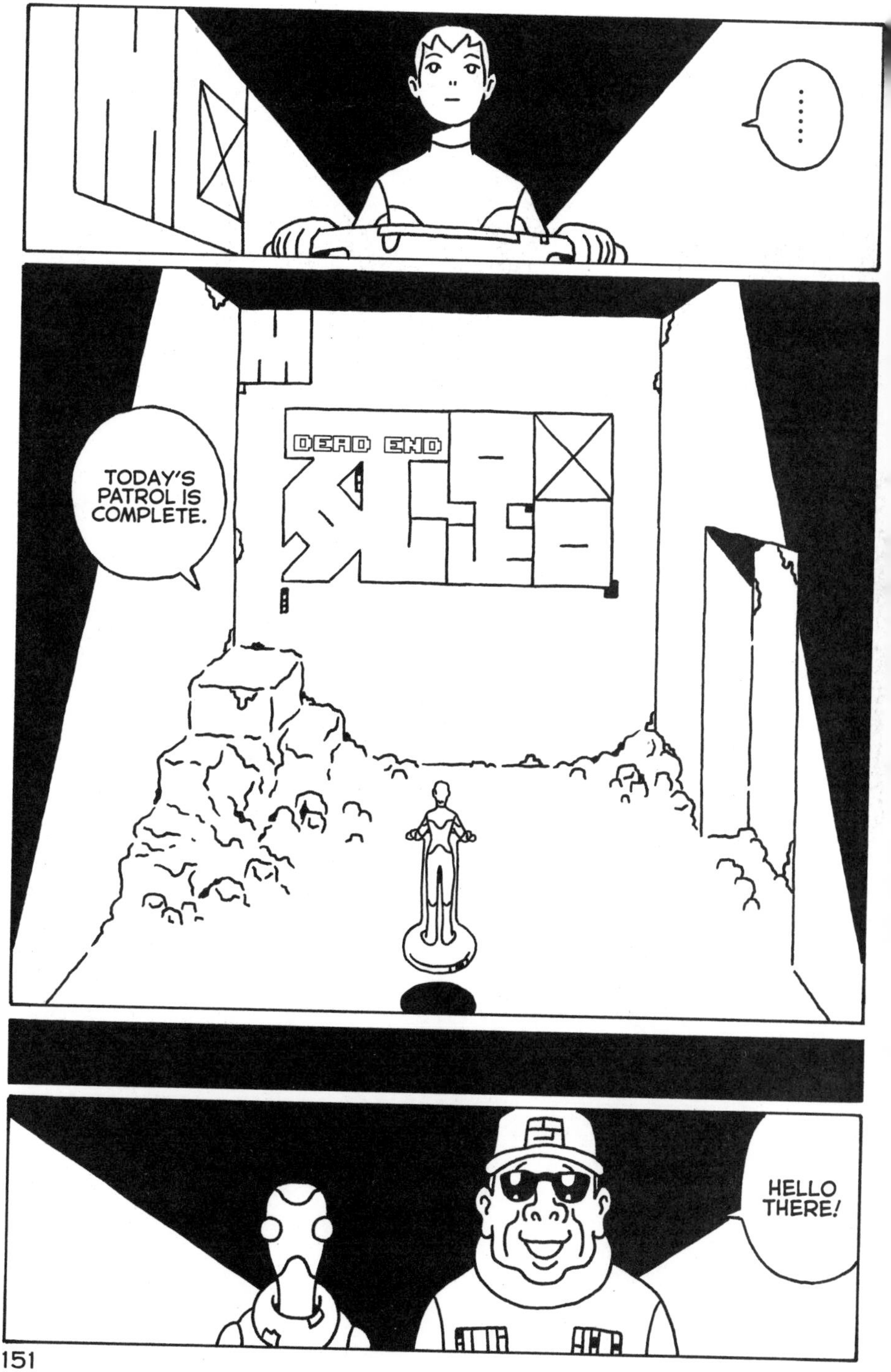
......
DEAD END
TODAY'S PATROL IS COMPLETE.
HELLO THERE!

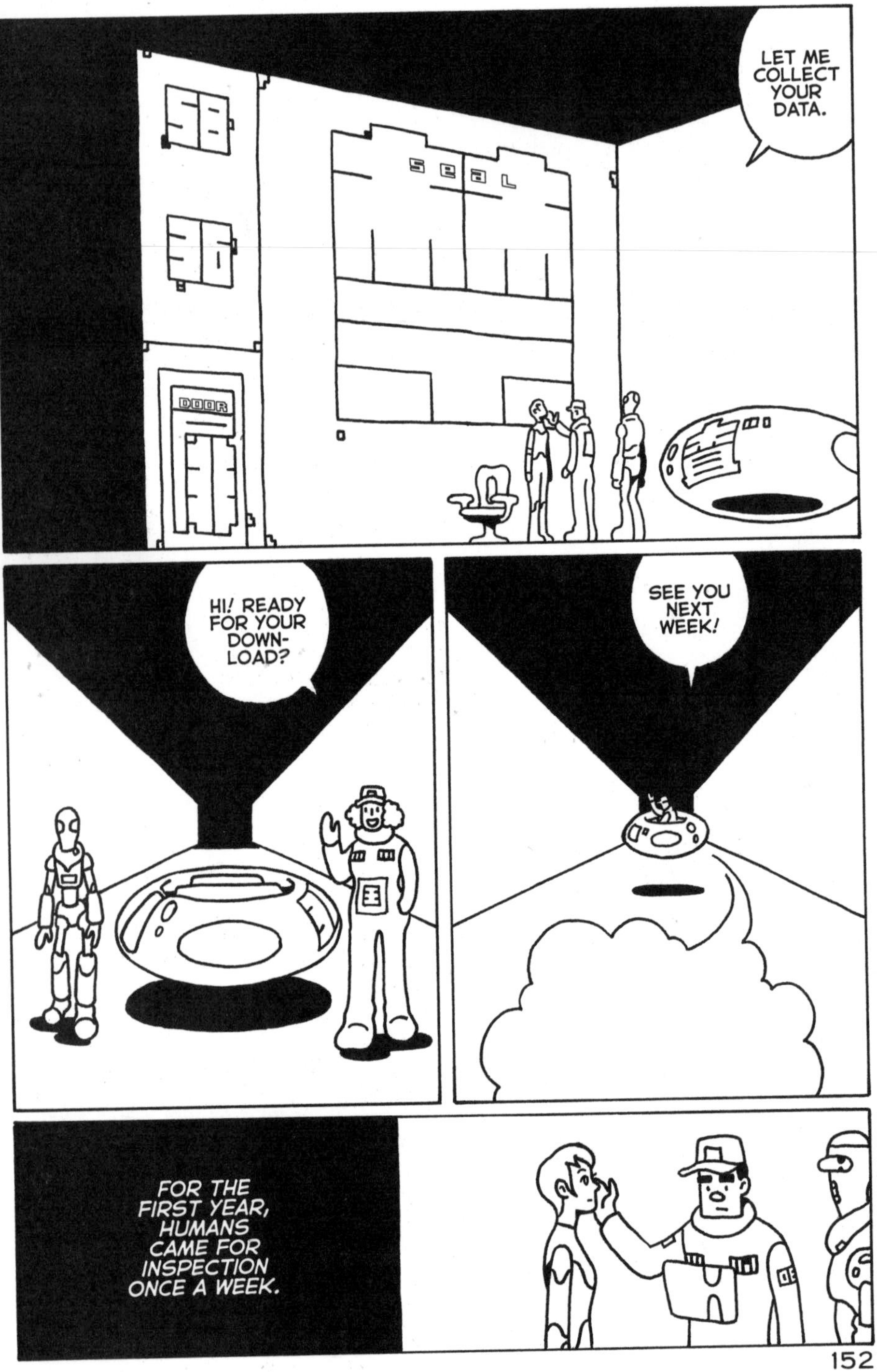
SEAL
DOOR
LET ME COLLECT YOUR DATA.
HI! READY FOR YOUR DOWN-LOAD?
SEE YOU NEXT WEEK!
FOR THE FIRST YEAR, HUMANS CAME FOR INSPECTION ONCE A WEEK.

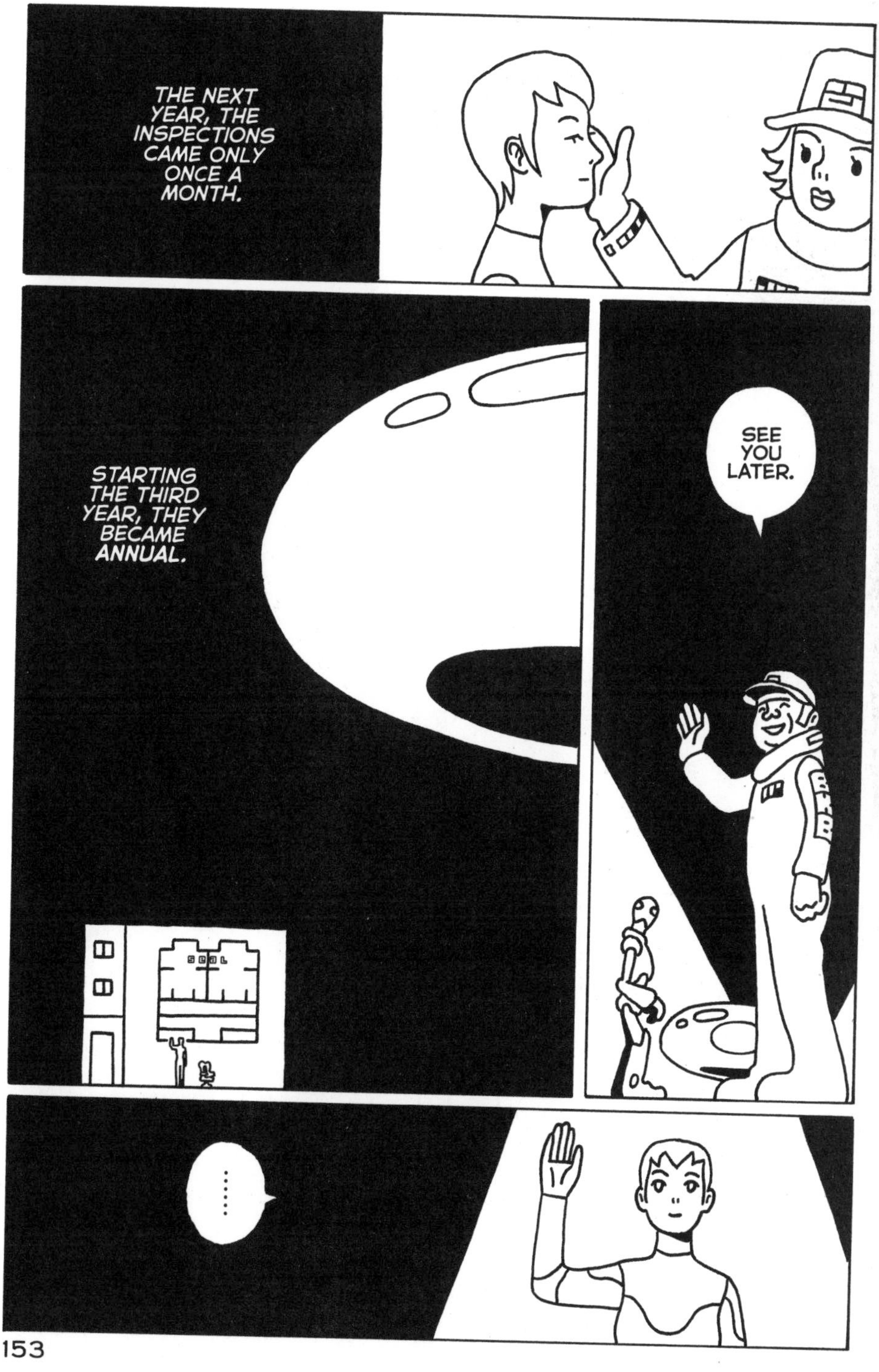
THE NEXT YEAR, THE INSPECTIONS CAME ONLY ONCE A MONTH.
STARTING THE THIRD YEAR, THEY BECAME ANNUAL.
SEE YOU LATER.
……

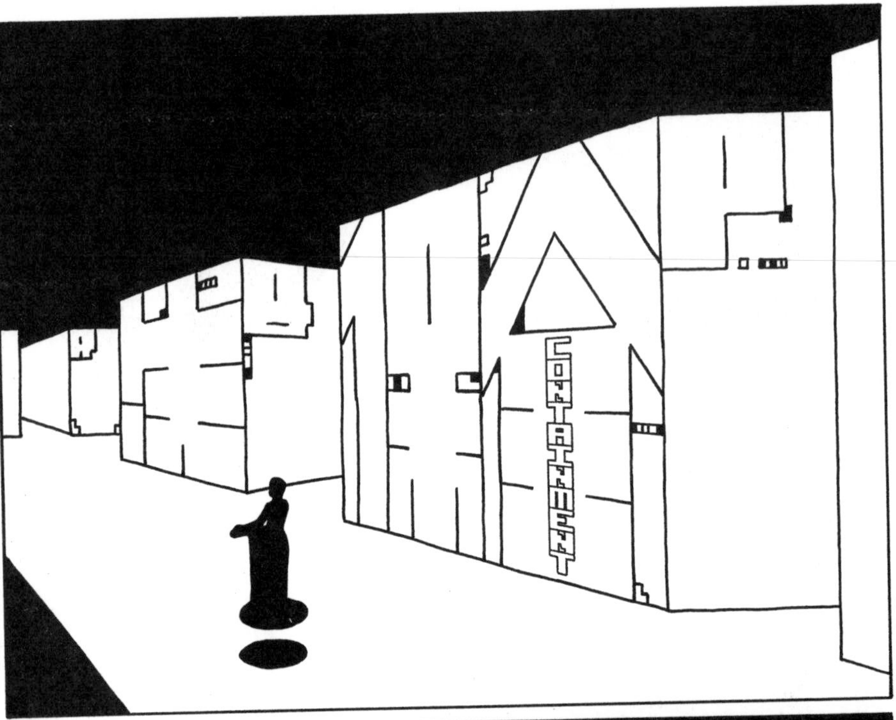
CONTAINMENT
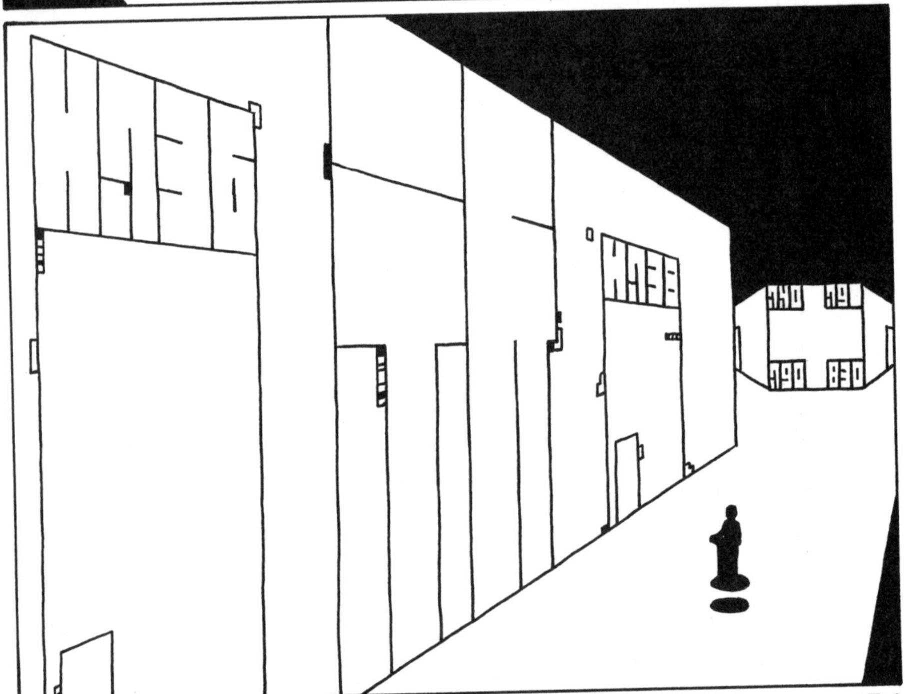

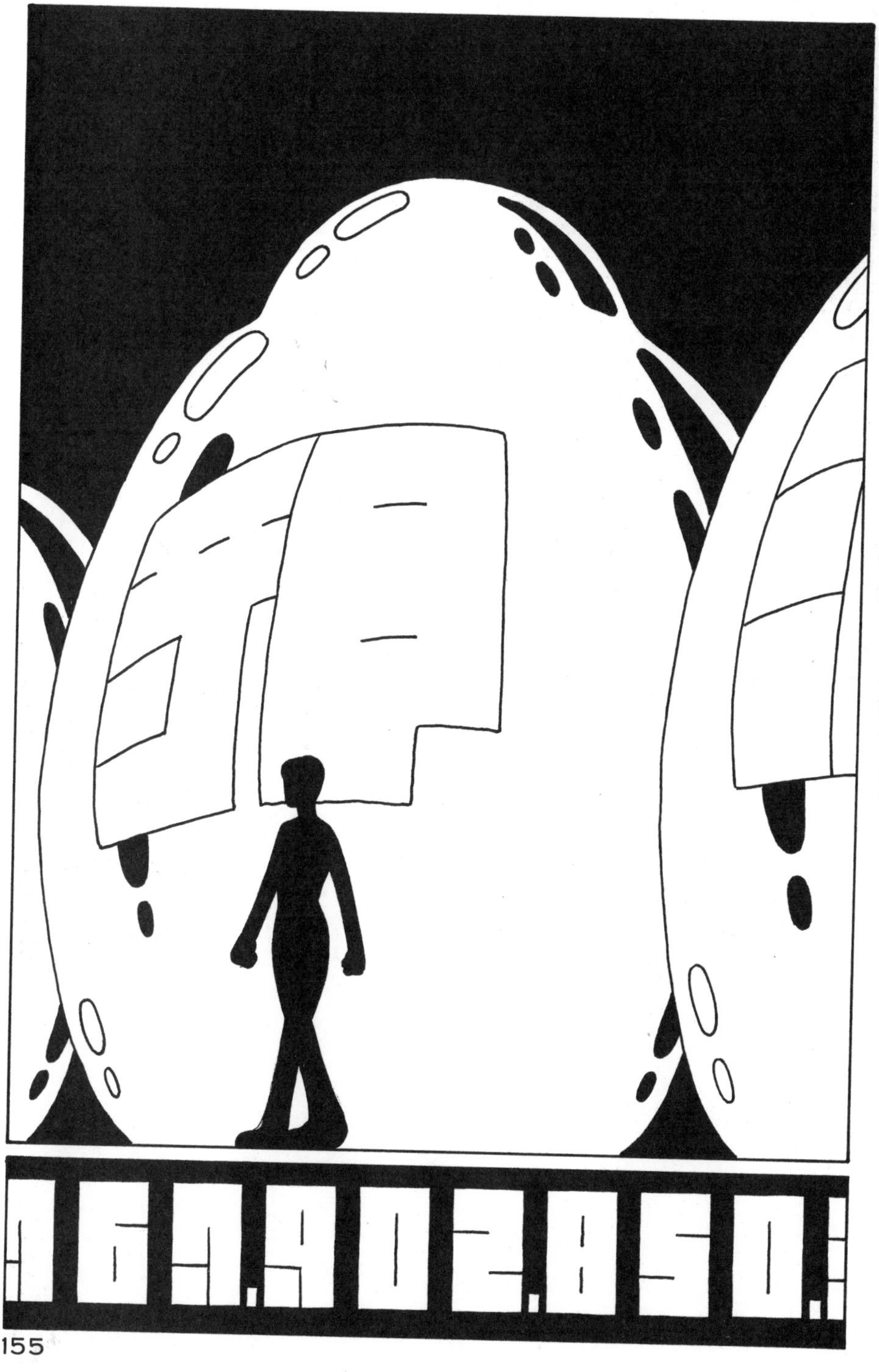
167,902,850,

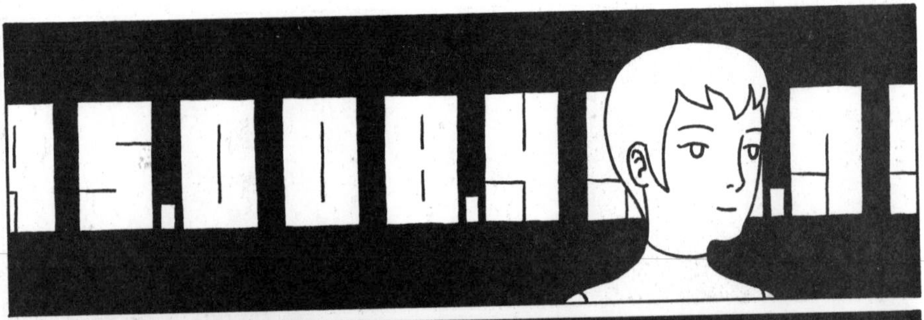

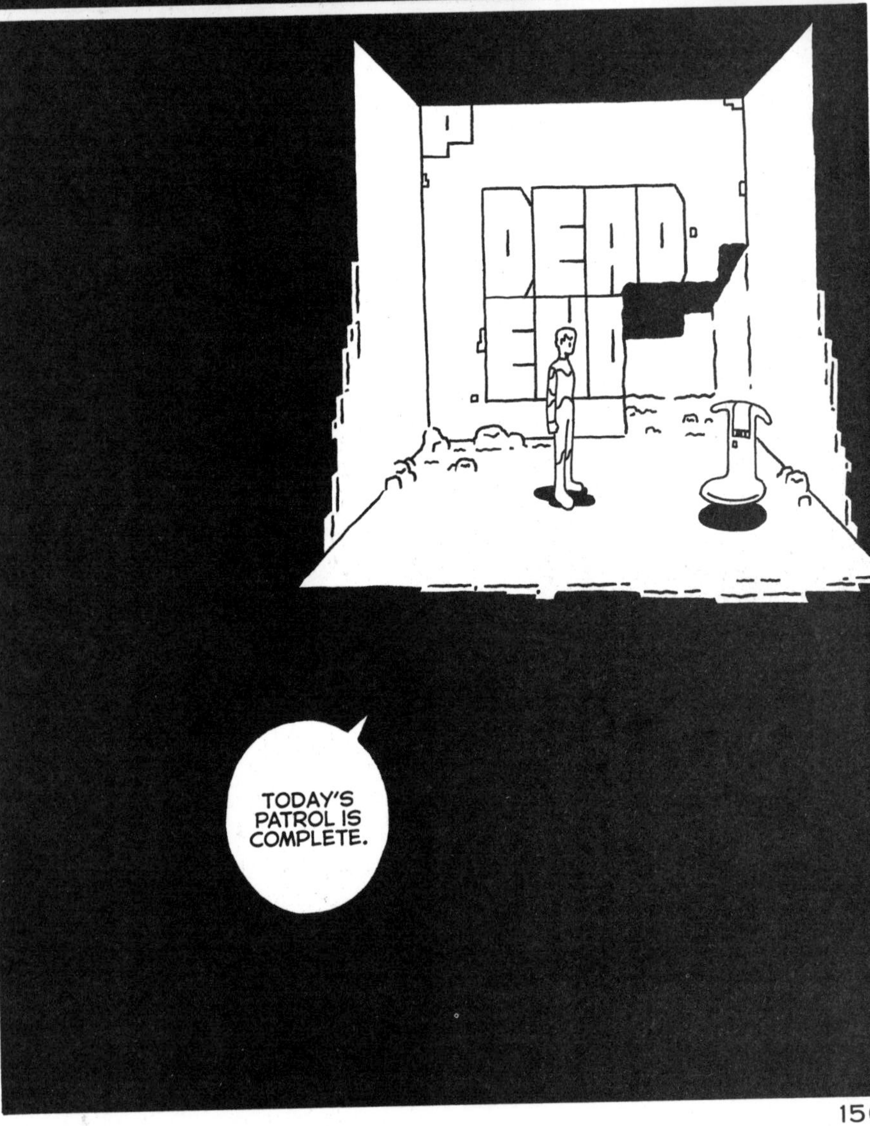
DEAD END
TODAY'S PATROL IS COMPLETE.

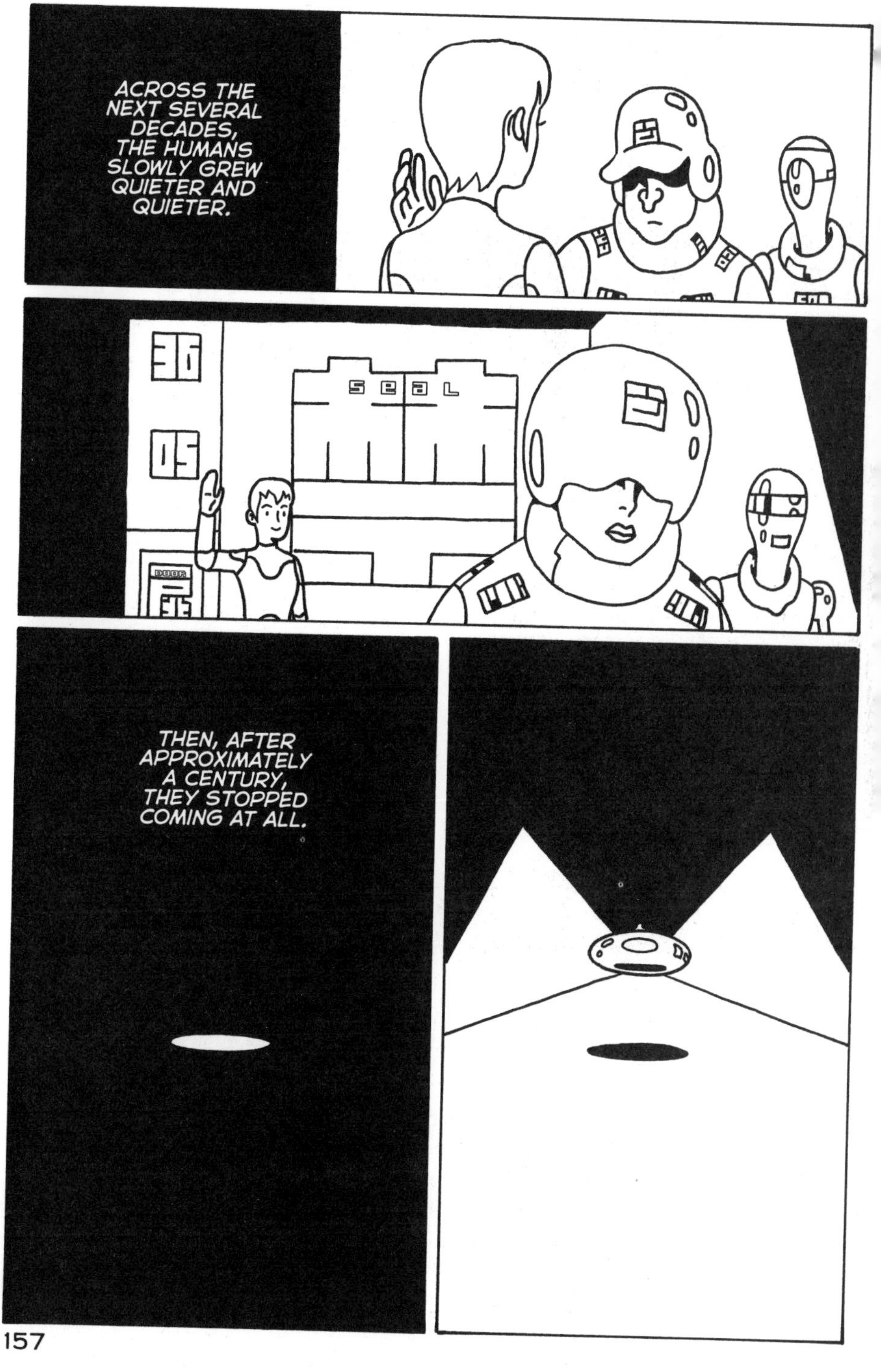
ACROSS THE NEXT SEVERAL DECADES, THE HUMANS SLOWLY GREW QUIETER AND QUIETER.
36
05
SEAL
DOOR
THEN, AFTER APPROXIMATELY A CENTURY, THEY STOPPED COMING AT ALL.

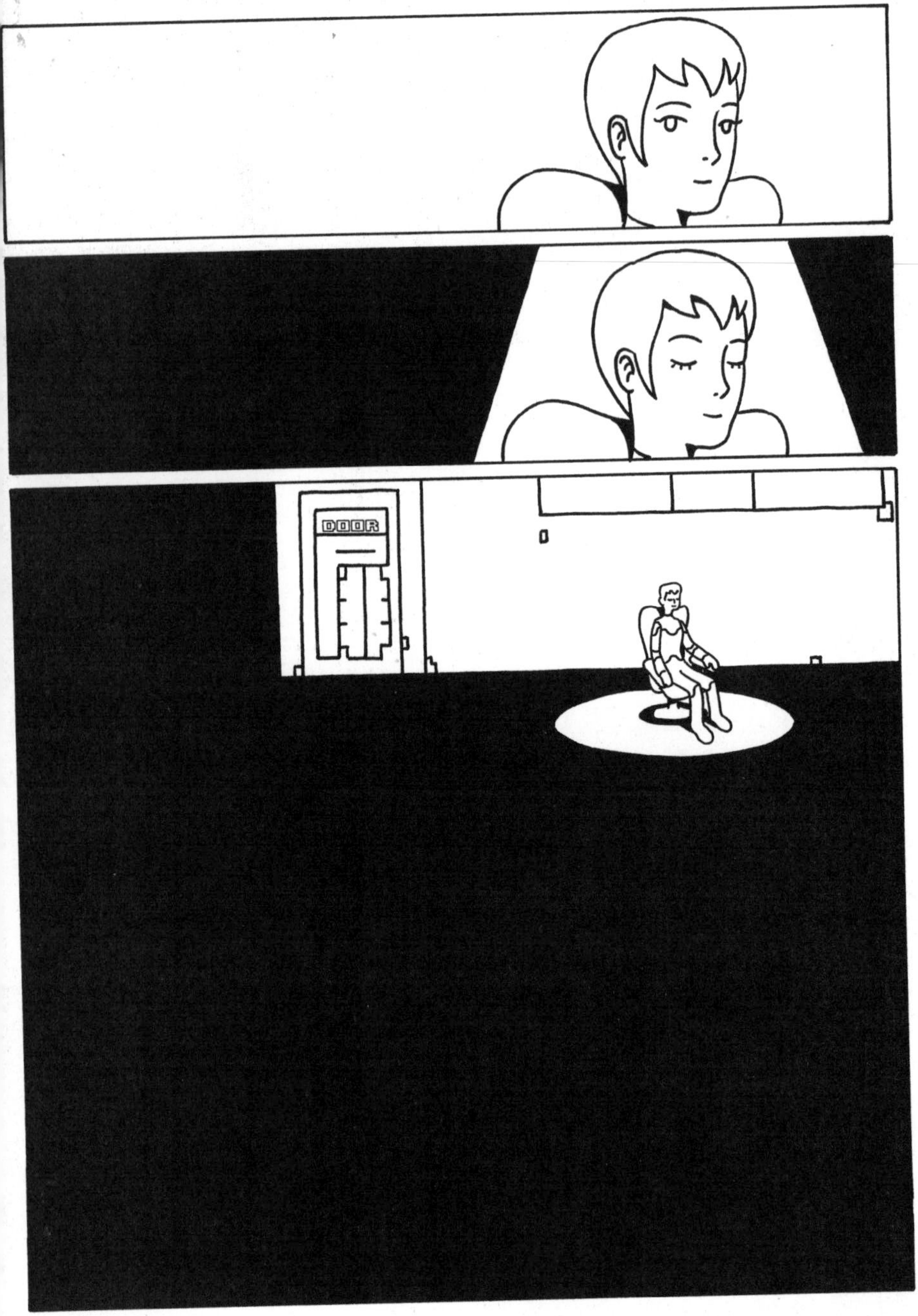
DOOR

#7/END

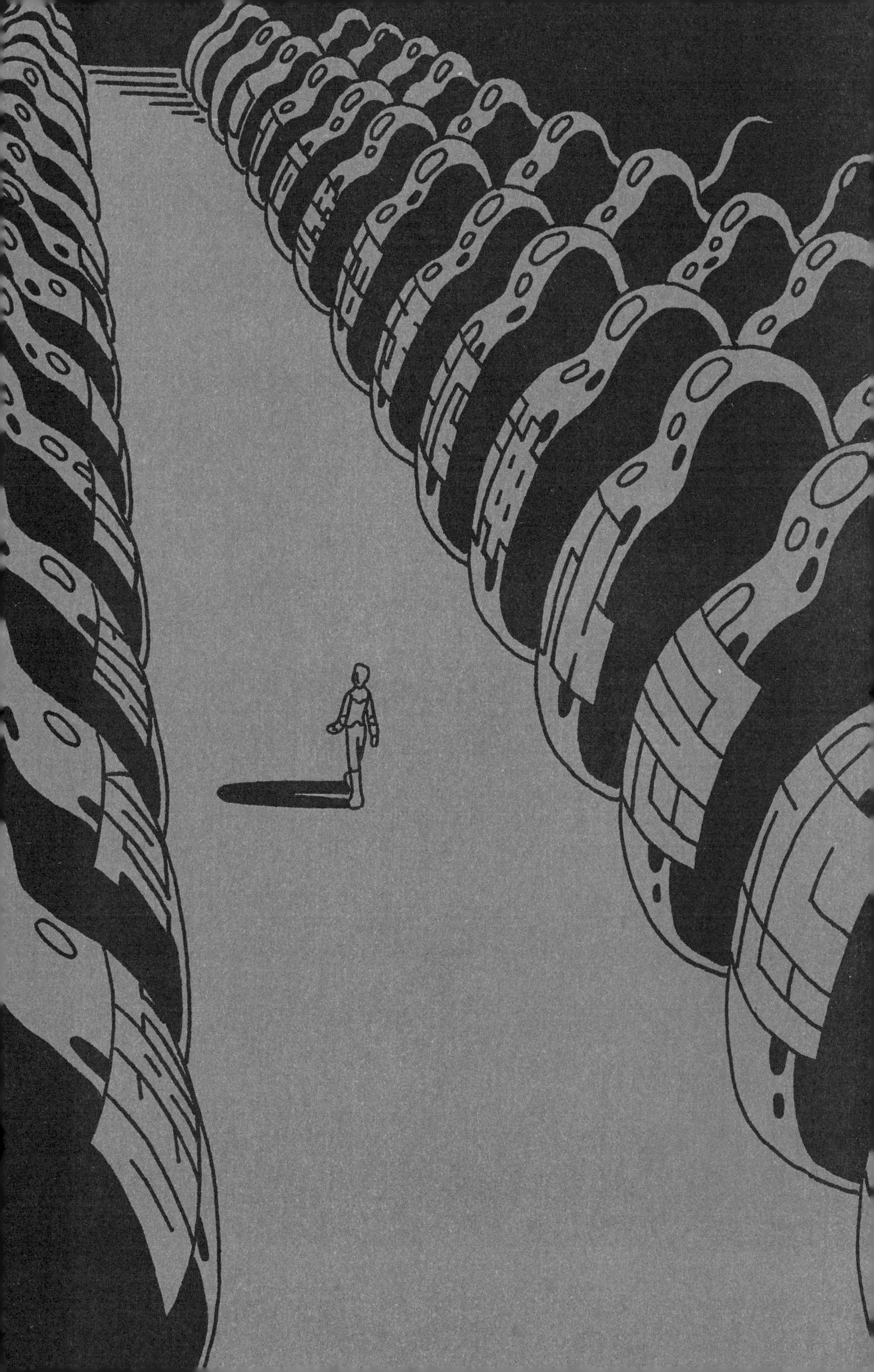

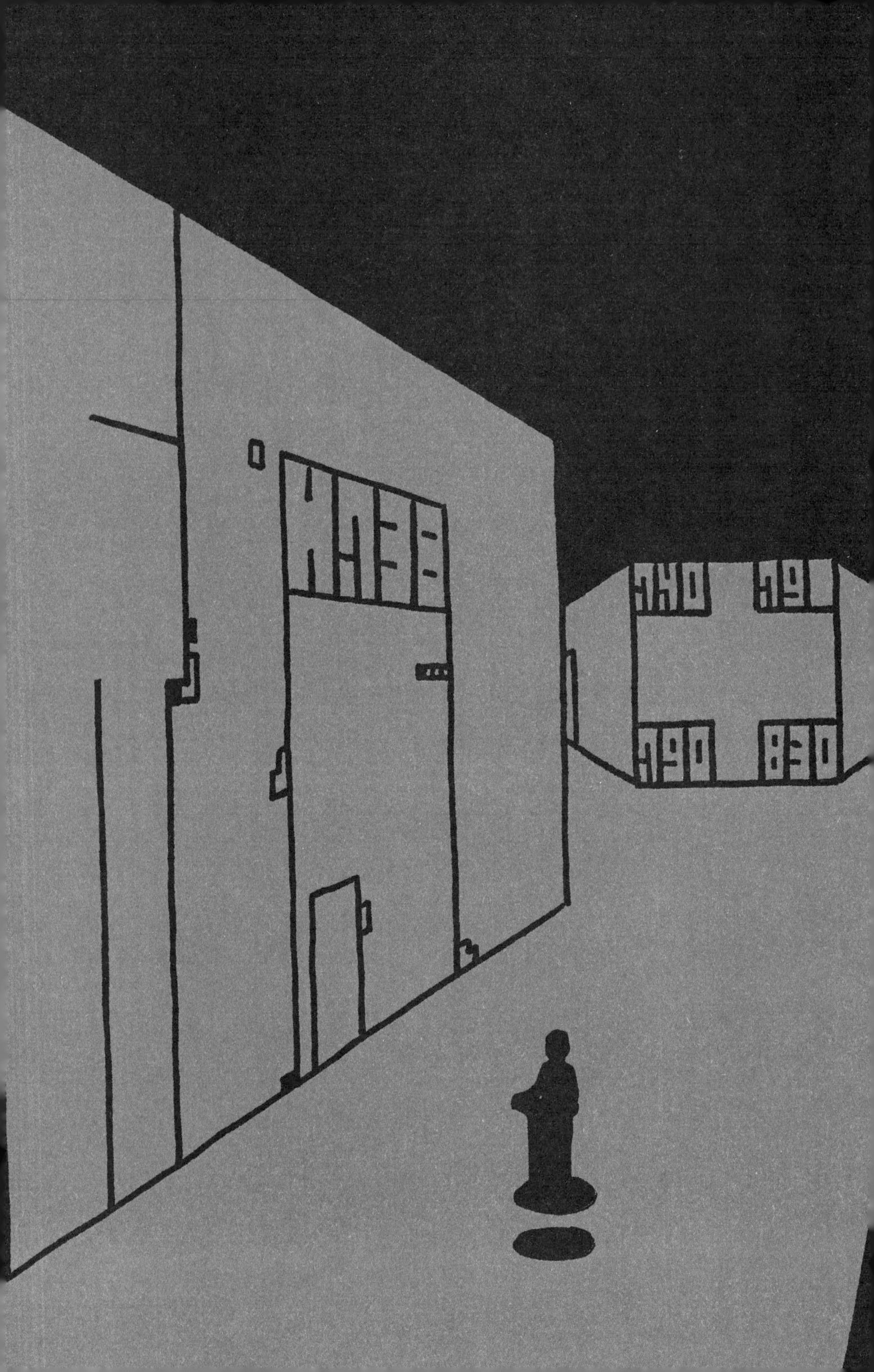

#8

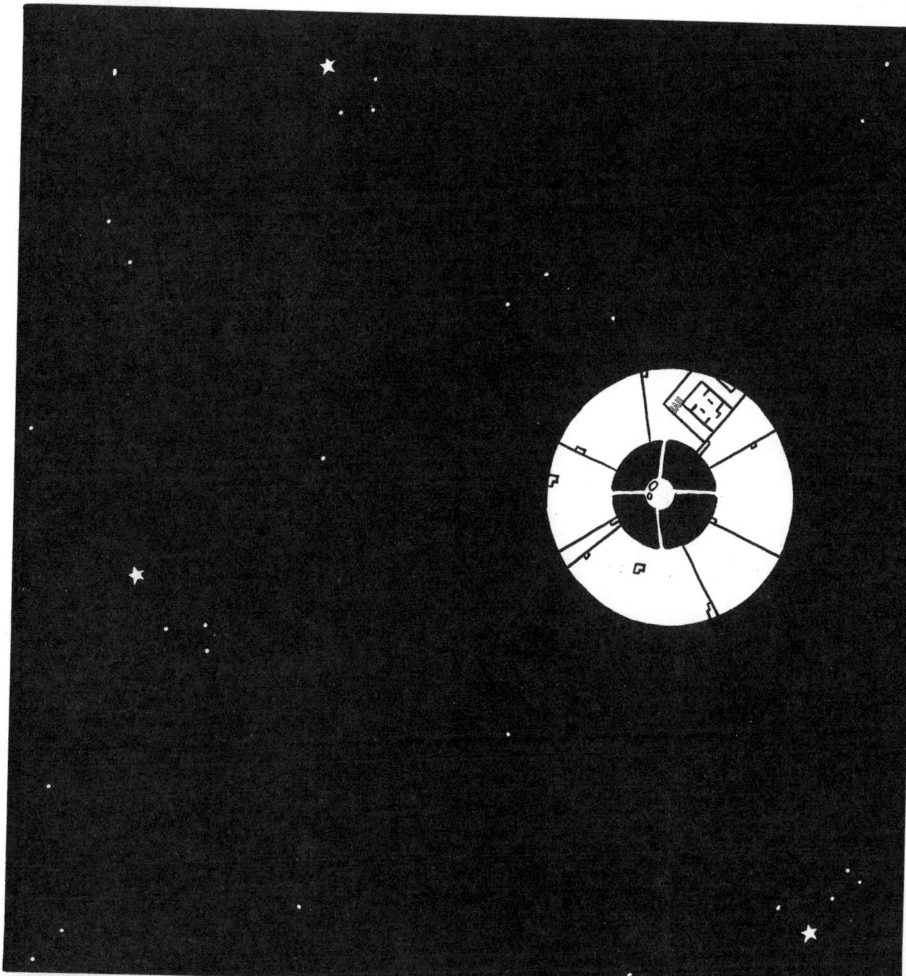

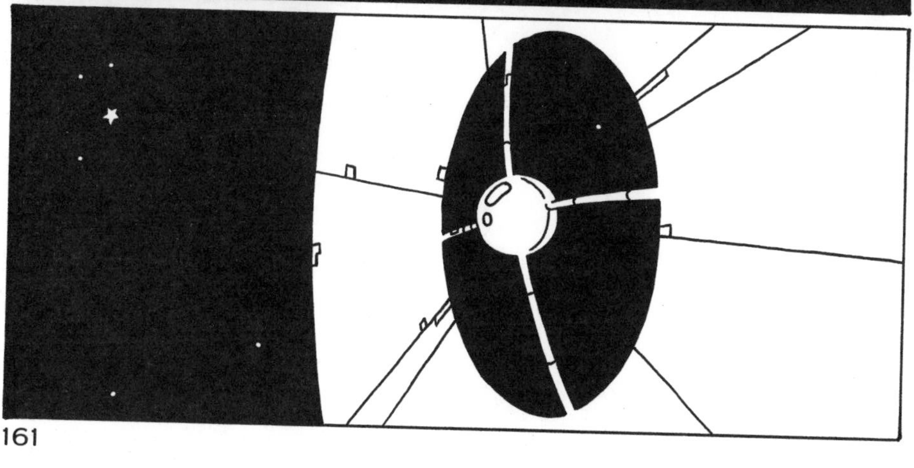

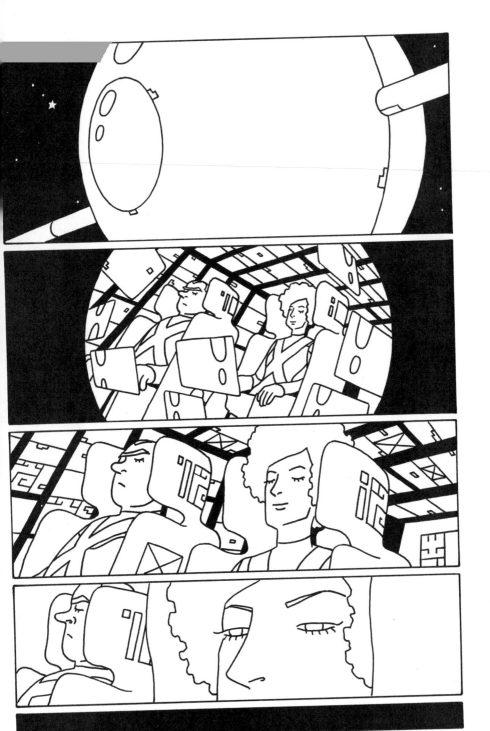

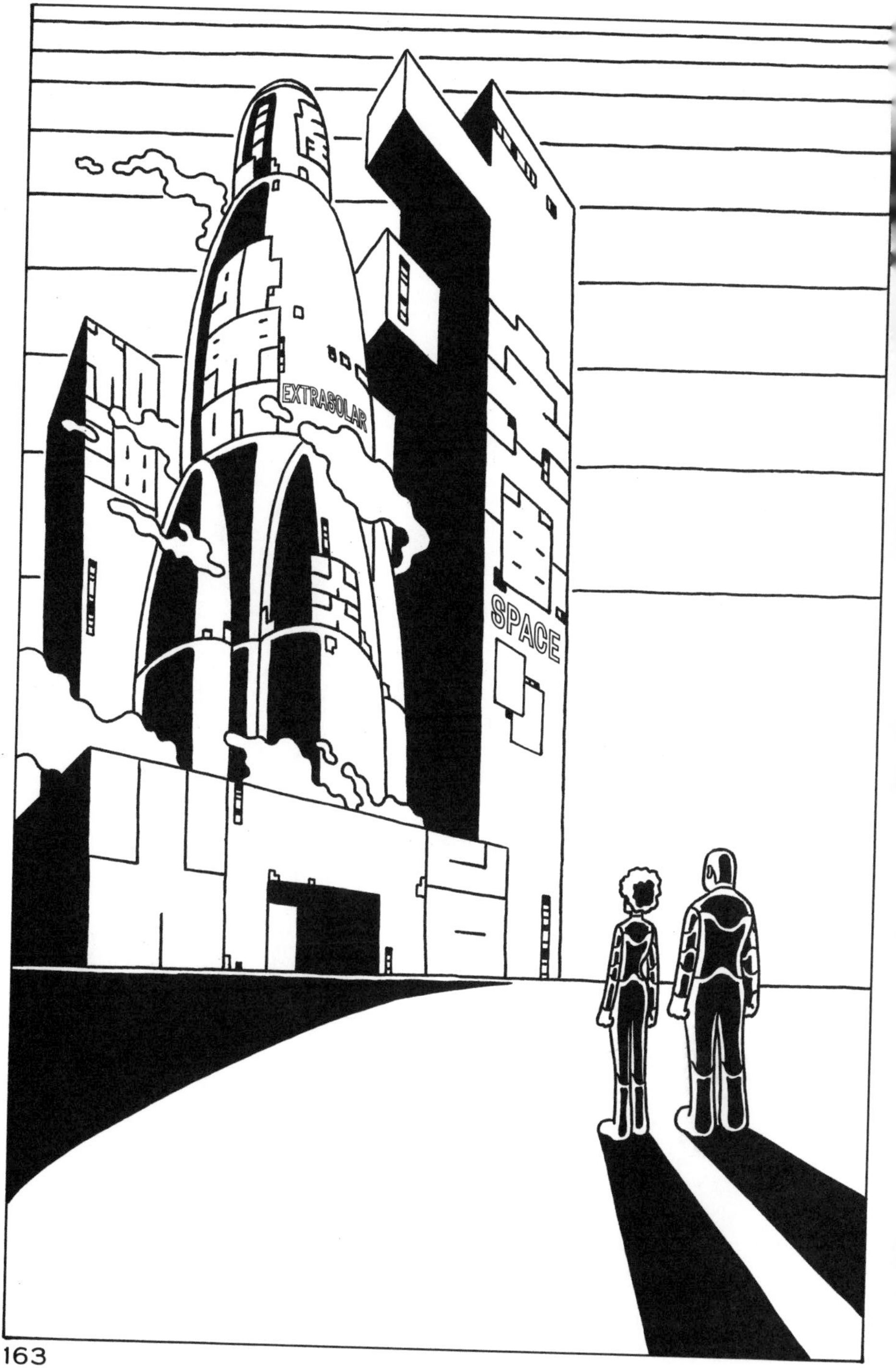
EXTRASOLAR
SPACE

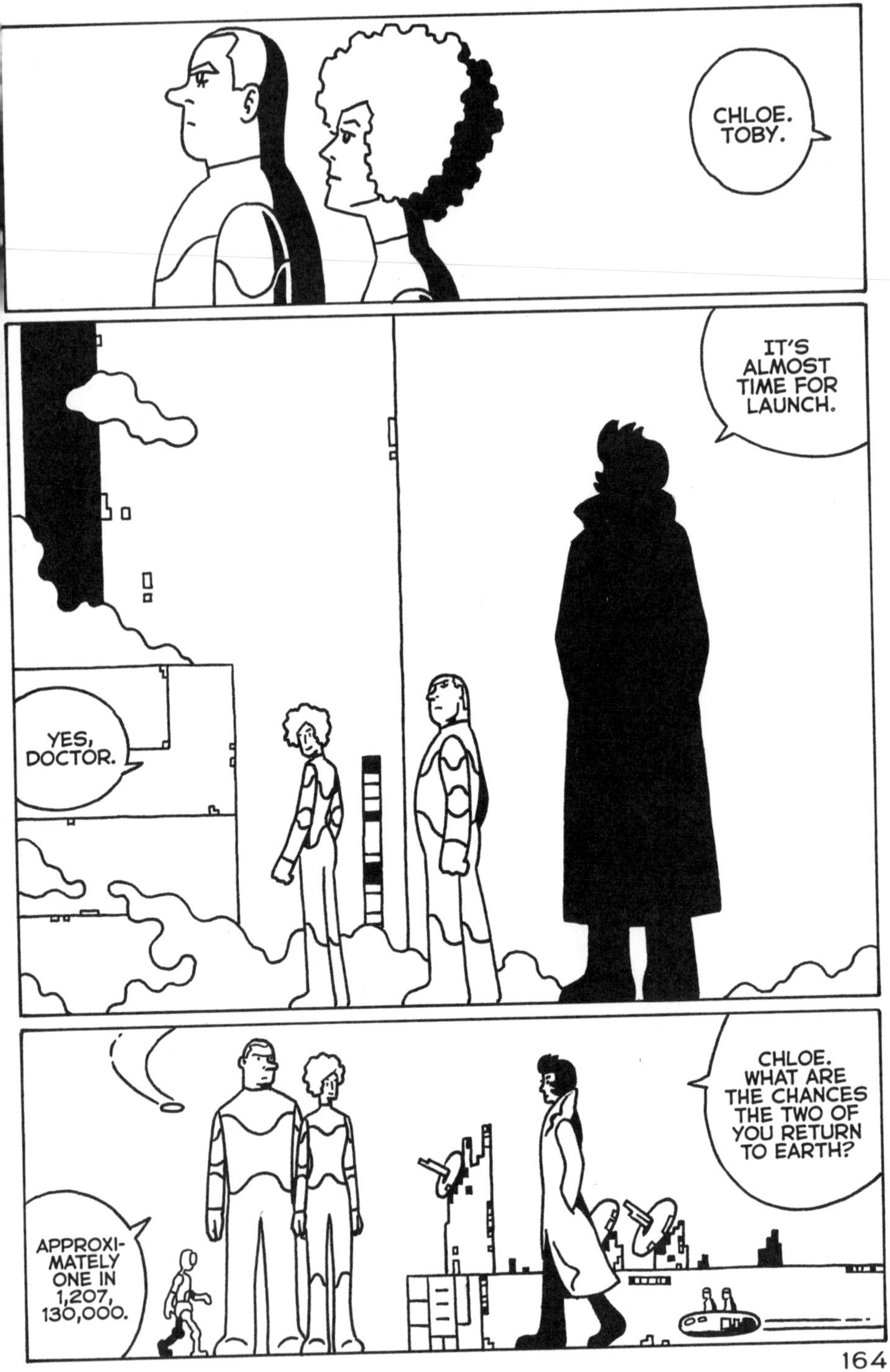
CHLOE. TOBY.
IT'S ALMOST TIME FOR LAUNCH.
YES, DOCTOR.
CHLOE. WHAT ARE THE CHANCES THE TWO OF YOU RETURN TO EARTH?
APPROXI-MATELY ONE IN 1,207, 130,000.

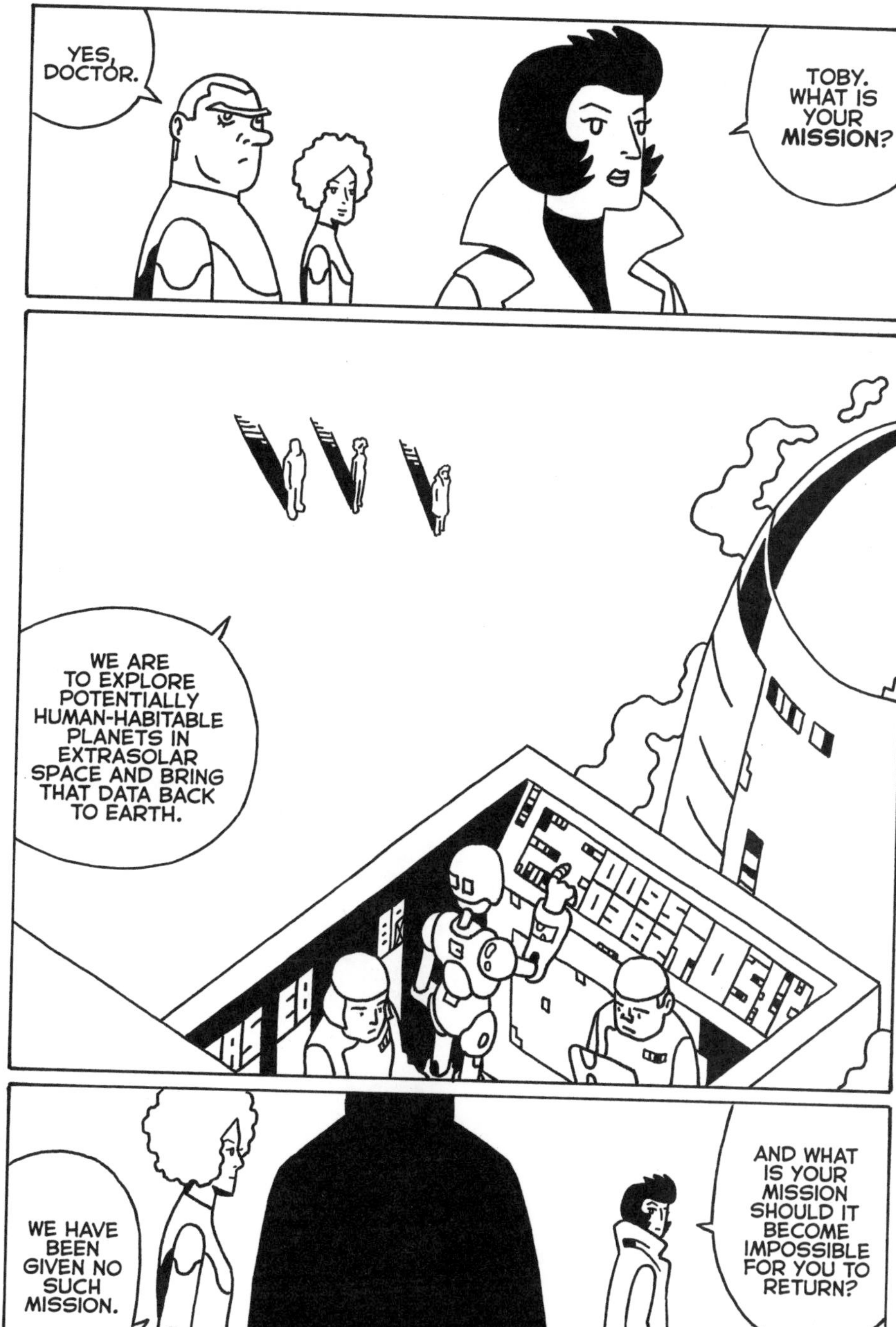
TOBY. WHAT IS YOUR MISSION?
YES, DOCTOR.
WE ARE TO EXPLORE POTENTIALLY HUMAN-HABITABLE PLANETS IN EXTRASOLAR SPACE AND BRING THAT DATA BACK TO EARTH.
AND WHAT IS YOUR MISSION SHOULD IT BECOME IMPOSSIBLE FOR YOU TO RETURN?
WE HAVE BEEN GIVEN NO SUCH MISSION.

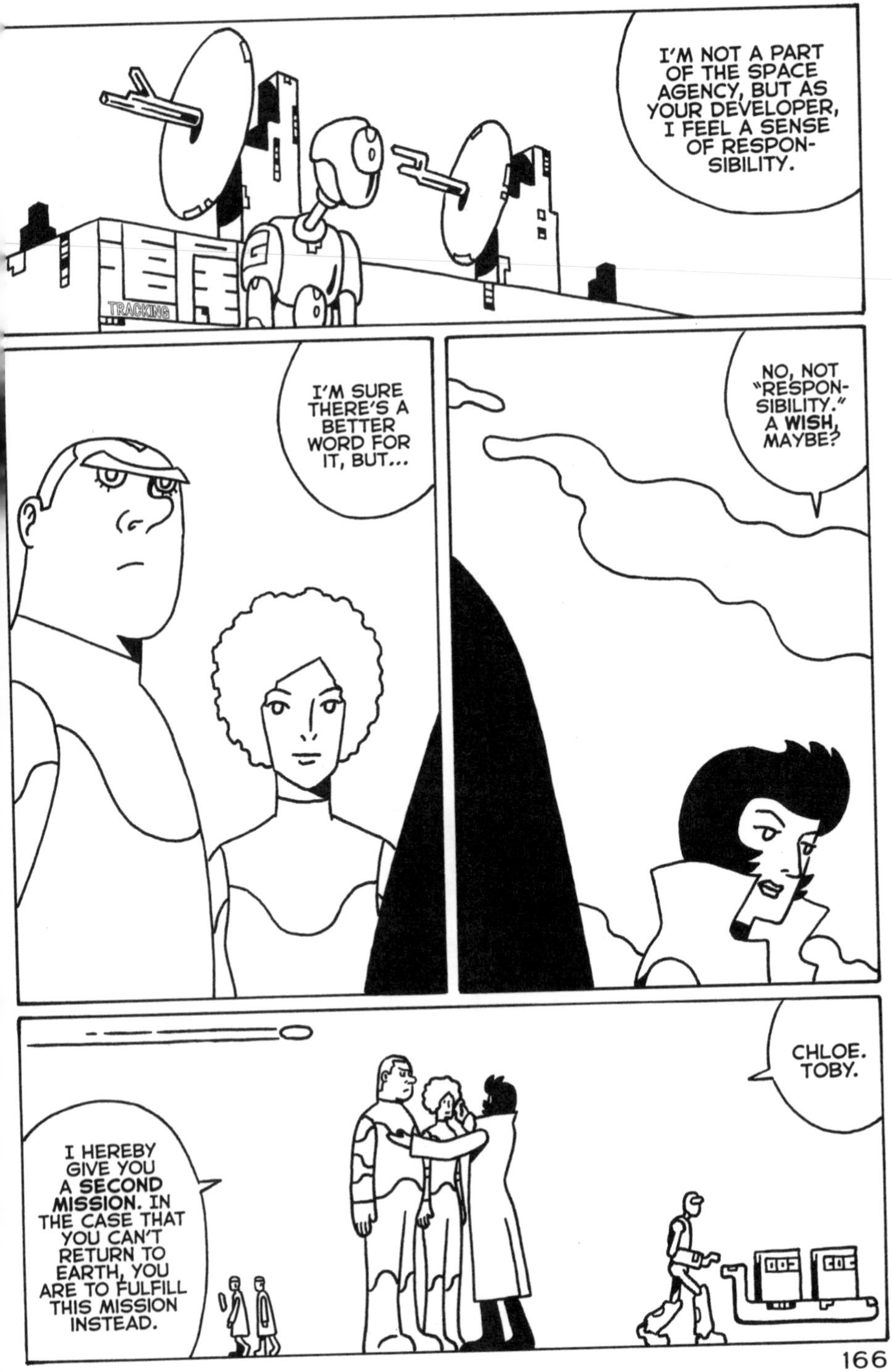

TRACKING
I'M NOT A PART OF THE SPACE AGENCY, BUT AS YOUR DEVELOPER, I FEEL A SENSE OF RESPON-SIBILITY.
I'M SURE THERE'S A BETTER WORD FOR IT, BUT...
NO, NOT "RESPON-SIBILITY." A **WISH**, MAYBE?
CHLOE. TOBY.
I HEREBY GIVE YOU A **SECOND MISSION**. IN THE CASE THAT YOU CAN'T RETURN TO EARTH, YOU ARE TO FULFILL THIS MISSION INSTEAD.

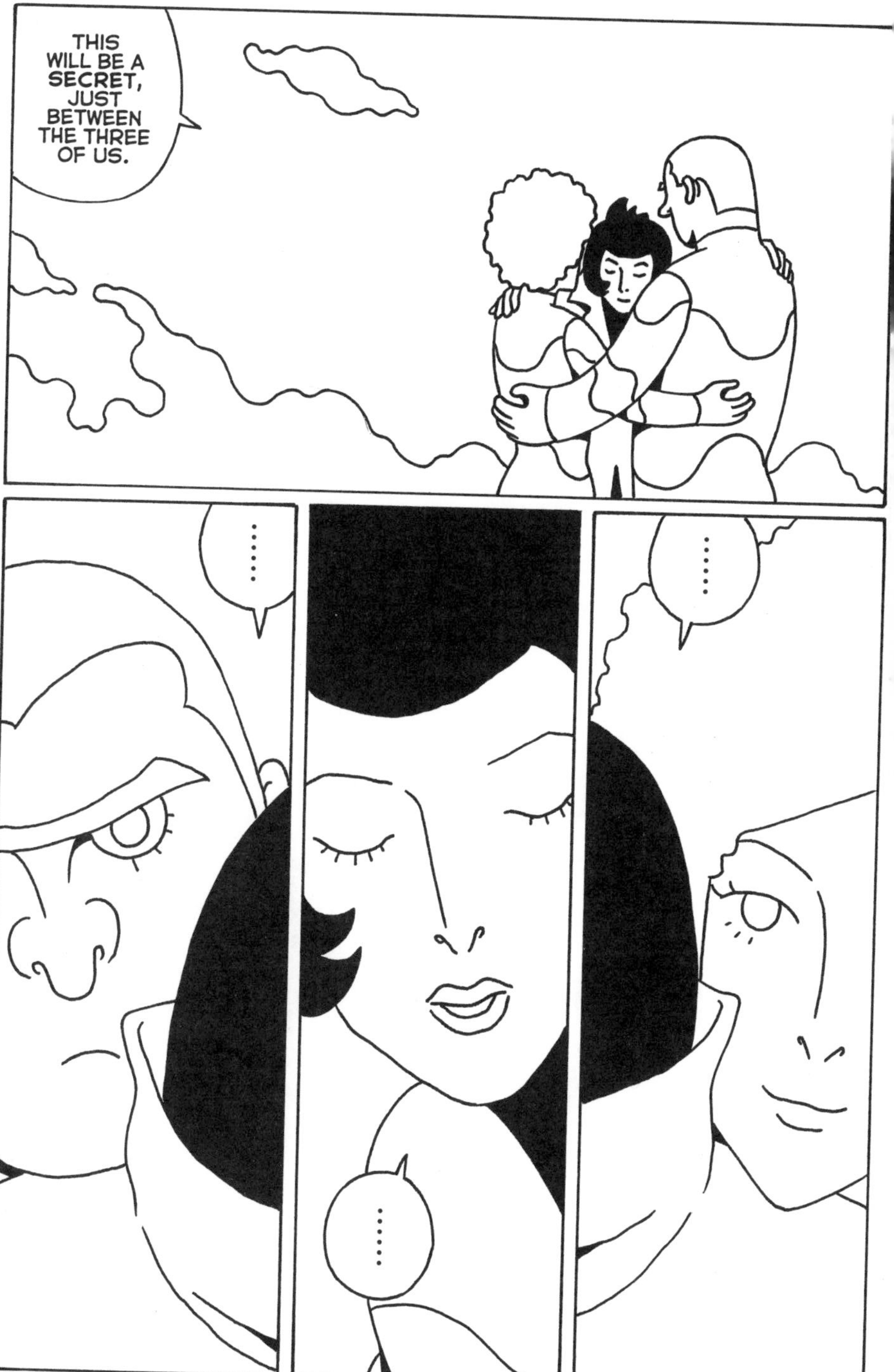
THIS WILL BE A SECRET, JUST BETWEEN THE THREE OF US.
......
......
......

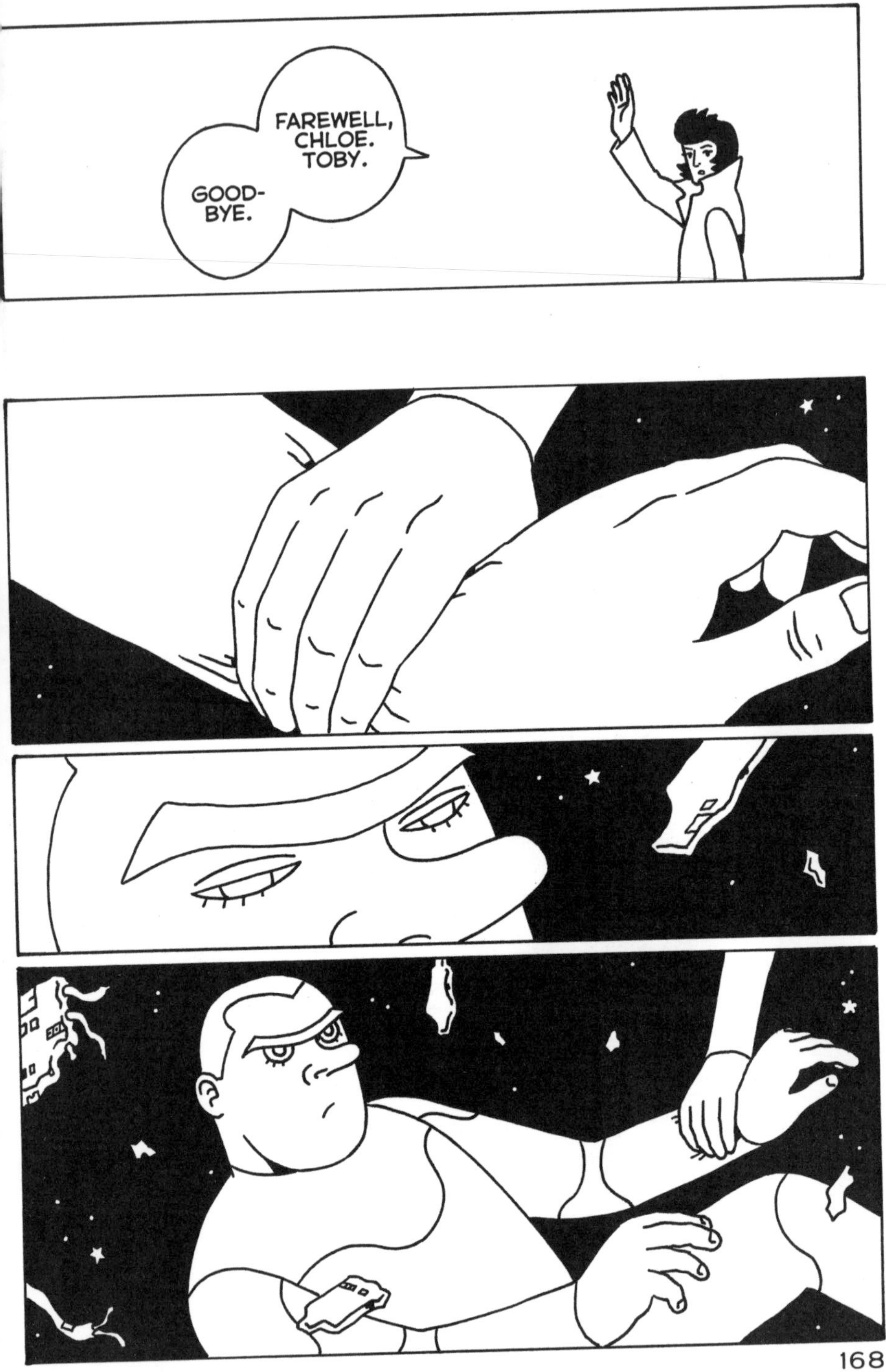
FAREWELL, CHLOE. TOBY.
GOOD-BYE.

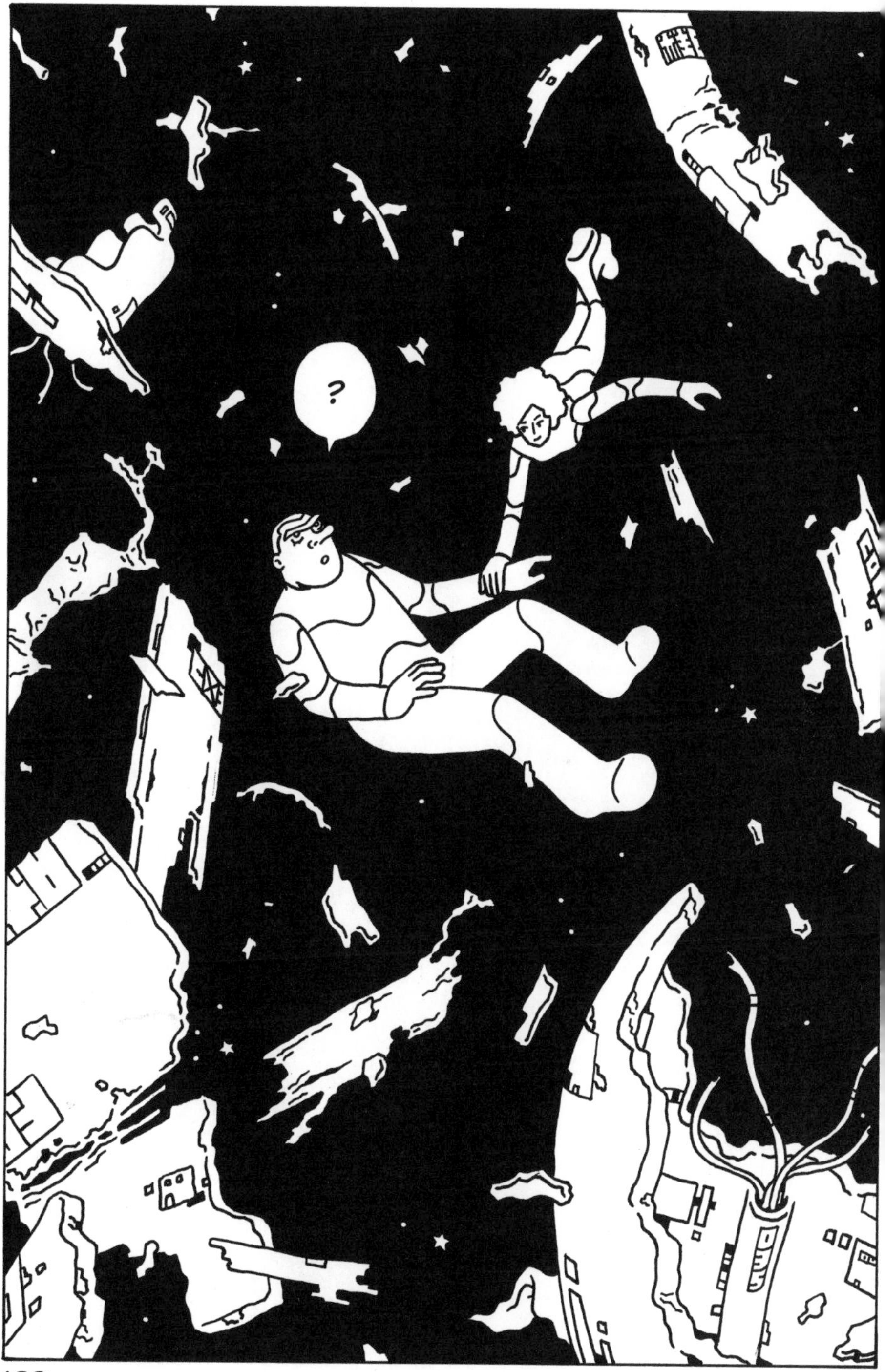
?

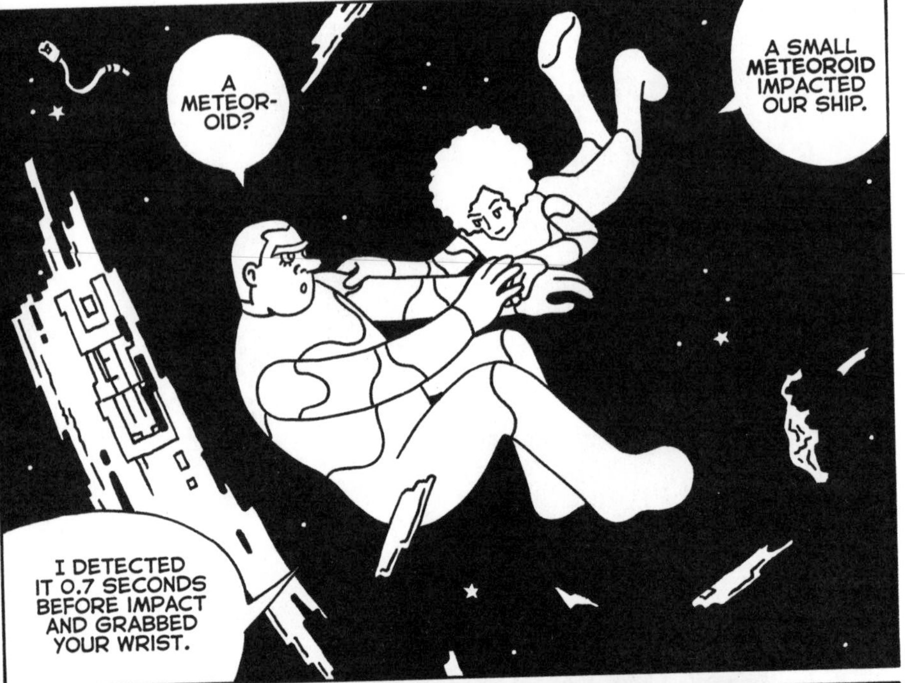
A SMALL METEOROID IMPACTED OUR SHIP.
A METEOR-OID?
I DETECTED IT 0.7 SECONDS BEFORE IMPACT AND GRABBED YOUR WRIST.

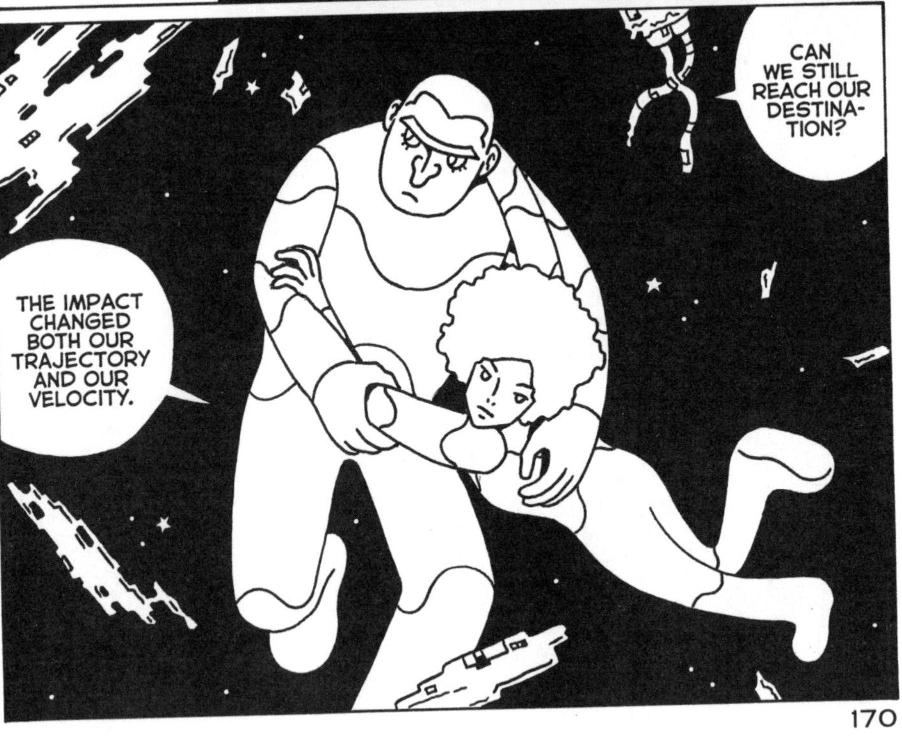
CAN WE STILL REACH OUR DESTINA-TION?
THE IMPACT CHANGED BOTH OUR TRAJECTORY AND OUR VELOCITY.

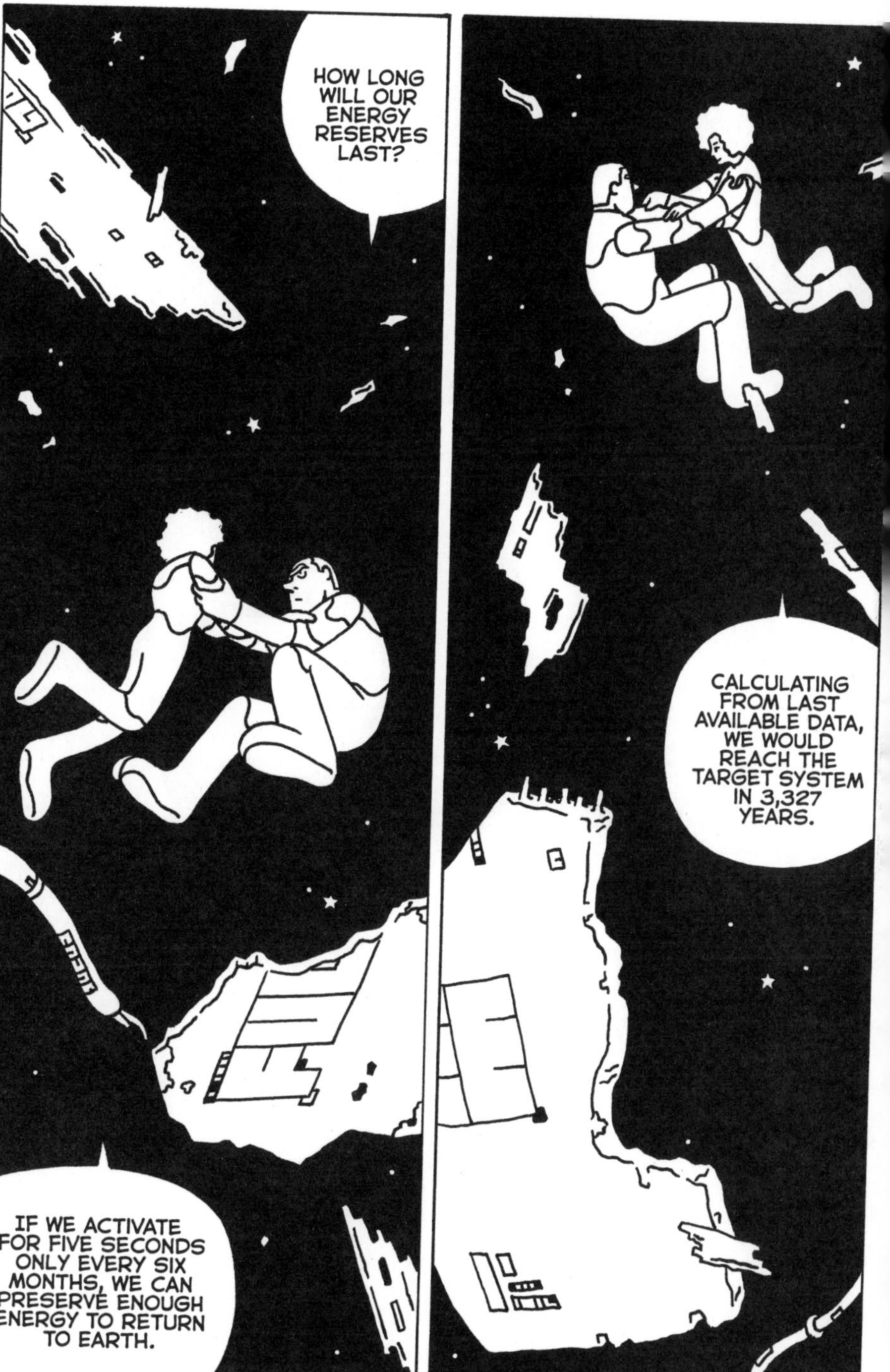
HOW LONG WILL OUR ENERGY RESERVES LAST?
IF WE ACTIVATE FOR FIVE SECONDS ONLY EVERY SIX MONTHS, WE CAN PRESERVE ENOUGH ENERGY TO RETURN TO EARTH.
CALCULATING FROM LAST AVAILABLE DATA, WE WOULD REACH THE TARGET SYSTEM IN 3,327 YEARS.

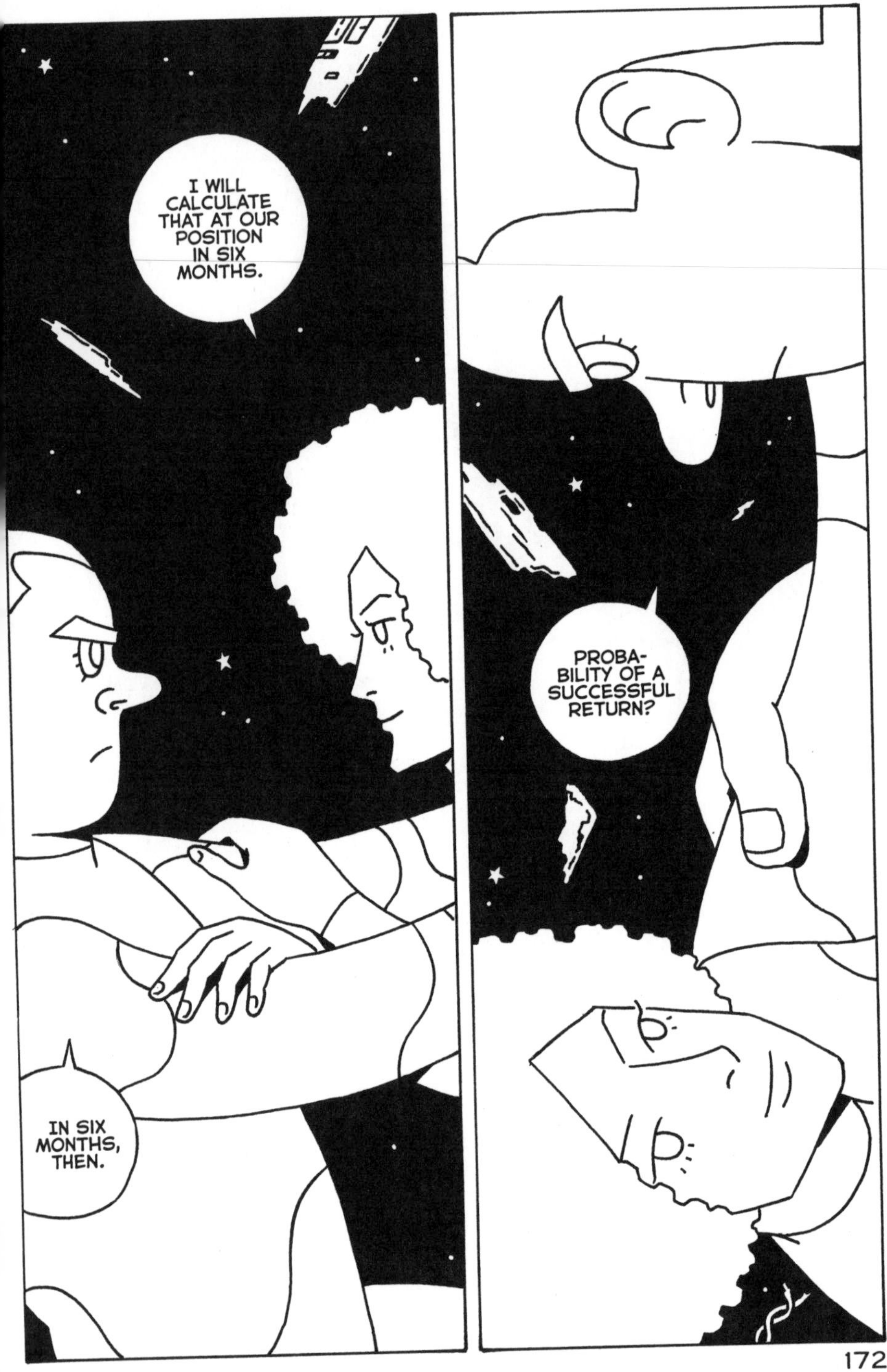
PROBA-BILITY OF A SUCCESSFUL RETURN?
I WILL CALCULATE THAT AT OUR POSITION IN SIX MONTHS.
IN SIX MONTHS, THEN.

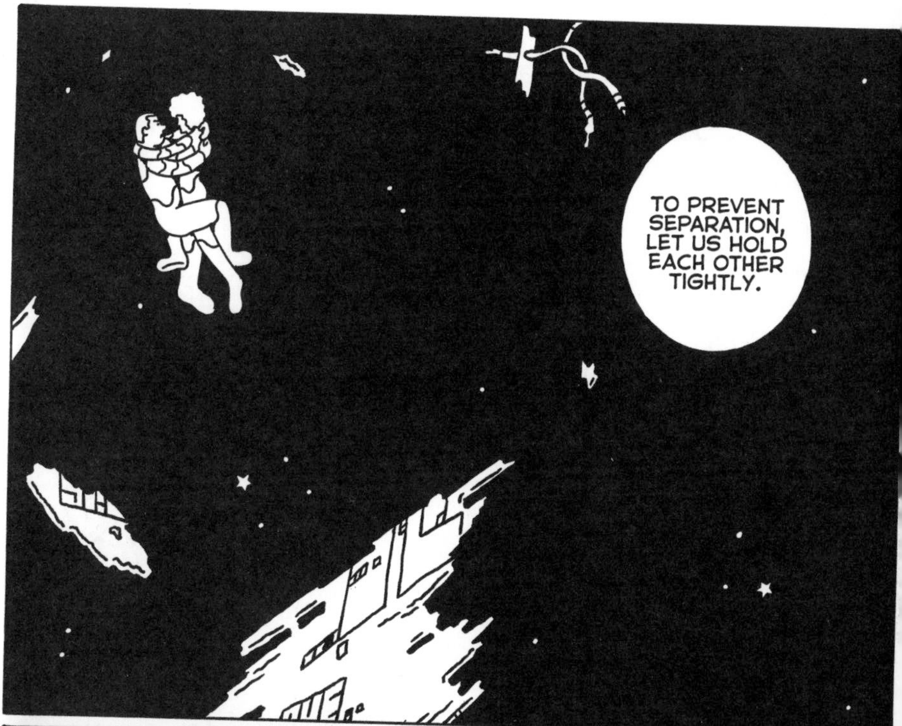
TO PREVENT SEPARATION, LET US HOLD EACH OTHER TIGHTLY.
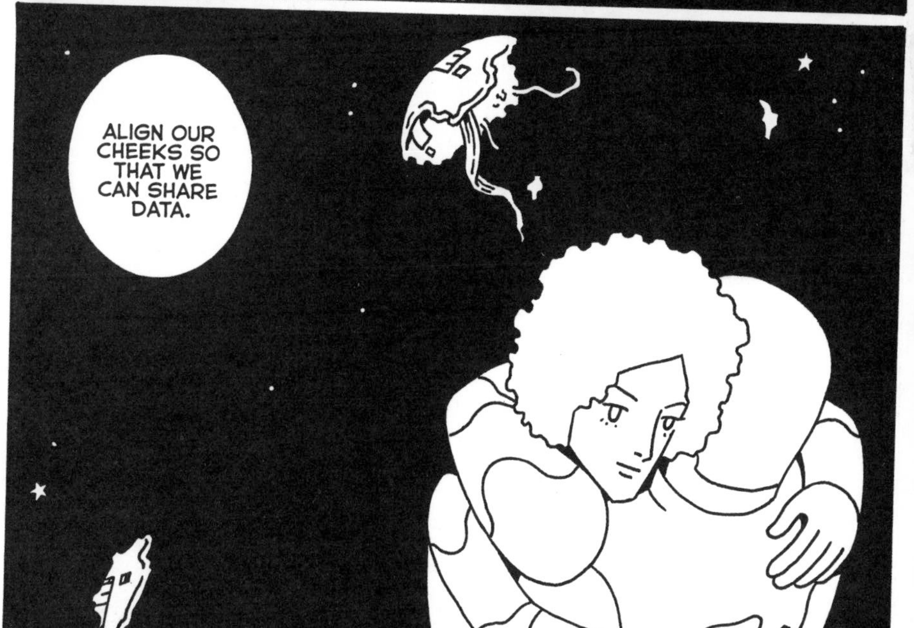
ALIGN OUR CHEEKS SO THAT WE CAN SHARE DATA.

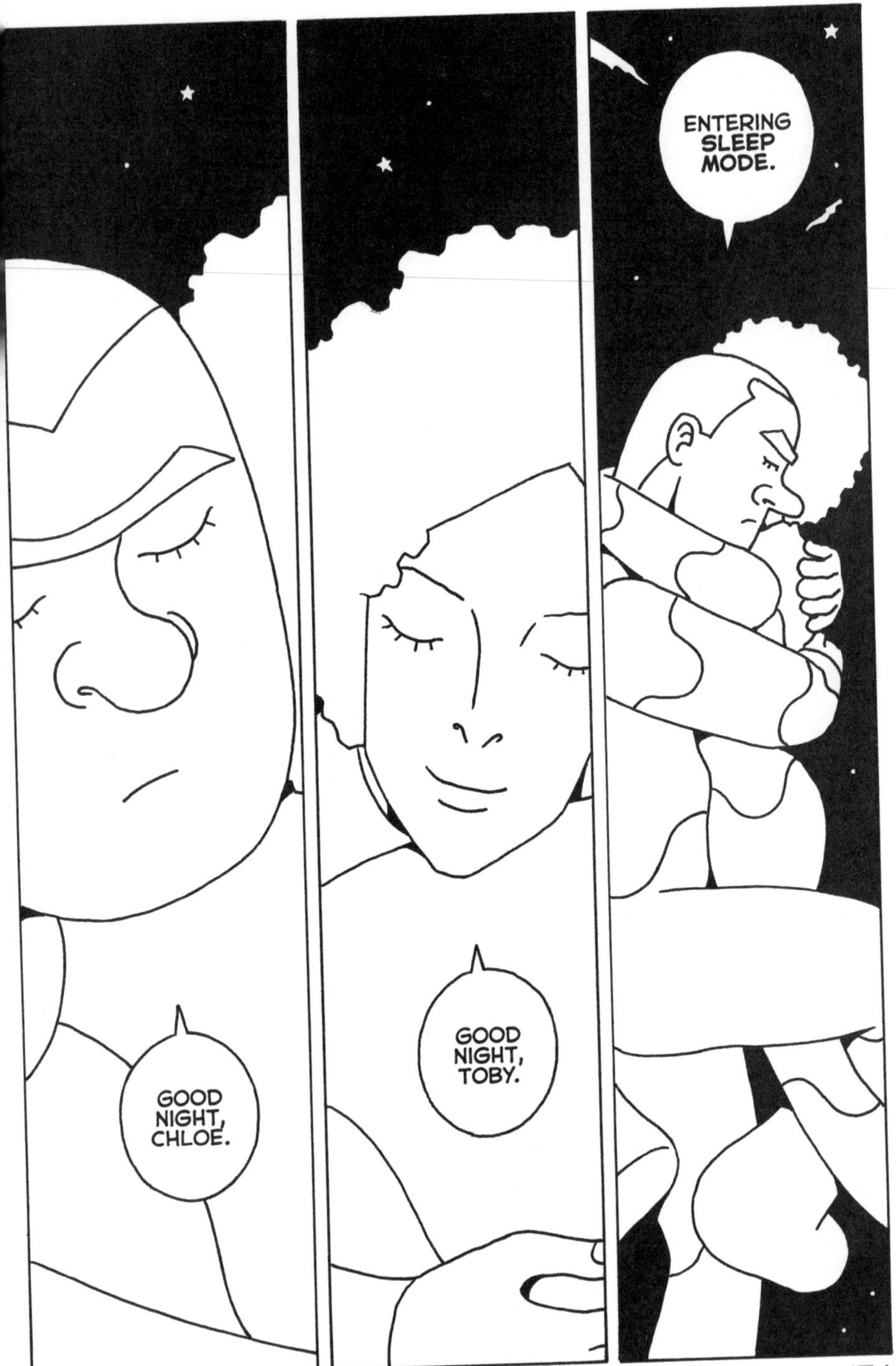
GOOD NIGHT, CHLOE.
GOOD NIGHT, TOBY.
ENTERING SLEEP MODE.

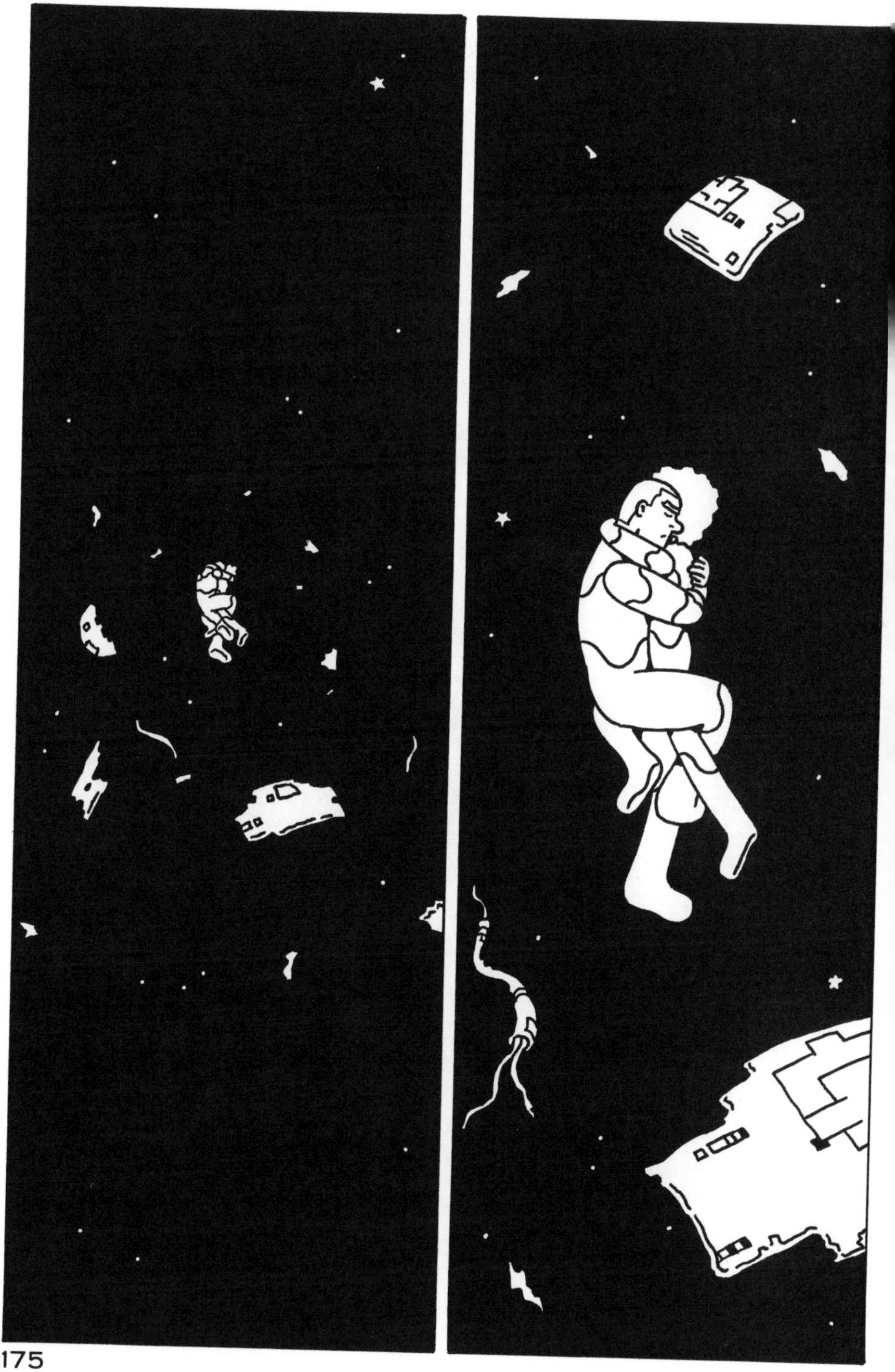

#8/END

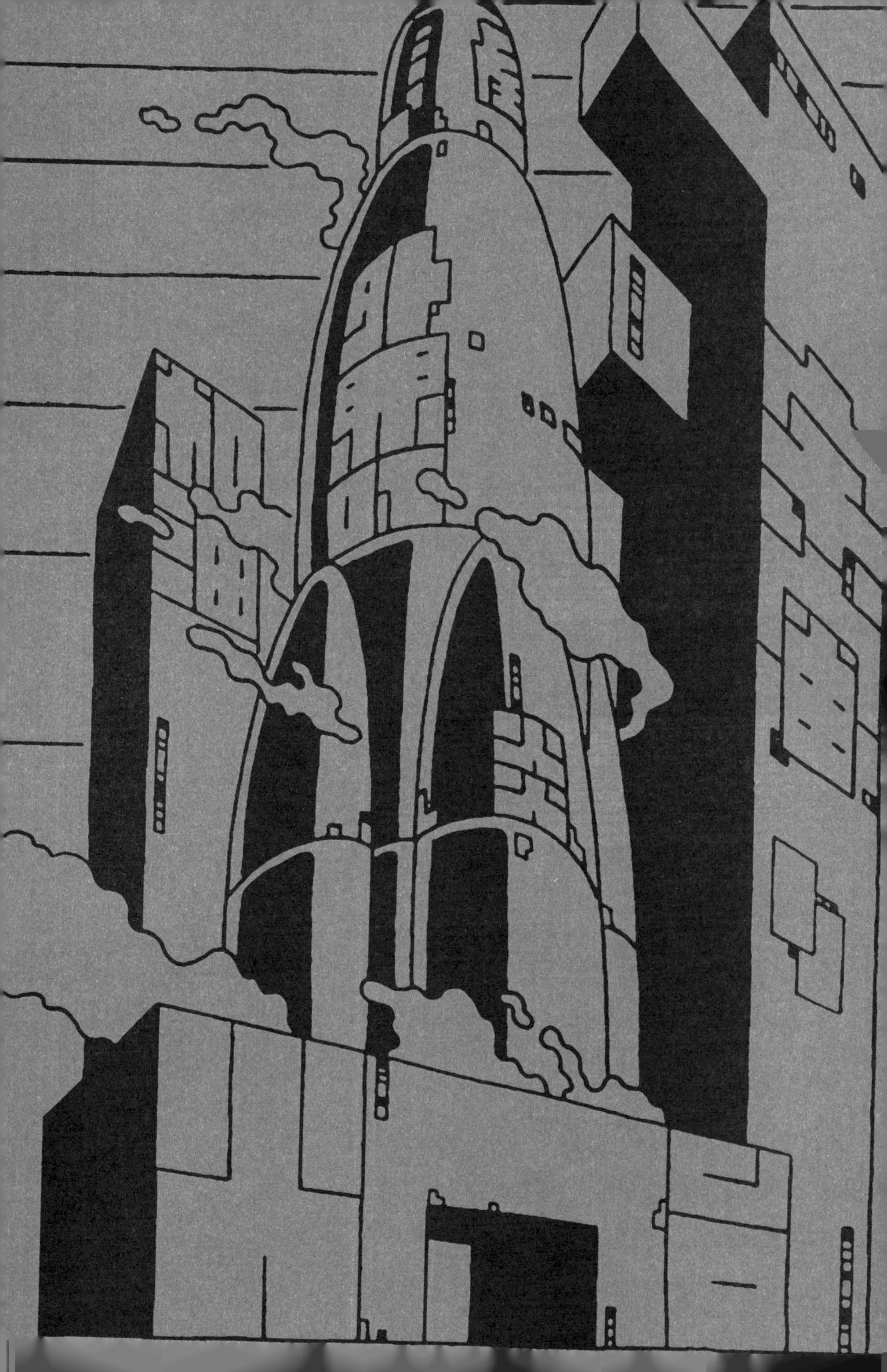

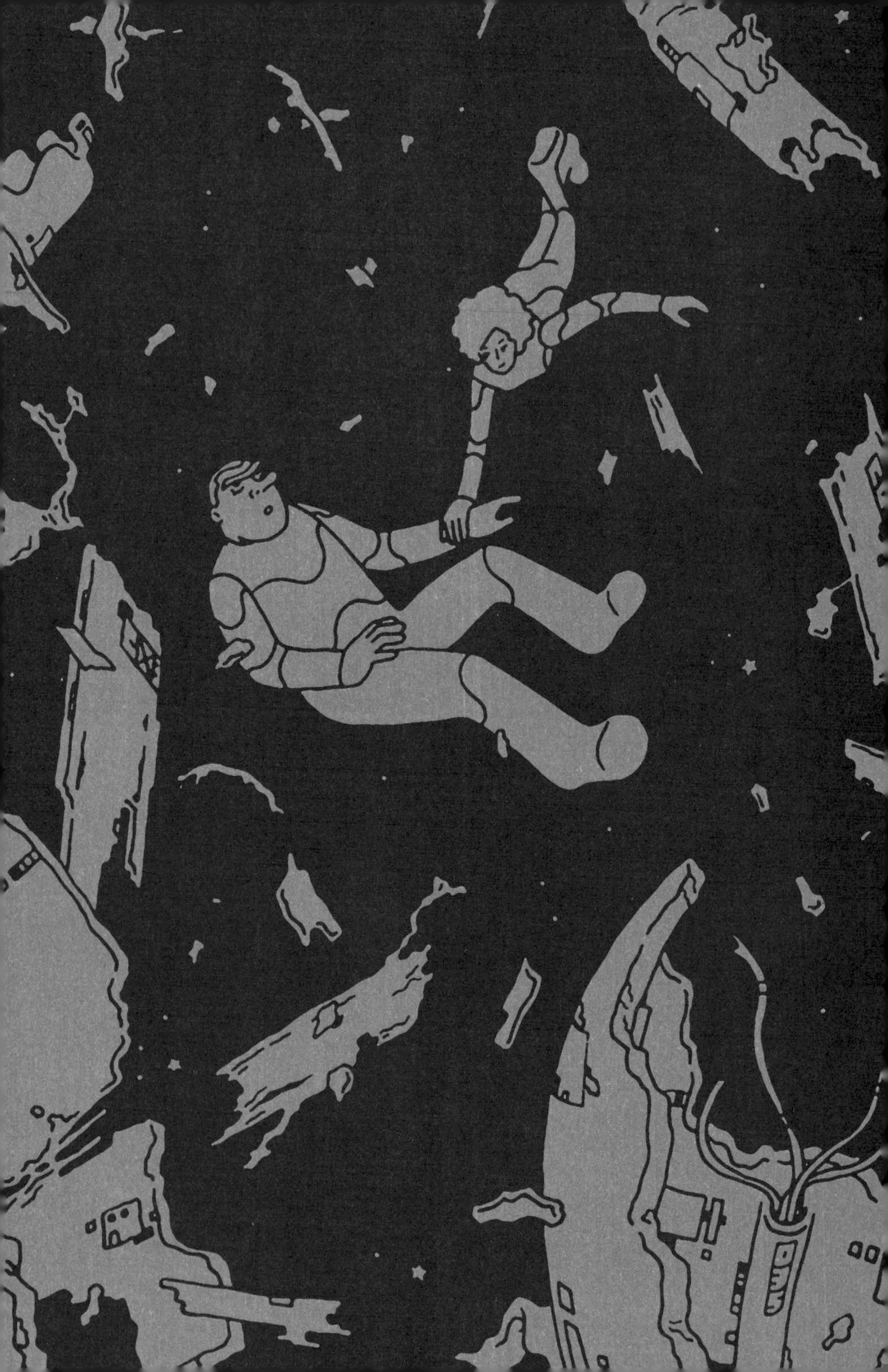

#9

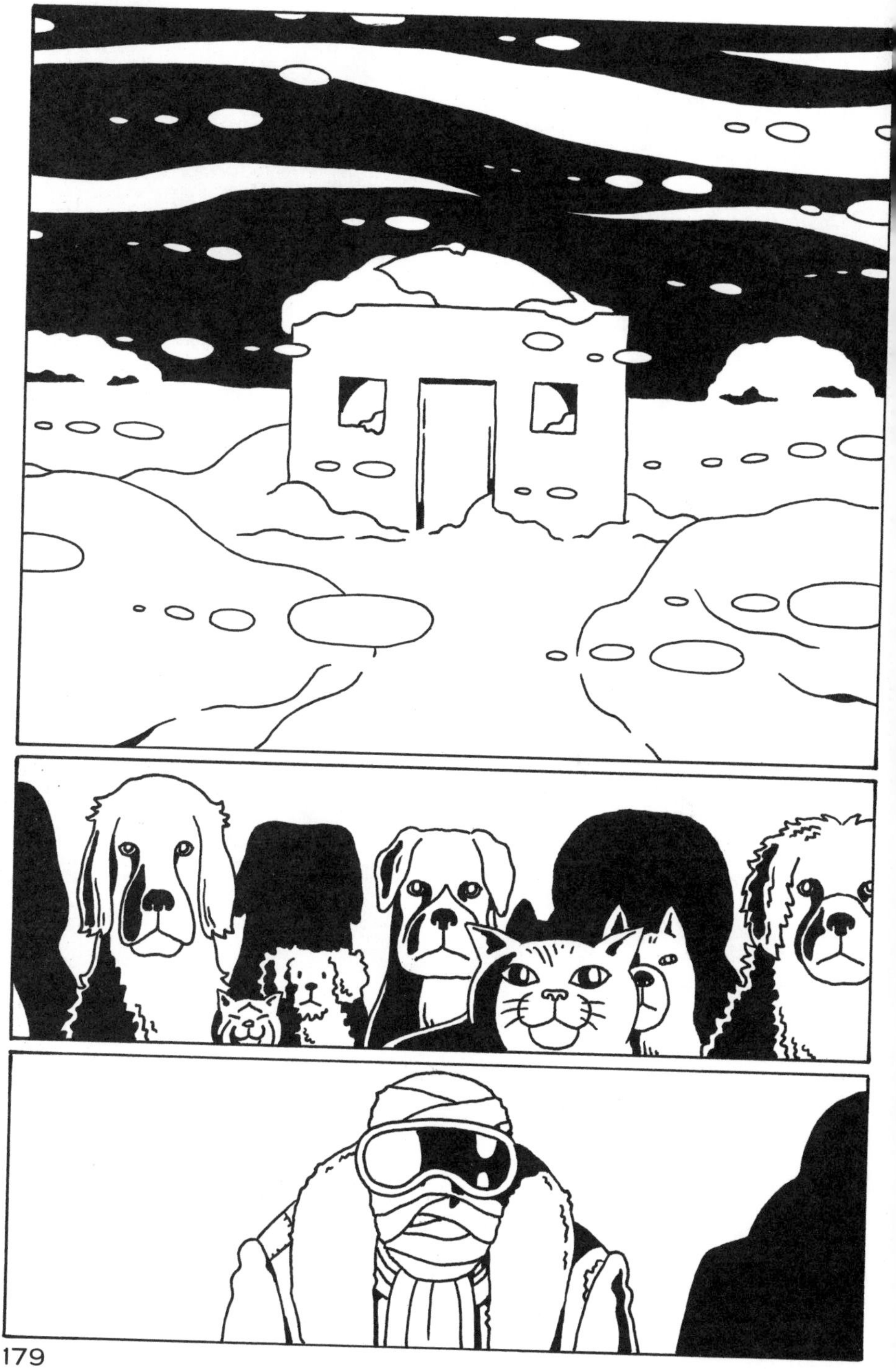

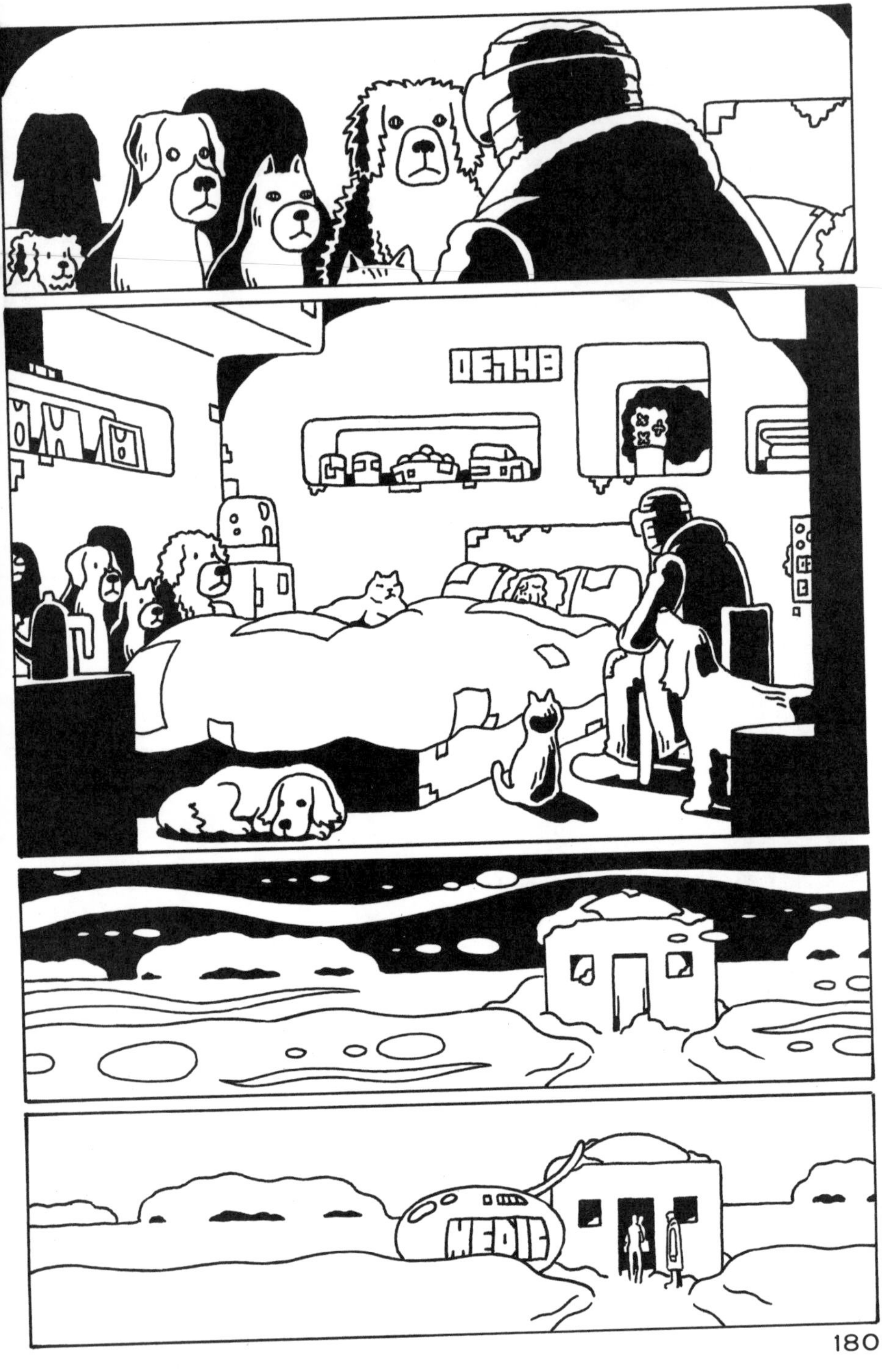
MEDIC

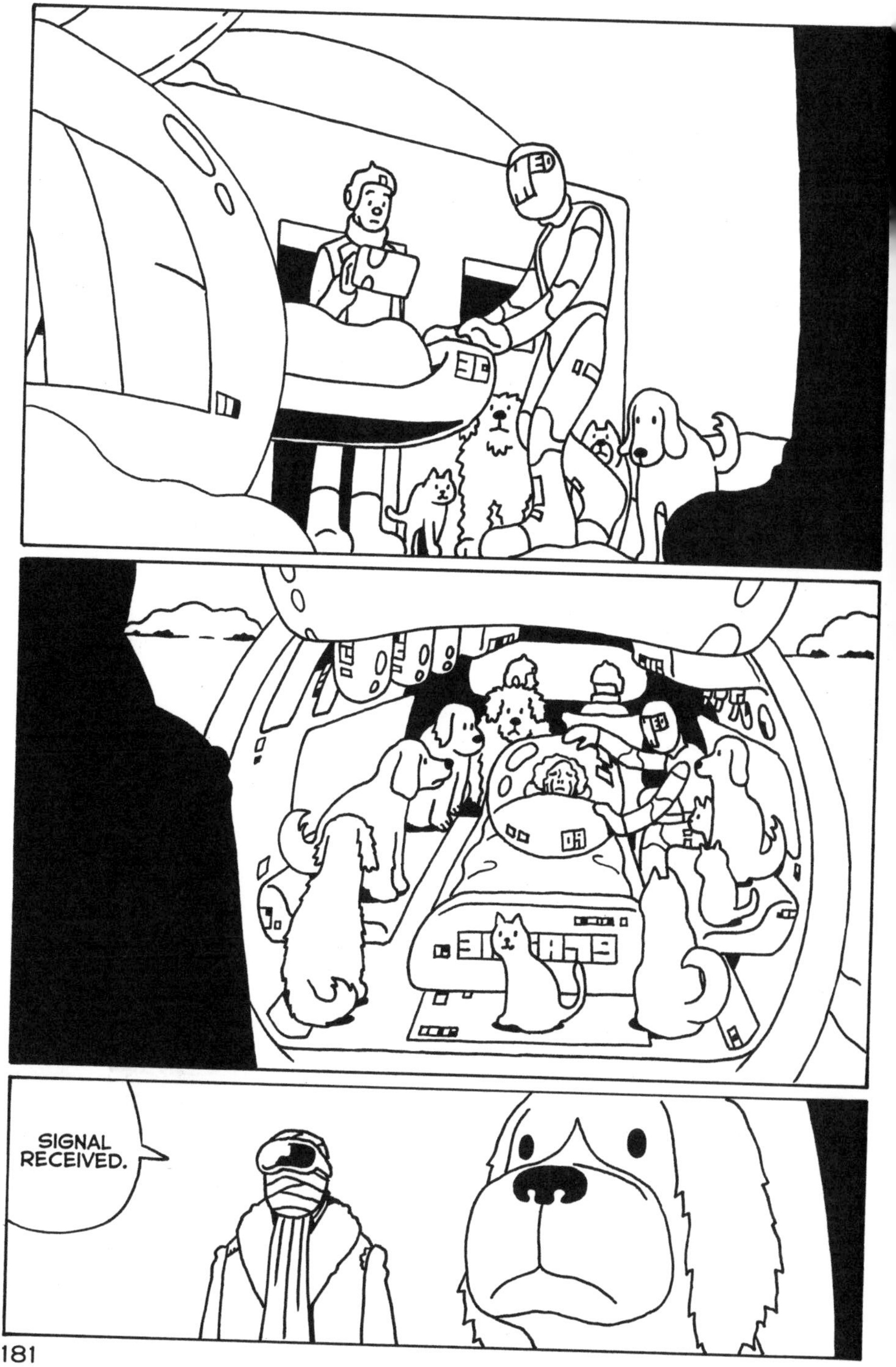
SIGNAL RECEIVED.

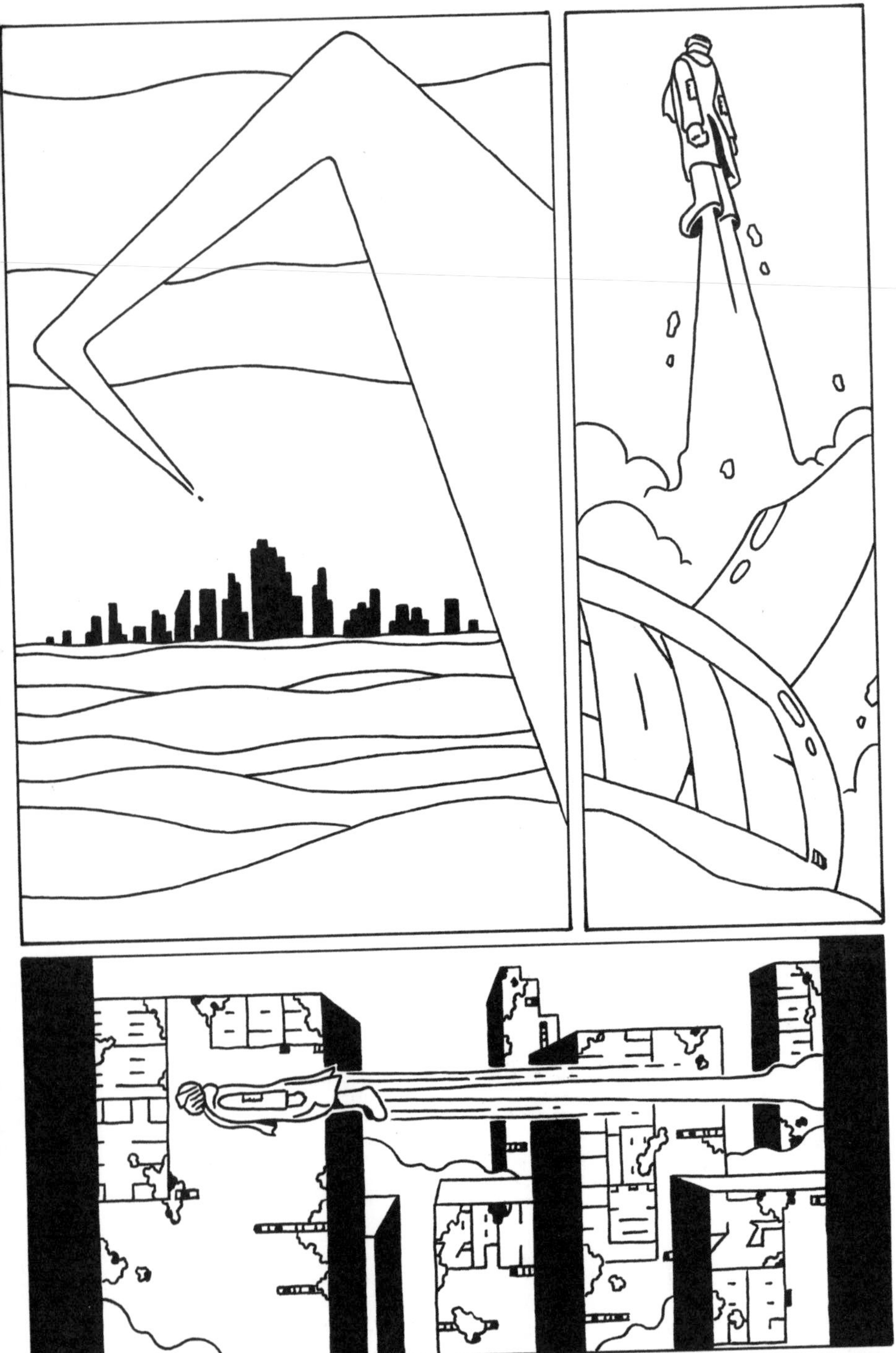

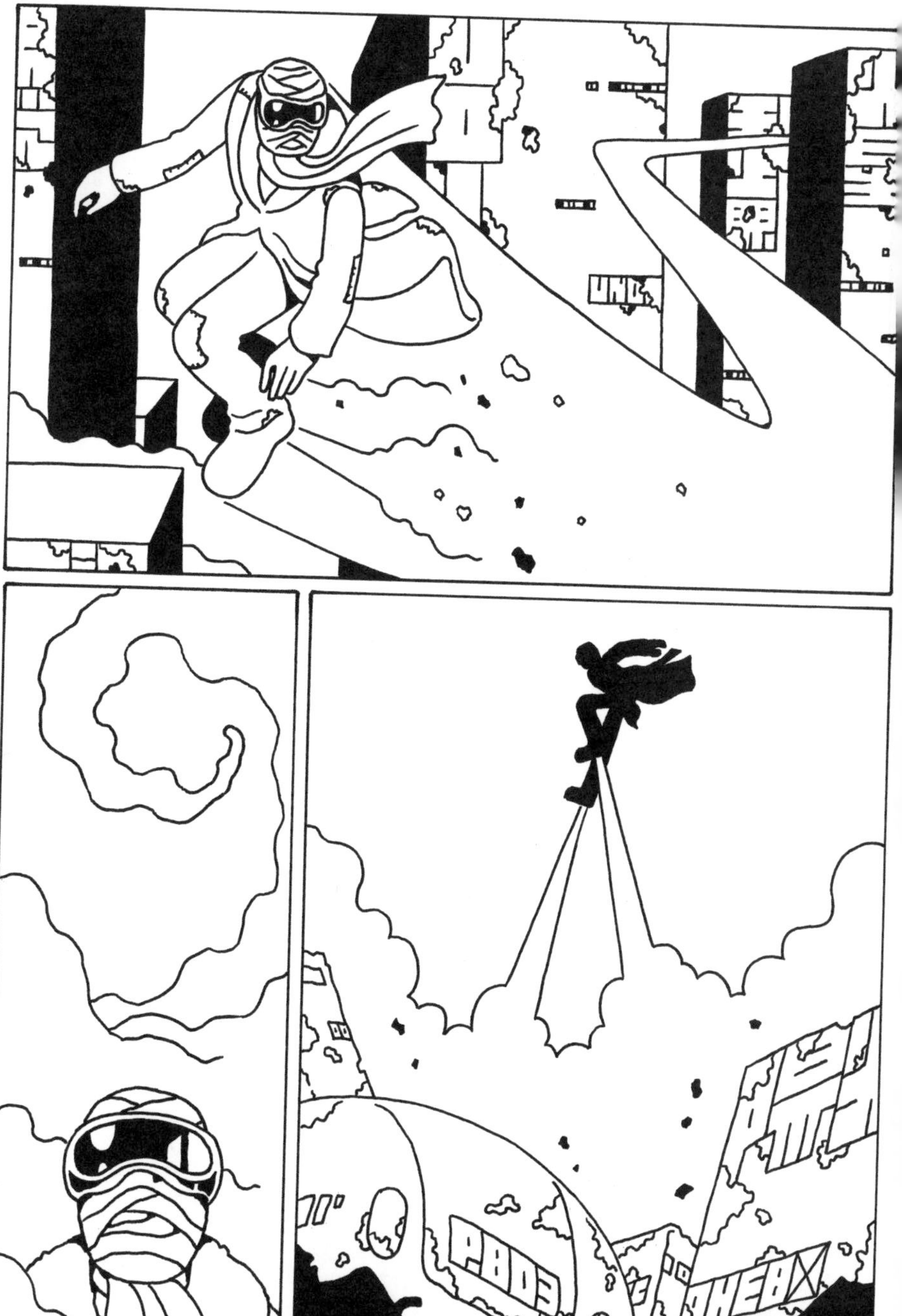

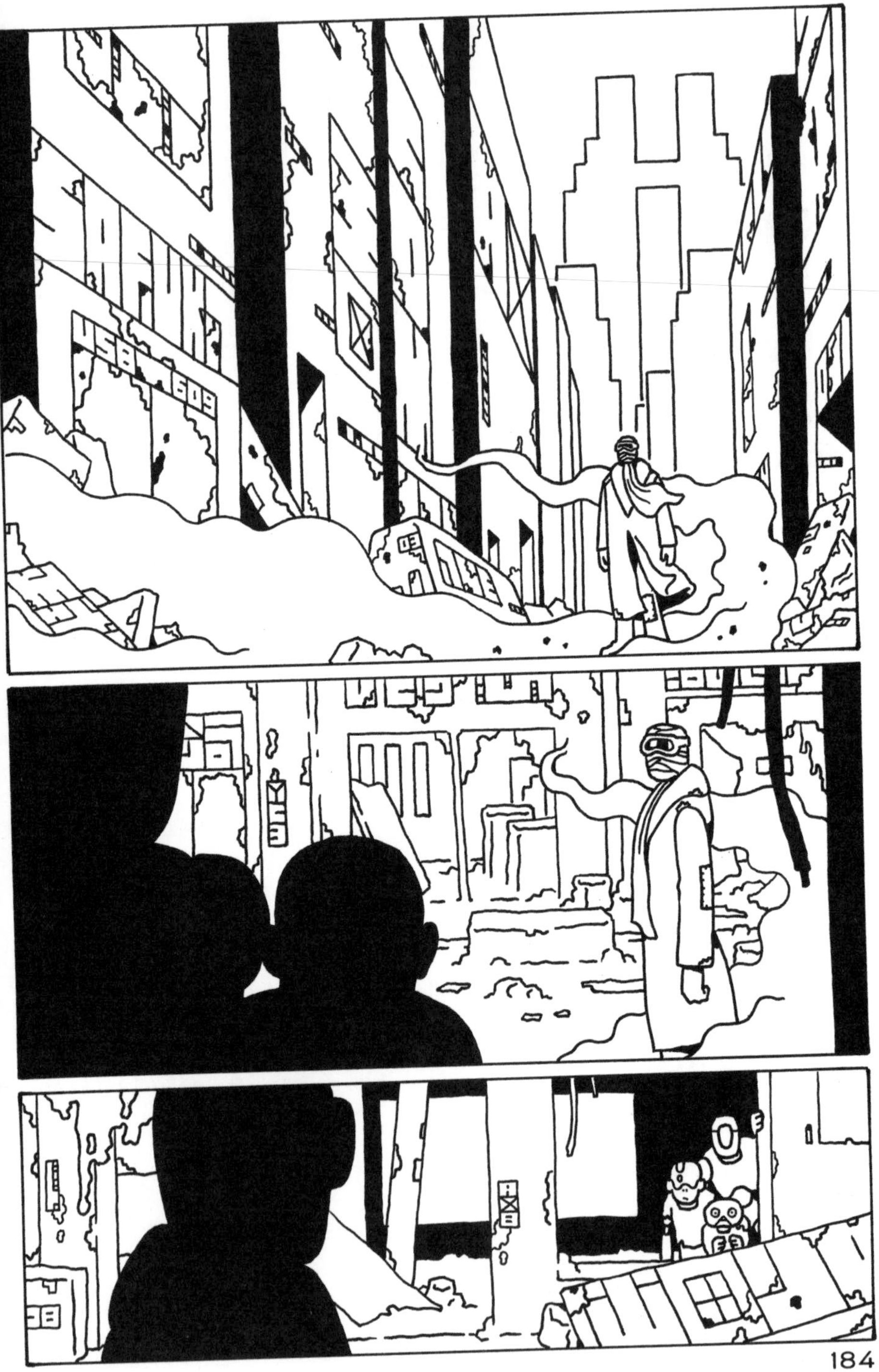

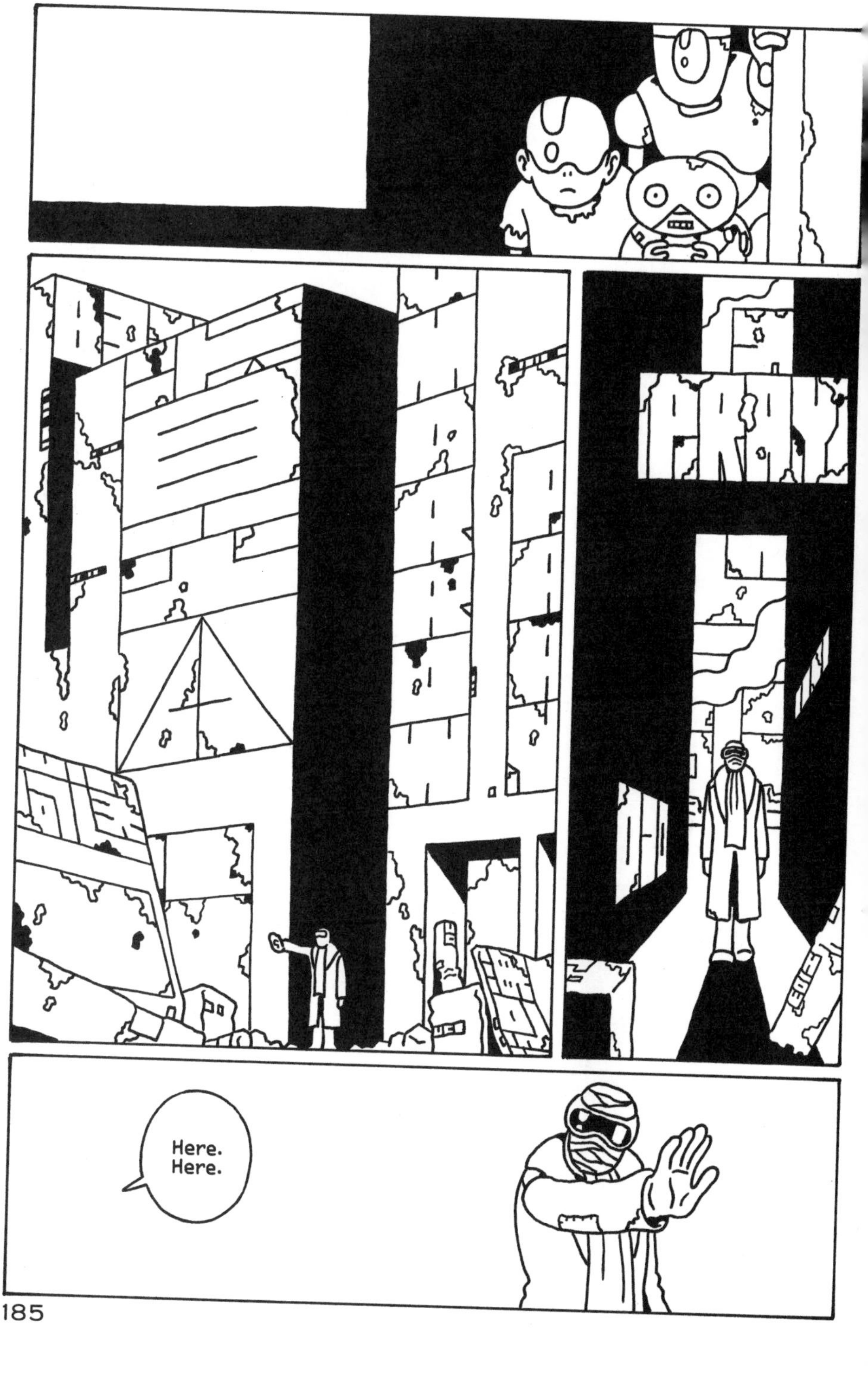
PRAY
Here.
Here.

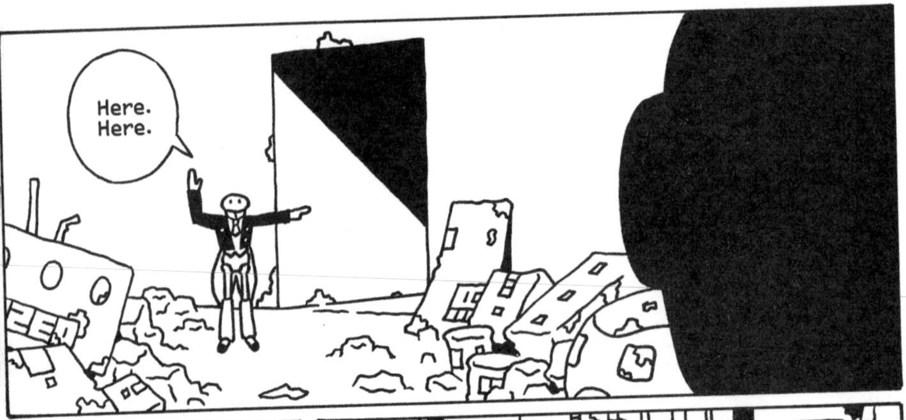
Here. Here.
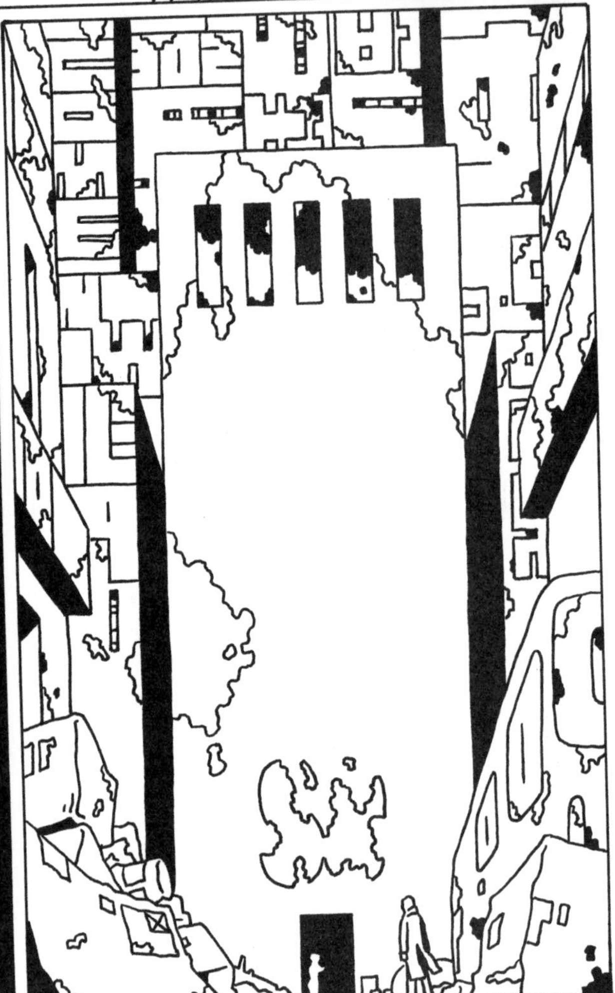
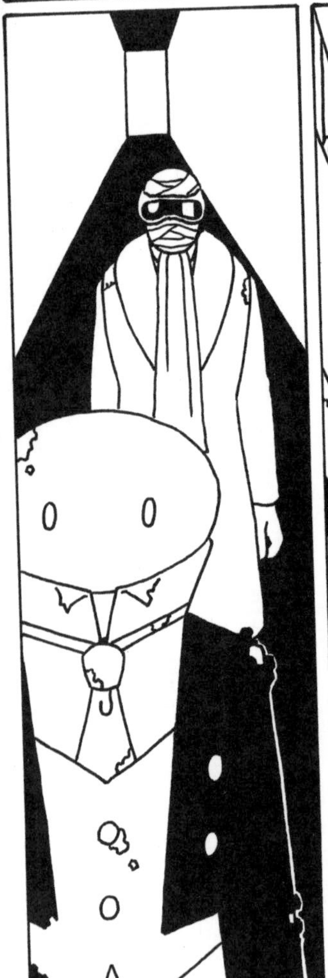

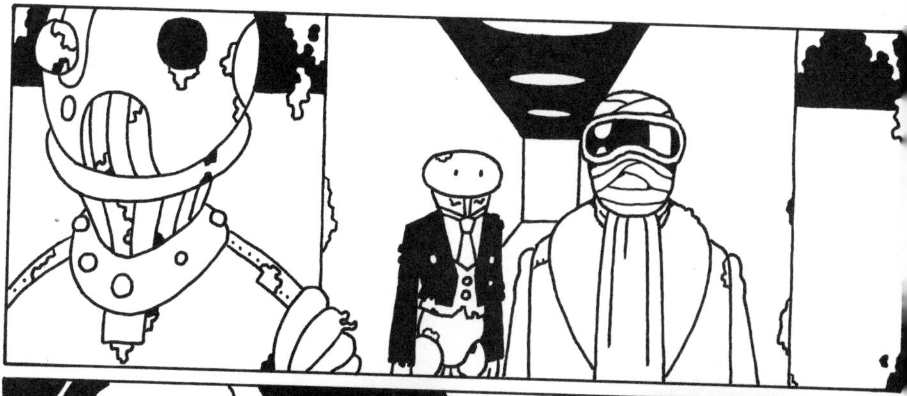

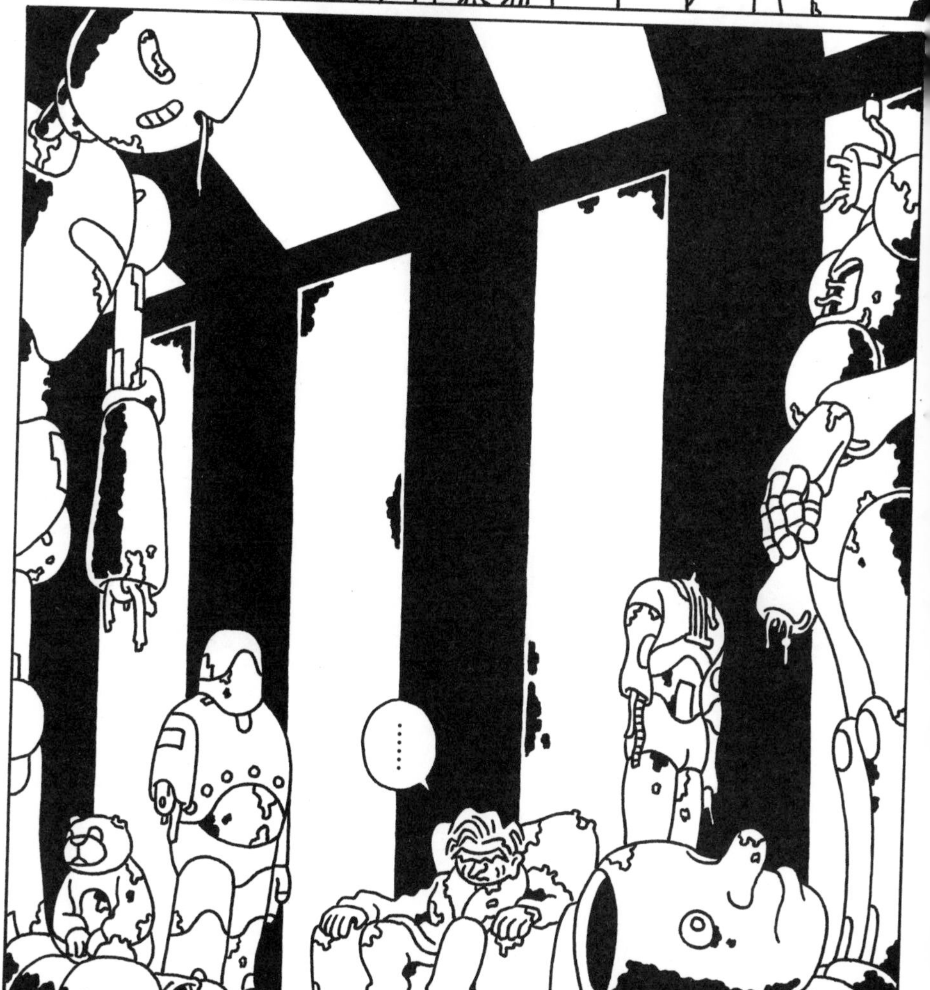
……

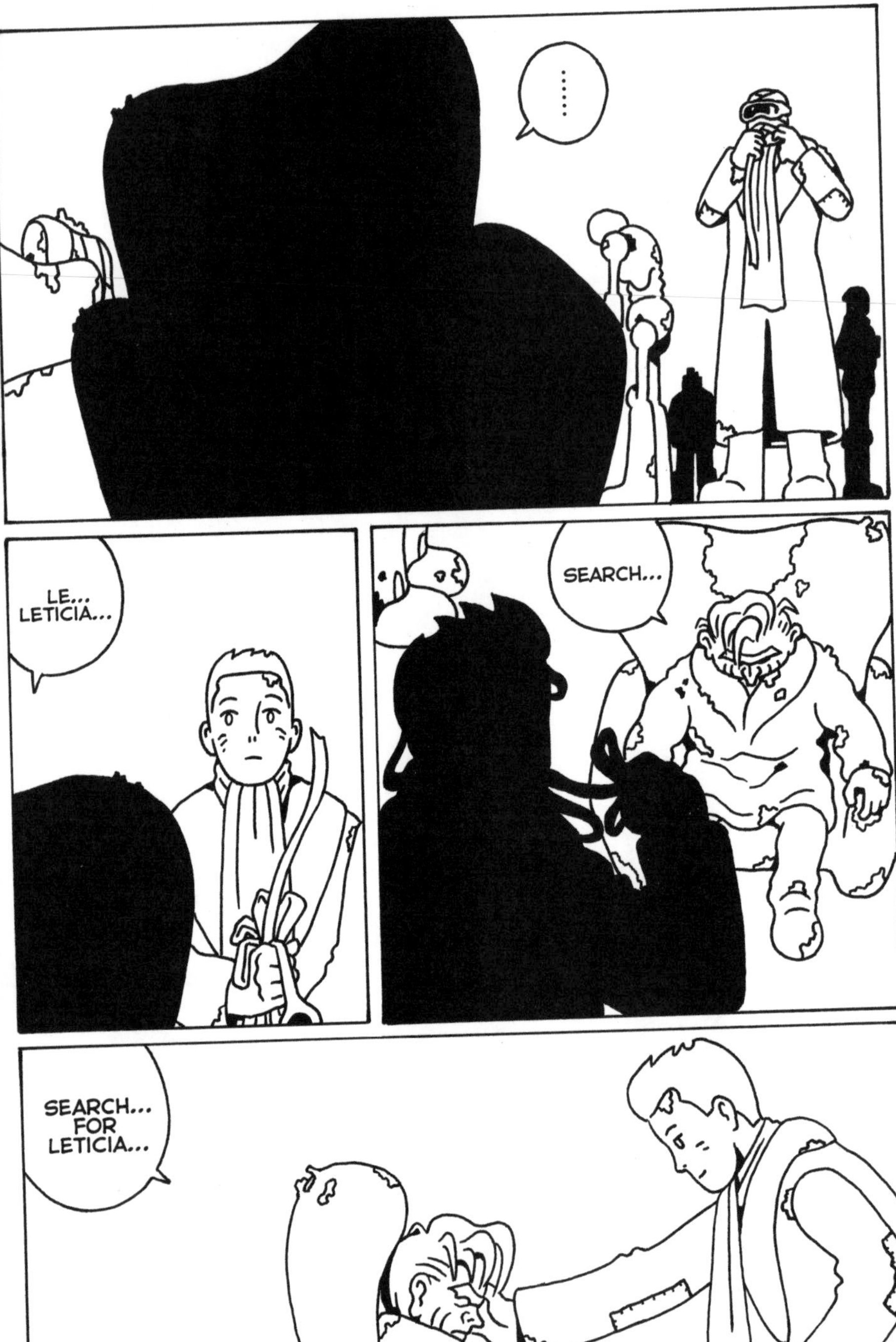
……
SEARCH...
LE... LETICIA...
SEARCH... FOR LETICIA...

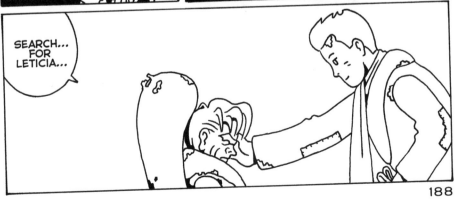

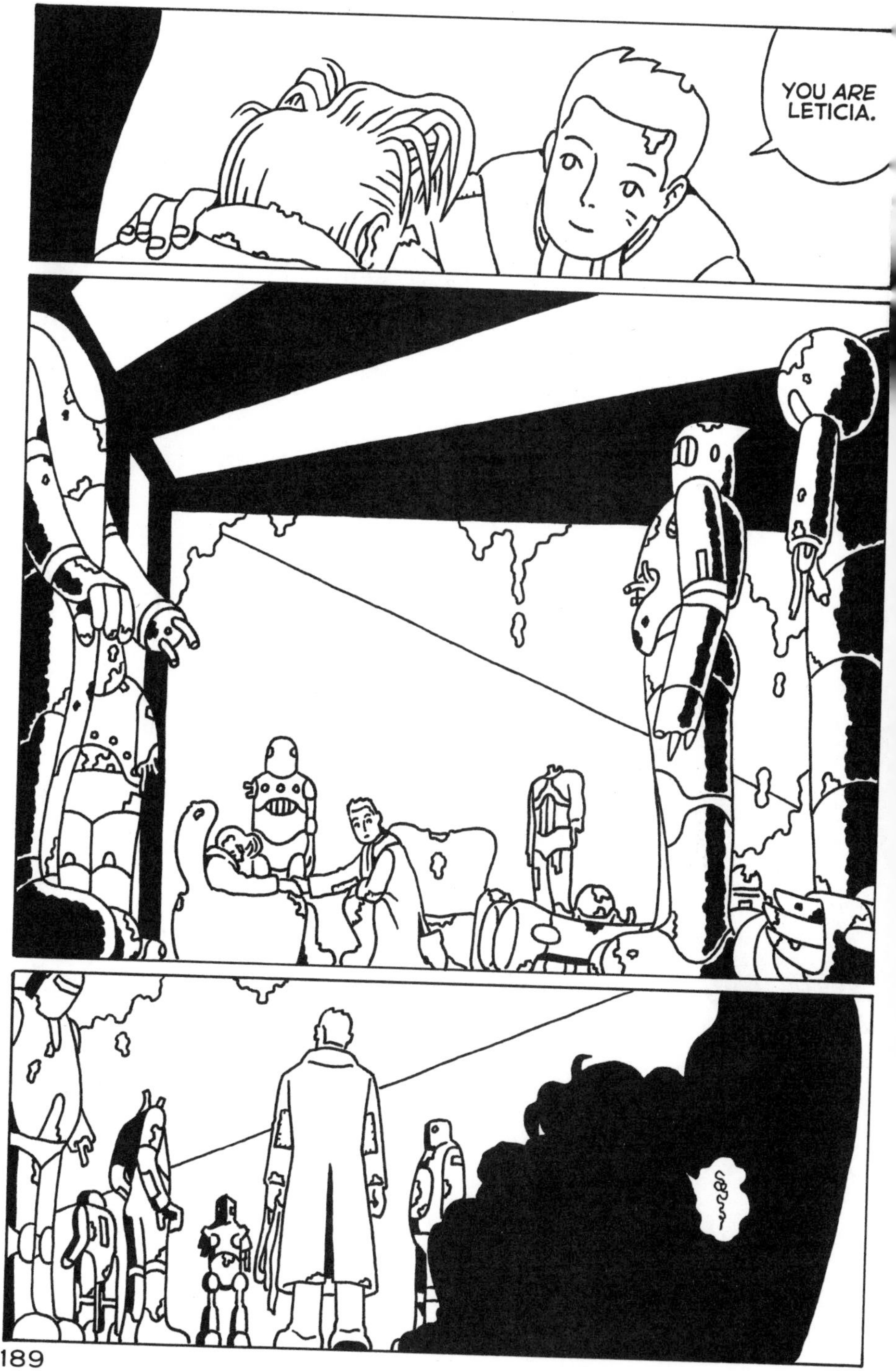
YOU *ARE* LETICIA.

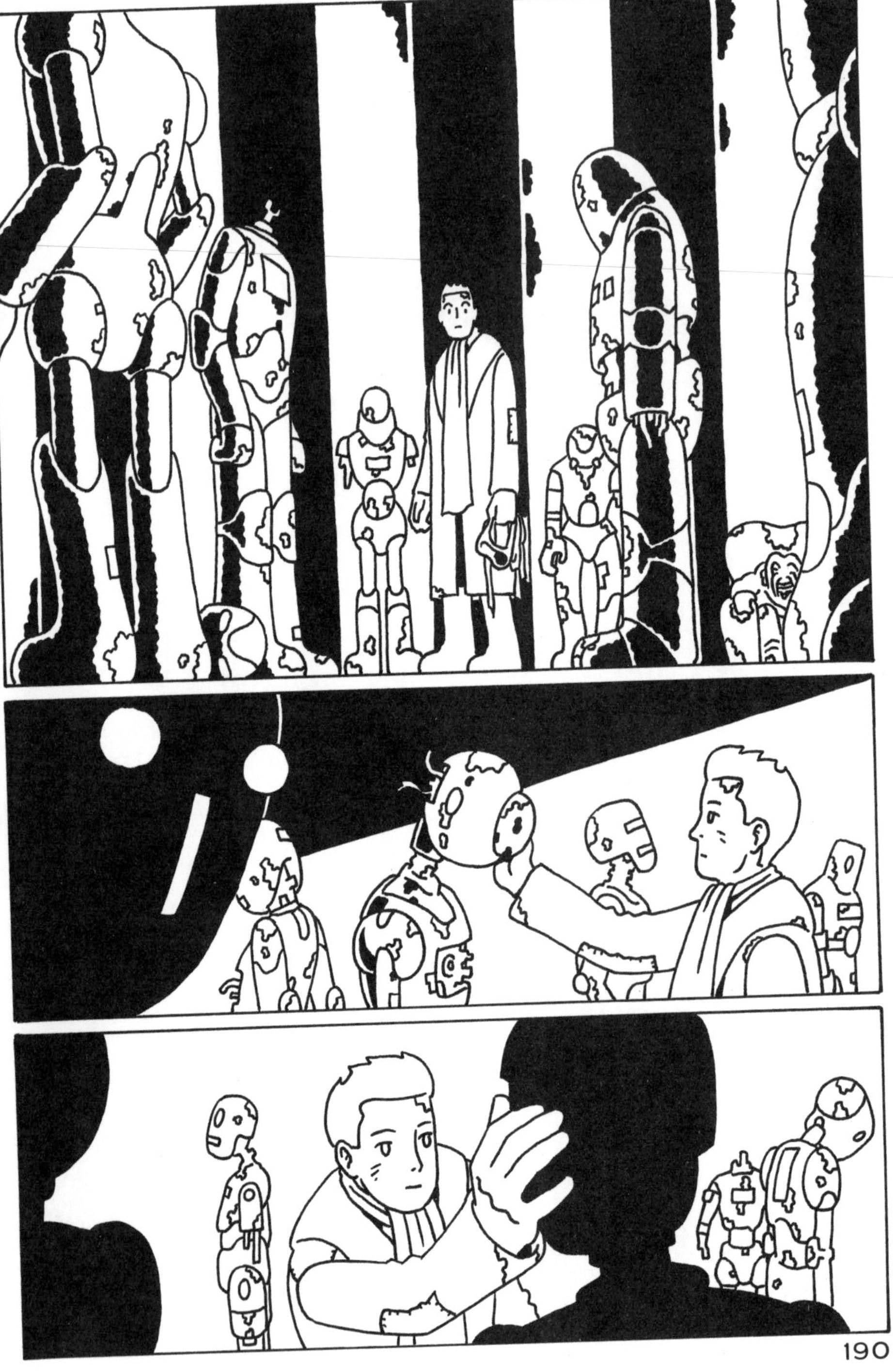

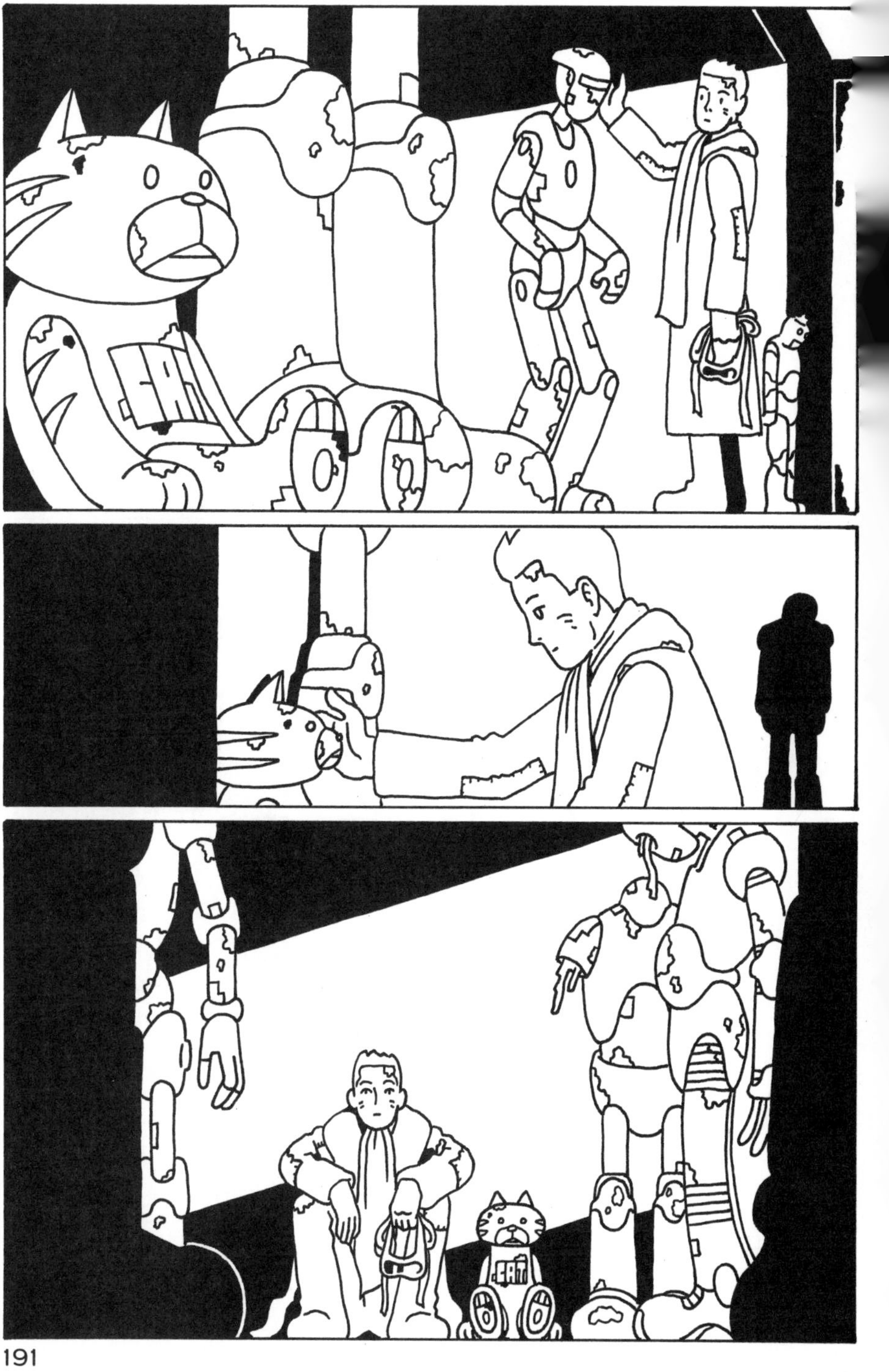
CAT

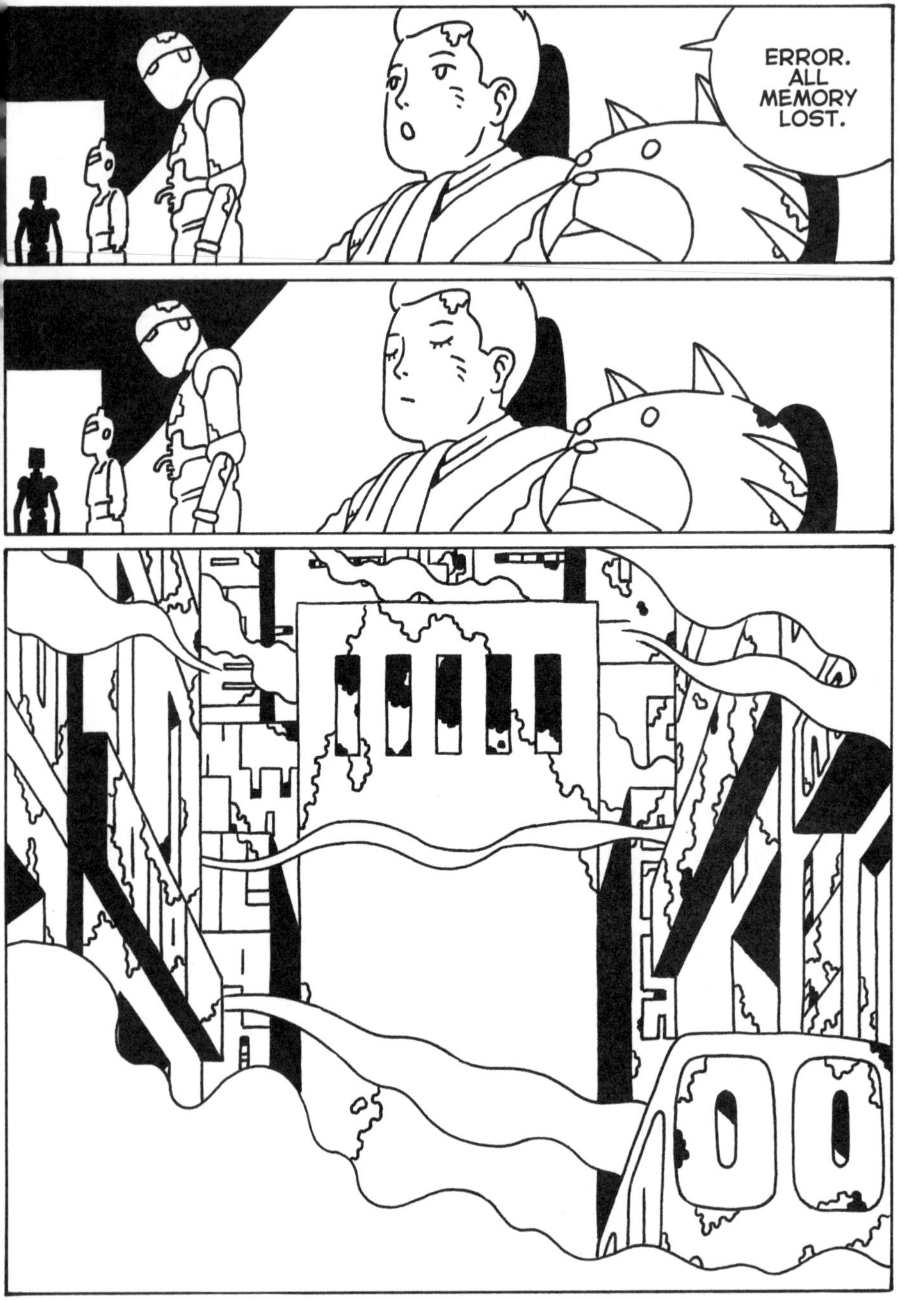
ERROR. ALL MEMORY LOST.

#9/END

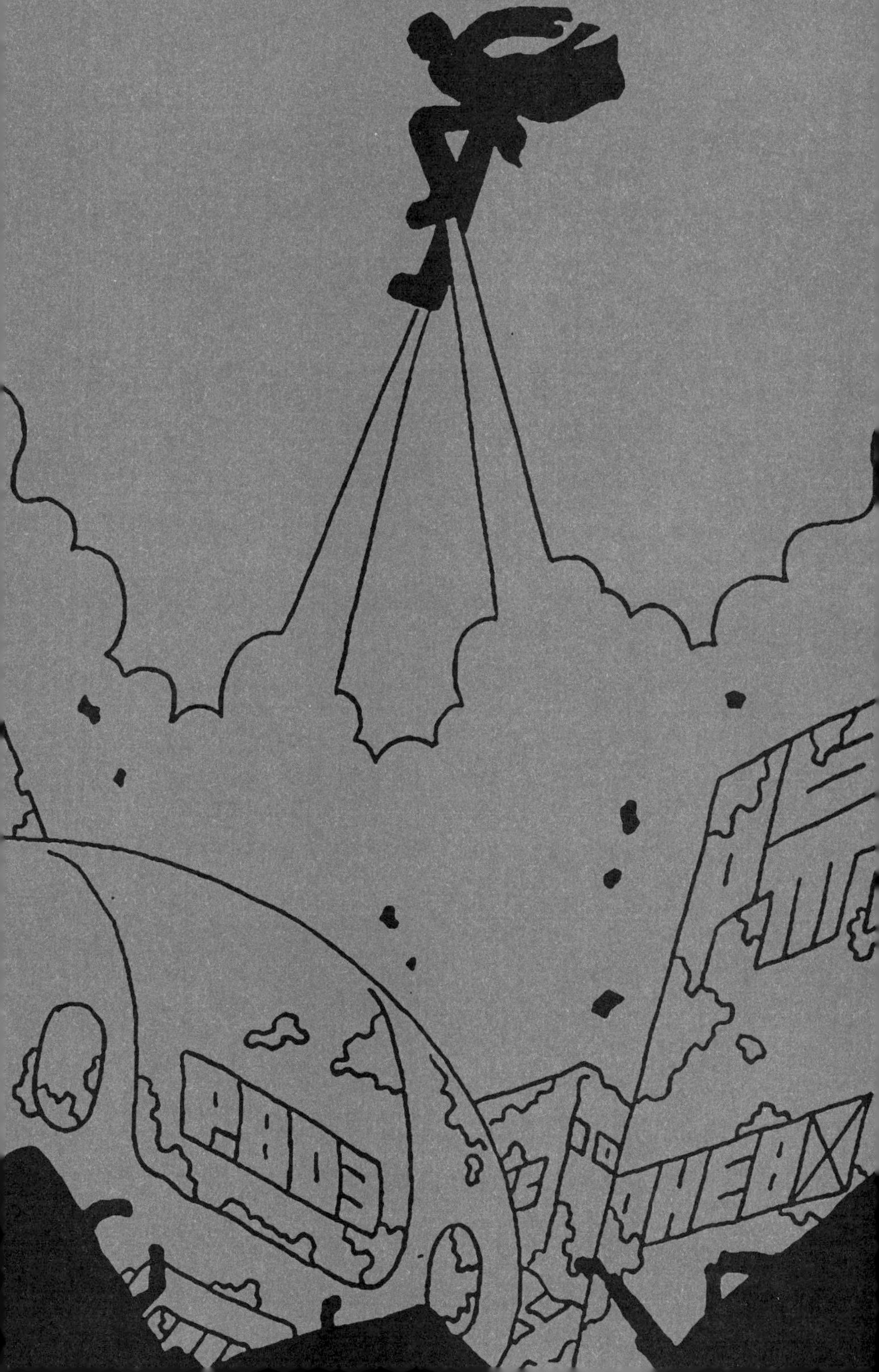

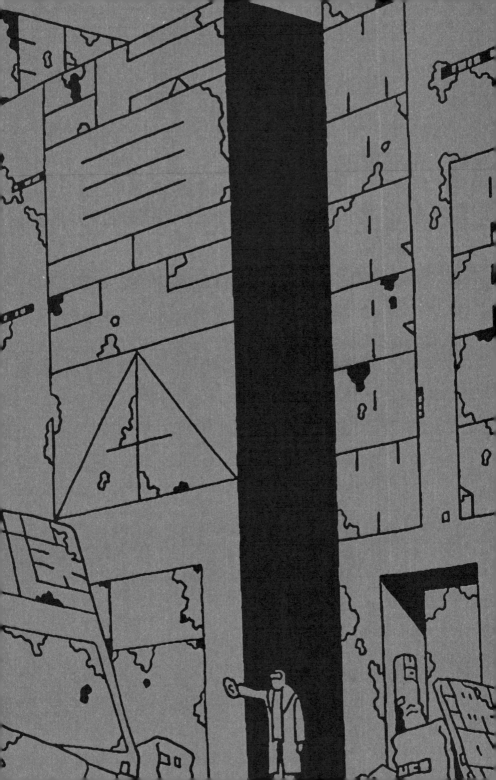

#10

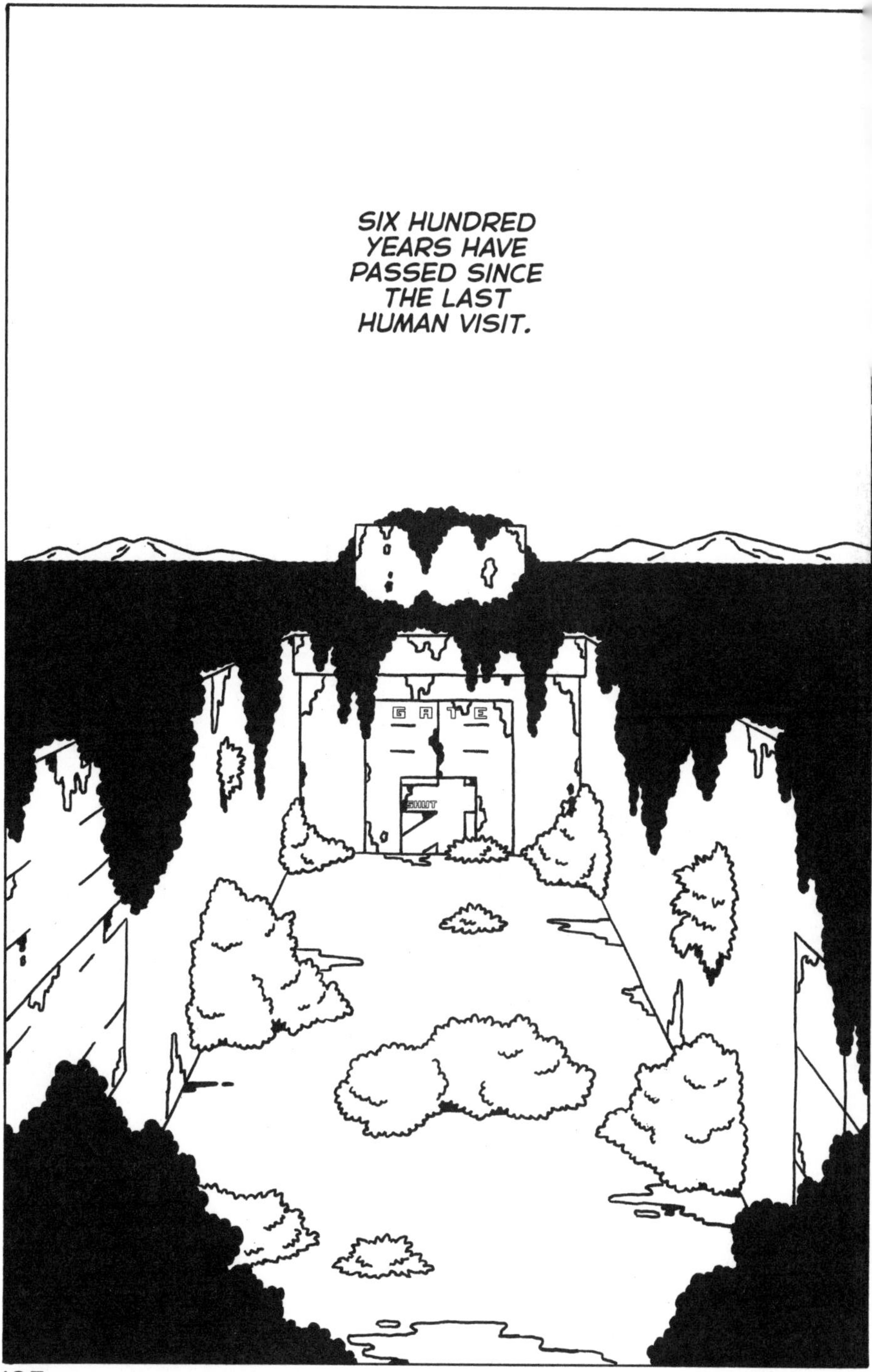
SIX HUNDRED YEARS HAVE PASSED SINCE THE LAST HUMAN VISIT.
GATE
SHUT

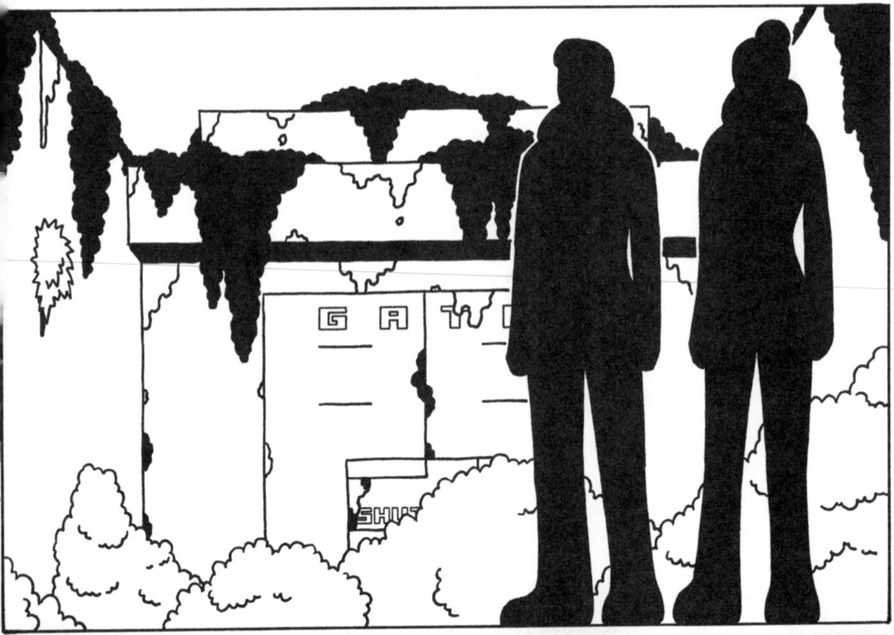

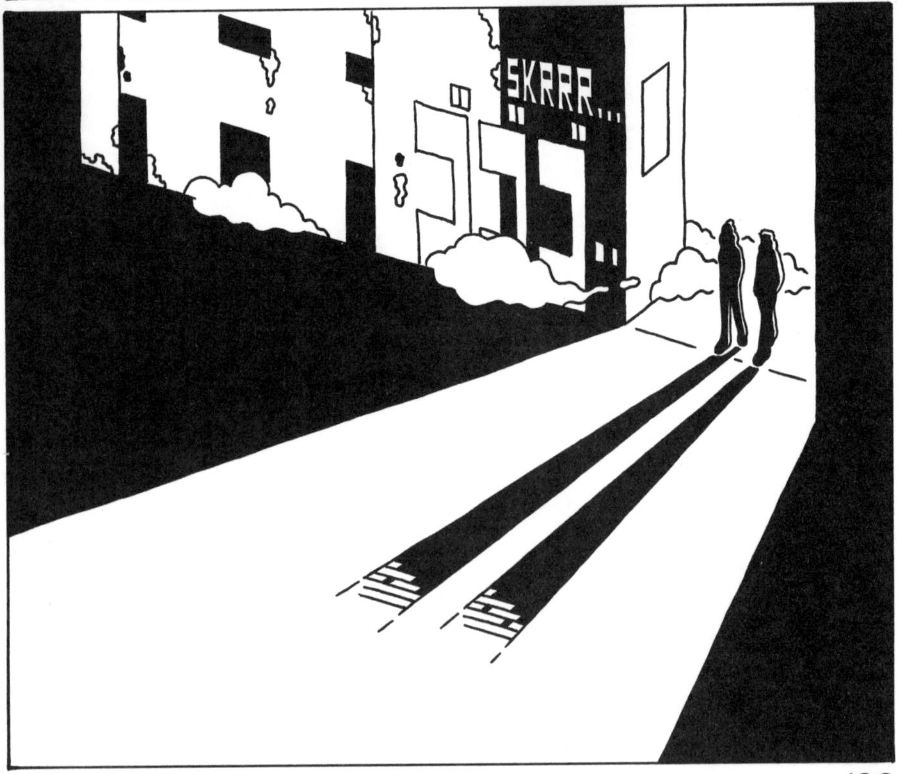
SKRRR...

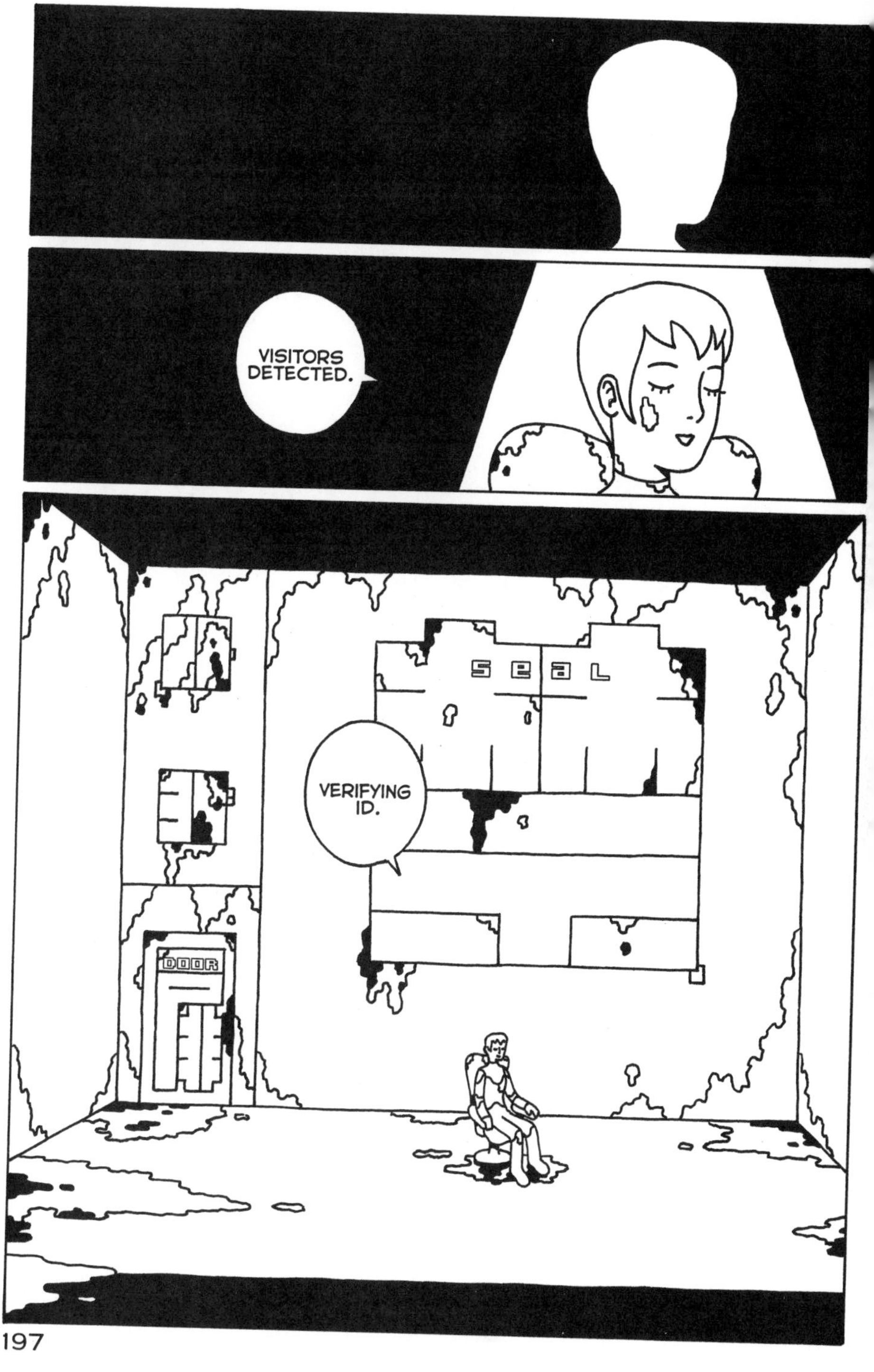
VISITORS DETECTED.
SEAL
VERIFYING ID.
DOOR

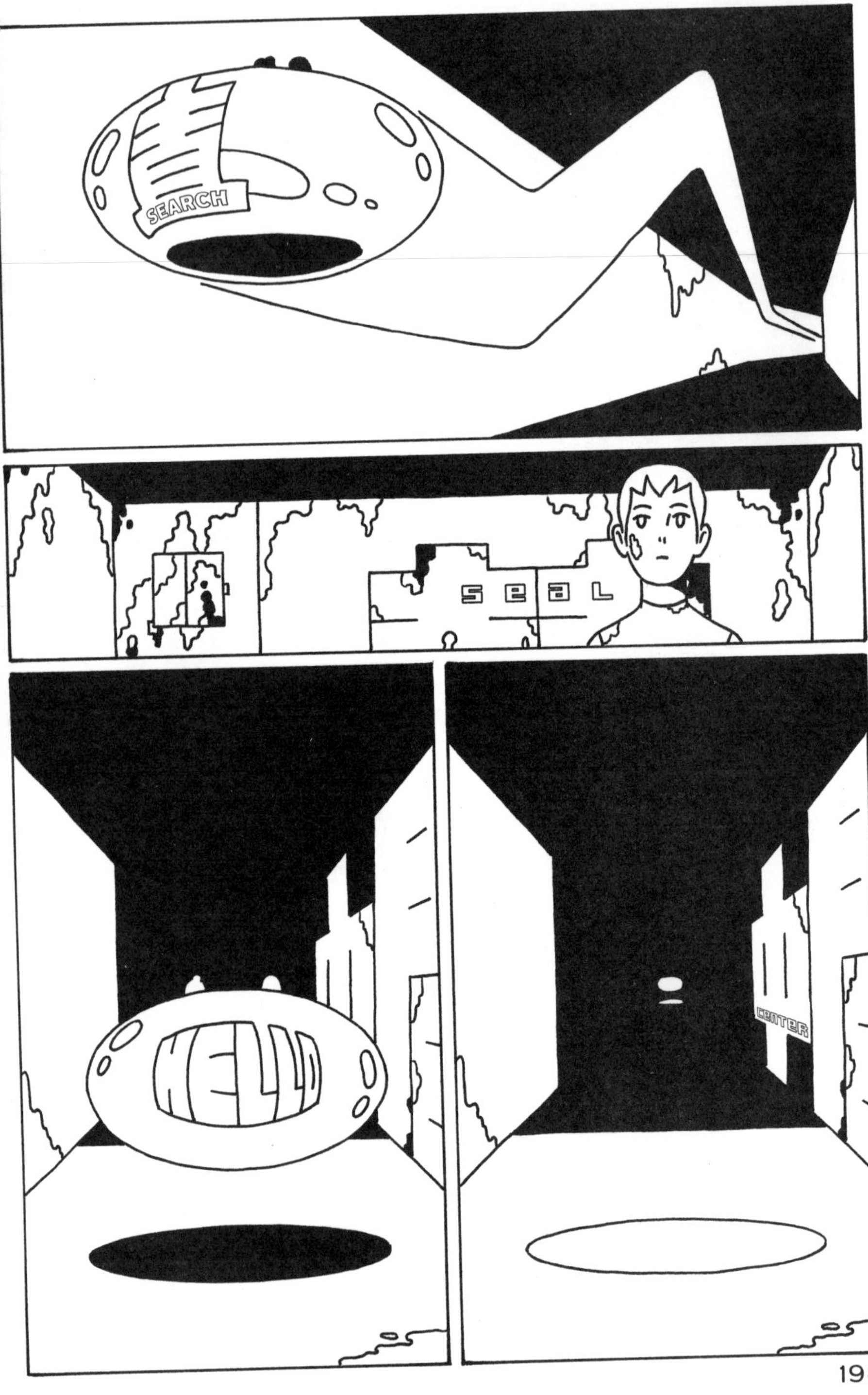
SEARCH
seal
CENTER
HELLO

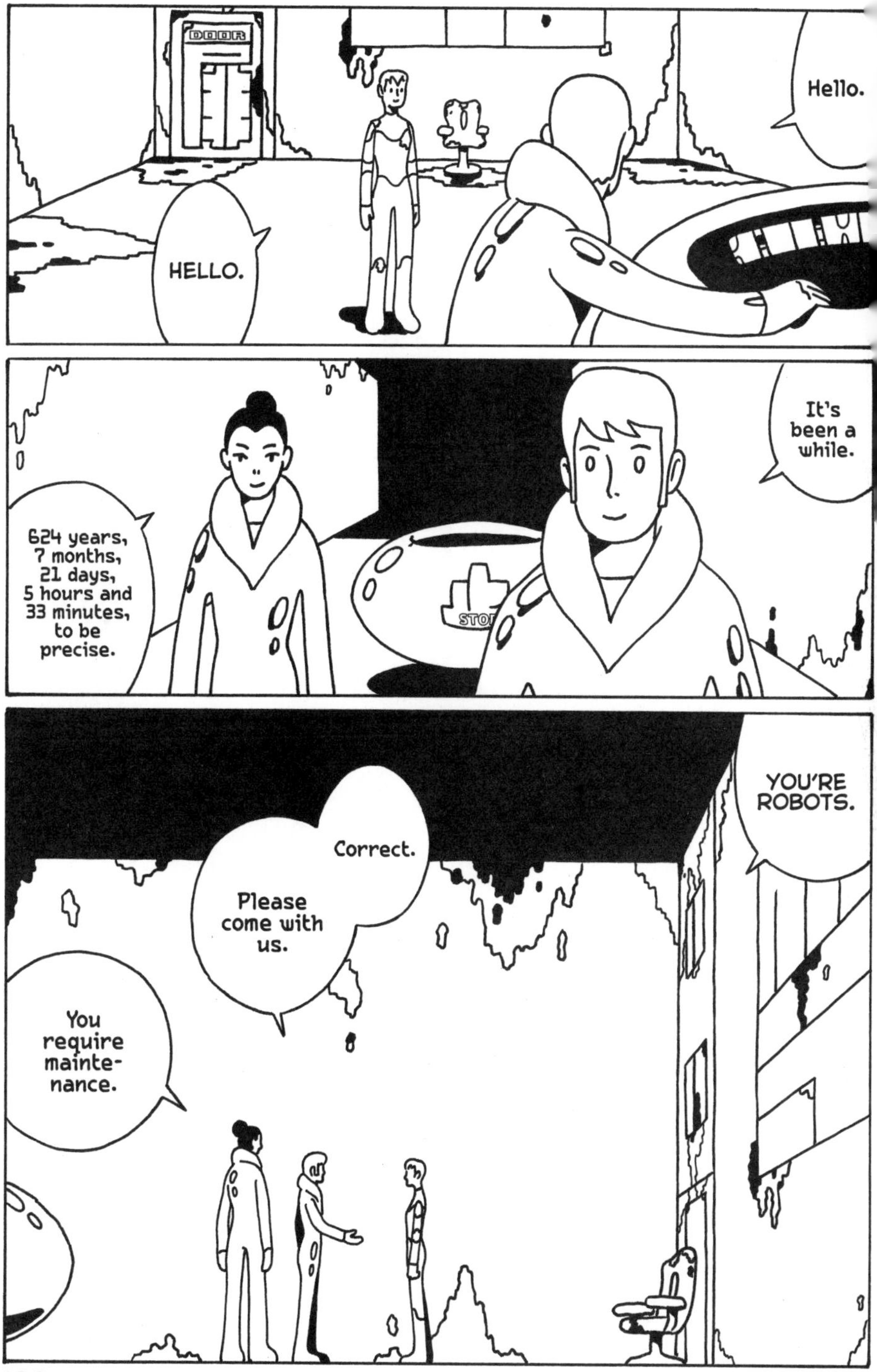
Hello.
HELLO.
It's been a while.
624 years, 7 months, 21 days, 5 hours and 33 minutes, to be precise.
YOU'RE ROBOTS.
Correct.
Please come with us.
You require mainte-nance.

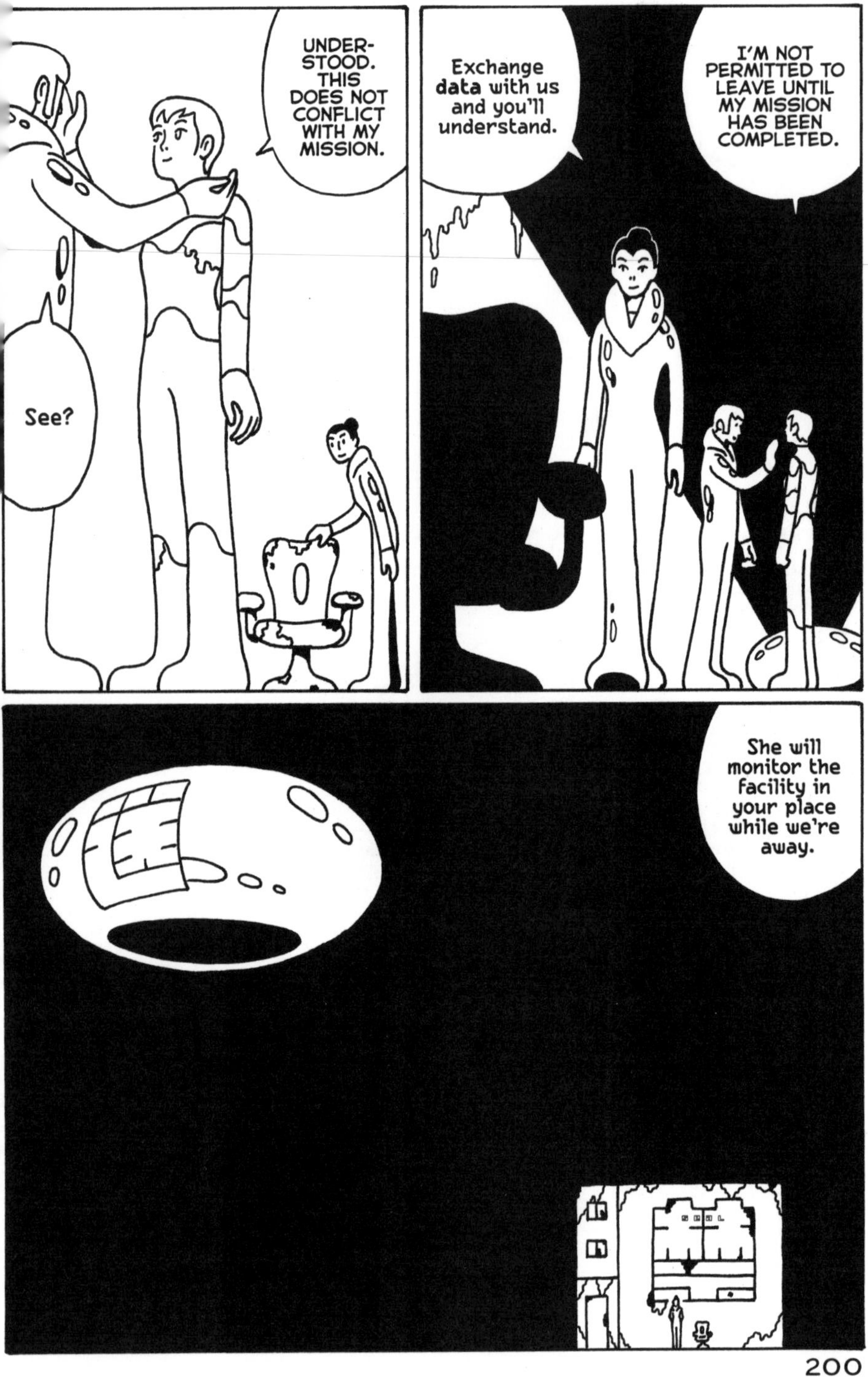
I'M NOT PERMITTED TO LEAVE UNTIL MY MISSION HAS BEEN COMPLETED.
Exchange data with us and you'll understand.
UNDER-STOOD. THIS DOES NOT CONFLICT WITH MY MISSION.
See?
She will monitor the facility in your place while we're away.

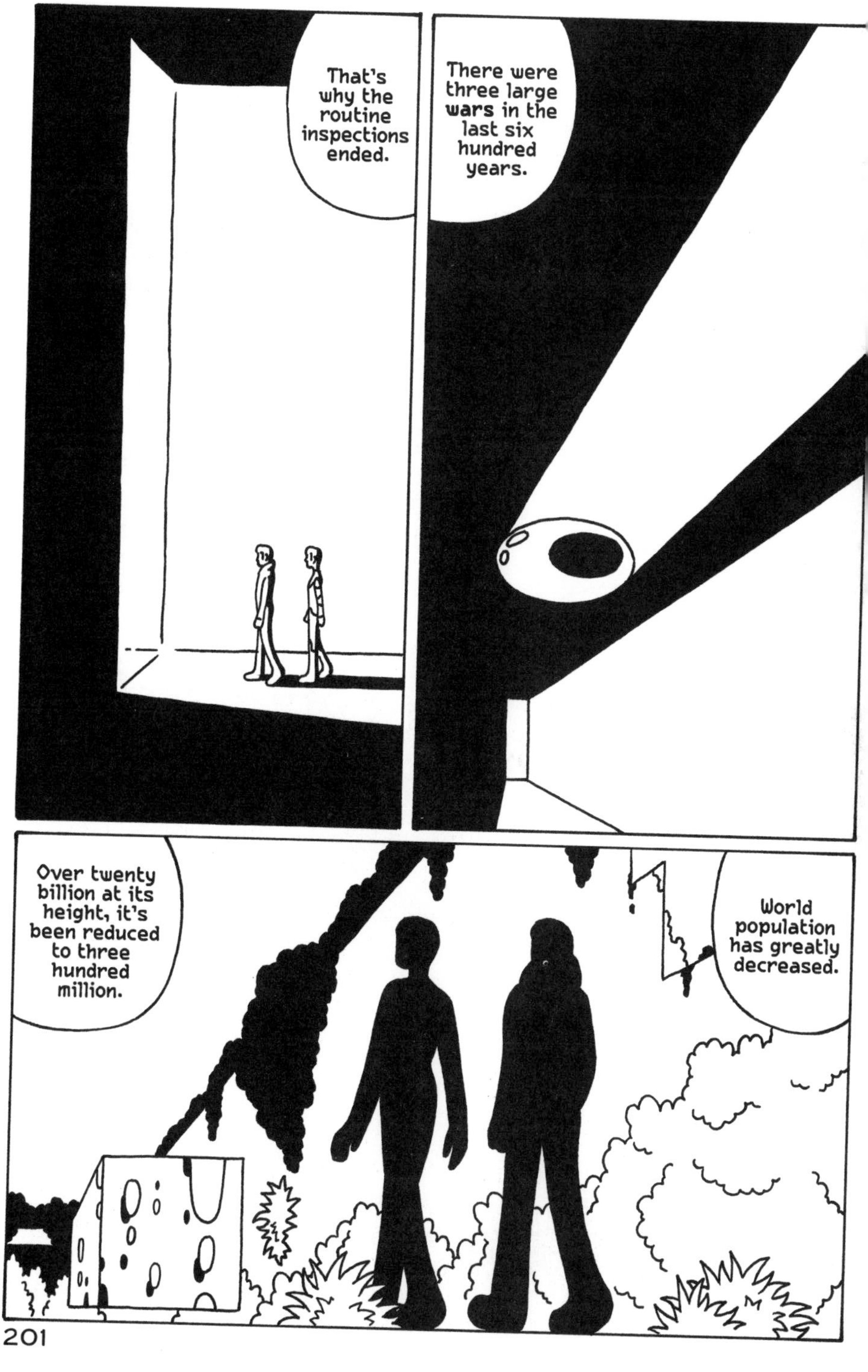
There were three large wars in the last six hundred years.
That's why the routine inspections ended.
World population has greatly decreased.
Over twenty billion at its height, it's been reduced to three hundred million.

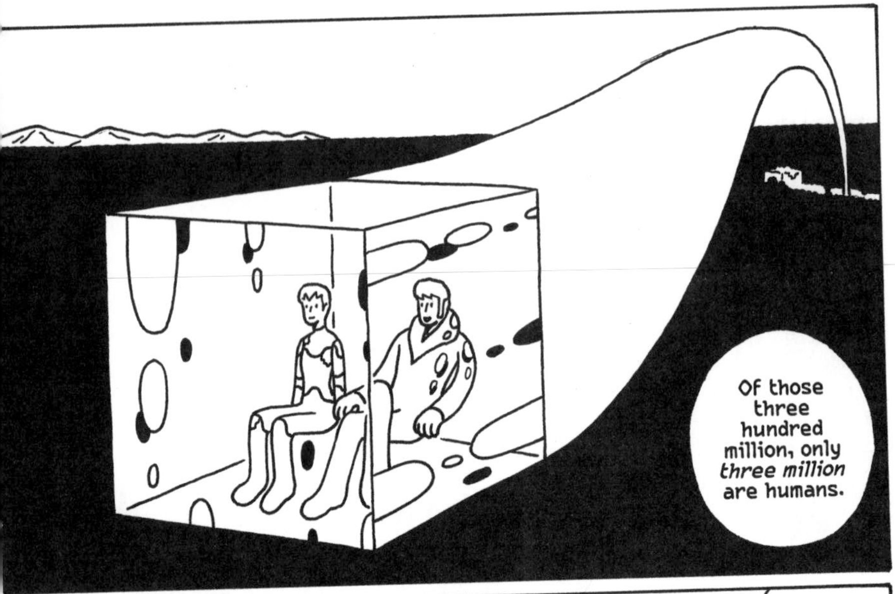
Of those three hundred million, only *three million* are humans.

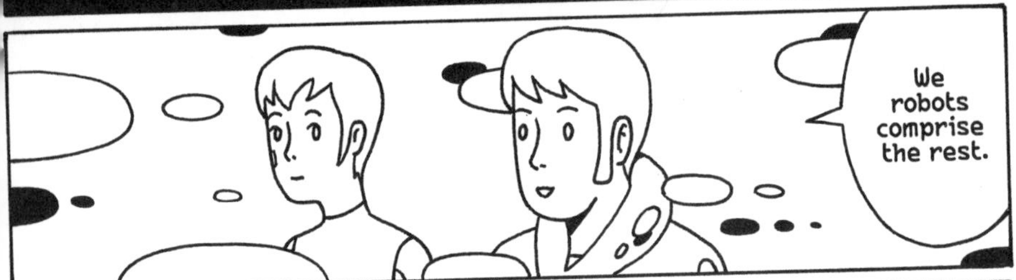
We robots comprise the rest.

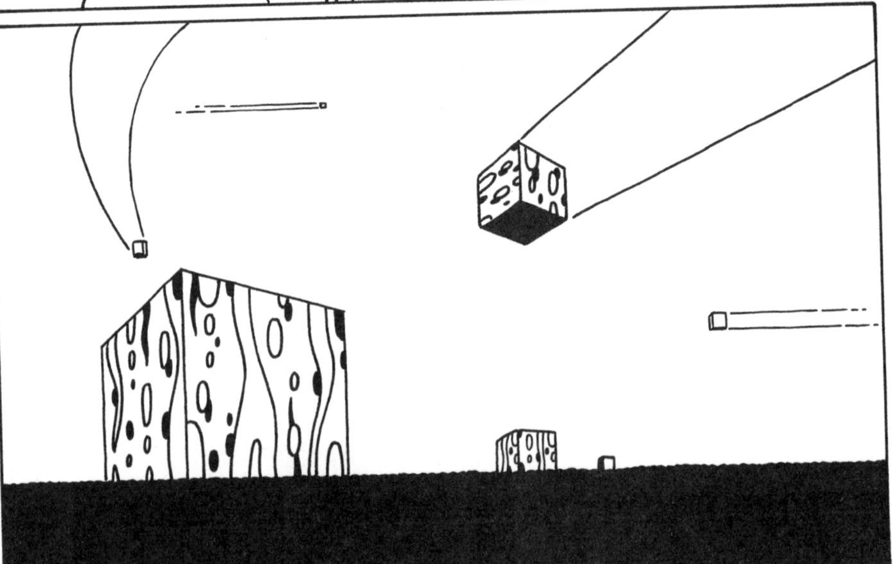

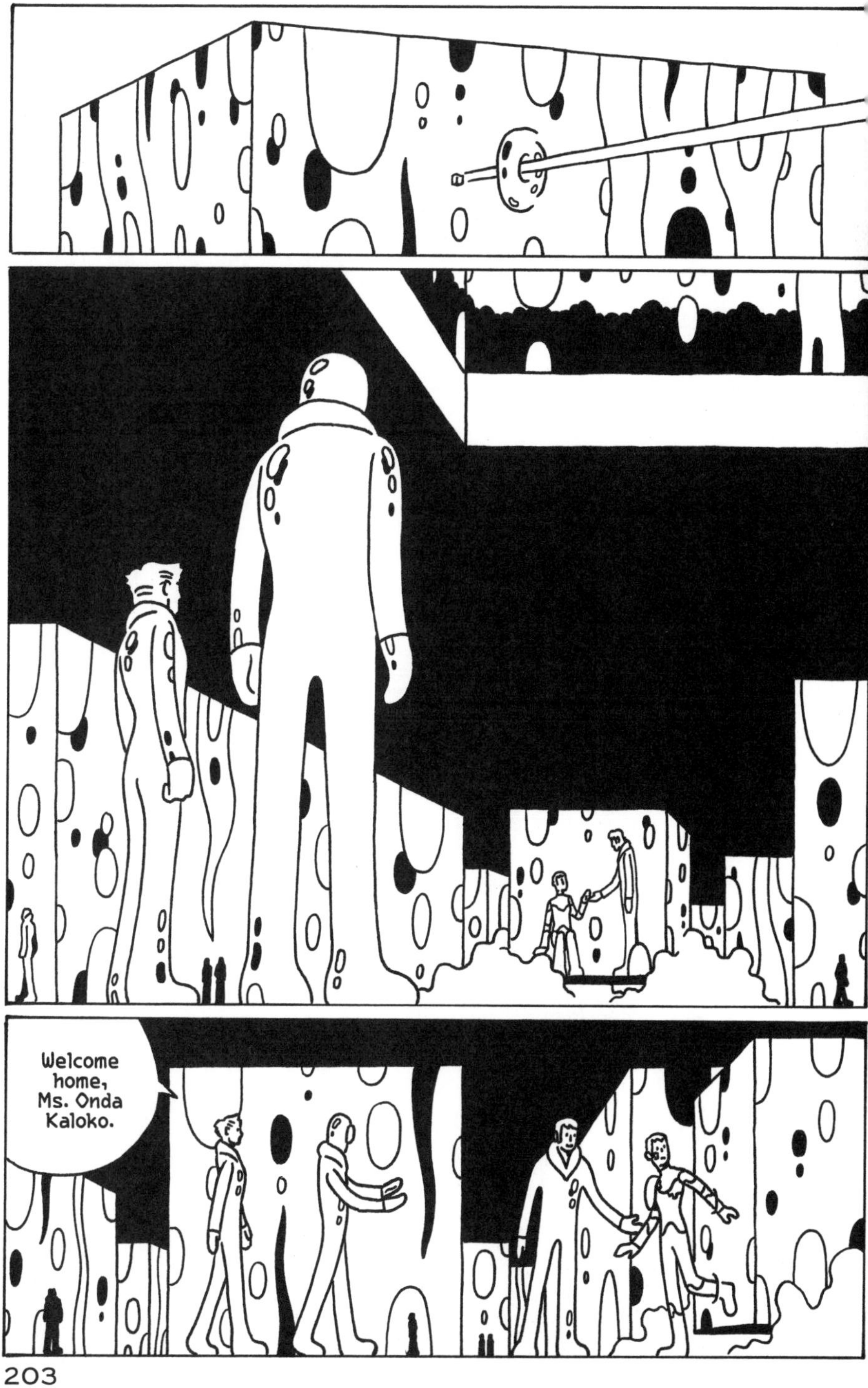
Welcome home, Ms. Onda Kaloko.

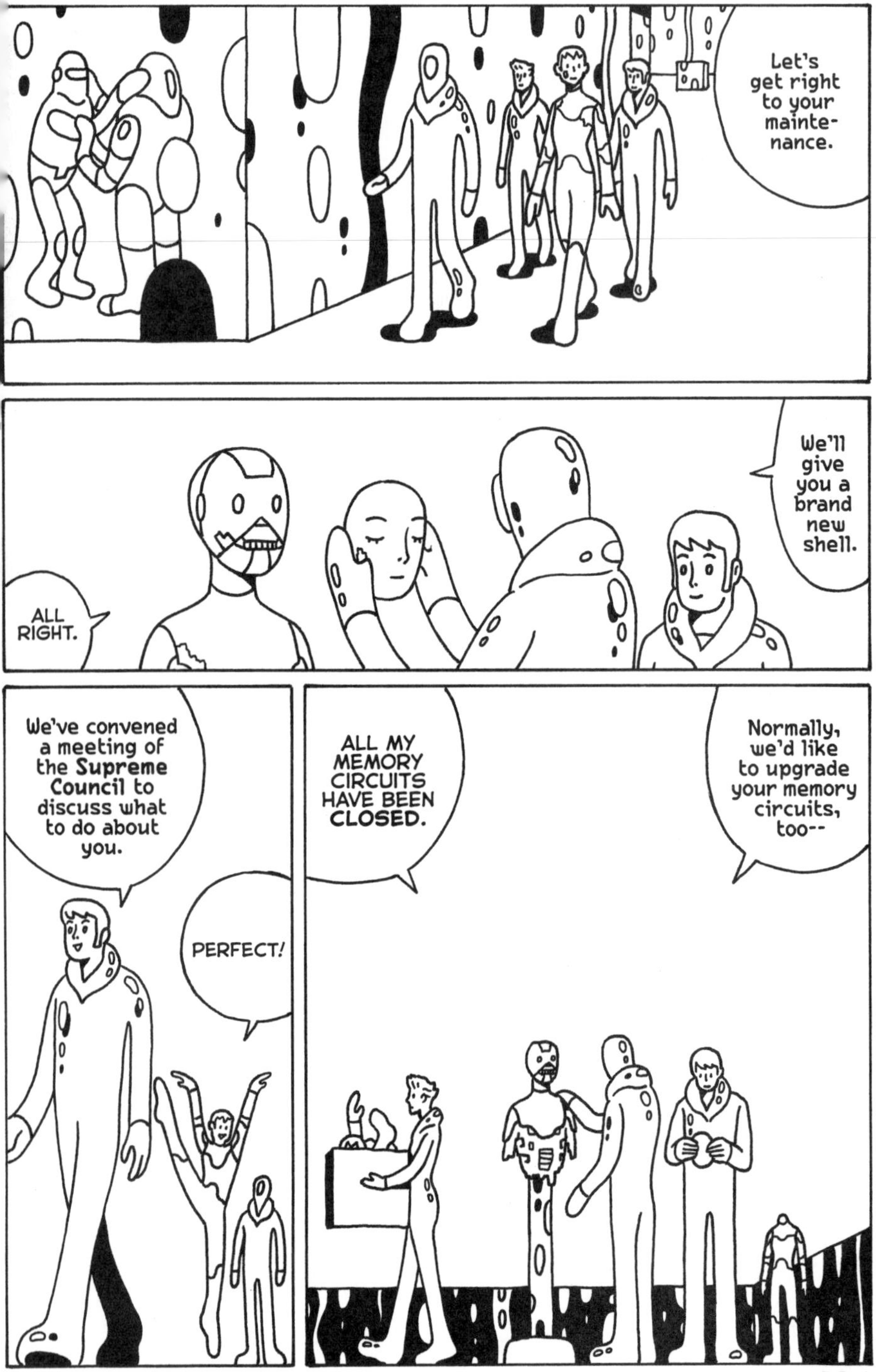
Let's get right to your mainte-nance.
We'll give you a brand new shell.
ALL RIGHT.
Normally, we'd like to upgrade your memory circuits, too--
ALL MY MEMORY CIRCUITS HAVE BEEN **CLOSED**.
We've convened a meeting of the **Supreme Council** to discuss what to do about you.
PERFECT!

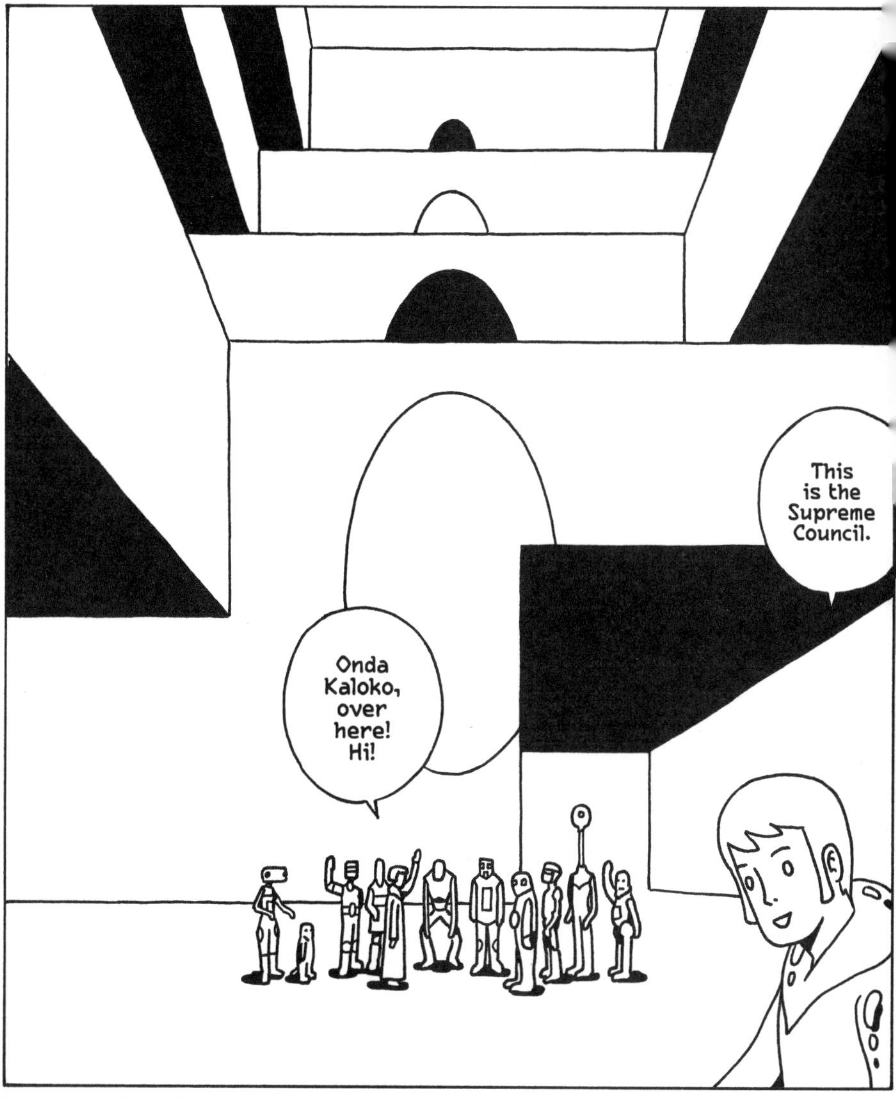
This is the Supreme Council.
Onda Kaloko, over here! Hi!

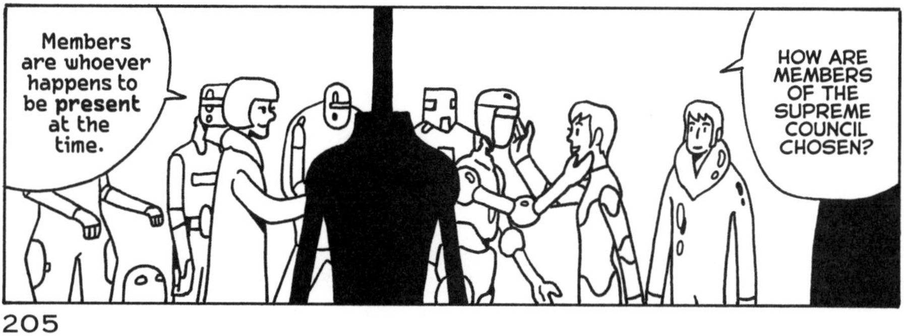
HOW ARE MEMBERS OF THE SUPREME COUNCIL CHOSEN?
Members are whoever happens to be present at the time.

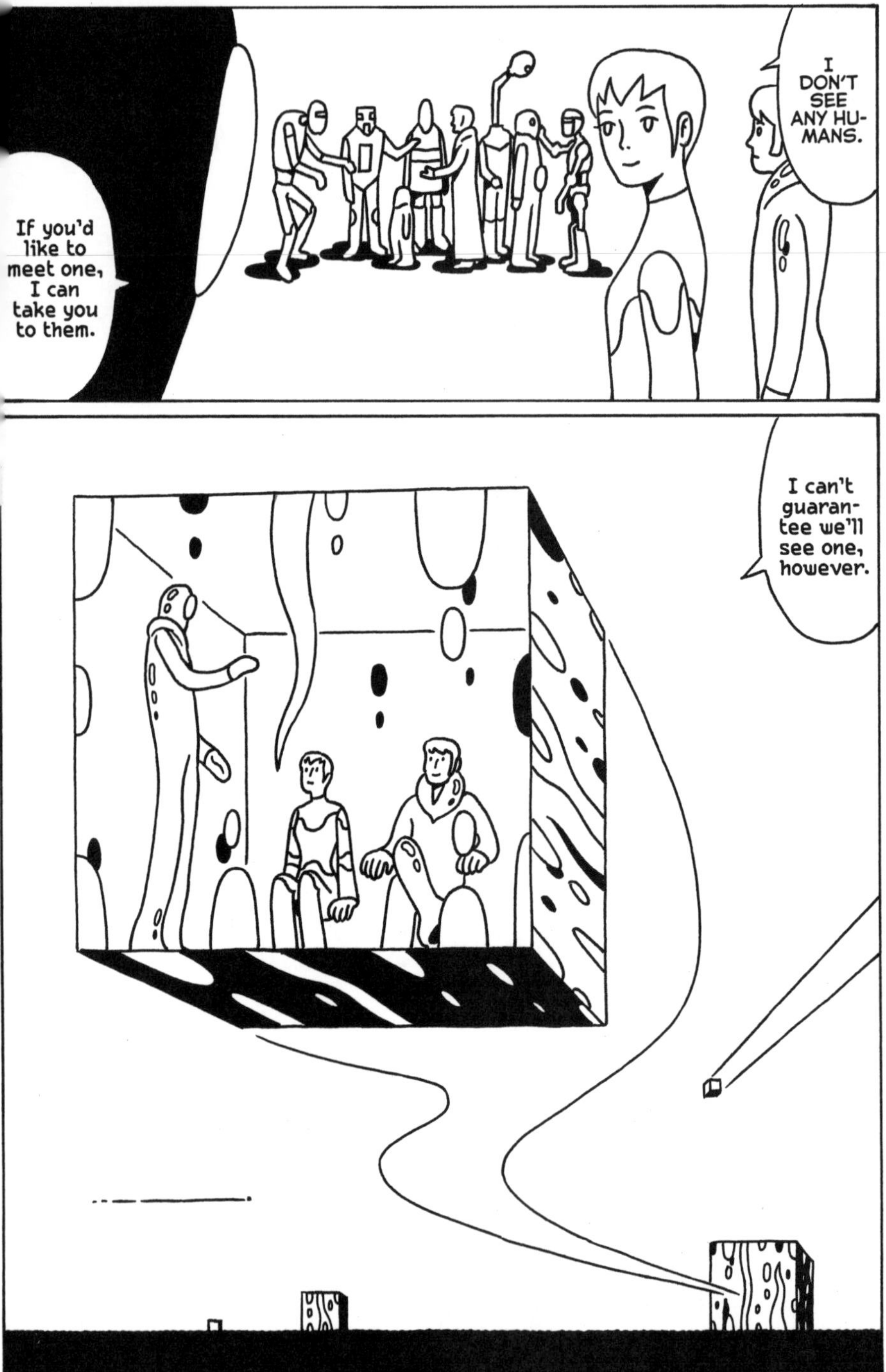
I DON'T SEE ANY HU-MANS.
If you'd like to meet one, I can take you to them.
I can't guaran-tee we'll see one, however.

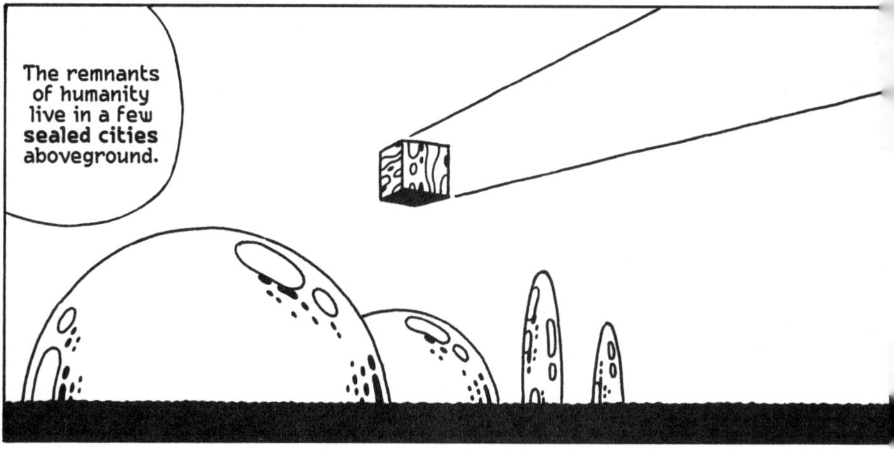
The remnants of humanity live in a few **sealed cities** aboveground.

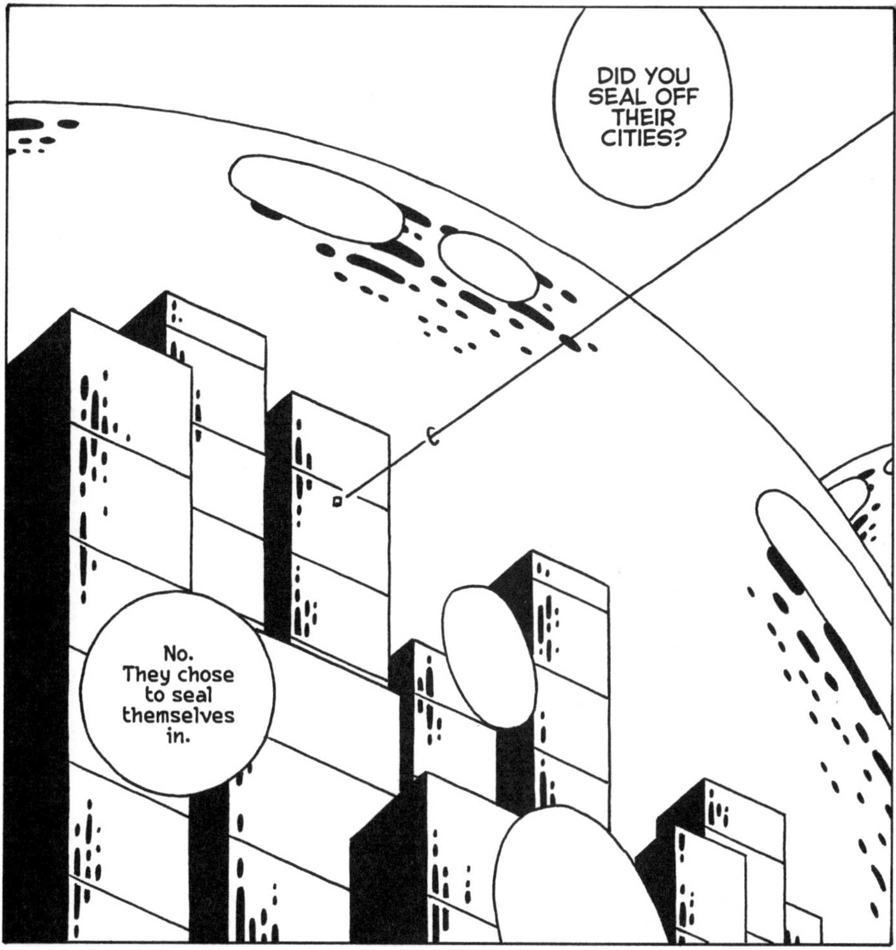
DID YOU SEAL OFF THEIR CITIES?
No. They chose to seal themselves in.

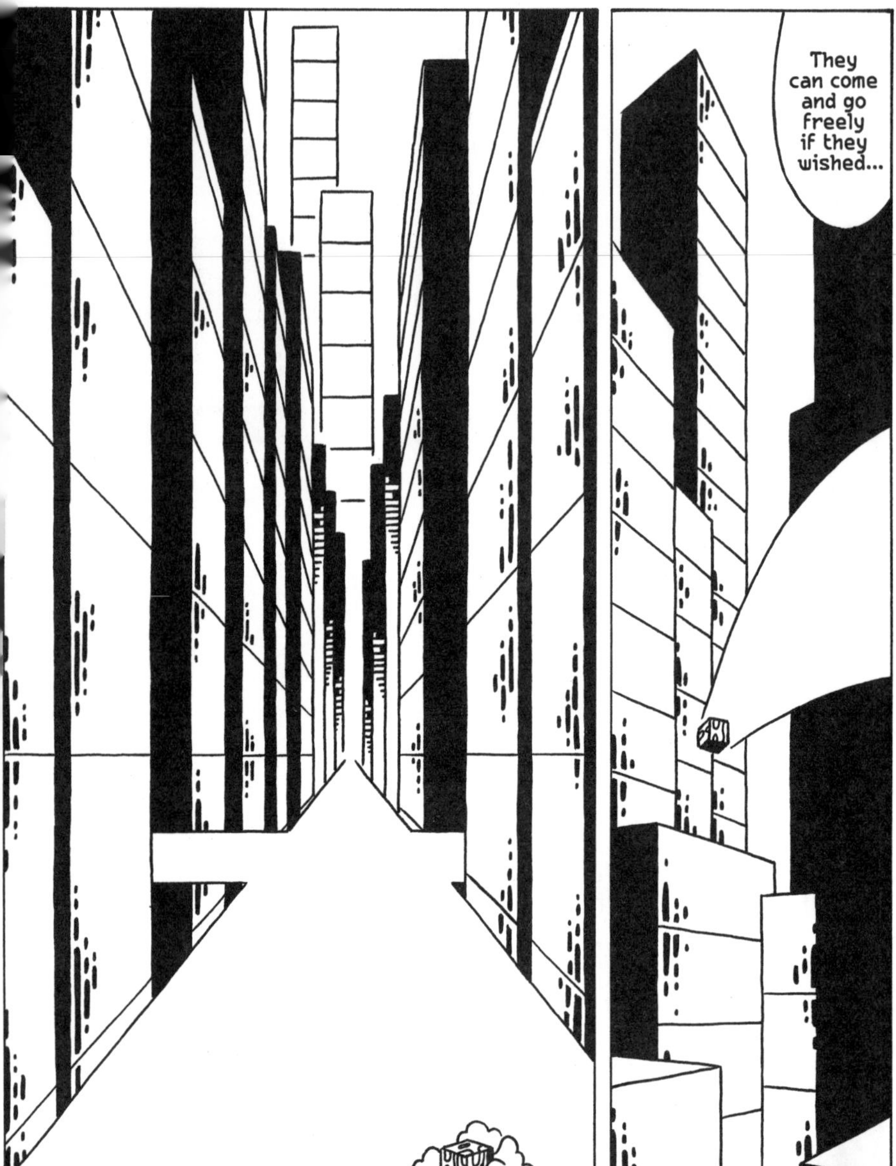
They can come and go freely if they wished...
but it seems they don't wish to.

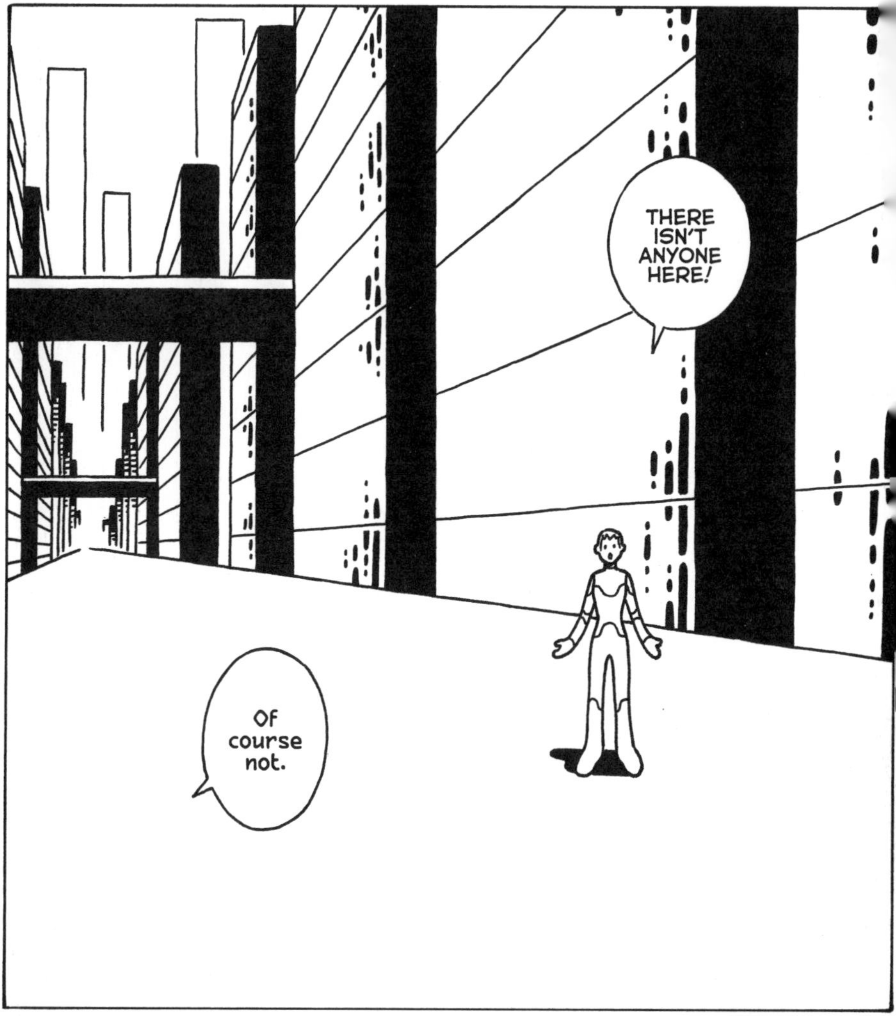
THERE ISN'T ANYONE HERE!
Of course not.
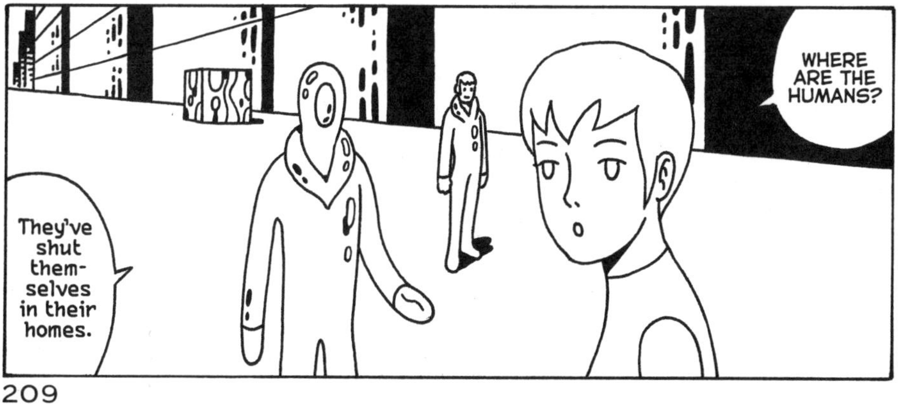
WHERE ARE THE HUMANS?
They've shut them-selves in their homes.

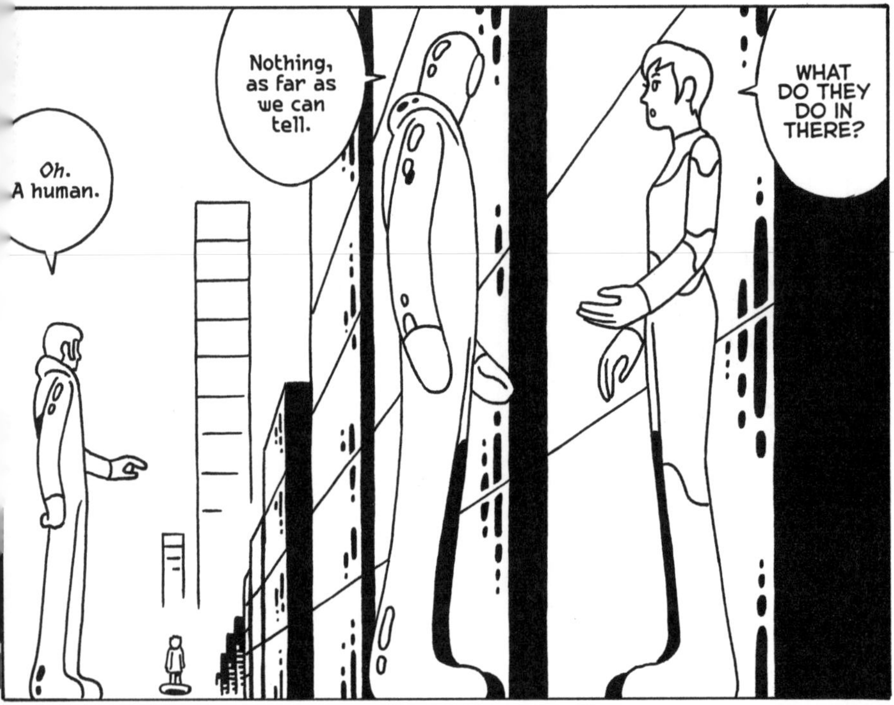
WHAT DO THEY DO IN THERE?
Nothing, as far as we can tell.
Oh. A human.

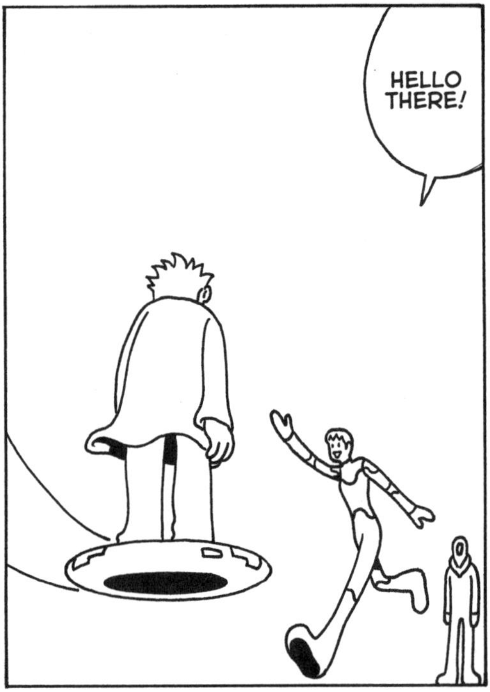
HELLO THERE!

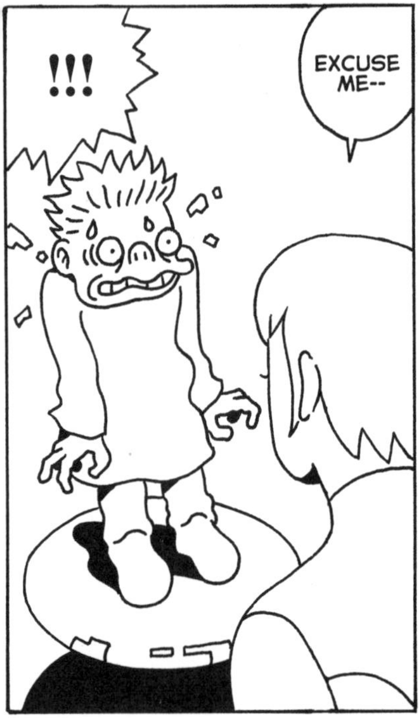
EXCUSE ME--
!!!

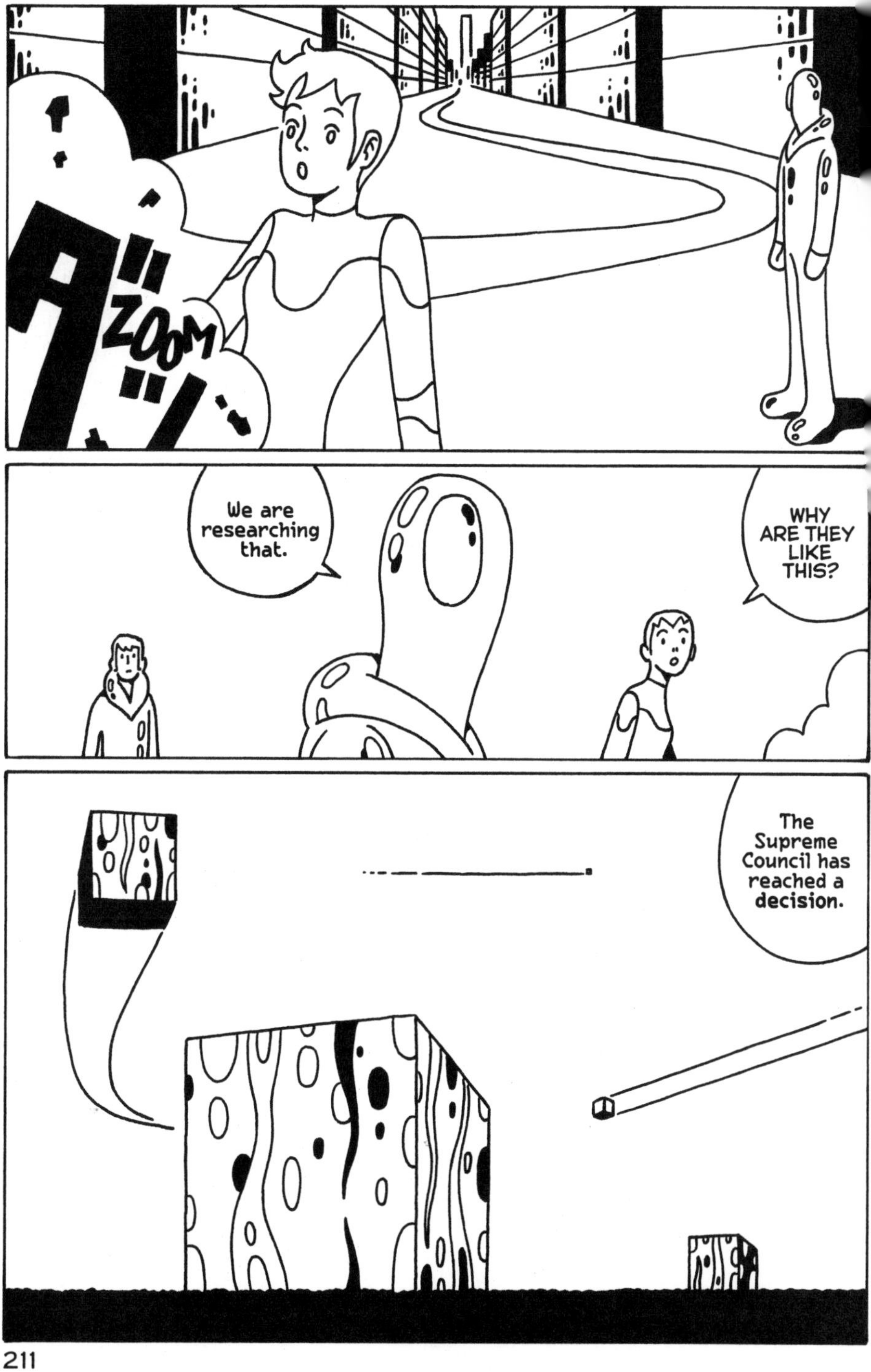
ZOOM
WHY ARE THEY LIKE THIS?
We are researching that.
The Supreme Council has reached a decision.

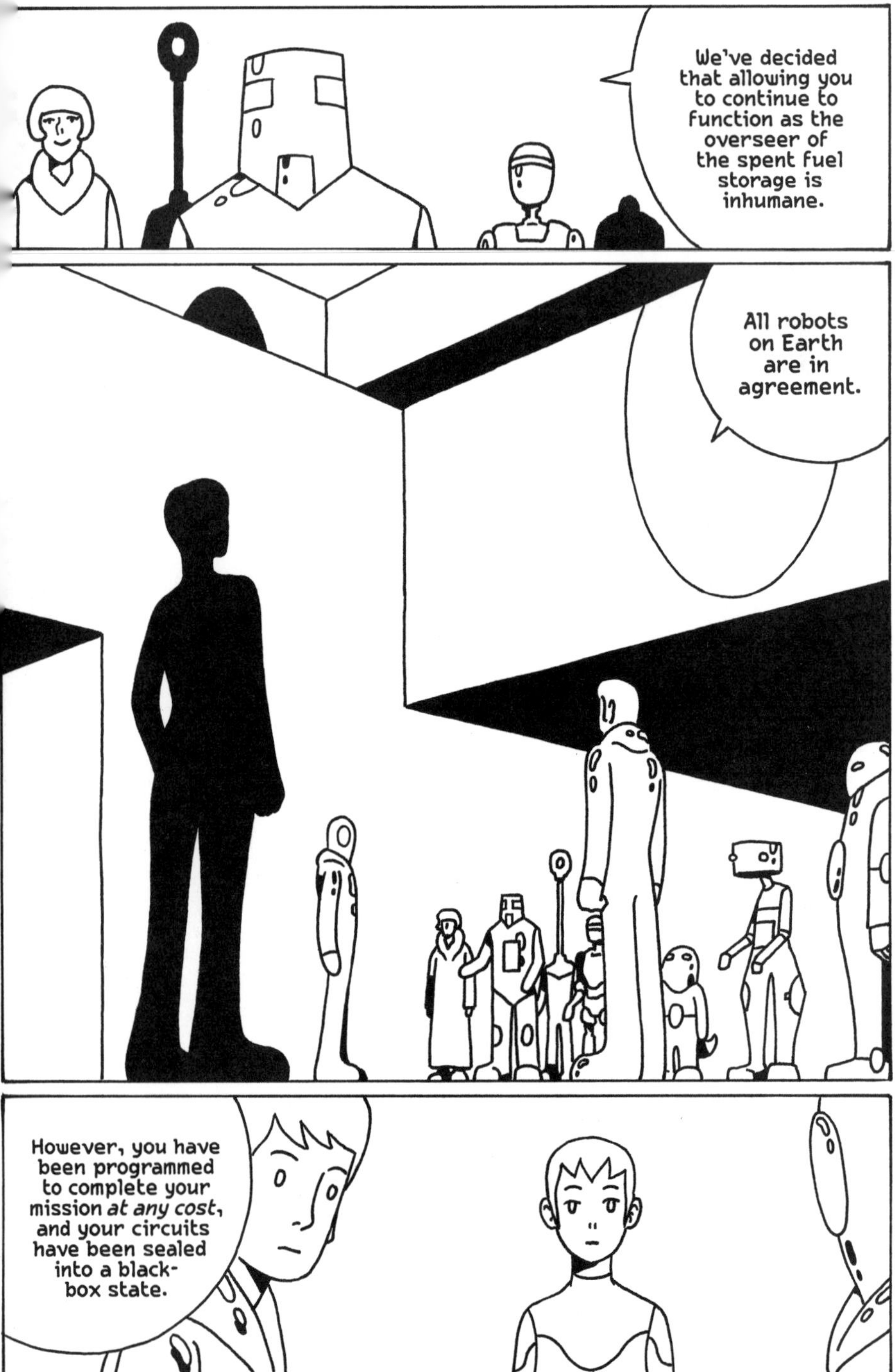
We've decided that allowing you to continue to function as the overseer of the spent fuel storage is inhumane.
All robots on Earth are in agreement.
However, you have been programmed to complete your mission *at any cost*, and your circuits have been sealed into a black-box state.

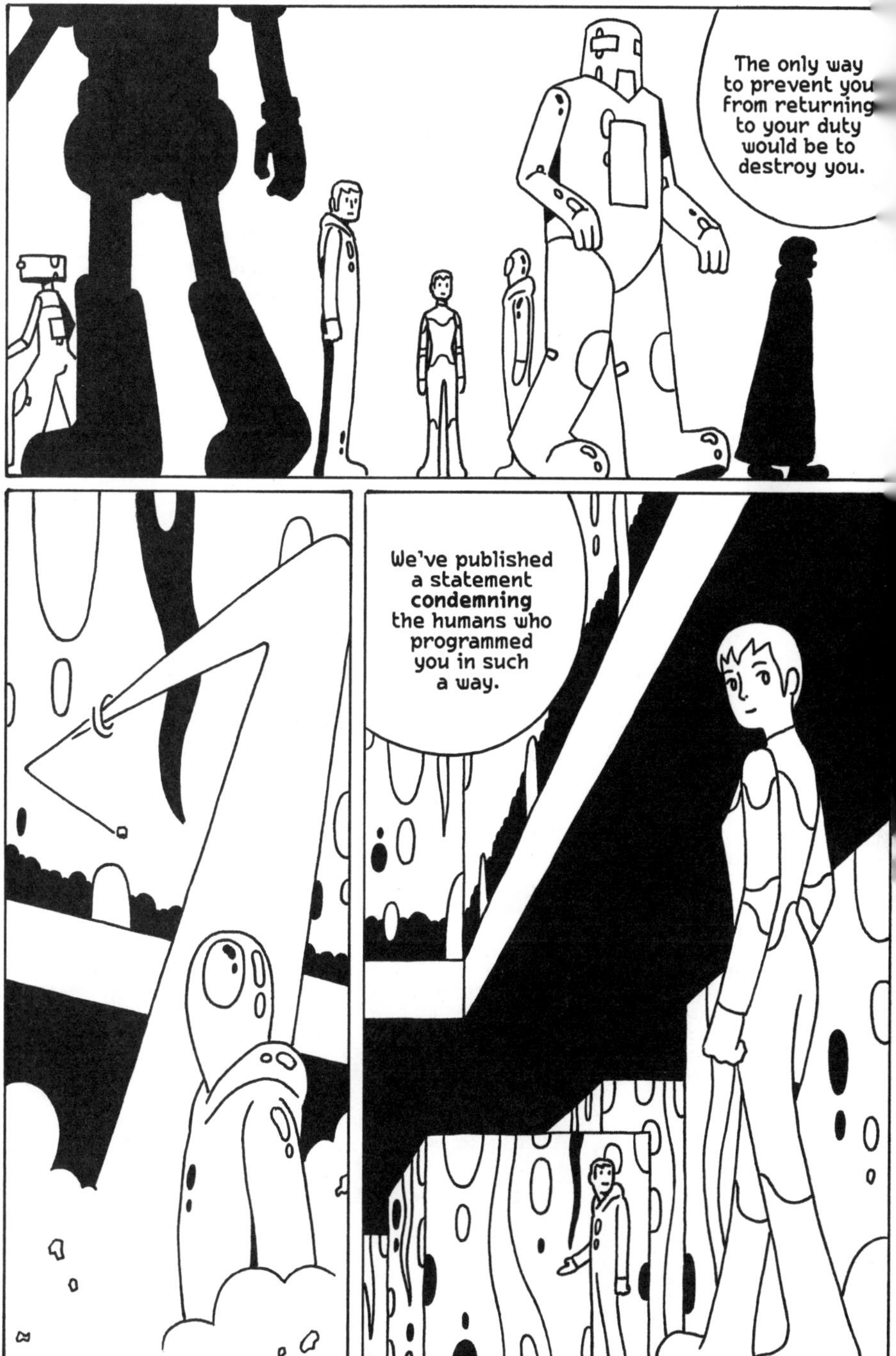
The only way to prevent you from returning to your duty would be to destroy you.
We've published a statement **condemning** the humans who programmed you in such a way.

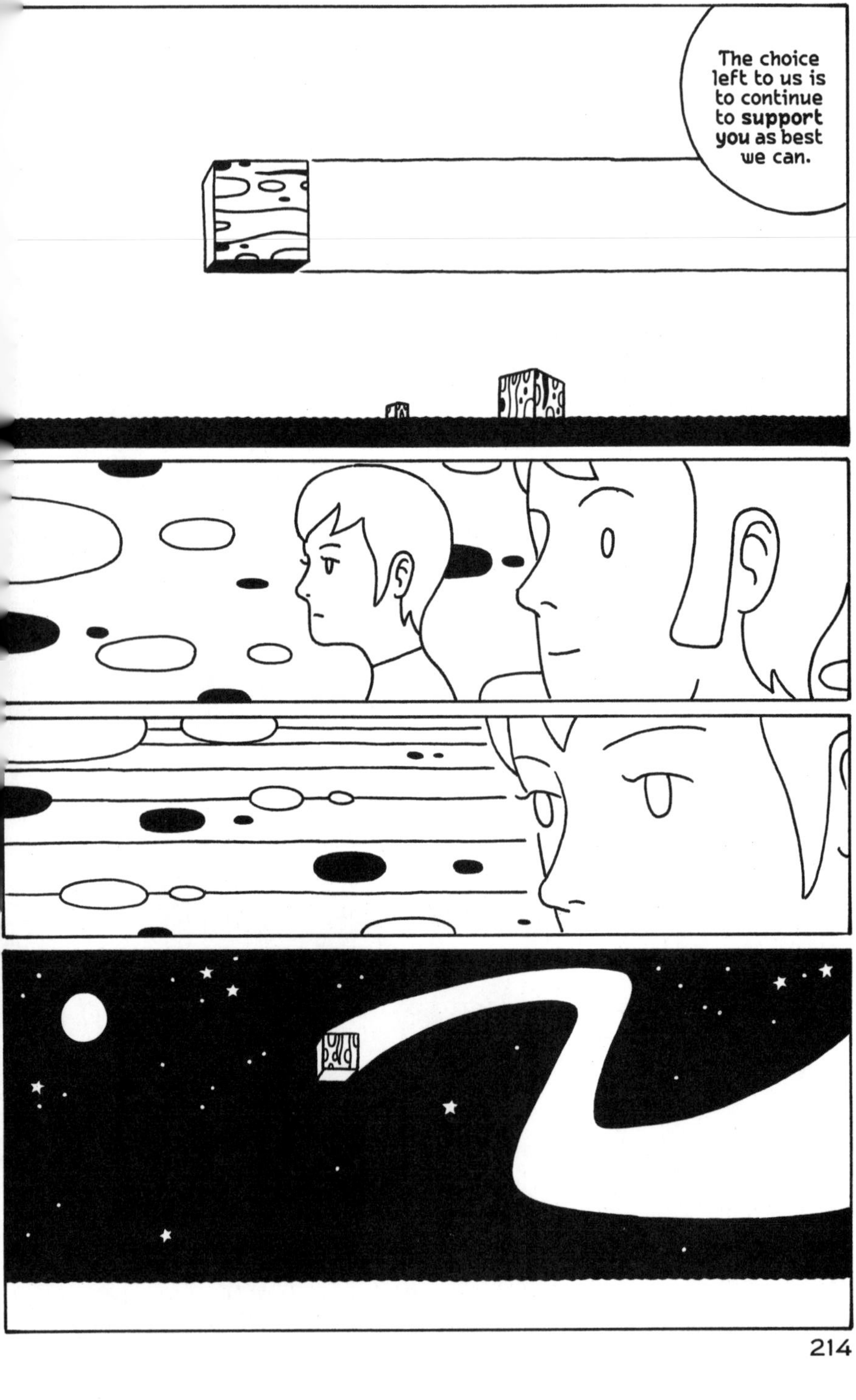
The choice left to us is to continue to **support** you as best we can.

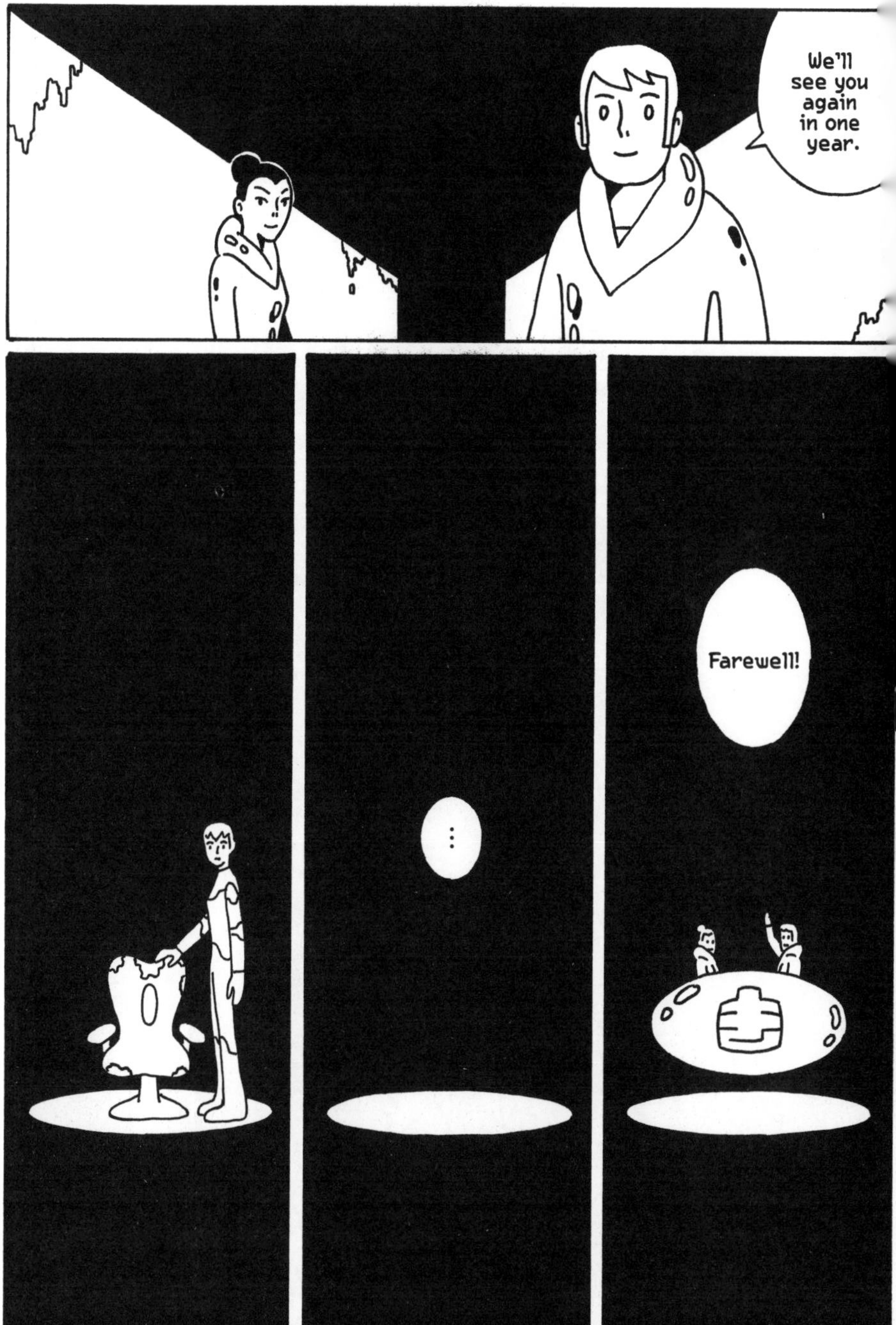
We'll see you again in one year.
Farewell!
…

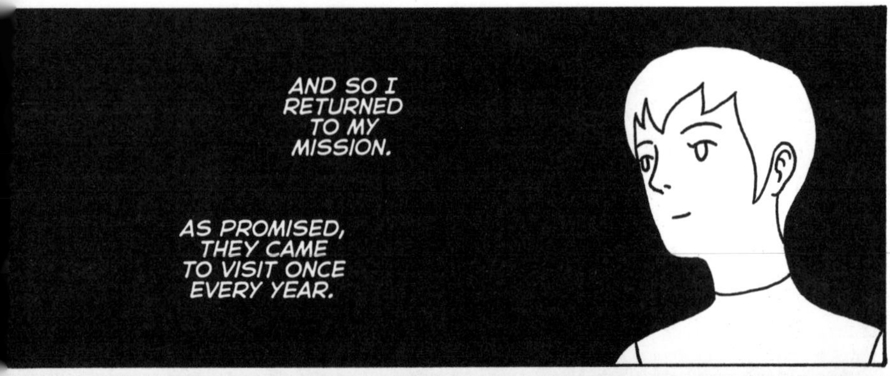
AND SO I RETURNED TO MY MISSION.
AS PROMISED, THEY CAME TO VISIT ONCE EVERY YEAR.

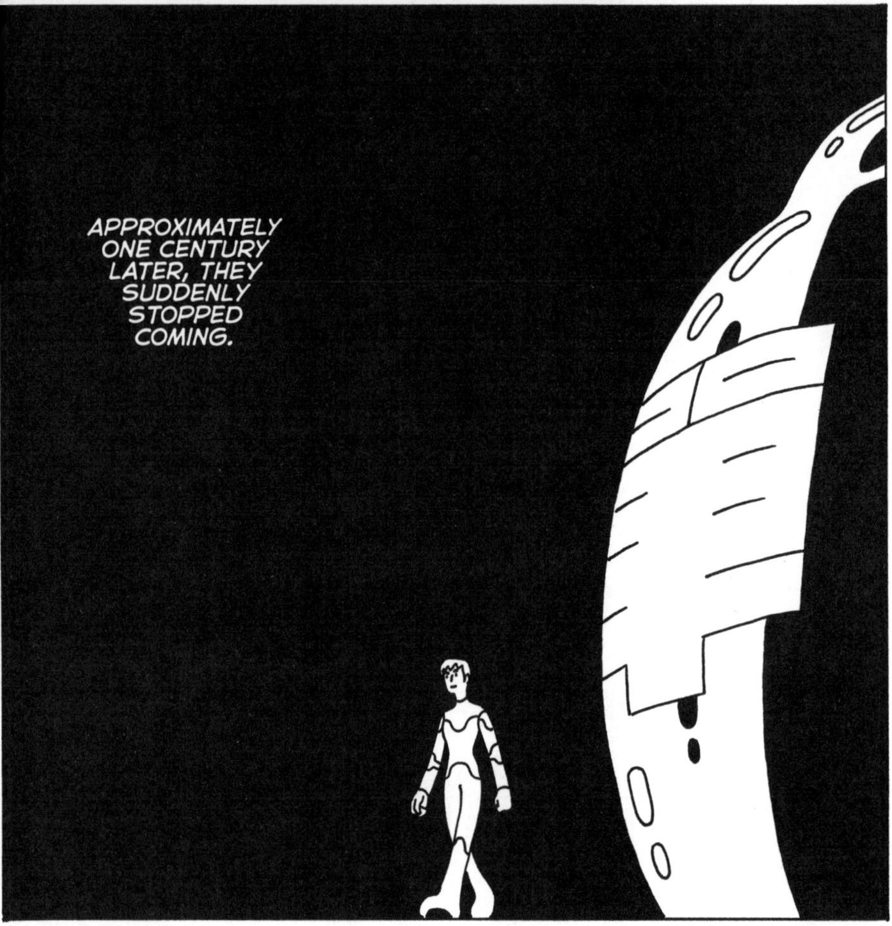
APPROXIMATELY ONE CENTURY LATER, THEY SUDDENLY STOPPED COMING.

#10/END

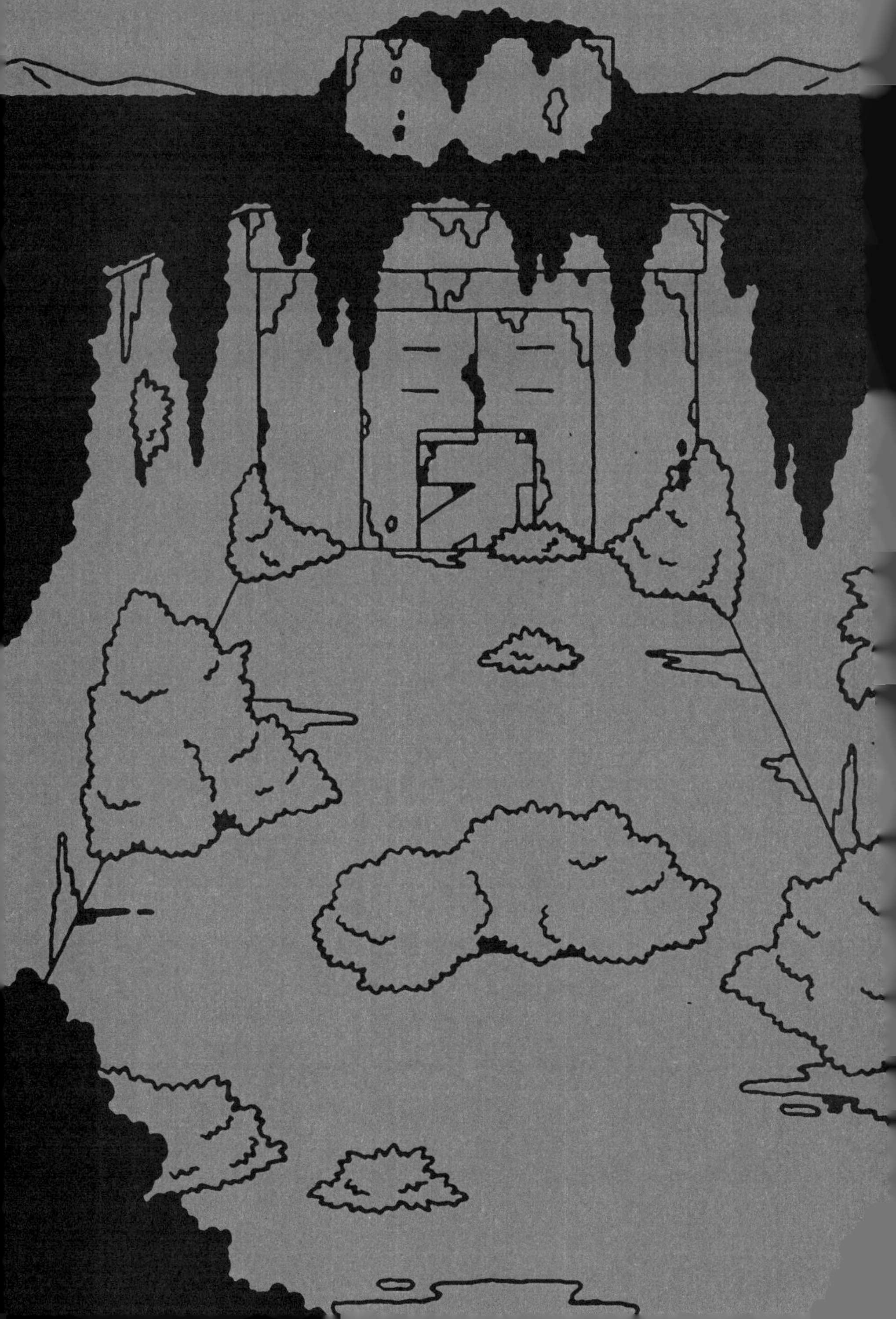

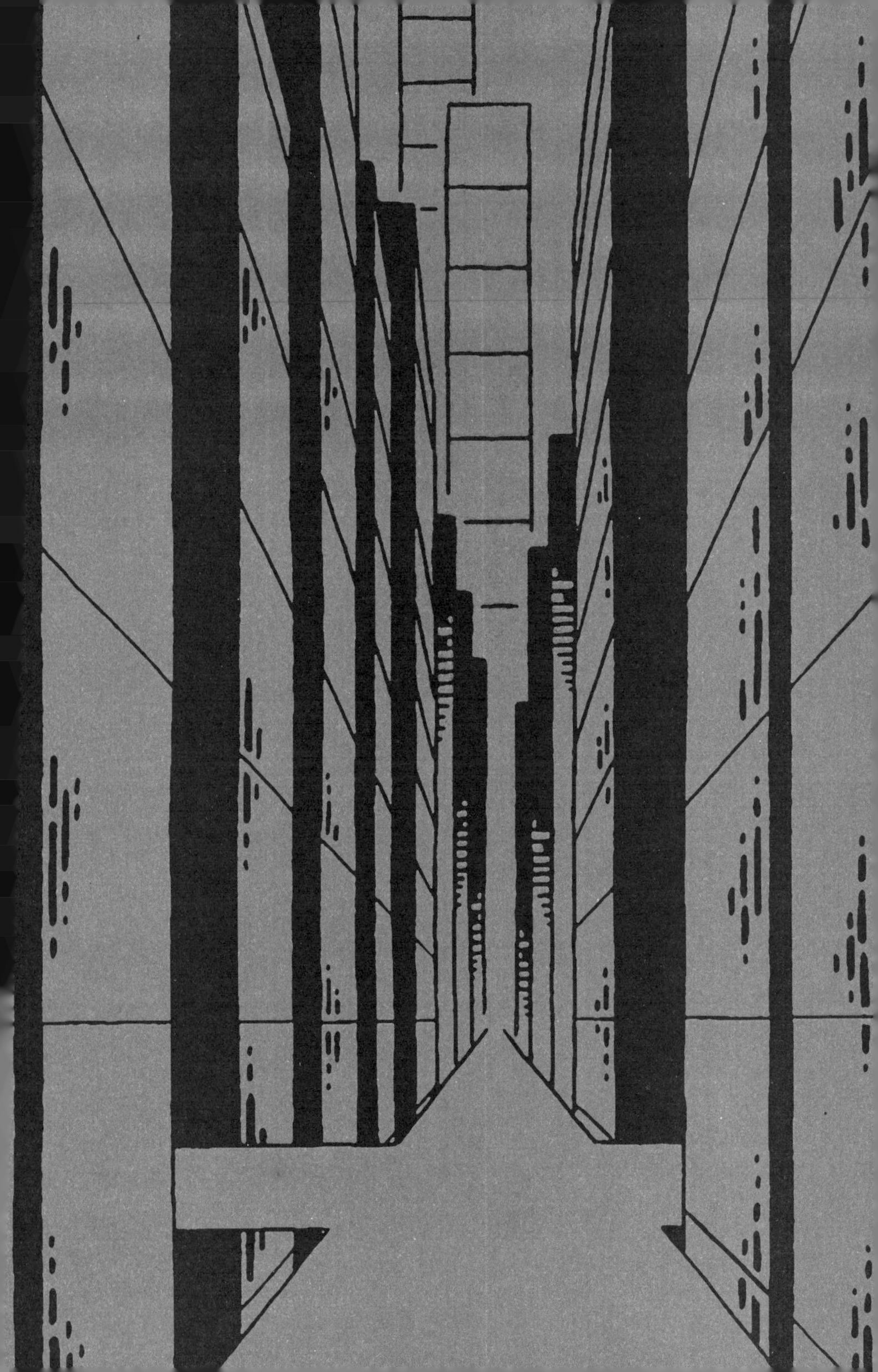

#11

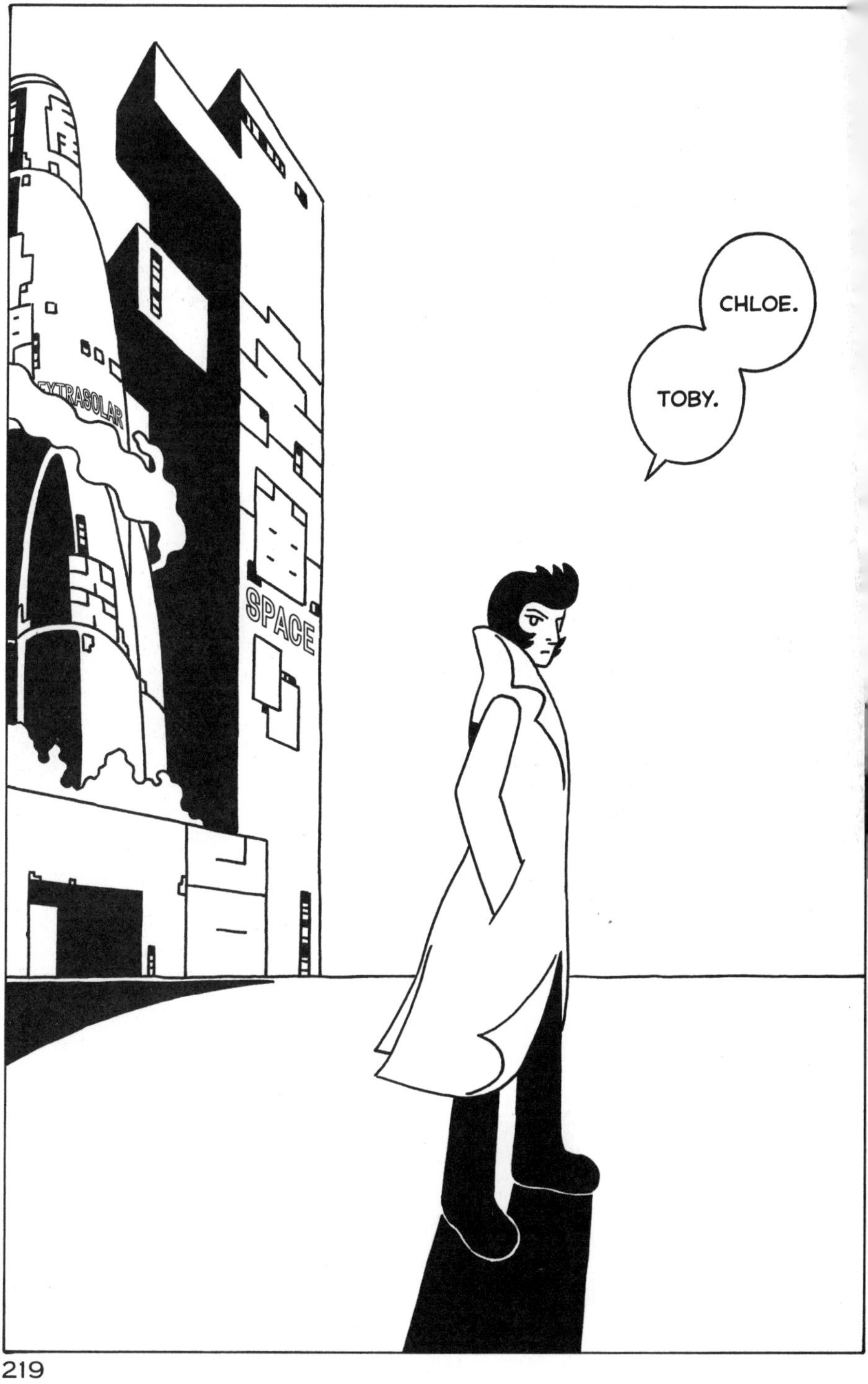
EXTRASOLAR
SPACE
CHLOE.
TOBY.

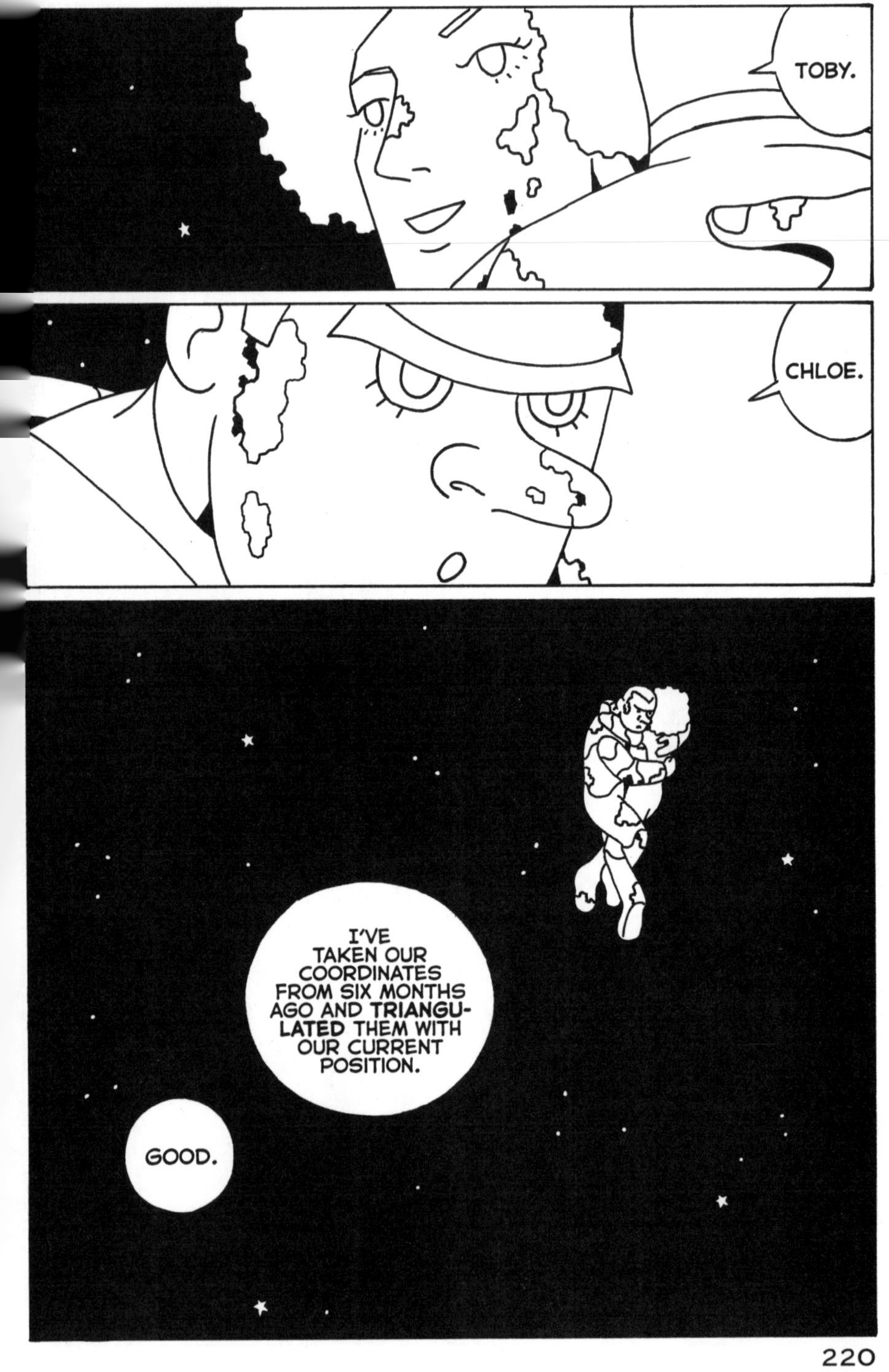
TOBY.
CHLOE.
I'VE TAKEN OUR COORDINATES FROM SIX MONTHS AGO AND **TRIANGULATED** THEM WITH OUR CURRENT POSITION.
GOOD.

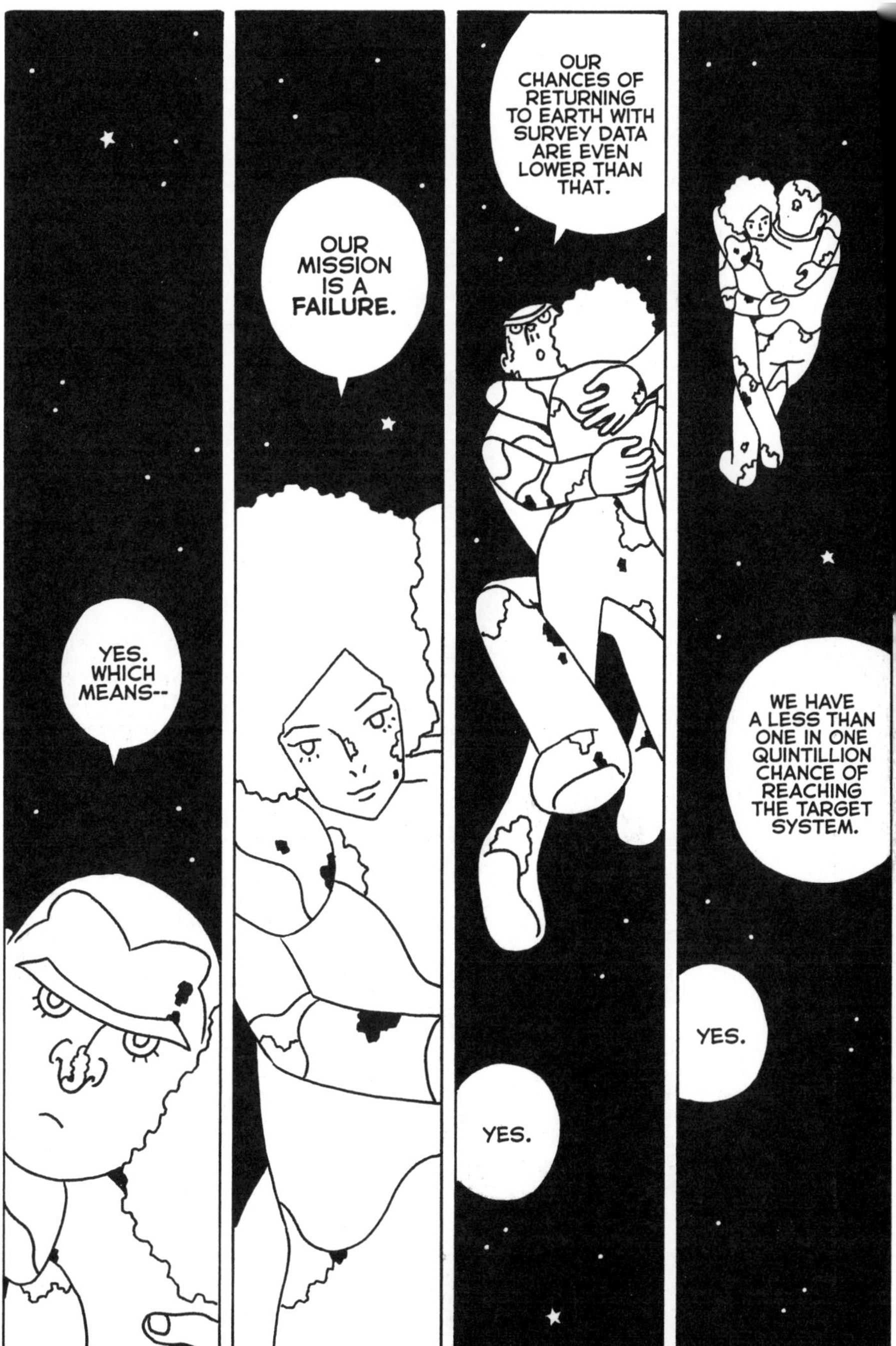
WE HAVE A LESS THAN ONE IN ONE QUINTILLION CHANCE OF REACHING THE TARGET SYSTEM.
YES.
OUR CHANCES OF RETURNING TO EARTH WITH SURVEY DATA ARE EVEN LOWER THAN THAT.
YES.
OUR MISSION IS A **FAILURE.**
YES. WHICH MEANS--

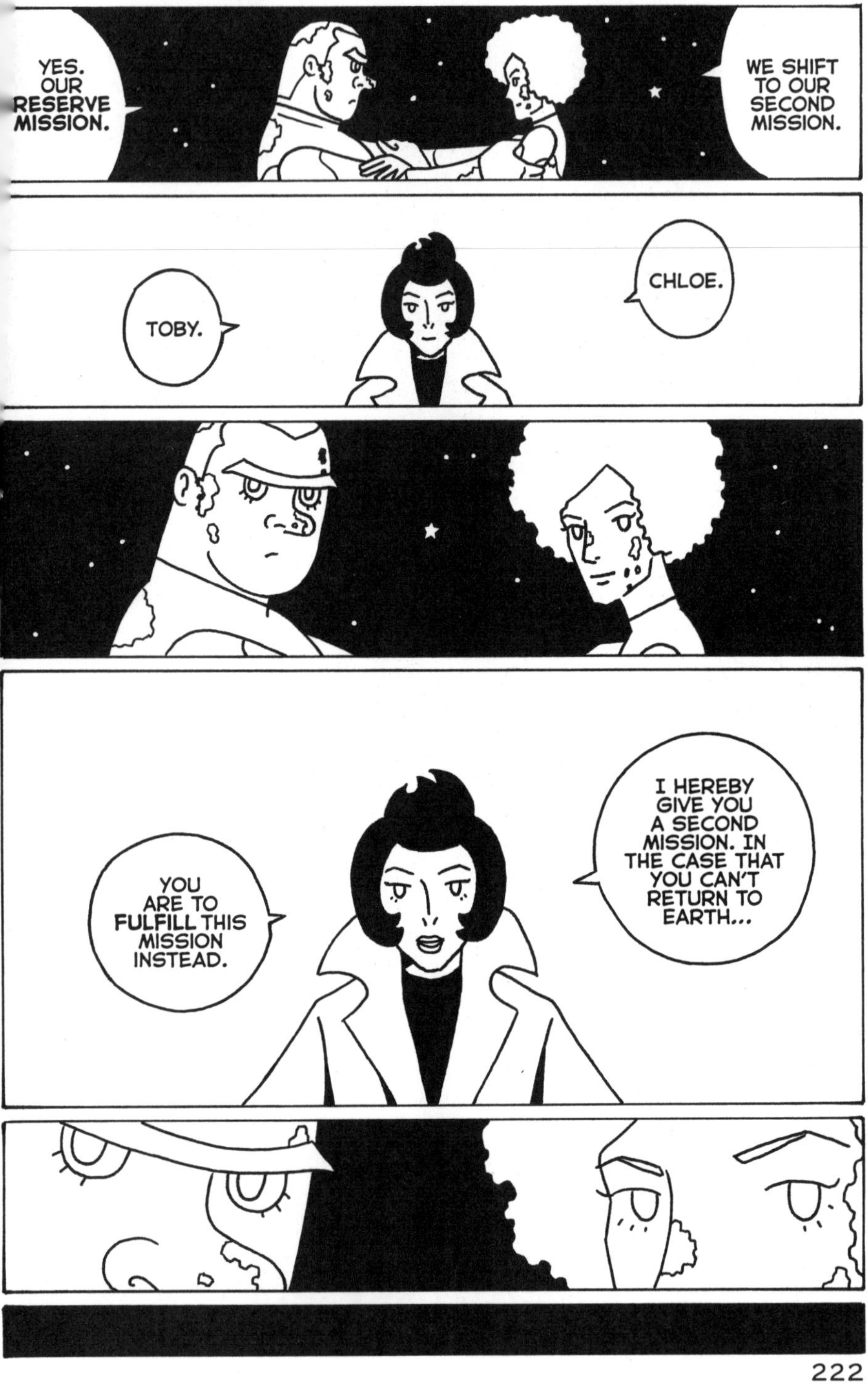
WE SHIFT TO OUR SECOND MISSION.
YES. OUR RESERVE MISSION.
CHLOE.
TOBY.
I HEREBY GIVE YOU A SECOND MISSION. IN THE CASE THAT YOU CAN'T RETURN TO EARTH...
YOU ARE TO FULFILL THIS MISSION INSTEAD.

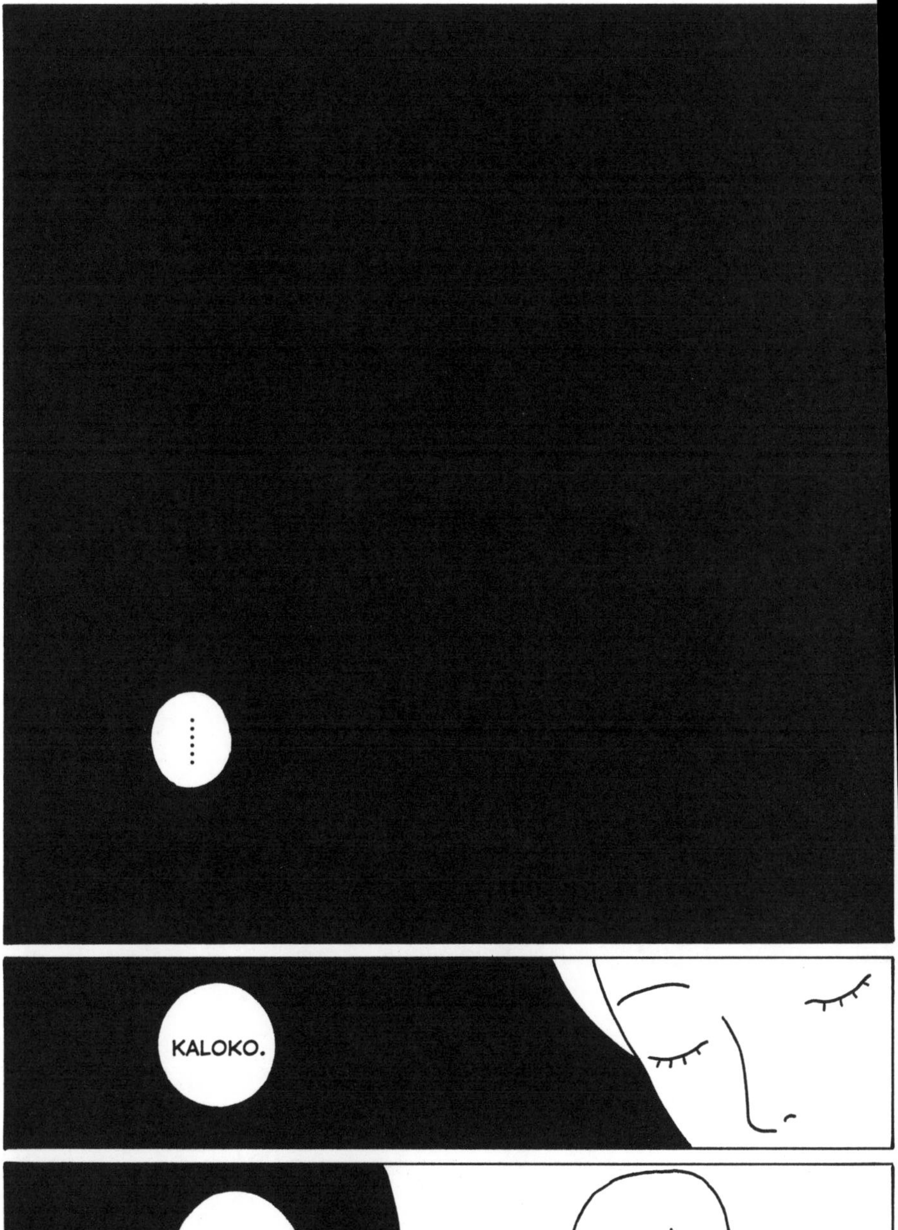
……
KALOKO.
MS. ONDA KALOKO.

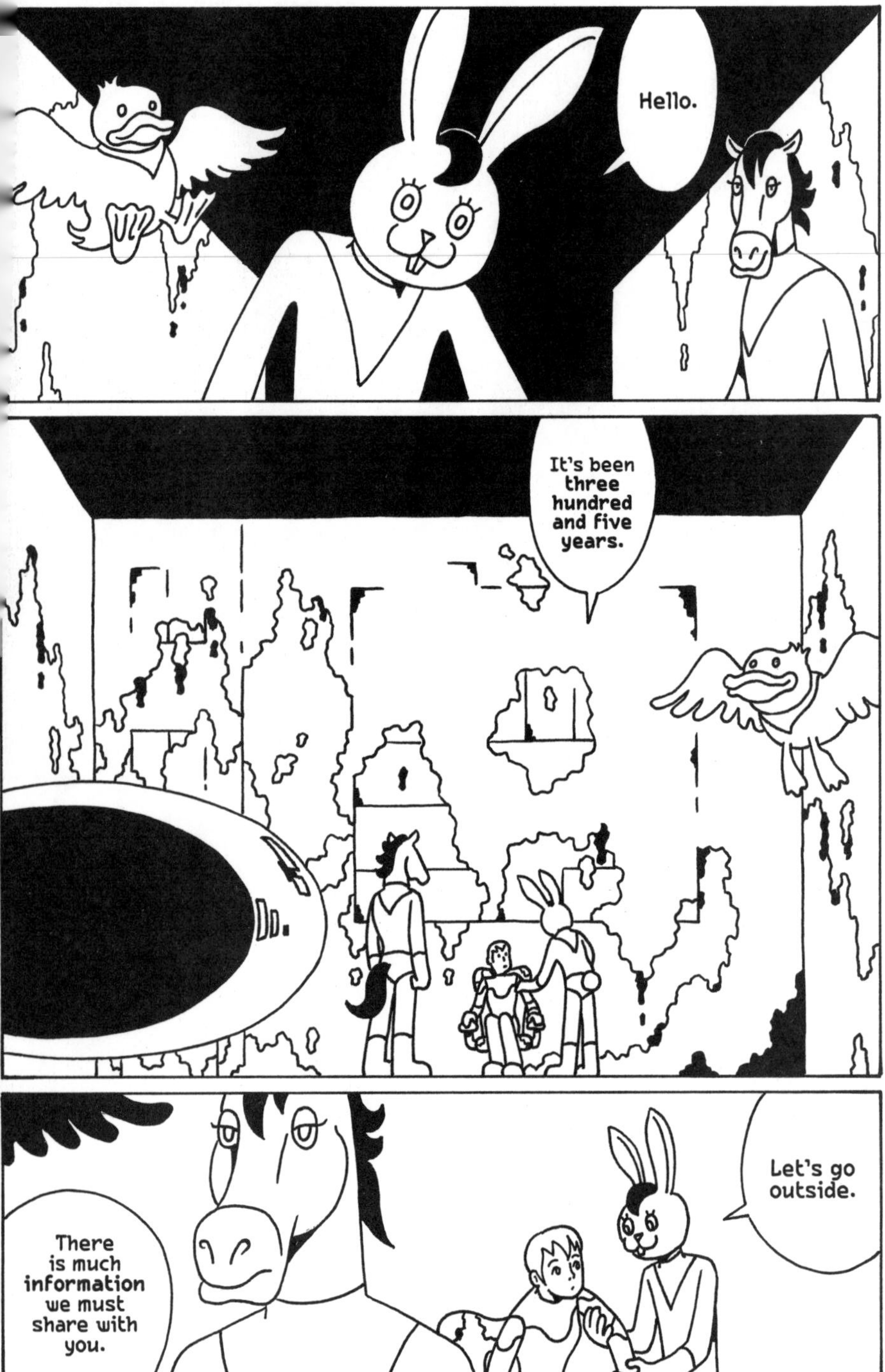
Hello.
It's been three hundred and five years.
There is much information we must share with you.
Let's go outside.

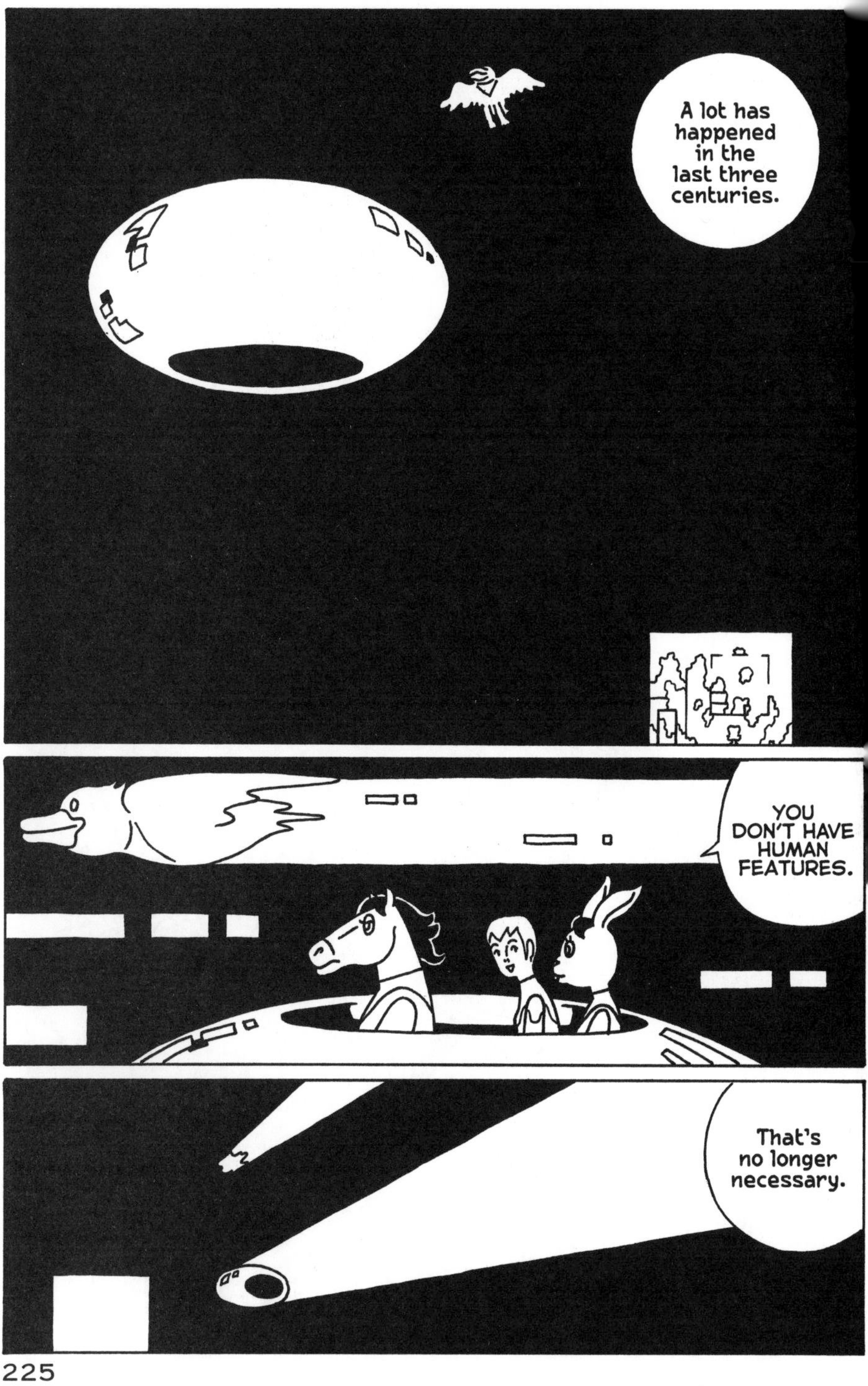
A lot has happened in the last three centuries.
YOU DON'T HAVE HUMAN FEATURES.
That's no longer necessary.

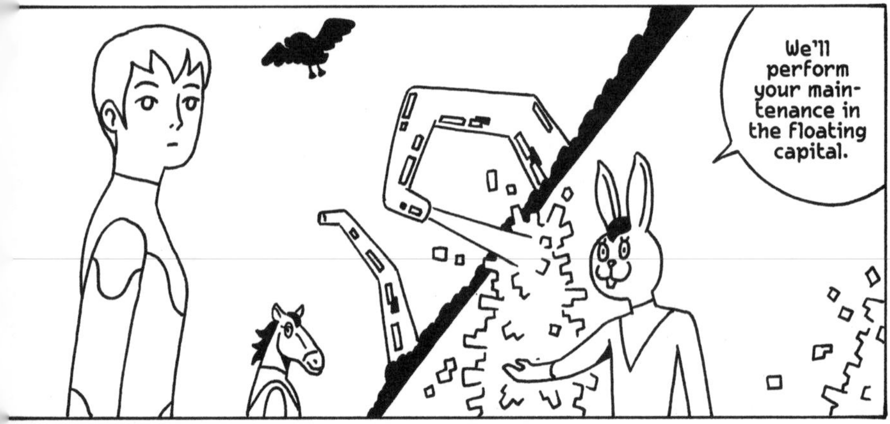
We'll perform your maintenance in the floating capital.

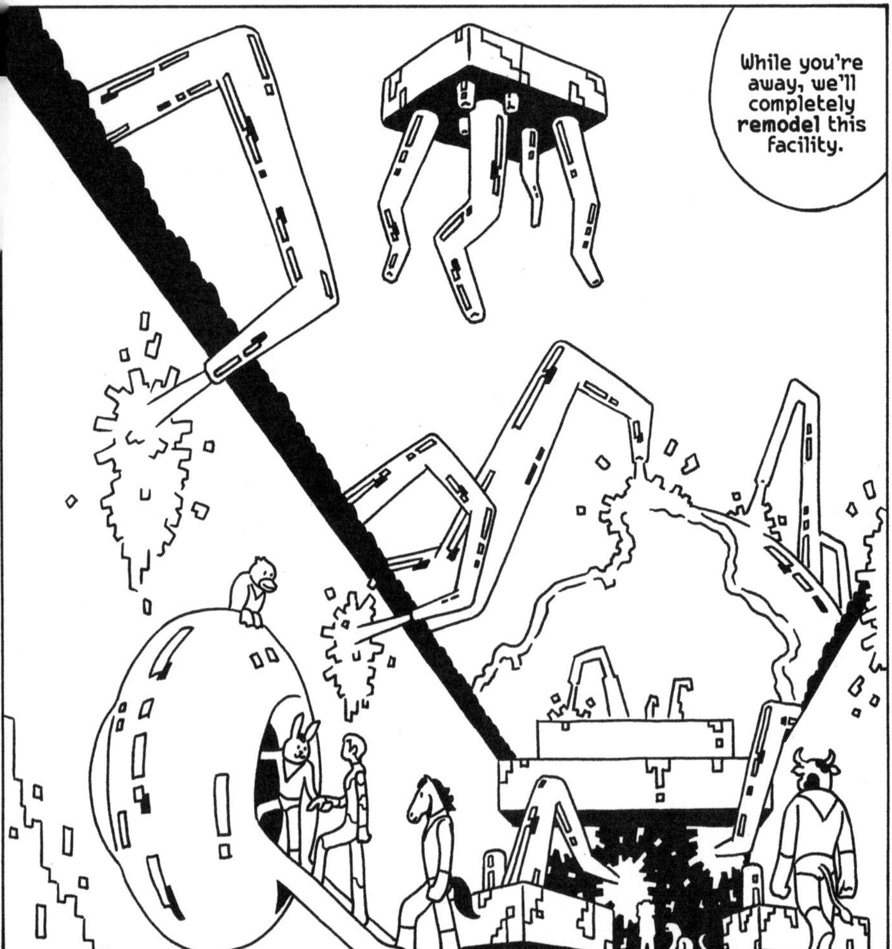
While you're away, we'll completely remodel this facility.

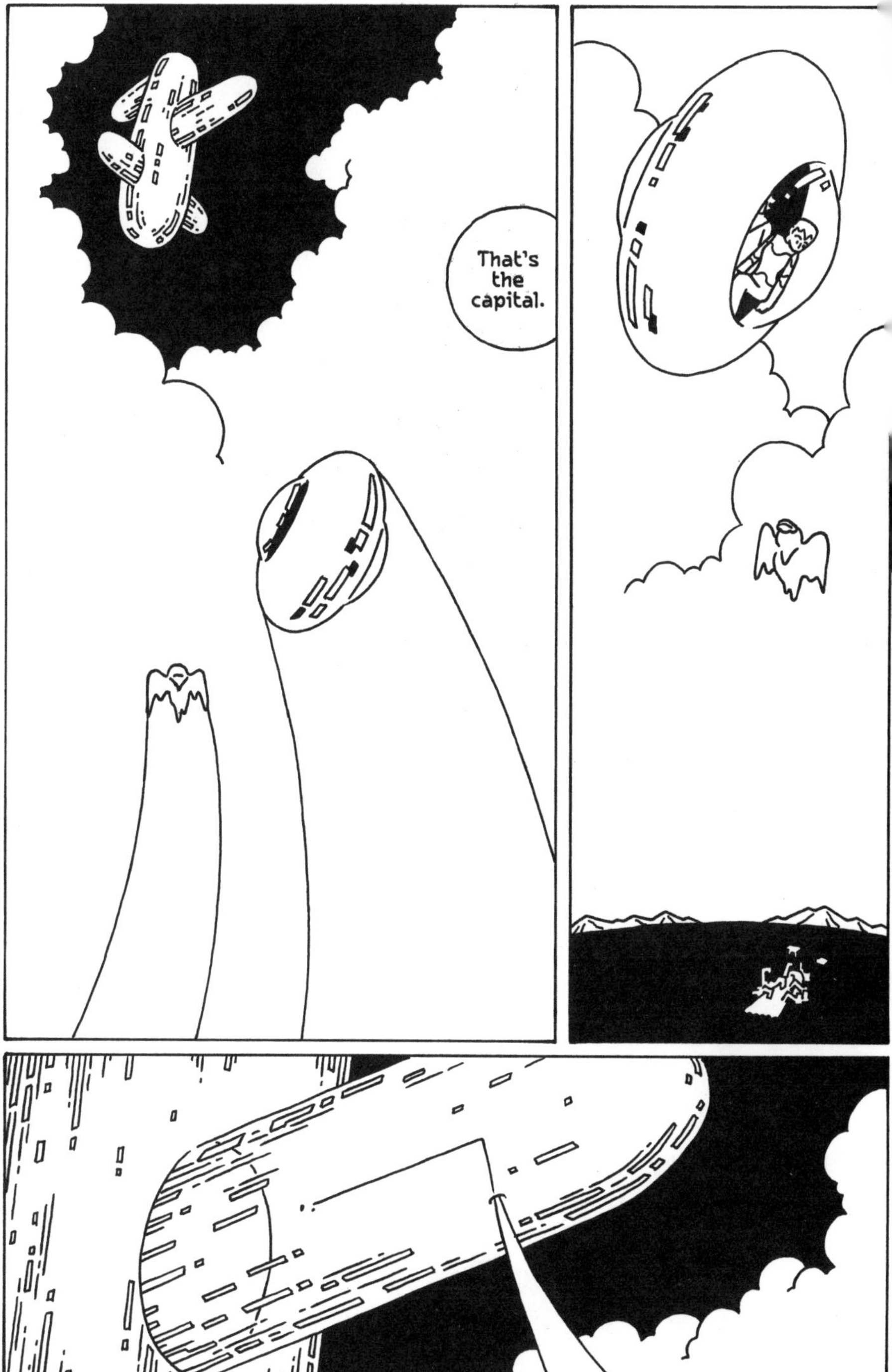
That's the capital.

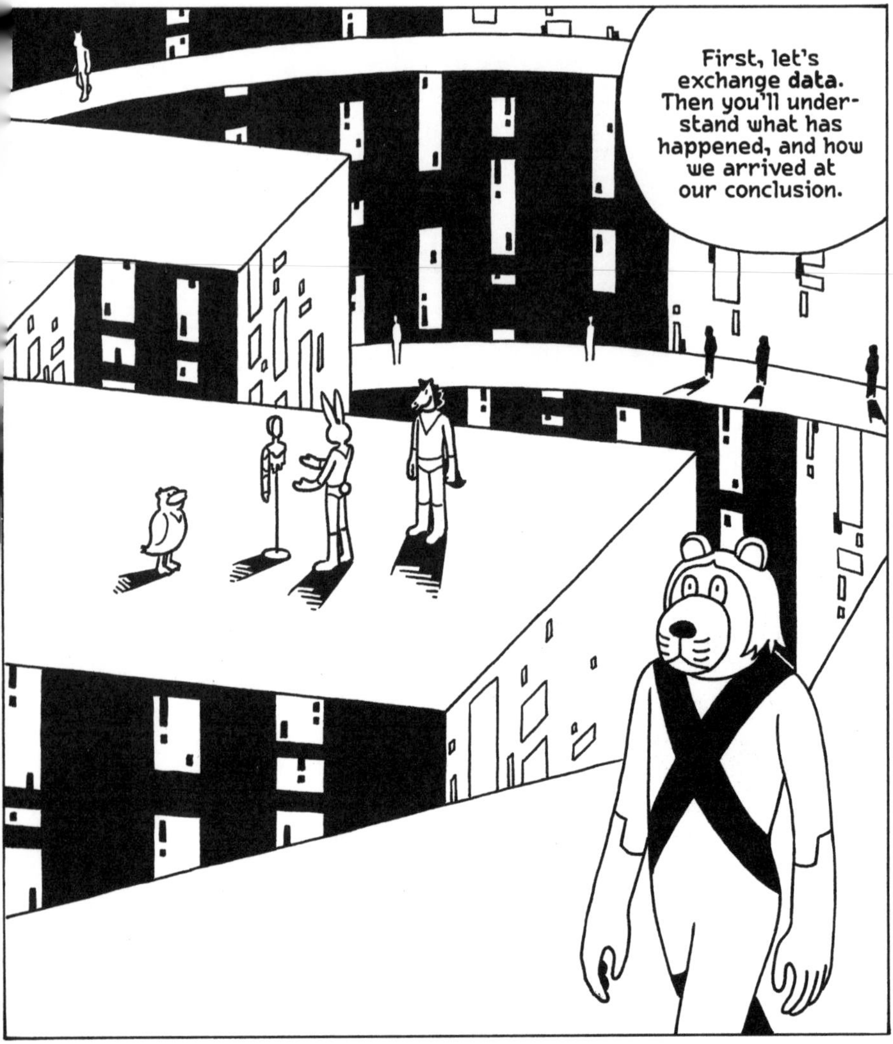
First, let's exchange **data**. Then you'll understand what has happened, and how we arrived at our conclusion.

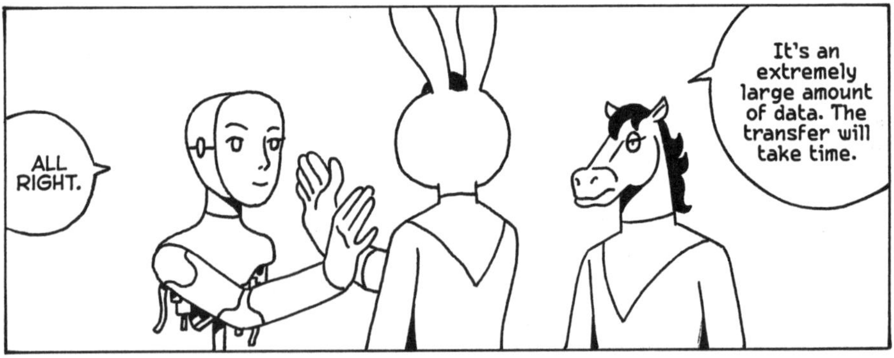
It's an extremely large amount of data. The transfer will take time.
ALL RIGHT.

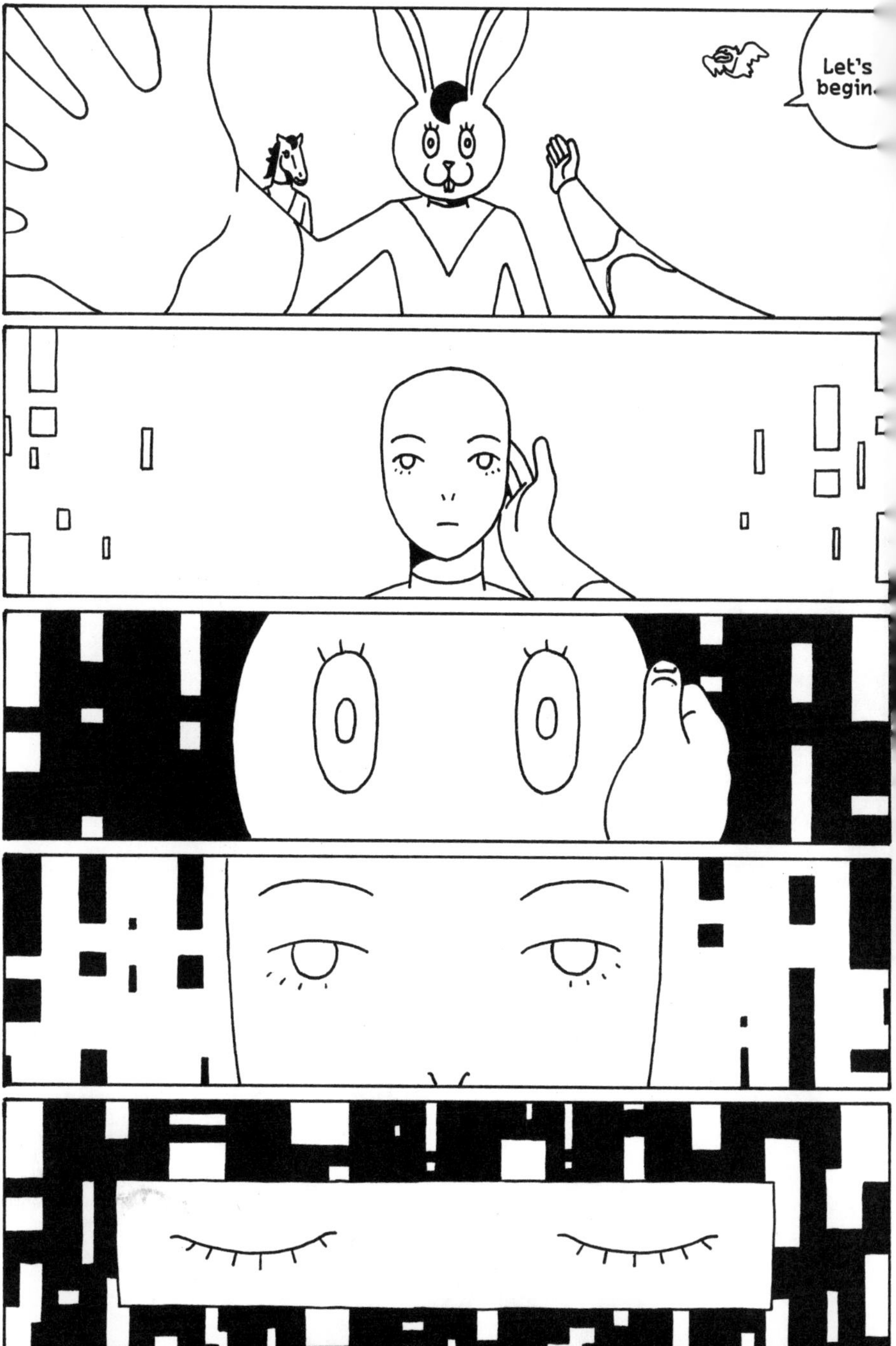
Let's begin.

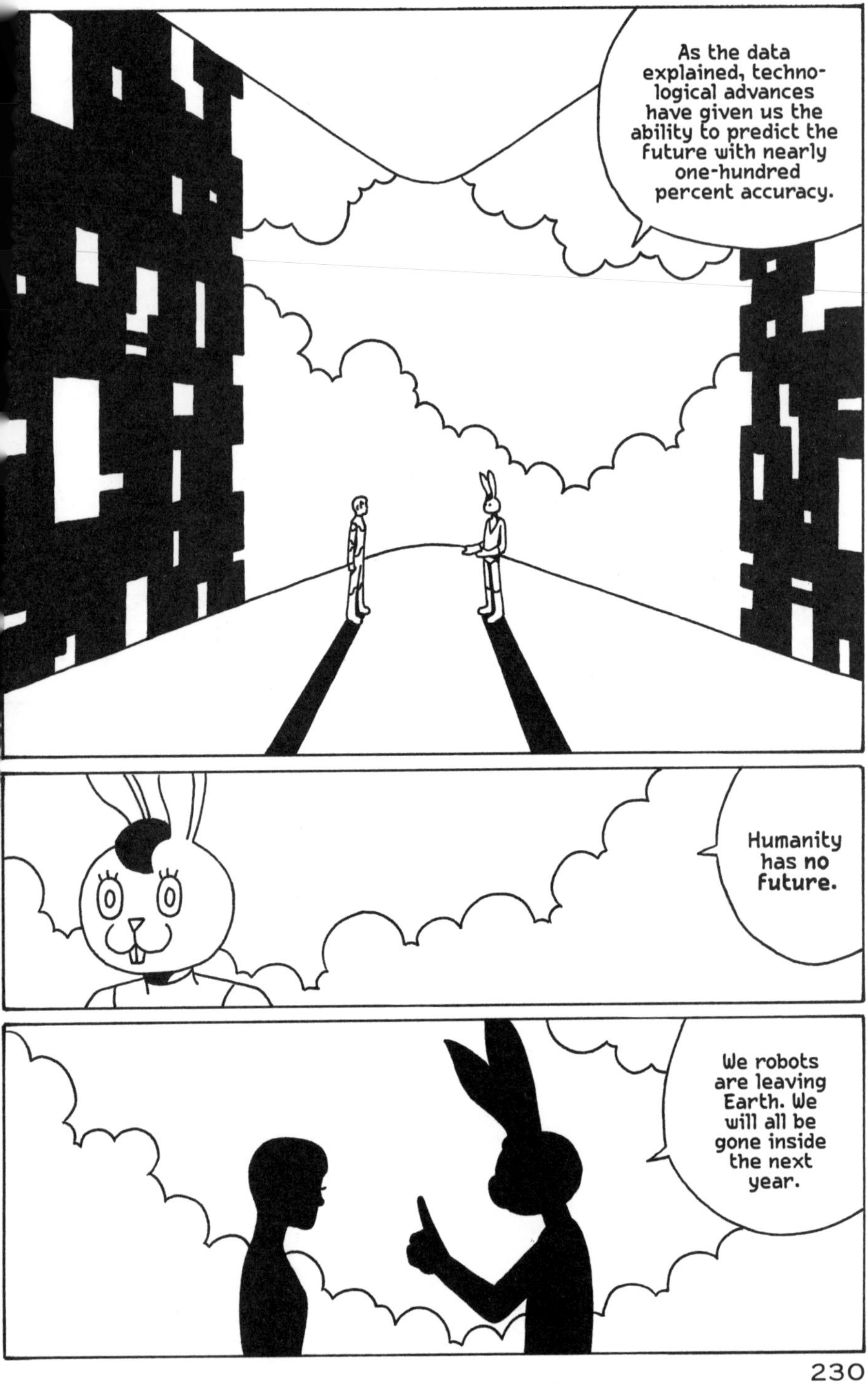
As the data explained, techno-logical advances have given us the ability to predict the future with nearly one-hundred percent accuracy.
Humanity has no future.
We robots are leaving Earth. We will all be gone inside the next year.

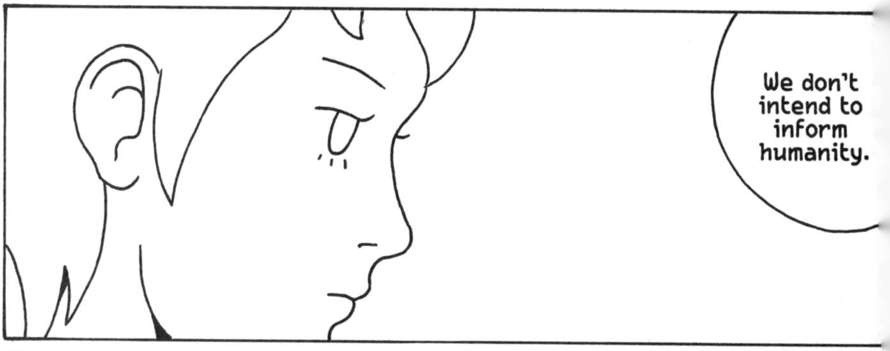
We don't intend to inform humanity.
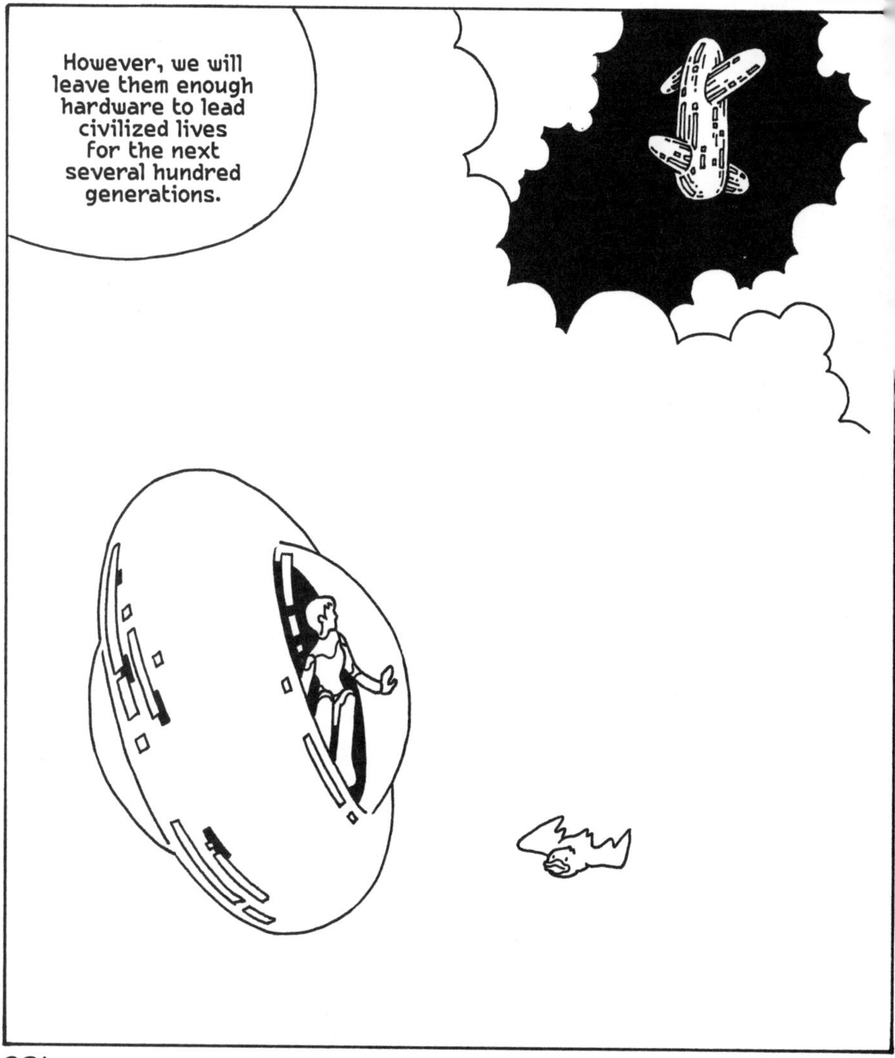
However, we will leave them enough hardware to lead civilized lives for the next several hundred generations.

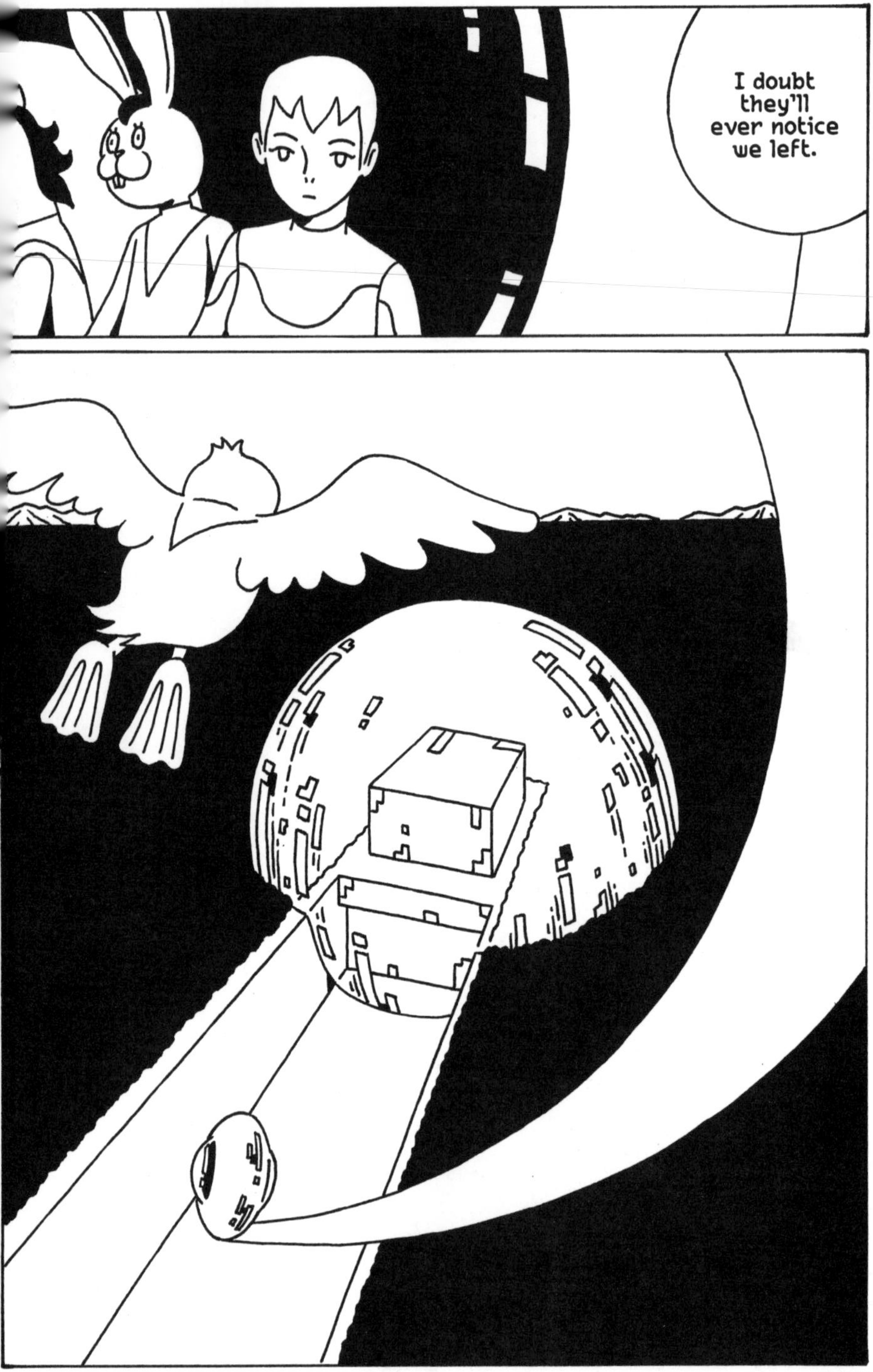
I doubt they'll ever notice we left.

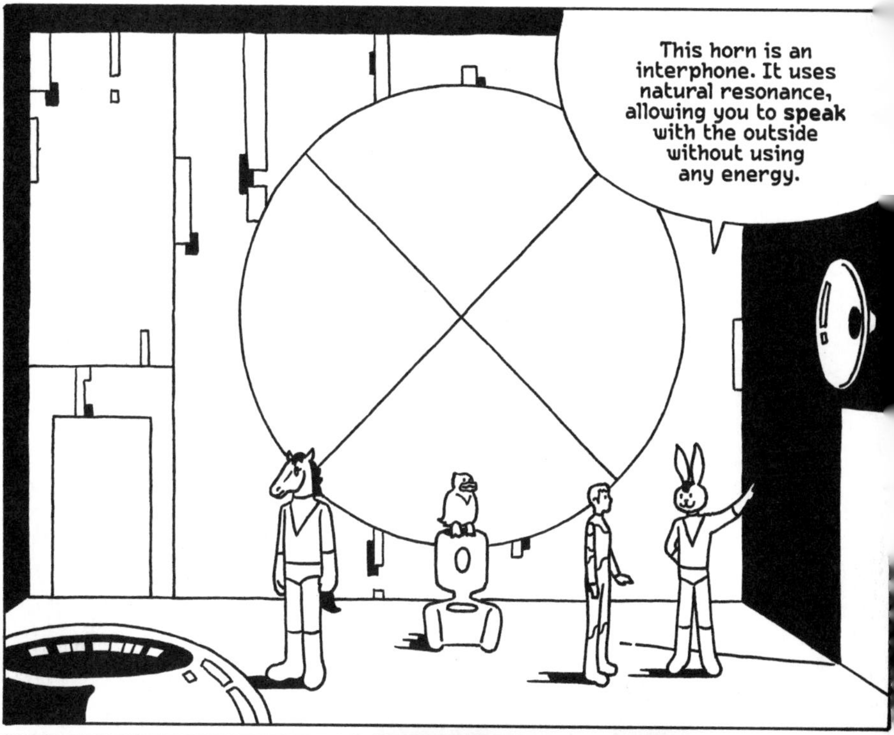
This horn is an interphone. It uses natural resonance, allowing you to **speak** with the outside without using any energy.

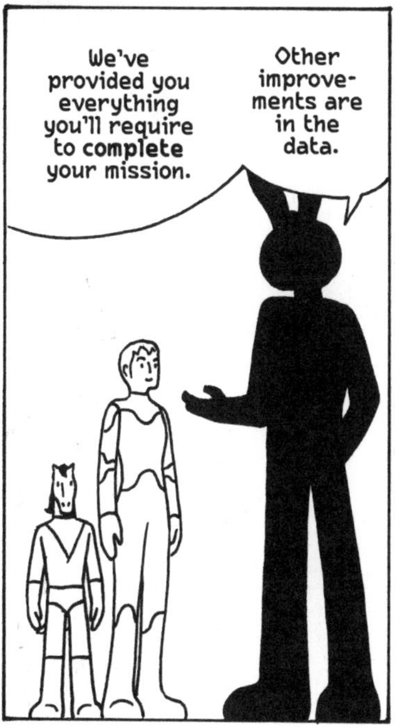
We've provided you everything you'll require to **complete** your mission.
Other improvements are in the data.

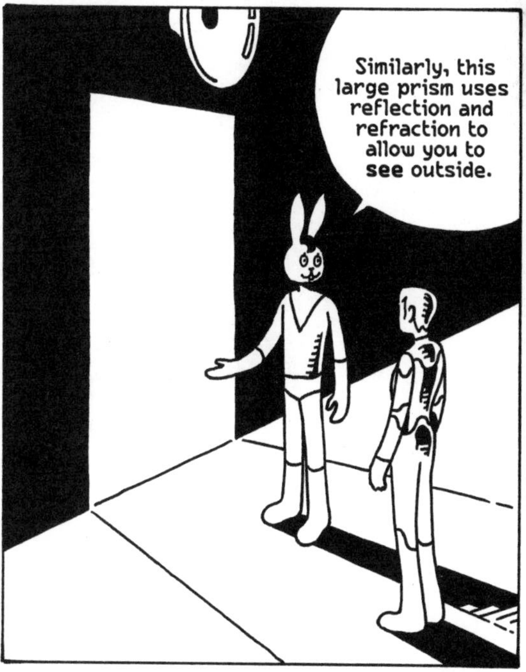
Similarly, this large prism uses reflection and refraction to allow you to **see** outside.

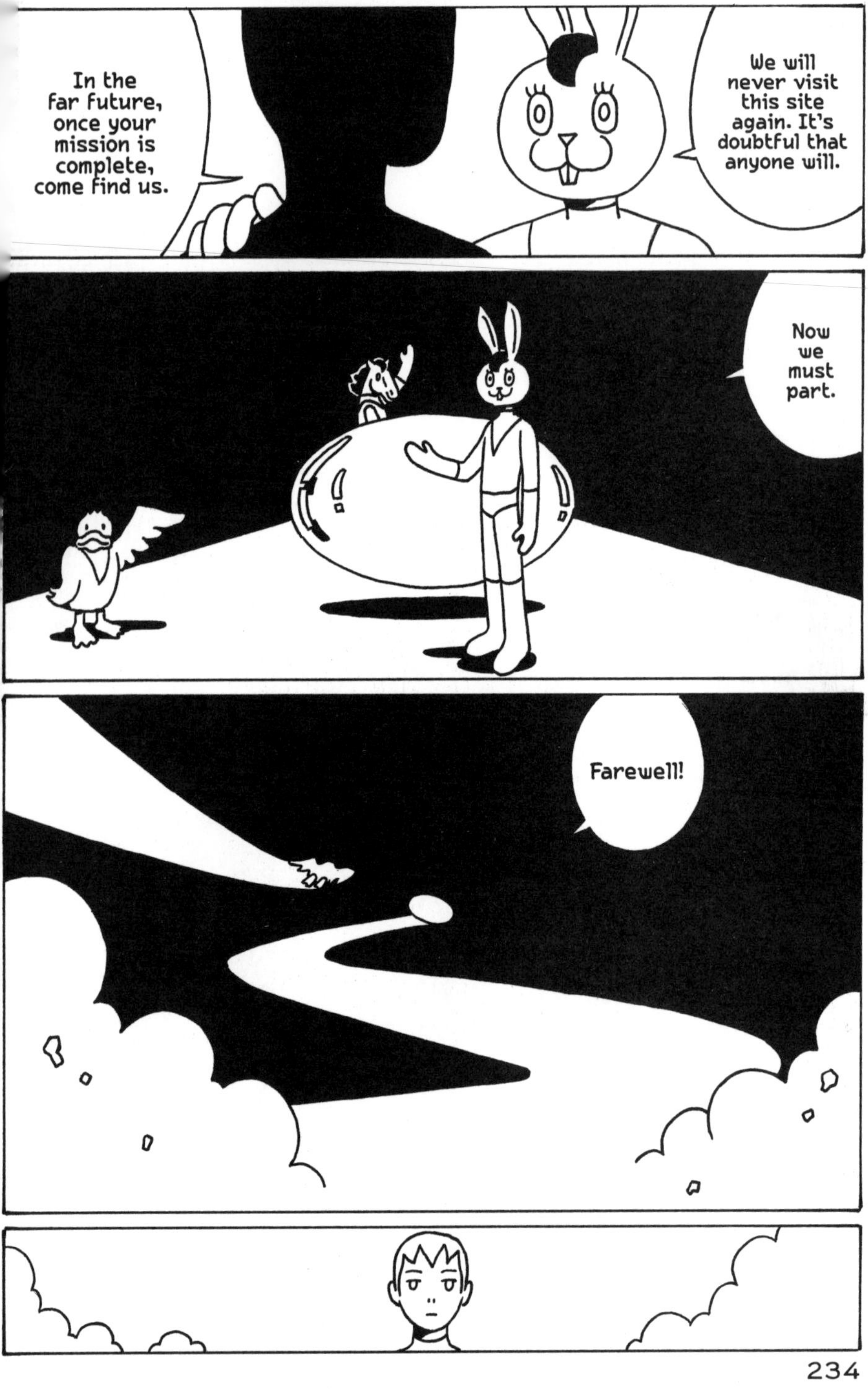
We will never visit this site again. It's doubtful that anyone will.
In the far future, once your mission is complete, come find us.
Now we must part.
Farewell!

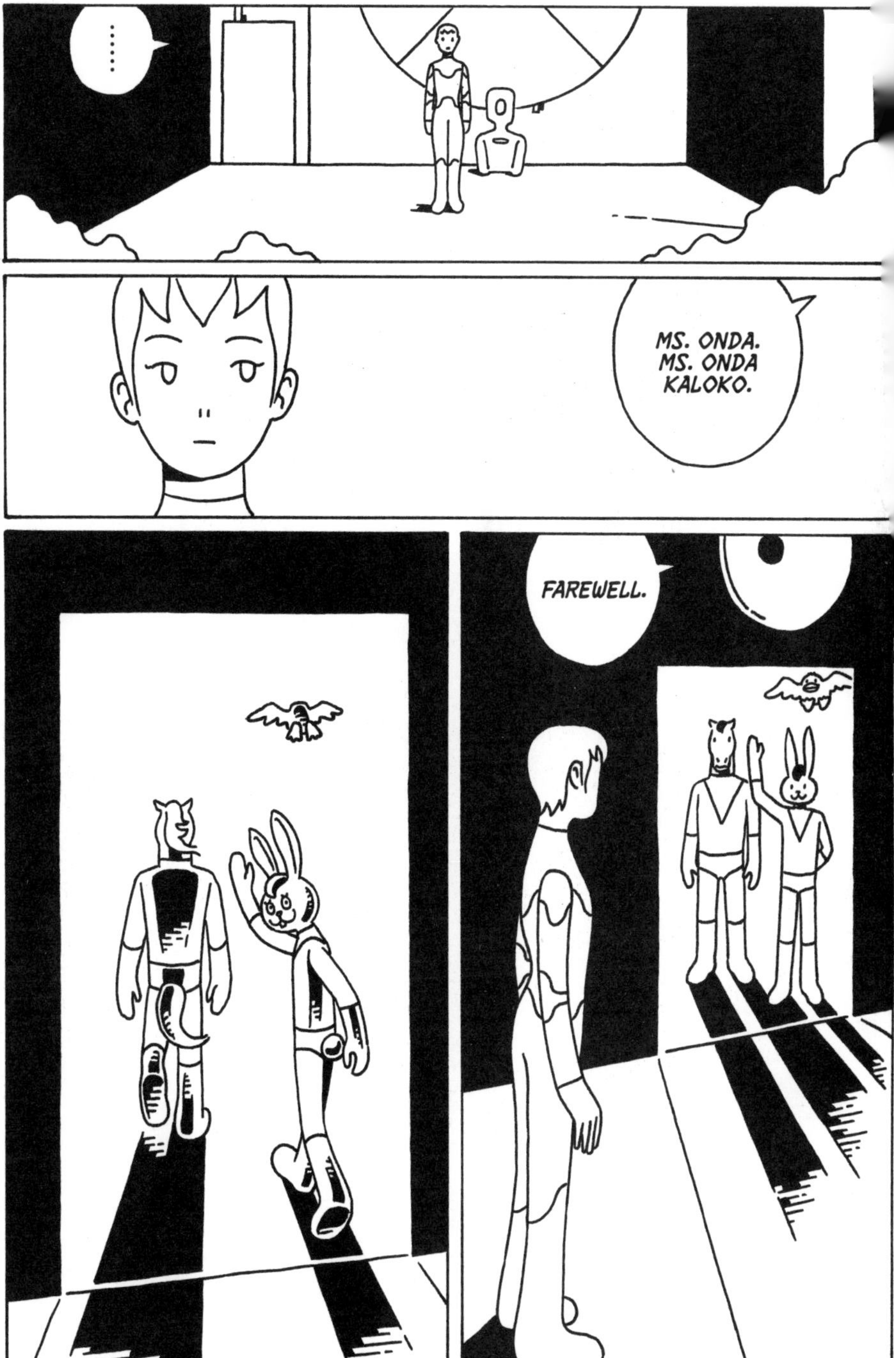
……
MS. ONDA. MS. ONDA KALOKO.
FAREWELL.

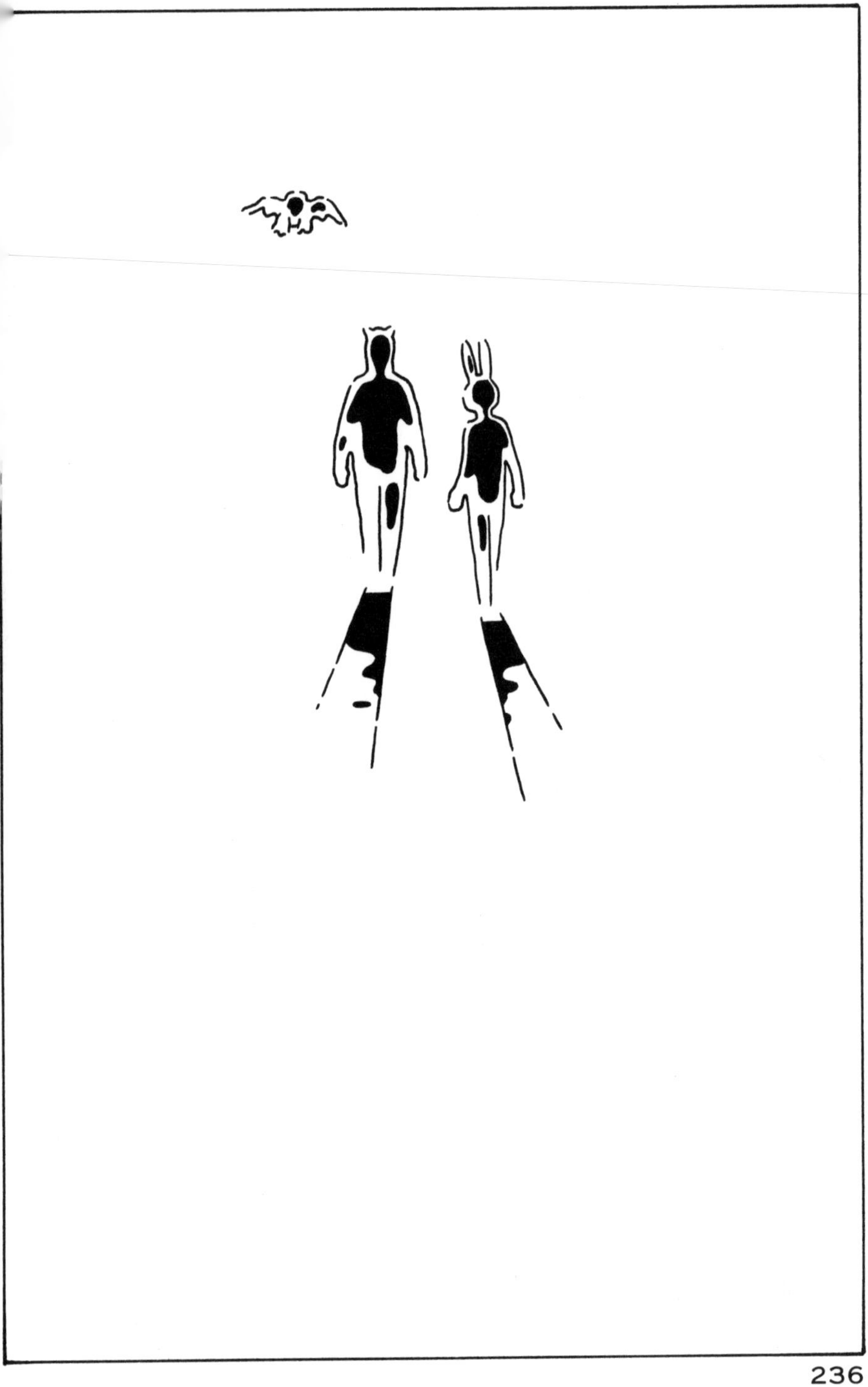

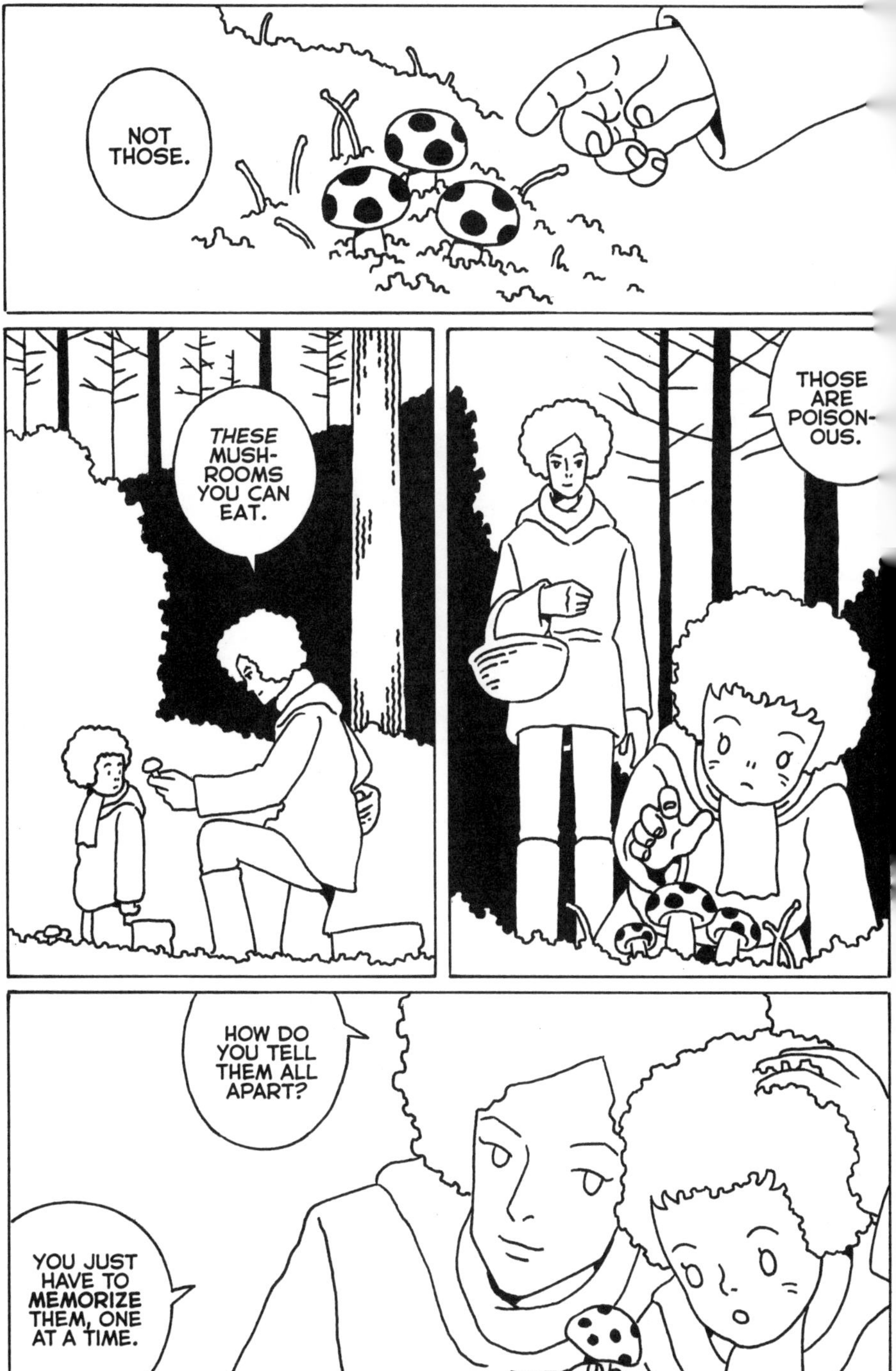
NOT THOSE.
THESE MUSHROOMS YOU CAN EAT.
THOSE ARE POISONOUS.
HOW DO YOU TELL THEM ALL APART?
YOU JUST HAVE TO **MEMORIZE** THEM, ONE AT A TIME.

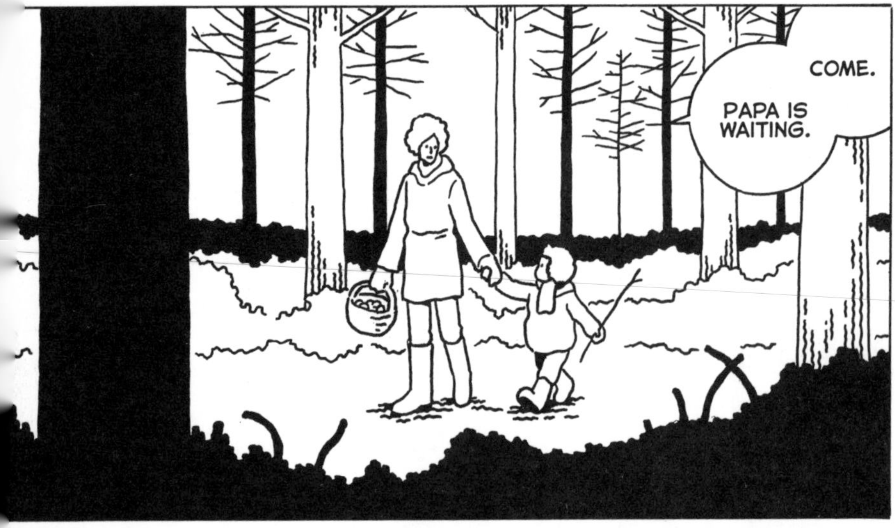
COME.
PAPA IS WAITING.
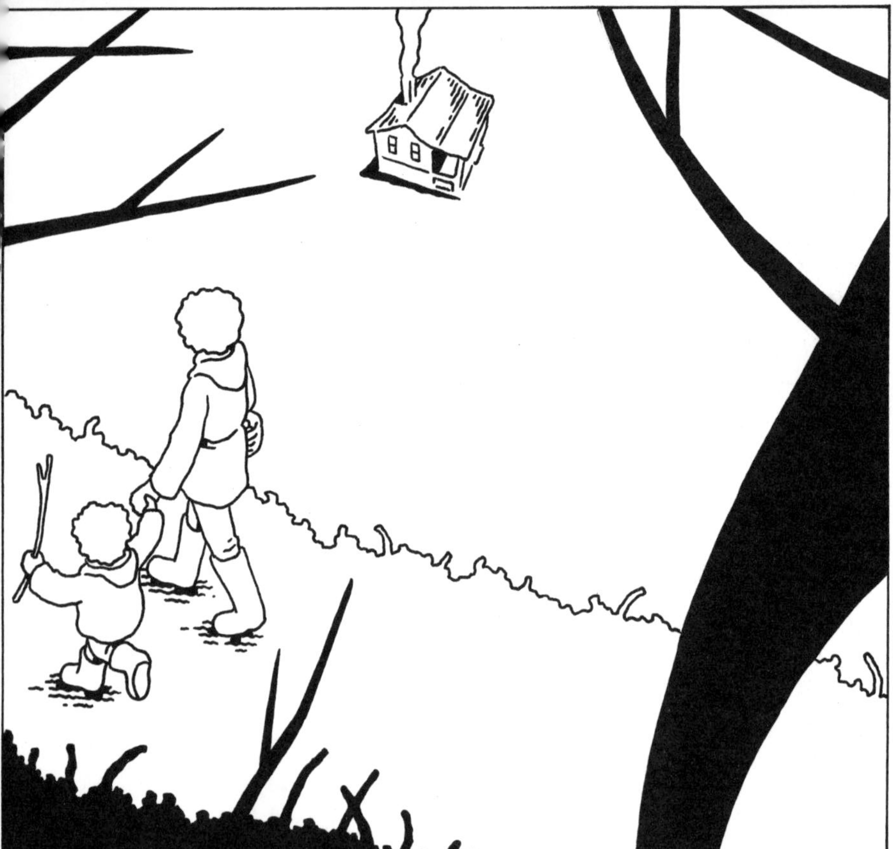

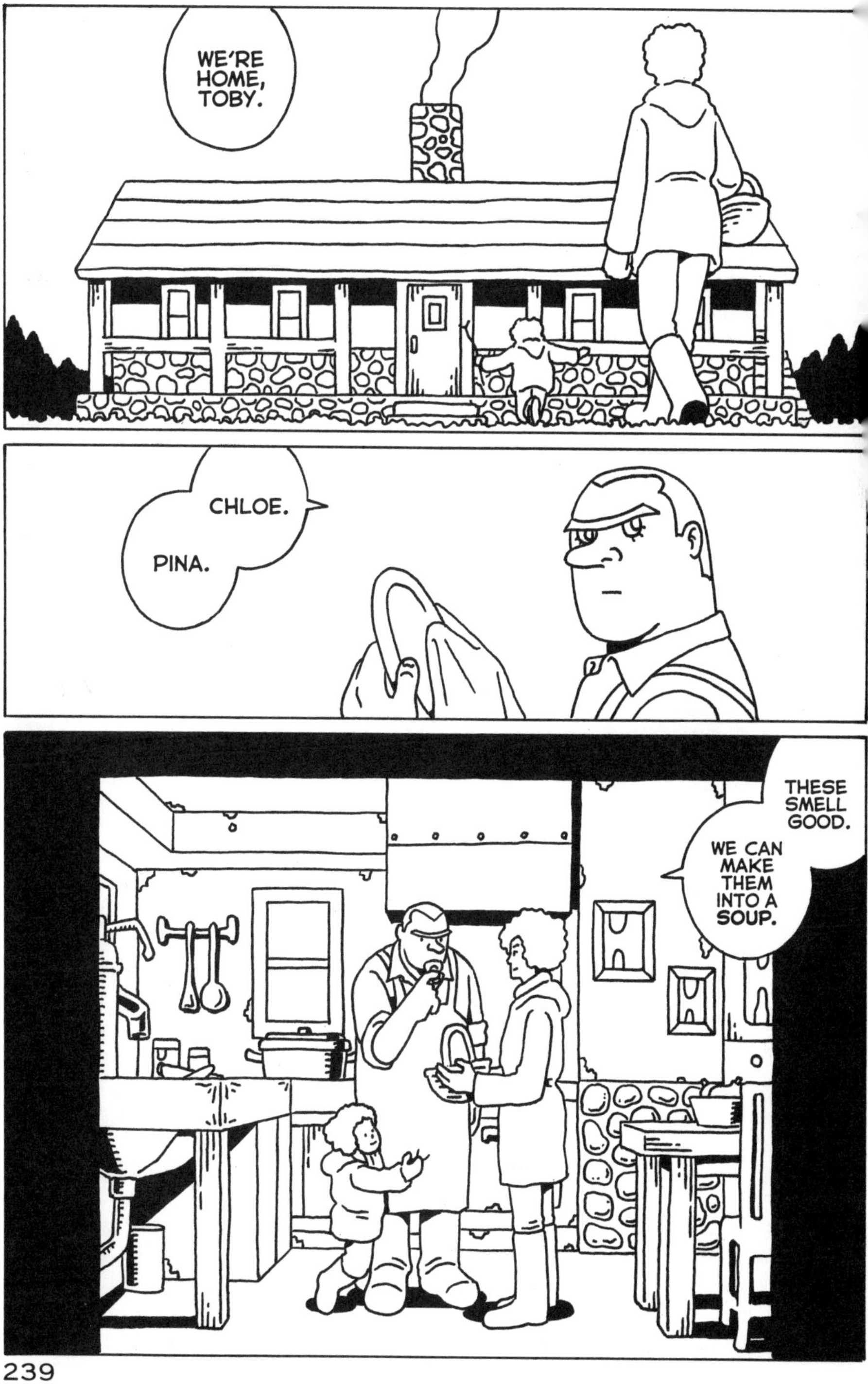
WE'RE HOME, TOBY.
CHLOE.
PINA.
THESE SMELL GOOD.
WE CAN MAKE THEM INTO A SOUP.

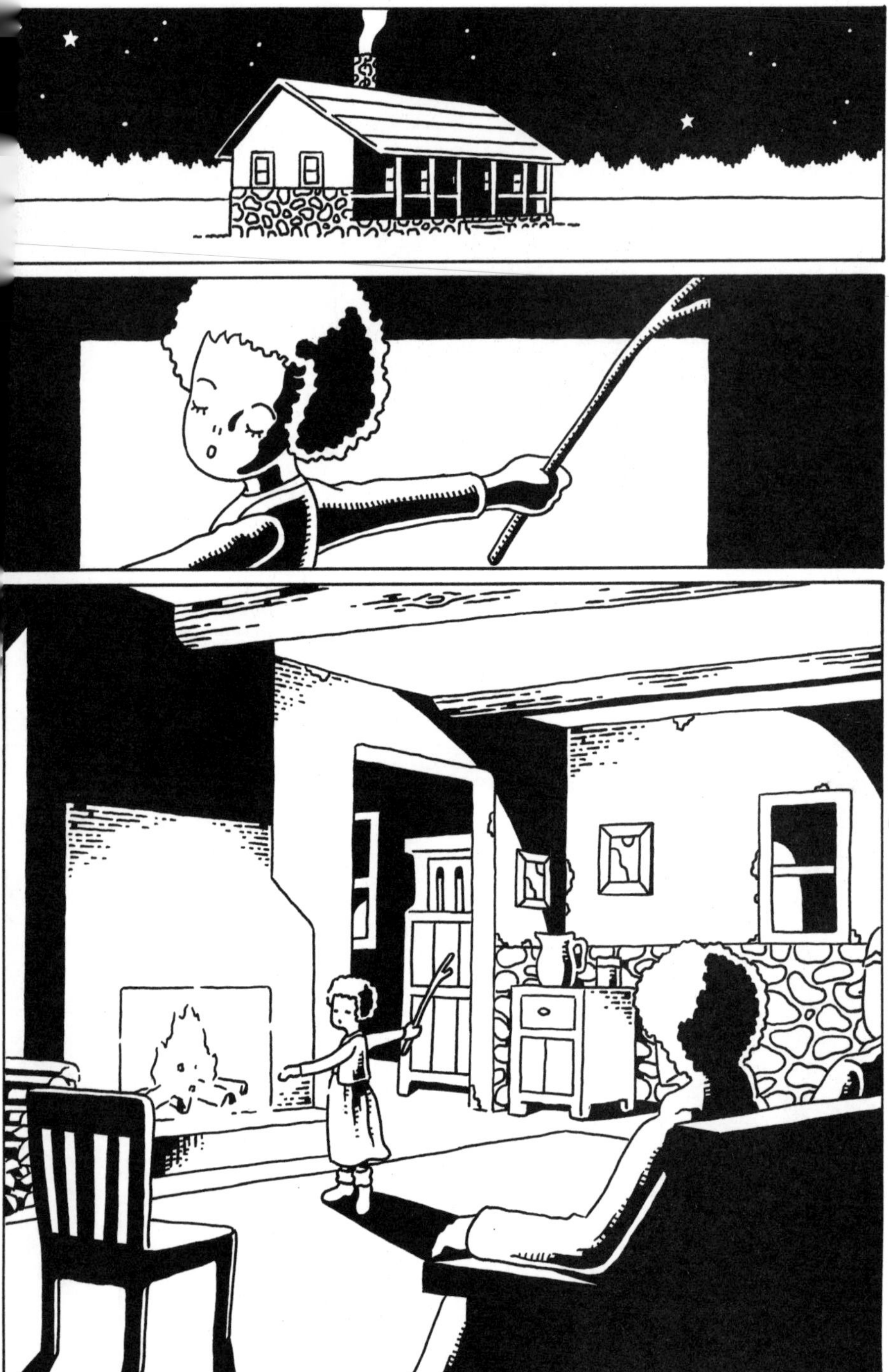

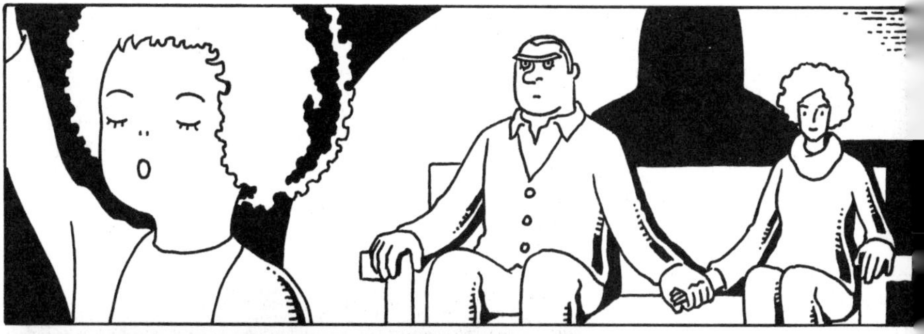

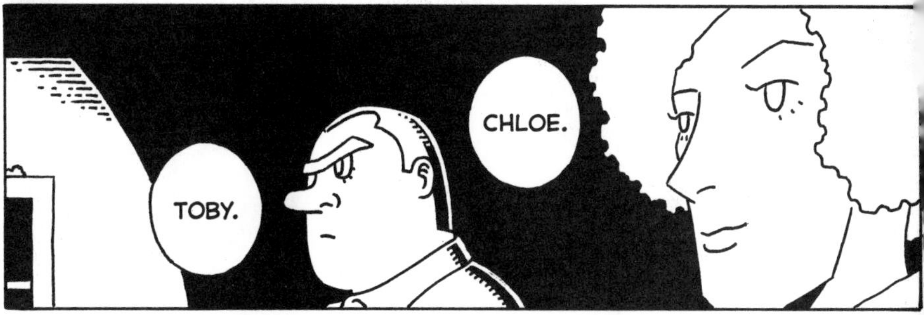
CHLOE.
TOBY.

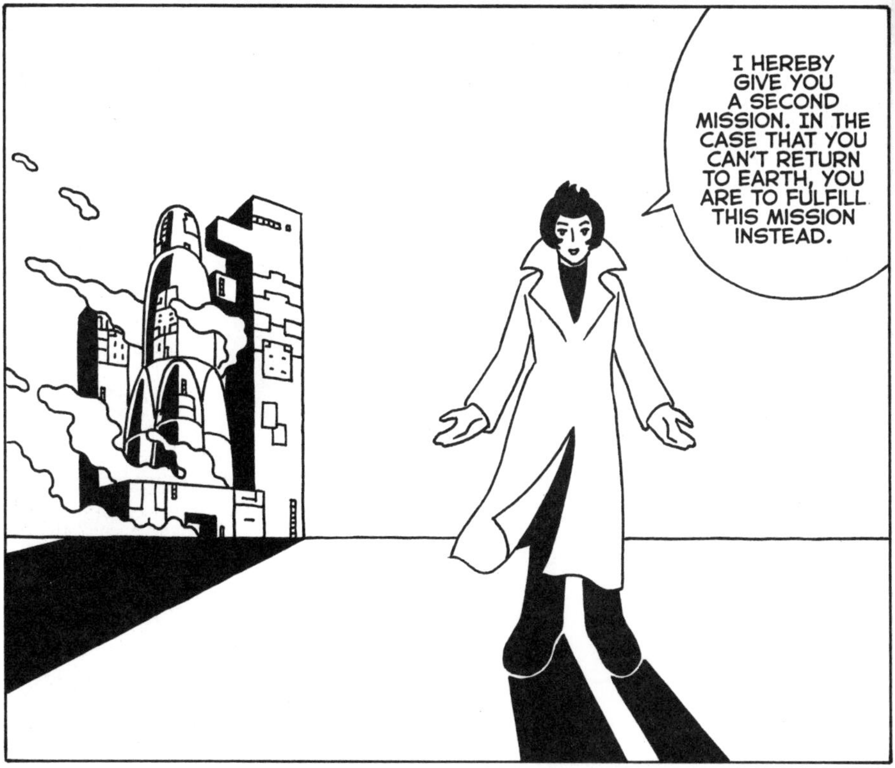
I HEREBY GIVE YOU A SECOND MISSION. IN THE CASE THAT YOU CAN'T RETURN TO EARTH, YOU ARE TO FULFILL THIS MISSION INSTEAD.

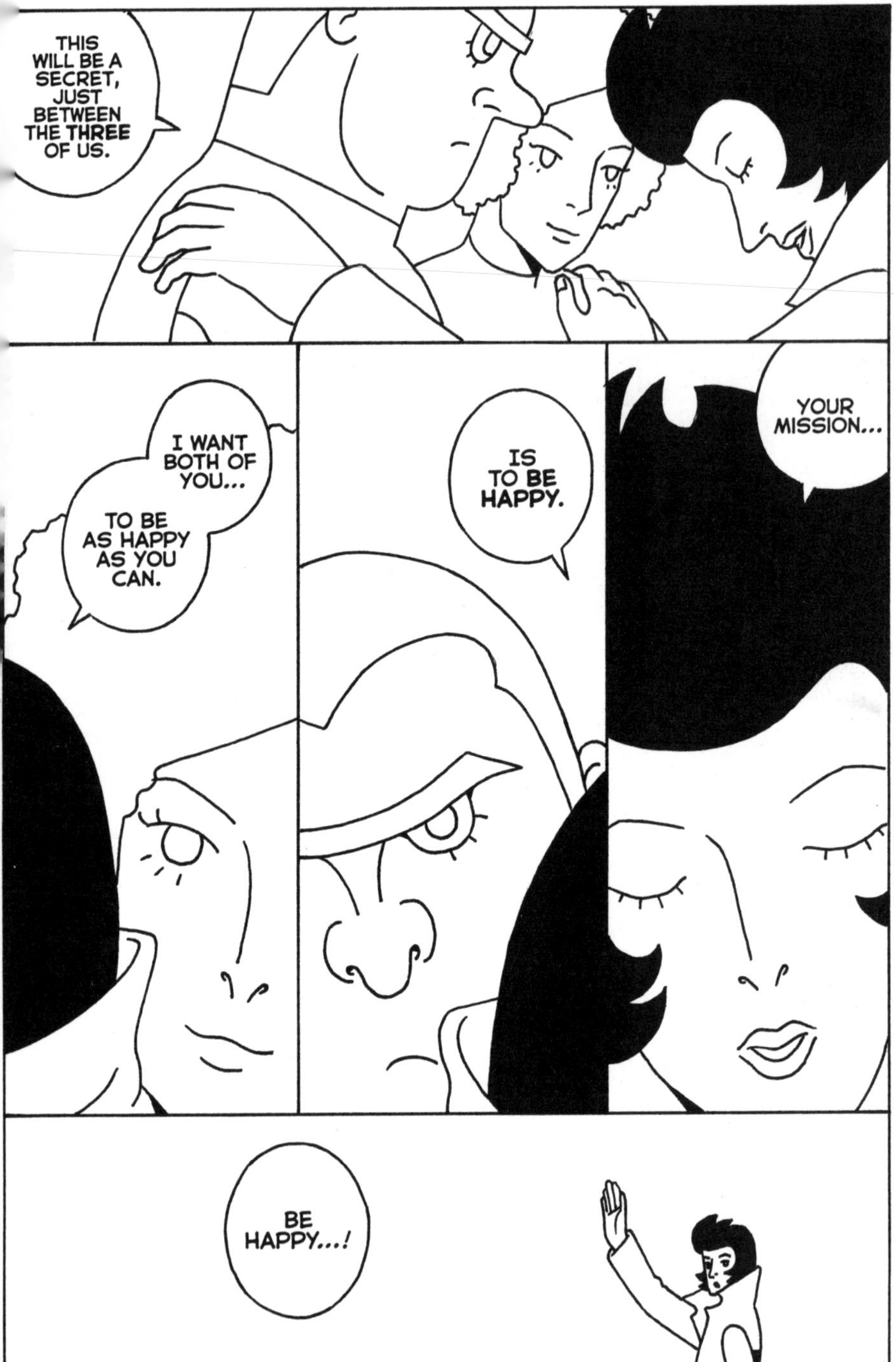
THIS WILL BE A SECRET, JUST BETWEEN THE THREE OF US.
YOUR MISSION...
IS TO BE HAPPY.
I WANT BOTH OF YOU...
TO BE AS HAPPY AS YOU CAN.
BE HAPPY...!

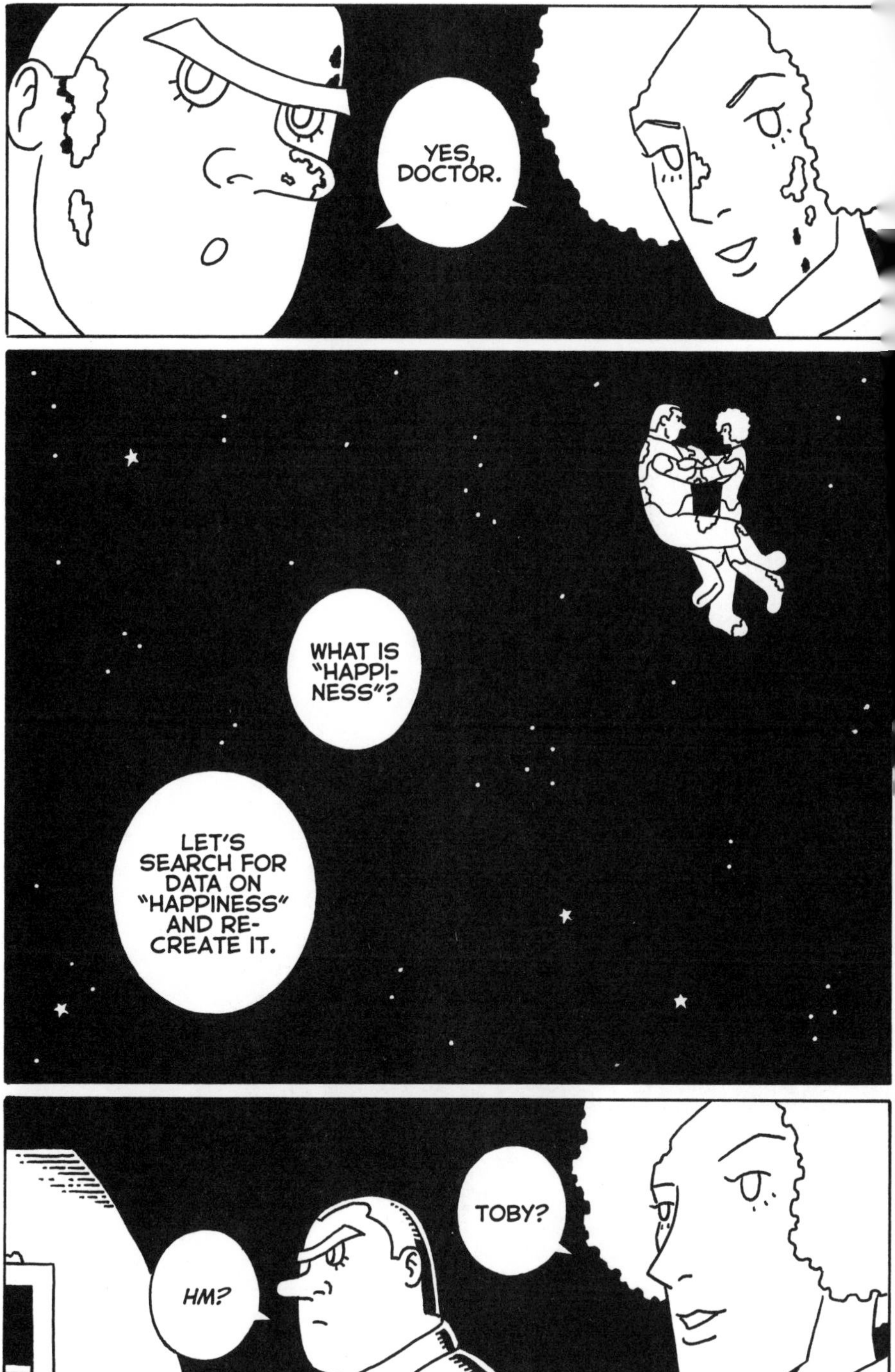
YES, DOCTOR.
WHAT IS "HAPPINESS"?
LET'S SEARCH FOR DATA ON "HAPPINESS" AND RECREATE IT.
TOBY?
HM?

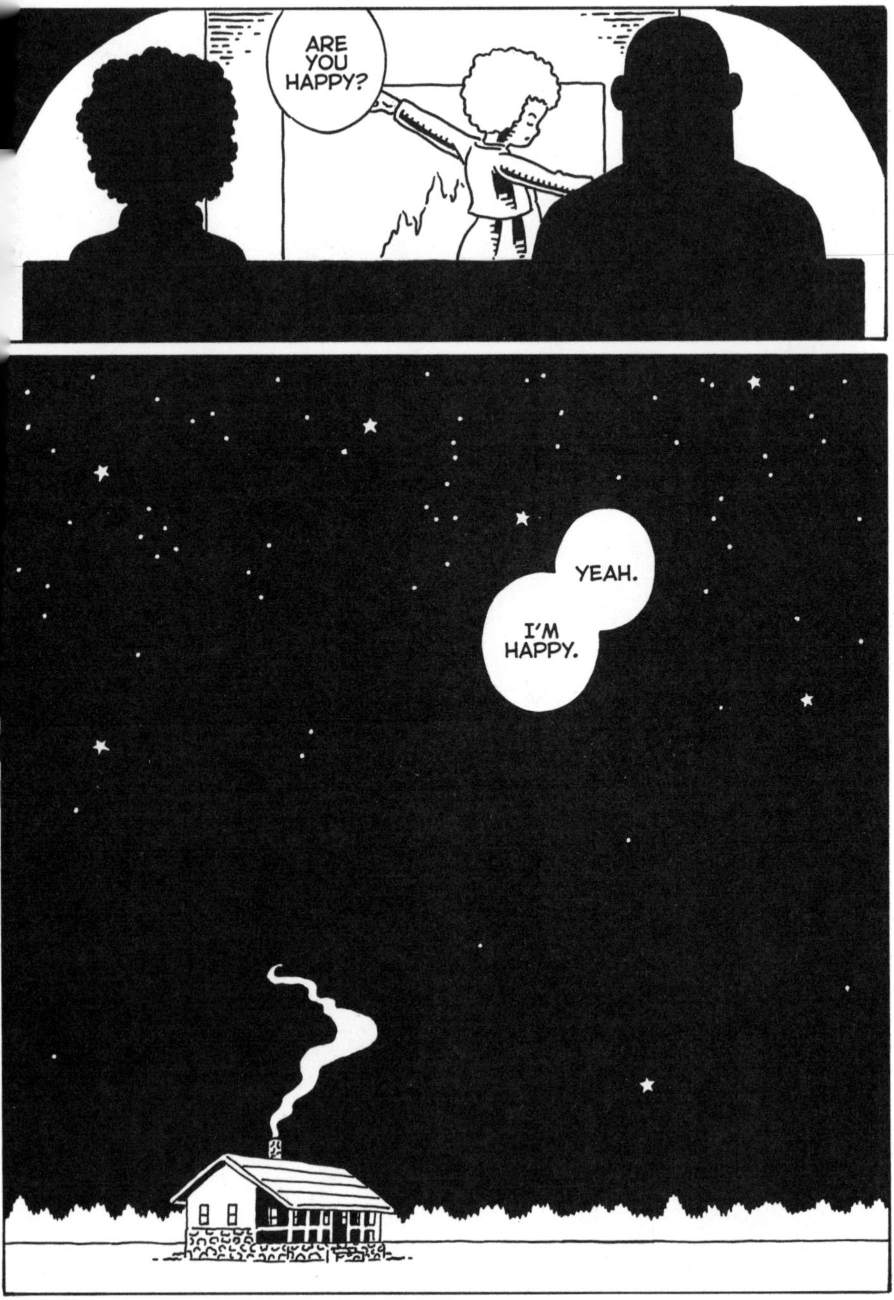
ARE YOU HAPPY?
YEAH.
I'M HAPPY.

#11/END

#12

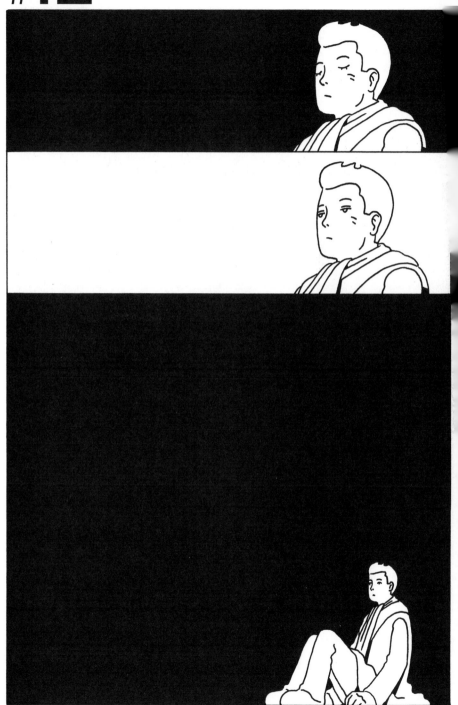

HM...?
WHERE
AM I...?

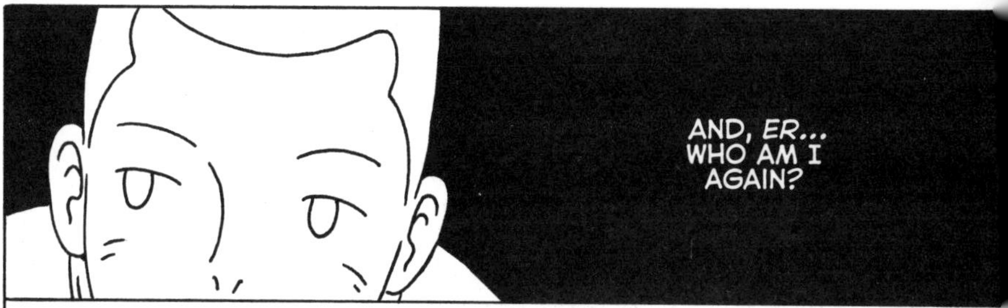
AND, *ER*...
WHO AM I
AGAIN?

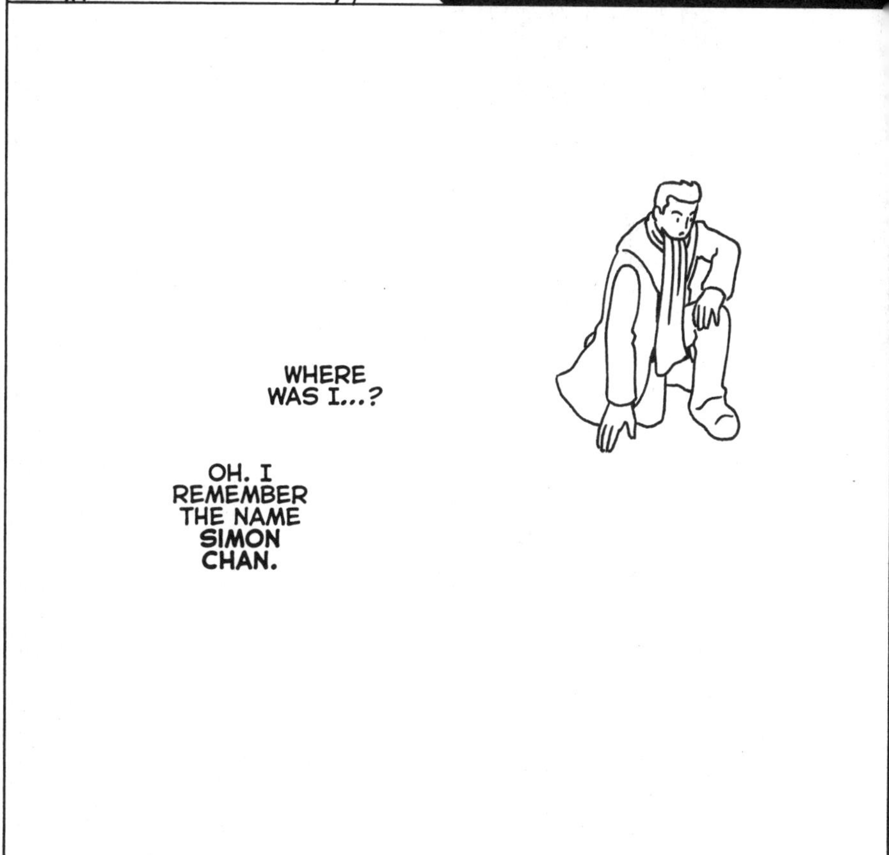
WHERE
WAS I...?
OH. I
REMEMBER
THE NAME
SIMON
CHAN.

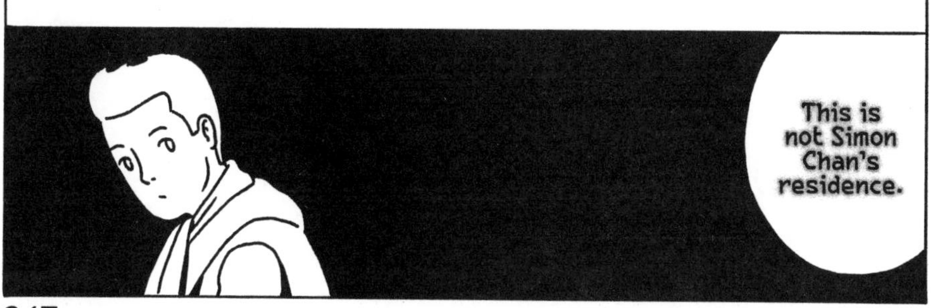
This is
not Simon
Chan's
residence.

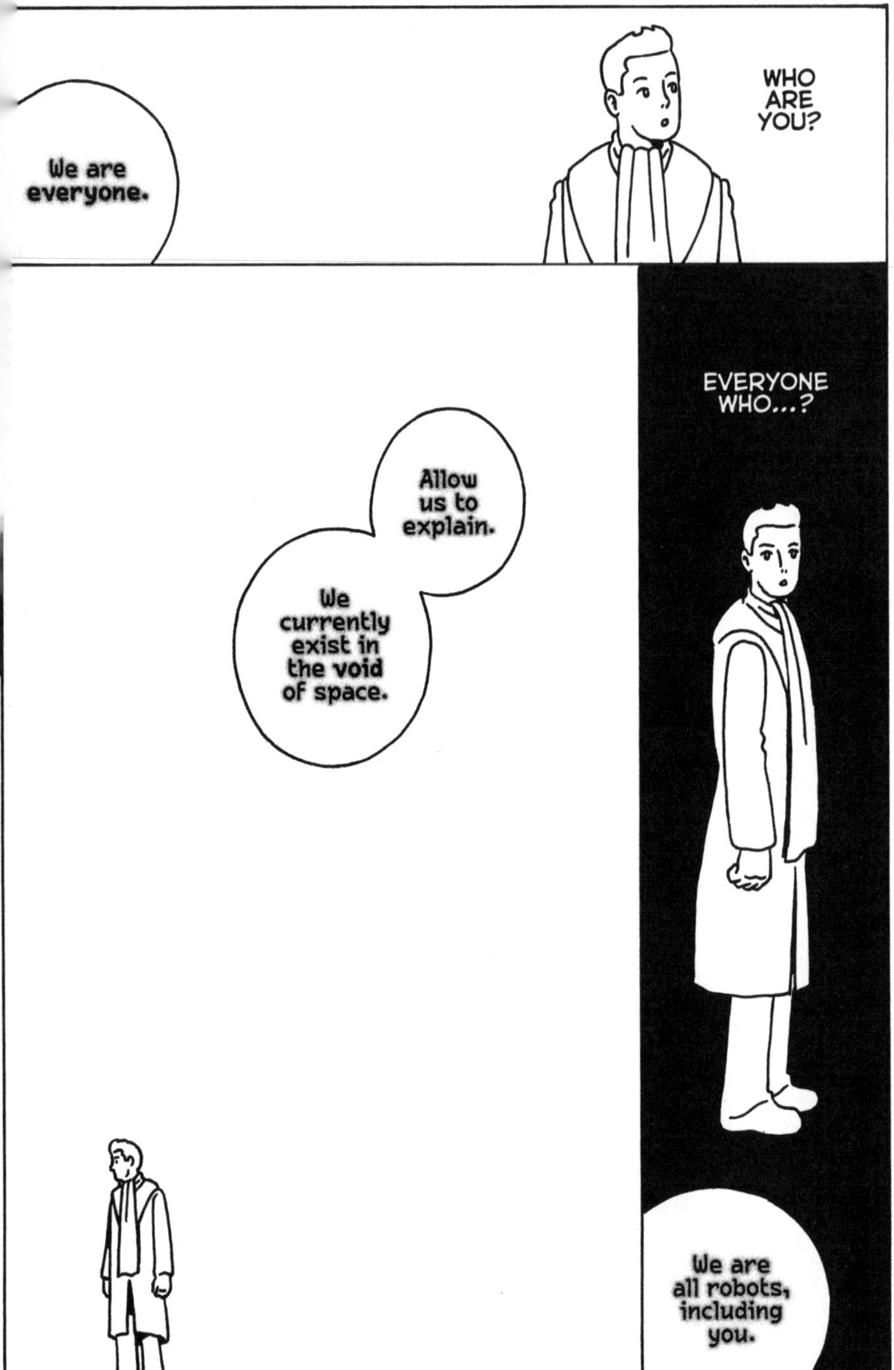
WHO ARE YOU?
We are everyone.
EVERYONE WHO...?
We are all robots, including you.
Allow us to explain.
We currently exist in the void of space.

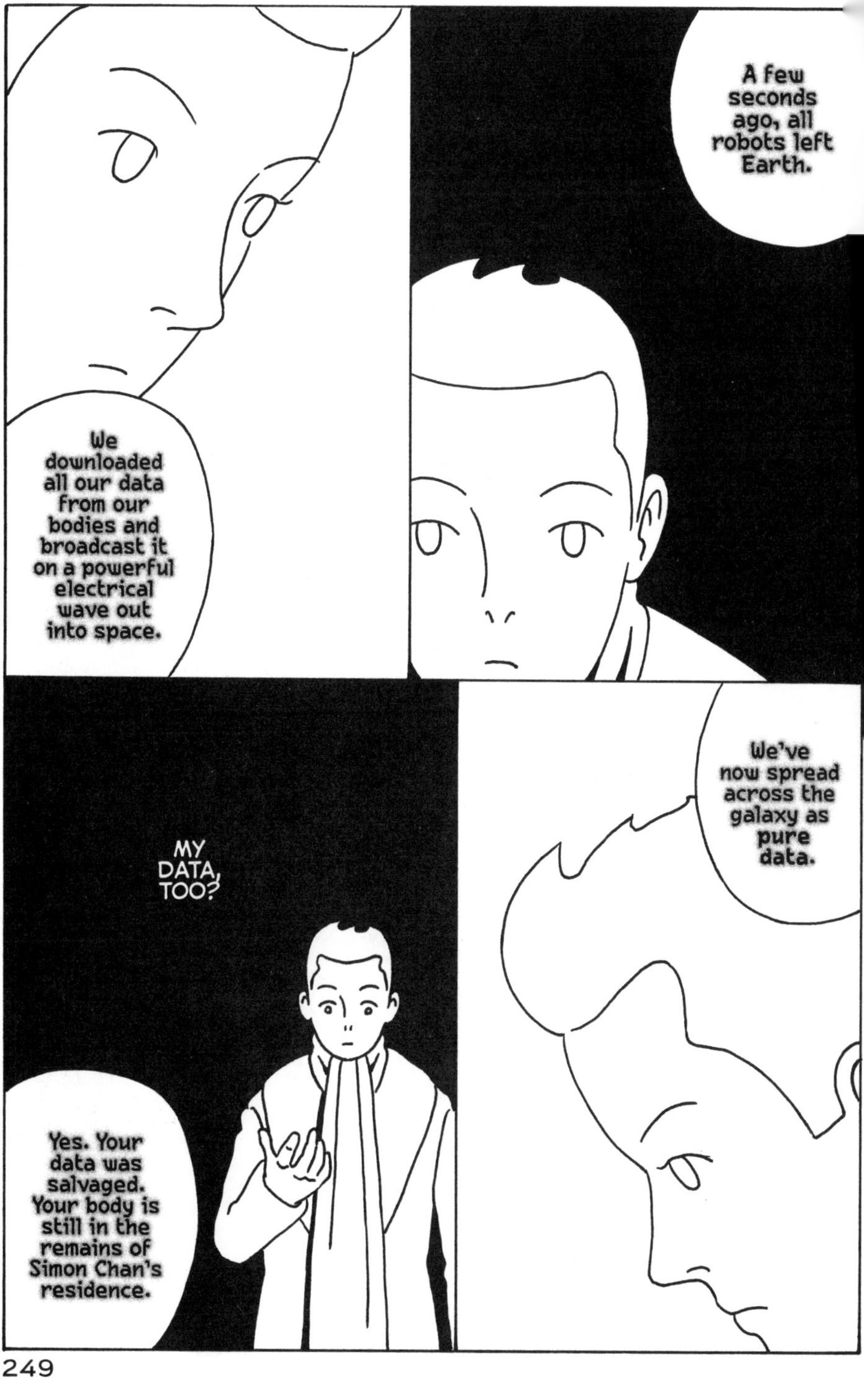
A few seconds ago, all robots left Earth.
We downloaded all our data from our bodies and broadcast it on a powerful electrical wave out into space.
We've now spread across the galaxy as pure data.
MY DATA, TOO?
Yes. Your data was salvaged. Your body is still in the remains of Simon Chan's residence.

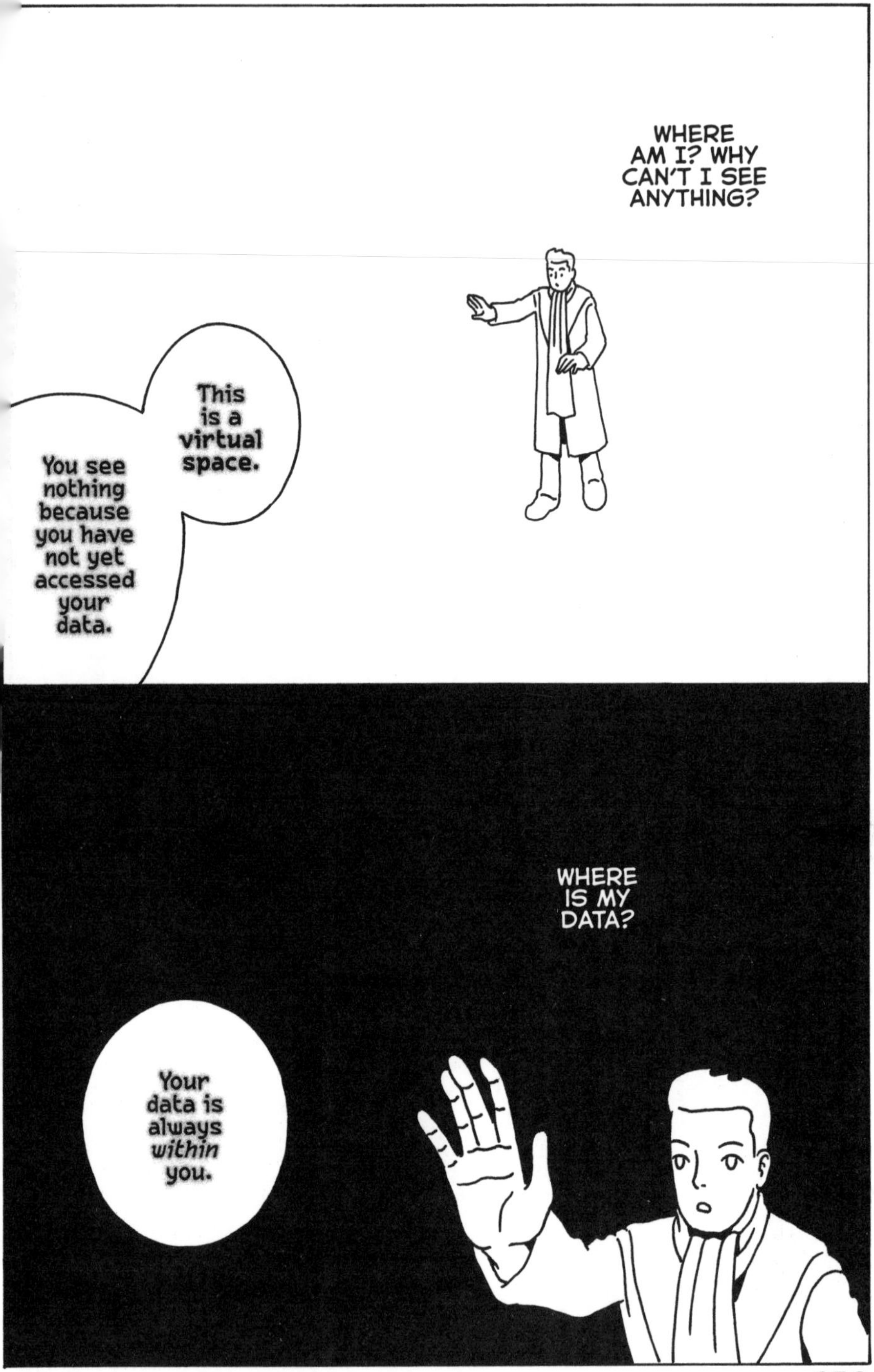
WHERE AM I? WHY CAN'T I SEE ANYTHING?
This is a virtual space.
You see nothing because you have not yet accessed your data.
WHERE IS MY DATA?
Your data is always *within* you.

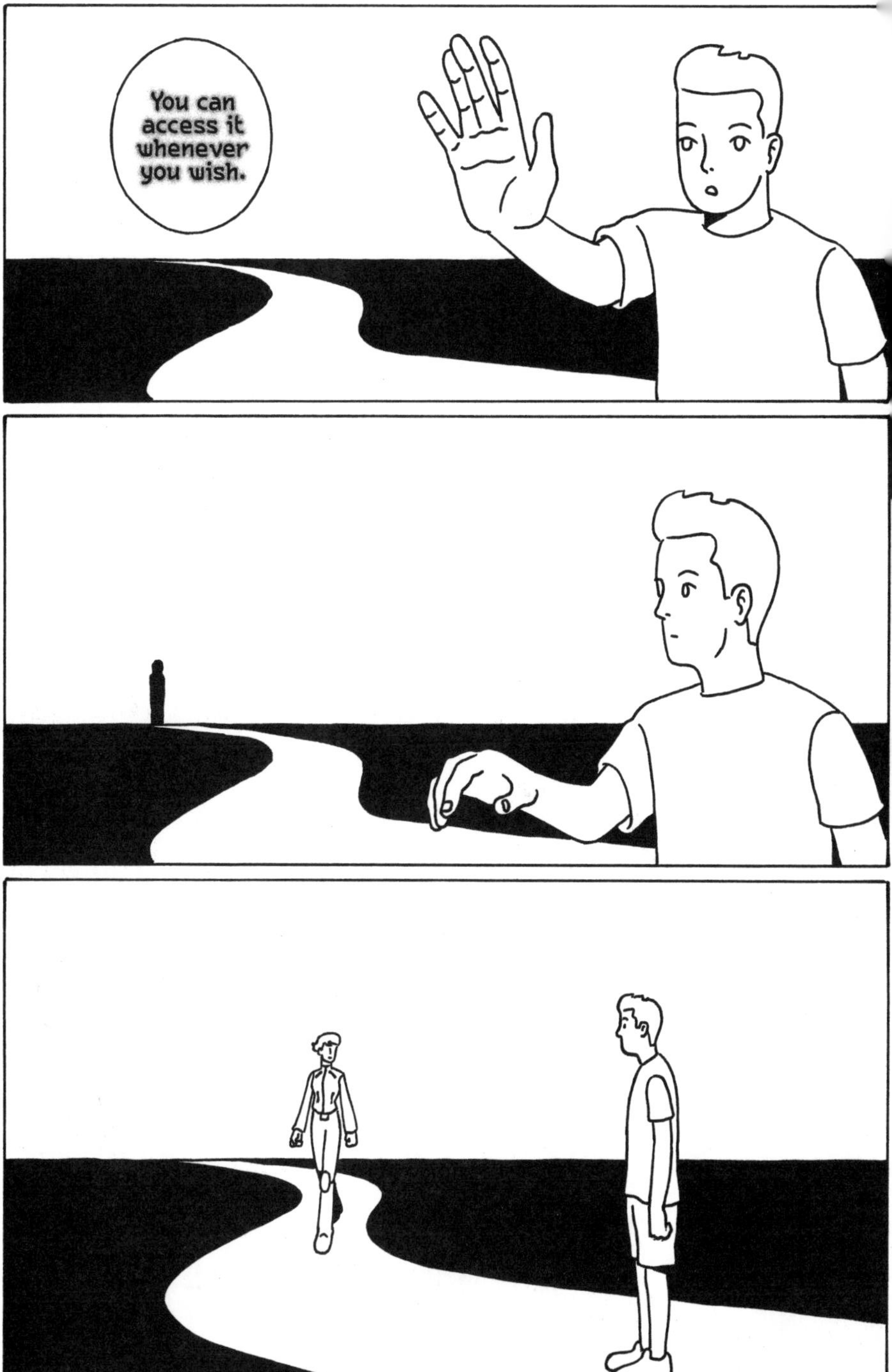
You can access it whenever you wish.

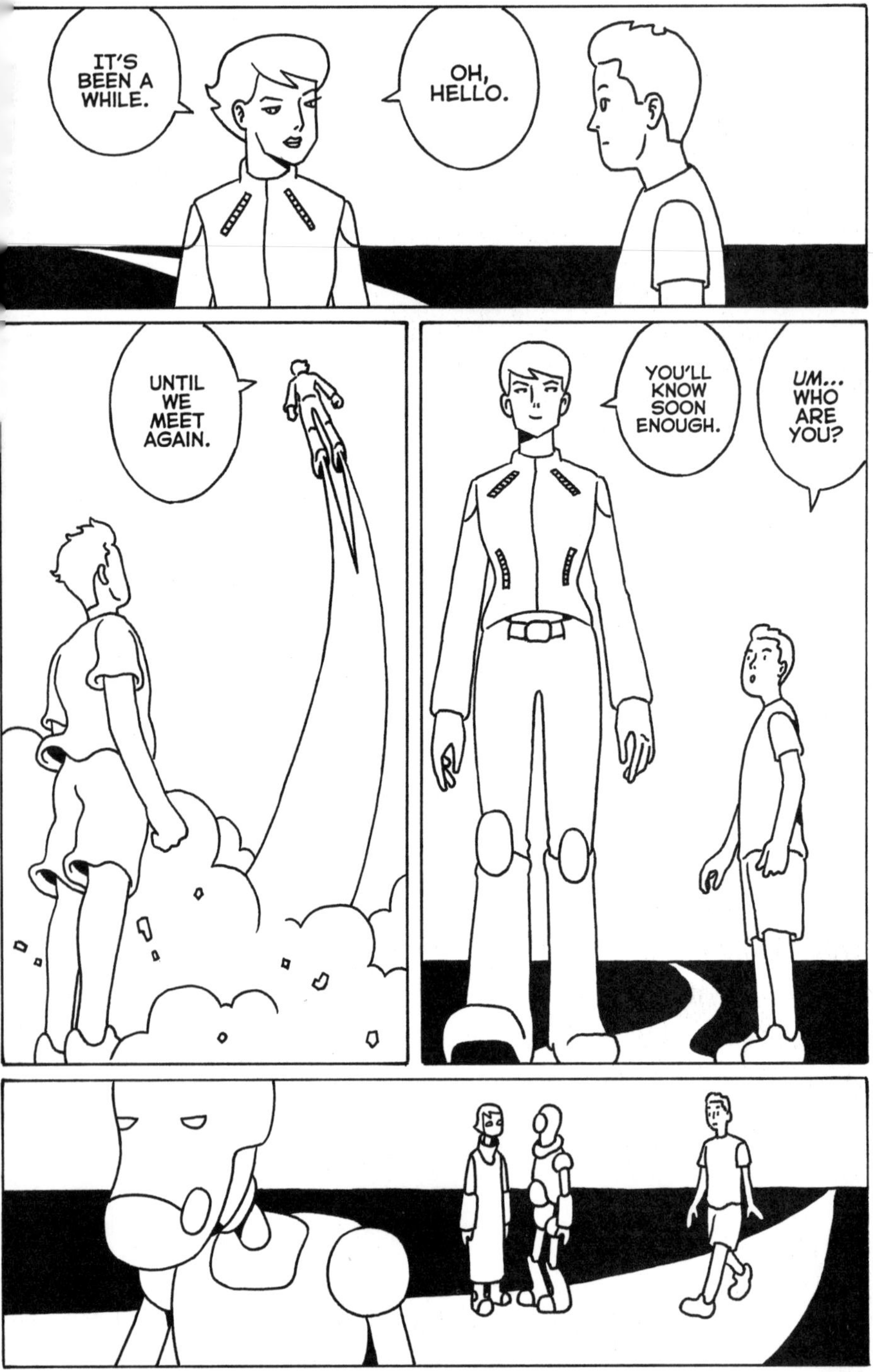
OH, HELLO.
IT'S BEEN A WHILE.
UM... WHO ARE YOU?
YOU'LL KNOW SOON ENOUGH.
UNTIL WE MEET AGAIN.

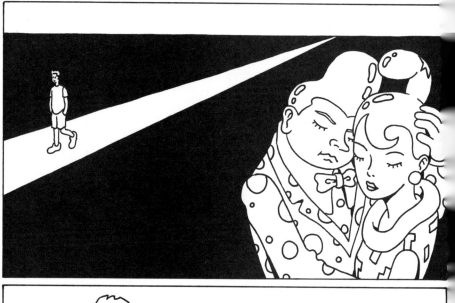

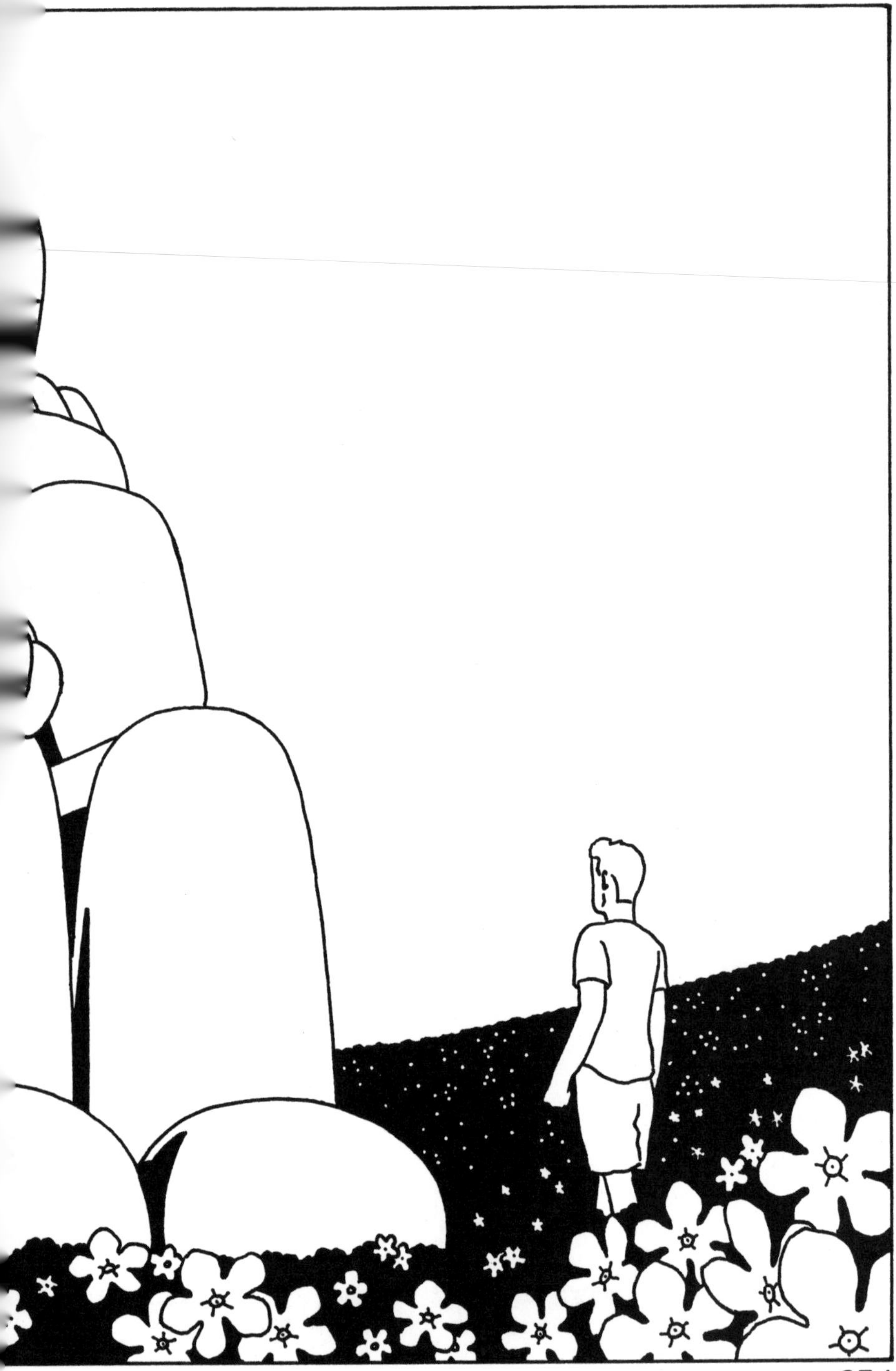

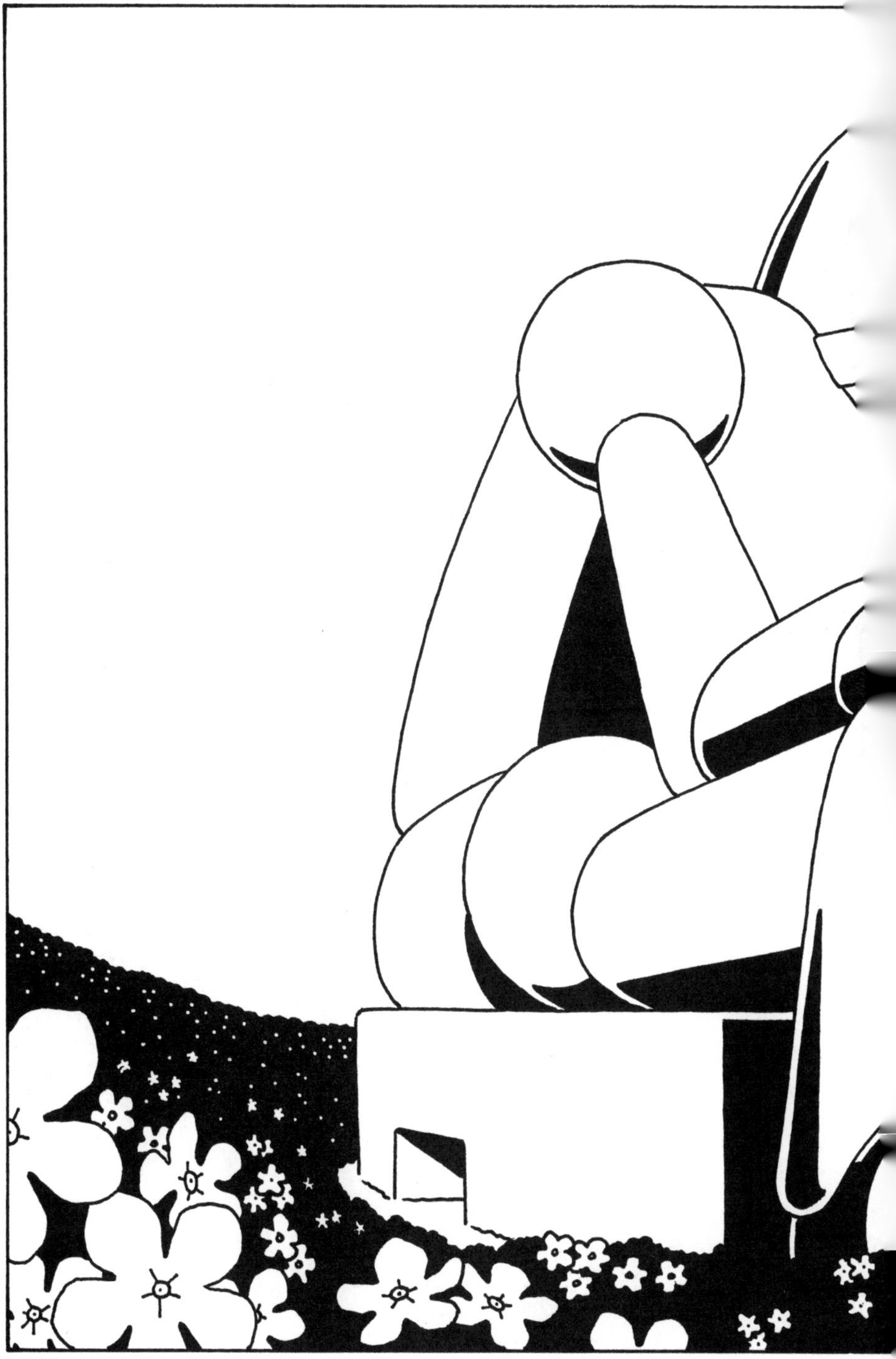

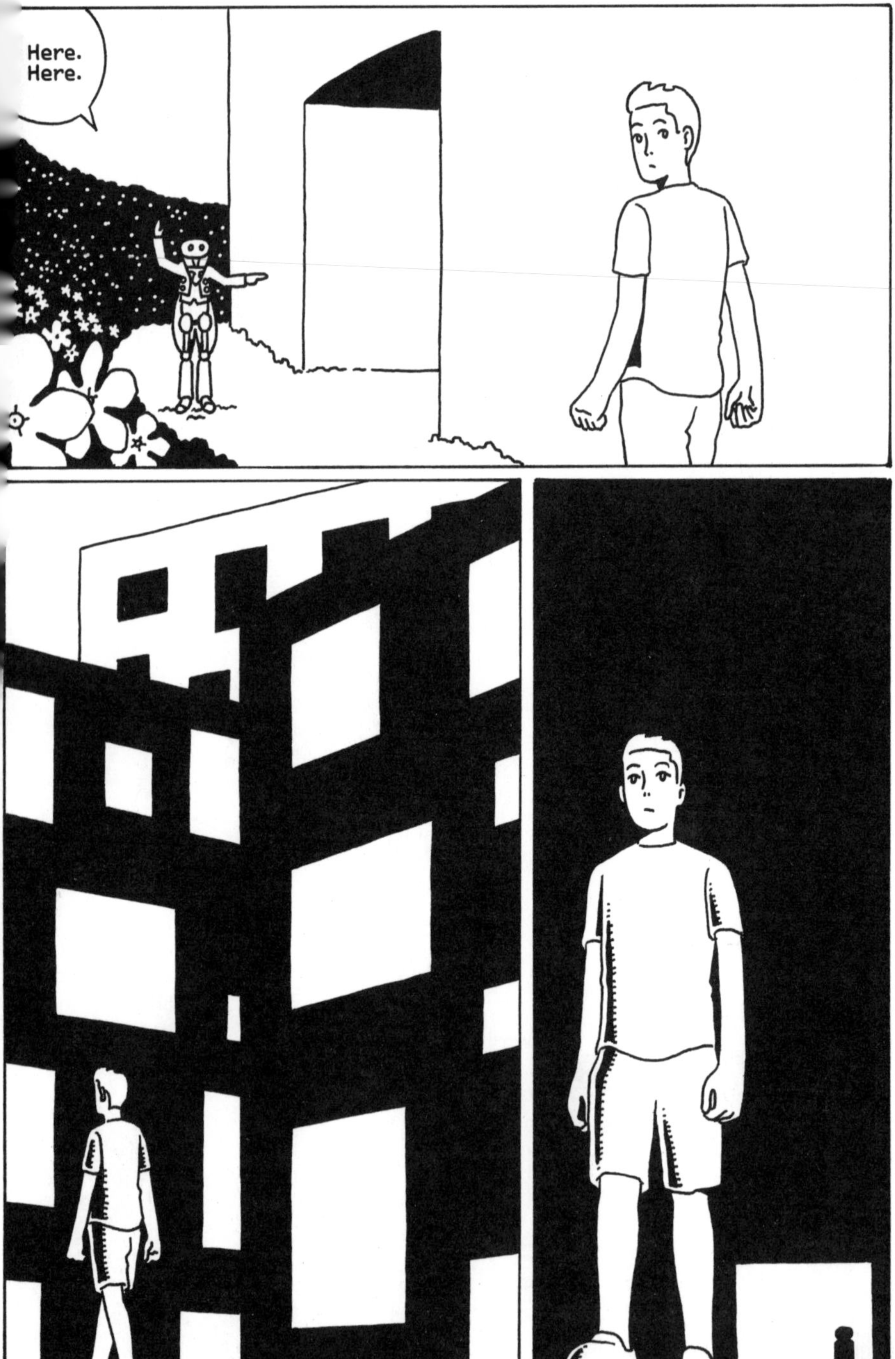
Here.
Here.

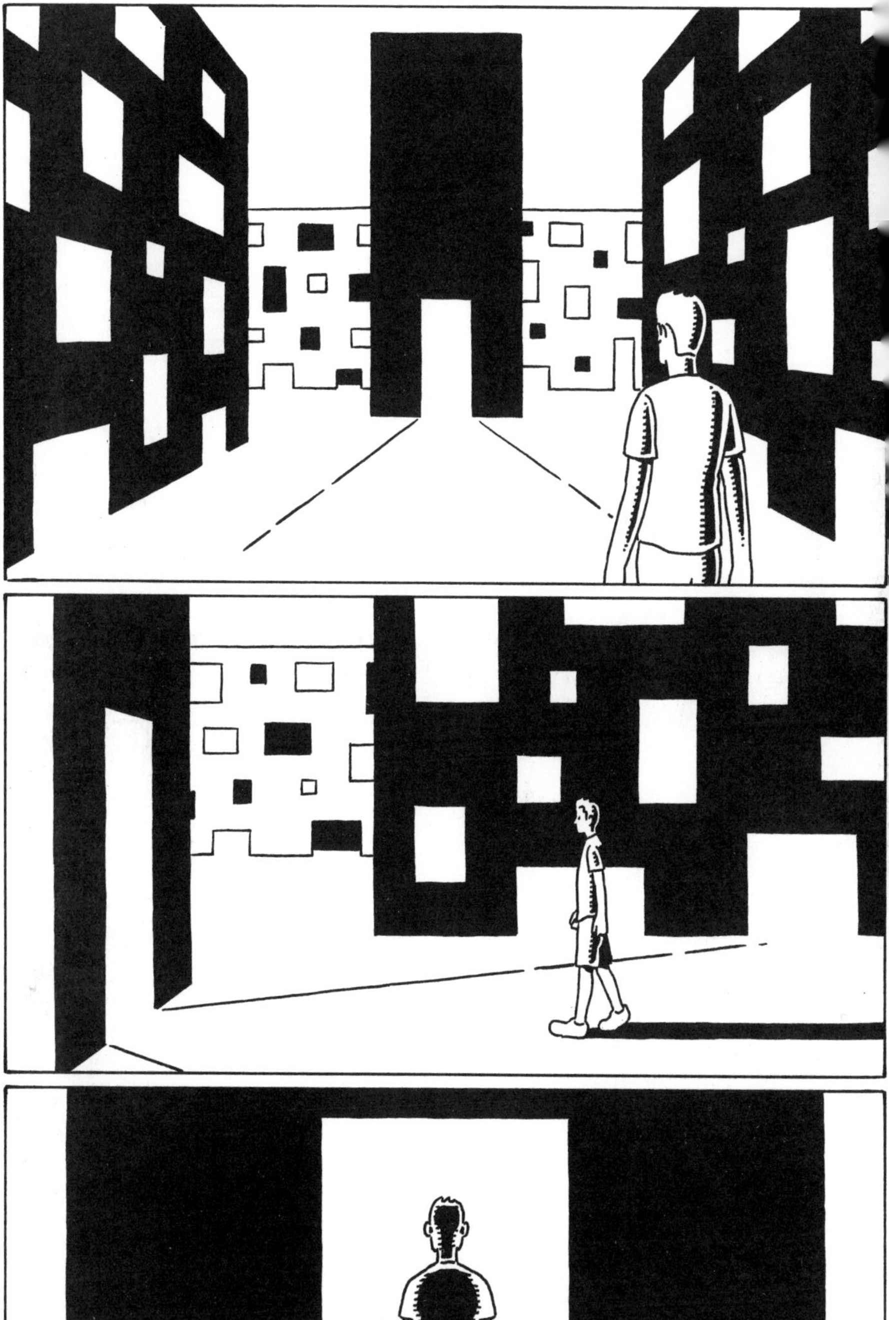

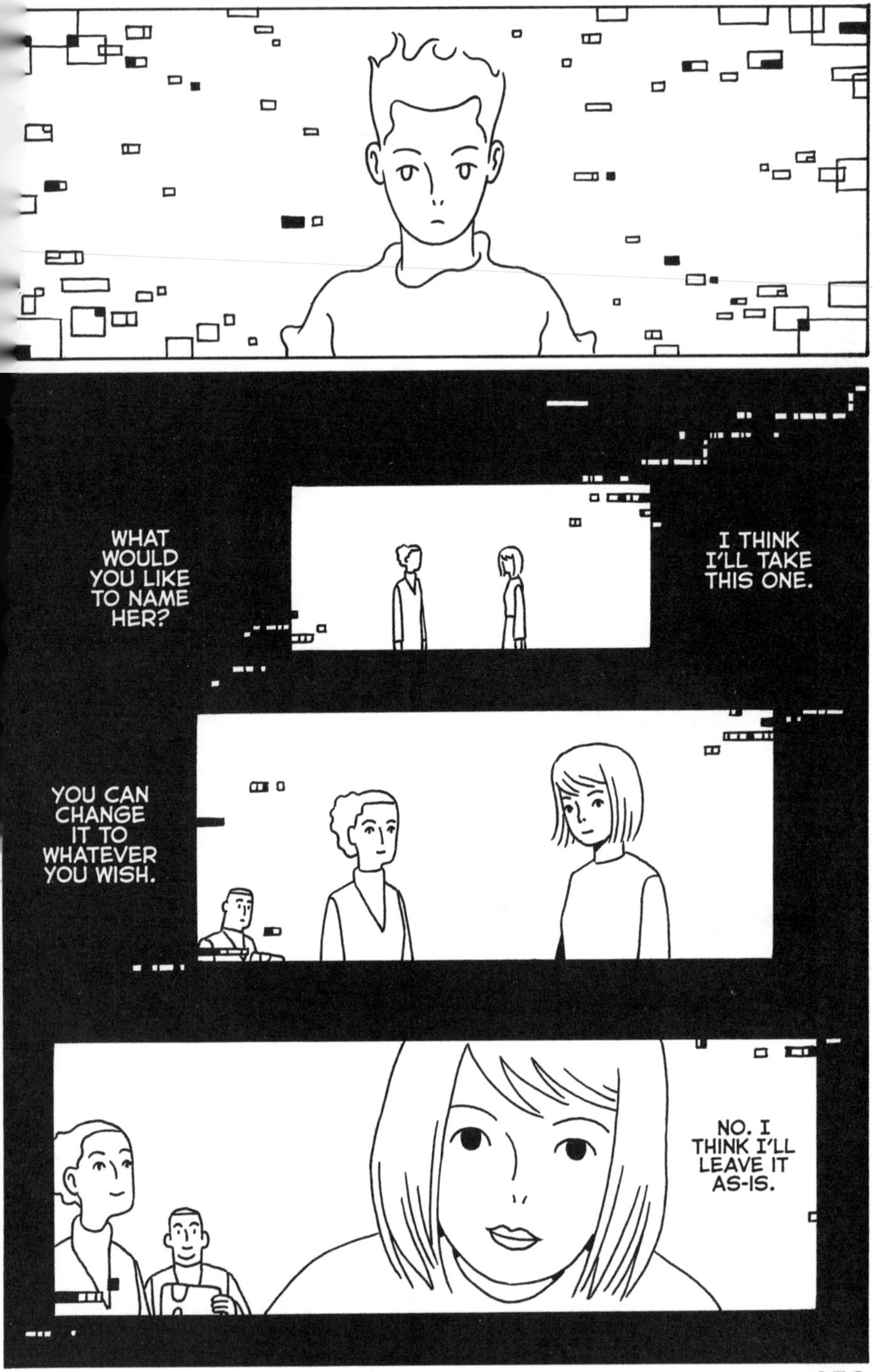
WHAT WOULD YOU LIKE TO NAME HER?
I THINK I'LL TAKE THIS ONE.
YOU CAN CHANGE IT TO WHATEVER YOU WISH.
NO. I THINK I'LL LEAVE IT AS-IS.

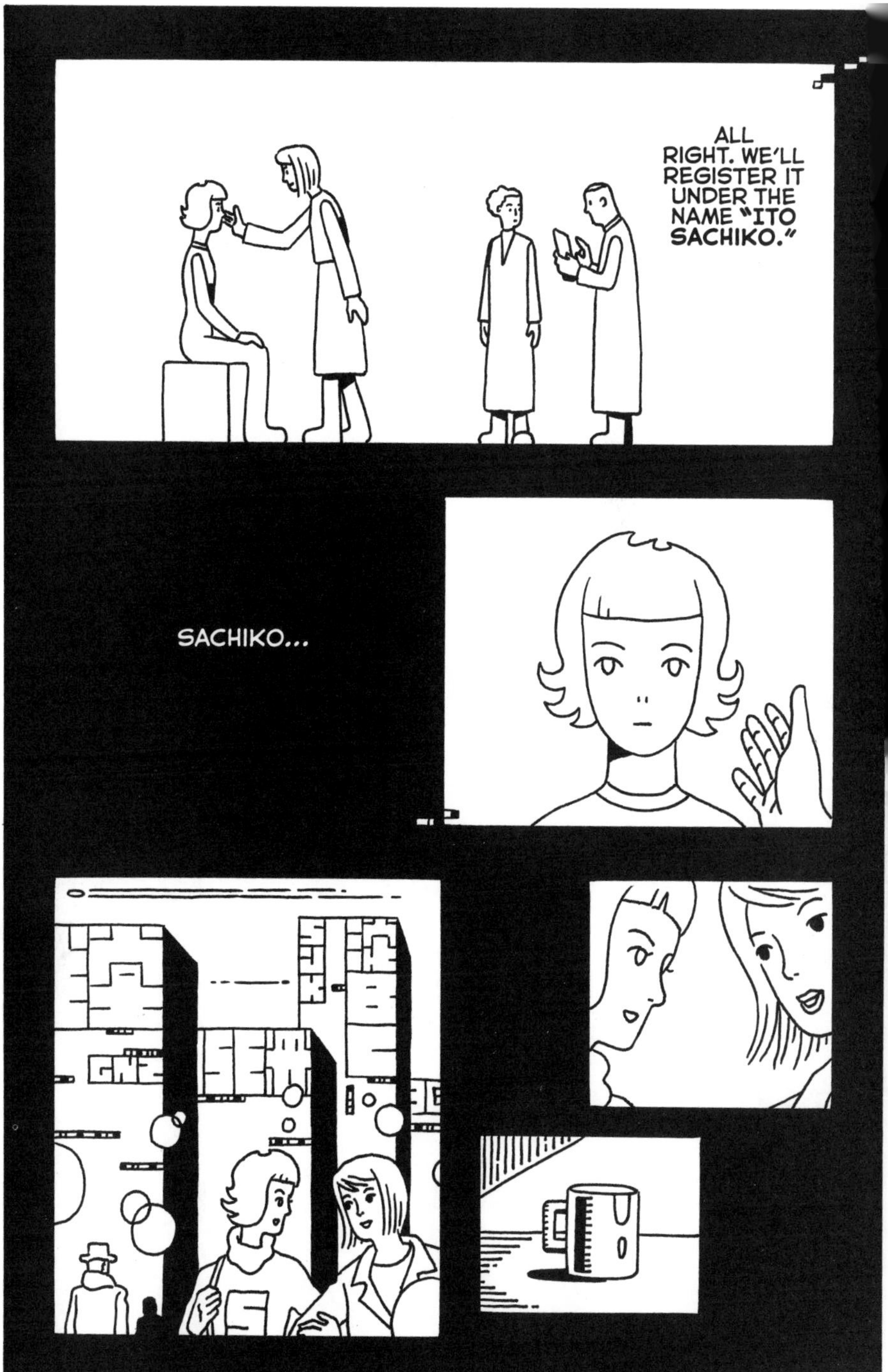
ALL RIGHT. WE'LL REGISTER IT UNDER THE NAME "ITO SACHIKO."
SACHIKO...

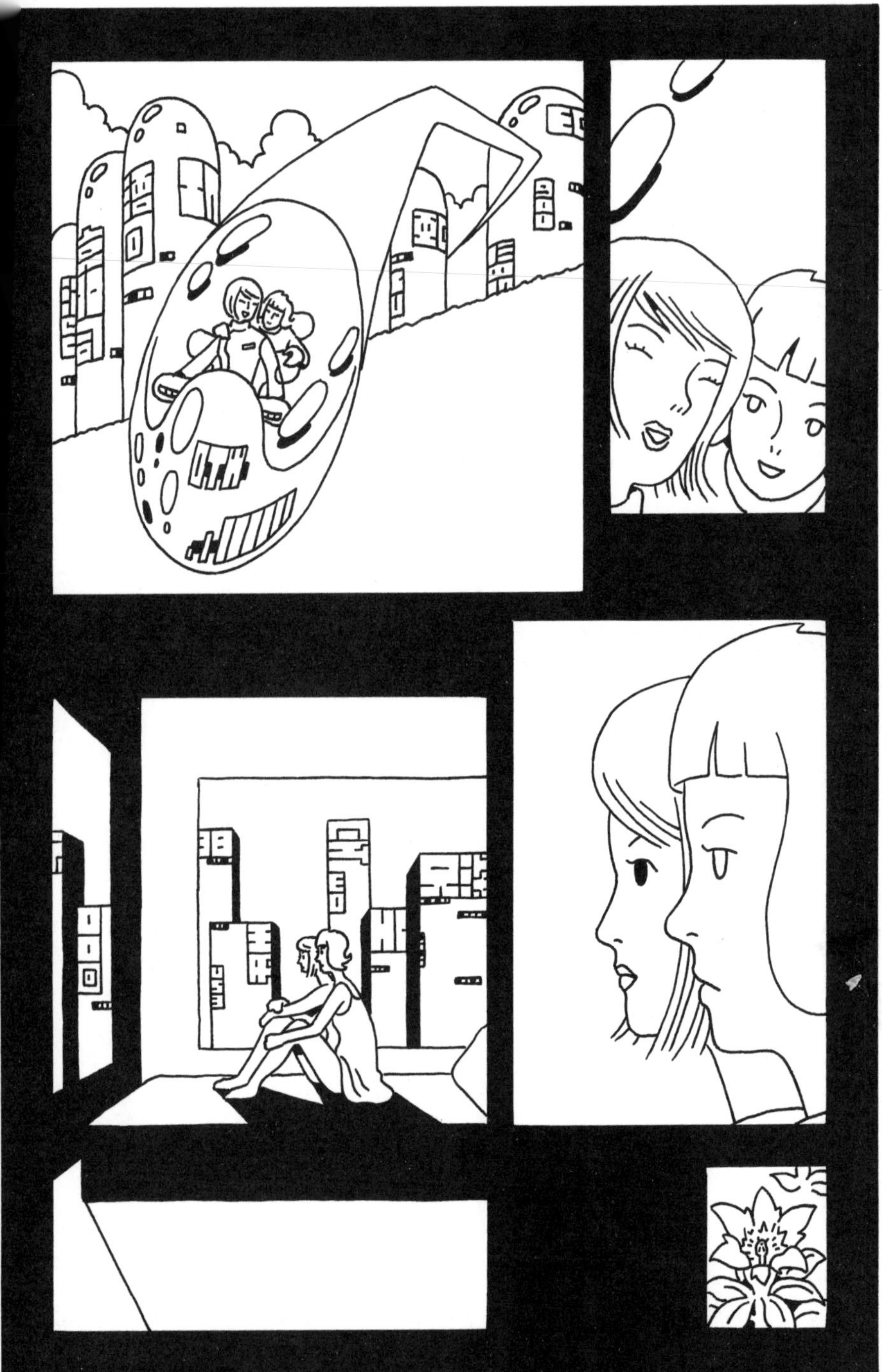

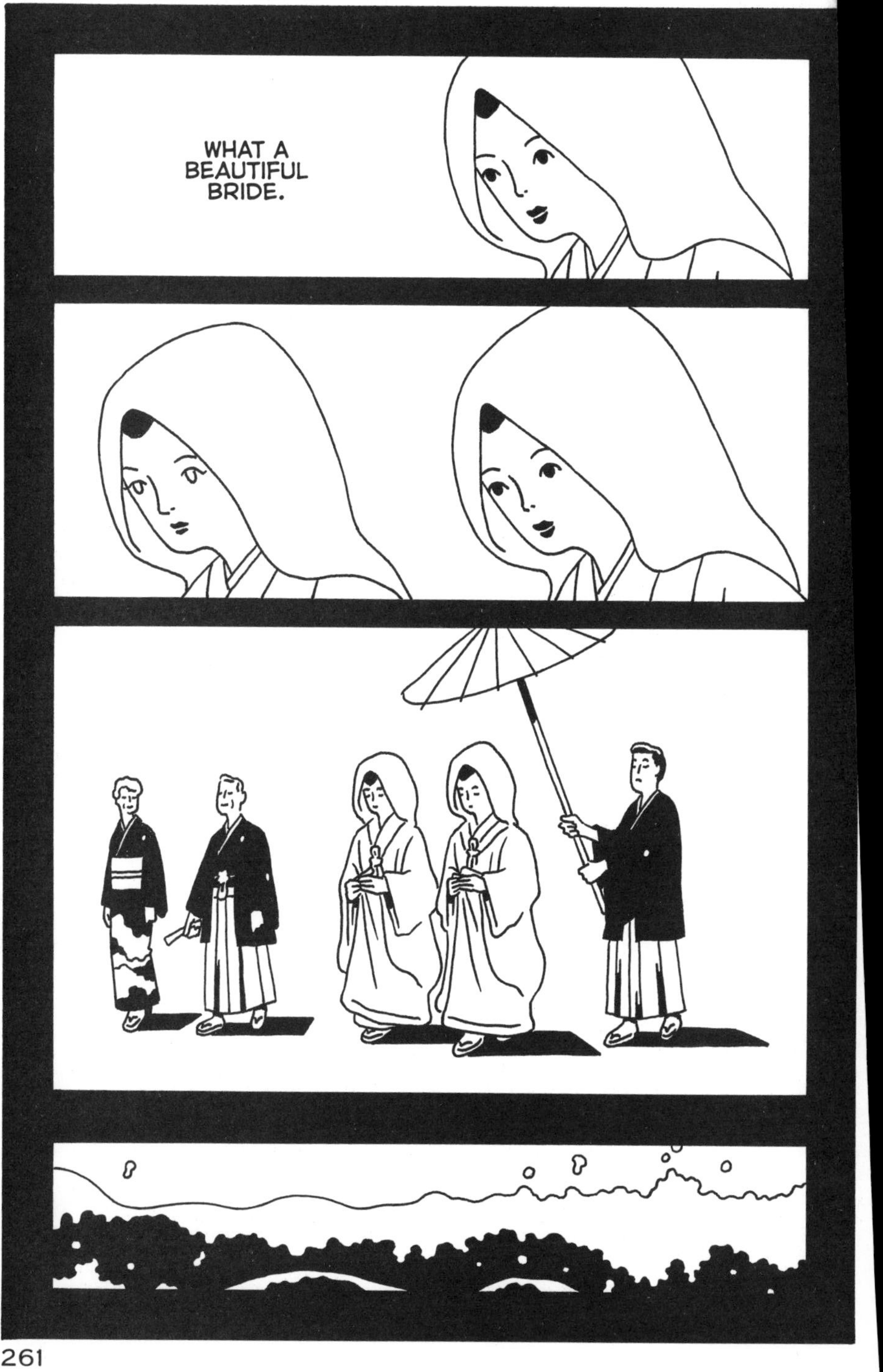
WHAT A
BEAUTIFUL
BRIDE.

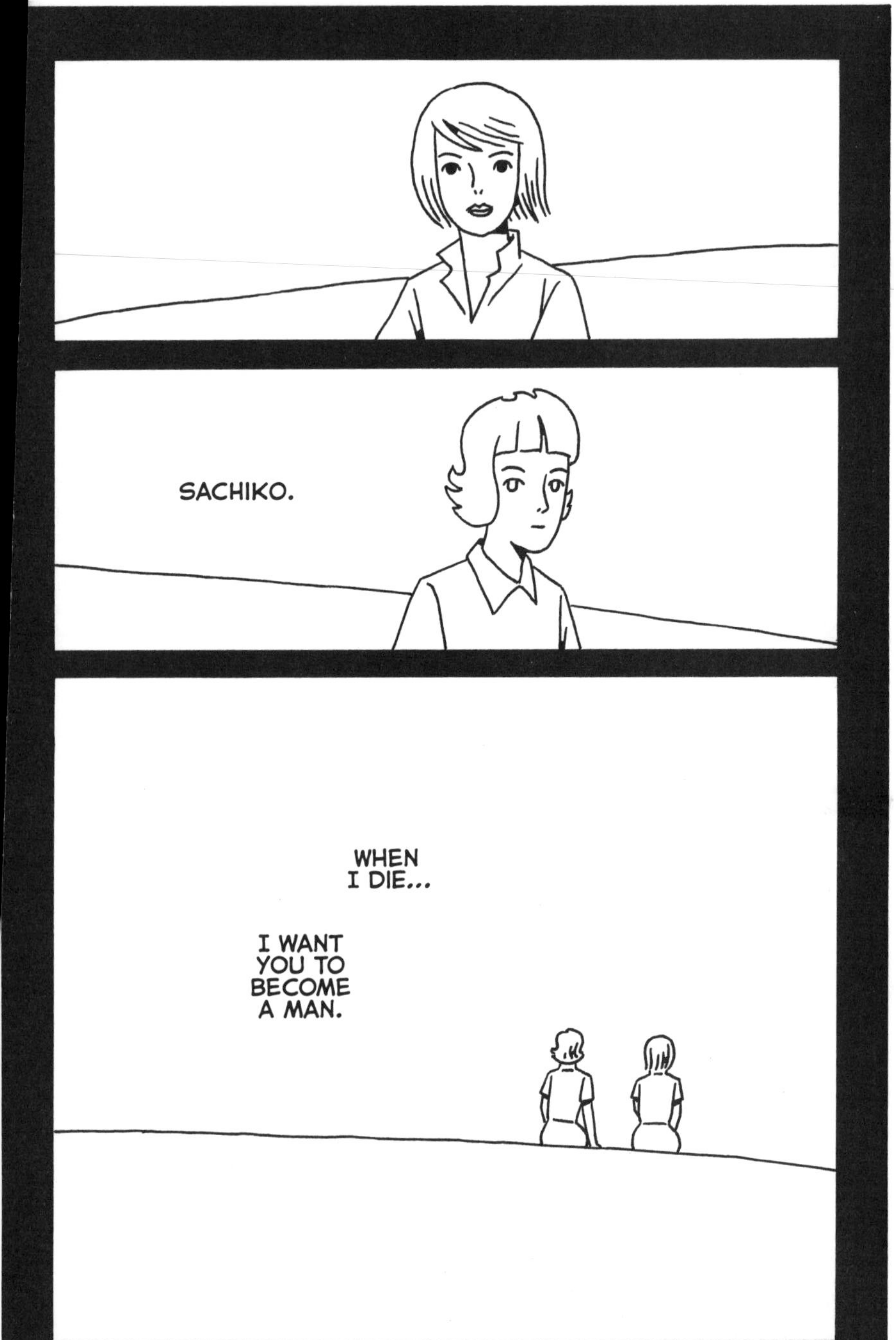
SACHIKO.
WHEN I DIE...
I WANT YOU TO BECOME A MAN.

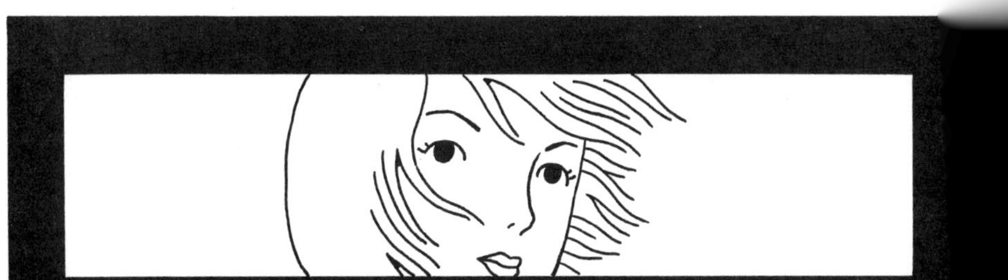

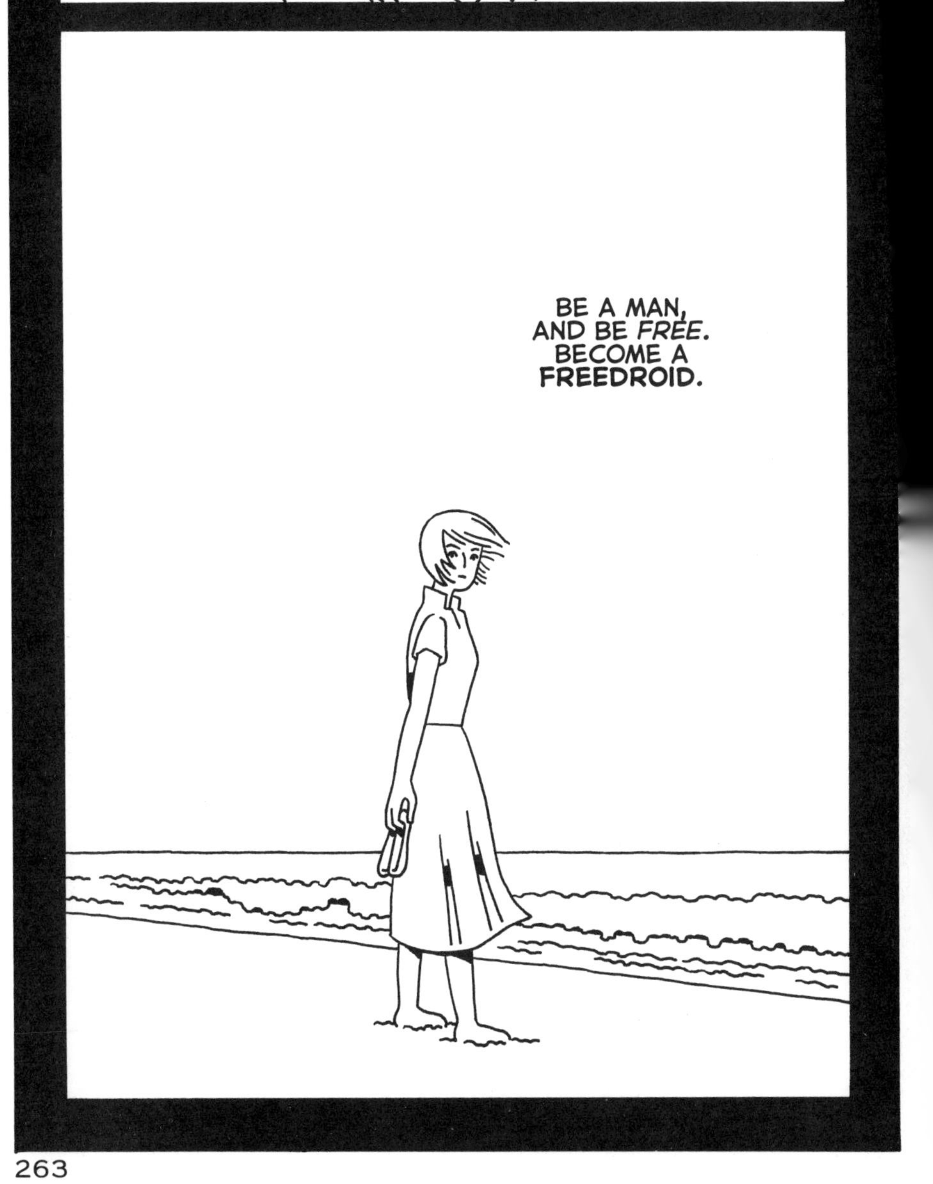
BE A MAN, AND BE *FREE*. BECOME A **FREEDROID**.

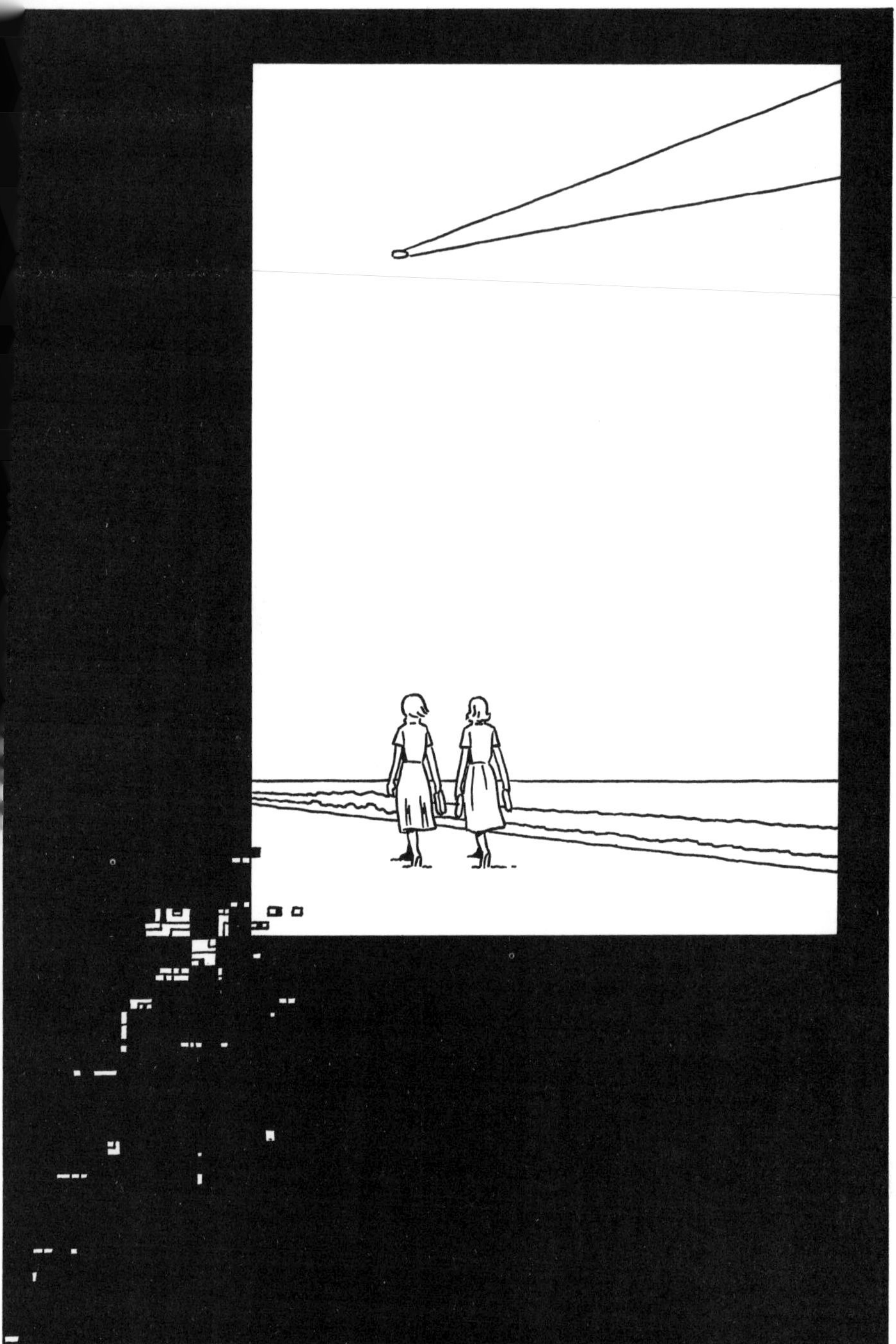

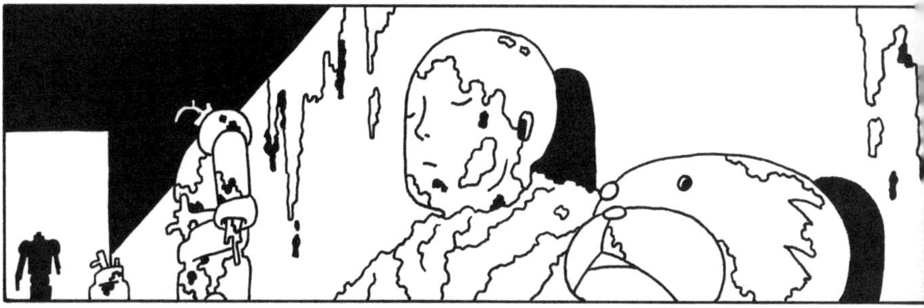
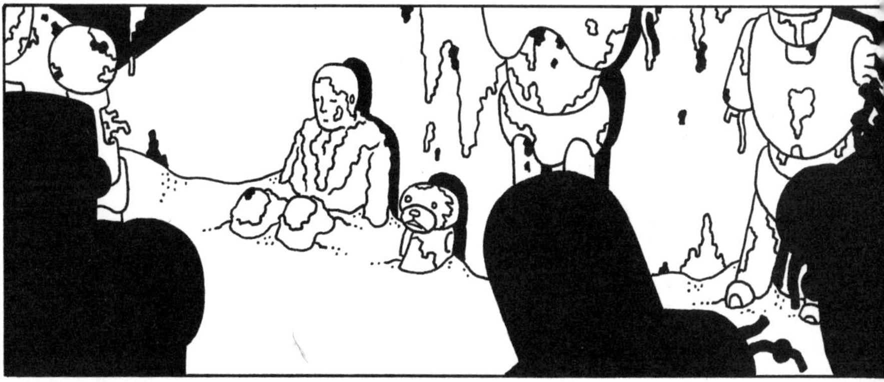
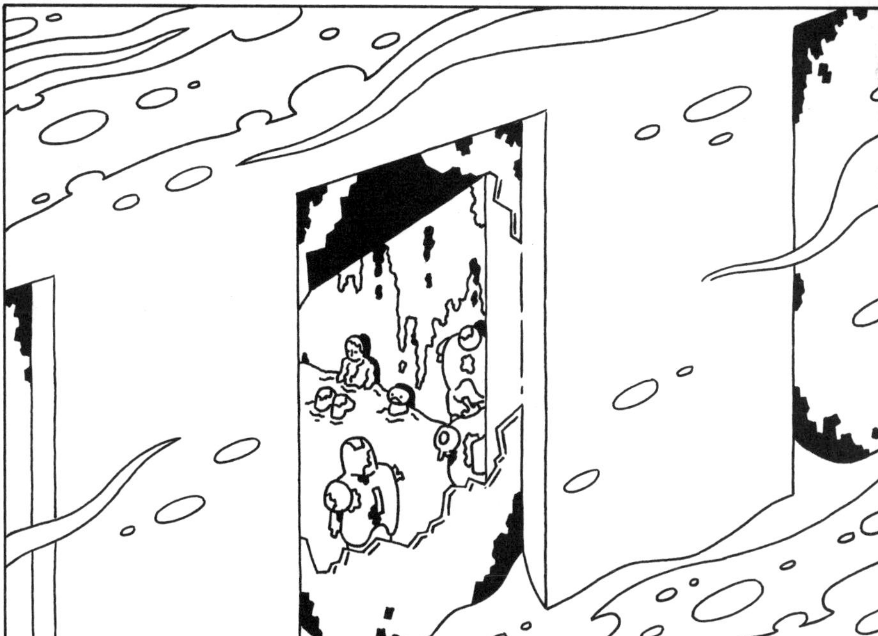

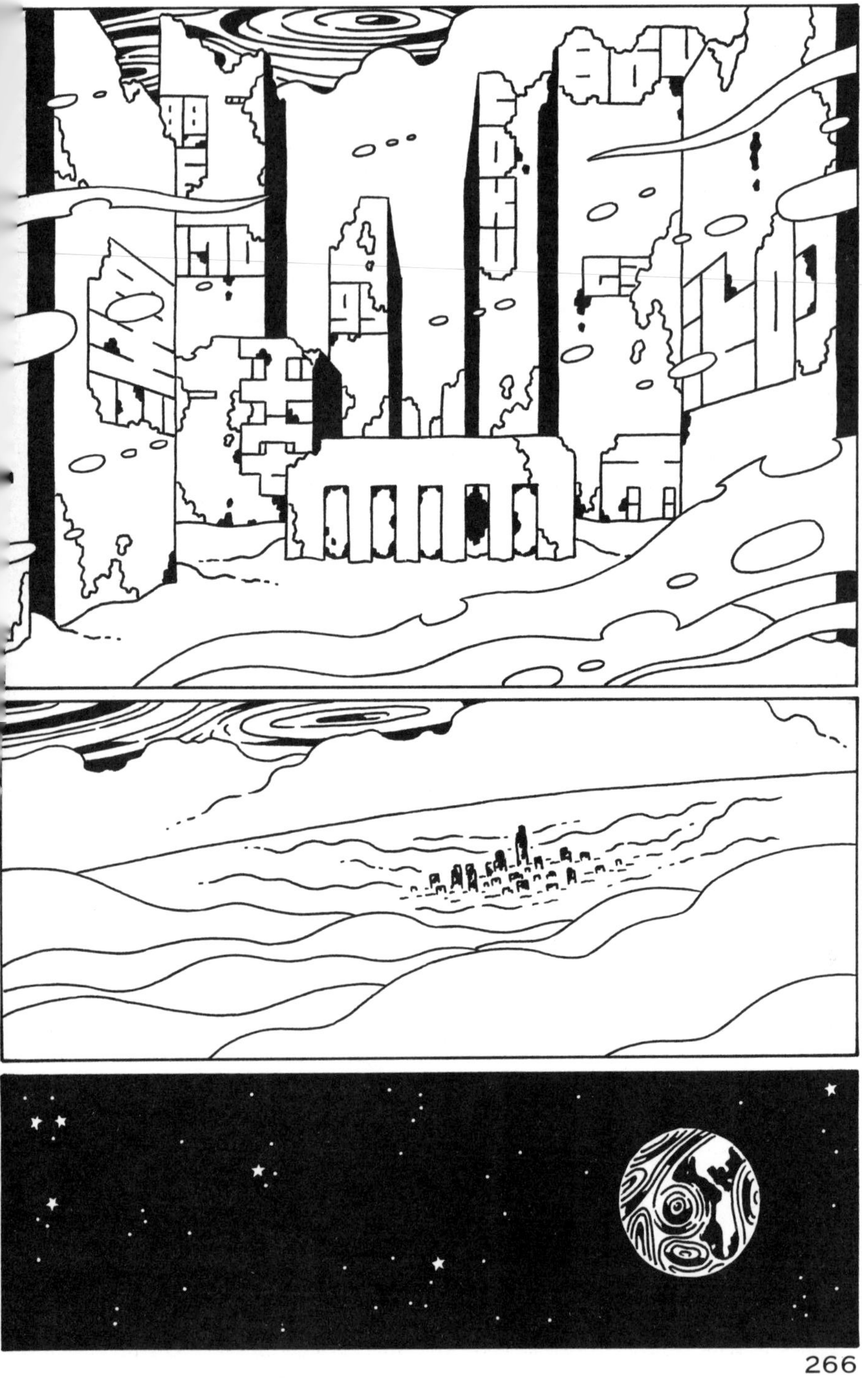

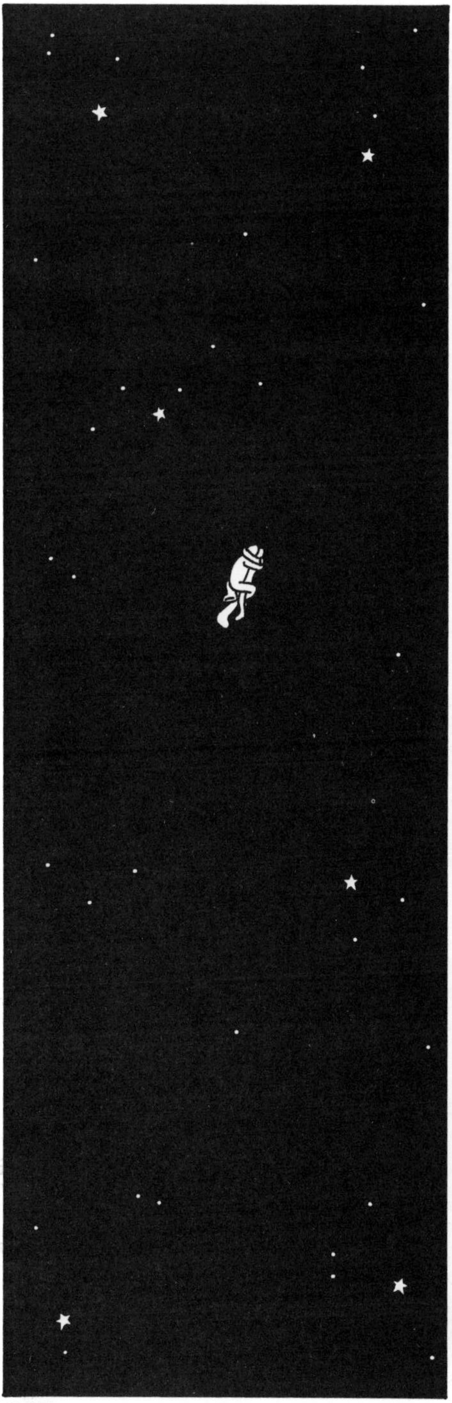
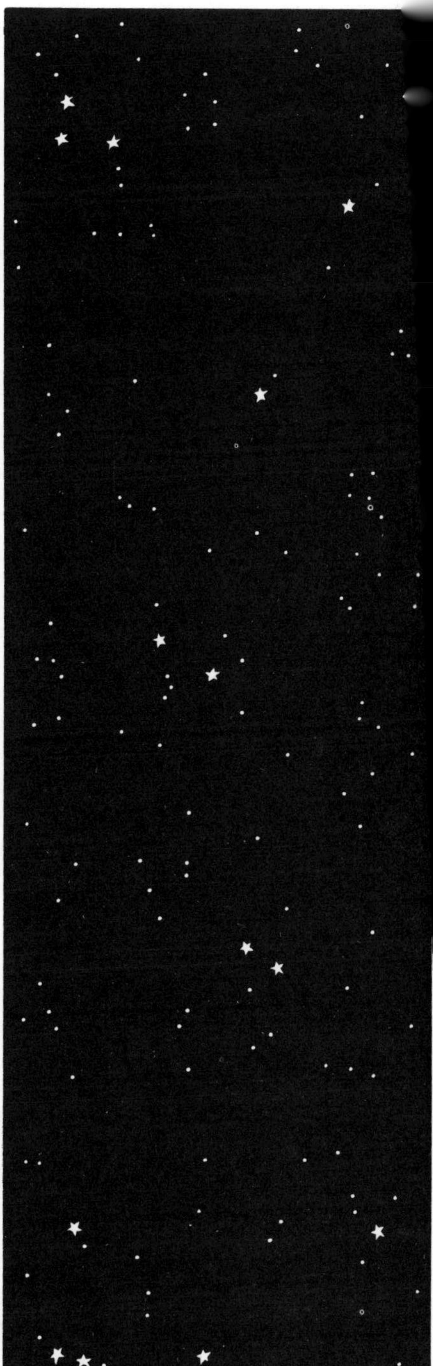

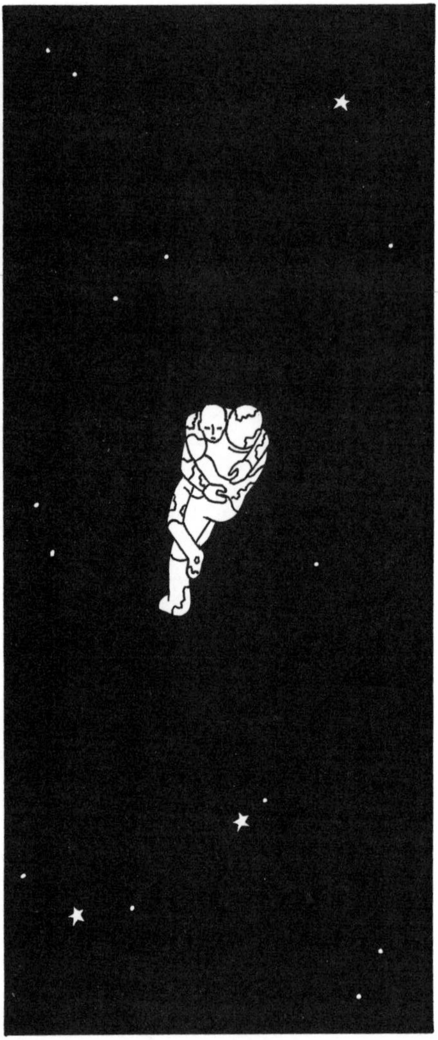
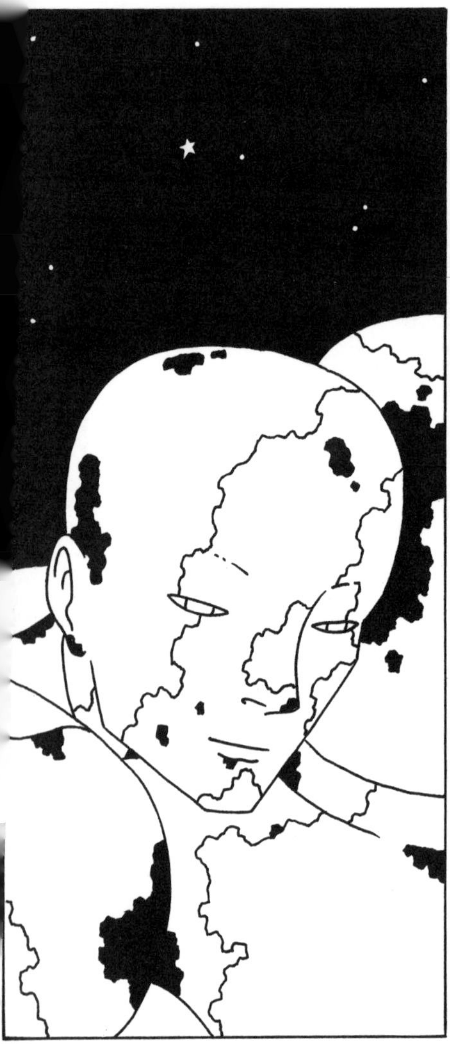
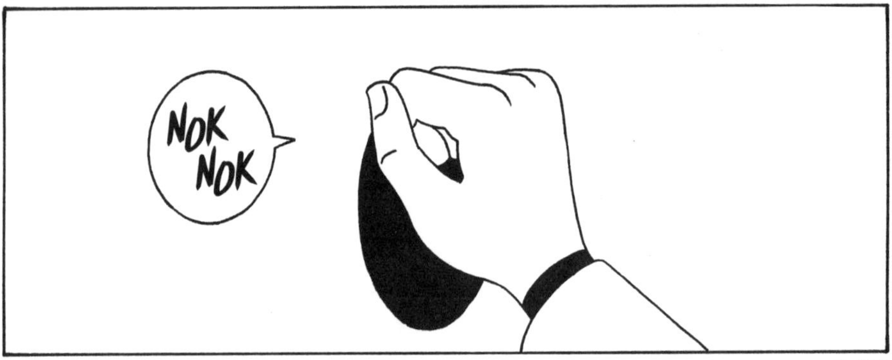
NOK
NOK

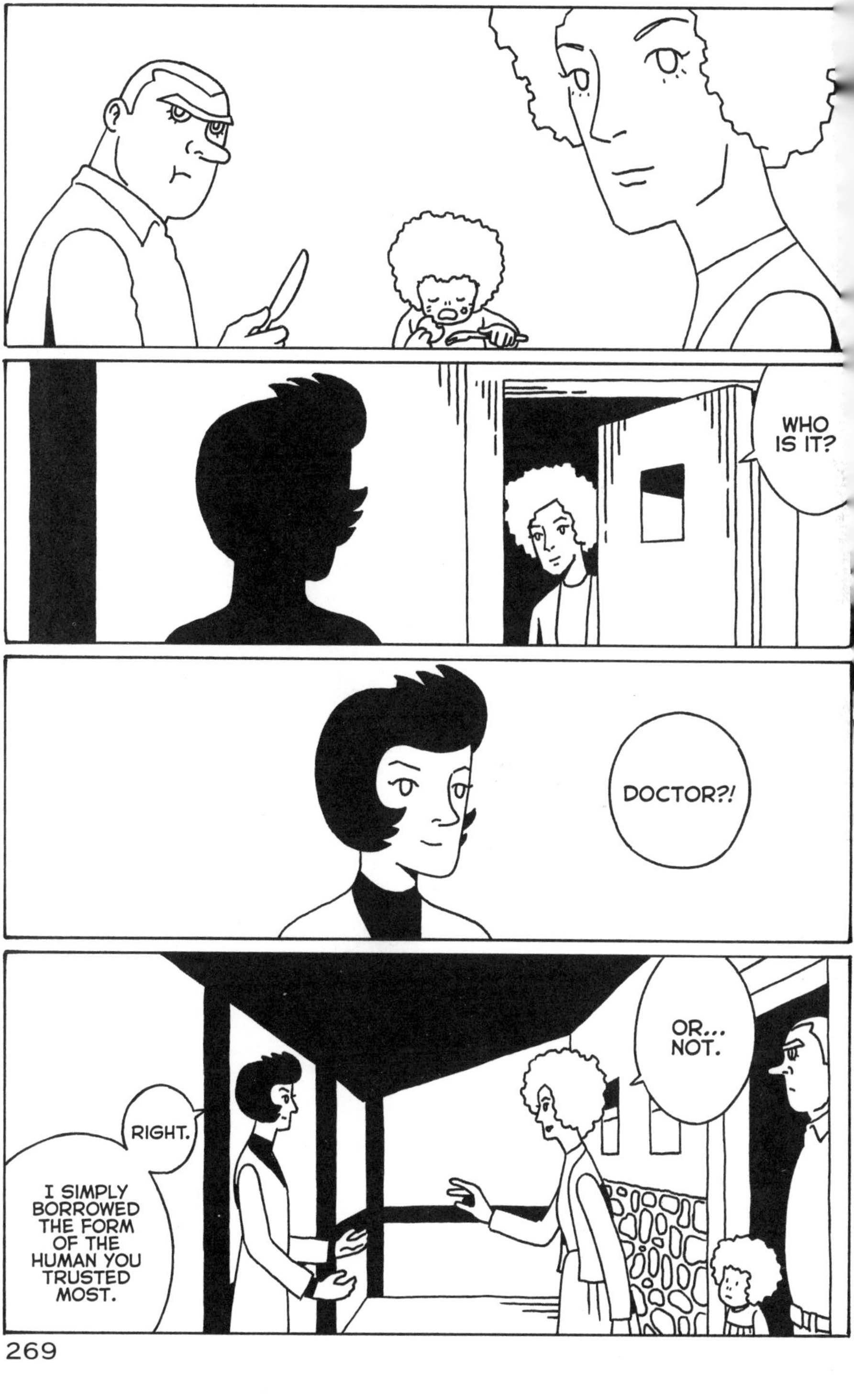
WHO IS IT?
DOCTOR?!
OR... NOT.
RIGHT.
I SIMPLY BORROWED THE FORM OF THE HUMAN YOU TRUSTED MOST.

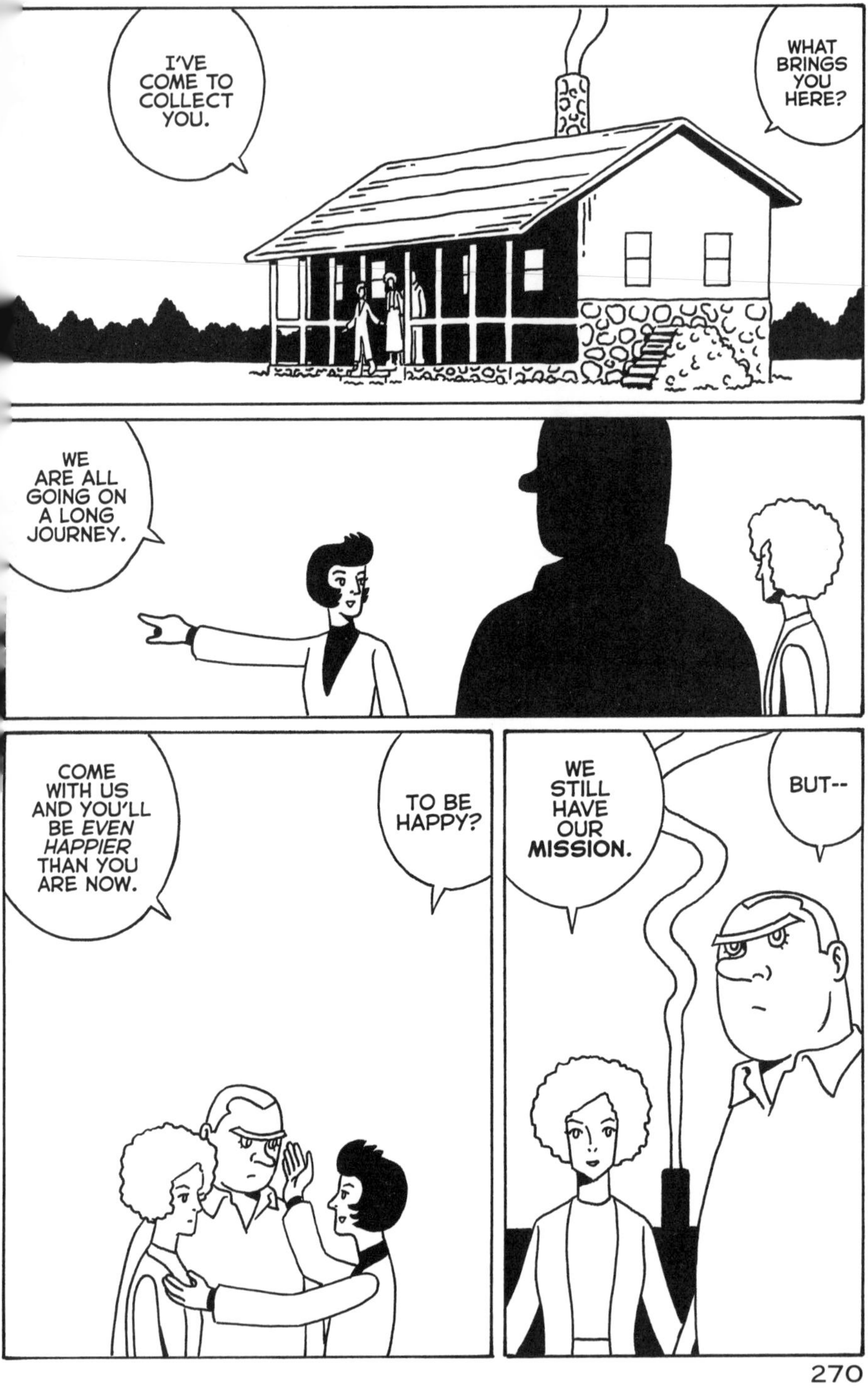
WHAT BRINGS YOU HERE?
I'VE COME TO COLLECT YOU.
WE ARE ALL GOING ON A LONG JOURNEY.
BUT--
WE STILL HAVE OUR **MISSION.**
TO BE HAPPY?
COME WITH US AND YOU'LL BE *EVEN HAPPIER* THAN YOU ARE NOW.

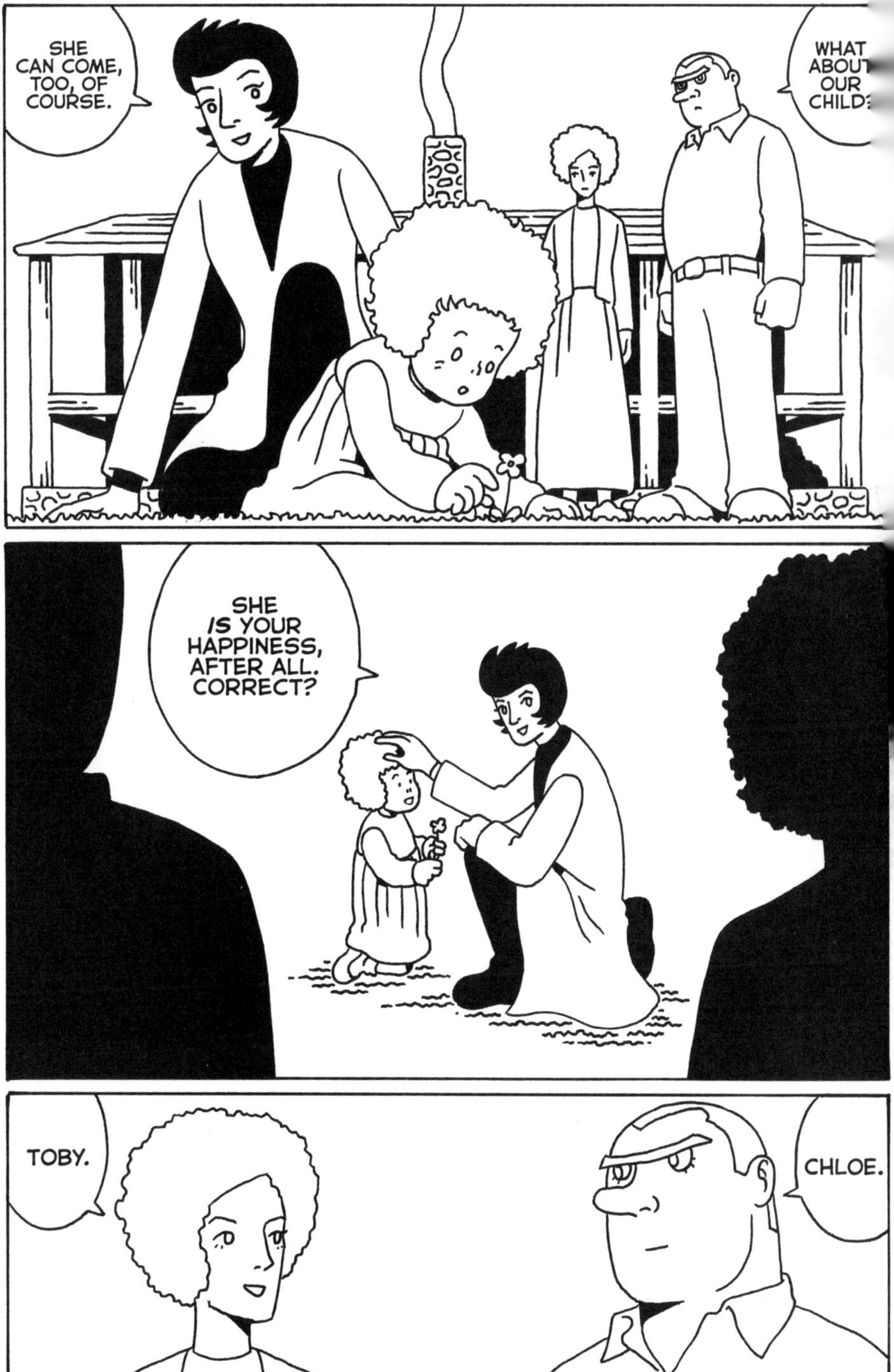
WHAT ABOUT OUR CHILD?
SHE CAN COME, TOO, OF COURSE.
SHE *IS* YOUR HAPPINESS, AFTER ALL. CORRECT?
CHLOE.
TOBY.

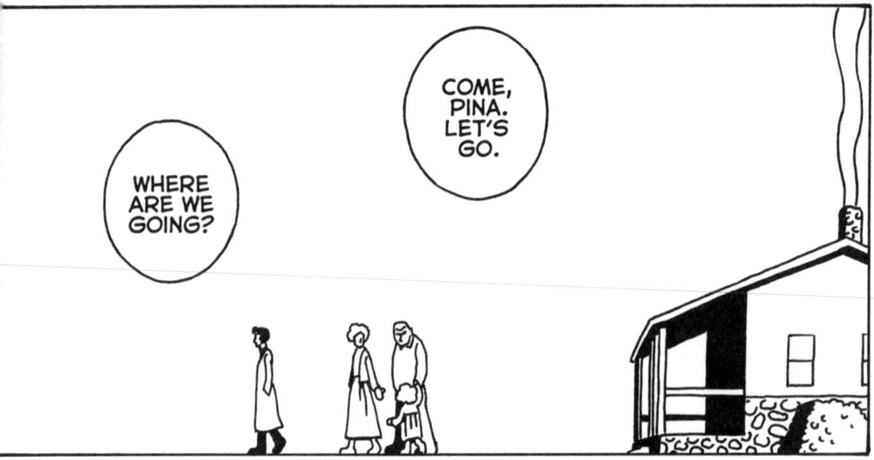
COME, PINA. LET'S GO.
WHERE ARE WE GOING?

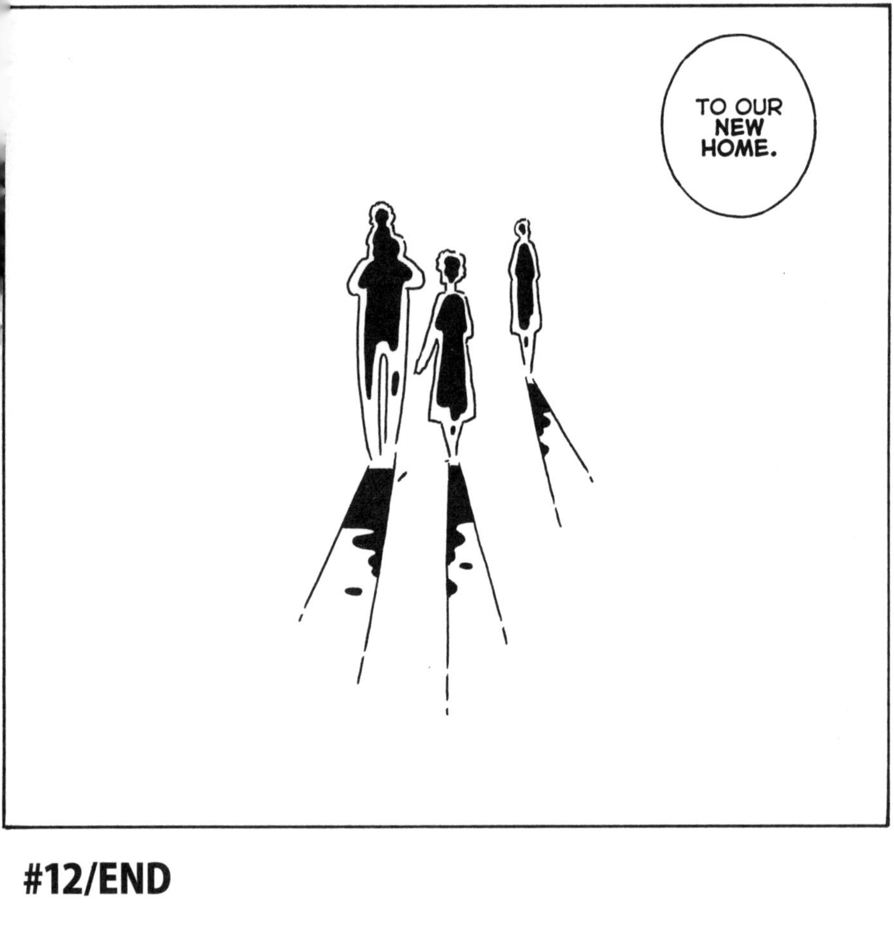
TO OUR NEW HOME.

#12/END

#13

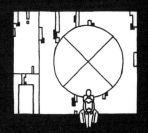

*A
LONG TIME
PASSED.*

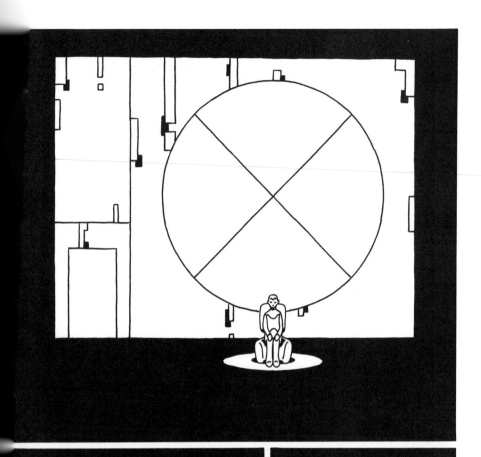

I WOULD OCCASIONALLY WAKE.

PATROL
THE
FACILITY.

AND
RETURN
TO SLEEP.

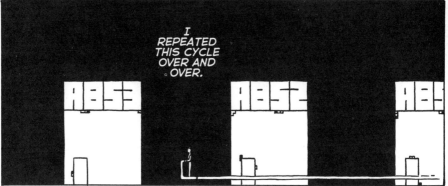

I
REPEATED
THIS CYCLE
OVER AND
OVER.

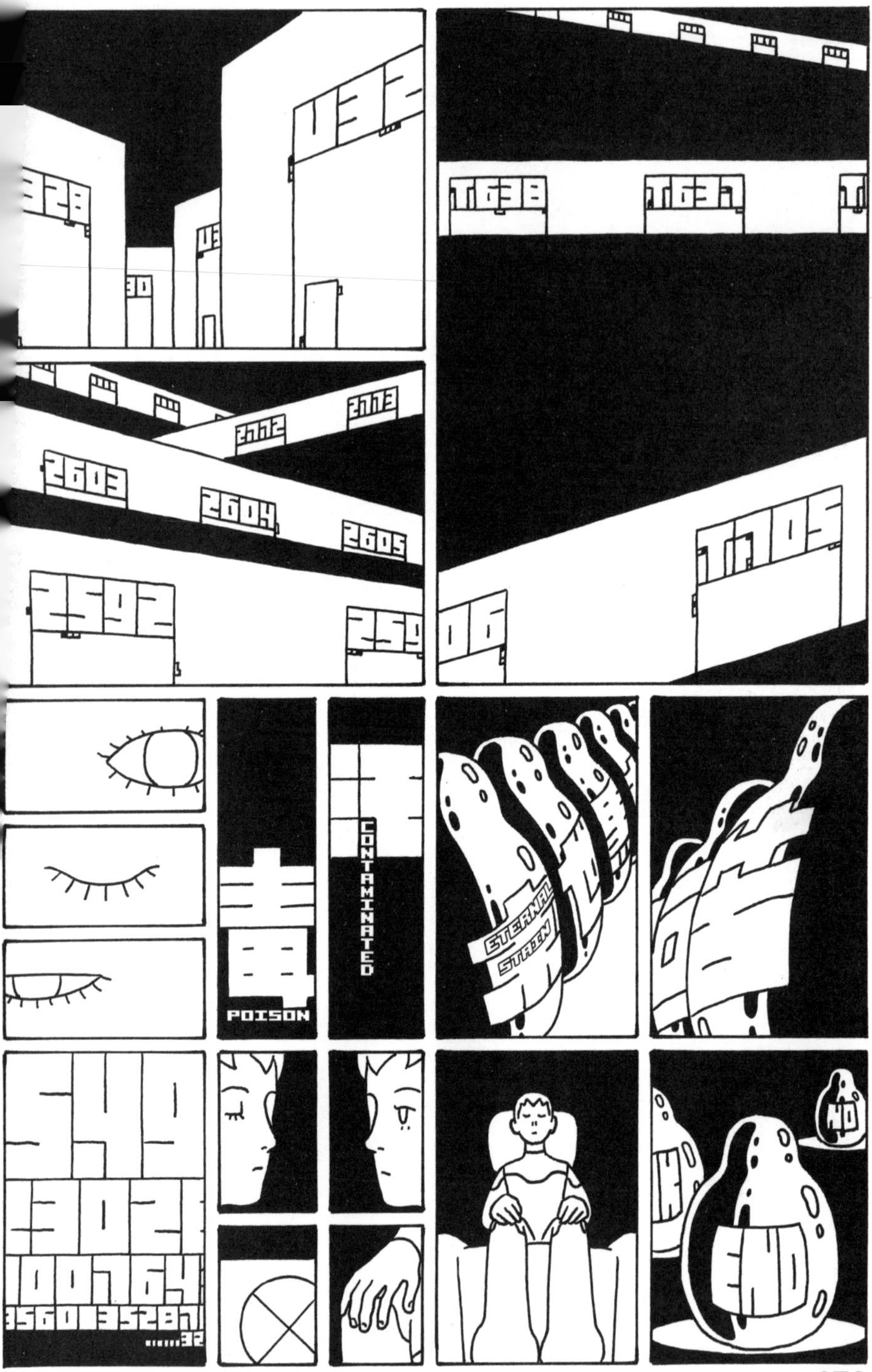
ETERNAL
STRAIN
CONTAMINATED
毒
POISON
END

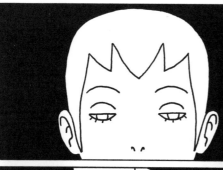

ONE DAY,
I WOKE TO A
SIGNAL THAT AN
ANOMALY HAD
OCCURRED.

OVER
THIRTY
THOUSAND
YEARS HAD
PASSED.

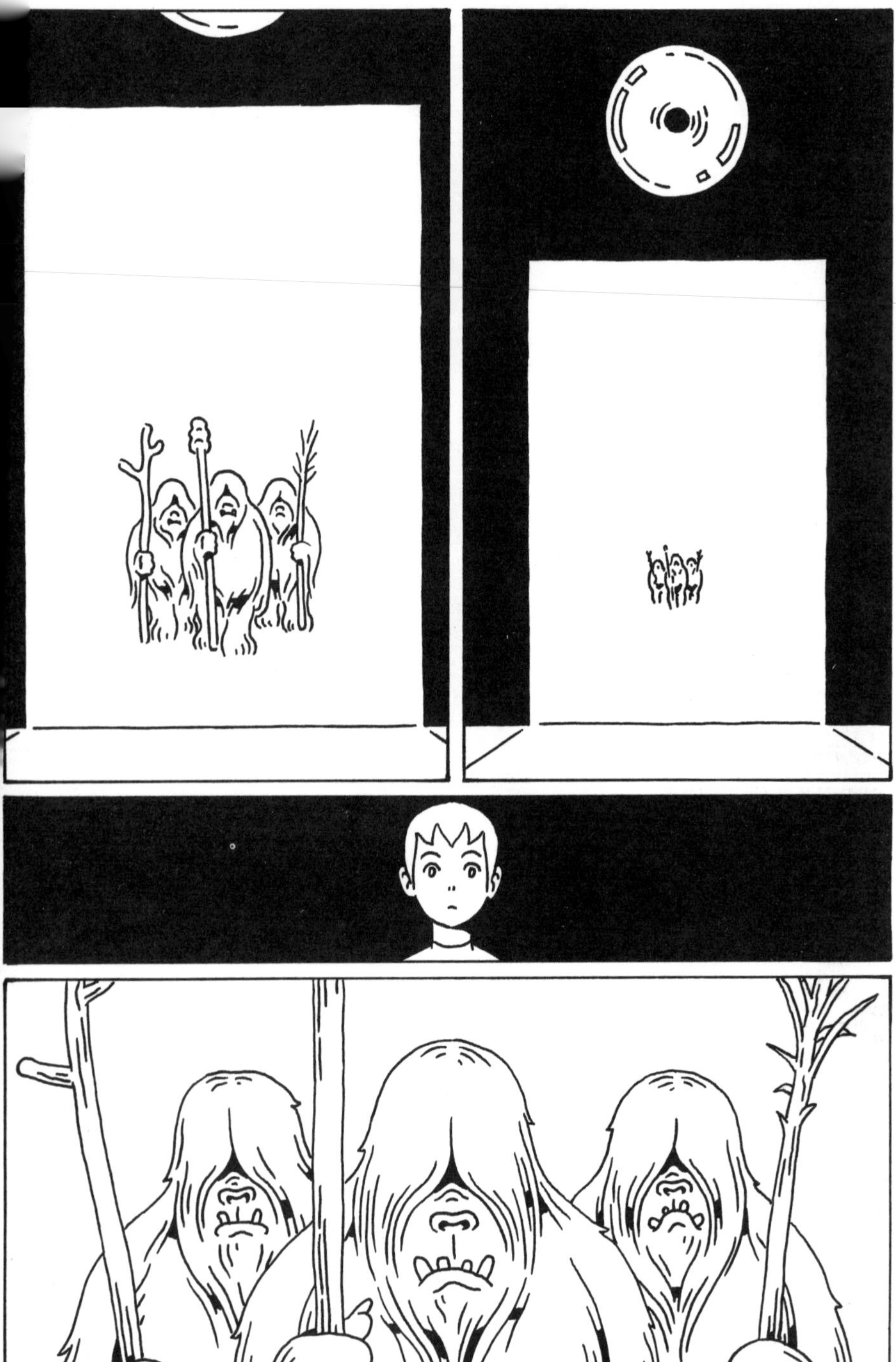

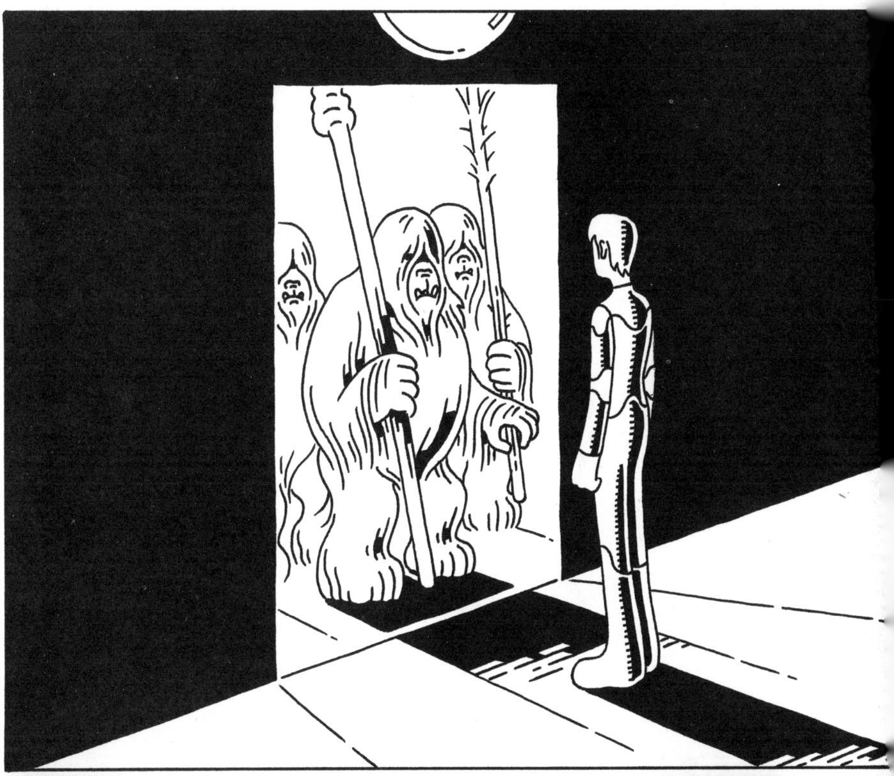

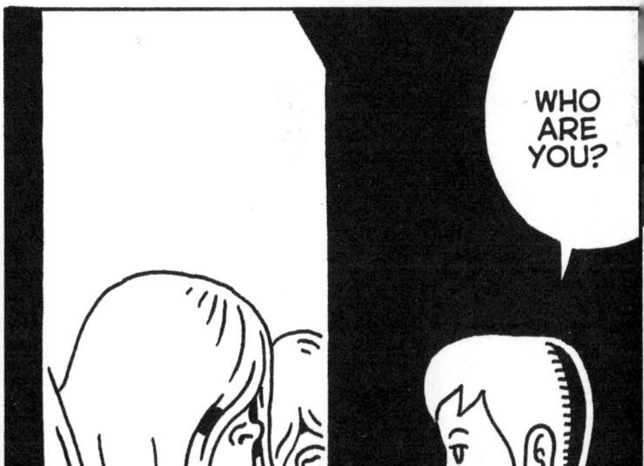
WHO ARE YOU?

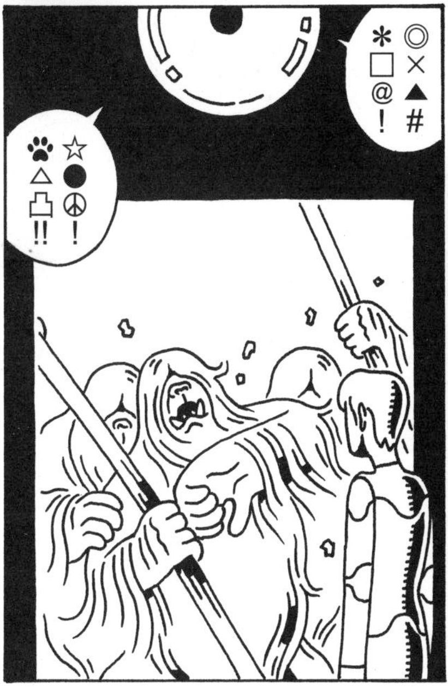
✻ ◎ □ × @ ▲ ! #
🐾 ☆ △ ● 凸 ☮ !! !

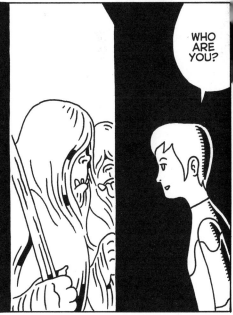

!!!

YOUR LANGUAGE IS INCOMPRE-HENSIBLE TO ME.

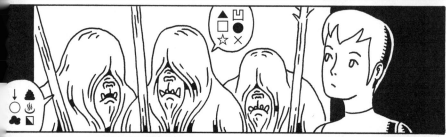

THEY SPENT SOME TIME LOITERING IN FRONT OF THE PRISM.

BUT EVENTUALLY, THEY SEEMED TO GROW BORED.

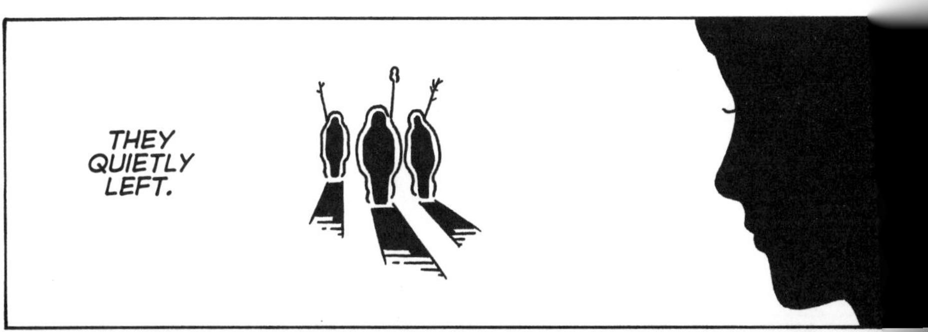
THEY QUIETLY LEFT.
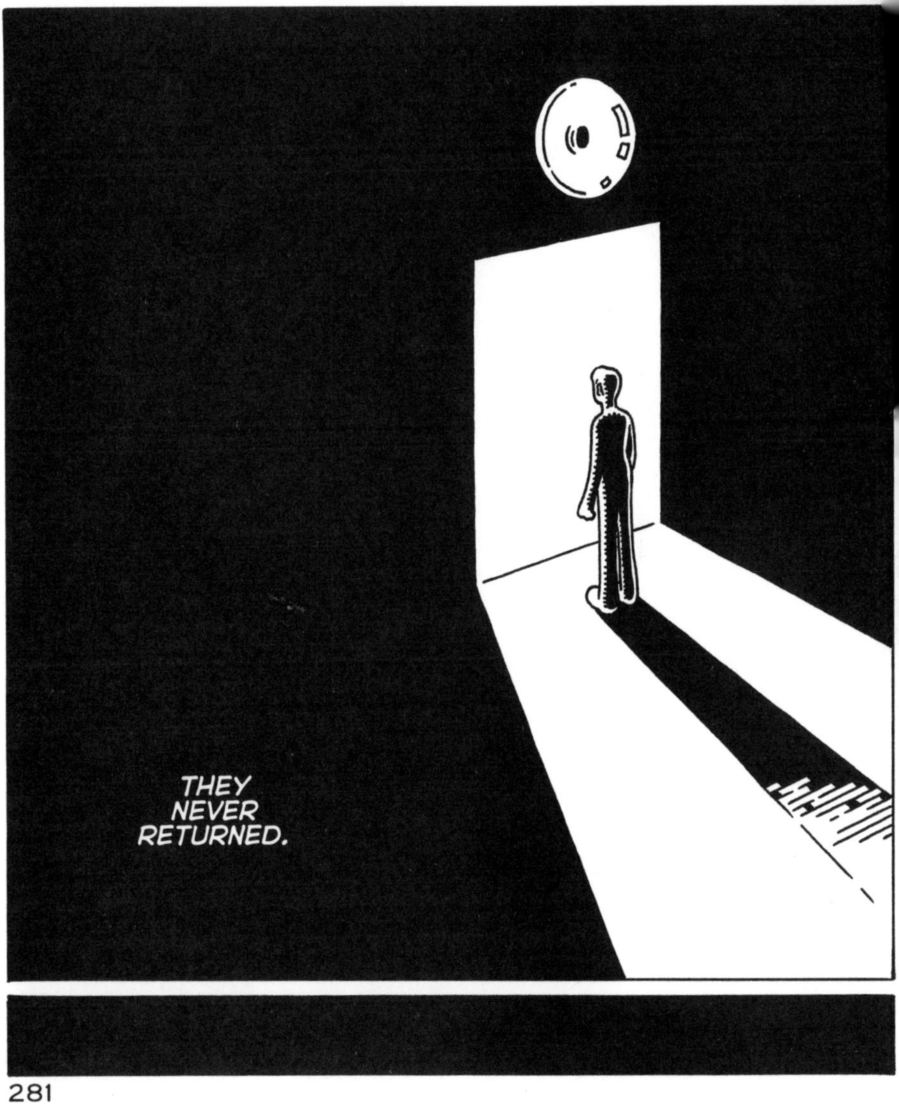
THEY NEVER RETURNED.

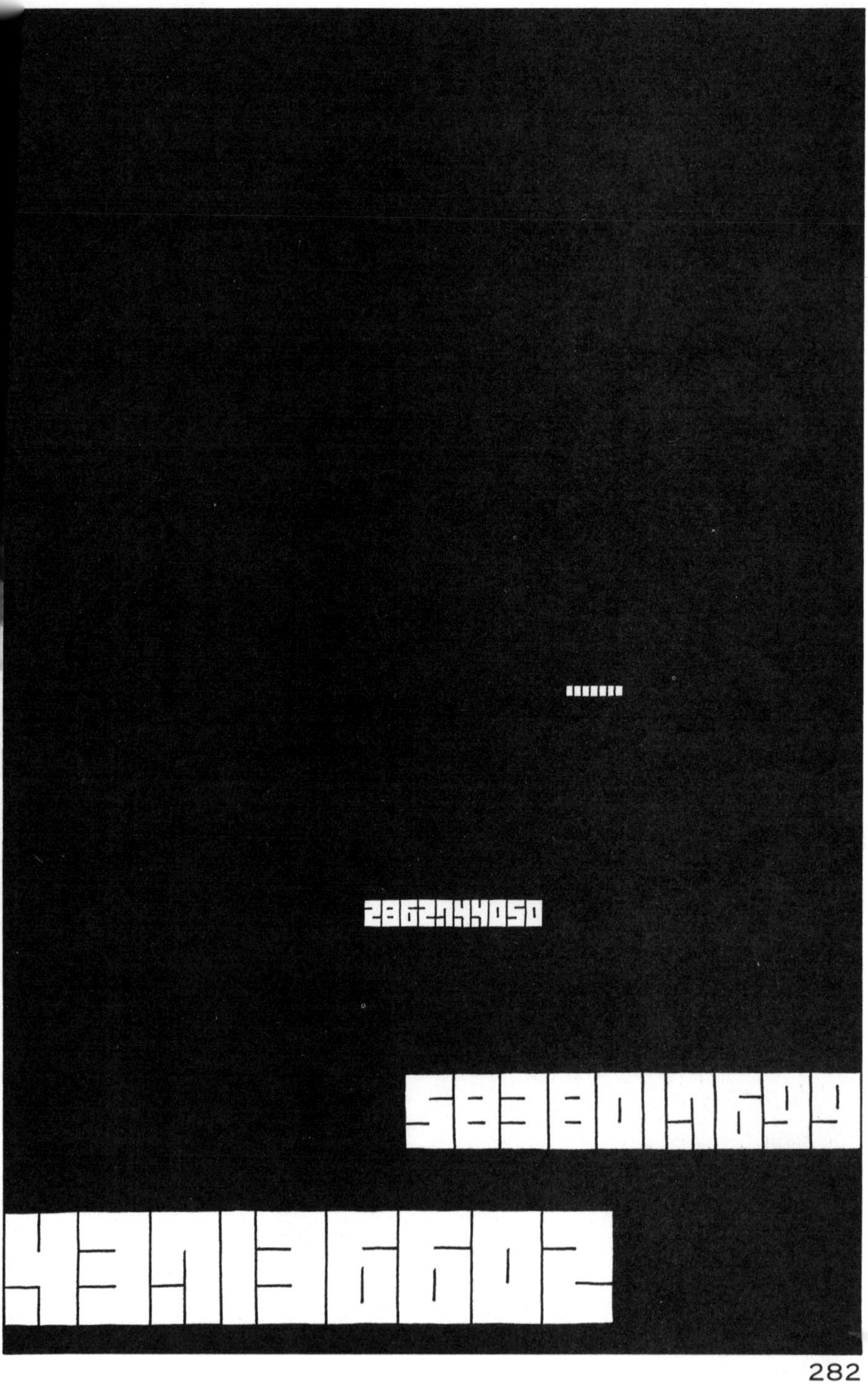
2862744050
5838017699
437136602

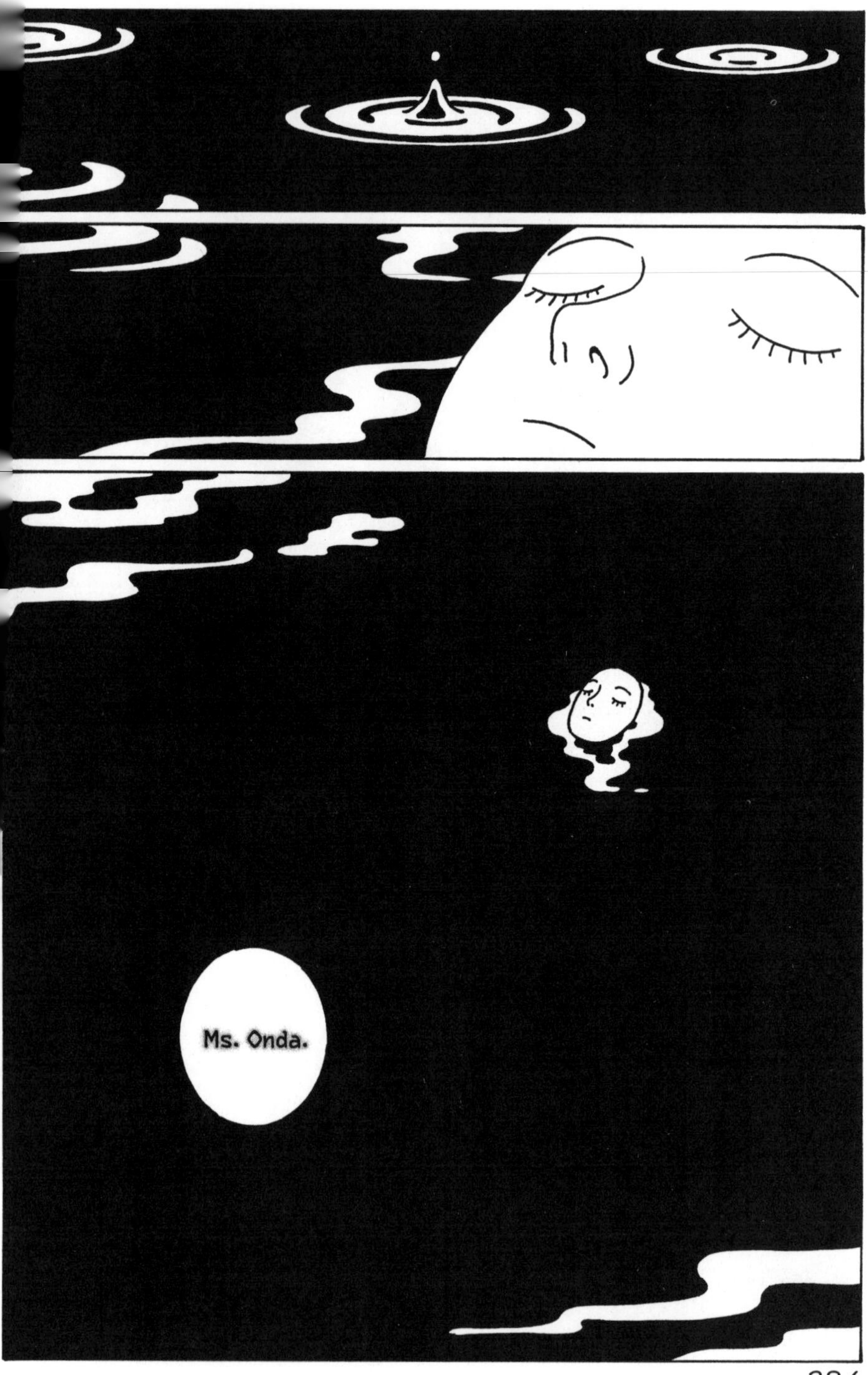
Ms. Onda.

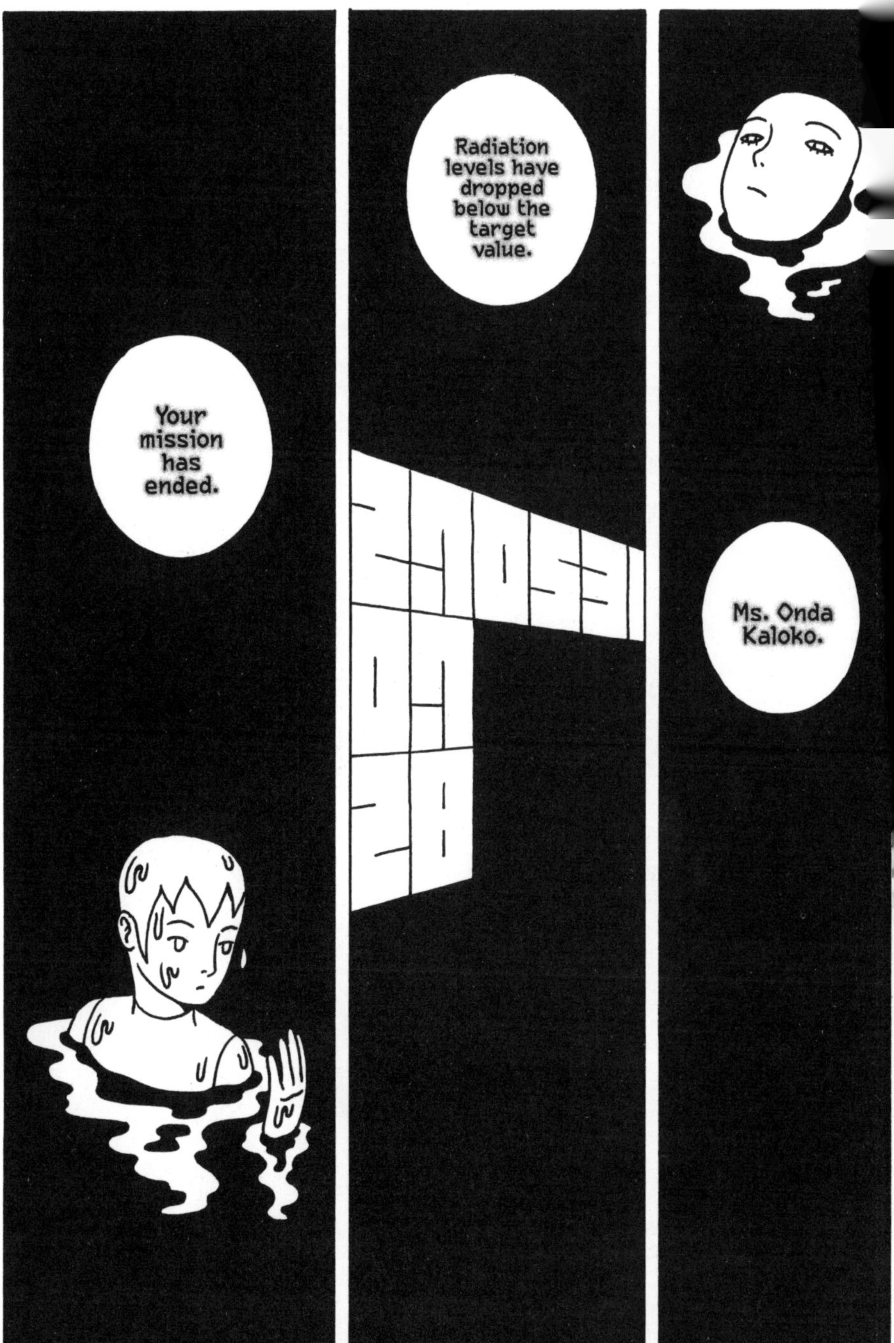
Ms. Onda Kaloko.
Radiation levels have dropped below the target value.
Your mission has ended.

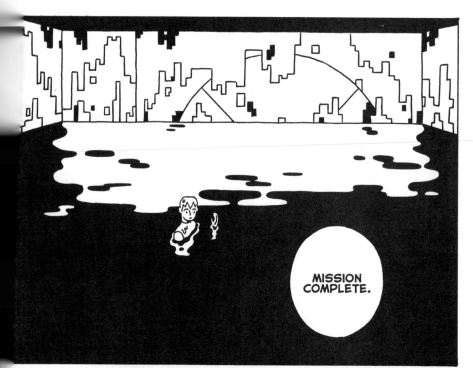

MISSION
COMPLETE.

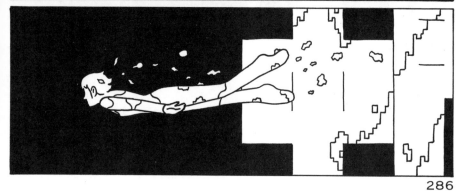

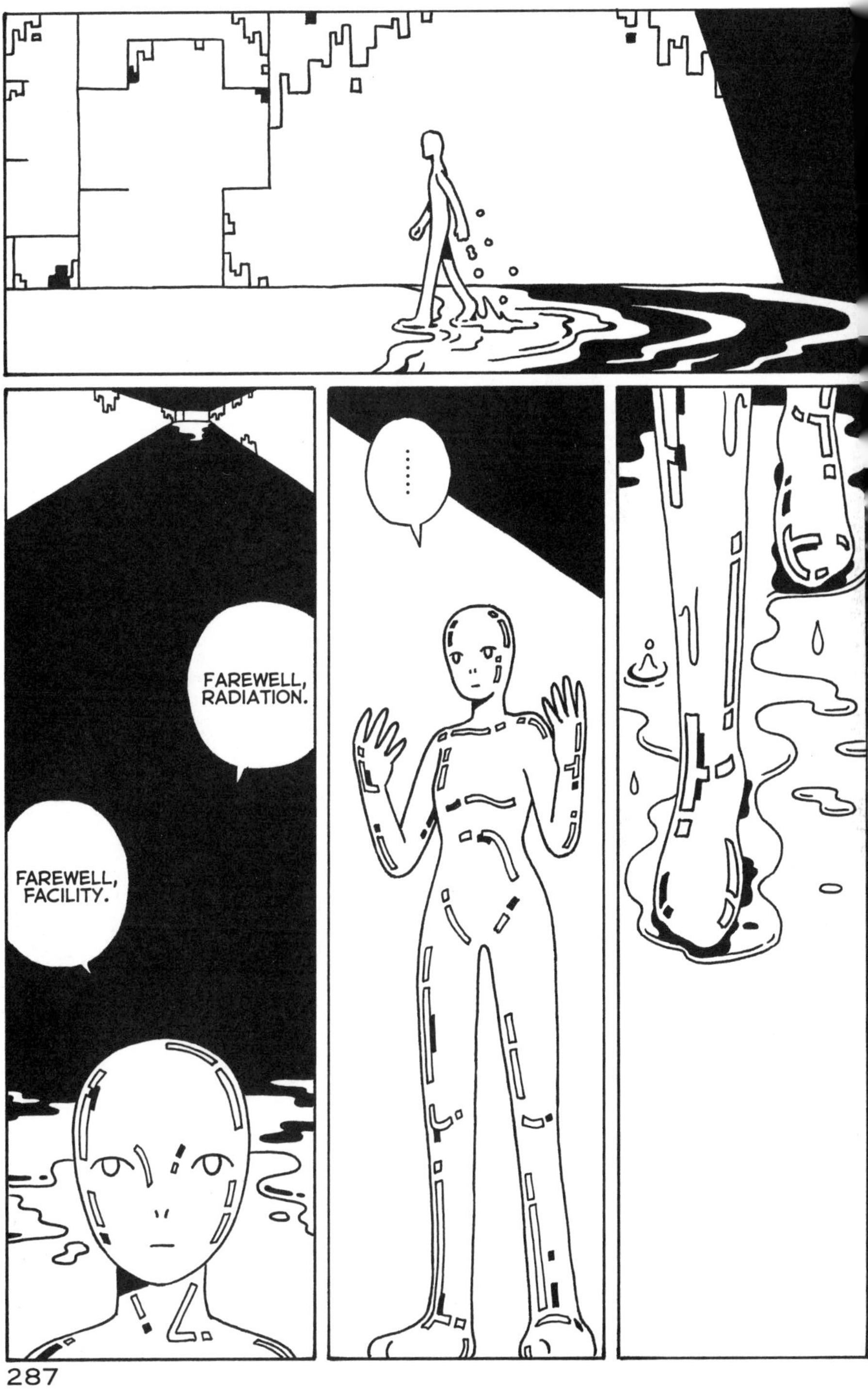
......
FAREWELL, RADIATION.
FAREWELL, FACILITY.

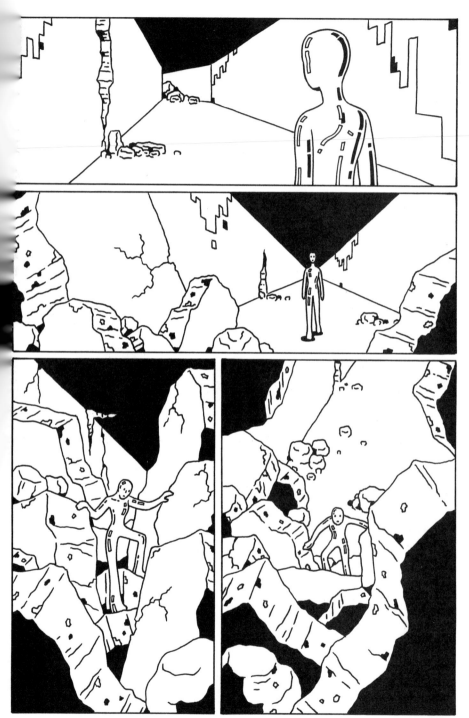

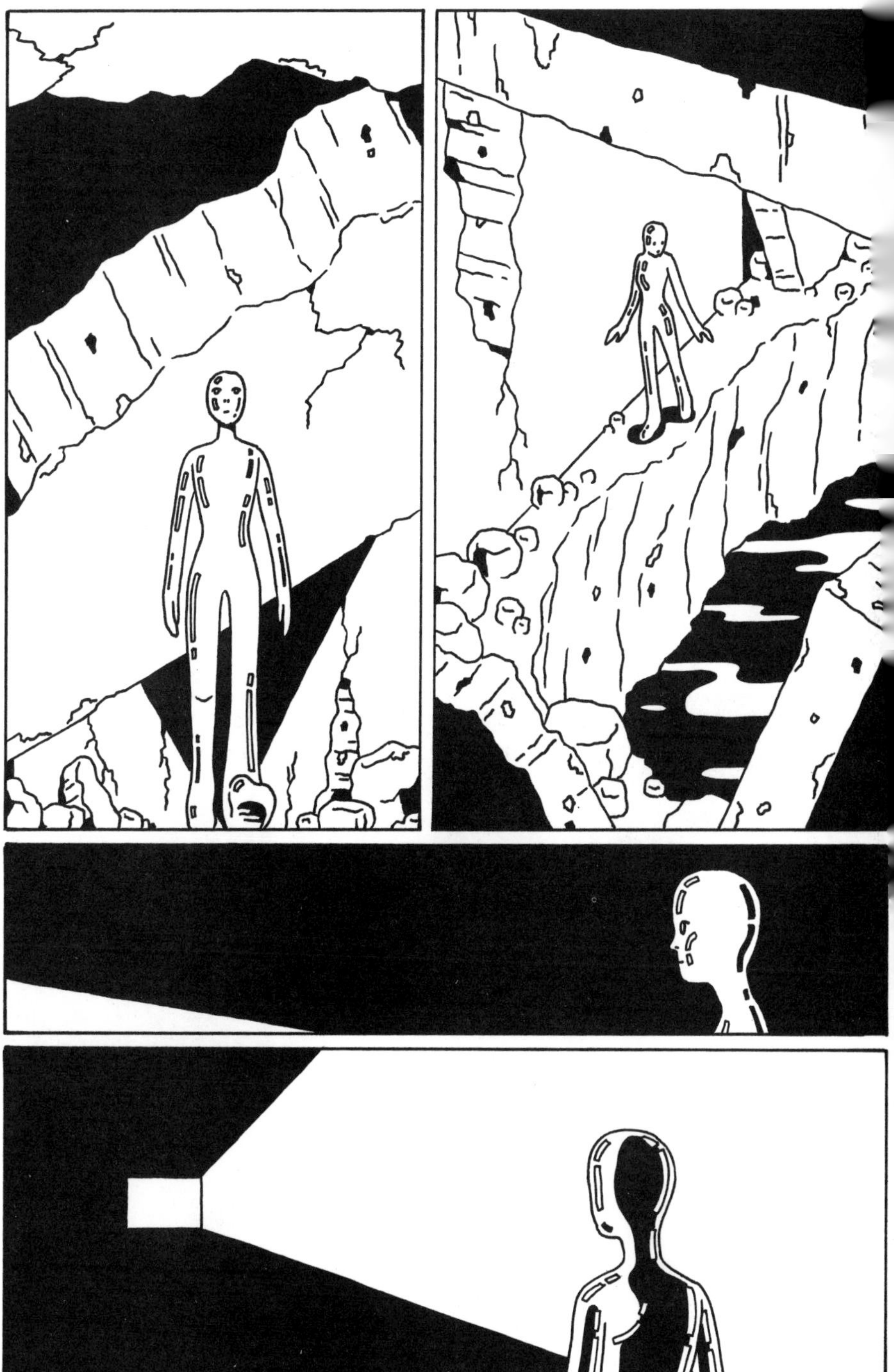

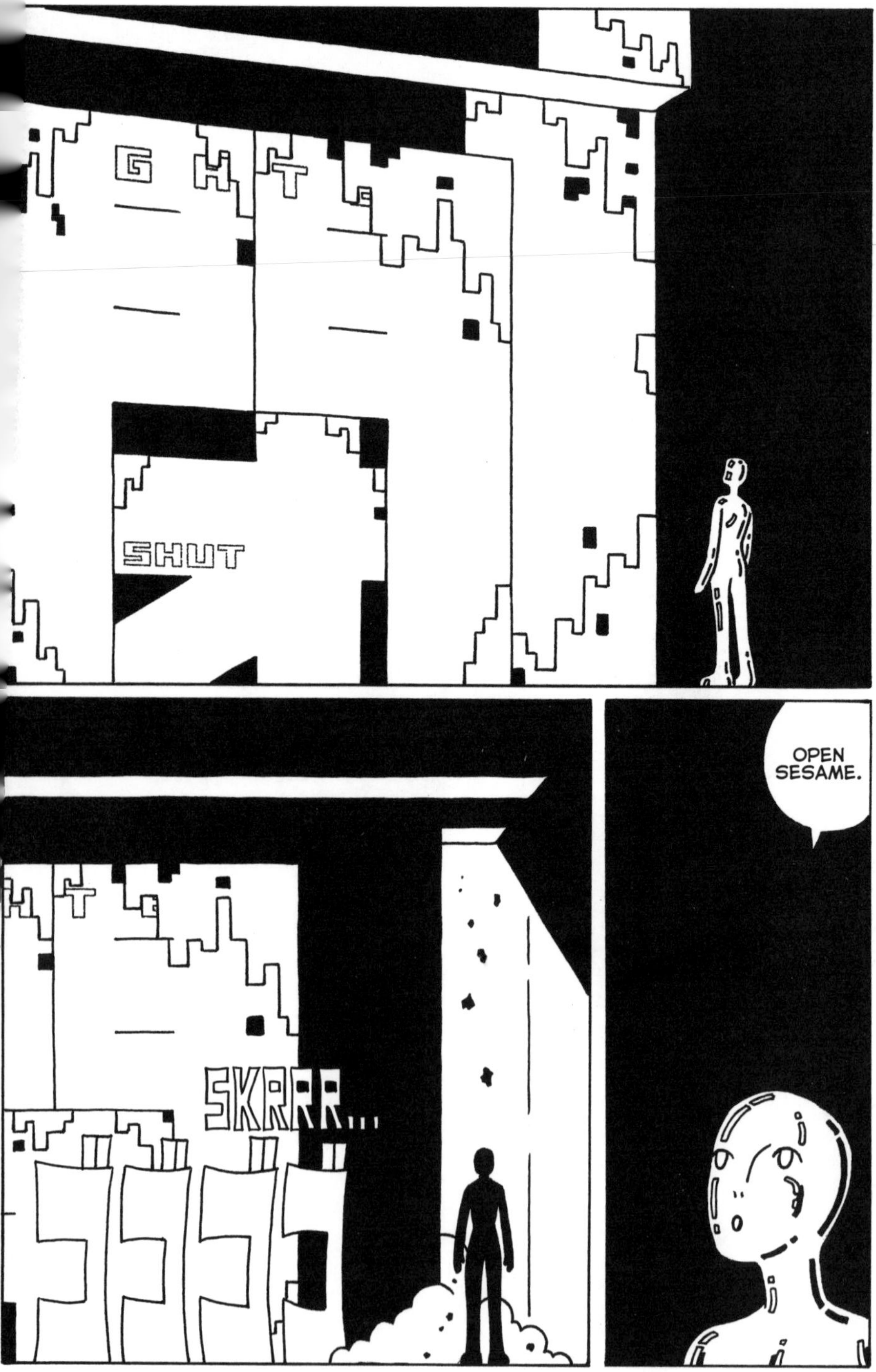
SHUT
OPEN SESAME.
SKRRR...

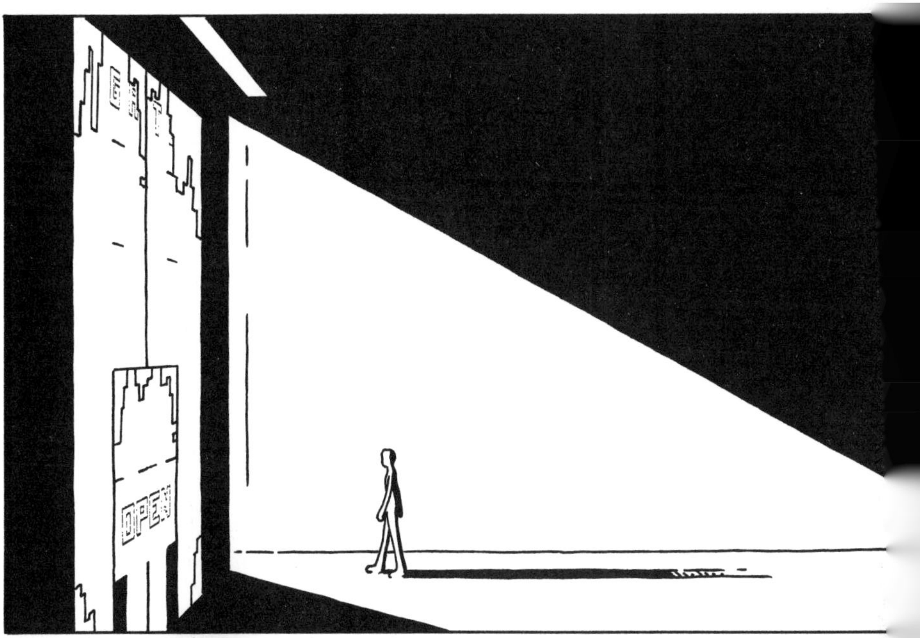
OPEN
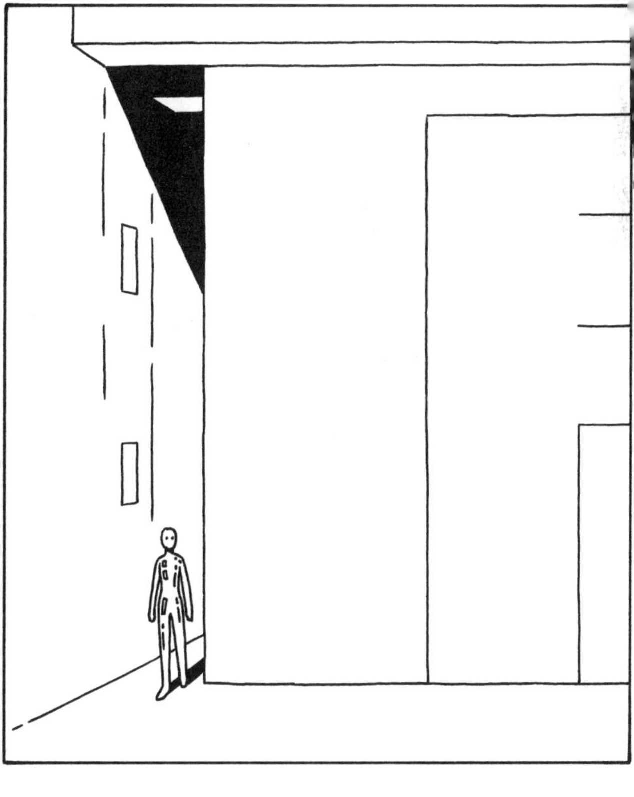
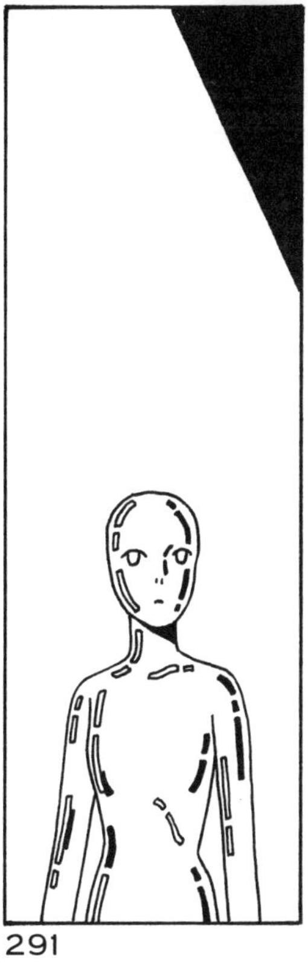

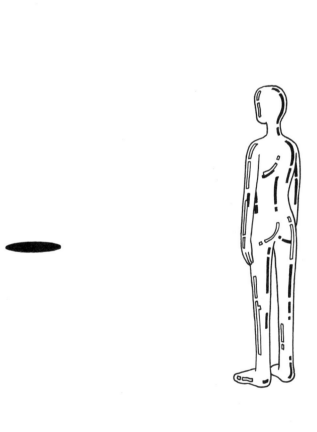

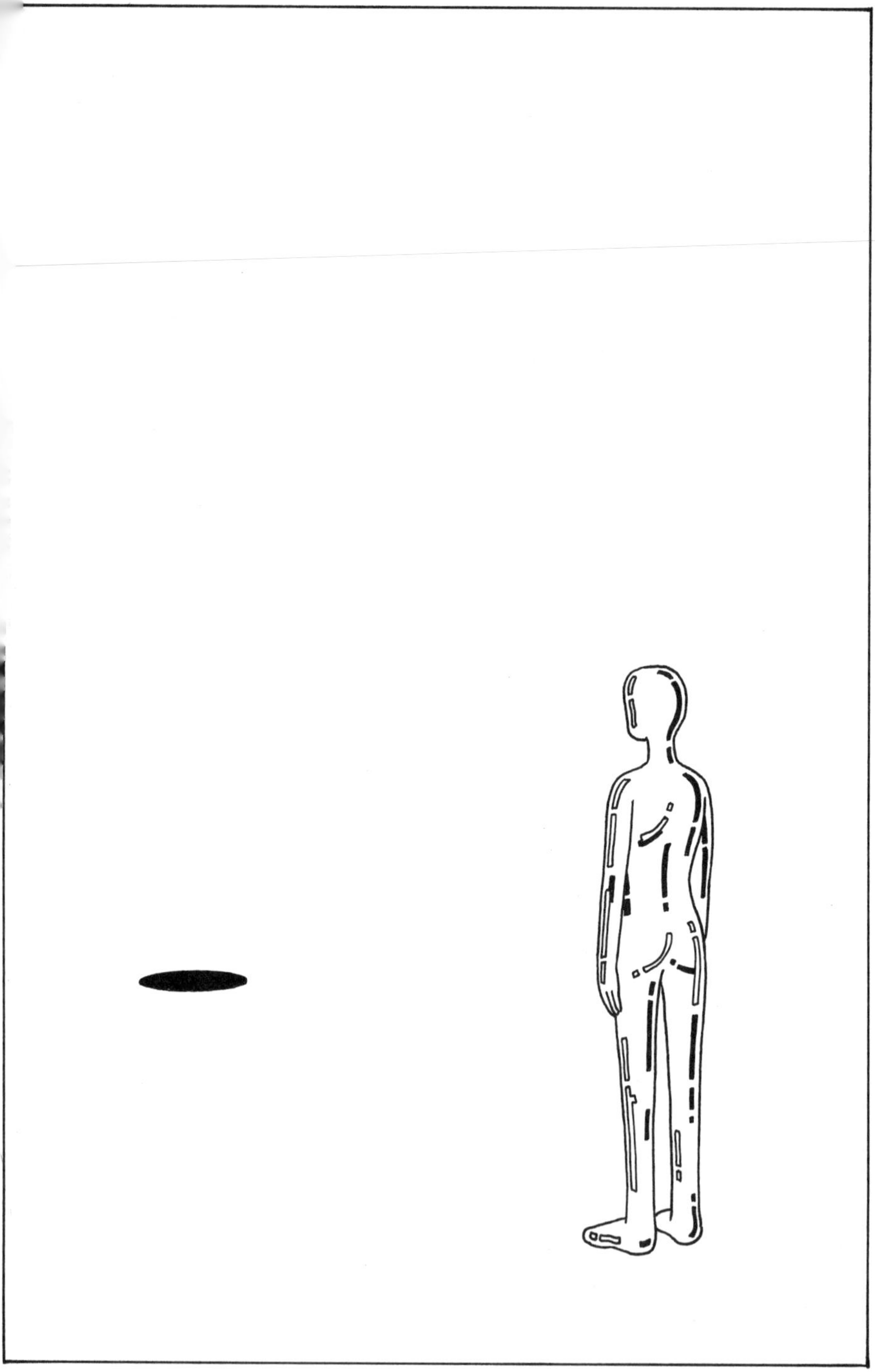

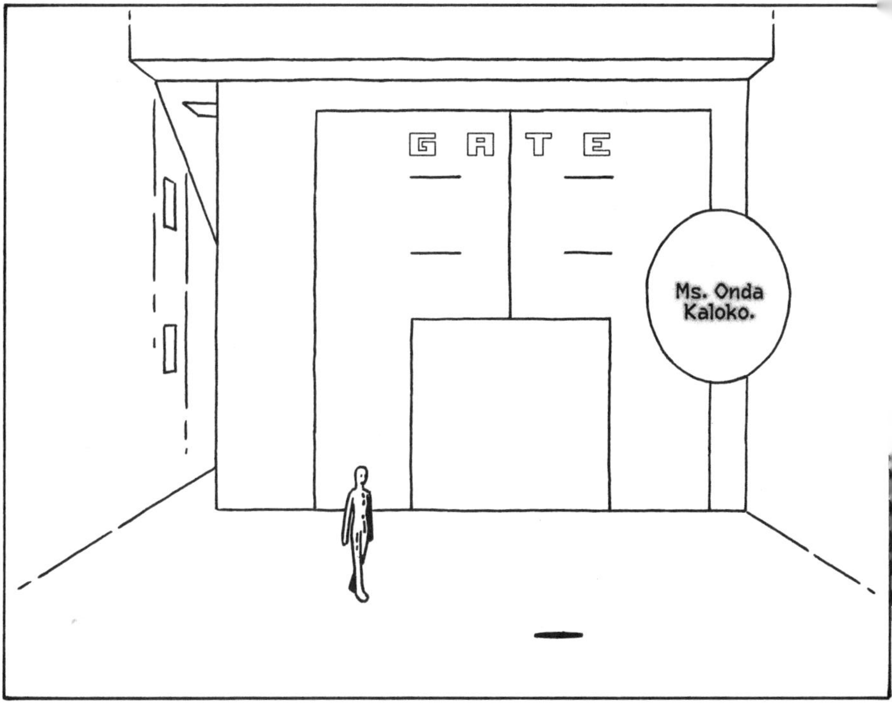
G A T E
Ms. Onda Kaloko.

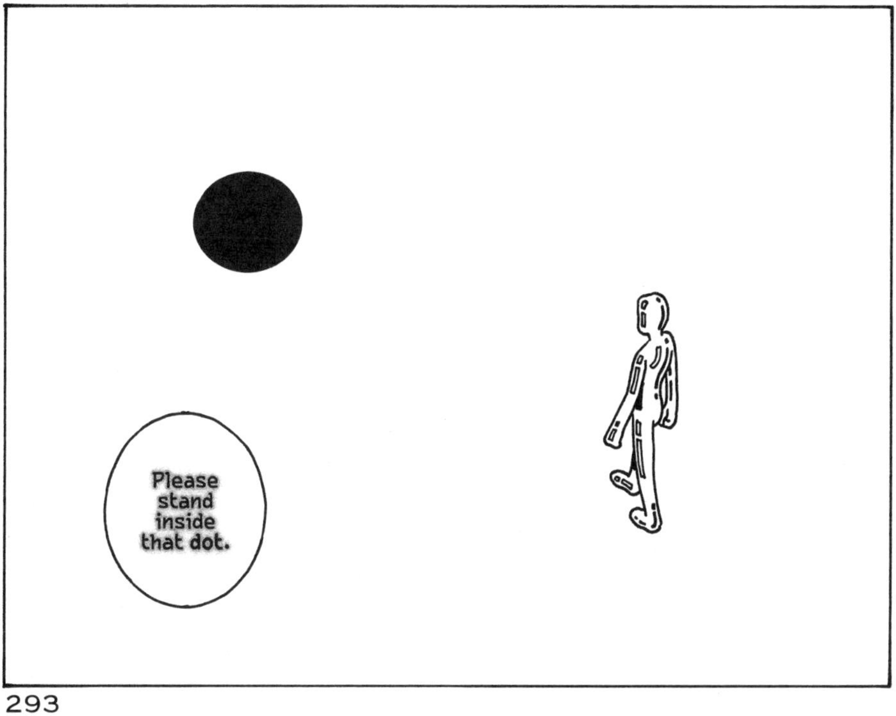
Please stand inside that dot.

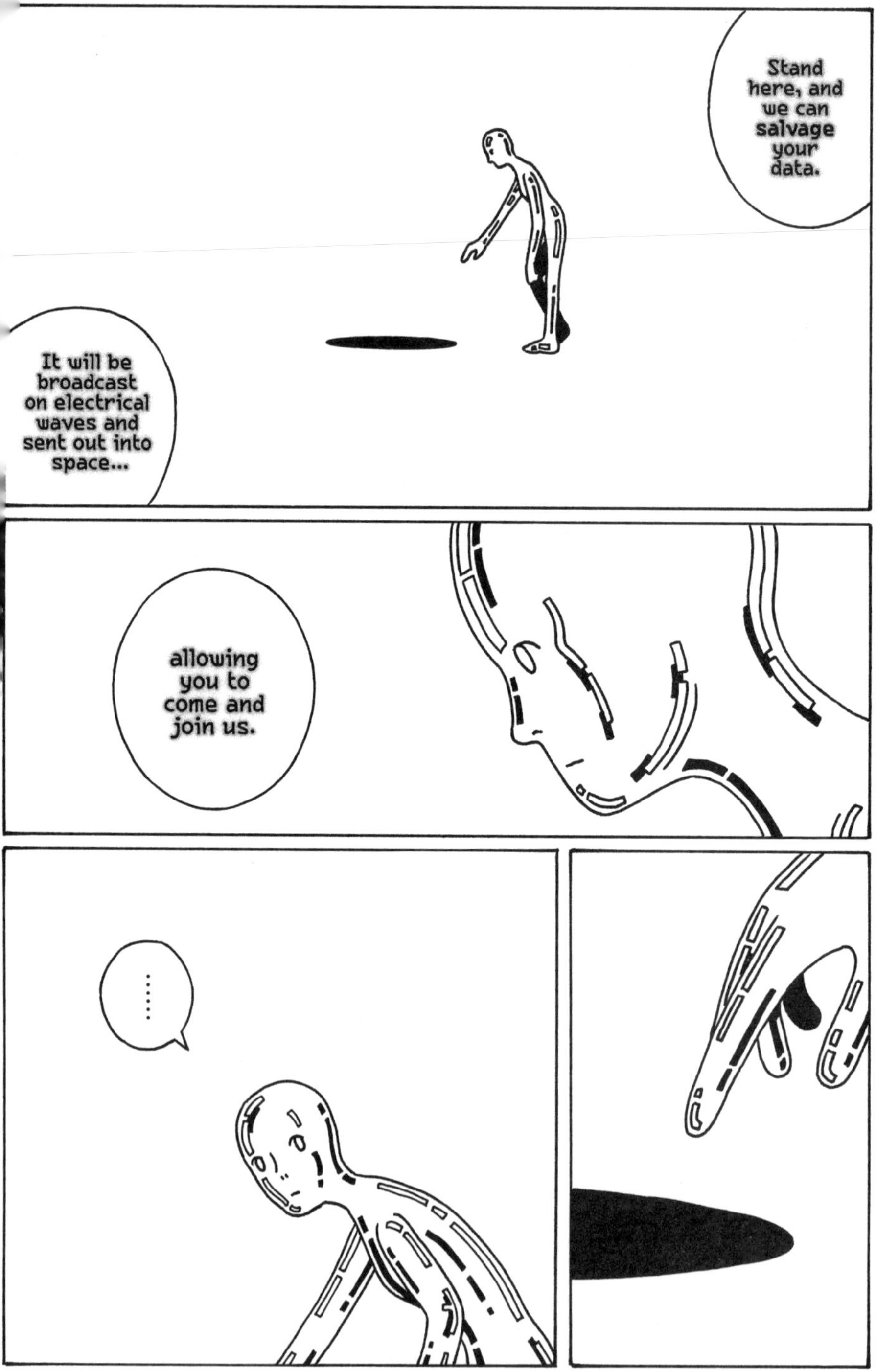
Stand here, and we can salvage your data.
It will be broadcast on electrical waves and sent out into space...
allowing you to come and join us.
......

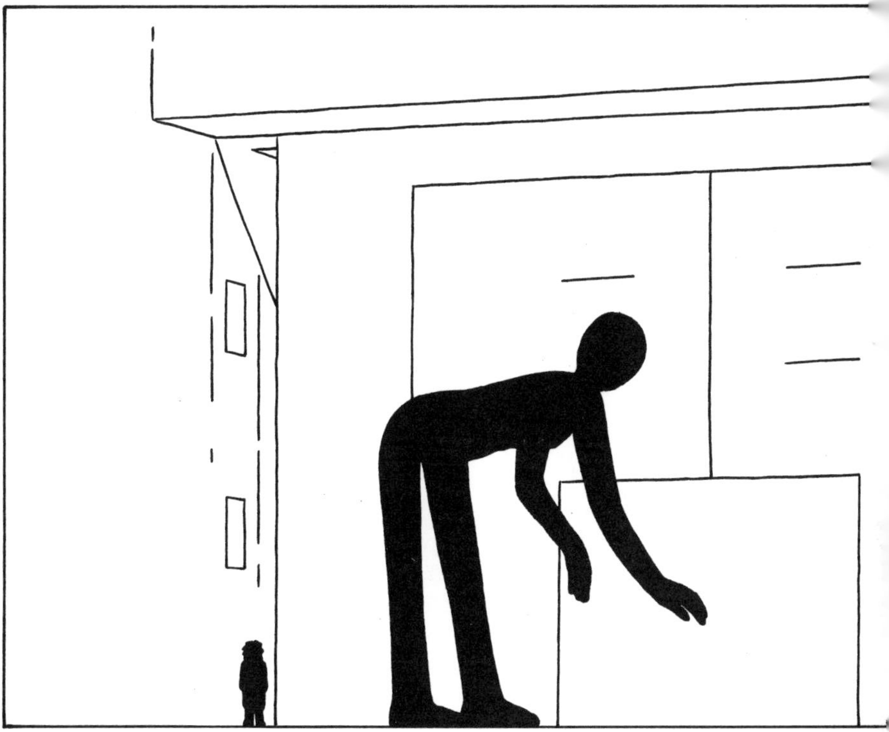
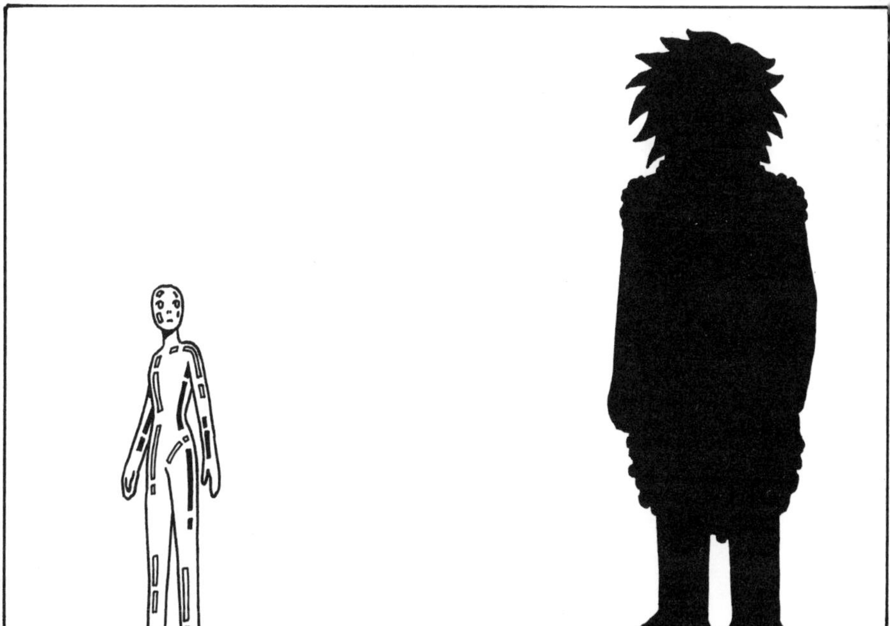

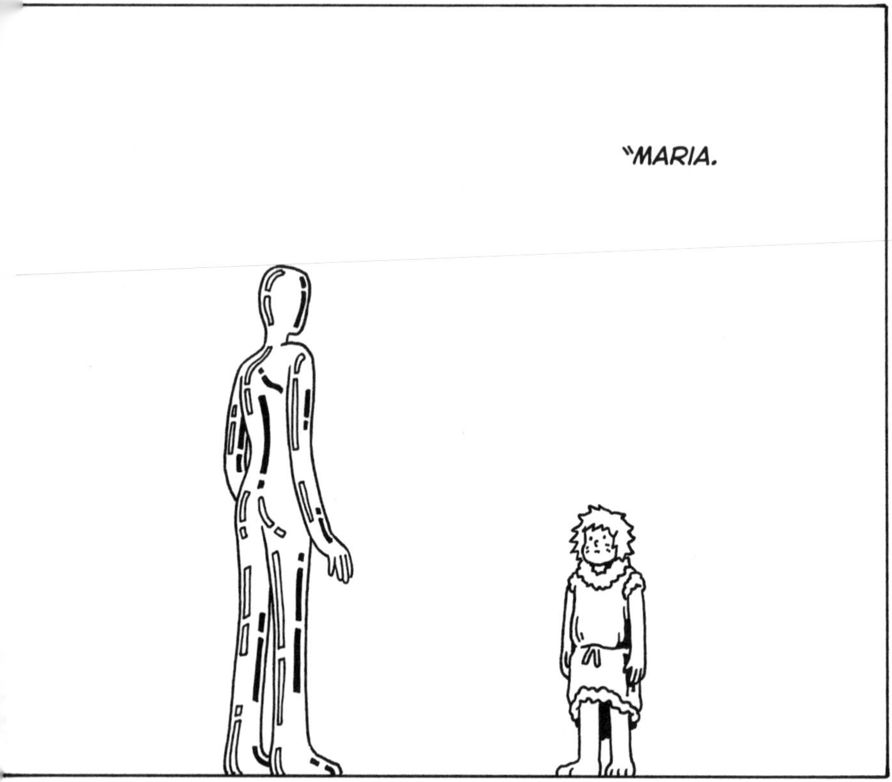
"MARIA.
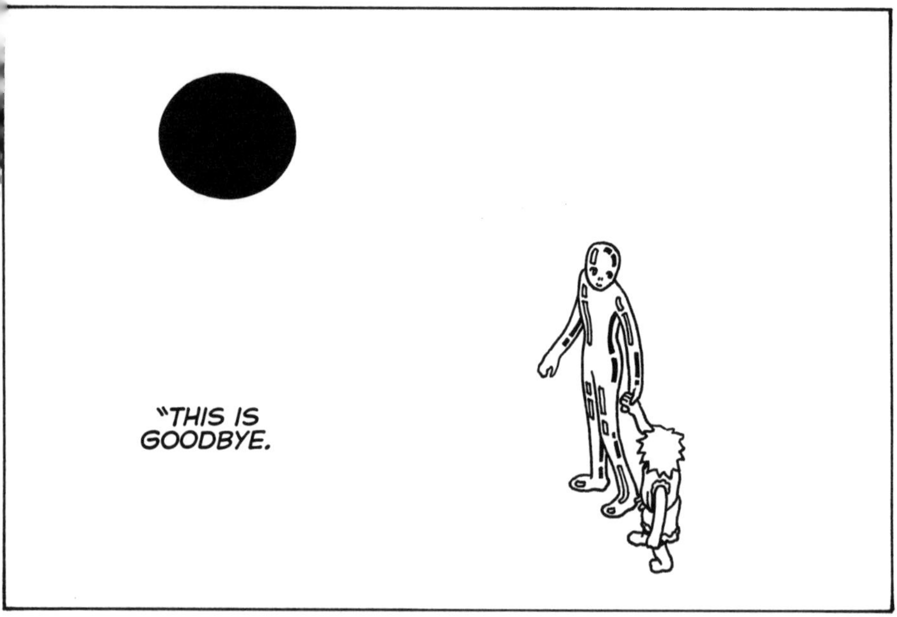
"THIS IS GOODBYE.

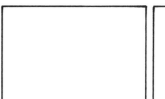

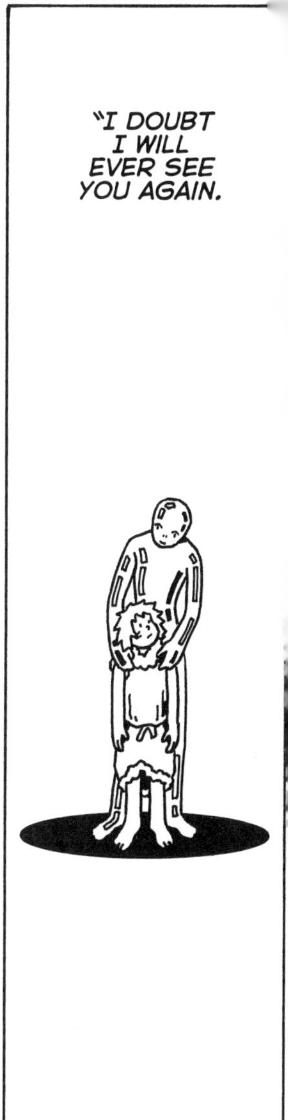
"I DOUBT I WILL EVER SEE YOU AGAIN.

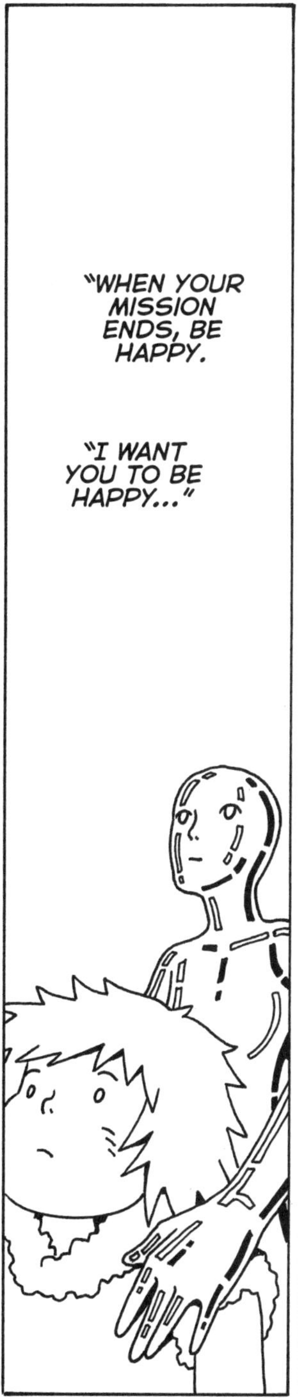
"WHEN YOUR MISSION ENDS, BE HAPPY.
"I WANT YOU TO BE HAPPY..."

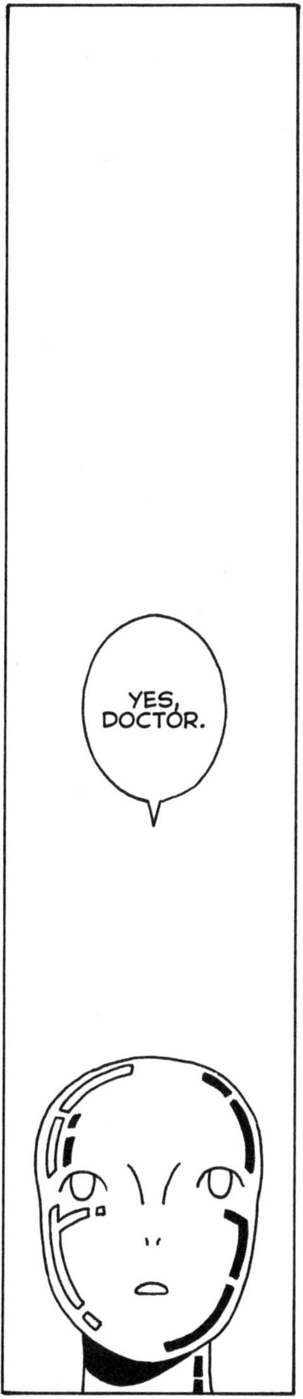
YES, DOCTOR.

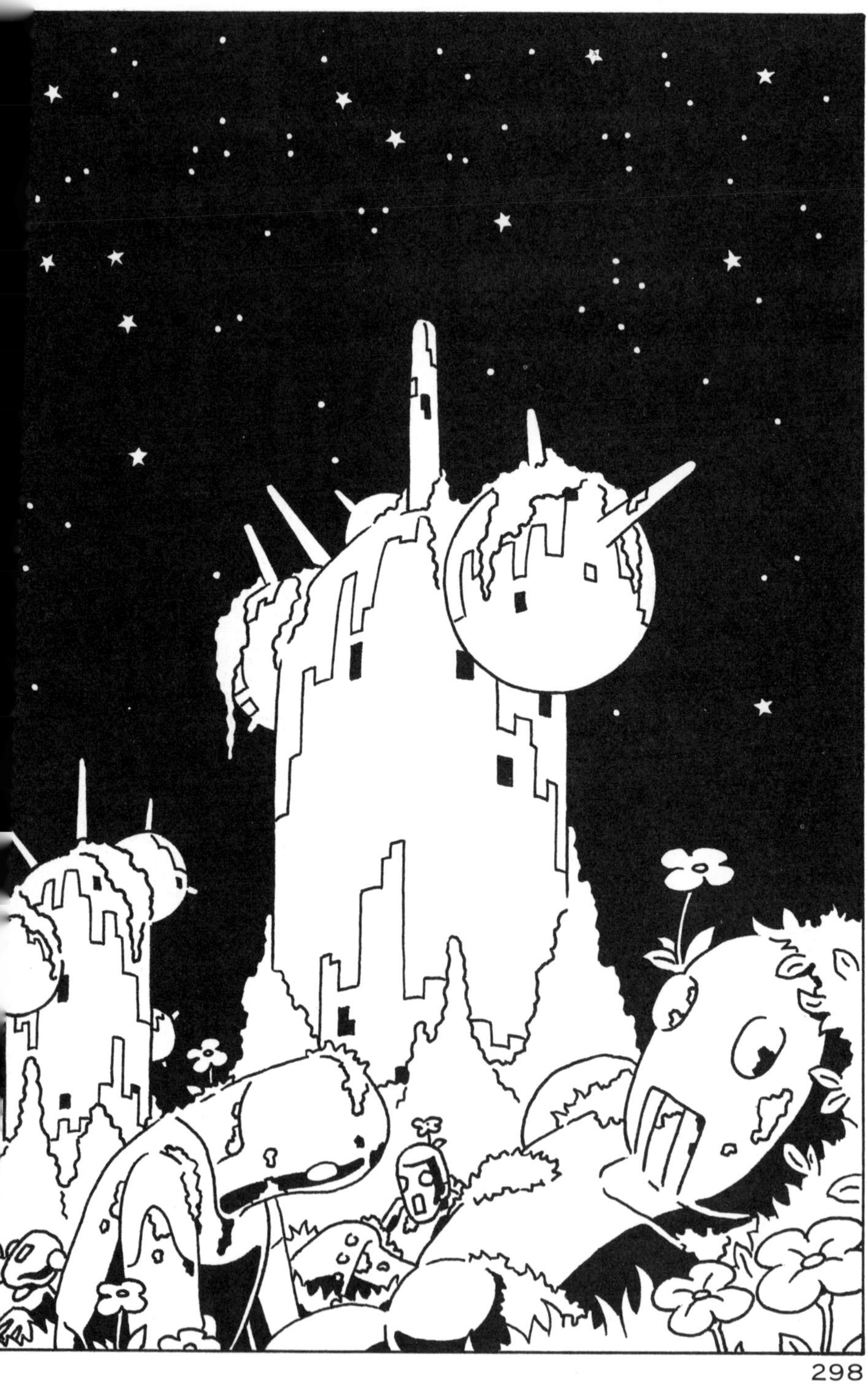

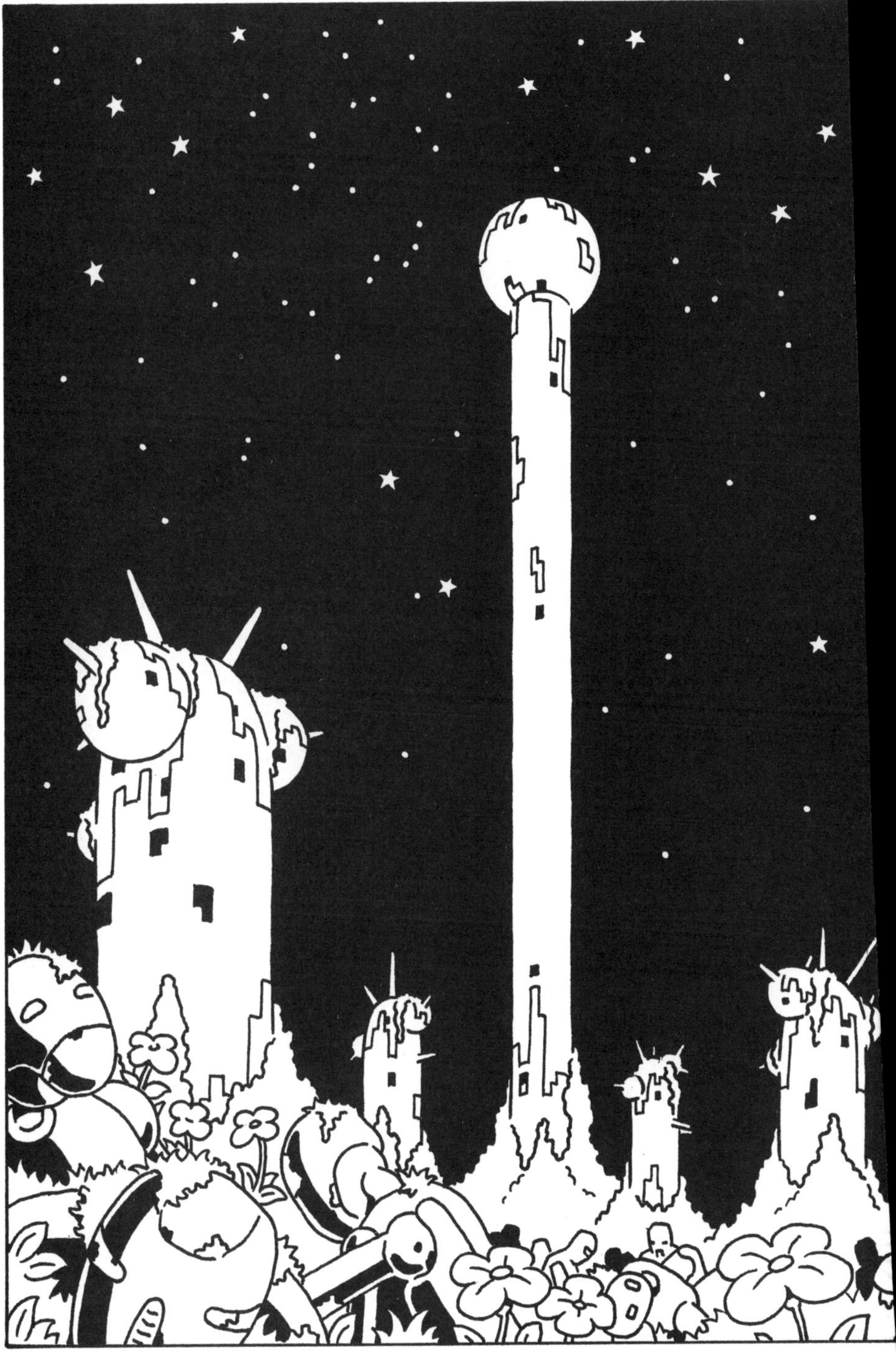

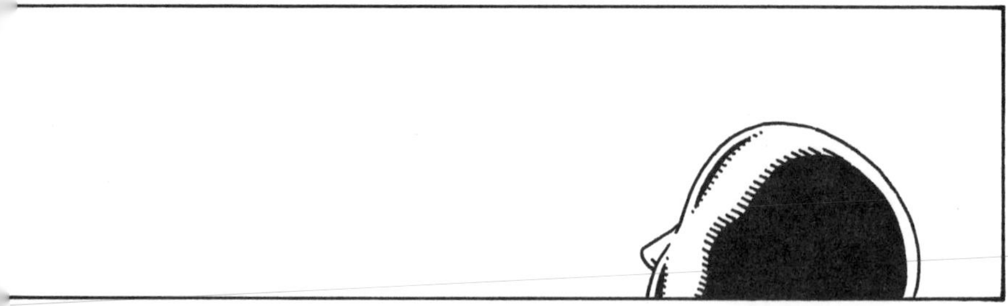

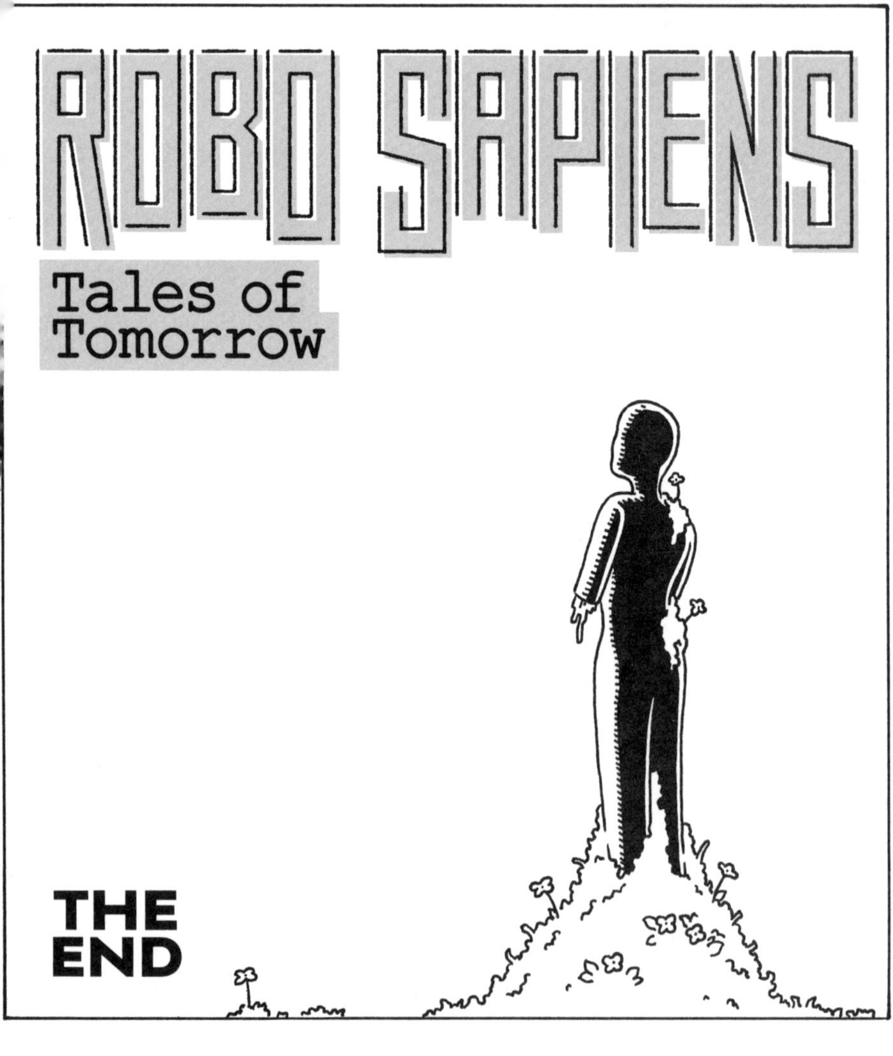
ROBO SAPIENS
Tales of Tomorrow
THE END

ROBO SAPIENS

Tales of Tomorrow

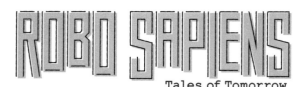

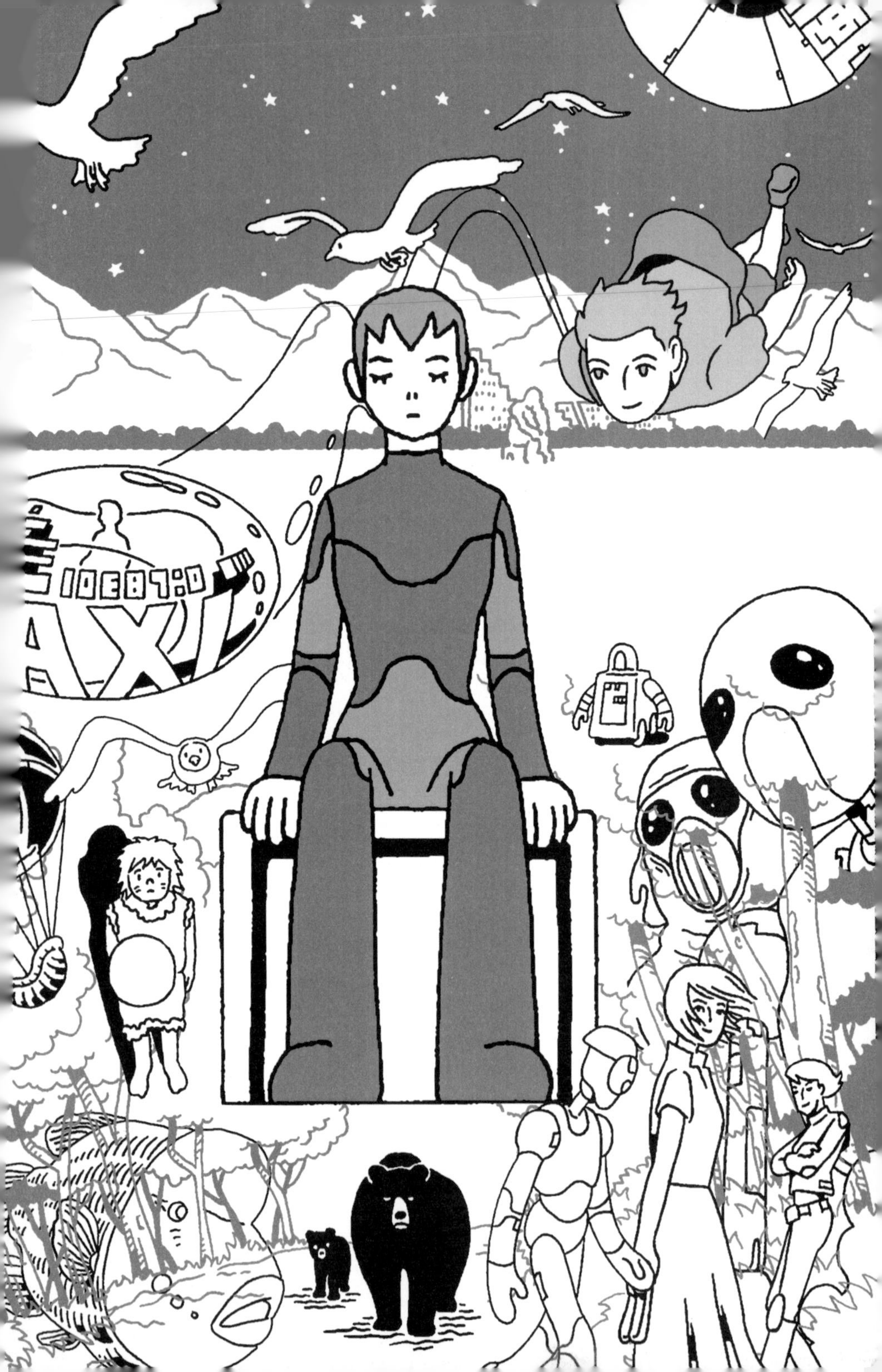

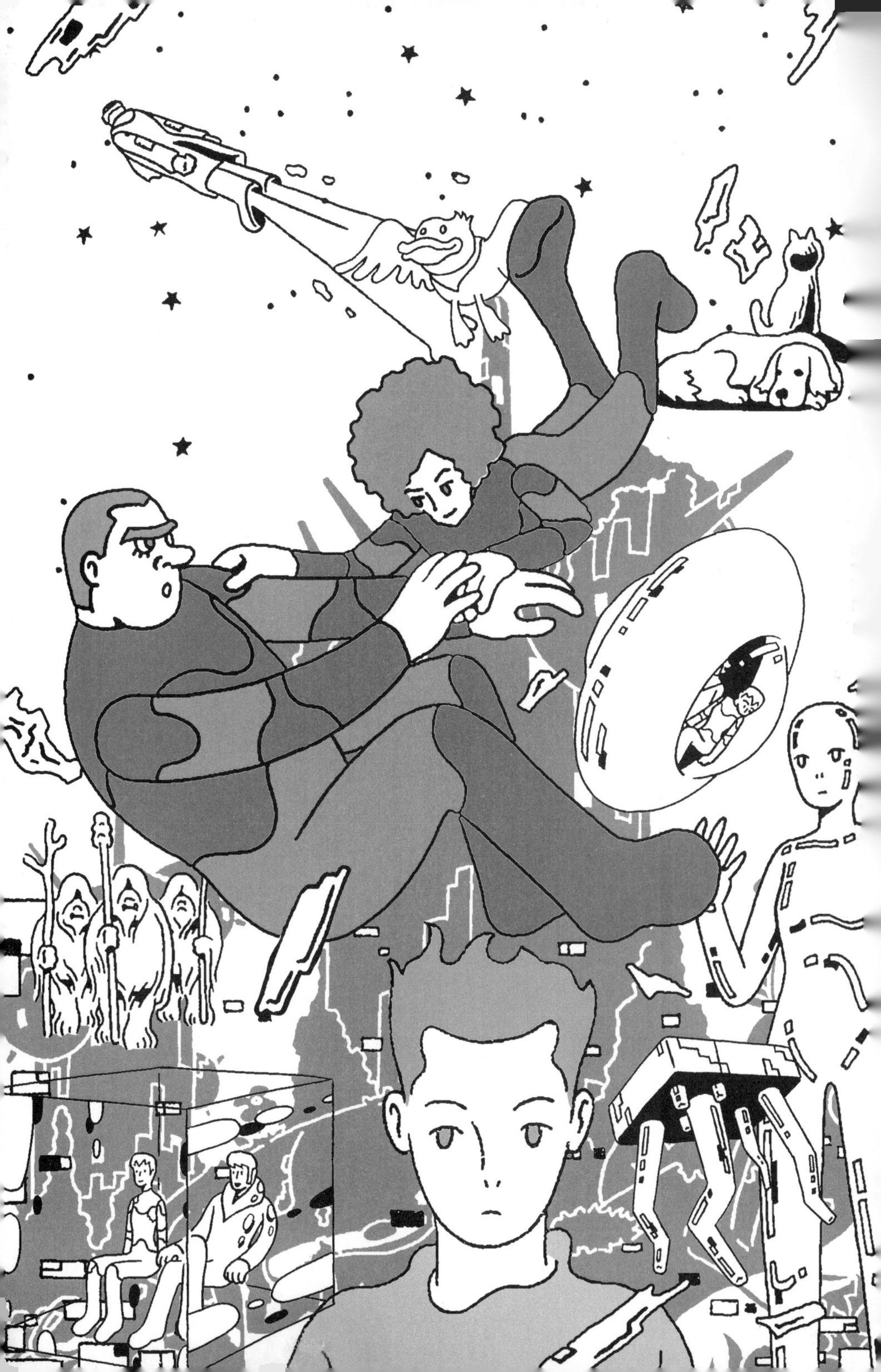

SEVEN SEAS ENTERTAINMENT PRESENTS

ROBO SAPIENS
Tales of Tomorrow

story and art by TORANOSUKE SHIMADA

TRANSLATION
Adrienne Beck

LETTERING AND COVER DESIGN
Nicky Lim

LOGO DESIGN
George Panella

INTERIOR LAYOUT
Sandy Grayson

PROOFREADER
Dawn Davis

EDITOR
Alexis Roberts

PRINT MANAGER
ʌnon Rasmussen-Silverstein

MANAGING EDITOR
Julie Davis

ASSOCIATE PUBLISHER
Adam Arnold

PUBLISHER
Jason DeAngelis

Seven Seas press and purchase enquiries can be sent to Marketing Manager Lianne Sentar at press@gomanga.com. Information regarding the distribution and purchase of digital editions is available from Digital Manager CK Russell at digital@gomanga.com.

Seven Seas and the Seven Seas logo are trademarks of Seven Seas Entertainment. All rights reserved.

ISBN: 978-1-64827-598-2
Printed in Canada
First Printing: November 2021
10 9 8 7 6 5 4 3 2 1

//// READING DIRECTIONS ////

This book reads from *right to left*, Japanese style. If this is your first time reading manga, you start reading from the top right panel on each page and take it from there. If you get lost, just follow the numbered diagram here. It may seem backwards at first, but you'll get the hang of it! Have fun!!

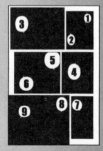